Psychology and You

Frank B. McMahon

Southern Illinois University
Edwardsville

Judith W. McMahon

Lindenwood College

Tony Romano

William Fremd High School

West Publishing Company

St. Paul   New York   Los Angeles   San Francisco

Copy Editor: Nancy Palmer Jones
Design: Janet Bollow
Photo Research: Stuart Kenter
Illustrations: Barbara Barnett, Tom Barnett
Composition: Alphatype

Cover: *Dunkles Land* by Willibrord Haas; reprinted with permission of the artist.

Credits appear after the index.

Library of Congress Cataloging-in-Publication Data

McMahon, Frank B.
  Psychology and you.

  Bibliography: p.
  Includes index.
  1. Psychology.   I. McMahon, Judith W.   II. Romano,
Tony, 1957–   .   III. Title.
BF121.M2945 1990   150   88–33869
ISBN 0–314–47357–2

 TEXT IS PRINTED ON 10% POST
CONSUMER RECYCLED PAPER

Contents

v

Chapter 4
Sensation and
Perception   77

Chapter 5
Motivation and
Emotion   109

Unit Three   Cognitive Processes   159

Unit Four   Human Development 243

Unit Five   Personality, Adjustment, and Conflict   343

Unit Six   Psychological Disorders

Unit Seven   Self and Social Influences 501

Preface

$\mathbf{A}$ preface gives us the opportunity to share our enthusiasm about this outstanding and unique high school psychology text. Its goal is to create active intellectual and emotional involvement by the student, not only in life, but in learning the science of psychology. Psychology encompasses broad areas of research about the human, information that should be available to all high school students who want to understand themselves and others better. Roughly twenty years ago we wrote our first introductory psychology text for college students that had as its central focus the student as a consumer. That is, uppermost in our minds was the belief that a book could be written that would be lively, entertaining, and fully scientific—all at the same time. That book is now in its sixth edition.

Given our love for the subject matter, we were excited to be approached by West Publishing to produce a book exclusively for the high school student. We were convinced at the beginning of the project—and are even more so now that it is done—that it was possible to produce something special for this select group. From the beginning we wrote with high school students uppermost in our minds. Learning abstractions and learning practicality do not have to be separate things. Almost every page ties in scientific issues with corresponding applications to daily life. We have also included special boxes—one for each chapter—called "Psychology in Your Life," which apply some of the principles found in the chapter directly to daily activity. We believe that we have produced a book that is sophisticated in its coverage, up-to-date, thorough, but at the same time exactly what the high school student needs and wants. There is a built-in rhythm to keep student interest high by the inclusion of anecdotes, historical facts, unusual events, everyday issues and concerns, humor—as well as a writing style that talks with the students, taking them step by step through the issues. These devices should keep interest high and improve retention.

We have not bypassed any areas covered by a college-level text, because we believe that with the proper examples and a feeling of enthusiasm one can convey most any concept to students, and they will not only learn it, but enjoy doing so. For example, normally the chapter on motivation and emotion is treated as heavy, ponderous subject matter, or is glossed over. But it need not be, and isn't. We begin it by covering some of the rather gross eating patterns found in people of early England to get the reader's attention, lead into some of the mechanisms of hunger and thirst, and tie these in with issues of concern that today's students have about over- or undereating. By the time the chapter is over, the reader has a well-rounded education in what we know today about such fascinating topics.

There clearly is one thing that we can say with no shyness: Along with each chapter are included learning devices and exercises that are phenomenal. We can say that because they were created by someone else, Tony Romano, a high school teacher of long standing who has a master's degree in psychology. Nowhere have we seen projects, discussions, and suggestions that equal the merit of what he has provided. We believe it would be impossible for any student not to come away from these exercises enriched and enlightened. Especially noteworthy are his In Focus segments, which condense and bring together subject matter that might be confusing or might lend itself to being forgotten. Mr. Romano has been active in setting up psychology science fairs for the counties in which he teaches, and his knowledge and skills in these activities come out clearly.

Tony Romano also developed the exceptional teacher's manual and test bank that accompany *Psychology and You*. The extensive test bank is available both on reproducible masters and in computerized form.

Barbara Wiggins, another high school teacher, has provided a student workbook that is outstanding and should be yet another backup to ensure that your students grasp the material.

A very exciting educational version of the highly acclaimed videotape "The Brain" is available to adopters. This two-hour video is indexed and referenced to *Psychology and You* for easy classroom presentation.

PSYCHWARE is a software package consisting of ten programs designed to help students better understand complex concepts. Psychware is self-booting, menu driven and operates almost effortlessly. It is complete with both a teacher's guide and student guide and runs on Apple II family microcomputers. Special pricing is available to adopters of *Psychology and You*.

Every effort has been made to be sure you are getting the best possible text. Twenty-five experienced high school teachers from across the country reviewed the manuscript. They followed us each step of the way, helping smooth over the rough spots and providing a heartwarming amount of support and encouragement for the project. We can't thank them enough.

Andrew F. Agosta
North Scott High School
Eldridge, Iowa

Bill Austin
Raytown South High School
Raytown, Missouri

Edward P. Blazer
Manheim Township High School
Lancaster, Pennsylvania

Don Ceynar
Lincoln High School
Des Moines, Iowa

Janice Crilly Daniel
East Mecklenburg High School
Charlotte, North Carolina

Harry L. DeVictoria
Seaside High School
Seaside, California

Emily Flowers
Greenwood High School
Greenwood, Mississippi

Jim Fuller
Box Elder High School
Brigham City, Utah

Robert J. Fullmer
Watertown High School
Watertown, Wisconsin

Terry Holdridge
Ankeny Community Senior High School
Ankeny, Iowa

Don Kober
St. Francis High School
Holland, Ohio

Jon Pederson
Parker High School
Janesville, Wisconsin

Edith Persing
Grand Haven High School
Grand Haven, Michigan

Michael A. Plessner
Washington Community High School
Washington, Illinois

Kent Quinn
Ventura High School
Ventura, California

William H. Randolph
Grove City High School
Grove City, Ohio

Frieda Rector
Turlock High School
Turlock, California

Ruth J. Regent-Smith
Pius XI High School
Milwaukee, Wisconsin

Shirley A. Roberts
Carroll High School
Corpus Christi, Texas

Tony Romano
Fremd High School
Palatine, Illinois

Faye D. Stearns
Wicomico Senior High
School
Salisbury, Maryland

Richard Timko
Collinsville High School
Collinsville, Illinois

Cindy Vivoda
Beloit Memorial High
School
Beloit, Wisconsin

Karl Weiss
Piper High School
Sunrise, Florida

Barbara G. Wiggins
Robert E. Lee High School
Montgomery, Alabama

We would like to thank West Publishing Company for its support of this book, particularly Clyde Perlee, Carole Grumney, and Lynda Kessler, who have worked on and believed in the project. We would also like to thank Janet Bollow, who designed the text, for her creativity and energy.

Finally, we once again express our hope that you and your students will find this book as exciting to use as we did to create.

Frank McMahon
Judith McMahon

Unit One

Approaches to Psychology

You are standing on a darkened street in a run-down part of town. It is three o'clock in the morning. You don't know how you got here, but you know you are in terrible trouble. Three men in leather jackets approach you. One of them has a knife, and the other two have chains wrapped around their fists. You have to run. But your legs don't work. You're immobilized. Suddenly you spring up in bed, sweating—it was a dream. How come you couldn't escape? Why this happens is studied by psychologists and will be discussed in this book.

Your friend is playing basketball. He or she runs down the court with the ball, tries to shoot a basket, but slips, and the bottom of your friend's head smashes onto the floor. After a short period of unconsciousness, memory seems to have disappeared. What happened to it? Psychologists study this, and why it happens will be covered in this book.

A woman is being attacked by a group of boys in a crowded shopping mall parking lot. There are dozens of people around, but not one of them comes to her aid. What causes this? Such behavior also comes under the jurisdiction of psychology and will be discussed later.

You have a friend who is one of the most negative people you've ever met. All she talks about is how terrible things are for her. She seems to get worse and worse and has major bouts of depression. What causes so much gloom and doom? We will discuss this, too.

On television you saw an amazing dog act. There were four dogs doing incredible things—dancing on their hind legs, doing somersaults, and jumping through hoops. And when the trainer pointed his finger at them as if it were a gun, they all fell down and stuck their paws up in the air. How does one train dogs to do this? We will cover the answer in the chapter on learning.

As you can see, psychology examines events and behaviors that explore just about all human and animal behavior. There are hundreds more examples, but you'll find them as you go through the book. We merely wanted to give you an idea of what the field is like before beginning.

Chapter 1

The Field
of Psychology

Be able to:

1. Define psychology and describe some of the work psychologists do.

2. Explain the influence the Greeks had on psychology.

3. Explain why the Renaissance was important.

4. Describe what Wundt was trying to accomplish with his laboratory work.

5. Give an example of and describe the five different approaches of present-day psychology to understanding human nature.

Global Look at the Chapter

Psychology began as philosophy because, in ancient times, this was the only known method by which people could understand themselves. But once science started to make progress, humans began to be viewed more as machines than as secret creatures. Since then, the human body and mind have been explored in detail. In this chapter, we cover some of these explorations, trying to establish human nature as it was seen in the past and as it is understood now.

The World of the Psychologist

For most people, a psychologist is someone who sits across from you, listens to your problems, and tries to help. There are more than 50,000 psychologists in the United States, and roughly a third do in fact deal with personal problems. But that leaves two-thirds of the group doing something else. What are the rest of them doing? Well, some try to understand what the world is like for children or adolescents or older people—that is, what are their worries, hopes, needs, and so forth. Some help design spacecraft cabins so dials and switches are in the right place and so the captain in an emergency won't hit the "up" button instead of the "down" button. Still others study the effects of various drugs, while some counsel alcoholics or drug abusers. Another group works with delinquents, but others try to figure out what causes delinquency in the first place. Psychologists work in educational systems. They try to understand exactly what we measure with an IQ test (since we're still not all the way sure); they try to keep the good students moving forward and help the bad ones get themselves together; they try to improve both teaching and learning. Some psychologists handle rape and suicide crises, while others try to figure out why such things happen and how best to prevent them.

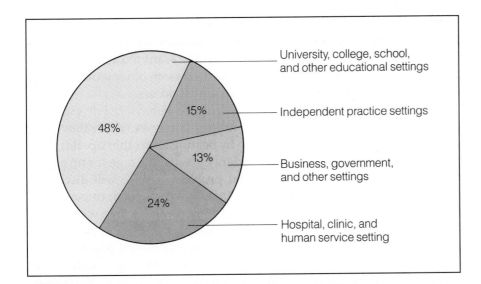

Figure 1.1
Approximate proportions of job
distribution among psychologists

University, college, school,
and other educational settings

Independent practice settings

Business, government,
and other settings

Hospital, clinic, and
human service setting

15%

48%

13%

24%

Figure 1.2
Representative areas of specialization
in psychology

Educational	Teaching
Military	Experimental
Adulthood and aging	Psychological testing
Engineering	Physiological
Rehabilitation	Developmental (children)
Community (problems and needs)	Personality and social behavior
Psychopharmacology	Clinical (abnormal)
Mental retardation	Industrial and organizational
Consumer behavior	Psychotherapy
Psychology of women	Environmental

As you have guessed by now, this list can go on and on. Figures 1.1 and 1.2 cover the major areas of psychology. And, at the end of the chapter, you'll find a fairly detailed outline of the tasks involved in some of the major fields of psychology.

Defining Psychology

At first, when we look at all the things that psychologists do, it doesn't seem possible to come up with a single definition for what psychology is. But there actually is one that fits them all: **Psychology** is the scientific study of human and animal behavior.* The term *behavior* is not used here in its simple, everyday sense. It refers to almost *any* activity. Thus, the

Psychology
The scientific study of human and animal behavior.

*Words throughout the book that are in dark **boldface** are terms that are important and for which you should know the definition.

blink of an eye is behavior, so is sweating, so is thinking. Behavior includes attitudes, thoughts, and physical changes, as well as emotional changes. We are studying behavior when we want to decide if people take drugs for psychological or physical reasons. In other words, studying behavior means trying to figure out why it occurs.

There can be many causes for a particular behavior. For example, people can be violent if they come from a family in which they have learned that arguments are dealt with by beating each other up. But there are also cases in which a person suddenly goes into a rage for no apparent reason. This might be a physical problem. As we will discuss in Chapter 3, there is a part of the brain that, when touched, causes a person to become extremely violent. About 15 years ago, a man with a brain growth that was touching this area climbed atop a tower at the University of Texas carrying rifles and ammunition and picked people off one by one. By the time the police got him, he had shot 44 people, killing 14 of them. So, psychologists study the physical as well as the purely psychological (Valenstein, 1973).†

Research Versus Applied Psychology

Depending on how close attention you were paying to the first paragraph, you may or may not have noticed that there are two basic types of psychologists. One group studies the origin, cause, or results of certain behaviors. Another group uses such information to deal with people and problems directly. Psychologists in the first group are called **research psychologists**. Since the second group makes direct use of ("applies") psychological studies, they are called **applied psychologists**. As we will discuss in Chapter 6, airlines have recently discovered a rather serious problem: Pilots are falling asleep in the cockpit as you ride along at 30,000 feet. Research psychologists who study sleep patterns and basic rhythms of the human have determined why this happens; applied psychologists consult with airlines and suggest ways to fix the pilots' schedules in order to avoid it.

Research psychologists
Those who study the origin, cause, or results of certain behaviors.

Applied psychologists
Those who make direct use of the findings of research psychologists; deal directly with clients.

History of Psychology

For our purposes, psychology has the goal of understanding the human being, how and why we operate the way we do. To understand what psychology is today and how it got there, you need a brief history. Some

†Psychology uses a special system for listing references. The last name of the author from whom certain information comes and the year he or she published that information appears in parentheses. These references are then listed in the back of the book under the author's name. (These are for reference only; do *not* try to memorize these names.)

of the things we talk about will seem downright weird. Some of the old beliefs about the world and the human were unusual, to say the least. For example, in about 3000 B.C., people thought that the moon, sun, and stars were kept in place overhead by a tin roof and that the planets were watching human beings' every behavior and controlling what happened to them.

How these beliefs came about is not hard to understand if you do a little mental experiment. In your mind, take a trip far away from where you are now into the middle of the desert where there is nothing at all within sight—no telephone poles, no soft-drink cans, no anything. Say that this is the only place you've ever known. Add to this that there are no newspapers, books, televisions—nothing. So, you are living there in the desert. Where exactly are you? How did you get there? What is it all about? You have *no* information at all; you don't know anything that we know today. Far above appear stars and an enormous moon. What are they? After a while, the sun appears, then again the stars and moon. Something so powerful is going on that it must somehow know about and control the people below.

Origins of Psychology

Psychology began as **philosophy**. Philosophy attempts to understand behavior simply by using reason, not observation or experiments. In other words, knowledge comes from arguing and discussing rather than from some kind of scientific proof. One of the most famous philosophers

Philosophy
The attempt to understand behavior by using logic and reason.

This is what the world must have looked like to the early people—there was nothing else at all.

of all time was Socrates. People out and about along a street in Athens, Greece, fifth century B.C., might run into a barefoot, flabby man shuffling along in a torn garment. This would have been Socrates. Aside from the fact that he looked so shabby, he was irritating because he kept asking, "What is it?" about everything. The problem was that he almost never gave any answers—just questions. Luckily he had a student, Plato, who did give answers about why we dream, where we came from, and how we operate (Hamilton, 1942; Wormser, 1962).

The Greeks   The Greeks were remarkable. They helped us to understand the universe and its planets, they developed scientific measuring instruments, they came up with solutions to problems of government, and they made some progress in understanding how human beings work. In fact, the word *psychology* comes from the Greek for the study of—*ology*—the mind or soul—*psyche* (SIGH-kee).

But trying to understand humans based simply on philosophy can cause a lot of mistakes, since philosophy does not have to deal with scientific proof. For example, the Greek philosopher Aristotle taught that the highest form of reasoning and thinking took place in the heart. This early claim is echoed today when a lover says, "My heart yearns for you." While the Greeks knew we had a brain, they thought of it as a big gland that was placed near the nose to help cool down the forces of life that descended from heaven and entered the body (Bergland, 1985).

The Greeks also missed on this one: If you take blood from a vein and let it sit in a glass, it separates into a blackish clot at the bottom, then a layer of yellow fluid, and finally a thin layer of white on top. This fact was the basis of the early belief that personality comes from what you have in your blood: If you have too much of the dark material ("black bile") flowing through your "tubes" inside, it makes you depressed and sad. The Greeks called this *melancholy*, a term we still use for someone who feels down and out. Too much yellow material, and you are bitter, angry, and hot-tempered. (Probably if you really did have yellow bile flowing through you, it would make you feel this way, but you don't.) Too much white material, and you become dull and sluggish. There is something to the third one, because the white part comes from cells that increase when you have an infection, which *can* make you feel thick. Still, white cells were not understood in those days, and there is no truth to this personality system (Bergland, 1985).

The Greeks thought personality could be changed by "bloodletting," using leeches or a knife to pierce the skin in order to allow evil spirits to escape. This could work—but not for the reason they thought. If you take enough blood out, a person weakens, and his or her personality seems to change for a while until he or she begins to recover. Then it's back to the old self. This removal of blood as a "treatment" was popular for a long time. George Washington in the late 1700s suffered from bouts of melancholy or depression unless he stayed active, so he often had blood removed, and he claimed that it made him feel better (Flexner, 1974).

While it is true that we can learn a fair amount about ourselves through philosophy, too many facts are missed. But you can't fault any of the Greeks because at that time there seemed to be no way really to study human beings. For one thing, no one knew how to begin, because humans were only a speck in a frightening universe. They felt overwhelmed and in the middle of something that was already beyond comprehension.

Meteorites and stars sailing through the skies were thought to be battles going on between the gods. Beliefs in such powers led to **astrology**, the prediction of human behavior by using the positions of planets and stars. Each day was controlled by one of seven different planets, in order, one after the other. This is where our seven-day week comes from: the sun—Sunday; the moon—Monday; the god of war, Mars ("tiw"-day in old English), translates into Tuesday, and so forth (Boorstin, 1983). The point is that the human was too "magical" to be fully understood, so we were lost in a world of unseen forces and magic numbers, such as the number seven (the seven planets). Rather than actually studying people, the safer way out was to make up things that sounded good even if they were not proven.

Astrology
The prediction of behavior based on the positions of the planets and stars.

Even today many believe the number seven is special. They believe there are both "lucky" and "unlucky" sevens. So many people stick "7" into their lottery choices that, if you win one with a seven in it, you often wind up sharing the pot with too many people. Try this experiment on classmates who are not in this course: Ask them to pick a number between one and ten. More than 90 percent of the time they will choose the number seven.

Almost everyone still enjoys horoscopes, which are supposed to predict your behavior based on planetary movements. As far as we know, they have no accuracy whatsoever.

The Dark and Middle Ages   From about 400 A.D. to 900 A.D., civil wars broke out all over Europe and the surrounding areas. Barbarians wandered the land killing and destroying. Chaos reigned. Greek thought, which had been so free and useful, was in danger of being lost forever. This period was called the **Dark Ages** because of its terrible effect on intellectual progress.

From 900 A.D. to 1400 A.D., various groups tried to restore order; in the process, they practically eliminated any freedom of thought. During this period, called the **Middle Ages**, science hardly moved at all. One scientist who claimed that blood circulated through the body was told that only planets could go in circles, so blood couldn't. He was given a trial, found guilty, tied to a stake, and burned alive (Bergland, 1985).

Dark Ages
400 A.D.–900 A.D.; period of chaos and civil wars when intellectual progress stopped.

Middle Ages
900 A.D.–1400 A.D.; period of little science.

The Renaissance   History seems to be a series of opposites: First things go one way, then the other, and then back again. In reaction to the Dark and Middle Ages, between 1400 A.D. and 1700 A.D. the **Renaissance** (a word meaning "rebirth") occurred. Greek thought came back, and with it came the freedom to explore new ideas as well as new places. Exploring, in turn, led to a number of scientific discoveries that are critical for understanding how psychology developed.

One of the most important findings was that the earth is not the center of the universe. Until this time, people had believed that the planets, sun, and moon were revolving around the earth for our benefit, which made humans very important. Not so. When this was found to be untrue, the human began to look a little less important in the overall picture. By 1620 the circulation of blood was finally proved correct. This finding made us look at least partly like a machine, and we no longer seemed too magical to be studied (Matson, 1964).

Further, until the Renaissance, medical information was to be found in 125 volumes, all written after studying slaughtered animals. These volumes contained such strange ideas as the belief that the human had 27 different kinds of pulse rate, including "wormlike," "wavelike," and "antlike," whatever those meant (Nourse, 1964). These medical books were all that was available. Even so, they made the human seem like a machine that could be "taken apart," so to speak. Dissection (cutting up corpses to see what is inside), which had been forbidden, began to come into its own. The business of robbing graves to provide bodies for experiments picked up. In fact, some "snatchers" pretended to be family members right after a death so they could get the body from the mortuary before the family showed up (Williams, 1987).

Moving Toward Modern Times

Psychology still had not really begun to be a science in the formal sense. But in the 1800s **Charles Darwin** went on a five-year sea journey around the world. He had two feet of walking space in his cabin and was seasick the whole time, but, when he was on land, he noted that animals he knew well at home in England had developed differently in other places according to climate or food sources. Eventually he suggested that animals, including humans, had evolved and changed. His theory has been causing argument since 1859 when it was first published. He was so worried about the effect his book might have on religion that he hid his manuscript from his wife for 14 years in fear that it would upset her (Stone, 1980; Adams, 1969). The true importance of Darwin's theory for our purposes lies not in whether it is right or wrong, but in the fact that it inspired scientists to study animals in an attempt to understand the human better, something psychologists still do all the time. Indeed, animals lower than humans do have a great deal in common with us. Although the individual units in the brain differ in size and location, the overall structure of the human brain is quite similar to that of the rat, cat, or dog. Since other animals are less complex than human beings, scientists of Darwin's era assumed that, if we understood how they worked, we could apply this information to ourselves. Thus, science was moving far beyond Aristotle, who claimed that you could tell the difference between humans and animals at least in part because we could laugh and wiggle our ears (Thomas, 1983). The rush was on to conquer both people and our world.

The Beginnings of Scientific Psychology

By the mid 1800s, then, things had really changed. It looked as if science was going to be able to understand almost everything—including the human. Our species was going to be examined and understood in detail.

This Rembrandt painting reflects a major breakthrough for science—dissection of the human body to understand how it operates.

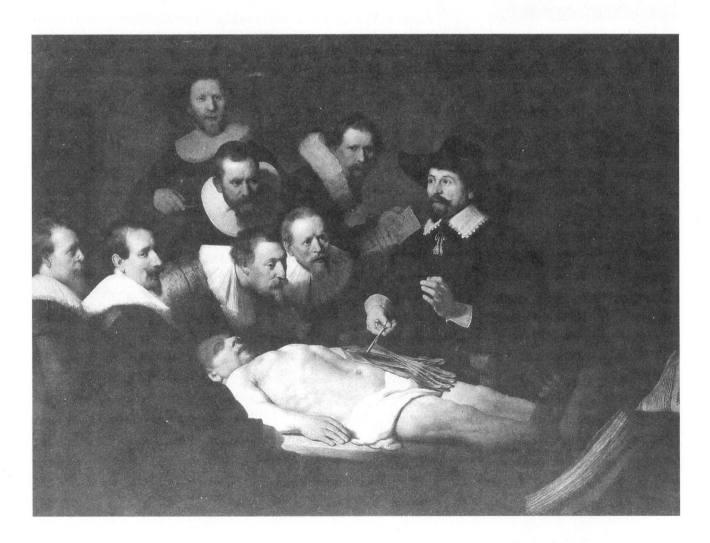

Wilhelm Wundt

At least that was the goal, but, as you know, people are more than a little difficult to pin down.

Wilhelm Wundt   **Wilhelm Wundt** (pronounced VUNT) is called the "father of psychology" because, in 1879, he started the first laboratory for studying humans. Like many famous people, he got off to a rocky start. Darwin's father, for example, had called his son a bum and had told him he was too lazy and stupid ever to amount to anything. Albert Einstein, one of the world's greatest mathematicians, kept failing high school math as well as college entrance exams. When he finally got through school, he claimed it had injured his mind. So, too, with Wundt: He spent most of his time in class daydreaming and failing, for which his teachers kept slapping him in the face (literally). Fortunately, a few teachers saw a promise of greater things in him and helped him to pull himself together. He eventually wrote so many books and articles that, if you read 50 pages a day, it would take you three years to get through them all (Adams, 1969; Snow, 1966; Fancher, 1979).

Because, in Wundt's time, sciences like chemistry were having success in breaking things down into parts, Wundt thought he might be able to break down the human mind in the same way. In other words, since chemists had found that water can be broken down into two parts of hydrogen and one part oxygen, maybe the same type of thing could be done with the human mind. If that was possible, psychology would understand the basics that go into making up our feelings and thoughts.

Wundt's idea was to train people to be very accurate in describing the sensations they got from objects they touched. For instance, if you pick up something like a shoe, what sensations (sights, smells) does it cause? What images or memories? What emotions (love, hate, distaste, and so on) does it bring out? Or, if you pick up a cat, what kinds of responses does it bring? Wundt hoped that, with responses to enough different objects, he would find certain things in common, and these would be the basic elements that humans use to build the thoughts they have.

Introspection   There is no question that Wundt had an excellent idea here. Unfortunately, it didn't work. The number of descriptions he and his assistant got kept getting larger and larger. At one point, they had 44,000 different sensations that people had described, with only a small number in common.

What went wrong? Actually, nothing. Wundt was learning that the human is so complex that mechanical measurement alone won't work. The only way anyone can deal with things like emotions and sensations is to ask people what they feel. This process is called **introspection**, which means "looking into" yourself and telling what is there (Bringmann and Tweney, 1980). Once you do that, though, rigid science becomes less rigid. Even today we have to rely on introspection when trying to get information about complex feelings.

But all was not a waste of time. Wundt and his followers showed that there are some things about the human that can be measured in a scientific fashion and that, if you are clever enough, you can get information in an objective fashion that is pretty reliable (Mueller, 1979).

Psychologists today will always try to be as objective as possible, even when they have to rely on introspection. But sometimes relying on introspection is not necessary. For instance, in Chapter 2, we will show you how an experiment is done. The issue we will deal with is an interesting one: Are males *really* better at playing video games than females? The results might surprise you, but we don't want to give them away here. In any case, such a study does not require introspection even though, as you will discover, it deals with very complex social and personal issues.

Present-Day Psychology

Since Wundt's 1879 laboratory, psychology has expanded dramatically. Many theories about what the human is and how we develop have arisen. Some have dropped by the wayside, but five approaches to the nature of the human being have survived up to the present. We will cover these theories here and again in more detail later in the book. But the first thing you will notice is that the different theories to some extent contradict one another. The fact that they do not agree is all right, however, since we don't have anything close to the final answers about human nature. Thus, each of them is a good guess with some support— but not the last word. Also, sometimes one theory will fit a particular situation where another might not. So, while most psychologists tend to lean toward one of the five theories, they often borrow here and there from other theories, making their own combination. This process is called **eclecticism** (ek-LEC-tuh-cism).

Eclecticism
The process of making your own system by borrowing from two or more other systems.

The Neurobiological Approach

Why do people behave as they do? While many view behavior in strictly psychological terms, it is possible to view behavior, as some psychologists do, as **neurobiological** (*neuro*—nerve cells + *biological*—physical, including chemical, muscular, and so on). Suppose you are on a camping trip and decide to find a secluded place under a tree just to enjoy nature. You sit down, leaning back against the tree. You are watching something to your left that has captured your attention. But then you hear a muffled noise and feel something on your right leg. You look down and, to your horror, see that a snake is using your leg as a pathway on its travels. You instinctively jump up, shaking your leg, gasping. Bad move.

While some psychologists would explain this extreme behavior as the result of learning, others (*neurobiologists*) see it differently. They explain

Neurobiological
Viewing behavior as the result of biology plus nerve cells.

The eclectic is like a child in a candy store who knows that getting only one kind of candy will not be quite satisfying enough.

it in terms of the physical changes that take place. Every time in the past that you have seen a snake or other slimy creature, your heart has started beating rapidly, you've become very nervous, and you've panicked. Over time your body has begun to respond more and more violently to seeing such creatures. In this case, the instant you saw the snake, your body took over and had a full emergency reaction.

Or, as can happen to almost anybody for no known reason, you are out shopping and are in the midst of a crowd, when all of a sudden you feel faint or dizzy. You think of the embarrassment of falling over. Nothing happens, but the next time you are at that spot in the store you begin to feel a little "funny." The second time, a neurobiological response has started. You are fearful or anxious that the dizziness might repeat itself. Again, this is not abnormal, but it does show how the body can control our feelings. As we will discuss in a later chapter, some people have let this type of thing get the better of them to the point where they have a full physiological fear response every time they try to leave the house. They have to keep returning in order to calm down (such an extreme case *is* abnormal). Thus, neurobiologists explain behavior in terms of chemical changes in the brain, such as starting a fear response when it isn't called for.

The Behavioral Approach

The **behaviorists** believe that we are the product of associations. We are the end result of all the different events we have been exposed to throughout life and of the types of responses we have made to them. Whether or not you get involved with drugs has to do only with the types of punishments or rewards that have been part of your life up to the time you make the decision. If the praise and rewards for *not* doing forbidden things have been great enough, this will successfully counteract the desire to do something forbidden, such as take drugs. On the other hand, if you have gotten attention over the years mostly for doing things that are not allowed, then the rewards for taking drugs can be greater than for not taking them.

The most famous behaviorist today is **B. F. Skinner**. His interests were away from philosophy and focused only on what could be seen. So he believed we are mechanically controlled by the environment in the sense that we become whatever the environment forces us to be—good or bad (Skinner, 1967).

In support of this theory, there certainly is evidence that we do a great number of things because we have been rewarded for them in the past. Such information is invaluable for those parents who are trying to figure out how to get started in making their offspring into reasonable human beings.

On the other hand, there are problems with this theory. For one thing, it takes away a person's "free will." In other words, if you decide "on the spur of the moment" to go get a pizza, the behaviorists say you really had no choice. Whether you went or not is the result of everything that has happened to you up to the present moment, not an impulse. Another problem is that this theory doesn't take into account what is going on in your life. If you are very attached to a person who does drugs or if you are part of a group that is involved in drugs, the pull you feel toward drugs is going to be greater than if you are close to people who don't do drugs. Thus, at times, previous learning is not as important as the present situation. Finally, the most uncomfortable aspect of behaviorist theory is that it sees us as little more than robots, a belief few of us want to accept.

Aggression: From faulty learning, unconscious impulse, or frustrated personal growth?

Behaviorists
Those who believe we are the product of associations.

B. F. Skinner

The Humanistic Approach

The **humanistic** approach to human behavior arose as a reaction to the problems we've mentioned about behaviorism. The term *humanistic* comes from *humane*. So, this group of psychologists believes that people are basically good and that our very nature is such that we could reach perfection—if all went right.

To the humanists, each of us is like the perfect seed: If we get the right amount of water, nutrients, and sunlight from the environment, we will become a perfect flower. Personal growth is internal and very individual. We are in control of our destinies, and all of us can make our lives worthwhile. Unlike the behaviorists, the humanists believe that the environment does not *force* us to become anything; instead, it acts as a background for our internal growth. How we handle the death of a loved one, for instance, is an individual thing in which we call on our own internal resources to make the best of it.

The most famous humanist was **Carl Rogers**. He was a minister for a while before he entered psychology. Possibly this influenced his beliefs, because he saw people as worthwhile creatures with free will and choice (Rogers, 1961). To him, every human had the potential to become great in his or her own (however small) way, with just a little guidance.

Carl Rogers

Some people find humanism a little too good to be true. Sometimes when we are alone and think about ourselves for a while, even the best and most "normal" of us can find thoughts and feelings inside that are quite removed from anything like the beauty of a flower.

The Psychoanalytic Approach

The best known of all theories, that of **Sigmund Freud** (FROID), considers our inner selves to be cesspools of forbidden desires. Freud developed a theory that centered around sexual and aggressive impulses that are hidden in our unconscious from early childhood. These impulses live below the surface of consciousness and from there control our everyday behavior in ways we are not aware of. For example, if you were very angry at your mother but knew better than to say anything, you might, when you call out to get her attention, say, "Oh, Bother!" The unconscious has replaced the "M" with a "B," showing your real feelings. Since these impulses are hidden, in order to understand them and have more choice about them, we have to *analyze* them with the help of a Freudian. Thus, this approach to our behavior is called **psychoanalysis**.

Sigmund Freud

Freud's theory has been popular since the early 1900s. In the last ten years, however, many psychologists have considered his theory to be too negative by itself, so they have combined it with other theories (eclecticism) that give the person more say-so in what fate has in store. In any case, Freud has been very important, and many of his ideas are still

In Focus: The Five Main Theories in Psychology

Neurobiology	Behavior viewed in terms of biological responses
Behaviorism	Behavior viewed as a product of learned responses
Humanism	Behavior viewed as a reflection of internal growth
Psychoanalysis	Behavior viewed as a reflection of unconscious aggressive and sexual impulses
Cognitive Psychology	Behavior viewed as a product of various internal sentences or thoughts

around. In a number of ways, he helped get much of psychology as a profession started, so he will be covered with the other theories as this book progresses.

The Cognitive Approach

The fifth and last approach is the most popular one in psychology today. It is called **cognitive psychology**. The word *cognition* refers to thinking or using mental processes. Once you understand that, the cognitive approach will be clear. For cognitive psychology, the most important human ability is that we can take information from the environment, analyze it, and come up with a solution to almost any problem. So, we are first and foremost thinking creatures able to compare the past with the present and make judgments. The human is special because we can change our thought patterns after looking at different problems and deciding on the best approach.

To the cognitivist, our personalities are, to some extent, made up of the different kinds of sentences (thoughts) we have inside our heads. If you pay close attention, you will notice that there are many times during the day when you are carrying on a conversation with yourself inside your head. In fact, you are, in a sense, sitting there listening while this goes on, even though it's coming from you. These sentences can sometimes get us in trouble, as when we keep saying, "This math is completely impossible to understand." The cognitivists believe that, if we replace such internal sentences with more useful ones like, "Joe Smaltz is stupid and *he* can do math; I am not an idiot, so I can, too," it will have an impact on how well we do (Hilgard, 1980; Haugeland, 1978).

A problem with the cognitive theory is that it badly downplays the effects of emotions on us. For most of us, hardly an hour goes by when we

Cognitive psychology
The study of how humans use mental processes to handle problems or develop certain personality characteristics.

don't get involved in something at least partly emotional. Hence, even though the cognitivists say we can control these by thought, they don't give enough credit to the effect of emotions on what we do.

Analyzing Your Neighbor

Strange things always go on next door or down the block. And everyone knows about them. So, we will look at the problem that John, who lives down the block, has, and we'll examine it, using each of the five approaches discussed. In this way, you'll get a better fix on how each approach views the person.

John is 40 years old and lives alone with his mother. He has never been married, but has a good job as an engineer. His life seemed to be going well—until one day a month ago his boss chewed him out for not doing something right. During the last month, John has been worried and depressed because he has started to forget things. He told his mother who told Ethel who lives next door, and now everybody knows. Here are examples of what has been happening to him: He was supposed to turn in plans for a new project, but forgot they were due. He had always remembered his mother's birthday, but it was a week ago and he forgot completely about it, hurting her, even though she pretended not to be upset. A month ago, a few days after the incident on the job, he met a woman he really liked and set up a date with her for later in the week. But he had forgotten that he was going to be out of town then, so he had to cancel the date.

Neurobiological Analysis

Psychologists know that memory is stored better if the learner is excited at the time of the event. Chemicals that aid in storage are much higher with excitement, anger, fear, or hope. But John's condition is such that just the opposite is going on: He is depressed. Depression lowers the level of brain chemicals that aid in memory. Therefore, John's memory problem is seen by neurobiologists as the result of a physical malfunction resulting from the trouble at work and other chaos in his life.

Behavioral Analysis

The behaviorists see the problem differently. When John was in grade school, he was comforted and hugged by his mother, not scolded, when he did things like forgetting to bring a book home to study for a test the next day. Not only that, but she let him stay home the next day because he "didn't feel well." So, over time, John has learned very bad habits from his early training. Something in John's present life is worrying him, just as an exam the next day used to. Now he is doing the same thing that worked well in the past: He is not forgetting textbooks, but he is forgetting other things to try to get love and attention from his mother.

Humanistic Analysis

For the humanists, John will soon continue with his fine work as an engineer. But his inner world has suffered a number of setbacks. It was going so well, but now he is more and more distracted. Exactly what is it that is causing John so much worry? His individual self has been injured. His personal growth has been slowed because he made mistakes and got upset about them and because he is starting to bring another woman into his personal life, which requires major adjustments. These distractions are causing the forgetting. But he still has the same basic internal strength and purpose. He will soon recover and get back on course if given patient understanding and a chance to regain his footing.

Psychoanalytic Analysis

The psychoanalysts focus on desires and needs such as sex and aggression. John is suffering from a conflict of wanting to stay with his mother, but knowing that, if he has a close relationship with the woman, which he also wants, he will someday have to leave home. Since the two desires cannot live side by side, he is getting more frustrated and aggressive toward others. This is shown by his forgetting his mother's birthday. But the more it goes on, the guiltier he gets, so he tries to forget this bad side of himself. He forgets many things in his effort to hide from the ongoing basic conflict raging in his unconscious.

Cognitive Approach

Cognitive psychologists focus on thinking skills rather than on previous learning or unconscious impulses. For them, John will have to sit down and take out a piece of paper and analyze (cognition) exactly what his life is like. He has to focus on the kinds of things he is saying to himself that are causing him so much trouble. For example, he is convincing himself he is forgetful. He is talking himself into hopelessness because he made a mistake at work. He is telling himself he can never do anything right. If, however, he makes a formal, logical plan of action and decides what he is going to do about this "other woman" in his life, then his memory will improve all by itself.

How to Study

SQ3R
Survey, question, read, recite, and review; a study technique that helps you organize, understand, and remember new material.

One of the most useful techniques for studying is called the **SQ3R** method (Robinson, 1941). These initials stand for survey, question, read, recite, and review. It might be of some benefit to you for us to go over the system here, with the hope that you might incorporate it into some of your own schoolwork. It may seem a little too much, but the more of these techniques you use, the better off you will be.

Survey Look over the chapter as a whole to get a feel for it. Don't try for detail at this time. First look at the major headings to see the overall outline. Then go back and look at the subheadings under each major heading. You will begin to form a general impression of the content and type of coverage the chapter includes. You are making a mental outline. You might read the summary, even though you won't understand all that it says as yet.

Question Take the topic headings and write them in question form on a separate piece of paper. Include any general questions you might have while doing this. Since you haven't read the material yet, you won't know the answers, but keep the sheets handy when you do read. Using a question format helps increase your sense of purpose or goal and makes the material more relevant to you.

Read Now read the material in order to answer your questions. To stay active and alive while you read, write down some of the answers to the questions you had. Take each major topic by itself, pausing for a short while between topics so you can keep the material orderly in your mind.

Recite During this pause between topics, *recite* (out loud—or at least mumble) to yourself the major points you have just covered. This will help you a great deal because it will make the material personal—as though it's coming from you—and it will put the material into your own mental framework where it is more likely to lodge. If you feel ambitious, an outstanding way to do this is to make up a little lecture of your own on the material.

Review After finishing the chapter, go over all the material you have written down, trying to bring it all together into a meaningful whole. Be sure you can answer all your original questions, including those from the beginning of the chapter that might have started to disappear by the time of the review. Using another person to ask you some of the questions can be helpful because it keeps your mind from drifting off the subject.

Being a Psychologist—Occupational Possibilities

In case you become interested in psychology as an occupation (which we hope will happen), here is a brief synopsis of some major areas in the field. Most of these occupations will require an advanced degree, meaning a master's degree (two to three years beyond the regular four years of college) or a doctorate (four to five years beyond the four-year college curriculum).

Clinical/Counseling Psychologists

This group works with people who have marital, personal, or mental problems, using specialized techniques to increase their clients' self-confidence and to reduce behaviors that are causing them trouble. These psychologists give psychological tests and help people to understand themselves and others better. They can work in private practice, in a mental hospital or clinic, in industry, or in a school system.

School/Educational Psychologists

This group works in the school setting. The tasks are varied. Some help design and improve the learning systems and curricula involved in education. Some work directly with the students, helping them with personal or learning problems or with the choice of a career. Others try to improve the quality of the school system as a

In psychology, one can find a job working with people of most any age group or type.

whole and act as educational advisers to the school administration.

Environmental Psychologists

This group works in industry or for the government. Their task is to study the effects of the environment on people. They look at the effects of disasters, of overcrowding, or even of toxic materials on the health and welfare of the population as a whole or on individual families. They also study such things as how best to design an environment (such as a prison) in order to benefit society by keeping those living there reasonably comfortable.

Developmental/Child Psychologists

As you will find when you read the chapter on child psychology, children live in a world all their own and have sets of rules often beyond adult comprehension. Psychologists in this area study child development, but they also often work in a clinic or private practice to help disturbed children or to help parents who are trying to understand the problems they face in living with and rearing these "foreigners."

Industrial/Consumer Psychologists

Psychologists in this area "take sides," so to speak. One group works with management to try to improve working conditions, to obtain greater efficiency from the work force, to increase sales, and to keep the corporation's image positive with the public. The other group works with the employees on any issues they might have, from difficult work conditions to problems at home.

Engineering Psychologists

Psychologists in this area work to design systems that help people become more efficient. These psychologists do everything from studying how to design the instruments on a machine or an automobile for greatest efficiency to figuring out the best physical design for a shopping mall so that people are able to get in and out efficiently and pleasantly.

Experimental Psychologists

These psychologists work in industry or universities. They perform research to understand better how the human operates physically or psychologically. This work may include the study of drugs, of physical reactions, and of the effect of certain laboratory events on human beings or animals. The goal of all of these studies is to add to the literature—the books and articles that are studied by other psychologists as well as made available to the public. For example, an experimental psychologist might try to answer the question, what leads to a heart attack?

Teaching

Teaching psychology can involve any of the above fields. That is what the authors of this book do. It's the most exciting field in the world. We hope some of you will try it someday. The rewards of communicating with others and helping them to understand are beyond belief.

Summary

1. Psychologists work in just about every setting you can imagine. About a third help people with personal problems.

2. Psychology is the scientific study of human and animal behavior. There are two basic types of psychologists—those who do research and those who apply the research.

3. The Greeks used the philosophical method to try to analyze the human. While their theories were often inaccurate, the Greeks are important because they supported freedom of thought and inquiry.

4. The Greek freedom disappeared for a while during the Dark and Middle Ages. It resurfaced during the Renaissance, the time of scientific rebirth. During this time, discoveries about the earth and the inner workings of the human set the stage for exploring the human in more detail.

5. Charles Darwin's theory in the mid 1800s suggested that animal studies might help us understand the human.

6. Wilhelm Wundt started the first human laboratory in 1879. He tried to break the human mind down into basic parts, but both our complexity and the need for introspection kept him from reaching his goal.

7. Today there are five approaches to the understanding of human behavior:
   a. The neurobiologists see behavior as mostly influenced by bodily and chemical processes.
   b. The behaviorists see us as creatures who are formed and controlled by what happens in the environment.
   c. The humanists see people as basically good and able to achieve almost anything. For them, each of us is special and in control of his or her destiny.
   d. The psychoanalysts, on the other hand, find us controlled by unconscious impulses, especially sex and aggression.
   e. The last group, the cognitivists, focus most on the thinking brain, which can talk itself into (and out of) almost any belief or behavior.

Key Words and Concepts

psychology	philosophy	Charles Darwin	behaviorioral	psychoanalysis
research	astrology	Wilhelm Wundt	humanistic	cognitive
psychologists	Dark Ages	introspection	Carl Rogers	psychology
applied	Middle Ages	eclecticism	B. F. Skinner	SQ3R
psychologists	Renaissance	neurobiological	Sigmund Freud	

Review Questions

Fill in the blank. Answer on a separate sheet of paper. (More than one word can be used.)

1. According to _____, knowledge is learned through arguing and discussing.

2. Psychologists who use research to solve practical problems are called _____ .

3. Psychologists who study the causes of behavior are called _____ .

4. The scientific study of behavior is called _____ .

5. _____ is considered the father of psychology.

True/False

6. Plato was one of the first ever to study behavior scientifically.

7. Astrology is a branch of psychology.

8. The human brain is remarkably similar to that of a rat.

9. The process of introspection helped Wilhelm Wundt categorize sensations into five main areas.

10. Eclecticism refers to a combination of psychological theories.

Matching (Answers can be used more than once.)

11. Rewards and punishments control behavior.

12. Physical changes are emphasized.

13. Humans are basically good.

14. The unconscious plays a great role in behavior.

15. The environment is all-important.

16. Humans control their own destinies.

17. One's thoughts are emphasized.

18. Chemical changes in the brain influence behavior.

19. Sexual and aggressive impulses control behavior.

20. Internal sentences directly influence personality.

a. behavioral approach

b. psychoanalytical approach

c. cognitive approach

d. neurobiological approach

e. humanistic approach

Discussion Questions

1. How could both a research and an applied psychologist possibly be involved, let's say, in reducing someone's fear of heights? Explain. Offer examples of what each type of psychologist might do.

2. In what ways is psychology similar to philosophy? In what ways is it different? Explain.

3. In your opinion, does it seem that your school promotes "Dark Ages" mentality or "Renaissance" mentality? Provide numerous examples to support your answer. Do not include any names.

4. If you were severely depressed for several weeks, would you rather have someone explain your depression to you using the neurobiological approach or the cognitive approach? Why? Explain.

5. Of the five main approaches to studying and understanding behavior (neurobiological, behaviorial, and so on), with which do you tend to agree the most and why? With which do you agree the least? Explain.

6. Maria wants to ask for a raise, but begins to sweat uncontrollably every time she even gets near her boss. Using the five approaches discussed in this chapter, briefly describe how each might explain this simple behavior.

7. You have just read about the SQ3R method of studying, and you probably have some reactions to it. Why will you or why will you *not* begin to use it? Be specific—and honest.

Activities

1. As discussed in the chapter, Socrates provided one of the initial sparks to studying behavior by asking a multitude of questions. For this first activity, we want you simply to write down 40 questions that you want answered by this text or this course. The questions can range from simple to personal to complex. Some examples: Why are my parents becoming grouchy lately—is it a midlife crisis? Do colors have any effect on a person's moods? Does ESP exist? Forty questions may seem like a lot at first, but you'll be surprised at how quickly you complete this activity, since psychology deals with so many interesting issues. Feel free to skim through the text for ideas. If your list of questions seems to end at about 25, leave it and come back to it in a day or two until you *can* complete it. It might be interesting to save this list or post it in the classroom, and at the end of the year check the questions that were answered.

2. Here's another simple activity to get you acquainted with the field of psychology. *Psychology Today* is a popular monthly magazine devoted entirely to exploring issues in psychology. It is well written, current, and highly interesting. Find a copy or two and read any three- or four-page article that interests you. Write a complete summary and include your reactions to the article. With which points do you agree, and with which do you disagree? Is the material merely research, or can it be practical, or is it both? Does the material relate to your own life in any way? In other words, make your summary *and* your reactions very detailed.

3. In the next chapter, you will learn about how psychologists gather information about behavior and the environment through scientific experimentation, and you will eventually conduct your own experiments. For now, we want you to gather information about the environment through informal observations. Visit two of the following sites (or choose your own sites): grocery store, train station, fast-food restaurant, factory, doctor's office, office building. For each site, take detailed notes on as many of the following categories as possible: (a) colors used; (b) music played; (c) arrangements of products; (d) arrangement of furniture; (e) other appropriate details you may notice.

Next, analyze your observations. *Why* does a store have red walls and low lighting? How will this influence your behavior? Does it make you want to hang around or leave quickly? Does it keep you awake or put you to sleep? Don't worry too much about the "correctness" of your analysis. The purpose of this activity is not to search for "right" answers, but merely to make you more aware of how "psychology" is all around you. One final suggestion: Some of the places you visit will be more thoughtfully designed than others, so use discretion when choosing your sites.

These are the kinds of observations you might note if visiting a grocery store: (1) Milk, located at the back of the store, is a popular item. As you walk through the entire store to get to it, you might buy other items. (2) Children's cereals are stacked on the bottom shelf so children, at their eye level, can point out the boxes to their parents. (3) Snack items are located at the checkout counter. These items are inexpensive and promote impulse buying.

You can present your analysis in one of two ways: (1) a written report where you list your observations and analyze each of them or (2) a chart on a poster that you will display in your classroom; the chart will include your list of observations followed by your analyses. Make a separate chart for each store. If you decide to do the charts, make them clear, colorful, uncluttered—and neat.

4. While reading the chapter, you were asked to try a mental experiment. Time to try another: Pretend that all your knowledge of human behavior has been completely erased. You don't know, for instance, that, traditionally, men in our society were trained to be dominant and women to be passive. Or you don't know that a clique tends to be exclusive and that its members are opposed to outsiders filtering in. You will observe all the human behavior around you as if for the first time, and you will try to arrive at some new understanding of these behaviors. Write a creative report describing your fresh observations from this point of view, and then draw some new conclusions from these observations. What you will be doing, in a sense, is developing your own psychological theory for understanding behavior based on these simple observations.

5. Ask your psychology teacher which chapter you will read next in this text. Then read that chapter using the SQ3R method of studying. The only way to determine whether this method is effective is to try it, so this will be a good opportunity. Also, you'll get a head start on your next reading assignment. Normally, when you use this method, the notes you take on a chapter will probably not be very neat since you will be the only one reading them. Just keep in mind that this time your teacher will also be reading your notes. Once you complete all the steps in the SQ3R method, write a paragraph or two describing your reactions to this method. Is it effective? Explain.

6. The end of the chapter lists several types of psychologists. Contact a psychologist who fits into one of the categories listed and interview this person. Have a list of questions prepared beforehand. Possible questions: (1) What kind of education is necessary for your particular job? (2) Would you recommend one kind of graduate school over another? (3) Are there many jobs available today in your type of work? (4) What would a typical day at work be like for you—or is there no such thing as "typical"? (5) What motivated you to enter this line of work? Write a report of your interview and include your specific reactions.

A psychological researcher in action.

Chapter 2

Methods of Psychology

Be able to:

1. Explain the overall purpose of using scientific methods.

2. Identify the independent and dependent variables, the experimental and control groups in an experiment.

3. Describe the advantages and disadvantages of survey methods.

4. Describe how naturalistic observation is done, and explain its usefulness.

5. Indicate the pros and cons of the interview method.

6. Explain what the case study method is used for.

7. Explain the purpose of the longitudinal versus the cross-sectional methods.

8. Discuss the pros and cons regarding the morality of experimenting with humans or animals.

To avoid bias and false conclusions, psychology, as a science, tries to be as objective and factual as possible in its studies. This chapter covers some of the methods that are used to gain information about people and animals without allowing the personal bias of the researcher to distort the conclusions reached.

Scientific Methods

In a year we consume roughly one *billion* dollars' worth of pain relievers such as aspirin. The forms these tablets take include buffered, coated, capsule, with "added ingredients," so-called nonaspirin aspirin (acetaminophen), and crystals or tablets that dissolve in water. You can see immediately that this is a big business involving an enormous intake of drugs. As a result, advertisers fight vigorously for every cent they can wrench from us. Their techniques often involve TV commercials with questionable "studies," using distorted charts, diagrams, and claims. How well do these products really work? The only way to find out is to perform an actual, unbiased study of the product.

Psychologists do these kinds of studies because the question immediately arises, "How much, if any, pill taking brings about a cure based on the power of suggestion?" In such a study, the goal of the researchers is to be completely objective. For instance, you would have to be careful about the age and sex of the subjects studied. Their overall health would have to be explored. If you happened to get a handful of people in the group you were studying who had a major illness or a disease that caused pain, the pain reliever would probably affect them differently than it would a person in good health but who has a headache. And you would have to determine whether it was actually the pain remedy that was responsible for the cure. As you can see, careful experimentation is very involved. Without it, we can draw no meaningful conclusions.

If we take an average of the studies in this area of pain relief, it turns out that roughly 50 percent of pain is "cured" by the power of suggestion (Frank, 1974). This is discovered when the experimenter uses one group that is given the real medicine and a similar group that is given a "medicine" with nothing in it that could cause a change. This second, "fake medicine" is called a **placebo** (pla-SEE-boh). By comparing the cure rate between the two groups, we discover that 50 percent are getting better just because they get a pill they believe will bring relief.

Placebo
A "medicine" that has no active ingredients and works by the power of suggestion.

Psychological studies provide broad scientific information about what we do, why we do it, and what changes go on during the process. Studies do not attempt to establish a "right" or "wrong" as much as to provide accurate information. For example, some people might decide that, since 50 percent of the people get better without the painkiller, this group should not take pills for a headache. That, however, would be a highly questionable judgment, because other studies show that, when people take a pill they *believe* will help them, their body chemistry actually changes to provide pain relief—even for those taking a pill that contains no pain reliever in it. Thus, fake pills can be necessary for triggering the body's own internal pain relievers.

One of our major goals in the first part of this chapter is to acquaint you with some of the terminology used in experimentation. This is best done by discussing a few different studies.

Effects of the Moon

An area of interest that has been around since ancient times is the belief that the moon influences our behavior. In fact, the word *lunacy* (insanity) comes from the word *lunar*, which means "moon."

One study compared mental hospital admissions with the phases of the moon to see if there might be some relationship between a full moon and abnormal behavior. Researchers compared mental hospital admission rates for ten days before the full moon with the rates for ten days

In this early drawing these people are being driven mad by direct influence of the moon.

after the full moon (Blackman & Catalina, 1973). They did find what seemed to be a relationship between the full moon and "lunatic" behavior.

Hypothesis

Hypothesis
A statement of the results that the experimenter expects.

We will use the above experiment to help you become familiar with the terminology used in experimentation. The researchers started with a **hypothesis** (hy-POTH-ah-sis), which is a statement of the results they expect to get. In this case, the hypothesis was that there would be a relationship between the occurrence of the full moon and an increase in mental hospital admissions.

Choosing Subjects

Subjects
People or animals on whom the experiment is conducted.

Subjects are people (or animals) on whom an experiment is conducted. In this study, the subjects were people being admitted to a mental hospital.

Variables

Variables
Factors that change in an experiment.

Every experiment has **variables**. The term *variable* refers to things that can change (vary). In the present study, the variables were the phases of the moon and the rate of mental hospital admissions. Researchers want to examine how, as one variable changes, the other changes. So, in this experiment, they asked, as the moon changes or varies, how does the admission rate vary?

Sometimes there are hidden or unexpected variables that you have to guard against. There was one in the moon study that was not discovered until after the study was over, and it invalidated the study. Hospital admissions drop over weekends. The time period right after the full moon happened to include a weekend. As a result, there was a sudden drop in admissions that was not connected with what was being studied—the moon phases. Hence, the study cannot conclude that the moon has an effect on people's mental health. When the experiment was run again, eliminating a weekend, the moon phases no longer showed up as having any influence on admissions. Researchers always have to watch out for this kind of problem (Pokorny & Mefferd, 1966).

The finding of the second study is disappointing because most of us like to believe in the exotic. To date, studies of many kinds have found that no clear connection exists between the moon and mental problems or criminal behavior, except in horror movies (Rotton & Kelly, 1985).

Some studies have so many variables that it can be difficult to know what the truth is. This is the reason that there is so much confusion about what really causes heart disease. Some scientists claim cholesterol and salt cause heart problems; others say that this is not necessarily so. The conflicting studies occur because there are likely to be hundreds of things that must fall into place to cause heart disease (weight, age, living style, family history . . .), only two of which might be cholesterol and salt intake. Since variables interact in knotty ways, sometimes salt or cholesterol shows up as a problem, sometimes not.

Most everybody believes it is possible to tell the difference between Pepsi and Coke even if blindfolded. That is not true; most people can't.

A Study of Social Behavior

To acquaint you with some more terms, we want to examine behavior when people buy or sell used cars. Aside from the terms, the information may be of some use to you. Everyone must be armed with either psychology or bravery to enter the lair of the used-car salesperson.

Research: Buying and Selling

Table 2.1 Effect of Asking and Selling Prices on Final Price Paid

Seller's Asking Price	Average Amount Buyer Paid
Extremely high	$1,302.60
Moderate	$1,189.13

Buyer's First Offer	Average Amount Seller Received
Extremely low	$1,221.01
Moderate	$1,368.78

Subjects in an experiment were divided into "buyers" and "sellers." They were to write down the prices that they wanted to buy or sell a used car for and pass them back and forth through the experimenters until both the buyer and seller agreed on an amount. Unknown to the subjects, the experimenters were substituting *their own* versions of the asking price or the offer, so they could study the effects of an extreme versus a moderate first request on the final accepted sales price. What happened is shown in Table 2.1, which gives the average prices that actually would have been paid.

As you can see, the accepted sale price largely depended on whether the original suggestion was extreme or moderate (Worchel & Cooper, 1983; Chertkoff & Conley, 1967). When the initial asking price was way too high, the buyers eventually paid more for the car than they did when the seller set a more reasonable or moderate price in the beginning. If the buyer's first offer was way too low, the sellers wound up getting less for the car than they did when the buyer made a more realistic bid to start with.

The psychology of this system works like this: If you offer someone $100 for something actually worth $300, the figure is seen as ridiculous, *but*, when you then offer $200, you have gone up a full $100 and seem to be really giving in, even though you're not. The seller is then put into the position of feeling ridiculous if you are willing to "give in" so much. The moral is to not be too reasonable at the very beginning—unless, of course, you are dealing with a friend.

Variables: Dependent and Independent

This study shows the importance of two special kinds of variables that are part and parcel of scientific experiments. The first is called the **dependent variable**, meaning that it will change depending on what some other factor does. For instance, does the final sale price depend on the original asking price? Clearly yes, so the final sale price is the dependent variable. In other words, the results you get depend on what else has happened. What has happened is that the **independent variable** has changed. In this case, as the experimenters changed the asking price or

Dependent variable
That which changes as a result of what the experimenter does with the independent variable.

Independent variable
That which the experimenter does that has an effect on the dependent variable.

first offer (the independent variable), the final price of the sale or purchase changed (the dependent variable).

Field Experiments

Not all experiments are carried out in the laboratory. If they are not, they are called **field experiments**, meaning they happen away from the laboratory or "in the field."

Field experiments
Research that takes place outside the laboratory.

Studying Jet Lag

As we will discuss in Chapter 6, a current and serious problem is the effect of the jet aircraft's speedy transportation on pilots and passengers. The disturbances created are called "jet lag" because the rhythm of the body lags behind (or runs ahead of) the time of day it would be at the person's place of departure. In other words a person is still on the time at home while engaging in activities being done on a different schedule at a different place (eating lunch at 4 P.M, for example). The body is very sensitive to any kind of shift in the time of day when we eat, sleep, or work. The result of major shifts in time are fatigue, stomach distress, dizziness, feeling "awful," and mental confusion.

This man avoided the pitfalls of jet lag by never getting off the ground.

One way that jet air travel causes disruption in the normal cycle of behavior is by flying across the ocean. Flights across the ocean are usually made at night. The airlines claim that the passenger will arrive at his or her destination "ready for a day's work." That's not really true. Here's what actually happens. If you leave from New York and are flying east, you will cross five time zones and arrive in Europe five hours out of synchronization with your own body's time. Thus, arriving at 9:00 A.M. London time actually has you at 4:00 A.M. at home. Your body is operating on home time. And 4:00 A.M. is the low point in the day for almost everyone; it is the time when your body is least able to cope with any kind of stress. It will take you at least several days to get into synchronization with London time, yet you are expected to operate at full efficiency right away, when you are weakest and least able to do so (Moore-Ede et al., 1982). So this shift in light and darkness and the changes in habits that it causes will create all the symptoms associated with jet lag. These effects have been demonstrated over and over and are the subject of considerable concern, even when they involve shorter time zone changes such as those that result from crossing the United States. But perhaps some people are still skeptical of these claims. How do we set up an experiment that will clearly show the problem comes from rhythmic changes rather than just from the fatigue of flying itself?

To examine whether the effects arise from disruption of body rhythms, the scientist uses the same experimental procedures that are followed inside the laboratory. To illustrate the effects are not from fatigue, the experimenters can look at the different reactions of two groups of subjects. The first group will fly to Europe, crossing the time zones. This group is called the **experimental group**, since the critical part of the experiment is being performed on them. A second group is needed, however—one that does *not* cross time zones. In this way, we can note how the two groups differ from the effects of the trip. So, we have to **control** the critical part of the investigation, the flying across time zones. "Control," then, refers to removing, for one group, the factor being studied. (Note that this was done in the study on pain relievers: One group was given a "medicine" that did not contain any medically active ingredients so that it could be compared with the group that received the real painkilling medications.) Thus, we form what is called a **control group** that flies an equal time and distance but to South America. The shift in light and darkness, and the alteration of sleep and eating times *do not* occur for this group because there is no time change.

What we discover is that the control group does not suffer the physical effects of time changes, which show up dramatically in the experimental group. Hence, we have demonstrated that the problems come from time changes, not the length of the flight itself.

To go over it once more: The independent variable is the alteration of the usual light-dark cycle by using a time-changing flight path, and the dependent variable is the result of the alteration: fatigue, trouble making decisions, and disturbances of the body's rhythmic cycles. The control

Experimental group
The group on which the critical part of the experiment is performed.

Control group
The group that does not participate in the critical part of the experiment.

group, which does not undergo the specific factor we are studying, is then contrasted with the experimental group—which *does* undergo the critical variable.

Fighting Insomnia

So many technical terms can be difficult to grasp at first, so we will review them with an additional experiment. In this one, we want to determine if people who have trouble sleeping (insomnia) can be helped by taking a "sleeping pill" before going to bed.

The experimenter assembles two groups of insomniac subjects and administers sleeping pills to one group and placebos to the other group. Here is the experimental set up and the results:

Hypothesis   *X* amount of sleeping pills helps the healthy but insomniac person to sleep better.

Subjects   The subjects of the experiment are two groups of people with similar physical health, age range, and sleep problems.

Independent Variable   (This is the variable that the experimenter changes.) The experimenter regulates the "medicine," with one group receiving genuine sleeping pills while the other receives a placebo.

Dependent Variable   (This is what results from the experimenter's varying or changing the independent variable.) The results can *vary* among better sleep, worse sleep, or about the same amount of sleep.

Control   (This is the removal of factors that might cause the results, even though they are not the independent variable.) The experimenter will not use people who are sick, people with severe allergies, or people who are very old. Any one of these factors could alter the real effects of the medicine in the average person with insomnia.

Control Group   (This group consists of the subjects who are like the experimental group except for the crucial part of the study.) The control group in this study consists of those subjects who receive a placebo, thinking it is a sleeping pill.

Experimental Group   (These are the people who participate in the crucial part of the study.) The experimental group consists of those subjects who get *X* amount of sleeping pills.

Results   The hypothesis turns out to be incorrect in a real-life study. Thus, we reject the hypothesis that those who receive the sleeping pill will sleep better. What is found is that subjects taking the sleeping pill over a period of days will still have the same insomnia, only worse. And the sleep they do get is worse (less restful) than the sleep the control group gets.

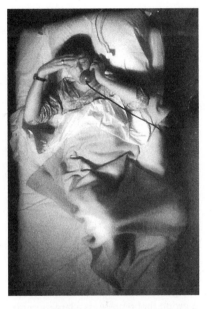

Insomnia can make the night so long we seek some type of social contact.

These results occur because most tranquilizers and sleeping pills interfere with dreams; they cause the person to feel worse because, without dreams, sleep loses most of its "curative effect" (Hartmann, 1984). This subject is discussed in more detail in Chapter 6.

Other Methods for Studying Behavior

In this section, we want to acquaint you with other methods that psychologists use to study behavior.

Survey Method

Survey
A method of research using questions on feelings, opinions, or behavior patterns.

A **survey** involves asking questions of a carefully selected group of people. This allows you to gather information on feelings, opinions, or behavior patterns. Surveys can be done by mail (using questionnaires), in person, over the phone, or via television using a responding device set up in the home. Which method is used is not as important as the kind of people chosen to participate in the research. Suppose we wanted to find out if people think that there is too much crime and that the prison sentences given criminals are too light. If, say, 30 percent of our sample is comprised of ex-convicts, we will get a distorted view of people's opinion on this subject—to say the least.

Sample
A group that represents a larger group.

Since we can't interview everyone, a **sample** must be chosen that represents the general population. The sample should be composed of a correct proportion of people from various races, sexes, social classes, and age groups. If properly selected, a sample can produce results that are amazingly accurate. The Gallup poll, for instance, is careful to include people from all the various groups. As a result, since 1950, the poll has missed the actual presidential election results only a remarkably low 1.6 percent of the time (Myers, 1983).

The way a question is phrased can also be of major importance. Advertisers are infamous for phrasing questions in such a way that they get results favorable to their point of view. For instance, an advertiser might ask, "Which aspects of car X [the advertiser's car] do you like better than car Y?" This question forces a biased answer. After the survey, the advertiser places ads that ignore the original question and how it was phrased and, instead, say something like, "Ninety percent of people surveyed said they preferred car X over car Y!" Such advertisers would be afraid to ask the more meaningful question, "Do you prefer car X or car Y?"

Using a questionnaire sent out through the mail can pose a big problem that may distort the results—namely, filling out the questionnaire takes time and trouble. Hence, many people will not bother to fill it out and mail it back. Usually only those with an ax to grind or a special devotion to the issue will go to the trouble of responding. Some surveys get as few as 20 to 30 percent of the questionnaires returned. It is hard to put much faith in such a low response rate. Too many opinions are missing.

Naturalistic Observation

In **naturalistic observation**, researchers secretly observe the subjects of the study—animal or human—in daily activity, carefully recording their behavior. The advantage to this method is that the creatures will behave as they normally do, since they don't know anyone is watching them. Both people and animals behave differently in the presence of an outsider. Thus, it is possible to get more realistic information on behavior through naturalistic observation. For example, observing male and female monkeys interacting with one another and as a "family" shows that males do a great deal more pushing and shoving of one another than do females, a situation similar to that found among humans. If the monkeys are in the laboratory or are aware of your presence, they do not act out their full repertoire of behavior. For humans, as we will discuss in Chapter 20, laboratory studies on the effects of violent TV strongly suggest that such TV shows cause violent behavior to increase. On the other hand, naturalistic observation of people after viewing violence yields results that don't always match the laboratory results; in some cases, people become less violent after a violent program. Thus, a whole different perspective is provided by this method.

On the other hand, one of the flaws with naturalistic methods is that the observer is not able to talk with or interact with the human subject. In some cases, the observer may be making an incorrect interpretation of exactly what is going on since the subject is never asked.

Naturalistic observation
A research method that involves studying subjects without their being aware that they're being watched.

Interviews

A common method for studying people and how they feel about things in the present is to **interview** them. Quite a bit of personal, detailed information can be obtained using this technique. The biggest problem here is trying to sort out fiction from fact, since the interviewee is going to be on his or her best behavior and will try to present information in the most favorable light. More often than not, for example, when people are asked what kind of television they watch, they will claim they are glued to the set viewing educational material on public TV rather than a soap opera or a blockbuster film filled with murder, mayhem, and mischief. If what they told us were true, public television would be making lots of money, which it never is, and the commercial networks would be broke, which they are not. Even so, a fair amount of reasonably accurate personal data can be gained through the interview.

Interview
A research method that involves studying people face to face and asking questions.

Another problem is that the interviewer always has to be on guard against his or her own biases in a face-to-face situation. All of us carry around subtle and not-so-subtle prejudices against certain types of people, certain age groups, certain modes of dress, and so forth. There is no doubt that these factors have an influence not only on the types of questions we ask but also, and more important, on the interpretation we give to an answer. An answer that might seem clever or original from interviewee A might be interpreted as flippant or rude coming from interviewee B.

Case Study Method

Case study method
Research that collects lengthy, detailed information about a person's background, usually for psychological treatment.

The **case study method** involves developing information about a person's long-term background for purposes of psychological treatment. The goal is to find out as much about how the personality has evolved from the early years as possible in order to shed light on what might be the origin of present-day problems. Again, this method is subject to the same distortion as the interview, but it is still a useful way to get a rough idea of how a person views the world. People who are very pessimistic might not know they are giving away the fact that they see most things so bleakly, but, if you talk to them for even a short period of time, you get clues that suggest the presence of this attitude. If you are lucky, you will also get some background information that suggests how they grew into such black-cloud creatures.

In real life, the psychological interview or case study method is most often used to get an overall sense of how a person approaches problems and of what his or her general feelings are; the psychologist generally doesn't rely too much on the specific content of what a person claims is the truth.

Psychological Tests

Psychological tests
Observation and measurement of the subject using objective measures (as opposed to an interview).

One way to overcome bias in an interview is to use objective **psychological tests**, such as the IQ test. All of us have experienced the phenomenon of being deceived by people we meet for the first time. They seemed to be very stupid (or bright), but later we discover that we have misjudged them just because they looked the way they did or dressed in a certain fashion. Problems of this kind can be avoided by using the IQ test, since it has a fixed set of questions *and* answers for scoring. It leaves no room for personal bias to enter into the interpretation of the results. The test takers either answered the questions correctly or they didn't. In a way, then, the psychological test is a kind of fixed, rigid interview with minimal opportunity for personal distortion. As we will discuss in Chapter 9, the test is a much better method than the interview for finding out a person's intellectual potential.

Tests of personality or job aptitude are again more objective than the interview, but, when we move into these rather vague areas, the tests often are not as useful as observation of a person on the job or in interaction with others. Too often people exaggerate the amount of information these tests provide. Such tests cannot predict behavior in the complex human with a high degree of accuracy, even though they can uncover important information that might be missed in an interview. The best of all worlds, then, is to combine and compare the results of both the interview and the psychological test.

Longitudinal and Cross-Sectional Studies

In addition to the fact that there are all these different methods for investigating behavior, you should be aware that there can also be different goals behind the investigation. For example, researchers might want to know what feelings large groups have regarding a problem that is current today, but they are not concerned with how the opinions developed or changed over time. Then there are other cases in which researchers want to examine a pattern over time in groups in order to observe the changes that might occur. For example, you may have heard that intelligence notably declines with age. This seemed to be true from early studies examining the issue. How were these studies done? Since the goal was to compare intelligence levels for people of different ages throughout the life span, the experimenters took subjects from different age groups, running from late childhood through old age, administered IQ tests to each age group, and then looked at how the results changed from one age group to another. This technique is called the **cross-sectional method** because a cross section (or representative sample) was taken from each major age group.

These findings on intelligence, however, turned out to be incorrect. There was a major flaw in the way the study was designed that no one saw at first. Using the cross-sectional method required that the researchers use different people from each age group. Therein lay the problem. The older people in the sample were from a generation that did not know as much as the generation following it. It seems that your generation will know more than we do, that we know more than our parents did, that our parents knew more than their parents, and so forth. (As long as we have to face up to this, we take some consolation in the fact that *your* children will know more than you do.) As a result, the cross-sectional method was measuring and comparing the older people, who had less knowledge to begin with, with younger people, who had more information. Thus, it *appeared* that, as a person got older, intelligence declined.

How was the error discovered? To understand, you need to know that there is another system of conducting studies, called the **longitudinal method** (lon-juh-TUE-di-nal). In the longitudinal method, the research-

Cross-sectional method
A method of research that looks at different age groups at the same time in order to understand changes that occur during the life span.

Longitudinal method
A method of research that studies the same group of people over an extended period of time.

In Focus: Methods of Research

	Advantages	Disadvantages
Laboratory Experiments	Researcher can be completely objective. Usually provides accurate information.	Often difficult to control all variables.
Field Experiments	Setting is more realistic than in a laboratory.	Often difficult to control all variables.
Survey Method	Can gather information on feelings, opinions, and behavior patterns. Can be amazingly accurate.	Survey's sample may not be representative of population as a whole. Questions used may not be phrased objectively. Results can be presented with distortions.
Naturalistic Observation	Behavior studied is completely natural.	Researcher cannot interact with subjects and may interpret subjects' responses incorrectly.
Interviews	Researcher can obtain personal, detailed information.	Subjects' responses may not be completely honest. Researcher's biases can influence behavior.
Case Study Method	Provides background information that may shed light on present behavior.	Subjects' responses may not be completely honest. Researchers' biases can influence behavior.
Psychological Tests	Provides accurate, objective information—little chance of distorting results.	Tests limited in the amount of information they can obtain.
Longitudinal Method	Necessary for certain kinds of research, such as studies on development.	Expensive and time consuming.
Cross-Sectional Method	Samples used are usually representative of population as a whole. Less expensive and less time consuming than longitudinal method.	Not appropriate for some types of research, such as studies on developmental changes over time.

ers follow the *same* group of people through the years, measuring them over and over from time to time. You can immediately see why this method is not used very often, given the great number of years and the expense involved. But sometimes it is necessary, as in this example about intelligence or in child development studies.

When the longitudinal studies were applied to the *same* group of people over the decades, researchers discovered that the cross-sectional studies were wrong. They found that, in general, people maintain approximately the same level of intelligence as they age. Of course, there is a slowing of reaction time and a moderate amount of memory loss when a person is quite old, but overall there is little decline in a person's mental abilities over the life span. Similar studies show that old people who are cranky, selfish, forgetful, and rigid in old age were that way when they were 30 and often when they were 15 years old.

Most psychological studies are cross-sectional, but every now and then longitudinal studies still appear today.

Ethics of Experimentation

Throughout this book, you will read studies that have required deception of subjects or the deliberate creation of frustration and anxiety in people to see how they react in certain situations. These studies are justified on the grounds that we are seeking more information about the human being. The more knowledge we have of ourselves, the better off we probably will be, and the more likely it is that we can be helped or that we'll understand problems that arise.

But serious issues come up with this kind of research. How far can and should an experimenter go in trying to find answers? For example, in Chapter 21, we will discuss an experiment designed to determine the causes of deplorable conditions in prisons. The experiment in question was performed with college students, and, for a time, it *literally* turned the college-student "guards" into vicious people and the college-student "prisoners" into helpless, miserable creatures. After the experiment, there was greater understanding of what causes prison conditions, but some of the subjects were psychologically scarred from finding out that they could act the way they did. Was it ethical and worth it? We don't know; the matter is still being argued back and forth.

Ethical Principles

The American Psychological Association has established ethical guidelines for experimenters. We want to cover the main points here so that you can make your own decisions about what is ethical (American Psychological Association, 1973).

1. *Human participants must leave the experiment unharmed either psychologically or physically.* This sounds straightforward enough, but it is sometimes hard to decide where harm to the person begins in the quest for scientific understanding. For example, is it legitimate to scare people in order to understand how the body responds to fear? Where do we draw the line?

2. *Openness and honesty are essential to experimentation.* Here is a typical problem in this area: Studies have been designed to examine under what circumstances a subject will cheat. The subjects are observed—unknown to them—in situations where cheating is possible. If the experimenter is honest with them, they will know they are being observed and will not cheat. How do we conduct this kind of study and still remain ethical?

3. *Subjects must always have the right to decline participation in an experiment.* This ethical principle is rarely violated. No one ever should be forced to take part in an experiment. Still, there can be that hidden pressure: "If I don't participate, what will the teacher think of me? Will he or she lower my grade?"

4. *The experimenter has the duty to see that any undesirable consequence of the experiment is removed before the subject is released from the study.* This rule covers the issue of any long-term effects from a study. If an experimenter does a study in which subjects are made to feel inferior (as would be the case with a deliberately difficult "IQ test"), then the subject must be told the true nature of the test at the end of the study. Sometimes, however, as in the prison-guard experiment, the damage has already been done, and there doesn't seem to be any way to help the person forget how he or she felt or behaved during the experiment itself.

Experimentation with Animals

People all over the country are expressing concern about experimentation with animals. Since animals have many things in common with humans, they are frequently studied in order to find out more about us. At the same time, since they do have things in common with us, they are not merely objects or abstract creatures with no feelings. Some people believe that any physical or psychological suffering caused an animal must be aimed at removing a problem in the human that is equal to or greater than the unpleasantness caused the animal (Fox, 1983).

Some have pointed out that, as the brighter creatures, humans have a moral obligation to protect animals rather than use them. Another concern about using them is that, since animals are part of the ecology of the whole planet, scientific researchers must show basic respect for them.

Otherwise, scientists will not be taken seriously as individuals trying to foster the greater good of the world (Fox, 1980b).

Fortunately, the bulk of evidence obtained about the majority of experiments in psychology suggests that animal treatment is humane, but humans must always be on guard against abusing their power over a helpless creature (Coile & Miller, 1984).

We hope you can tell by reading this book that we love psychology but that we also love animals. We have tried to avoid mentioning experiments that seemed cruel because we don't want to give any more publicity to people who would do such things. In a few cases, however, we have not been in a position to decide for certain whether an experiment involved cruelty; in these cases, we have given the researcher the benefit of the doubt. We report only those studies that seem to be useful—and then we cross our fingers and continue to worry about it.

Socialized Sex Differences?

There is no hotter topic among the general population as well as in the scientific world than the one regarding the differences between the sexes. We will discuss this in some detail in Chapter 12, but overall we find that there are far more similarities between the sexes than differences. One area of difference does stand out, however, and this is called **spatial ability**. Spatial ability is the ability to imagine how things look in space and to manipulate these objects mentally or physically. Thus, playing video games is a good measure of this characteristic. By and large, males take delight in the fact that females, as a group, don't compare well with males on this task. While we can't disagree with this fact, it clearly requires a more detailed examination. One of the major criticisms of the suggestion that innate differences are involved is the possibility that females either aren't interested in tasks involving spatial skills or, more likely, that society puts pressure on them to stay away from such activities.

We want to go through a real experiment on video games and male-female skills. The goal is to try to help you think through the basic problem and some of the issues that come up along the way in such a study. Then we'll give you the results of the study (Gagnon, 1986).

Fifty-eight students at Harvard University participated in the

Are females really inferior in video game-playing skills?

study, 34 males and 24 females. The purpose of the exploration was to determine if practice made any difference in video-game skills. If females don't play the games very often, could this be a factor in their relatively poor performance? In the study, one of the tasks to be performed was to play a video game called "Targ," which involves moving a spaceship through a maze while fighting off enemy ships.

As we proceed, asking each question, try to answer it for yourself before reading on.

What is the first step in the experiment?

First an hypothesis is formed and subjects are selected. In this case, subjects were categorized as "expert" or "novice" on video-game playing to form a background for analyzing their results later on.

Do you need a control group?

Yes. A control group was used that got no practice after a pretest of their skills on the machine. Using a control group reduces the possibility of any other factors influencing the results. The control group, then, took the pretest on the machine to establish a starting point, did nothing in between, and then took a posttest on the machine. The experimental group took the pretest, got two and a half hours practice on the machine over the period of a week, then took the posttest on the machine to detect whatever changes might have occurred.

Here is what the experiment looked like in diagram form:

Experimental group: Pretest → 2½ hours of playing → Posttest

Control group: Pretest → wait during week → Posttest

Before starting, the experimenter would not have done the task properly if she hadn't obtained as much information on the subjects' school histories as possible. *What might she need to know, given that society might be influencing the results? That is, what school courses does society consider "masculine" and might be related to these skills?*

The experimenter obtained from the subjects information regarding the math, science, or "engineering"-type courses they had taken, since these courses could be related to spatial skills.

What were the results of the study?

With practice, the improvement rate for females was such that there was no significant difference in learning between males and females. In other words, females clearly can learn such skills rapidly. The second finding suggested: Spatial skills are something that improve with practice and that cumulatively get better over time. Third finding: The number of math and science courses taken is related to improvement in video-game skills. Fourth: The control group did not improve in their skills (which was to be expected, but was a necessary check).

This study has clear social significance. It strongly implies that we are dealing with a socially-induced difference in spatial skills between males and females rather than with some kind of innate difference. In and of itself, the study is not conclusive, but it adds a bit of information to the broad study of male and female differences and helps call into question the assumption that females are less capable of dealing with so-called masculine pursuits of this type.

Summary

1. In the scientific method of psychological experimentation, first the hypothesis is formed and the subjects are chosen; then they are divided up into an experimental group and a control group.

2. A variable is any factor in an experiment that changes. The variable that is regulated by the experimenter is the independent variable. The second variable is the dependent variable, which is the change that occurs as a result of what the experimenter does with the independent variable.

3. Field experiments are conducted away from the laboratory, but they still adhere as much as possible to the rigid rules of experimentation.

4. A survey is used to ask questions of carefully selected people in order to understand opinions and feelings. The questionnaire is one such method, but it may not be too effective if administered by mail.

5. Naturalistic observation avoids interfering with the subject's behavior and focuses on hidden observation in order to record how the creature behaves when not aware that it is being watched.

6. The interview involves the face-to-face collection of people's ideas, actions, background, or behavior. The case study is somewhat similar in that it collects specific background information covering greater period of years in order to help develop a picture of the person, usually to aid in psychological treatment.

7. Psychological tests are completely objective methods of gathering information about people. The questions are determined beforehand, and the range of answers is restricted.

8. The longitudinal method of research requires considerable time and expense. The same group of people is examined over and over during a lengthy period of time, often many decades. The cross-sectional method also studies the effects of time, but it uses people from different age groups and tests them all at the same time in order to provide the desired information.

Key Words and Concepts

placebo
hypothesis
subjects
variables
dependent variable
independent variable

field experiments
experimental group
control group
survey
sample
naturalistic observation

interview
case study method
psychological tests
cross-sectional method
longitudinal method
spatial ability

Review Questions

Read the following sample experiment and fill in the blanks. Answer on a separate sheet of paper.

Psychologists wanted to find out if people are less likely to help in an emergency if there is a full moon. An "emergency" situation (a flat tire) was staged for 20 males and 20 females, all in cars. One-half of the subjects (group A) was tested when there was a full moon. The other half (group B) was tested when the moon was not full. Helping was defined as "seeing the flat tire, stopping, and getting out of the car to assist in any way."

1. Hypothesis = _____
2. Subjects = _____
3. Dependent variable = _____
4. Independent variable = _____
5. Control group = _____
6. Experimental group = _____

True/False

7. Placebos have some medicinal ingredients but not enough for the brain to detect.
8. The experimental group is exposed to the independent variable.
9. The control group is exposed to the dependent variable.
10. The control group is not exposed to the independent variable.

Matching: Choose the answer that best *fits the description. (Answers can be used more than once.)*

11. Results can be easily distorted to mislead others
12. Minimizes the chance of personal bias distorting results
13. Researcher has to be careful about own biases
14. A representative sample from each age group is taken
15. Subjects can act "normally"
16. Subject's past is studied in order to help with present problems

a. psychological tests
b. interviews
c. longitudinal method
d. survey method
e. naturalistic observation
f. cross-sectional method
g. case study method

17. Not very useful for studies on long-term development
18. Able to study only a sample of the population
19. Can be expensive
20. Information is gathered objectively
21. As this is a face-to-face situation, subject may put up a false front
22. Gathers lengthy information about a subject's background
23. Subjects studied for a long period of time
24. Researcher does *not* interact with subjects

Discussion Questions

1. In your own words, explain the conclusion of the "buyer and seller" experiment. Then provide an example of how you could apply this information to your own life. For example, a teacher who decides that he or she really wants students to work hard may assign an enormous amount of homework. When students finally complain, the teacher reduces the workload quite a bit—which makes him or her seem flexible—yet the workload is *still* high, which is what the teacher wanted in the first place.

2. Let's say that you started off conducting an experiment on why people do not help in emergencies. Immediately after the experiment is completed, you decide to interview those people who did not help. What potential problems might you have with these interviews? Explain.

3. The chapter describes several methods that psychologists use in their research. If you wanted to study the effects of alcoholism on the family, which of the methods described would you use to study this and why? Explain. Briefly describe how you might conduct this research. Why would you probably *not* conduct your research in the laboratory?

4. Which method of research would you probably use to study the effects of mild stress on job performance? Explain. Briefly describe how you might conduct this research.

5. Leo is an animal rights activist. He believes we should stop *all* experimentation on animals and find alternative means. He argues that, if animals somehow could choose, they certainly would not choose to be part of the experiments. They suffer; they are part of the ecology; they should be given greater rights. Sam, on the other hand, believes we should experiment on animals as much as we like. He argues that only with this attitude will we ever find vaccines and cures that will improve the quality of life. He admits that animals will obviously not experience this quality life at first, but, in the long run, even they will benefit. Both of these views are extreme, but with whom do you tend to agree and why? Explain.

6. The chapter presents the stereotype that males are better than females at video games and then explains that, if males *are* better, it is because they have had more practice. List three other stereotypes about sex differences; then tell whether you believe each is true and explain why or why not.

Activities

1. The magazine *Psychology Today* often includes reports on experiments that have been conducted recently. Skim through several issues of the magazine and find information about three experiments. Briefly summarize each experiment, and then identify the following: the hypothesis, the subjects, the dependent variable, the independent variable, the control group, and the experimental group. Do the experiments seem to meet the ethical guidelines established by the American Psychological Association? Explain.

2. Here's a chance to conduct your own experiment! Reread the "buyer and seller" experiment described at the beginning of the chapter. Instead of having your subjects buy or sell a car, you will have them buy or sell an album or a compact disc—whichever you choose to use.

Part One Procedure: Get a friend to sit on one side of you, and another friend to sit on the other side. Assign one to be a buyer and the other a seller. Read the following instructions to them:

> *"Seller, you bought an album, but when you got home and played it, you realized that you didn't like it at all. You now want to sell it to the buyer here. You will write down an amount that you want to sell the album for,*

> *show it to me, and I will show the amount to the buyer. Buyer, you will then return with another amount and show it to me, and I will show the price to the seller. You will both continue doing this until you can agree on a final price. In other words, you will both be negotiating for the best price possible for yourselves, and I will be relaying your prices back and forth. Neither of you can talk throughout the negotiation."*

You will have your own little pieces of paper on which you will write the prices. The seller will show you his or her first price. Regardless of what the price is, you write "$25—no tax," and show it to the buyer. Next, flip this sheet to the bottom of your stack so no one sees it. Then, from this point on, accurately relay all the prices given to you. Record the final selling price. Repeat this entire procedure two more times on four other friends. In other words, you will use six friends altogether for this part of the experiment, and you will record three final selling prices.

Part Two Procedure: Use six new subjects. Follow the same procedure as for Part One, but this time change the seller's initial selling price to a more moderate "$8" instead of "$25—no tax." Again, record the final selling prices.

What was the average amount that the buyers paid in Part One? In Part Two? Compare and contrast these two amounts. Did you get the same results as in the experiment described in the chapter? Draw several conclusions as to why you think you got the results that you did. Were there any particular problems you had with conducting the experiment? Explain.

Since this is your first experiment, a few general comments are in order. For an experiment to be valid, subjects should be chosen randomly; therefore, you would not use your friends as subjects. So, when we suggest that you conduct an experiment and then we tell you to use your friends, we are using the term "experiment" lightly. Also, more than 5 or 10 or 15 or 50 subjects are usually needed for an experiment to be considered representative of the population as a whole. If we were to enforce these and all the other strict guidelines needed to conduct a valid experiment, it would probably take most of the fun out of it for you. So, what we have done for this experiment— and for all the other suggested experiments·in the activity sections in this book—is to encourage you to use a certain degree of correct standards without (we hope) going too far.

3. The following experiment is a direct variation on the one in number 2. Follow the same procedures and answer the same questions at the end, except use the following instructions instead:

"Seller, you bought an album, but when you got home and played it, you realized that you did not like it at all. You now want to sell it to the buyer here. Buyer, you will write down the amount that you want to buy the album for and show it to me, and I will show the amount to the seller. Seller, you will then return with another price and show it to me, and I will show it to the buyer. You will continue doing this until you can agree on a final price. In other words, you both will be negotiating for the best price possible for yourselves, and I will be relaying your amounts back and forth. Neither of you can talk throughout the negotiation."

Half the time (for three of your buyers), you will write down "$5" as the buyer's initial offer; the other half of the time, you will write down "$.50" as the buyer's initial offer.

If you decide to do both this activity *and* the one in number 2, compare and contrast your results.

4. As noted in this chapter, surveys gather information on feelings, opinions, or behavior patterns. Write your own ten-item survey to find out the feelings and opinions of at least 50 freshmen and 50 seniors at your school. The survey should deal with a single subject of your choice. For example, it might be interesting to find out how freshmen view dating and to contrast that with how seniors view it. Other possible subjects: parents; clothes; friendship; work; studying. Once you decide on a subject, write ten objective questions. Objective questions are those that have multiple-choice answers. Do *not* include open-ended questions that allow participants to fill in the blanks. You might get 100 different answers in these blanks, and responses would then become difficult to analyze. Or consider using a scale similar to this one:

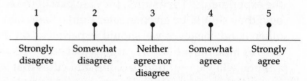

1	2	3	4	5
Strongly disagree	Somewhat disagree	Neither agree nor disagree	Somewhat agree	Strongly agree

Then you would write ten statements below the scale and have participants place a corresponding number next to each statement. Sample statements: "The male should initiate and pay for the first date." "A movie theater is a good place to go for a first date."

Draw a simple chart summarizing all your responses and then analyze your results. Compare and contrast the freshmen responses with the senior responses. Any surprises? Were there any questions that could have been phrased more carefully? Explain.

5. One of the most controversial issues in psychological research involves animal experimentation. Find an article that presents more than one side of the issue and write a brief summary. Then write an argumentative paper either for or against animal experimentation. Include in your paper information from the article that you have summarized.

Unit Two

Brain, Body, and Awareness

A CAT scan of a human brain.

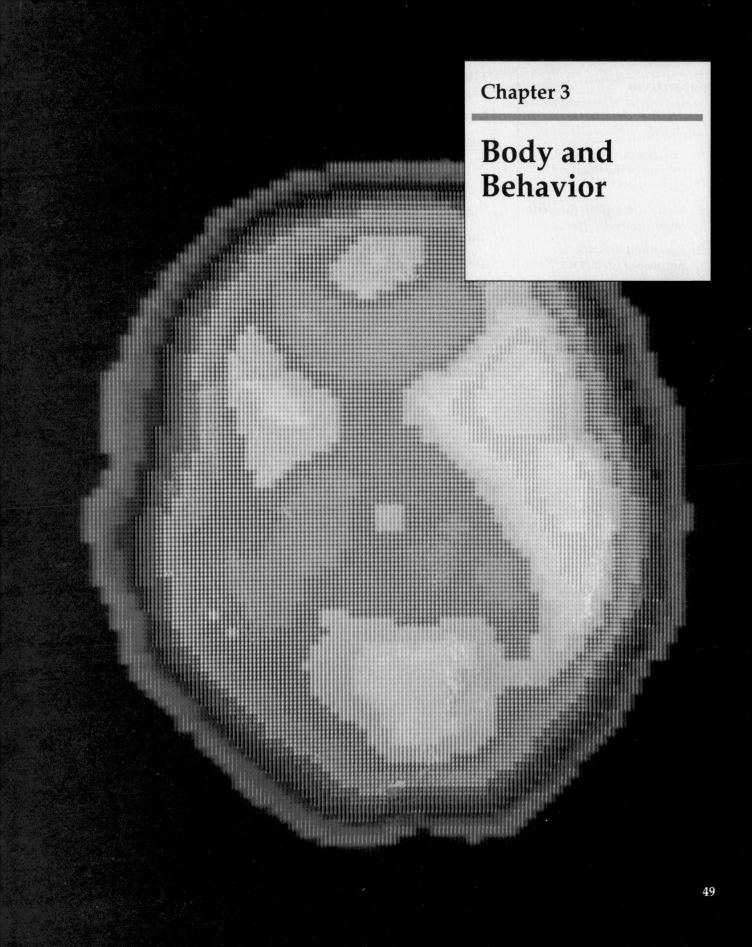

Body and Behavior

Global Look at the Chapter

Many behaviors that seem "psychological" are in fact the result of some activity of the brain or endocrine system. The human brain is remarkable in what it can do. It allows a combination of animal-like behaviors to come from the "lower" brain and very elaborate thought processes from the higher brain. This chapter will show that the brain plays an important part in everything we do.

Observing the Brain in Action

Let's start with an experiment. You need to put the book down to do the task, so you have to learn it first. Here it is: You are to stand up and put your right arm straight out, palm downward. Next, bring your hand in toward your head and put your finger gently into your right ear, saying, "I stretch my hand forth; I bring my hand back." Finally, take your finger out and sit back down. Once you know the procedure, put the book down and do it. Then we'll continue.

You have just done something that is almost beyond belief it is so remarkable. Here is what happened: Your brain analyzed the instructions. It sent a message to your body to get up. Next it sent a message to your arm. Then it called on the area that controls hand movements and put your finger into your ear. It didn't miss the ear and make you wind up with a finger in your eye or nose. While that was going on, the brain searched through the memory banks for the words you needed, put them together, and then used the speech areas of the brain to make those words. Finally, when you sat back down, it controlled your balance. When the upper part of your legs touched the chair, the brain received this sensation, you made a slight adjustment to be seated properly, came on down, and finally relaxed.

The experiment is not all the way over, though. Probably if you sense you were tricked into doing something weird, you now feel stupid, or irritated, or puzzled. These are emotions coming from yet another part of the inner brain. The brain decides whether or not you were treated fairly and triggers an emotional response that will vary, depending on how you interpreted the experiment.

There were a couple of reasons for our "experiment." First, in daily life, we all too often take for granted the wondrous thing that we are. In truth, it is worth considering how amazing it is that you are able to do what you just did. Second, as we move through the chapter, we wanted to be able to use a concrete example of something you have done, rather than talk in general terms about the workings of the brain.

Examining the Brain

Psychologists study the brain in detail because it is the part of us that controls every thought, action, and feeling. The brain is the most demanding organ of the body. If you spend a long time studying, it takes more energy and causes more aches and pains than jogging. The brain uses 20 percent of all our oxygen, eats up most of the sugar we take in, and operates on 20 watts of electrical power. Even though very elaborate, its workings are not hard to understand if you follow the description in this chapter step by step. Still, most students have trouble getting an image of how the brain is set up—even with many drawings. So here's an image for you to use: Assume that the brain is a large grapefruit. Imagine that we take the grapefruit and cut about a third of it off and throw that away. Now there is a flat side you can put on a table. If you look at it as it sits there, you have something that comes pretty close to what the skull looks like. The first thing we need to do is take off the grapefruit peel, which represents the hard skull. Once that's done, we have a floppy, moist mass of material that roughly represents the real brain, except the brain itself looks more like tightly compressed macaroni.

The Hemispheres

Before we continue, stuff two imaginary olives into the grapefruit. These should be about an inch apart to represent the eyes. Now you can keep the "brain" oriented at all times by aiming the "eyes" straight ahead, making them the farthest part away from you.

Next cut the grapefruit mass in half. Hold the knife straight out so that as you cut downward each half with an eye falls, one to the right and one to the left. The real brain is similar; it has two halves—it is not a whole unit. Each half is called a **hemisphere**. "Hemi" means half, so we have two halves of a sphere. These are referred to as the right and left hemispheres as you view them with the eyes farthest away from you. Inside a real skull, the hemispheres are held together by nerve bundles running

Hemisphere
One-half of the two halves of the brain; the right hemisphere controls the left side of the body while the left controls the right side.

back and forth between the two halves. Next, we have to glue the two halves of the grapefruit back together. It was worth it though, because now you know there are two halves that together look like one unit but actually are not. In real life, the left hemisphere controls the movements and feelings on the right side of the body; the right half controls the left side of the body. (We don't know why this is. It just is.)

With the brain back together, move your fingers along the top of the left hemisphere, about one-half of the way forward. You will find two rectangular areas that sit side by side, with the long parts running downward. These are called the **sensory** and **motor strips** (see Figure 3.1). The one farthest away from you is the motor strip. Every part of the body that can move is represented on this strip. That is why it is called *motor*: Motor means "relating to movement." During surgery, if the real brain is ex-

Sensory strip
The rectangular band running down the side of the brain that registers and provides all sensation.

Motor strip
The rectangular strip running down the side of the brain that controls all bodily movements (called motor functions).

Figure 3.1
The sensory and motor strips

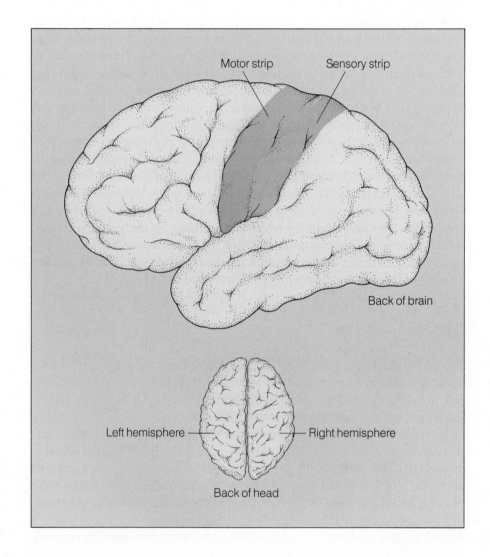

Motor strip   Sensory strip

Back of brain

Left hemisphere ——   —— Right hemisphere

Back of head

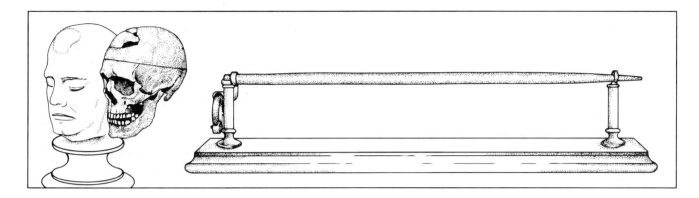

Life mask and skull of Phineas P. Gage and the tamping iron that did all the damage.

posed this way, the surgeon can stimulate different parts of this motor strip with an electrically-active wire, and, depending on the area touched, the arm will move, the leg, the finger, the nose will twitch, and so forth.

Now bring your hand back toward you but stay on the hemisphere. You will find what is called the *sensory strip*. If this is stimulated on an exposed brain, the person feels a sensation in different areas—in the leg, ear, mouth, and so forth—depending on the area of the strip that the electricity hits. So, for the experiment you did at the beginning, you used the sensory strip to register as your legs cleared the chair, to tell you when your finger actually hit your ear, and to control sitting back down by telling you when you had touched the chair again. The motor strip registered as you moved your arm out, brought your finger in, and sat back down. A similar set of sensory and motor strips is found on the right hemisphere for the other half of the body.

If you go straight back from the lower end of the sensory strip, you will find a circular area whose job is to create sentences. This is the area that helps (and often fails) those trying to get a good grade in English composition. It organizes sentences so they can be understood. If someone is unlucky enough to damage this area of the brain, he or she can still speak, but what is said is a jumble of words that make no sense. Connected to this part is a circular area a few inches forward (see Figure 3.2). This forward area controls the physical part of speaking, so it makes the words, using the motor strip and other parts. If it is damaged, a person can still think of the proper sentences, but they don't come out when the person tries to speak. So, when you said the little speech about your hand at the beginning of the chapter, the speech was made up by the first unit and actually spoken by the second unit, even if you didn't say it out loud. When we are "talking" silently to ourselves, as we all do, the same units are involved, because the actual sounds that others hear come only when you activate your voice box in the throat.

For most people, these speech areas are only in the left hemisphere. But about 25 percent of left-handers have them only in the right hemisphere. We'll talk about "lefties" shortly.

Interpretation by the Brain

When you were reading the first part of this chapter, the words you saw went through the lens of the eyes and landed on the back of the eyeball. What was received was then sent through nerves to the back of the brain, the area of the grapefruit closest to you. This back part of the brain interprets everything we see. It is the **visual area** (see Figure 3.2).

The brain sits in a fluid that acts like a shock absorber, giving it some room to move back and forth and sideways. Sometimes that isn't enough, however. If you've ever been hit really hard in the front part of your head, you saw all kinds of images in front of you for a second (seeing "stars"). This is because the blow sent the brain sloshing backward, crashing the back visual part into the skull. The collision stirred up the electrical system of this visual area, and it made these strange images. If you've never been hit, you can still see this area in operation. Lie on the bed in a dark room for about ten minutes. Then open your eyes and *VERY GENTLY*(!) touch the edges of your eyeballs. This will send electrical impulses to the back visual area that will create odd images "right before your very eyes" (Oster, 1970).

Visual area
The area at the back of the brain that interprets everything we see.

Figure 3.2
View of left hemisphere with skull removed.

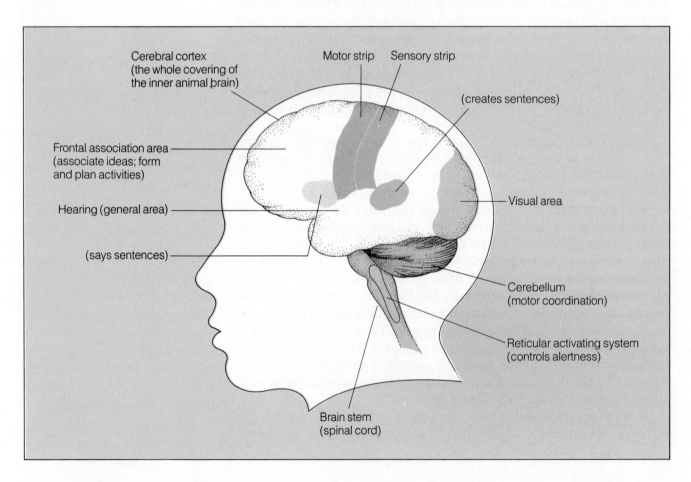

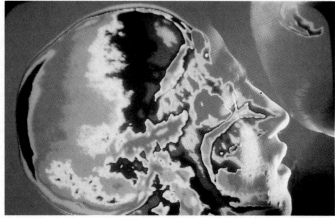

In the photo at right, the darker and red portions of the visual area at the back of the brain are showing electrical activity from colliding with the skull.

The Frontal Association Area

Once the words you received while reading were processed by the visual area, this information was sent all the way straight ahead to the forehead area. As you can see in Figure 3.2, this part is called the **frontal association area**, since it is located in the front part of the brain. The frontal association area is very heavily packed with nerve cells because its task is very complex: to interpret what is going on and tell us what to do and what to feel. It decided how you reacted to our "experiment," for example. In many ways, the frontal area seems to form the core of a person's personality, since so many decisions are made there.

In the 1840s, a railroad worker with the unlikely name of Phineas P. Gage was injured in a freakish accident, which gave us clues into the nature of the frontal area. He was pushing some dynamite into a hole with a four-foot-long iron bar in the shape of a toothpick, about an inch in diameter. The dynamite went off, firing the bar upward through his jaw, through the frontal area, and on out. Remarkably he survived because none of the vital parts that control breathing, movement, or physical control had been damaged. Still, the injury to his frontal area made some *major* changes. While he had been friendly and normal, suddenly he became someone who swore all the time, undressed wherever he felt like it, went to the bathroom anywhere in public, and had temper tantrums. Thus, this complex area of the brain must play a large part in what we call social control as well as in our basic personalities.

The frontal area also tries to make sense of the environment. Someone who has major damage in this part of the brain can know what is happening, but not be able to bring together all the aspects of the situation. For

Frontal association area
The forward portion of the brain that engages in elaborate associations or mental connections; it plays an important part in integrating personality and in complex thoughts.

A famous "leftie," Paul McCartney, who presumably is using his talented right hemisphere.

example, a man with damage here can watch someone: (1) take a bullet; (2) put it in a gun; (3) cock the gun; and (4) aim the gun at him. He will not show any concern. He understands each act by itself, but is not able to put it all together (Jouandet & Gazzaniga, 1979).

The size of the frontal area likely reflects intelligence level from one species to another. Since we can't "talk to the animals," we will probably never know for sure, but it is interesting that the amount of the brain devoted to the frontal part depends on how advanced the animal is. Thus, for the dog, it is 7 percent, 15 percent in the chimpanzee, and 30 percent in the human.

If you want, you can actually see the frontal area in operation. Try this experiment, but pick someone who is a reasonably pleasant person. While the victim is standing in a line, go up to where he or she is and bump him or her from behind. Wait five seconds after the person turns around before you apologize. Note that the person will spend this time (a *long* time for the brain) looking at you, mentally "waiting," going back and forth mentally, while the frontal area decides if what you did was on purpose or not and whether he or she should get mad.

Hemispheres and Handedness

Ten percent of the population is left-handed. Because they are different from others statistically, people wonder how "they got that way." Earlier we mentioned that the left hemisphere controls the right side of the body and vice versa. That *is* true, but we were referring only to major body movements. When dealing with small, fine movements, such as putting your finger in your ear or writing, one hemisphere has **dominance**. In other words, one hemisphere is always the preferred one to use. Most people are left-hemisphere dominant and right-handed. But, if the right hemisphere is dominant, then the person will be left-handed for all fine movements.

Left-handedness does not seem to be inherited—at least not in the same sense as something like eye color, which follows a clear family pattern. Sometimes in identical twins, who come from the same egg and have exactly the same heredity, there will be one left-handed twin and one right-handed (Corballis & Morgan, 1978).

The genetic instructions that make the brain have got to be complex beyond imagination. We suspect that, for some reason, accidental or otherwise, the part of the "program" that develops the brain gets slightly different signals for the left-hander and shifts the dominance to the other hemisphere. Or, if the shift isn't all the way complete, a very few become what is called "ambidextrous" (both-handed people). The instructions got "stuck" in the middle of the two hemispheres, so to speak.

The intelligence of right- versus left-handed people is about the same; that is, there seems to be about the same number of bright, average, and dull people in both groups. But statistically the left-hander will probably do better in art, music, and mathematics. And the odds increase that the speech areas will be in the right rather than the left hemisphere (Annett, 1978). They also tend to be better actors: Try keeping track for a while of the number of leading men and women in movies and TV who are left-handed. We will explain why this is in a few paragraphs.

Before going on, though, there is a myth that, if a left-hander is forced by the parent to use the right hand in childhood, it might cause insanity. That's not true. But what a nuisance it can be, and so uncomfortable. People used to think that something was wrong with left-handers (there isn't anything wrong, any more than with right-handers) and tried to change their children. It's hard enough to grow up as it is without adding the burden of making children uncomfortable trying to do an "unnatural" act (Geschwind, 1983).

Tasks of the Hemispheres

Scientists have wondered for hundreds of years about why the brain has two halves. There must be some reason. Only recently have we begun to understand why this might be.

We have already mentioned that nerve fibers hold the two hemispheres together. In fact, there are about 3 million of them going from one side to the other. They run across in bundles and are used to pass information from one half to the other and back again (Myers, 1984). The bundles are so dense that they have their own location and name. Note in Figure 3.3 that this unit is called the **corpus callosum** (KORE-pus kah-LOH-sum), and sits toward the middle bottom of the brain, inside the split in our "grapefruit."

Corpus callosum
The massive bundle of nerve fibers that connects the two hemispheres of the brain.

The difference between hemispheres was noted with patients who had to have the corpus callosum cut surgically to stop electrical disturbances of the brain. Experiments were set up in which information was fed through part of the eyes that led to only one hemisphere or the other. This was possible because, with a severed corpus callosum, most communication between the two halves is cut off. Hence, only one half of the brain gets the message.

In the first experiment (Figure 3.3), using a woman with a split brain, her right hemisphere was shown a photo of a nude woman (the left hemisphere "saw" nothing). The woman blushed and laughed nervously. When asked why she was blushing, she said she didn't know! In a second experiment, a picture of a spoon was shown to a man's left hemisphere. He was asked what he had seen and correctly said, "Spoon." But, next, the picture of a spoon was shown to his *right* hemisphere. He was asked what he saw. He couldn't *say* what it was. But he could pick a spoon from objects on the table to indicate what he saw (Gazzaniga, 1970). What do these findings mean?

Figure 3.3
The hemispheres and the corpus
callosum.

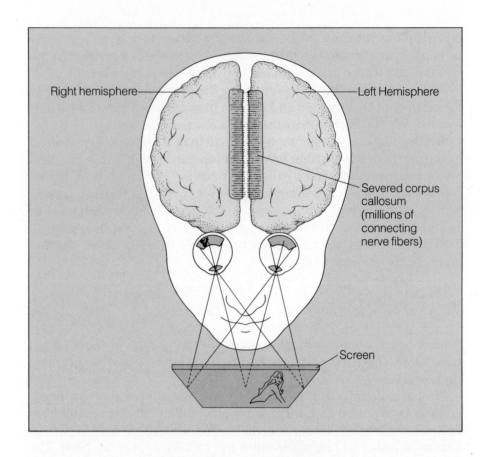

It seems that the left hemisphere (for right-handers and most left-handers) handles verbal or speech material (see Figure 3.4). So, when the man saw the spoon only with the right hemisphere, he couldn't *say* what it was (left hemisphere). The right hemisphere deals with objects in space, art, music, mathematics, as well as emotional material. Hence, the woman had an emotional reaction because of what she saw in the right hemisphere, but couldn't say what it was (left hemisphere). For those who are left-handed, since the right hemisphere will dominate, the odds increase that they will be better at and deal more with their right hemispheres. This, in turn, increases the chances that they will do well in art, music, mathematics, architecture, or the physical and emotional art of acting—all *non*verbal activities (Springer & Deutsch, 1985).

The Cerebral Cortex and the Lower Brain

There is one task left with the grapefruit before we drop the image. Turn the grapefruit over, keeping the "eyes" farthest away from you. With an imaginary tablespoon, gouge out a crater that starts about half an inch from the edge and runs away from you to about the middle of the grapefruit. At its deepest part, it should be about three inches. The grapefruit you are holding in your hand is what we call the **cerebral cortex**. While

Cerebral cortex
The 100-billion-nerve-cell unit that covers the lower brain and controls very high-level thought.

we haven't formally said so, all the parts discussed so far (hemisphere, frontal area, and so forth) are part of the cerebral cortex. This unit controls very high-level thought (*cerebral* means "relating to thought or intelligence"). In the human, the cerebral cortex is made up of roughly 100 billion (100,000,000,000) nerve cells all packed into the macaronilike material. If it is untwisted and spread out, the cortex is about the size of a large bath towel. We know of nothing in the universe that can equal it. These nerve cells can connect with one another in so many ways that, if you emptied dump trucks full of computers night and day until you'd filled up a football stadium, this pile would not even come close to equaling our brain power. In fact, some people have estimated that the number of possible different connections the brain can make is greater than the number of particles in the universe (Sagan, 1977).

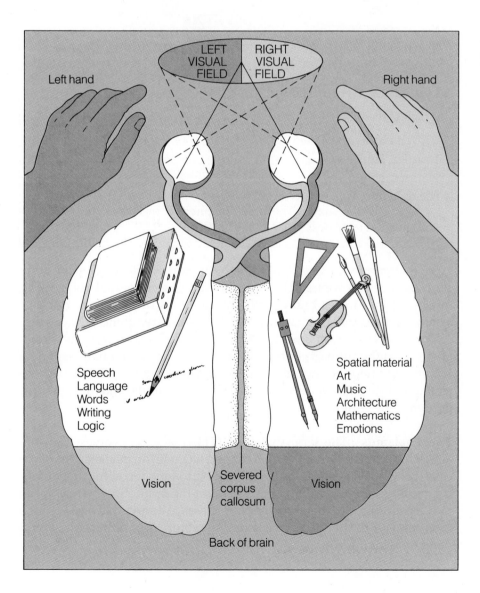

Figure 3.4
Assumed areas of "specialization" in the brain.

In Focus: Tasks of the Two Hemispheres

Typical Right Hemisphere Task

Which of the pieces, above right, would fit into space 4 on the left?

Typical Left-Hemisphere Task

Which of the following is correct?

a. I wish I was a rich man.

b. I wish I were a rich man.

The right hemisphere specializes in spatial functions such as piecing together a jigsaw puzzle. The left hemisphere specializes in the verbal skills needed to answer a "language" question.

No matter how fantastic it is, though, the cortex will not keep the body running. For that we need a "lower" brain. The crater that you gouged out holds this **lower brain**, with the cerebral cortex fitting over and around it. The word *cortex* means "bark," as on a tree; hence, the cerebral cortex covers the lower brain like a layer of bark. Use Figure 3.5 as we talk about the different parts of the lower brain. For most human responses (except automatic behaviors such as withdrawing a hand from a hot object), the cortex influences the animal-like lower units, and they, in turn, influence the cortex.

The Thalamus   The term **thalamus** (THAL-ah-mus) comes from the Greek for "couch." Note that it is shaped like one, an oval mass of nerve cells (Brown, 1976). It acts as a relay station to send incoming and outgoing messages to and from various parts of the brain. So, if you want to move your big toe, the brain sends a message to the thalamus, which then sends it to the correct place on the motor strip. Otherwise, you'd wind up blinking your eye.

Lower brain
Basic "animal" units common to animals and humans that regulate basic functions such as breathing.

Thalamus
The portion of the lower brain that functions primarily as a central relay station for incoming and outgoing messages from the body to the brain and the brain to the body.

The Cerebellum   The **cerebellum** (sera-BELL-um) looks like a ball of yarn a little larger than a golf ball, and it hooks onto the base of the brain below the visual area. Its job is complex. Whenever you move, it makes sure you stay in balance, remain coordinated, and get where you want to go. It was responsible for you getting your finger into your ear. Here's another example: Think back to the first day of class this year. You had to go to different rooms from the ones you did the previous year, and all was chaos trying to remember the right ones. But, within a week, the cerebellum had programmed itself to take you to every class in sequence, and you no longer had to pay attention to where you were going. In fact, often you now go from one class to the other, turning right, left, right, and so forth, while you are talking to someone—and you "magically" arrive at the right place. The cerebellum also contains thousands of nerve cells lined up in rows like the spokes of half a wheel with the cerebellum

Cerebellum
The portion of the lower brain that coordinates and organizes bodily movements for balance and accuracy.

Figure 3.5
The Parts of the Lower Brain (left side of cortex removed)

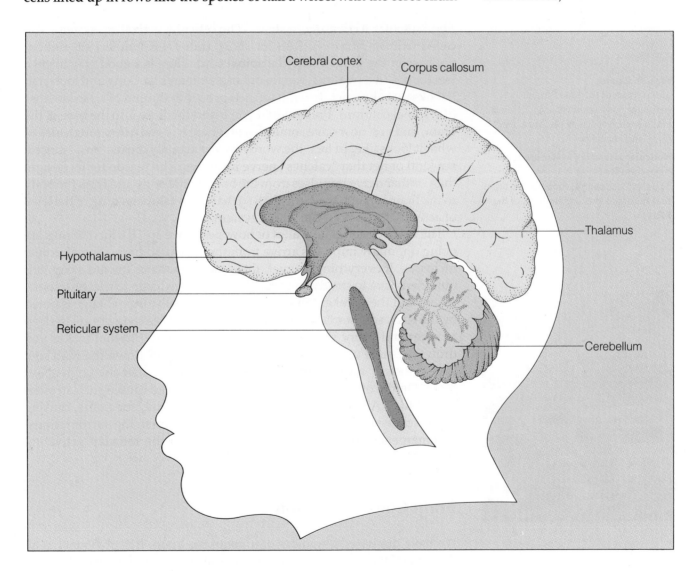

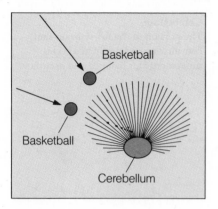

Figure 3.6
Symbolic representation of nerve network in cerebellum: Dots inside are nerve cells firing in sequence to indicate speed and direction of oncoming ball.

Hypothalamus
The portion of the lower brain that regulates basic needs (hunger, thirst) and emotions such as pleasure, fear, rage, and sexuality.

Reticular activating system/reticular formation/RAS
The alertness control center of the brain that regulates the activity level of the body.

core as the center (see Figure 3.6). When someone throws a basketball to you, your eyes cause firing of cerebellum cells one after the other as the ball is tracked on its path toward you. The cerebellum calculates speed and direction as the cells fire, signals through the thalamus to the motor control, and your hands will automatically go to the correct place to catch the ball (Llinas & Pellionisa, 1979).

The Hypothalamus   The **hypothalamus** (*hypo* means "below") sits below the thalamus. While only the size of a large pea, it helps control rage, pleasure, hunger, thirst, and sexual desire. Thus, if it is electrically stimulated in the rage center, it can cause a person to go wild and start smashing things. We will discuss this unit in Chapter 5 when we talk about motivation and emotion.

The Reticular Activating System   The **reticular activating system**, also called *reticular formation*, RAS for short, (reh-TICK-you-ler) sits right at the base of the brain inside the spinal cord. Here is a good way to get a feel for it: Cut a two-inch square out of a woman's stocking and look at it. It looks just like a net. Insert it an inch or so into the end of a garden hose (the spinal column). Pretend that you insert the hose into the base of the brain, and you now have some idea of where it is and a *very* rough idea of what it looks like. In fact, the word *reticular* actually means "net," since it *is* a kind of net that "catches" nerve impulses. The reason for its design, then, is that nerve impulses from the brain to the body and from the body to the brain pass through the RAS so that it can take a reading of the level of activity throughout the whole system.

The RAS regulates how alert or how sleepy we are. If a lot of things are going on, many impulses arrive from the body and brain, and alertness increases. If everything is quiet, this system heads us toward sleep. It is quite sensitive to steady sounds. Thus, if you go listen to a lecture somewhere and the speaker talks very slowly and dully, little change is noted by the RAS, so it starts to put you to sleep. If you are trying to get to sleep at night and count sheep passing by, that endless rhythm makes you drowsy. Drugs used for surgery dramatically slow down the RAS so it "doesn't care" about pain signals and thus won't alert the brain about them. On the other hand, a major blow to the head causes such an overload of the RAS circuits that they shut off completely for a time, causing unconsciousness. A continuous change in rhythm in the surroundings, an emergency, or emotional thoughts stir up the reticular activating system.

Brain Communication

We have discussed a number of units of the brain. It is obvious that all these parts have to communicate with one another. Thus, the eye must send information to the visual area of the brain, the foot to the motor strip, the cerebellum to and from the muscles and body, and so forth. We have already noted that there is electricity in the nerve cells, but now the question is: How do we get the parts to "talk" to one another? One way might be to string nerves directly from one part to another. In the 1700s, scientists believed this was the case, but they were very wrong (Bergland, 1985). Why won't this work? Think about it for a minute. If you connect all the parts together and turn on a "switch," *everything* will go on at the same time, which would be a hopeless mess. So that can't be the answer.

Another problem is that the brain has to be able to join different ideas. But even using separate nerves for each unit still won't work. For instance, the brain stores the idea of *red*. If we connect a nerve from *red* to the idea of *rose*, that connection would work, but then how could we get the idea of *red* to the idea of *car* without triggering *rose* at the same time? Or how do we get the hypothalamus to signal rage without also sending out a signal for thirst, which would cause us to drink instead of yell? To solve these problems, we need many nerve cells that are separate but still able to alternate signals from one circuit to another. We certainly have more than enough of them, since each of our 100 billion nerve cells has thousands of connections to the others (Craik, 1979).

The Neuron

Each nerve cell, then, is separate, one from the other, and is called a **neuron** (NYOOR-ron). As you can see in Figures 3.7 and 3.8, the body of the cell has a number of fibers sticking out from it. One of these fibers is very long; it is called an **axon**. The axon carries the message *from* the cell to other neurons. At the end of the axon are thousands of terminals, each sitting opposite a receptor (receiver) for another neuron. The receptors sit on what are called **dendrites**, a word meaning "tree," since they look like branches. So, the message comes from an axon of one cell over to a receptor on a dendrite of another cell, goes through the cell, and then out that cell's axon if the message is to continue on.

Neuron
A nerve cell, which transmits electrical and chemical information (via neurotransmitters) throughout the body.

Axon
The part of the neuron that carries messages away from the nerve cell to the dendrites on another nerve cell.

Dendrite
The part of the nerve cell that receives information from the axons of other nerve cells.

The Synapse

If you look carefully at Figures 3.7 and 3.8, you'll see that there is a space between the endings of the axon and the waiting dendrites. This space is called the **synapse** (SIN-apse), which means "junction point." Since the neurons work by electricity, we now have another problem: Electricity will not go over a space, so it stops. And we have yet another problem: All electricity is the same. If you cut your finger and an electrical impulse goes up to the brain, how is the brain supposed to know it is a "pain message" and not a message to kick your foot?

Synapse
The junction point of two or more neurons; a connection is made by neurotransmitters.

Figure 3.7
Artist's diagram of how parts of nerve cells look and connect.

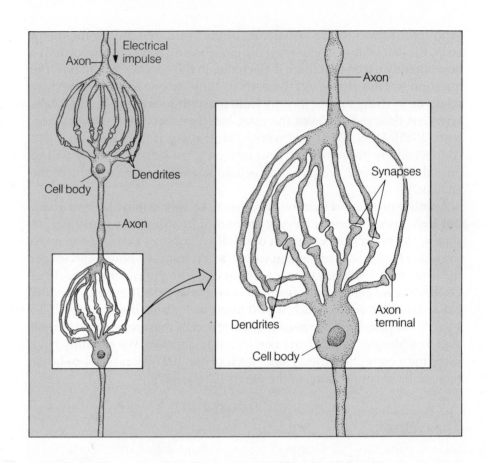

Figure 3.8
Close-up drawing of parts of nerve cells.

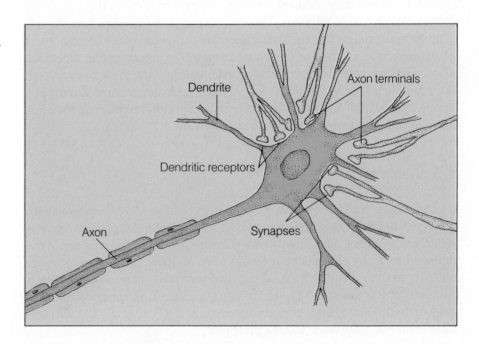

Neurotransmitters

The solution to these problems lies in an amazing system of communication. Where the axon ends, just before the synapse, the area is filled with small containers that look like bubbles. Inside each of them sit thousands of chemical "messengers." Since chemical molecules can be any size or shape, they are not like electricity—you can identify them. So, if a circuit is for pain, the molecules inside that container will have a unique shape that means only "pain message" to the brain. If the circuit is for moving your arm, the container holds different-shaped molecules that will be used to signal only the movement circuit. These molecules are called **neurotransmitters** because they send (*transmit*) nerve (*neuro*) information from the end of the axon over the synapse to the dendrite receptor. Use Figures 3.9 and 3.10 to follow this discussion. Each circuit contains a specific different molecule for each activity that circuit controls: movement circuits, pain circuit, pleasure circuit, and so forth.

Here's what happens: You think, "Move my arm." The electrical impulse in the circuit for movement goes down the axon to a nerve ending (a terminal). The electrical impulse stops at the synapse, but, when it arrives close to that area, the chemical containers holding molecules for "movement"are designed to float toward the synapse, where they lock onto a terminal and open up, flooding the open space with neurotransmitters for "movement." Once in the open space, the chemicals then float to the appropriate dendritic receptors for movement—in other words, each receptor is designed to accept only a specific type of chemical molecule (the "movement" molecules, in this case). Once accepted by a movement circuit, these molecules excite the dendrites there, which

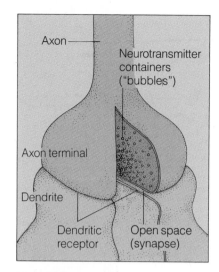

Figure 3.9
Close-up detail of axon ending.

Neurotransmitters
Chemicals in the endings of nerve cells that send information across the synapse.

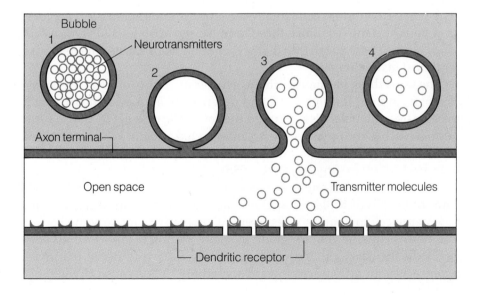

Figure 3.10
Single container moving (1–4 is the same one) as the neurotransmitter is deposited into the receptor.

In Focus: Sizzling Neurons

The A-B-Cs of Neurons!

Imagine that each tiny nerve cell, or neuron, is one complete firecracker. Imagine further that we have a bunch of these neurons, or firecrackers, lined up next to each other throughout our bodies. When one of these neurons is stimulated, it begins a chain reaction.

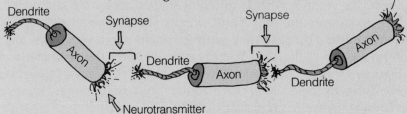

The wick (dendrite) receives the incoming message. The message is then carried along the length of the firecracker (axon). By the time the message gets to the end of the firecracker, it causes a chemical to leak (a neurotransmitter). This chemical is responsible for bridging the tiny gap (synapse) between two firecrackers; it sends the message across the gap and lights the next wick.

The nice thing about all this is that you can use the wicks and firecrackers over and over again!

Acetylcholine
Neurotransmitter that regulates basic bodily processes such as movement.

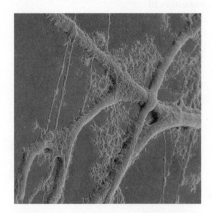

The startling complexity of a single nerve cell is shown under extremely high magnification.

starts an electrical impulse through the new cell as the process repeats. The process continues until finally the impulse ends at muscle receptors, and your arm moves. Since these impulses go at about 120 yards a second, none of us is so tall that this presents a time problem. The response is almost instantaneous.

The same thing happens with the neurotransmitter for pain. Messages travel from a cut through a cell and down an axon to dendrites that will receive its pain molecules, through the cell to the next axon, and so forth until it reaches the brain where it is interpreted as pain. We now know of 40 different neurotransmitters, but we will probably eventually find hundreds of them (Snyder, 1984; 1986).

The most common and well-studied neurotransmitter is called **acetylcholine** (a-SEE-til-KOH-leen). One of its uses is to send information from one nerve cell to another whenever we get ready to move some part of the body. Thus, if you are going to move your arm (as we've just described), the acetylcholine will *very* rapidly fire every nerve cell in sequence as your arm moves toward something. It will cause all the muscles in the arm to expand and contract, as necessary, so you can get the job done swiftly and accurately.

One final thing might have occurred to you. If you were breathing in and had no way to turn the muscles off, you wouldn't be able to exhale. Similarly, since the reticular activating system has to slow down in order for you to sleep, there must be a way to turn some of its cells off. There is. Some dendritic receptors are designed so that, when a neurotransmitter arrives, the cell turns *off*. An example of this occurs when people drink too much. The alcohol molecule resembles a neurotransmitter that the body uses to turn cells off. So, when the alcohol gets into the system, cells begin to shut down. Cells turn off in the RAS, making the person sleepy; in the speech area, making him or her slur; in the cerebellum, causing him or her eventually to fall over; and so forth.

The Spinal Cord

All the nerve impulses to the body from the brain and from the brain to the body must enter and leave the **spinal cord**. Figure 3.11 shows what is called a *cross section* of this unit. The drawing illustrates how the spinal cord would appear if you were cut in half and you looked down on the

Spinal cord
The part of the body that functions as an automatic "brain" in its own right and is a relay station for impulses to and from the higher brain.

Figure 3.11
The spinal cord

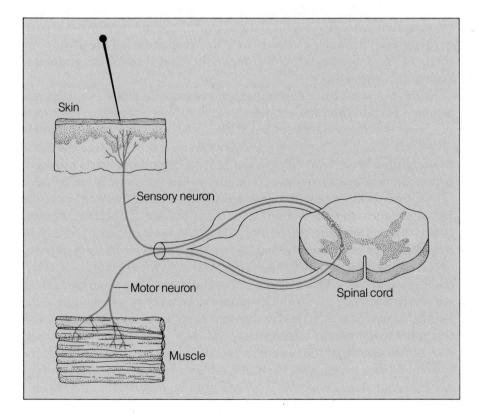

Skin

Sensory neuron

Motor neuron

Spinal cord

Muscle

bottom half. Sometimes, for our survival, the spinal cord must activate the muscles long before we are even aware of it, a behavior called a **reflex**. In the first stages the brain does not act but the spinal cord does. This happens in a close call when driving. You are about to hit another car, but, "before you know it," you have swerved and missed it. The spinal neurons are short, direct, and very powerful in order to get us out of such messes (Thompson, 1967). They have very few synapses to slow them down—just enough are available to send a message to the brain about what happened.

In theory, the spinal cord could operate by itself. For example, a frog has a very small cerebral cortex. If the frog's head is cut off, some of the parts of its body still work. If the foot is pinched, what is left of the frog will still draw its leg up—for an hour or so. But can the head still work? In a really gory experiment in France years ago, scientists tried talking to the heads of men who had just had them cut off in an execution. The heads did not answer (Von Frisch, 1963).

Looking at the Glandular System

Communication by neurons is speedy and efficient, but it doesn't last very long. Some messages need to stay in the system longer. These messages come from chemicals called **hormones**, which are passed through the body using the bloodstream. *Hormone* comes from a word meaning "to activate," since that's what it does: Hormones can turn on other parts of the body. These chemicals are held inside **glands**. All the glands and their chemical messages together make up what is called the **endocrine system** (EN-doh-crin).

Hormones work like neurotransmitters in that they have a special molecular structure that must match the structure of a receptor. For example, there is a hormone-receptor pair designed only for a woman about to give birth. When the time comes, the hormone is sent through the blood to the proper area, where it locks onto its receptor and starts muscular contractions. If a woman never has a baby, this hormone is never used.

In the near-miss accident discussed in the previous section, once the message gets to the brain about what is happening, it declares an emergency that will require the body to be active for a period of time. The hypothalamus uses neurotransmitters to signal the pituitary gland (discussed next). The pituitary then sends out hormones through the endocrine system. They arrive at the adrenal glands (also discussed later), which stir the body up for the emergency. When you get enough of the adrenal hormone in your body, you start to shake all over and feel sick—this is the worst part of a near-miss.

In the sections that follow, we look at the major parts of the endocrine system. Be sure to note that the brain, our inner selves, the body, and the environment all work together; no one of them ever works all by itself.

Hormones
Chemical regulators that control bodily processes such as emotional responses, growth, sexuality.

Glands
Units of the body that contain the hormones.

Endocrine system
The system of all the glands and their chemical messages taken together.

The Pituitary Gland

The **pituitary gland** (pi-TUE-i-ter-ee) is called the master gland of the body. In Figure 3.12, you will see that it is a small bean-shaped unit that is attached to and controlled by the hypothalamus. Physicians many centuries ago thought that mucus running from the nose came from this gland. "Pituita" was a taboo slang word used for this substance, and everyone who heard the word was disgusted. They were wrong about what it does, but the term stuck. The pituitary has two jobs: (1) to send messages that will start other glands going and (2) to decide how tall or short we will be (Bergland, 1985).

Pituitary gland
The master gland of the body that activates other hormones and controls the growth hormone.

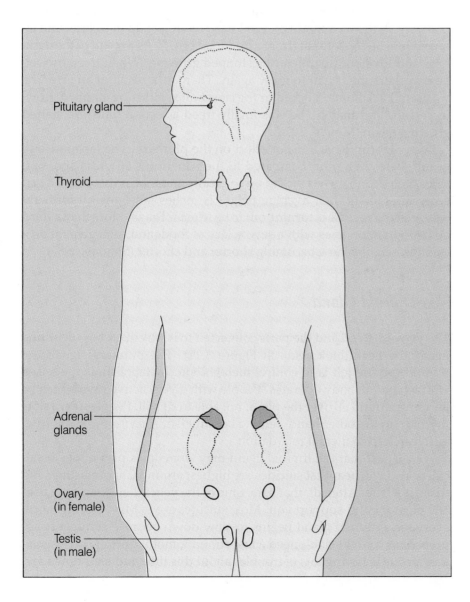

Figure 3.12
The glandular system.

The effects of the pituitary are clearly shown here. Entertainer David Frost stands between the world's smallest and largest men.

The pituitary makes a **growth hormone**, but it does it in fits and starts. Even those who grow to a proper height can suffer greatly along the way because of this gland. Sometimes its action is delayed, causing people in the growth phase to worry that they will never reach a proper height. On occasion it seems to start too soon, creating youngsters who feel too tall and "not quite right."

Most of the time, these starts and stops in growth lead to a reasonable height. But not always. When things are not working properly, there can be incredible growth: The tallest person in history was 8 feet 11.1 inches. He died at the age of 22, partly as a result of this defect. The shortest known person was 23.2 inches tall when she died at age 19. Today's medicine can handle most such problems if caught early enough, but these cases show what happens if the pituitary goes awry.

Like all body systems, the pituitary requires a normal environment. In one very sad case, a mother locked her growing child in a closet and allowed him out only to eat (from a dog-food bowl). As a result of the darkness and his poor treatment, he stopped growing. When freed by welfare workers, he began to grow again. Then, as a result of an error, he was sent back home. Locked in the closet once more, he stopped growing again. Fortunately, he was finally freed a second time and started growing again (Money, 1974).

Even diet can have a major effect on the pituitary. The Japanese as a group were very short compared to the Americans 30 years ago, but, since their economy has picked up so greatly and food is more varied and accessible, today their average height is inches taller than it formerly was. Just the reverse is turning out to be true for Brazil. More than a third of its population lives with a severe lack of food, and each generation's average height is now becoming shorter and shorter (Simons, 1987).

The Thyroid Gland

The **thyroid gland** and the parts connected to it look like a bow tie sitting inside the neck (look again at Figure 3.12). The pituitary signals the thyroid, whose job is to control **metabolism**. Metabolism is the speed with which the body operates. People with a very active thyroid can be jumping around all over the place, not able to sit still. People with a slow thyroid, on the other hand, tend to be sluggish. A *very* slow gland from birth can lead to mental retardation.

We suspect that the thyroid gland may sometimes play a role in suicides. You will hear that suicides are highest around Christmastime, but that's not true. After all, that's the time of the year when people are usually pleasant and support you. Most suicides are in May. During April, everyone's thyroid gland begins to slow down because summer is approaching, and we don't need a fast-running motor during that season. If someone is having lots of troubles about this time and feels down and out, it may well be that the body slowing down will make him or her feel even more depressed and unable to cope, and this may tip the scale toward suicide (Zung & Green, 1974).

The Adrenal Glands

The **adrenal glands** (a-DREE-nal) are located on the right and left side of the body, slightly above the navel and to the back. When they operate at full force they create an overexcited body, which none of us wants. But we don't go long without triggering them. In the near-accident example, the quick-acting spinal nerves make us swerve the car to avoid it. For a moment, we sigh with relief. But, when all the activity gets to the reticular formation and then goes to the cerebral cortex, we begin to think about what *could* have happened. The cortex signals a major emergency to the hypothalamus, which tells the pituitary, which sends hormones to the adrenal glands. The adrenal glands then dump **adrenaline** (a-DREN-a-lin) into the bloodstream. Adrenaline prepares us for an emergency: We begin to breathe rapidly, blood pressure goes up, muscles tense, sugar is dumped into the body for energy, and we are so excited that our armpits and feet sweat. This system is amazing: It even sends out a chemical that will help the blood clot faster just in case we get cut! These reactions are not designed by nature to deal with traffic problems, but the body can't tell the difference between a real emergency (such as an accident we *don't* manage to avoid) and one we just think about. For instance, the whole emergency system is set into motion if we have to talk in front of a group or, for many of us, if we are about to take an examination. Hands tremble, armpits and feet drip, we can hardly breathe, the heart is jumping, all saliva is gone so that we feel like we are choking, and we know for sure we are going to die right in the middle of the talk or the test.

Adrenal glands
The glands that cause excitement in order to prepare the body for an emergency or for some important activity.

Adrenaline
The chemical that prepares the body for emergency activity by increasing blood pressure, breathing rate, and energy level.

The Gonads

The **gonads** are the sex glands; they make the sperm or eggs used for reproduction. The male sex hormones are called **androgen**, and the female ones **estrogen**. *Both* males and females have *both* hormones in their bodies, but, for the male, there will be more androgen and, for the female, more estrogen. These hormones make us look either male or female. For example, if a female is injected with extra androgen, she will grow body hair and a beard. Androgen also starts the sex drive for both males and females, but the sex drive doesn't really become very active until people are in their middle teens.

Earlier we mentioned that mind and body affect one another. Nowhere is this more clear than in the case of sex hormones. If you neuter a

Gonads
The sex glands that make sperm or eggs for reproduction.

Androgen
The male sex hormone.

Estrogen
The female sex hormone.

dog, it will lose its desire to reproduce. That is *not* the case with an adult human. Even after an accident that removes the source of the hormones, the sex drive can remain for years. So, even though our sex drive is at one time started by hormones, it is then taken over by the cerebral cortex, which makes it a social, symbolic behavior as well as a physical one. Many find this hard to believe, but, because the cortex controls it, sex must actually be learned by humans. It is not like hunger or thirst. This fact is often a source of real confusion for adolescents because it takes a long time for anyone to understand what sex is all about. To add to the problem, all of their friends of the same age *pretend* they already know all about it. The presence of the cortex, however, does give humans the feelings of love, hope, warmth, respect, and care that can be attached to the sex act. On the other hand, the presence of the cortex also means that the opposite feelings—fear, anxiety, and psychological pain—can likewise occur regarding sex.

Brain Control

Endless television shows, movies, and science fiction books suggest that it might be possible to control people's brains. But what is the real, scientific evidence that we might be taken over and turned into robots?

It is startling to think about someone going berserk if a portion of the hypothalamus is electrically stimulated. We mentioned that event earlier because it shows what *can* happen. What we did not talk about, though, is the fact that the hypothalamus for each one of us is slightly different from that of another person. This is true of all parts of the brain and body. For example, each of us has a different-shaped stomach, and each person's stomach is located in a slightly different place. You can see the problem: It would take endless hours of work to locate the pleasure or rage center in the hypothalamus of one single person. You can imagine the impossible task of putting electrical control devices in enough people even to get a small mob going, much less control a larger group. To make it more difficult, humans are so complex and variable that some of us respond with pleasure where the anger portion of the hypothalamus is supposed to be! So, you can rule out this method of controlling us (Deutsch, 1973).

But what about drugs? You have probably heard about a drug called a "truth serum." When it is administered (in the movies), the subject suddenly starts blurting out all his or her secrets. Surely that would be a good way to "get" things on someone and control him or her in that way. Well, no. Again the whole thing is exaggerated. The so-called truth serum only slows down the reticular activating system so that the victim is drowsy and fuzzy. This condition makes us all more suggestible in the sense that we don't worry as much about telling the truth. But such is not the case for those who have something to lose! Tests show that people lie all the time, if they need to, under this drug. Others make things up; for example, they confess to crimes they couldn't possibly have committed (Brown, 1973; Frank, 1966). So we have to rule that one out, too.

What about "confessions" given by prisoners of war or victims of the police? If enough psychological torture is used, sometimes prisoners will confess to things they didn't do. Historically, more often they will not do so. In any case, they have not really been "brainwashed" because, as soon as they are free, they go right back to whatever they felt and believed before the torture. In fact, often the "confessions" from war camps are written in strange English to say the opposite of what the foreign captors think they are saying (Johnson, 1971).

We discussed the railroad worker who had an iron bar fired through his brain. That certainly changed his personality, didn't it? Not exactly. There's a big difference between *changing* a personality and damaging the brain so much that the person doesn't work right anymore. The iron bar had cut the connections between his frontal area and the lower "animal" brain. Hence, the frontal area was no longer able to maintain control, and he acted like an animal. Strictly speaking, he was not turned into another, different, person. Likewise, someone on drugs will behave strangely, possibly even violently, but, when the drugs are removed, the basic person remains. We know of no method that will create major personality changes in an orderly, permanent fashion so that you can get a robot or make a different person.

Exotic as such ideas might seem, in most cases we are what we are and believe what we believe after years of a certain life style (Brown, 1976). While we clearly can change bad habits and stop some of the awful things we do, there is no evidence at all that our brains can be taken over or altered to such an extent that we are not the same old person we've always been.

Summary

1. The upper outer covering of the brain is the cerebral cortex. The cerebral cortex is divided into two halves, called hemispheres. The halves are connected through the corpus callosum. The left half controls the right side of the body and vice versa.

2. The cortex is divided into sections. The frontal association area integrates the environment and carries on very complex analyses. The visual area at the back of the head organizes visual information. One the side of the cortex are areas controlling speech, sensation, and motor movements.

3. The lower brain controls basic bodily activity. The thalamus is a relay station to and from the cortex and the lower brain. The cerebellum guides coordination and balance. The hypothalamus is part of a system controlling rage, pleasure, hunger, thirst, and sexual desire. The reticular activating system keeps us alert or puts us to sleep.

4. Parts of the brain are connected to one another through neurons. The neurons have electricity running from the dendrite through the cell to the axon and on out to the synapse. The brain is connected to the body through neurons. Communication through the synapses is actually handled by neurotransmitters, chemicals that regulate different systems such as muscle movement or pain.

5. The endocrine system uses hormones to provide a longer-lasting method of chemical communication than the neurons can provide. The pituitary is the master gland that guides growth, but it also signals the thyroid for metabolism, the adrenal glands for emergencies, and the gonads for sexual activity.

Key Words and Concepts

hemisphere	lower brain	synapse	growth hormone
sensory strip	thalamus	neurotransmitters	thyroid gland
motor strip	cerebellum	acetylcholine	metabolism
visual area	hypothalamus	spinal cord	adrenal glands
frontal association	reticular activating	reflex	adrenaline
area	system	hormones	gonads
dominance	neuron	glands	androgen
corpus callosum	axon	endocrine system	estrogen
cerebral cortex	dendrite	pituitary gland	

Review Questions

Fill in the blank Answer on a separate sheet of paper. (More than one word can fit on a line.)

1. The cerebral cortex is divided into two halves called
   _____ .

2. The _____ connects the two halves of the cerebral cortex.

3. The _____ forms the core of a person's personality.

4. Most of our movements are controlled by the _____ .

5. The touch of a feather on your skin is registered by the _____ .

Matching: Match the function with the proper part of the lower brain.

6. Controls balance

7. Controls hunger and thirst

8. Sends messages to various parts of the brain

9. "Catches" nerve impulses in order to register activity level

    a. thalamus

    b. RAS

    c. cerebellum

    d. hypothalamus

Matching

10. Receive electrical messages from other nerve cells
11. The spaces between nerve cells
12. Carry electrical messages to the end of the nerve cell
13. Chemicals that send messages from neuron to neuron
14. Nerve cells

a. synapses
b. axons
c. neurons
d. dendrites
e. neuro-transmitters

For each of the following, answer T for thyroid gland, A for adrenal gland, and P for pituitary gland. Each answer will be used twice.

15. Regulates metabolism
16. Activated especially during emergencies
17. May cause general sluggishness
18. The master gland
19. Helps regulate blood pressure
20. Helps determine height

Discussion Questions

1. Suppose you met a blind person whose corpus callosum had been cut. If you were to put a comb in this person's left hand, would he or she be able to tell you what was in his or her hand? If yes, explain. If no, what other way could the person communicate "comb" to you? Explain. What if the comb were put in his or her right hand?

2. How do you suppose alcohol would affect each part of the lower brain (thalamus, hypothalamus, cerebellum, RAS) and each part of the upper brain (frontal association area, visual area, motor strip, sensory strip)? Explain.

3. Describe several situations where you might want your neurotransmitters to operate very efficiently and quickly. Describe several situations where you might wish your neurotransmitters to work inefficiently and slowly.

4. The "brain transplant" is a common science fiction theme. Just for fun, imagine that the procedure has just become possible, and you have been chosen as the first candidate. Discuss the following:

   a. Whose brain would you choose? Why?
   b. If you had to choose between a smart, somber brain or a simple, happy brain, which would you choose? Why?
   c. Regardless of your choices in (a) and (b), *who* would you be *after* the transplant? Would your identity be the same as it was before, because you would occupy the same body? Or would your identity be that of the new brain? Explain.

5. Which of the three glands discussed in the chapter would probably be most affected by the aging process? Explain your reasoning and provide supporting examples. Which of the three glands would be least affected by age? Explain.

6. The chapter explains that our sex drive has both physical and social aspects and that sex must be learned by humans. Other than actual experience and heart-to-heart talks, how *do* we learn about sex? Through TV? Through the media in general? Who or what teaches us? And what is the message being taught?

Activities

1. Several advertisers explicitly use the theory of left- and right-hemisphere dominance to promote their products. For example, they openly claim that their products appeal to the left hemisphere and then supply statistics; at the same time, they claim that their products appeal to the right hemisphere and then supply vivid, emotional pictures. (Yes, they actually use the terms "left and right hemispheres" in their ads!)

   Other than these obvious examples, *do* advertisers direct their sales pitches to one hemisphere or another? To find out, collect ten magazine ads that appeal primarily to the left hemisphere, ten that appeal to the right hemisphere, and ten that appeal to both hemispheres. Neatly type each ad onto a sheet of paper and provide captions explaining why you chose the ads that you did.

2. An alternative to the activity in number 1 might be to videotape at random 10 commercials and then analyze each one. Which ones appeal to the left hemisphere? To the right? To both? Explain your reasoning.

3. Contact a local hospital for information on the latest techniques for studying and examining the brain. Ask

about MRIs, CAT scans, PET scans, and EEGs. Find out the advantages and disadvantages of each technique and under what conditions each would be used. Also find out the actual costs of each technique.

4. Conduct research on lobotomies, the surgical procedure for removing or disconnecting the frontal association area. Find out why lobotomies became popular and why they were eventually discontinued. Find out if any versions of lobotomies are still performed today. Compare your findings with any ideas about lobotomies that you may have had before you did this research.

5. Find out how the human brain compares with the brains of other animals. Compare size, development, and structure. One of the more important areas you should compare is the ratio of brain size to body weight. Do any animals have a better brain-body ratio than humans? Another area you can compare is the cubic centimeter capacity, or the volume, of the brain.

6. Find a teacher or counselor or someone at school who has a great deal of medical knowledge about drugs. Find out how various drugs, both legal and illegal, affect the body's neurotransmitters.

7. Some fascinating research is being conducted today on how to repair damaged nerves. Find out what discoveries are being made and particularly focus your research on one of the following areas: (a) burn victims, (b) people with lost limbs, or (c) paraplegics.

8. What common expressions are hidden in the following puzzles?

   a. NOON GOOD   **b.** HE'S HIMSELF

The answers, of course, are: (a) "Good afternoon" and (b) "He's beside himself." Although these particular puzzles are not extremely difficult, the skills of both hemispheres are needed to solve them. The left hemisphere needs to *read* the words, while the right hemisphere needs to determine the *spatial relationship* between the words (for example, the word "good" appears *after* the word "noon").

Here's a more difficult example: **c.** ii ii / ooo ooo

Why are some people better than others at solving these kinds of puzzles? One answer might be that some people have thicker and more efficient corpus callosums, allowing the two hemispheres to work together well. Another answer might be that, in some people, one hemisphere does not dominate over another; these people have developed an efficient "balance" between the hemispheres. In fact, there seems to be some evidence that left-handed people are more likely than right-handed people to have balanced brains. If this is true, it may be safe to assume that "lefties" would do better at solving the puzzles we've shown.

Conduct an experiment to find out if these assumptions are correct. Put together a list of about 20 puzzles, similar to those shown here. Either create your own or get them out of the comics section of a newspaper or *Games Magazine*, which regularly publishes these types of puzzles. Find ten "righties" and ten "lefties" to solve the puzzles (lefties are relatively rare, but you should be able to find ten). Allow each subject two minutes to solve the puzzles. Tally the correct answers.

Do "lefties" perform better? What conclusions can you draw?

An alternative to this activity might be to compare the performance of males and females on these puzzles to see which sex has a more balanced brain.

Incidentally, the answer to puzzle (c) is "Circles under the eyes."

A micrograph of rods and cones in the retina.

Chapter 4

Sensation and Perception

Global Look at the Chapter

Sensation and perception form our world. Without them we can make no sense of what is happening around us. Perception is controlled psychologically in the sense that we can change the incoming stimulation (sensation) to fit our needs or desires. Still, the basic information from sensation is processed by remarkable receptors designed just for each task.

Sensory Processes

We are so used to processing information from the senses that we take this ability for granted. Nonetheless, our ability to understand what is going on around us is truly remarkable. Our brains set up all kinds of methods for handling this complex information. If you receive information that is deliberately confused—well, let's see what happens. We will give you a sentence, and you try to figure out what it says. We have put the "translation" of it somewhere in the next couple of paragraphs. Don't look for it until you have tried to figure out what it says. Here it is:

ThEcOwgAvecOla

This is really a sentence, but you have trouble processing it because the normal shape and boundaries of the words and letters have been rearranged. Everyone must rely heavily on these shapes to be able to read as fast as we do. The eye skips and jumps from one part of the sentence to another; if a word is very common, like "and" or "the," we take only a glimpse of it as the eye looks at clumps of words all at one time. The normal method for reading is to focus on the beginning letters of a sentence and determine what basic *shape* the rest of the words in the sentence have. If everything looks familiar, we assume, after a very slight pause, that the words are known; if, as we read on, the sentence doesn't fit with what comes next, we stop and go back to find out what we missed. If you actually had to read every letter and word on this page, it would take you more than 20 minutes to read it and about eight hours to read this chapter—a fate no one deserves. So what is it we've done to make the example sentence so confusing? We've changed its physical structure. Here is the sentence written in something close to the normal structure; now you should have no trouble whatsoever with it: TheCowGaveCola (Dunn-Rankin, 1978).

All incoming sensation must be interpreted by the brain. As a result, quite often we see what we want to see and hear what we want to hear (or don't see or hear, according to what we really desire). So sensation is not merely a physical event—it can be very psychological. Here is a simple example of making something what it isn't. Read the following sentence from *right to left*, once, without stopping. *Don't* read it again yet.

".rat eht saw tac ehT"

Everybody reads one of two versions: "The cat saw the rat." or "The cat was the rat." Both of these are wrong. You made this mistake because, if you had read the sentence backwards the way it really is written, it wouldn't have made sense to you. Read it again, this time very carefully, and you will see what we mean (Dunn-Rankin, 1978).

One more example: We assign a symbolic "top," "bottom," and "side" to most objects we know, and we keep them that way, regardless of their position. Cut out a piece of paper with four equal sides, put it up on the wall, and call it a "square." Tilt your head and view it. It is still a square. Move your head around some more. It is still a square. Now, cut out the same basic square and call it a "diamond" before you put it up on the wall with one corner at the top. Tilt your head to the point where it actually looks like a "square." Is it? No, it remains a diamond in your mind.

In these examples, what started out as light energy coming into your eyes and going from there to the brain has been given a meaning not contained in the actual source of the light energy.

In this chapter, we will analyze some of our most incredible abilities: (1) **sensation**—the process of receiving information from the environment—and (2) **perception**—our interpretation of what the incoming messages mean. These two processes actually go together and are intermixed. To make it easier to learn about them, however, we will divide the chapter into two sections, starting with sensation.

Sensation
The process of receiving information from the environment.

Perception
A person's interpretation of what an incoming sensory message means.

Sensation

In this section, we will look at the workings of each of the five human senses—sight, hearing, feeling (as in touch), smell, and taste.

Vision

Vision dominates the human senses. We always believe what we see first, and only secondarily do we accept information from taste, smell, hearing, or feeling. Thus, if you are brave enough to eat a green-colored steak, it will taste funny to you even if it has only been colored by a tasteless food dye. Despite the fact that your sense of smell says it is all right, that will make no difference in how it tastes.

White light
Light as it originates from the sun or a bulb before it is broken into different frequencies.

Light Light movement is based on the same principle as snapping a whip. In a whip snap, the energy starts at the wrist and is sent in the shape of a wave down to the end of the whip. Depending on how hard the whip is snapped, the waves can vary from long and slow to short and fast. Light starts out from the sun (or a lightbulb) as **white light**; color is seen only after the waves of white light hit objects and bounce back to us at different speeds. There really is no such thing as "color": We give different light wavelengths certain names (see Figure 4.1). "Color" is seen because the eyes have different "color" receptors for different wavelengths. Some speeds (such as that of ultraviolet light waves) are too slow for our eyes to be able to see the light, but these light waves can be used by other creatures: The bee seeks out flowers using ultraviolet light waves, for example. The waves that are too fast for us to see (such as infrared light waves) are used by snakes to see at night (Manning, 1967).

The key to color, then, is white light waves hitting various objects in the environment and bouncing off at different wavelengths, which in turn hit receptors in our eyes. A good analogy is what happens if a shotgun is fired at the side of a hill: Some of the pellets hit dirt and are absorbed. Some hit leaves and are deflected. Some hit rock or other material and come back at us at different speeds. If these last pellets were light waves, they would be the ones we use for vision. Their speed of movement will vary depending on the texture and solidity of what they hit. For instance, snowflakes are built like crystals, so they have many flat surfaces. Sunlight, which is white, hits the slick flat surfaces of the flakes and bounces off without breaking up, so we see the snowflakes as white. In the same way, a polished wood surface gives out almost-white streaks where the bright light hits the glossy spots (directly reflected light), but, if the end of a board is broken off, we can see a number of different colors. The light hitting the broken board breaks into different wavelengths, depending on which part of the board the light hits and how flat each part is. Water molecules are very strangely shaped and complex. Because of this, they absorb (remove from our vision) the energy at the red end of Figure 4.1, which would be the yellow and red light waves. This leaves two sets of rays that bounce back from water: green or blue. And this is why bodies of water look green or blue to us (Nassau, 1980).

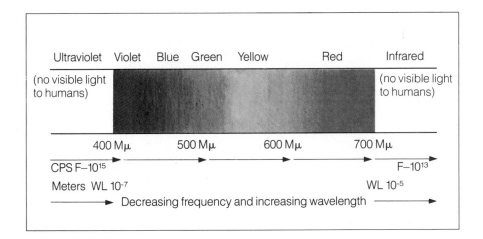

Figure 4.1
Energy waves arranged by frequency and wavelength ("CPS F" refers to the cycles per second of the frequency).

Structure of the Eye Figure 4.2 shows a top view of the eye if the eye were cut in half and the top taken off. The **cornea** (KOR-nee-ah) is a clear outer covering behind which is a fluid. If you look at your eyes in a mirror, they seem shiny because you are seeing a reflection from the fluid behind the cornea. Next comes the portion of the eyes that lovers focus on. It is called the **iris** (EYE-ris), which is actually a colored circular muscle that opens and closes into larger or smaller circles in order to control the amount of light getting into the eye. To see it in operation, face a mirror, cover one eye, and turn on the light. Stand so that the light will hit the covered eye when you remove your hand. Remove your hand, and watch how the iris, which had opened because it was dark behind your hand, quickly closes to a very small circle. When you leave a movie matinee, your irises are wide open to catch the limited light in the darkened theater; as you walk out into the sun, the light seems blinding at first because the irises aren't able to close fast enough; they let in too much light to too many receptors.

The **lens** of your eye is very much like a camera lens; it helps you to focus the objects you see onto the back of the eye where there are receptors. If the lens is not shaped correctly, the image coming in will either overshoot or fall short of the receptors at the back of the eye, and this causes images to blur. Eyeglasses are designed to change the angle at which the light hits the lens, causing the incoming light waves to land properly on the receptors. The lens automatically adjusts to whatever object we want to see. As the muscles controlling the lens make the adjustment, they give the brain information about how much they have moved, and this is one way we learn to judge how far away from us an object is.

What is the black circle in the middle of your eye? Nothing. The **pupil**, as you can see in Figure 4.2, is just an opening that changes size as the iris muscles move to cover and uncover the eye. Since it is dark inside your

Cornea
The clear outer covering of the eye behind which is a fluid.

Iris
A colored circular muscle that opens and closes, forming larger and smaller circles to control the amount of light getting into the eye.

Lens
The part of the eye that focuses an object on the back of the eye.

Pupil
The opening in the eye.

Figure 4.2
Cross section of the eye as seen from the top.

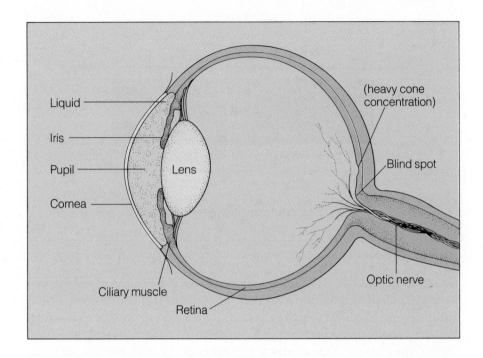

eye, the opening of the pupil looks black, but, if you flash a light inside, the colors coming back through the pupil can vary across the whole range, depending on how the light is bent and what it hits in there.

Psychological factors can control the iris muscles and thus the size of the pupil. The pupils of our eyes get smaller if we see something unpleasant; they get larger if we see something we really like (Millodot, 1982). Those who learn this think they might be onto something. Since the pupils enlarge if someone likes you a lot, checking out pupils may be a way to make sure. In fact, years and years ago about the only way most women could survive was to marry someone. If they found a passable male, they would put a few drops of medicine made from a poisonous plant called *belladonna* into their eyes, causing the pupils to widen. The woman couldn't see very well until it wore off, but long before science, nature knew what wide pupils meant and the men began to fall in love with them, not quite knowing why. *Belladonna* means "beautiful lady." Lest you go off thinking this is foolproof, best to tell you that the pupils open up all the way when someone is *afraid* also, because this makes it possible to explore the threat in the environment better.

The light entering the eye gets to the back of the eyeball and hits the **retina** (RET-in-ah). Millions upon millions of receptors are embedded in the retina. We will discuss them in a moment. Before leaving the overall structure of the eyeball, note in Figures 4.2 and 4.3 that there is a place where all the nerve cells leave the eye in what's called the optic nerve. Retinal receptors are to the right and left of this point, but there are none where this nerve bundle leaves. This is called the **blind spot**. We can't

Retina
The back of the eye, which contains millions of receptors for light.

Blind spot
The portion of the retina through which the optic nerve exits and where there are no receptors for light waves.

see anything when light waves hit that point. Still, the eyes dart back and forth so rapidly that we normally never notice it. If you want to find your blind spot, use Figure 4.4.

Receptors in the Retina Go outside as twilight approaches. Take a chair, a blue object, and a red object (or go where there are some blue and some red flowers). Sit in the chair, put the objects down, and watch them as darkness approaches. The red objects will turn black and disappear, but the blue objects will not turn black until it is almost completely dark outside.

What you are experiencing is the fact that the retina is made up of two different kinds of receptors. The first type of receptor is called a **rod** because it is shaped like one (see photograph, p. 84). The second is called a **cone** because that's the shape it has. Rods are very sensitive to the violet-purple range of wavelengths, but we will only "see" black and white with them because they have no color chemicals in them. There are about 100 million rods in the retina, and they are used for night vision because they respond very well to low levels of light. Since the rods are turning on as it darkens, they are keeping the blue objects visible. The cones are shutting off; so the red objects disappear. Thus cones are used for color and daylight vision and respond best to wavelengths in the red range and shut off at night. You can see color on a highway when you are driving through the city at night because the light level is almost as high as during the day. But, if you watch carefully when you turn away from a populated area and drive down a dimly lit street, you will notice that the images you see are no longer sharp except where the headlights hit. This is because the cones, which provide sharpness of vision, have shut off, and rods by themselves only provide a rough outline of objects. Rods are very heavily packed into the sides of the retina. If you are trying to see

Rod
A visual receptor most sensitive to the violet-purple wavelengths; very sensitive for night vision; "sees" only black and white.

Cone
A visual receptor that responds during daylight; receives color.

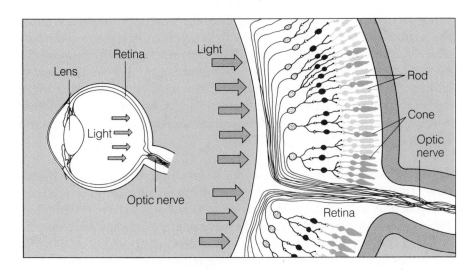

Figure 4.3
Rods and cones transmitting impulses through the optic nerve

Figure 4.4

Finding the blind spot. (a) With your right eye closed, stare at the upper right cross. Hold the book about one foot from you and slowly move it back and forth. You should be able to find a position that causes the black spot to disappear. When it does, that is your blind spot. (b) Repeat this process, but stare instead at the lower cross. When the white space falls on the blind spot, the black line will appear to be continuous because your brain will fill in details for the place it can't see.

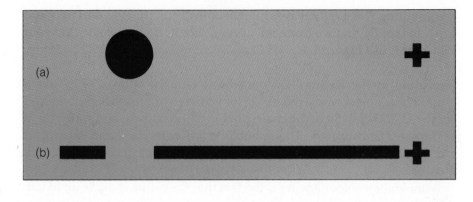

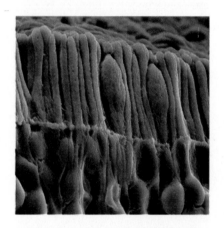

The visual receptors, rods and cones, are named for their shapes. The rods are the long, thin cells on the left; the cones are the roundish cells in between the rods.

something in a dark area, look *away* from where you think it is, and the rods on the sides of your retina will pick up its shape. Or have a friend sneak up on you in the dark and notice how you can spot him or her if you are approached from the side, but you have trouble if he or she moves toward the center of your line of sight, since the cones that have shut off are located mostly in the center of each retina. In daylight, on the other hand, the rods shut off, so, when you enter a darkened movie theater, you can't see anything at first, since the cones can't handle darkness.

Fire departments take rods and cones very seriously. Fire trucks used to be red. Today only a few are. Too many accidents occurred at twilight because automobile drivers couldn't see the red trucks very well. Most trucks today are a yellowish green, which is right in the middle of the color chart (Figure 4.1) between violet on one end and red on the other. This compromise coloring provides the best visibility for both day and night.

Color Vision   This is how **color vision** works: All the colors we see are red, blue, green, or a mixture of these three. You can understand the principle of mixture if you take red, blue, and green spotlights and shine them on a white wall. By mixing the lights, you will get every color possible. Throughout the center part of the retina are millions of cones connected together. Some receive red, some green, and some blue wavelengths. Depending on the texture of the objects we are viewing, light from each part of the object will bounce back at different wavelengths, and the brain will mix these wavelengths, making the object appear a specific color (Normann et al., 1984).

Color Defects   A number of people have a defect called **color blindness**. The most common form of this problem is found in those who can see color only in the yellow-blue range and cannot see red or green color. The receptors *do* respond to the light wave energy, but they *don't* see it as "colored." About 8 percent of males have this inherited defect, only 0.5 percent of females. For these people, the red or green cone system does

(a) Photo and chips as seen by normal person

(b) Photo and chips as seen by red-green blind person

(c) Photo and chips as seen by yellow-blue blind person

(d) Photo and chips as seen by totally colorblind person

not work (in terms of seeing color). They still have a third color-receiving (cone) system that responds only in the yellow-blue area (Mollon, 1982). In all other respects, their vision is completely normal.

Truly "color-blind" people are very rare. They respond only with rods. Even a moderately bright light can be very painful for them because all the rods are responding in unison to white light, something they are not designed to do.

People sometimes make things up out of nowhere and pass on the misinformation from one generation to another. You may hear that dogs and cats see everything in gray because they have no color vision. This is simply not true. Both animals have very elaborate rod and cone systems, just as we do (Muntz, 1981; McFarland, 1981). And you will hear that bulls go crazy when they see a red matador's cape. Bulls and cows have full color vision, but the idea of red inflaming them doesn't make sense. The bull is responding to movement, not color. If you don't believe us, try getting in a ring with one and waving a black or green or purple or whatever cape and see what happens.

Afterimages All physical systems strive to stay in balance. If we are cold, we shiver to increase circulation; if hot, we sweat to cool down. The same principle applies to the cone network of the eyes. If you stare at a colored object for a minute or so, the chemicals in the cones for the colors you are seeing will be partially used up as changes in the chemicals cause electrical impulses (signals to the brain). The chemicals for all the colors you are *not* seeing are still intact. No message has been sent to the brain for them because you haven't seen these colors. As a result, the cone system is not in balance. If you look away from the object and stare at a white piece of paper, you will see the object in opposite colors. This **afterimage** results from the remaining "unused" cones firing so that all the cones can restore themselves to equal chemical levels at the same time. The same process will occur if you stare at a television for a while and then look at the wall.

You do not see these afterimages during normal viewing because you keep replacing one image with another, and each image fires a different set of cones (Hurvich, 1974). Figure 4.5 gives you the chance to see the afterimage principle in action.

Hearing

In hearing, or **audition** (aw-DISH-on), the energy form is sound waves, which have a much slower range of speeds but move in roughly the same fashion as do light waves. Many animals use sound more than humans do. The dolphin, for instance, sends out clicks, and the echoes that come back tell it the size and shape of what the sound waves have hit— whether the object is food, something dangerous, or a place of refuge (Fobes & Smock, 1981). Bats are amazing. They use sound waves to find

Afterimage
The firing of the cones not used after viewing something steadily in order to bring the visual system back in balance.

Audition
The sense of hearing.

Rod and cone behavior is illustrated by these two fire engines. Note that in daylight or bright artificial light, both engines are visible. Now move this picture to very dim light, and stare at the center of the red fire engine for about four minutes. Because the image is falling on the center portion of the retina, which is mostly cones, the red engine will disappear, while the blue engine (rods in dim light) can still be seen.

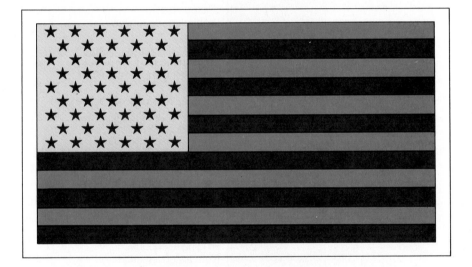

Figure 4.5
To prove the afterimage effect for yourself, take a sheet of white typing paper or other flat white surface, and put it aside. Focus your eyes on the last star (the one in the lower right-hand corner), and stare at it for one minute. Now quickly move your eyes to the white paper, and you should see the flag appear in red, white, and blue.

extremely small flying insects by bouncing sound waves off them. Nature has given their favorite food, the bat moth, a built-in detector for the high-frequency sounds emitted by the bats, so the moths can try to escape.

Pitch and Intensity Different sounds vary in terms of **pitch**, which means how high or low the sound is. Most men have a lower pitch to their voices than women do.

Sounds also vary in terms of **intensity**—how loud they are. Intensity is measured in **decibels** (DES-e-bels). When sounds reach a decibel level

Pitch
How high or low a sound is.

Intensity
How loud a sound is.

Decibels
A measure of how loud a sound is (its intensity).

beyond 130 (see Figure 4.6), they can become painful. Continuous loud noises will actually impair hearing by killing receptor cells in the ear (Bohne, 1985). Sleep is disturbed by noise as high as that of a refrigerator (70), but helped by a continuous sound of roughly 50 decibels (Gilbert, 1985).

Structure of the Ear   "My, what big ears you have, Grandma!" said Little Red Riding Hood.

"The better to hear you with, my dear." Actually, the wolf is wrong. Ear size makes no difference, but the shape does have a purpose. The cupped design of the outer ear catches the sound waves and funnels them in toward the **eardrum** (see Figure 4.7), a piece of skin stretched

Eardrum
A piece of skin stretched over the entrance to the ear; vibrates to sound.

Figure 4.6
Decibel chart showing sound levels of various objects and events.

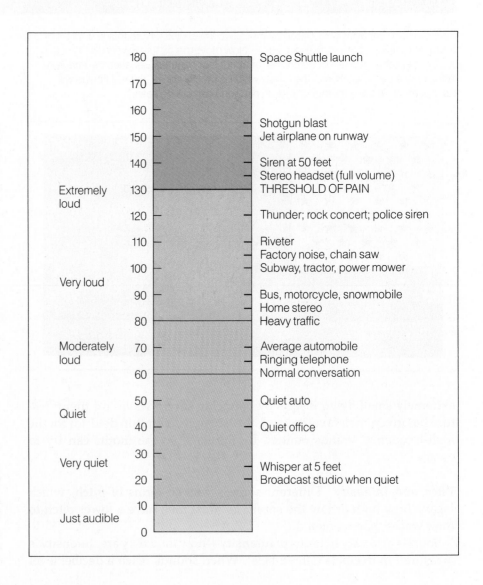

180	Space Shuttle launch
170	
160	Shotgun blast
150	Jet airplane on runway
140	Siren at 50 feet
	Stereo headset (full volume)
Extremely loud — 130	THRESHOLD OF PAIN
120	Thunder; rock concert; police siren
110	Riveter
	Factory noise, chain saw
100	Subway, tractor, power mower
Very loud	
90	Bus, motorcycle, snowmobile
	Home stereo
80	Heavy traffic
Moderately loud — 70	Average automobile
	Ringing telephone
60	Normal conversation
50	Quiet auto
Quiet	
40	Quiet office
30	
Very quiet	Whisper at 5 feet
20	Broadcast studio when quiet
10	
Just audible	
0	

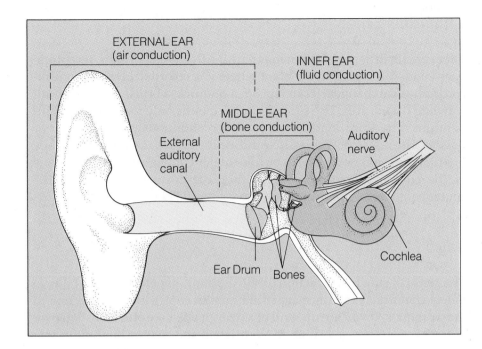

Figure 4.7
Structure of the ear ("conduction" means movement of sound by air, fluid, or bone vibration).

tightly—just like a drum—over the entrance to the rest of the ear. When the sound waves hit the drum, it vibrates. This vibration causes a small bone to vibrate. This bone is attached to another bone and acts like a lever, causing it, in turn, to vibrate. A third bone is attached to a snail-shaped unit called the **cochlea** (KOKE-lee-ah). The cochlea is filled with fluid and small hairs, called *cilia*.

The key to hearing is the existence of these 20,000 **hair cells**, which we gradually lose as we age. They are lined up in the cochlea and "tuned" to receive different frequencies just as the strings are tuned on a musical instrument. The hair cells will respond to movement of only a *trillionth* of an inch, about the space between two atoms. As this movement occurs, it causes a flow of electrical particles in the nerve cell connected to each hair (Loeb, 1985). The electrical impulse goes through the **auditory nerve** to the brain where the sound pattern is interpreted. How strong a sound is and when it arrives at one ear is contrasted by the brain with the strength and arrival time at the other ear, and the difference between them helps us locate where the sound is coming from.

Sound can have strong psychological implications. For instance, some cells specialize; that is, certain cells recognize specific important sound patterns. Thus, a bird mother makes sounds to her offspring inside the egg, so she can be recognized later; the infant bird will then follow her sounds as it moves about. Newborn human babies relax when hearing tapes of the mother's voice or heartbeat, so this must be a human phenomenon also.

Cochlea
A snail-shaped part of the ear, filled with fluid and small hairs that vibrate to incoming sound.

Hair cells
Same as cilia.

Auditory nerve
Bundle of nerves carrying sound to the brain.

Cutaneous Senses

Cutaneous receptors
The nerve receptors in the skin that account for the sense of touch.

There are three types of **cutaneous** (cue-TAIN-ee-us), or skin, **receptors**. Each sends a message to the brain where it is recorded. The first one records physical changes. It can register a pinprick, a bruise, or even an ant crawling up the arm. The second kind responds only to changes in temperature. The third kind remains active continuously to an injury or poison. These last receptors cause the feelings we all dread, because they fire for hours and hours after a burn or major cut. Figure 4.8 shows some of the cutaneous receptors. (Lest there be any confusion, "touch," "cutaneous" and "skin receptors" have essentially the same meaning.)

Smell

Olfaction
The sense of smell.

The sense of smell, or **olfaction** (ol-FAC-shun), depends on the ability to detect chemicals, and once again the human comes in a poor second to most animals. If you are upwind of a deer, it will take off before you ever see it because it is sensitive to your smell (no matter how often you bathe). A shark uses your odor molecules in the water to decide if you are worth eating.

Smell is the most animal-like of the human senses. Odors are very hard to define using words, but when an odor is associated with an emo-

Figure 4.8
The skin senses include touch, pressure, pain, cold, and warmth. This drawing shows different forms the skin receptors can take.

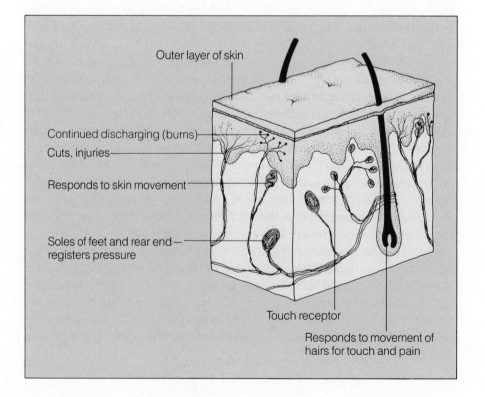

Outer layer of skin

Continued discharging (burns)

Cuts, injuries

Responds to skin movement

Soles of feet and rear end — registers pressure

Touch receptor

Responds to movement of hairs for touch and pain

tional event, we never forget it. If we ever happen to smell that odor again, it will recreate a complete and very strong emotional memory (Engen, 1987).

Mechanisms of Smell   Inside the nasal cavity (Figure 4.9), embedded in a layer of mucus, are microscopic hairs called **cilia** (SIL-ee-ah) that collect molecules of odor. When the odor molecules attach to the hairs, an electrical signal is sent to the **olfactory bulbs**, which generate a "code" that is sent to the brain for interpretation (Rivlin & Gravelle, 1984).

Cilia
Tiny hairs (that receive odor molecules). Some act as receptors in the nose.

Olfactory bulbs
Units that receive odor molecules and communicate their nature to the brain.

Smell Communication   The most critical use for our sense of smell is information about food heading toward the mouth. In fact, smell is more important in eating than is taste. If you don't believe this, try holding your nose when you eat. The food will have almost no taste at all.

Animals use smell to communicate sexual interest. An animal's body sends out odor chemicals, called **pheromones** (FER-oh-moans), in order to reach a possible partner. Whether humans have such sexual communication is not clear. A few studies find some possible connection, but not all of them. Since almost all creatures communicate this way, it seems probable that the human would too. This is difficult to study because human sexual interest is a complex mixture of things like clothing, perfumes, fads about body shape, and so forth. There is no evidence, however, that "musk" perfumes do anything to make the male more attractive but instead make it difficult to get near him. As a matter of fact, musk works best in cockroach courtship (true). Even so, there actually *was* a study in which the researchers found that people could tell male from female by smelling sweaty T-shirts (Russell et al., 1977).

Pheromones
Odor chemicals that communicate a message.

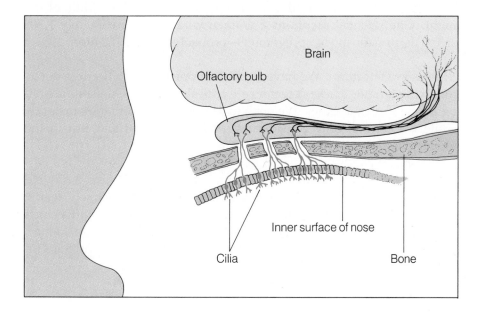

Figure 4.9
Mechanisms of smell

Taste

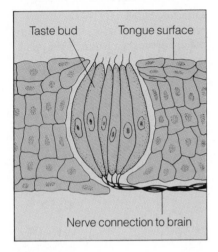

Figure 4.10
Taste buds

Taste receptors operate by chemical communication. The major receivers are the little red spots (because of their rich blood supply) on the tongue. These are called "taste buds" because they resemble flowers (see Figure 4.10). The mucus and saliva in the mouth cleanses the buds, but it takes a while to do so, as you may have learned on Thanksgiving if you have ever eaten some cranberries and followed them by a drink of milk— a horrible combination. There are four types of receptors—*sweet, sour, bitter,* and *salt.* These combine sensations much as the cones in vision do to give us the subtle differences between, say, barbecued ribs and sweet-and-sour pork (Rivlin & Gravelle, 1984).

Salt Needs   Salt is necessary for survival. It operates nerve cells, helps keep body chemistry in balance, and is used for muscle contraction. A very low-salt diet can make you dizzy and sick. In healthy people, excess salt is quickly and efficiently removed from the body in the urine with no ill effects (Beauchamp, 1987). While some uses of salt may be learned (such as salting some cooked foods), the evidence suggests humans are born with a fixed sequence of need. The newborn does not like salt. But, from the age of a few months onward, youngsters want salt. Until late childhood, this interest in salt remains high, while, on the other hand, children dislike spicy, sour, or bitter food. This is why the children's menu at fast-food chains tastes like cardboard with salt on it. That's all they want to eat (Cowart, 1981). The desire for salt gradually tapers off with age. But then, much later in life, it reappears. Old people love chili dogs with mustard, onions, pepper, salt, and almost anything else around, because their taste receptors are not as sharp as they once were. Pregnant women seek an extra supply of salt for the fetus; you will hear of a pregnant woman suddenly needing a pickle in the middle of the night. One scientist mentions a woman who ate approximately 1,500 salted herring during her pregnancy—probably a record (Denton, 1983).

Bitterness Detectors   We have more than one type of bitterness detector on the tongue. These detectors are critical. Almost all poisons are bitter in one way or another. We need to process this information instantly while we are still only considering swallowing what was put in the mouth (Bartoshuk, 1978).

Sugar Needs   Most animals need sugar. Human newborns a day old can tell when something has sugar in it, and they will actively seek it (Cowart, 1981). Sugar is vital for energy to run the body. Too little sugar makes a person tremble, feel faint, and causes mental confusion. Hence, the desire for something sweet is built in, even if it presents problems for those on a diet.

Perception

The truly remarkable thing about the world "out there" is how stable and organized it seems. You go to the parking lot and put the key into the right car. You don't try to put it into a Honda if you own a Buick. At the supermarket, you buy three small grapefruit if that's what you need. You don't come back with three very large lemons. You go to another room to get a certain book. If the book is sideways, upside down, lying on the floor, whatever, you don't decide it is not the same book. But, in every one of those positions, the book looks entirely different to the eye. What amazing creatures we are! Through a combination of inborn abilities and experience, we gradually are able to handle billions of bits of information correctly. We make the world make sense. This is **perception**. Perception is the process of assembling sensory information to understand what the incoming energy means. Perception is always a matter of *interpretation* and *expectation*. For example, experimenters have had subjects smoke dried-up weeds from a pasture rolled in brown paper, and the subjects report that the "marijuana" sensations are extraordinary. Benjamin Franklin used to entertain his friends by hooking himself up to an electrical laboratory apparatus; then they all held hands, supposedly getting a wonderful sensation. Everyone laughed and thought it was delightful. Like the weeds, it was but a matter of suggestion (Oster, 1970).

Perception
Assembling sensory information to understand incoming sensory information.

Perceptual Constancies

Our world is always in motion. So are we, in relation to the world. Things change from one split second to another. The word "constancy" means holding steady. And this is what we must do to the world in order to maintain order and control, to make sense out of our environment.

Size Constancy   In the 1500s, Spanish explorers arrived at the Grand Canyon, something the likes of which they had never seen before. According to their records, they stood atop the south rim and looked across at the other rim, in some places more than ten miles across. They looked down at the river and estimated its width at six feet across. The Indians in the area knew better because they had been down to the bottom and had discovered that the river was about two miles wide (Hawgood, 1967). Thus, when the Indians stood on the rim of the canyon, they perceived a two-mile-wide river that looked smaller "because it was far away"; they were using what is called **size constancy**, the ability to retain the size of an object no matter where it is located. This skill is so important that it appears in an infant only a couple of weeks old (Pribram, 1971).

It is possible, though, to trick the brain, and this allows you to see size constancy in operation: The average cigarette pack is about three and

Size constancy
The ability to retain the size of an object regardless of where it is located.

The river winding below in the Grand Canyon is the one the Spanish thought was six feet wide.

three-eighths inches high. In a laboratory, a specially constructed cigarette pack only two inches high is put in front of people. They are asked to judge how far it is from them. They will claim the pack is much farther away than it is. Why? Because they know its usual size and it appears smaller. Hence, their brains tell them that it *must* be more distant—things get smaller only with more distance.

Color Constancy   As discussed, we have three different color receptors (for red, blue, and green) that blend varying energy waves together to give an object color. But notice that, if you take an apple from a bright kitchen into a darkened room with just the TV on, the apple still seems exactly the same color. It hasn't turned darker. The light being reflected from the apple cannot be the same in the two locations. So how do we hold the color constant? The visual network works all by itself once we have decided what color something is. It has the ability to increase or decrease *mentally* the internal firing of visual receptors to equal what the brain tells it the color is (Mollon, 1982). This is called **color constancy**, but it only works—like the Grand Canyon example—when we already know what color something is.

Brightness Constancy   Possibly color constancy can be better understood after we look at **brightness constancy**, which follows roughly the same principles. Find a familiar black object. Look at it indoors, then take it outside on a very bright sunny day. The level of brightness reflected from the object is extremely high outside, yet it looks to be about the

Color constancy
The ability to perceive an object as the same color regardless of the environment.

Brightness constancy
By taking an average, the human visual network keeps brightness constant as an object changes environment.

In Focus: Size Constancy

If we stand on a railroad tie and look down the track, the railroad ties in the distance actually seem to get smaller. But because of size constancy, we're not fooled for a moment. The *eyes* record the railroad ties in the distance as tiny, but the *brain* S T R E T C H E S them out to "normal" size.

Depth perception
The ability to see objects in space.

Visual cliff
A large table with Plexiglas, used to demonstrate depth perception in small children.

Binocular disparity
The difference between the image provided by each eye. When the images are brought together in the brain, they provide a sense of depth.

Space constancy
The ability to keep objects in the environment steady.

same color as it did inside, rather than "bright black." The brain causes the rods and cones to compensate for the brightness. If the object seems too bright to match our concept of "black," some of the visual nerve cells shut off.

To see the brain in action, look at Figure 4.11. We assume the light is hitting the object from the left side. This makes the right side darker, as it would be in real life. But, if you cover the "shadow" at the lower right, the picture no longer makes sense in terms of a belief that light is coming from the left. It now looks like an open book, one side of which could be dark regardless of light direction. Further, since a book is printed, note that your visual system makes the "page" look much darker once you cover the shadow (Land, 1977; Beck, 1975).

Space Constancy The most common type of auto accident is the "rear-ender." Despite many warnings, people don't take "not following too closely" to heart—because they don't understand perception. We have to keep objects in the environment steady in order to survive. This is called **space constancy**. But we must allow some motion. There are two types of motion: *self-motion* and *object-motion*. We must choose between allowing ourselves to move in reference to the environment and allowing the environment to move in reference to us. If we allow both at one time, severe dizziness results. For example, we can focus on telephone poles as we move along in a car (object motion), or we can focus on ourselves and the inside of the car (self-motion), letting the poles blur. Usually when we drive, we are aware of our own movement. When that is the case, we must hold the cars in front of us steady in our minds. As a result, only a *major* change in the speed of the cars will be noticed. A small change, such as occurs during a normal stop, will not be perceived well

Figure 4.11
Depending on your assumptions regarding light direction, the brightness changes. See text.

(Probst et al., 1984). This is why auto manufacturers were forced to put a third brake-warning light at eye level starting with 1986 cars.

Depth Perception **Depth perception** is the ability to see objects "out there" in space. It is built into a baby from a very young age. This was shown by an experimenter who was on a picnic one day at the Grand Canyon. She wondered if her baby would crawl over the canyon rim or already "knew better." She sensibly decided not to try it at the canyon itself in case the baby failed to stop. So, in a laboratory, she constructed what is called the **visual cliff** experiment (Figure 4.12). This experiment uses a large table with retaining walls of wood on three sides. The fourth side is left open. A piece of heavy, clear Plexiglas covers the table and extends many feet beyond the open edge. To the baby's eyes, it looks as if anyone going beyond the end of the table will fall into space. Babies from 6 to 14 months old were placed on the table and enticed by rattles and goodies to leave the table and "fall" over the fake cliff. But the babies wouldn't go beyond the edge onto the Plexiglas (Gibson & Walk, 1960). This showed that humans have depth perception almost from the beginning.

Depth perception requires a number of brain skills. First, there is **binocular disparity** (di-SPAR-i-tee). There is a difference (disparity) between the images received by each of your eyes (binocular means "two eyes"). Hold your finger steady in front of your eyes; first close one eye, then the other, and notice how the finger shifts. This is the result of each eye seeing a different image. We have to bring these images together in our brains in order to see them correctly. In the process of doing so, we judge and "see" distance and depth (Poggio, 1984).

Another cue to distance is called **visual texture**. "Texture" refers to how smooth or rough something appears to be—that is, how clear its de-

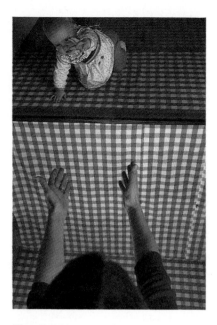

Figure 4.12
The "Visual Cliff." The baby likes to crawl to the mother, but is not about to fall over a cliff to get to her.

Visual texture
Depth perception based on how rough or smooth objects appear.

Figure 4.13
Binocular stereoscopic pictures

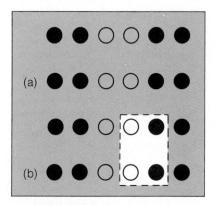

Figure 4.15
Similarity

Similarity
A perceptual cue in which we group like things together.

Closure
The process of filling in the missing details of what is viewed.

Illusion
An inaccurate perception.

tails are. Note, in Figure 4.14, that we gauge the distance of flowers in each row by how clearly we can see them. Since we can see the individual flowers at the bottom of the picture, we know they are close. As they become more distant, we see much less detail, and they appear "smooth," blending together, so we know these are "way out there." Others that we can't tell apart at all are "way, way out there."

Other Perceptual Cues There are other examples of how we organize the world so that it makes sense. We interpret things the way we feel they *should* be, not in terms of how they actually are. One example of such perceptual cues is **similarity**, in which we group like things together. In Part A of Figure 4.15, you perceive three squares, one of white circles and two of black circles. You won't see squares made up of white and black circles (highlighted in Part B). We group like things together to keep the world organized.

Another process is called **closure**, in which we fill in (close) the details that aren't there to complete the picture. For example, in Figure 4.16, we see a complete word, although it obviously isn't one.

Illusions

Illusions occur when we perceive something inaccurately. They are misperceptions. Nonetheless, they are important because they show how we construct the world. A striking illusion is the "Room of Mystery" found at carnivals and amusement parks. When you go into one of these rooms, you seem to be walking at a very steep angle and feel like you might fall over if you don't hold onto something. Guides claim there is a mysterious magnetic force involved. Actually, if you look at Figure 4.17, you will see the unique construction of this room. It is built in such a way that you can't tell it from a normal room; everything in the room is glued or nailed down. The room *is* on a slight angle, but, since you expect to be able to walk and stand straight up, the mixed signals your brain is getting make you feel as if you are going to fall over. You are actually walking only at about the angle required to get to a higher level at a sports stadium. But because your eyes and your body are sending mixed signals to your brain, it decides you are in danger, which increases the effect. Try going through one of these or similar distorted rooms with a friend (you trust) and keep your eyes closed. Now it's simple because you aren't getting mixed signals.

Most people think of illusions as "mistakes" that we make. That is not really the case. Instead, over the years, each of us learns to change what we see so that the world makes more sense. It is truly fascinating to see the eye-brain mechanisms perform some of these changes. We will use what is called the **Müller-Lyer illusion** (MUE-ler-Liar) to illustrate the point. Look at Figure 4.18 and decide which of the two lines is longer. The "arrowhead" line looks much shorter. It is not; measure them. Some have thought the effect results from the arrowheads drawing the eyes in, but that is not the explanation. If the figures are flashed to the eyes faster than the eyes can move, the illusion remains (Bolles, 1969). So, how do

Figure 4.16
Closure

Müller-Lyer illusion
Two pictures in which one inner line seems longer than the other but really isn't.

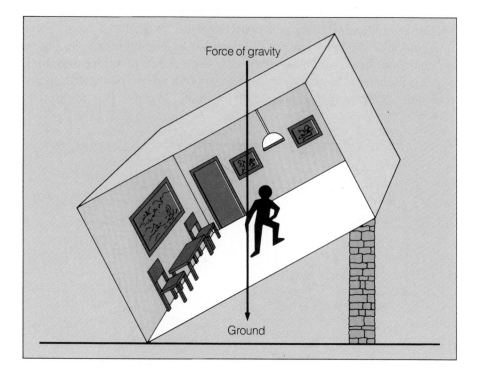

Figure 4.17
Tilted room: objects are glued to the walls and floor causing the eye/brain mechanism to think the room is at a really *severe* angle.

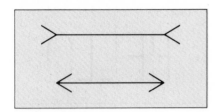

Figure 4.18
Müller-Lyer Illusion: both lines are the same size.

we explain it? The Müller-Lyer effect is an excellent vehicle for understanding what is going on.

Suppose you take two identical books and place them on a table, as shown in Figure 4.19. Stand them on their ends and align them side by side so that one book has the open pages facing you and the other has the cover facing you. Sit down in a chair directly in front of the books and look at them on the table from a distance of about six or seven feet. Next, ask yourself the length of each book's spine. Are they the same length? You will see them as being so, even though the images arriving on the back of the eye are *not* the same length. The images arriving at the eye can't be the same size since the spine of one book is seven or eight inches farther away from you than the other one. You are experiencing size constancy. Both spines appear the same length. This happens because we know both books are the same size.

Now, Figure 4.19 has been tampered with by an artist. Both lines representing the spines in that drawing are identical in length. Try measuring them. Follow this carefully and you will see how the eye-brain mechanism works: (1) Two identical lines for the spines arrive at the eye. (2) If the lines are the same length—which they are—then the spine of the book with the pages open and facing you is made longer by the brain since, in real life, if the lines were equal then that book has got to be bigger than the other one. Again, if the images of the spines are the same length, the books can't be the same size because the spine of one book has to be farther away than the other. Hence, the eye-brain mechanism makes the line in the book that is open toward you look longer than the other one—just as it would have to be if the books were real.

Finally, turn the page sideways and you will see that the books form a Müller-Lyer illusion. Now you know why the "arrowhead" part of that illusion looks shorter than the other part. The eye-brain system has so much experience in real life with seeing these kinds of angles and interpreting their lengths that just seeing part of a whole picture triggers a complete analysis of the length of the lines. We use this method to

Figure 4.19
(Both book spines are the *same* length.

analyze the height or length not only of books but also of buildings, fences, windows, and so forth (Gregory, 1968).

Many illusions come from the need for us to make sense about our surroundings. We make guesses in the context of what we think should be the case (Gregory, 1981). For instance, suppose you see a small dot far away on the opposite side of the highway coming toward you. You assume this is a regular-sized car. Next, suppose you are in a field with no roads anywhere, and, across the field, you see a round object the same size as the one you saw before moving at the same speed, just at eye level, coming right toward you. Can you imagine your panic? Since it can't be a car, it must be—what? An enormous bee? A hawk? In any case, you form opinions about the nature of objects and then they look that way to you—at least for a while. This is the case with what is called a **reversible figure**. Since the shape of the object shown in Figure 4.20 is such that it can be more than one thing, the eye-brain mechanism keeps "changing its mind." First you assume that it is a vase, but then all of a sudden the faces of two men nose to nose appear; then it looks like a vase again, and so forth. Obviously, something that appears to be an illusion is really the brain doing the best it can with an ambiguous figure, wanting to make certain it doesn't miss something important.

Figure 4.20
This vase creates the face-goblet illusion.

Subliminal Perception

There are all kinds of videotapes on the market today that claim they can reach your unconscious with messages that can control diet, eliminate smoking, and help you be more popular. During the playing of the tape, a message, such as "Don't eat chocolate," is flashed on the screen over and over so fast that the conscious mind is not aware of it, but it is still registered.

A lot of attention was given to this process in the 1950s when an advertiser very rapidly flashed "EAT POPCORN" on the movie screen at a theater. The advertiser claimed that popcorn sales increased 50 percent. What is interesting is that studies since then have not been able to duplicate these results. In fact, some experimenters have flashed words on a screen and offered a lot of money to students who could say what the words were. No student turns down money, but none of them was able to tell the researcher the words (Moore, 1984; McConnell et al., 1958). We know the brain registers anything seen, but it doesn't pay much attention to this so-called **subliminal perception** (sub-LIM-uh-null). The reason may be obvious: The brain does not consider a faint message as important as one that is there for a while. Still, people buy many of these videotapes. (By the way, subliminal comes from the word "limen," which means a line that marks off a boundary; hence, *sub*—beneath—the limen would mean that the thing seen is below the level of everyday consciousness.)

Reversible figure
An illusion in which the same object is seen as two alternate figures—first one, then the other.

Subliminal perception
Stimulation presented below the level of consciousness.

Do You Have ESP?

Most people you meet, possibly even you, will have had an experience similar to this one: You feel as if you have gotten a message that a friend is sick or lonely and needs you. You call and check—and it turns out to be the case. Was this mental telepathy? That is, did the two of you actually communicate in some special way?

Most psychologists don't believe in the phenomenon of **extrasensory perception**, or ESP (receiving information without the aid of our "normal" senses—vision, hearing, and so on—hence, *extra* sensory, or even beyond normal awareness). Nonetheless, there have been a number of carefully done studies that suggest that this type of communication is possible. Here is where the difficulty lies: Many scientists say that the biggest problem with the existence of ESP is that there isn't any way to get the message from one person to another. For example, suppose you wanted to send a message to someone who is now in New York or California (that is, across the country, depending on where you live). How can it get to that person? Even if you got the message to the proper state, how do you guide it to the right street address? Since the brain is run by electricity, today's sensitive measuring devices can pick up electrical impulses about three or four inches from the skull, but beyond that they measure nothing. So electrical impulses don't seem to

One would hesitate to not agree with whatever Madam Mae says.

be the answer. Another problem is that the ESP ability seems to come and go; it is not consistent. Those who claim to have it on one day may not have it on another. That makes it difficult to study. Yet another problem is that most ESP demonstrations are fake. Stage shows in which someone "reads" another's mind are preplanned and use a stooge. Popular acts, such as bending a key with psychic forces, are magic tricks, not ESP.

Even though most scientists doubt that ESP exists, there are people who keep claiming they have these special powers. Maybe

even you do. Never say "never." After all, most people believed the radio would never work. Next people were certain television was impossible. Television certainly seems impossible. As you sit in a room reading this, all the shows on television are going through the air in the room (can't be!?). It is extremely important to remember that we (you, we, scientists, researchers, whoever) know almost nothing in comparison to the vast intelligence of our universe. We can't even understand the smallest ant. If you take an ant apart, it's almost impossible to find a "brain" as we know it, yet ants can walk, communicate, build houses, carry, dig, breathe, avoid obstacles, see, and even interpret.

Here is something interesting to try: A few people are so sensitive that they can tell a difference in an object's color and pick the right one using only touch (Youtz, 1968). Try it. You may be one of the *very* few who can do it. Have someone take three or four different-colored squares—all of exactly the same type of colored paper—and put them under a thin piece of plastic so you can't tell differences by texture alone. Blindfold yourself and try to tell one color from another using just the tips of your fingers. It has been done—in one case, with 68 percent success in telling blue from white. Good luck!

In Focus: ESP

Extrasensory perception
The receipt of information without the aid of the "normal" senses such as hearing, seeing, feeling, and so on.

Four Types of ESP Commonly Studied

1. **Telepathy:** (te-LEP-e-thee) Reading someone's mind.
   Example: Your best friend is thousands of miles away. He hurts a foot, and at the same time your own foot starts to hurt. You have "read" the pain in his mind.

2. **Clairvoyance:** (klar-VOI-ence) Seeing or knowing something without being there.
   Example: Your best friend hurts her foot, and at the same time you "see" her do it. So you call her up, and she is amazed!

3. **Precognition:** (PRE-kog-NISH-en) Predicting the future.
   Example: You realize hours before he does it that your friend will hurt his foot.

4. **Psychokinesis:** (SIGH-koe-ki-KNEE-sis) Moving objects with your brain.
   Example: You concentrate and concentrate and you *cause* a log to move, over which your friend stumbles and hurts her foot. (Let's be thankful that there is no scientific evidence so far to support the existence of psychokinesis.)

Summary

1. Sensation is the process of receiving information from the environment.

2. Vision is our most powerful sense. It uses light waves from the environment, which go through a lens in the eye and hit the retina. Information is then forwarded to the brain. The receptors in the retina are rods for night vision and cones for daylight color vision.

3. Audition uses sound waves to stimulate the eardrum. Sound varies in pitch and intensity. The intensity is measured using decibels. Hair cells in the cochlea are tuned to receive the information and forward it to the brain.

4. Cutaneous senses respond to three basic types of stimulation: physical changes, temperature, and some type of injury.

5. In olfaction, the olfactory bulbs receive information from the tiny hairs (cilia) in the nose and send this information to the brain.

6. Taste receptors respond to sweet, sour, bitter, and salt. Sugar and salt are necessary for human survival. Bitterness receptors are used to detect poisons.

7. Perception is based on interpretation and expectation. To organize the world in order to understand it, our perception holds it steady by using size, color, brightness, and space constancies.

8. Depth perception arises from binocular disparity and visual texture. We also order the world by using similarity and closure.

9. Illusions are misperceptions, but they show how we organize the world. The Müller-Lyer illusion is an example of how we evaluate objects like a book to determine their shape and size.

10. Subliminal perception does not work according to most studies. Still, people continue to believe in it.

11. ESP may be possible, but we cannot figure out any method by which it could be accomplished.

Key Words and Concepts

sensation
white light
cornea
iris
lens
pupil
retina
blind spot
rod
cone
color vision
color blindness

afterimage
audition
pitch
intensity
decibels
eardrum
cochlea
hair cells
auditory nerve
cutaneous
  receptors
olfaction

cilia
olfactory bulbs
pheromones
taste receptors
perception
size constancy
color constancy
brightness
  constancy
space constancy
depth perception
visual cliff

binocular disparity
visual texture
similarity
closure
illusions
Müller-Lyer
  illusion
reversible figure
subliminal
  perception
extrasensory
  perception

Review Questions

Matching

1. Responsible for focusing
2. Muscle that controls amount of light that hits the eye
3. Located at the back of the eye
4. Black circle in middle of the eye
5. Outer covering of the eye

a. pupil

b. lens

c. retina

d. cornea

e. iris

For each of the following, answer R if "rod" applies, C if "cone" applies.

6. Used for night vision
7. Responds best to red wavelengths
8. More sensitive to violet-purple range of wavelengths
9. Used for color and daylight vision

Multiple Choice

10. If someone is said to be color blind, it usually means that:
    a. he or she can see no color at all
    b. part of his or her cone system is not working
    c. his or her system of rods is not working.

11. For people who are truly color blind:
    a. none of their cone systems is working
    b. none of their rods is working
    c. neither cones nor rods are working.

12. Cutaneous refers to the:
    a. nose   **b.** ears   **c.** skin   **d.** eyes.

13. The hairs inside the nasal cavity are called:
    a. pheromones   **c.** cilia
    b. bulbs   **d.** bulb cells.

14. Smell chemicals are called:
    a. pheromones   **c.** cilia
    b. bulbs   **d.** nasalines.

Matching

15. Loudness
16. How high or low a sound is
17. Measurement of loudness
18. Hearing
19. Bone in ear

a. audition

b. decibels

c. intensity

d. pitch

e. cochlea

Fill in the Blank. Answer on a separate sheet of paper. (More than one word can be used.)

20. Sally kisses John in a dark room. Although his face looks crimson, she knows it's really a bright red; this is an example of _____ _____ .

21. Ballet dancers who spin a lot in circles don't get dizzy because of _____ _____ .

22. Flying in an airplane, you look down at the "tiny" cars, but you don't perceive them as tiny because of _____ _____ .

23. The fact that one of our eyes actually sees something different than the other is called _____

_____ .

24. We perceive objects that are outside in the same way whether it's cloudy or sunny because of

_____ _____ .

Discussion Questions

1. Briefly define *ultraviolet* and *infrared* wavelengths. Describe how the world might be different if humans had receptors for these wavelengths. Be specific.

2. Which of your senses is most important to you? Explain. If you had to give up one sense, which one would you give up? Why? What if you had to choose between giving up hearing and giving up seeing?

3. What if you could magically improve the performance of one of your senses? Which sense would you choose to improve? Why? Could you improve the performance of this one sense without magic? How? Be specific.

4. If we compare the performance of our senses as human beings to the senses of other animals, what conclusions can we draw? Do humans rate poorly, average, or above average? Why? Explain.

5. Each day our senses are bombarded with stimulation from the environment. What do you suppose would happen if we were *completely* deprived of this stimulation for two or three days? List several possible side effects. *Hint*: Try finding someone who has driven alone on the highway at night; how did the person feel once fatigue set in?

6. The chapter explains that ESP may be an extra sense. Do you think human beings have any *other* extra senses? To answer this question, you might research kinesthesia, circadian rhythms, and equilibratory senses.

7. Assume you are an experimental psychologist. Someone who claims to have ESP asks for an appointment with you in your laboratory. What kinds of questions would you ask? What types of experiments would you conduct?

8. Do you think that subliminal messages have *any* influence on people? Explain. Assume that these messages do influence people in some way; should the messages be regulated by law? Do you see any dangers in their use?

Activities

1. Conduct a taste test on 10 to 15 people (your "subjects") to demonstrate how smell contributes to taste. *Procedure*: Blindfold a subject and place four pieces of food in front of her or him. Don't tell the subject what foods you're using. The pieces can be taken from: (1) an apple, (2) a potato, (3) a pear, and (4) a carrot—or choose your own food groups. Guide the subject's hand to the first piece of food; tell the subject to hold her or his nose with the other hand while eating the food and to continue holding it until she or he has guessed what the food is. Repeat this for each piece. Repeat the entire procedure for each subject.

   Predict beforehand which kinds of foods the subjects will most often guess correctly. Which will they most often guess incorrectly?

   After conducting the test, consider this: Since your subjects could not use smell to guess what they were eating, they had to rely on other cues or hints. What were some of these cues? Explain.

2. Look in a phone book to find a center for the blind. Find out if there are any blind speakers who would like to talk to a high school psychology class. If this is inconvenient, conduct your own interview with a blind person, and report what you learn to your class. Possible questions: Have your other senses become stronger? (This question wouldn't apply to someone blind from birth.) Do you dream in sounds, smells, or images? What's the most difficult part about being blind?

3. Describe an experience where a smell has had such an impact on you that you still remember it vividly and with emotion. Try to recreate the experience for your reader by providing vivid details.

4. Create your own illusion. Take a small sheet of paper. Make three cuts in it as shown in the diagram on page 106. Hold the paper in your hand. With your left hand at the top of the left (shaded) side of the paper, turn this side over by pulling it toward you, so that your left hand ends up at the bottom, still on the left side of the paper. Put the paper down. The "FLAP" should now be sticking straight up. You can help to straighten it by folding it up and down. A top view of the finished illusion should look like the small drawing on page 106. The illusion may not seem like an illusion to you since you have created it. But try it on your friends and family. They'll insist that you used glue or two pieces of paper. In other words, what you have made *seems* impossible to make with a single sheet of paper.

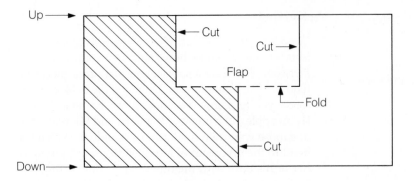

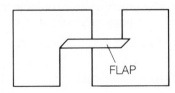

Without offering your friends any instructions, give them a sheet of paper and let them try to create the illusion. What steps do they take? What problem-solving strategies do they use? Refer back to the chapter on brain hemispheres (Chapter 3). Which hemisphere *should* play a greater role in solving the illusion? Why? Which hemisphere do you think your friends primarily used? Why? Explain.

5. When you walk through a grocery store, do you avoid the generic sections? Do you perceive generic products as being inferior to brand name products?

Conduct a test to see if people, because of their perceptions of labels, prefer brand name products over generic products. *Procedure*: Buy a jar of peanuts (or another snack item). Empty half the peanuts into a brand name jar; empty the other half into a jar labeled "generic." Have people taste a peanut from both and decide which tastes better. Don't tell them you are conducting a psychology experiment or they will figure out that the peanuts are identical.

Analyze your results. Did people's perceptions affect their preferences? Discuss. To help with your discussion, you might look up some *Consumer Reports* issues on food products.

6. Most of us have a favorite color; we decorate our rooms with that color; we wear clothes of that color. In other words, we perceive that color as being the best.

Conduct a test to find out if colors and our perceptions of colors affect not only our preferences but also our thinking ability. *Procedure*: Take two pieces of different-colored typing paper and write a list of ten mathematical equations on each of them. The equations on both sheets should be identical; the only difference between the two sheets is the color. Then get 30 people to try to solve the equations; give half of them one color; give the other half the other color. Time them while they take the test.

Analyze your results. Did the first group solve the equations faster than the second group, or vice versa? If there was a big difference in time used, do you think that color was a factor? Or were there other factors involved?

Why did you choose the colors that you did? What results do you think you would have gotten with other colors? If time permits, conduct the test again with two different colors.

7. Which of the two lines below is longer?

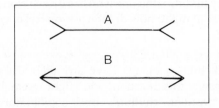

If you answered that the two lines are the same length, you were probably affected by your expectations: You just finished reading a chapter that included a discussion on illusions, and you expected to be fooled. Even if one line did look longer to you, you expected equality in the lines and so you perceived equality.

Look again. Line B is a full half-inch longer than line A.

Try the following experiment, where you create different expectations in others and see whether these expectations influence their behavior. *Procedure*: Ask 15 people, one at a time (this is important), to look at the above lines and decide which line is longer. Before you do this, however, give them different directions:

1. Tell the first five: "We're studying illusions in psychology. Look at these lines. Which is longer?"
2. Tell the next five: "We're studying intelligence and IQ in psychology. Look at these lines. Which is longer?"
3. Tell the last five: "Look at these lines. Which is longer?"

What are *your* expectations of the results you'll get? Which group of subjects will do best? Worst? Make a note of your answers to these questions before you begin the experiment.

Finally, after you conduct the experiment, analyze your results. Were your expectations correct? What conclusions can you draw from your results?

Who can say what motivates some
people to reach for the heights?

Chapter 5

Motivation and Emotion

Be able to:

1. Describe how symbolism is tied in with basic drives.

2. Describe the difference between motivation and emotion.

3. Explain the physical basis of hunger and thirst.

4. Explain the problems with extrinsic motivation.

5. Explain Maslow's hierarchy of needs.

6. Describe each of the three theories of emotion.

Global Look at the Chapter

Motivations and emotions are intricately guided by physical processes. Even so, human needs, desires, and feelings can become quite complex because we are also guided primarily by symbols and rituals.

Symbolism, Motivation, and Emotion

At first glance, both motivation and emotion seem reasonably straight-forward, but nothing could be further from the truth. We will define and explore each of them shortly. But first, to illustrate how complex things can become, we will focus on hunger (a motivator) for a few moments. Satisfying hunger can be a mixture of social, psychological, and physical factors.

Visitors to the birthplace of Shakespeare, Stratford-upon-Avon, England, are fascinated by some of the items on display. In an old tavern, there is a dining table from Shakespeare's era, the late 1500s and early 1600s. The table surface looks like it was worked on by a chain saw. Its appearance is the result of thousands of travelers in those days gouging and stabbing at food laid directly on the table after they had removed it from "community" bowls. Some people carried with them their own wooden plates, but others just attacked bread and meat on the table. At upper social class functions, soup was served in individual bowls, but in places like this one the same bowl was passed from person to person so that each could eat a spoonful as it continued its circular trip around the table. The fork was forbidden because it was considered an instrument of the devil; it did not come into general use until the mid 1700s. The French king, Louis XIV, prided himself on being the best in his kingdom in one respect: He was able to eat chicken stew with his fingers without spilling a drop. The famous French author of the time, Michel de Montaigne, complained that he often found himself eating so fast he was constantly biting his fingers. Two customs of that era survive today: (1) the napkin (a real necessity then) and (2) hand washing between courses (this now takes place only at fancy restaurants) (Braudel, 1981).

Note how, as you read this discussion, you had emotional responses—mostly negative—to the different behaviors mentioned. Why? Because satisfying hunger is not just a basic motivation. We attach rules and regulations to the process. What appears to be a basic "animal" behavior—eating—is elaborate and filled with all kinds of symbolism. Eating is a special ritual. If we have something to celebrate or if we desire companionship, we go to a special place and are served food in a formal way. For both the Jewish and Christian religions, eating and drinking wine have deep religious significance. (Next time you see a painting of the Last Supper, look carefully at the table—no forks.) Note also our rituals of drinking different substances from different-shaped glasses. There are beer steins, water glasses, martini glasses, wineglasses, and so forth. And almost anyone who wants to drink Coke out of a glass is considered weird. Further, different drinks have different meanings. For example, wine is often served at a formal Thanksgiving feast; many people think that serving beer or Pepsi with the meal would seem very much out of place.

The higher brain of the human operates by complex symbolism and ritual. We even have uniforms to wear while satisfying hunger. The higher brain takes itself seriously about such things in that it thinks symbols are real, not imaginary. Here is a good experiment to demonstrate that. Ask a parent why it isn't acceptable to wear a clean pair of Levis to a dinner party. The answer you get will probably resemble "It just isn't done," or "It would embarrass us and you." There is no real answer that makes sense. It is a rule based on symbolism. Ask some friends who aren't taking this class why—*really why*—it would be weird for someone to wear a dress or a suit when the group plans on getting pizza and spending the evening talking. They will come up with similar reasons, especially the circular one, "Well, it's just weird, that's all," which only proves our point and doesn't answer the question.

Finally, eating behavior in its most symbolic form consists of *not* eating. People with important causes go on hunger strikes to call attention to things they feel need correcting. Eating is so important that they are able to attract attention by not doing it.

Using the hands is a necessity in conveying strongly felt emotions.

Motivation and Emotion: Physical Factors

Motivation is what drives us to seek a specific goal. Hence, we are motivated to drink, eat, make friends, and so forth. **Emotion** is a state of the body that causes feelings, which vary according to how we view a situa-

Motivation
The need to seek a goal, such as food, water, friends, and so on.

Emotion
A state of the body causing feelings of hope, fear, love, and so on.

Figure 5.1
Major brain areas involved in motivation
and emotion.

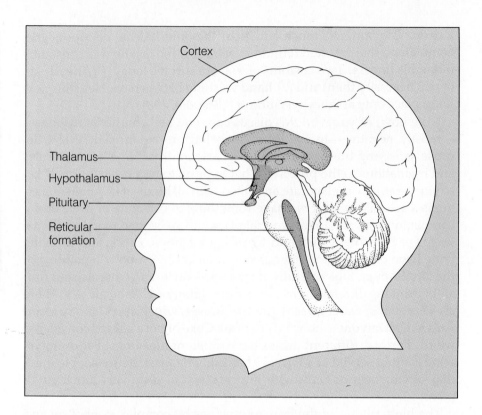

Cortex

Thalamus

Hypothalamus

Pituitary

Reticular
formation

tion—with fear, hope, love, and so forth. Motivation and emotion involve both physiological and psychological factors. We will start with the parts of the body that are involved. Use Figure 5.1 so you get an image of what we are talking about. In that figure, the head has been sliced down the middle vertically so you can see the inner structure of the brain.

The Hypothalamus

Hypothalamus
A part of the inner brain that controls such basic needs and desires as pleasure, pain, fear, rage, hunger, thirst, and sex.

Attaining pleasure and avoiding pain are often cited as primary motivators in human behavior. Scientists have located the centers for both pain and pleasure in a unit called the **hypothalamus** (high-po-THAL-ahmus). Humans and animals alike have such centers. This unit also contains fear, rage, hunger, thirst, and sex centers.

Sending electrical stimulation through a small wire to the hypothalamus can produce any of these motivators or emotions, depending on which part is touched. Animals receiving stimulation to the pleasure center if they push a lever have been known to stimulate themselves for up to 20 days at 20 responses per minute for a total of 576,000 pushes. Some of them prefer this to eating or drinking and have died as a result (Valenstein, 1973; Olds, 1956).

Studies of the fear-rage portion of the hypothalamus have had their wilder moments. One experimenter connected a miniature radio receiver to the fear area of a bull's hypothalamus, and then he got into the ring with the bull. The experimenter was armed only with a radio transmitter. When the bull charged, he pushed a button sending an impulse to the bull's fear center. Fortunately, the bull came to a screeching halt (Delgado, 1969). The experimenter was taking quite a chance because, right next to the fear area is an area of rage, which could well have been activated if the receiving wire had been off by a millimeter or so.

The Reticular Formation

Almost any emotional or motivational state involves taking some kind of action. Whether we run, fight, or seek something we need, we require an increase in activity level. Anyone who sits through a sporting event with no change in heart rate, blood pressure, or speech level has not been very involved in it. The **reticular formation** (re-TICK-u-lar) shown in Figure 5.1 is at the base of the brain inside the neck. It controls not only sleep but also how high or low the level of activity in the body is.

The Pituitary Gland and the Adrenal Glands

Neither the reticular formation nor the hypothalamus can do its work all alone. Both frequently call on the chemical system of the body to get us going. The controller of chemical responses is called the **pituitary gland** (pi-TUE-i-ter-ee), a small structure just below the hypothalamus. The bodily reaction when a person gets highly anxious, excited, or emotionally involved is controlled at least in part by the pituitary. When we see someone we love so intensely they seem to be gradually killing us, the hypothalamus tells the pituitary, which uses chemicals to signal the **adrenal glands** (a-DREE-nal)—there are two of them, one on each side of

Damage to the hypothalamus has resulted in this extraordinarily heavy rat which lost the ability to stop eating.

Reticular formation
The unit in the inner brain that registers and controls activity level, increases excitement, and helps generate sleep.

Pituitary gland
The controller of other glands and hormones, as well as the producer of its own hormone that regulates growth.

Adrenal glands
Glands that secrete adrenaline, which stirs up the body, changing the breathing, perspiration, heart rate, and so on.

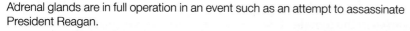

Adrenal glands are in full operation in an event such as an attempt to assassinate President Reagan.

Figure 5.2
Significant physiological areas in
emotion and motivation.

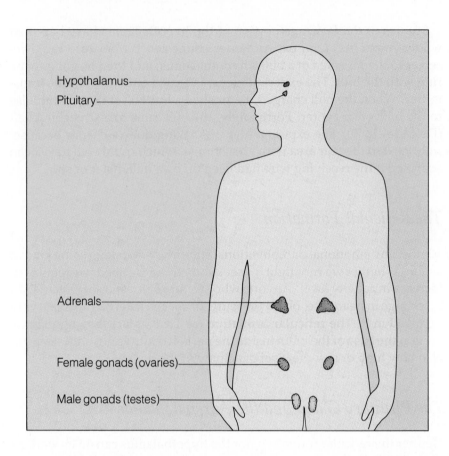

and about even with the belly button (Figure 5.2). These glands secrete
the chemical *adrenaline* (a-DREN-a-lin), which makes the heart beat
faster, breathing increase, and perspiration break out when we see the
loved one—or when we are faced with an emergency.

The Gonads

Gonads
The sex glands.

Testes
The male sex gland; makes sperm.

Ovaries
The female sex gland; makes eggs.

The sex glands, called **gonads**, are of two types: the **testes** in the male and
the **ovaries** in the female. They produce sperm and eggs, respectively, as
well as sex hormones. The hypothalamus signals the pituitary, which, in
turn, causes the gonads to produce the sex hormones that will make a
fetus into either a male or a female. Prior to birth, just a slight error by the
hypothalamus can change the amount of sex hormone released, and the
result, on occasion, is an infant who has both male and female sexual organs. This problem is usually handled well today with surgery and hormone supplements. When the physician discovers it, a decision is made
regarding which sex the child should be. Most infants with this abnormality have physical parts that belong more to one sex than those that belong to the other. So hormones for the desired sex are administered, and
eventually surgery is performed to make the child look like and feel like

the determined sex. Most such children turn out well both physically and psychologically (Money, 1980).

Sexual interest is controlled by the male hormones, called **androgens**. The female hormone, **estrogen**, seems to have the primary goal of regulating the reproductive cycles of the body. There is some indication that estrogen plays a limited role in sexual interest for the woman, but the androgens are the key to starting sexual interest in both males and females. Thus, both sexes have both male and female hormones. Obviously, the male hormone dominates in the male, and the female hormone dominates in the female.

Once someone starts to experience sexual interest, usually at the beginning of adolescence, all the symbolism of the higher brain enters the picture. For humans, sexuality, as opposed to hunger or thirst, is almost exclusively mental and symbolic, with the physical part playing a secondary role. This is why some individuals can give up sex and lead a celibate life. This certainly could not be done with hunger or thirst. The average person can go about three days without water and 60 to 70 days without food. You may have heard that, if a person does not use the sex organs, the organs will gradually waste away. Or that, each time they are used, people lose a little more of their "life energy." Neither of these rumors is true.

Androgens
Hormones that control sexual interest in both males and females.

Estrogen
The hormone that controls the female reproductive cycle.

Motivational Forces

Motivation is thought to result from **drives**—that is, forces that push the organism into action. For example, if you are thirsty, you have a need for water and are driven by the body to seek it.

Drive
Forces that push an organism into action.

Two male elephants trunk wrapping, trying to establish dominance.

Hunger

In the middle 1800s, a man had part of his stomach left exposed after a shotgun accident. Experimenters talked him into becoming a guinea pig for their research on how the stomach worked. A see-through covering was placed over the wound so the effects of various foods and other activities in the stomach could be viewed. After a while, the man got fed up with all this and fled to Canada, where he hid out. Later, when word came that he had died there, a doctor in the United States planned to try to get his body for a medical museum. The family heard about it and warned the doctor with a classic in telegrams. It said, "DON'T COME FOR AUTOPSY. YOU WILL BE KILLED" (Rosenzweig, 1962). Being extra cautious, the family kept the body exposed a long time so it decomposed and became useless to any museum. Because of the stench, it had to remain outside during the funeral.

During the time the man was studied, however, his stomach provided much information on how the **digestive system** functions. For example, when people feel depressed, the amount of acid in the stomach drops noticeably and salivation slows, both of which are needed for digestion. This may be one of the physical reasons why depressed people don't want to eat. On the other hand, when we are angry, the opposite occurs: The stomach's mucous membranes become red and engorged with blood, acid production more than doubles, and the stomach begins violent contractions. You may have learned this from trying to eat during a family argument at the dinner table. Aside from the possibility of choking, the increased acid causes nausea.

What Causes Hunger? Researchers are still trying to understand fully how we know it is time to eat or why we feel satisfied after a meal. The earliest suggestion was that the stomach growled and contracted when it was empty. To see if this was the case, in the early 1900s experimenters had people swallow deflated balloons that were attached to a recording

The subject pushes a key to indicate when stomach sensations are felt. This is then compared with actual stomach contractions.

In Focus: Feeling Hungry?

Here are four possible reasons why

1. Your stomach is contracting.

2. Your blood-sugar level is low.

3. Your taste receptors are "on."

4. You've lost weight, and shrunken cells are signalling you.

device. Then they were inflated to touch the stomach walls, so each stomach contraction was recorded. The experimenters found that, when a person is hungry, the stomach does indeed contract, *but* it also contracts at other times (Cannon, 1939). So contractions might be part of the answer, but certainly not the complete one.

A problem with the contraction theory arose when it was discovered that people who had operations in which the stomach had to be removed still experienced hunger. How were they getting signals of hunger? In the 1960s, it occurred to some researchers that the hypothalamus might be involved. Following up on this hypothesis, the researchers discovered that electrical stimulation of the side part of the hypothalamus would cause eating behavior even in animals that were full. Similarly, damage to a lower portion of the hypothalamus would cause the animal to stop eating (Margules & Olds, 1962).

Still, knowing that the hypothalamus is involved doesn't explain *how* it works. A clue appeared years ago but was not understood for a while: You may have noticed that, if you skip a number of meals, you begin to feel weak and sometimes dizzy. This is caused by a low **blood-sugar level**, a term referring to the amount of sugar (called **glucose**) in your blood. A low amount can be corrected for a short while by eating a candy bar or drinking a soft drink, because either will flood the body with straight sugar. But then your blood sugar zooms downward again. Eating something like meat, chicken, or pasta is a better solution because the body will convert part of it into a steady source of glucose. In any case, researchers found that the hypothalamus contains *glucose monitors* within it, which determine the level of blood sugar. If the level starts to fall too low, these monitors send out signals that make you feel hungry (Arkes & Garske, 1982). If you skip a meal, your hunger disappears after an hour or so because the body will dump some of its stored glucose into the system to tide you over until the next meal.

There are other factors involved. If you pay close attention the next time you eat, stop after five minutes or so and examine how you feel. Notice that you already are less hungry. But there hasn't been time for all

Blood-sugar level
The amount of sugar contained in the blood, which indicates the level of hunger.

Glucose
Another name for sugar in the blood.

Something is very wrong with this man's set-point. Obesity at this level is almost always physiologically caused.

Set point
The body-regulating mechanism that determines a person's typical weight.

you have eaten even to get to your stomach, let alone to change your blood-sugar level. How can this be? The tongue, learning, and chemical responses all seem to play a role. From experience, we discover that food on the tongue means we will be satisfied. That is the learning part—previous association. When food hits the tongue, it communicates to the brain that you are eating. What if you stopped eating at that point? You would not be hungry for a while; in the intestines and stomach, however, there are other receptors that release a chemical to say when *they* are satisfied. As a result, since what you have eaten won't satisfy them, you will begin to feel hungry again (Whalen & Simon, 1984).

Taste is also a most important factor. It is critical to eating, a fact discovered in another unlucky event. A ten-year-old drank some boiling soup that fused his esophagus shut so he could not swallow. This was in the early 1940s when surgery was primitive. Nothing could be done for him except to insert a feeding tube through the area above the belly button into the stomach. The man lived a full life this way, but he found he didn't feel satisfied without taste. Hence, he would put a small amount of his (liquid) meals into his mouth first, spit that out, and then pour the rest into his feeding tube (Wolf & Wolff, 1947). As we continue to eat, the taste receptors begin to shut down so that we will stop eating. Notice toward the end of the meal how tasteless your food has become.

Factors Controlling Weight   Because obesity is so often a topic of concern, there has been quite a bit of research on the problem. One of the most prominent theories suggests that the very heavy person is not able to read accurately the internal cues provided by the hypothalamus, blood sugar, and stomach—cues that would help him or her decide when and how much to eat. Instead, such people operate on external cues. In other words, if an item *looks* interesting or tasty, some obese people pay little attention to whether they need food at the moment, but are carried away by its availability. There is a reasonable amount of evidence that this is the case in *some* obesity problems (Schachter & Rodin, 1974).

We all know people who can eat enormous quantities of food and never gain an ounce, while others seem to enlarge after eating a single M & M. One explanation for this is that people differ in what is called their **set points**. A set point is the body's regulating mechanism that determines what an individual's own weight should be (Bennett & Gurin, 1982). If you have a high set point, the body will keep moving upward in weight to that point, and vice versa if you have a low set point. Set points vary from one individual to another. You may have noticed that, when you have tried to gain or lose weight, there is a specific weight that is very difficult for you to get above or below. That is your set point. A set point *can* be changed, but only with considerable work. A regular program of exercise will gradually change the set point to a limited degree in the case of those who are too heavy or add muscle to those too thin (Thompson et al., 1982). Your set point is to some extent determined by your fat cells, which vary in both size and number from one person to another. Some people have trouble losing weight because, as they start dieting, the cell size shrinks and sends hunger signals to the body (Brownell, 1984).

It is risky to give an excuse to those people who want one for overeating, because overeating is almost always unhealthy. Still, the evidence is that a fair number of people are overweight based partly on their heredity and their metabolism, the speed with which the body uses up energy in the form of fat. Some people store fat more readily and have a slower body speed than is needed to use it up.

What we eat seems also to have some hereditary basis. Taste receptors can vary from one person to another as the result of inheritance. One inherited factor that can arise if both the mother and father have a dominant gene for it is a horrible, bitter taste when eating green, leafy vegetables (Rodin, 1984). This may help explain why some children have such an aversion to vegetables; many are just being "difficult," but a handful will actually experience a horrible taste from them.

Two researchers have reviewed more than a hundred studies on obesity and find that no single factor shows up consistently. Obese people seem to be quite variable in physical structure, psychological motivation, and eating behavior. Exceptions are those who are *very* obese—150 percent or more over their normal weight. These people probably have something physically wrong, as well as a tendency to respond to most food items, even a picture of a sandwich (Conger et al., 1980). In one extreme case, a girl was injured, damaging her hypothalamus. On her first day up and around in the hospital, her physician went with her to the cafeteria. On the way he asked her if she was hungry, and she said no. But when she got there, she ran behind the counter and started grabbing handfuls of food, pushing them into her mouth (Pribram, 1971).

Thirst

Humans are roughly 65 to 70 percent water. As mentioned earlier, we can't go long without water. Whereas we have storage units for excess fat in case of an emergency, there is no place to put water, and we always need a ready supply. The amount of water we need is determined by units that "count" the number of water molecules in certain body cells surrounding the hypothalamus. When the count gets low, the desire for water increases.

While a dry tongue and the need to make it moist are important in thirst, there are also receptors in the intestine to make certain that this vital fluid actually gets into the body. Most animals have such receptors on the tongue, but we don't (Maddison et al., 1980). Instead, humans respond to temperature receptors on the tongue, which trigger a desire for cold drinks in summer and hot ones in winter (Kapatos & Gold, 1972). Thus, dryness of tongue, temperature of water, and balance of water in the body cells are all registered by the hypothalamus.

For most of us, water intake is controlled by learning rather than by a physical signal. Over time we learn the amount of water we need and the amount we tend to drink on a fairly regular basis. For example, studies show that, right after playing tennis—before the bodily signals have been activated—the tennis player will gulp just the right amount of water to compensate for the loss that will be signaled shortly (Pribram, 1971).

A sometimes serious side effect of such learning is that we can come to associate eating food with the relaxation and grogginess it can produce or drinking alcohol with the same type of feeling. As a result, many times people get into the habit of eating and drinking at the first sign of any type of pressure or anxiety, trying to offset the upcoming upset. People with this problem must fight it by restricting drinking (of alcohol) and eating to only certain times of the day and for only a brief period (Bellack et al., 1973). We have also learned that children must never be given food as a reward for doing something good, or food will take on an abnormal interest that can, over time, become a dominant one for the child. This behavior can carry into adulthood. Best to give the child some other reward whose power as a motivator is not as likely to increase as the drive to eat is. On the other hand, infants are supposed to be chubby and should not be put on a diet except in the case of medical crisis or a disease.

Psychological Needs

We humans do a good job of taking basic needs and making them symbolic. The brain never seems content with leaving things basic. For example, we have a psychological need for change. There is always something "new" that we want to do, such as rearranging our rooms, changing the decorations or the colors, and so forth. This constant need for cerebral (brain) changes is one of our stronger needs, even though it is not critical to survival. This section looks at just such psychological drives.

Curiosity Motives The strong psychological need to see new, odd, or different things is not confined to humans, but is also found on a limited basis in "lower" animals. We have a German shepherd, for example, that drives us crazy with this **curiosity motive**. Naming it doesn't help. He has learned to open closet doors to find out what is new in there. We might as well not even have doors on the closets because he opens them every time he is in the house. Discipline is not a solution because he would have to be beaten into submission to obey and we are too softhearted to do that. In humans, one of the most noticeable bits of evidence

Curiosity motive
A drive that moves a person to see new and different things.

of this motive is the fact that in rush-hour traffic people will slow down and jam things up hopelessly in order to view even the most minor accident.

Manipulation Motive   When we move up the scale from the dog or cat to the *primates* (such as monkeys, chimps, and humans), we find what are called **manipulation motives**. Monkeys, for instance, love complicated mechanical puzzles of hooks, latches, and sliding bolts—just to have something to play with or examine. They will manipulate such things for hours with no other reward (such as encouragement or petting). Monkeys will work especially hard to be able to open a door and see a toy train going around in a circle, satisfying both curiosity and manipulation needs (Harlow et al., 1956). Monkeys and other higher primates also love new human inventions such as the videotape machine. When a foot switch is rigged to turn on a video player, monkeys will hold it down 60 percent or more of every hour merely to be able to enjoy the show. This is especially true of males, who will watch tapes of female monkeys about 75 percent of every hour if they are given the chance (Swartz & Rosenblum, 1980).

The important factor in these findings seems to be a desire for some type of change. Animals that are in very elaborate cages, such as a psychedelically decorated one, eventually prefer a simple cage, and the reverse is true for those in simple cages. Apparently, change, in and of itself, helps meet some need of the brain and possibly the body (Eisenberger, 1972).

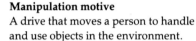

Manipulation motive
A drive that moves a person to handle and use objects in the environment.

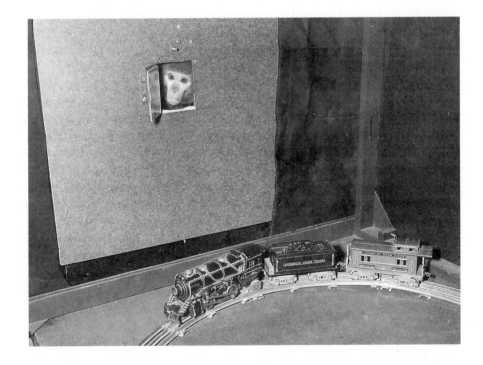

The monkey's curiosity motive is very strong. They will work hard to get a chance to see this train in operation.

Hooks, latches, and sliding bolts are among monkeys' favorite things.

Intrinsic motivation
Satisfaction that comes from within the individual for certain behavior.

Extrinsic motivation
A reward from outside the organism for certain behavior.

Intrinsic Versus Extrinsic Motivation As mentioned, monkeys will play with latches and hooks endlessly if left on their own. But what happens if you start giving them a reward, such as a banana, for doing so? Something unexpected: They will lose their incentive to play and start to focus on the reward instead. If it doesn't arrive, they quit playing. We explain this situation by what is called **intrinsic** versus **extrinsic motivation**. "Intrinsic" means coming from within the organism. "Extrinsic" means coming from outside.

You may remember how, as a child, you were curious about almost everything. Often, now, the reverse is true. This is one of the heavy prices we pay for having to organize and structure things into a formal school system. When we give people external rewards (such as grades and praise), we are using extrinsic motivation and to some extent removing intrinsic motivation. Thus, too many students begin to act like the monkeys, no longer able to get really deeply involved in what they're learning. But give these same students a problem outside the classroom, and they will work for hours on it (intrinsic). So what is the solution? The school structure is so big and so formalized that it won't work to take away grades (extrinsic). We need to find a way to add intrinsic motivation for students. If all of us were stuck on a desert island, it wouldn't be long before we were actually begging for a chance to learn something new.

Need for Stimulation All animals must have physical stimulation in order to develop properly. Monkeys that have not been handled while they were growing up become cold, aloof, and unfriendly not only to others but also to their own offspring. Such monkeys can be partially "repaired" over a period of about six months if placed with other monkeys, but the fact that it takes so long shows the devastating effects of no stimulation (Suomi, 1983).

Psychologist **Harry Harlow** showed this need for **contact comfort** dramatically in a series of studies with monkey babies. Monkeys were placed in a cage with two fake mothers (see Figure 5.3). One of the "mothers" was made of wire and had a bottle attached to it where the monkeys could feed. The other mother was covered with terrycloth but provided no food. Once the animals had adjusted to having the two mothers, a fear test was performed.

While a mechanical, wind-up, teddy bear is fascinating to a child, it is very frightening to a monkey, so it formed the basis for the test. The mechanical teddy bear was put into the cage. The monkeys panicked. Here is the key point: Even though the monkeys were fed by the wire mother, they consistently ran to the cloth mother for protection and comfort. This indicates the importance of contact comfort in development. While we would expect the monkeys to go to the mother that fed them, they found pleasant physical contact of the cloth made them feel far more secure (Harlow, 1959).

There are parallel situations in humans. In one study during World War II, infants who were reared in an institution where there was almost no personal attention in the form of touching or holding were compared with infants who were reared in a prison nursery where they had contact with their mothers. The results were frightening: 37 percent of the institution children died within a year, despite being fed and kept clean (Spitz, 1946).

There is even physical evidence of these needs. At the base of the brain is a unit called the *cerebellum*, which registers and controls bodily movement and sensation. (For more detail, see Chapter 3.) The cerebellum has a number of connections to emotional systems. Without enough rocking and touching, the cerebellum does not develop properly, which is likely to create permanent emotional and physical scars (Prescott, 1979). We suspect that nature sees to this need, giving mothers the desire, almost automatically, to rock their infants.

Contact comfort
The satisfaction obtained from pleasant, soft stimulation.

Figure 5.3
This monkey gets the best of both worlds—contact comfort with the soft "mother" and food from the other one.

The Theory of Needs

Psychologist **Abraham Maslow** developed a theory called the **hierarchy of needs**. A hierarchy (HI-er-arc-ee) is a system that ranks items one above the other in importance. His goal was to put human needs into such an arrangement. The most obvious needs are at the base of the pyramid shown in Figure 5.4—the physiological, or physical, needs. These **physiological needs**, such as hunger and thirst, must be met first.

Hierarchy of needs
A system that ranks needs one above the other with the most basic needs for physical survival at the bottom of the pyramid.

Physiological needs
The bottom of the hierarchy: hunger and thirst.

Figure 5.4
Maslow's hierarchy of needs

Safety needs
Part of the hierarchy: shelter, nest egg of money.

Belongingness needs
Part of the hierarchy: friendship, closeness with another.

Self-esteem needs
Part of the hierarchy: liking and respecting yourself, feeling important and useful.

Self-actualization
The top of the hierarchy: establishing meaningful goals and a purpose in life.

When people are starving or thirsty, this will almost always dominate their thoughts and behavior.

Once the physiological needs are satisfied, however, we move upward. On the next level are the **safety needs**. Once we have food and water, we begin to experience other, less-critical but still basic needs, such as trying to provide a little shelter and possibly a small nest egg of money so that we are "safe" over the long run.

When we are reasonably safe, we seek contact and love with another. This is called the **belongingness need**. We cannot survive very well over time without friendship and closeness, so these needs appear after safety.

It is very hard for anyone to feel important in the scheme of things unless at least one other person cares about him or her. So, once we have satisfied the need to belong, we begin to feel acceptable. Now we need to develop that self-acceptance into a sense of being more than a cog in the machinery—a sense of being a real person. These are the **self-esteem needs**, with self-esteem meaning liking and respecting yourself (in the positive sense, not in the sense of being "stuck up").

Having attained the needs of the bottom four levels of the hierarchy, we are in a position to go on to even greater things—the need to establish meaningful goals and a purpose in life, called **self-actualization needs**. The term refers to our ability to put into practice (actualize) whatever skills and talents we possess. If you have carpentry skills, then these are used to make a fine product, the best you can—not something shoddy that barely hangs together. If you have musical talent, then you develop it so that you can sing or play an instrument beautifully and meaningfully (Maslow, 1954).

Psychologist Abraham Maslow.

In Focus: I'm Stuck in a "Hole"

Let's compare Maslow's five hierarchy needs with a set of five building blocks. Once we arrange the first block to our satisfaction, we add the second block, and so on. A problem arises, however, when we can't arrange a particular block just the way we want.

For example, in the diagram shown here, someone has arranged the first two blocks pretty well. The third block, however, keeps falling over. This represents the fact that the person feels that he or she can develop no close or intimate relationships.

What's the solution? One obvious solution is to recognize that the stack of blocks is incomplete, that there is a "hole," and to keep trying to fill the hole. For instance, maybe this person doesn't really feel deeply safe, and this is why he or she finds it hard to reach out to people, to be open with them. The person needs first to try to understand why he or she doesn't feel safe, and then to try to fill that second-level need, before he or she can go on to work directly on making friends. As we all know, this is not always easy, but it is usually worthwhile.

Another "solution" is just to keep fiddling with and focusing on the first two blocks, thinking that this will take care of the falling block—that this will fill the hole. This behavior is typical of anorexics, who feel that they're not loved, so they compensate by becoming obsessed with food (or rearranging the first block over and over again).

Still another "solution" is to forget the third block and put the fourth block on the stack. The "hole" is still there, but it becomes less noticeable. This is typical of workaholics who try to attain self-esteem strictly through their jobs, at the expense of a meaningful private life.

To sum all this up: If a person feels stuck in a "hole," he or she may work directly to fill it or may compensate by becoming obsessed with some other more accessible need.

Maslow's theory has had a beneficial effect on the business world. Employers now provide more meaningful tasks for employees whenever possible because a self-actualized group of people produces a far superior product and has a lower absentee rate. Maslow's theory has also had an effect on our understanding of people who have trouble in life. They may lack a sense of purpose because they have failed to satisfy their needs at one of the lower levels. For example, someone stuck at the belongingness level has a "hole which has to be filled, an emptiness into which love [needs to be] poured" (Maslow, 1968, p. 39).

Emotions

Emotions are part of our physical survival system. Without anger and fear, for instance, we could not protect ourselves. In this sense, we are very much like animals. Again, however, humans often express themselves in a social and symbolic context. Thus, rioters have been known to destroy police cars because the cars are a symbol of authority, not because the cars pose an immediate life-threatening danger to the rioters.

It would be helpful if we could list the basic emotions. But scientists have been arguing for centuries about what emotions we have and the differences between them. Try sometime to define a clear difference between anger and frustration, and you will see how hard it is to do.

Cognition and Emotion

Cognition (symbolic thought processes) is intimately involved in the emotions we feel. Thus, in laboratory experiments, when one group of people is led to believe they will experience pain, that group becomes far more anxious than another group whose members are told they will not be hurt. If the first group receives a minor shock, they overestimate how agonizing it is—just from the expectation of pain. Or take the sensation of starting to fall forward or backward. All of us immediately panic as we try to correct for it. But, if we label the sensation as *fun*, then we don't react that way to the same sensations. Example? A roller coaster ride. Imagine how you would respond if all those sensations were present while you were sitting in class. So, how something feels becomes a matter of interpretation.

Often physical arousal cannot be identified as a specific emotion until we label it. For example, two people meet face to face, about to get into a fight. One is seven feet tall and weighs 275 pounds; the other is five feet tall and weighs 75 pounds. Both are fully aroused physically, but devices that measure bodily responses wouldn't show a difference between them. Even so, aren't they feeling different emotions?

Theories of Emotion

A *theory* tries to explain how something works. This may seem strange to you, but it is *not* necessary that a theory be absolutely correct. A theory gives us a framework in which to study things. For example, suppose one person says that a caterpillar moves along the ground by using some kind of magnetism; another says that it moves by using some kind of temperature sensing; a third says that wiggling "scoots" it along the ground. Until we find an answer, all three theories can be used as a basis for research, each researcher trying to find support for his or her own

Cognition
Symbolic thought processes.

According to opponent process theory, this type of behavior becomes addictive after a couple of hair-raising trials.

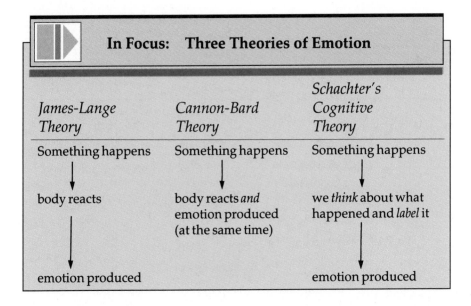

In Focus: Three Theories of Emotion

James-Lange Theory	Cannon-Bard Theory	Schachter's Cognitive Theory
Something happens	Something happens	Something happens
↓	↓	↓
body reacts	body reacts *and* emotion produced (at the same time)	we *think* about what happened and *label* it
↓		↓
emotion produced		emotion produced

theory. Theories provide structure. We will discuss three theories of emotions in the sections that follow. At present, our understanding of emotion is still incomplete, so all three theories can stand side by side as possible "answers," even though they are different. And one theory might fit a particular set of circumstances to which another one doesn't even apply. (The caterpillar examples are fictional, by the way, created just to make a point.)

The James-Lange Theory   The **James-Lange theory** (Lang), named after the two men who proposed it, is simple. But it can be confusing unless you pay close attention. The theory suggests that emotions operate in reverse of the way most of us assume. In general, people think that we see a snake, feel an emotion, then run. These two men claimed that we see a snake, our bodies respond, we run, and *only then* do we feel an emotion because the body is so keyed up. They arrived at this theory because they believed that just thinking about or seeing a snake has no real effect until *after* the body has responded. So our physical feelings *are* the emotions.

James-Lange theory
For emotion, first the body responds, *then* one feels the emotion.

The Cannon-Bard Theory   The **Cannon-Bard theory** of emotion is again named after two scientists. Their theory arose after the discovery of the thalamus as a physical unit of the brain that can instantly transmit messages (Chapter 1). They claim that, when an emergency is perceived, both the bodily reaction and the emotional system respond at the same time. So, while James-Lange waited for the body to respond first, in this theory both occur together.

The Cannon-Bard theory might fit many cases, but for some the James-Lange would fit better. For instance, in a near-accident, we respond physically first, by reflex, and then later we start feeling panic. In this

Cannon-Bard theory
The bodily reaction and the emotional response to an event occur at the same time.

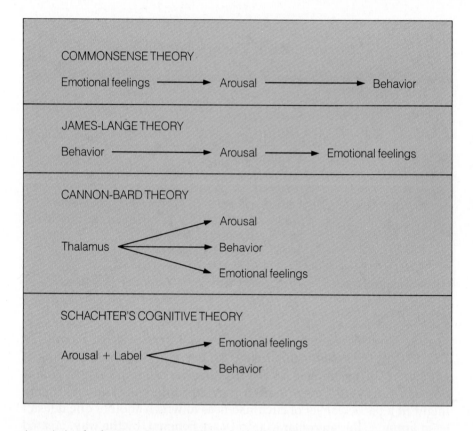

COMMONSENSE THEORY

Emotional feelings → Arousal → Behavior

JAMES-LANGE THEORY

Behavior → Arousal → Emotional feelings

CANNON-BARD THEORY

Thalamus → Arousal
→ Behavior
→ Emotional feelings

SCHACHTER'S COGNITIVE THEORY

Arousal + Label → Emotional feelings
→ Behavior

situation, the brain takes roughly two seconds to respond, a *long* time in an emergency. Hence, what we are feeling over the near accident comes after the body is stirred up.

Schachter's Cognitive Theory The psychologist **Stanley Schachter** (SHACK-ter) performed experiments to support his **cognitive theory**—the belief that we label our bodily responses as being certain emotions. His subjects were injected with adrenaline, which speeds up the body's processes. One group of subjects was told that the drug would make them feel "high" or on top of the world. The other group, which got exactly the same drug injection, was told the drug would make them feel angry. Subjects were then put in a room with stooges who were to act in a fashion that would support what the subjects had been told about the drug's effect. Thus, the subjects who were told they would feel high were surrounded by very happy stooges playing games and laughing. The "angry" subjects were placed in a room with stooges who complained, moaned, and groaned about almost everything. The experiment showed that the subjects, once the drug had taken effect and stirred up the body, began to feel and act the way they had been prompted to—either high or angry. In these results, Schachter finds support for his theory that we tend to (cognitively)label our behavior and control our feelings in terms of those around us and how they are acting (Schachter & Singer, 1962).

Cognitive theory (Schachter)
We label a bodily response by giving it the name of an emotion we think we are feeling.

Anorexia nervosa
A disorder that involves loss of weight to the point of imminent starvation and death.

Bulimia
A disorder that involves trying to avoid gaining weight by throwing up or using laxatives.

Trying to Survive Body Size

The average wolf weighs about 80 pounds. It is not unusual for it to eat up to 18 pounds of meat at one sitting (Lopez, 1978). Yet it would be rare to find an obese wolf, even in areas of plenty. Humans, on the other hand, have made the process of eating and not eating so complex that it often involves nothing but chaos, anxiety, and a great deal of injury to both psyche and body. If you have been trying to make sense out of all the conflicting claims in this area and have gotten lost, join the club. At best, things are murky. Some scientists say too much salt and cholesterol are bad; others say they are irrelevant. Some say too much fat is bad; others say it is not necessarily harmful. Eskimos in Alaska used to put a premium on obesity in both male and female marriage partners, while, every decade or so, people in the other states try to turn themselves into walking sticks with a cell or two hanging onto them. We want to outline here some of the things that seem to be pretty well established with the hope that at least a few partially reasonable facts will be available to you.

Most rats know better than to keep eating the same thing over and over and over. Some variety of foods seems necessary for humans too. Certain types of food groups have been well established as providing vitamin and mineral needs. These can be found, with no preaching or discussion, in one of the half-dozen annual almanacs

To the average Eskimo male, the heavier Eskimo woman is far more appealing than the skinny Anglo woman below.

(such as *World Almanac* or *Information Please Almanac*) sold for a couple of dollars at drugstores and in supermarkets.

There is nothing inherently wrong with fat, salt, or sugar. They are all necessary for survival. And, when the body doesn't have enough fat or sugar, it will make its own. On the other hand, we humans do not seem to have very good detectors for telling us when we are overdoing any of the three. We must have had these detectors at one time, but somehow over the centuries their effectiveness has been destroyed. The body still does show some wisdom in terms of a need for fruits and vegetables, since many people still get a craving for them. But we must remain skeptical of something like a "craving" for a hot dog.

Food can act in a fashion similar to a narcotic in that it can relieve tension by making a person groggy. This is especially true of chocolate, which has a chemical composition that makes us sleepy. Hence, many can fall prey to using food much as someone would use alcohol or drugs.

One of the toughest decisions many slightly heavy people have to make is what to do if the fashion of the moment is to be skinny. Set points are just plain higher for some people than for others. But there can be so much social pressure that it is hard to know how to handle it. One of the most serious dangers of losing too much weight is a disorder called **anorexia**

In the 1950s, Marilyn Monroe typified the "perfect" figure.

nervosa (ano-REX-ee-ah/ner-VOS-ah). This problem occurs most often among teenage females who are trying to develop the "perfect" body. People with this problem become so obsessed with dieting that, even when they are below a healthy weight, they still see themselves as too fat when they look in a mirror. Over time, the body gradually adapts to lower and lower weights until eventually it is impossible to eat much of anything, and many die of starvation because they simply can't hold food.

Another sign that things are serious is a disorder called **bulimia** (bu-LEE-me-ah), in which the person eats a heavy meal and then throws it up or takes heavy doses of laxatives in order to avoid gaining weight.

"Speed" or amphetamines make people so jumpy and nervous that they don't want to eat. While weight loss is possible by taking these drugs, the odds are very great that the users will become addicted to them and wind up with much more serious problems than they had at the beginning.

If you want to make money, write a diet book, because there is always one on the best-seller list. They often suggest dangerous paths to follow, though. Some fad diets can kill you by depriving you of absolutely necessary nutrients. Most people who go on one of these diets get off it within about six months anyway. A fad diet is not worth the risk. About the only consistent and safe way to lower weight is by exercising and eating less food (and, of course, not gorging on fat and sugars). If you are *actually* overweight, for a while, try eating at mealtimes only and see what happens. Or try eating a little less on a consistent basis.

None of this may help, but maybe it will. A couple of final ideas to make life a little better for everybody: Try to look at your body in a positive way; we *all* have our good points and bad points. And every one of us has such oddities as hair follicles, funny-looking nostrils, and all the rest. If your weight is honestly out of control—either too thin or too heavy—you are not alone. But something needs to be done. One of the most comfortable ways to handle it is to join a group of other people who are working together on the same problem. You'll get plenty of support from the group as you work to improve your health.

Summary

1. Motivation consists of drives that make us seek specific goals. Emotion involves various states of the body that cause feelings; these feelings vary in terms of how we view a situation.

2. The hypothalamus contains centers for pleasure, pain, rage, sex, hunger, thirst, and fear. It controls other units of the body when we seek satisfaction or respond to certain feelings.

3. The reticular formation controls the level of bodily activation. Given a need, it increases the body's activity noticeably.

4. The pituitary gland works under instructions from the hypothalamus and secretes chemicals that stir up the body.

5. The gonads control which sex the fetus will be, and, later in life, they trigger sexual responses.

6. Hunger is signaled by the hypothalamus after taking into account stomach contractions, intestinal receptors, taste, and blood-sugar level.

7. A set point is the body's determination of what weight each individual should be.

8. Thirst is also controlled by the hypothalamus; here the dryness of the tongue and the amount of water in body cells are also registered to determine if water is necessary.

9. Curiosity and manipulation motives seem to be heavily psychological—that is, needs of the brain. The evidence is clear that physically we also need stimulation and contact comfort.

10. Abraham Maslow's hierarchy of needs ranks our needs in a pyramid of importance. Most basic are physiological and safety needs, followed by belongingness and self-esteem, and at the top is self-actualization.

11. The James-Lange theory of emotion claims that the body is stirred up first and then the emotion is felt. The Cannon-Bard theory says that the thalamus causes both the body and the emotion to be stirred up at the same time. Schachter's cognitive theory suggests that we call a particular excited state of the body by a label or name, so emotion is actually a cognitive process.

Key Words and Concepts

drive
motivation
emotion
hypothalamus
reticular formation
pituitary gland
adrenal glands
gonads
testes
ovaries
androgens
estrogen
drives
blood-sugar level
glucose
set points
curiosity motive
manipulation motive
intrinsic motivation
extrinsic motivation

Harry Harlow
contact comfort
hierarchy of needs (Maslow)
Abraham Maslow
physiological needs
safety needs
belongingness needs
self-esteem needs
self-actualization needs
cognition
James-Lange theory
Cannon-Bard theory
cognitive theory
anorexia nervosa
bulimia

Review Questions

For each of the following, answer R for reticular formation, P for pituitary gland, and A for adrenal glands.

1. Helps us react in an emergency
2. Regulates level of activity in the body
3. Signals other glands to release chemicals
4. Located just below hypothalamus
5. Releases chemicals that affect heart rate
6. Controls sleep

Fill in the blank. Answer on a separate sheet of paper.

7. The female hormone is called _____ .
8. Sex glands are called _____ .
9. _____ regulates the female reproductive cycle.
10. Male hormones are called _____ .

For each of the following, answer yes if it does cause hunger, no if it does not.

11. Taste
12. Stomach contractions

13. Low blood-sugar level

14. High blood-sugar level

15. Cell size

True–False

16. We are born with certain set points, and they do not change with age.

17. A person's set point is partly determined by fat cells.

18. Inherited factors may lead to weight problems.

19. The hypothalamus regulates both hunger and thirst.

Matching

20. Bank accounts
21. Self-acceptance
22. Hunger
23. Doing your best
24. Friendship

   a. belongingness needs
   b. self-actualization needs
   c. safety needs
   d. physiological needs
   e. self-esteem needs

Matching

25. Body's reaction and emotion occur simultaneously

26. Emotions are produced through labeling them

27. Body reacts first, then emotion is produced

   a. James-Lange theory
   b. Schachter's cognitive theory
   c. Cannon-Bard theory

Discussion Questions

1. The chapter mentions that eating is a special ritual. Analyze your own family meals, taking into account both past and present gatherings. What "rituals" does your family seem to follow? What do these rituals say about your family? Have the rituals changed over the years? What does this say about your family?

2. Do you think that, in general, motivation changes as you get older? If so, in what ways does it change? Be specific. If not, provide examples to show that motivation does not change.

3. Imagine that your parents gave you $100 for each A that you received on your report card. First, do you think that the money would motivate you? Why or why not? Second, assume that the money did motivate you. Would you actually learn more? Why or why not?

4. Besides money, what motivates your parent(s) to go to work every day? Explain. Which motivators are more important—money or the ones you've just listed? Explain.

5. Briefly define extrinsic and intrinsic motivation. Then analyze Maslow's theory and decide which of his hierarchy needs are extrinsically satisfied, which are intrinsically satisfied, and which, if any, are satisfied in both ways. Explain.

6. Compare Maslow's hierarchy of needs to your own life. Which needs have you adequately satisfied? Explain. (If you have indeed satisfied these needs, you don't spend much time thinking about them.) Which needs are you currently trying to satisfy? Explain. (These are needs that you *do* spend a great deal of time thinking about.)

7. According to Maslow, self-actualizers are people who strive to do their best, strive to reach their potential. If you look around, you'll probably agree that very few people consistently choose this path. Why not? Offer several reasons or explanations.

8. Think of a time when someone rejected you (for a job, a date, a favor, whatever). Which of the theories of emotions best describes how you felt after the rejection? Explain.

Activities

1. The chapter explains that hunger is a product of both internal and external cues. Make a list of everything that you ate yesterday. Next to each food item, write *I* if the item was eaten primarily because of internal cues (for example, you were hungry), and write *E* if the item was eaten primarily because of external cues (it was time to eat, everyone else was eating, the food was there, and so on). For some items, both *I* and *E* may apply. In this case, pick the cue that seemed dominant, or stronger, at the time.

Analyze your list. Is there a pattern? Which cues seem to play a greater role in your eating habits? Explain.

If there is a pattern, this may have something to do with your family life. To find out, conduct a brief survey. Interview the person who does the grocery shopping and/or cooking for your household. Have this person make a list of everything he or she ate the day before. After the list is made, explain to this person about internal and external cues, and then have the person mark each item *I* or *E* just as you did for yourself. Urge the interviewee to be honest.

Did a pattern develop in your interviewee's answers? Compare these answers to your own answers. Can you draw any conclusions? Is there too much food in your house? The wrong kinds of food? Explain.

2. Conduct an experiment to find out the influence of visual external cues on eating. Buy a package of cookies or some other snack that your family likes. One day, leave the snack on the table, the kitchen counter, or somewhere else very visible, and see how many cookies are eaten by the end of the day. Wait a few days, and buy the same snack. This time, make sure somehow that everyone knows about the snack, but stick it in a drawer or in the refrigerator or somewhere else that is *not* very visible. But don't hide it; everyone should know where it is. Again, count how many cookies are eaten by the end of the day. Compare your results. Discuss your conclusions.

If you're ambitious, you can contact a local fast-food restaurant and have the owner conduct a similar experiment. In this case, the owner one day would put up pictures of, let's say, a hot dog, and the next day he or she would put up no pictures.

3. The chapter mentions that Maslow's theory has had a beneficial effect on the business world—this, of course, includes the world of advertising. To understand how, collect 20 magazine ads, all for different products. Then take a sheet of paper, number it from 1 to 20, and divide it into three long columns. Label the columns as follows: *Product*; *Need That the Product Satisfies*; and *Needs* (notice plural) *That the Ad Appeals to*. For example, the first entry might look like this:

Product	Need That the Product Satisfies	Need That the Ad Appeals to
1. Brand "X" soda	physiological needs	belongingness needs self-esteem needs

In other words, soda satisfies a basic physiological need: thirst. Advertisers, however, in order to sell their products, appeal to our belongingness needs: They present images of friends having a good time. Also, they appeal to our self-esteem needs: They use slogans like "It'll make you feel better about yourself."

Next, analyze your chart. Are the second and third columns identical or vastly different? Do any patterns develop in either column? If so, how do you account for this? Did your results turn out as expected, or were you surprised? Explain.

4. An alternative to the activity in number 3 might be to watch 20 television commercials or listen to 20 radio commercials, and then follow the same directions and answer the same questions. In this case, when you're analyzing the third column—*Needs the Commercial Appeals to*—you might take into account background music, narrator's voice, and dialogue.

5. This next idea will count as two activities (just in case your teacher is counting). Do *both* of the activities in numbers 3 and 4; that is, fill out a chart for magazine ads *and* a chart for television commercials. In this case, skip the questions listed, and focus instead on comparing the two charts. Do advertisers use different appeals in magazines than they do on television or radio? Explain. Point out numerous differences and similarities.

6. This activity may seem simple, but, combined with creativity and thoughtfulness, it can be worthwhile. Take Maslow's theory and create a collage that will bring it to life. For example, you could take a poster and cut it to form some kind of pyramid (see Figure 5.4) and then attach pictures at each level. Level one might include a steaming dish of spaghetti; level two could include a savings account book; and so on. But don't be restricted by these suggestions. Be creative—satisfy your self-actualization needs!

7. Conduct research on anorexia nervosa and/or bulimia. If you use books or magazines, write a brief report on causes and treatments of these disorders. Or you can gather your information through personal contacts. Either interview an acquaintance or a friend who has recovered from an eating disorder, or contact a therapist in your area who treats people with eating disorders. You'll be surprised how eager many therapists are to grant interviews for this type of assignment. In general, find out what motivates people not to eat and what treatments seem to work best. For either type of interview, be sure to have a list of questions ready beforehand. After writing out your interview, write a brief paragraph describing your reactions to what you have learned.

It is possible to enter an altered state of consciousness through meditation.

Chapter 6

States of Consciousness

Be able to:

1. Describe consciousness and its levels.

2. Explain chronobiology and biological clocks.

3. Describe circadian rhythm and explain its influence.

4. Explain the importance of REM.

5. Describe the content of and different kinds of dreams.

6. Explain what hypnosis is; explain why it is not a special state of consciousness.

Global Look at the Chapter

In daily life we continuously change from one state of consciousness to another. The unseen world of body chemistry controls our levels of awareness as well as our bodily processes as we go through the day. We never remain in the same state of consciousness for very long.

Defining Consciousness

Years ago a teacher told one of us that we couldn't prove that a rock rolling down a hill didn't know where it was going. The whole class sat there and looked at him. We didn't know what to say. In a way, though, he had a point. Exactly what is consciousness? It is a lot harder to define than you might think at first; we can't touch it, find it, or pick it up. It is a **construct**. A construct is a belief in something that cannot be seen or touched but that, according to evidence, actually is present.

The ancients (1500s) came up with an idea for measuring consciousness. They took people who were obviously dying and put them on large scales. Researchers were stationed in front of the scales at all times. The moment the person died, they watched the dial in order to measure any weight difference when the "soul" or "consciousness" left the body. As you might have guessed, no change occurred. Consciousness must not weigh anything—or at least it is so light we don't have any way of recording it. Yet it seems obvious that it is there.

We will do the best we can with a definition: **Consciousness** is the awareness of, or the possibility of knowing, what is going on inside or outside the organism. This definition fits the fact that we can receive stimulation, analyze it, and then take some action.

Construct
A belief in something that cannot be seen or touched but that seems to exist.

Consciousness
The awareness of, or the possibility of knowing, what is happening inside or outside the organism.

Consciousness: Map of the Self in Relation to the World

Consciousness (for both humans and animals) is believed to come from our making a "map" of where we are in space and then more or less seeing ourselves on this map (Jaynes, 1976). Notice that, when you think about something you did a while back, you actually seem to be watching yourself from the outside. Or, if you want to, you can move inside the "you" that you are remembering and "look out" as you imagine doing what you did before. We think consciousness results from just such a series of stored and viewed images of ourselves. In other words, as we move about, different scenes, some from the environment, some from memory, flash before us, then fade and are instantly replaced by the next scene. Some of them are stored in memory for later use. This situation is a great deal like a motion picture at the theater. Movies are nothing more than a series of thousands of fixed images (in each "frame") flashed one after the other on the screen so it looks to us as if the people are alive and moving. Thus, all day long, we combine millions of brief memory images of ourselves with our current images of the world, and we call this consciousness (Casler, 1976; Griffin, 1976).

Levels of Consciousness

We are not necessarily conscious of everything we do. For example, experiments show that sometimes, when we are going to reach for something or get up and walk around, our brain circuits for these acts may fire *before* we consciously know we are going to do anything (Libet et al., 1983). Likewise, if a "forbidden" word is flashed on a screen in front of people very rapidly and then removed, the people's brains respond electrically even if the people claim they didn't see the word (Posner et al., 1973). The level of awareness here is called the **subconscious**, meaning consciousness just below our present awareness. Some people believe that we also have a much deeper level of awareness called the **unconscious**, which contains thoughts or desires about which we have no knowledge and which we will never know about directly.

An example of subconscious thought would be a very vague feeling that, for some unknown reason, the people around you at a party are acting strangely toward you. You don't put the feeling into words, and, for the most part, you ignore it; still, you feel vaguely uncomfortable or worried. You don't even realize that you have *noticed* people's strange behavior toward you until you get home and you start to wonder why you didn't have a very good time at the party. Then you remember what your subconscious had picked up (and you wonder if maybe you had bad breath or something).

Subconscious
Consciousness just below our present awareness.

Unconscious
Thoughts or desires about which we can have no direct knowledge.

Unconscious thought is very easy to see in children: For example, a jealous brother keeps undoing the bolts on his brother's bicycle, but, when caught, he really can't explain why he does it—even to himself. We will discuss the unconscious in greater detail in Unit 5, where we look at personality.

Chronobiology and Unseen Forces

Many of us spend money to be scared out of our wits by a horror movie. If you stop and think about it, what makes the horror movie so exciting is that there are things hidden in the background—the unseen. We have a similar show going on around us all the time—and it's not only free but far more fascinating than the best of horror films. This is because it is real: All creatures are controlled by forces that none of us can see or feel.

This area of study is called **chronobiology** (KRON-oh + biology). *Chronology* refers to time, so the focus of chronobiology is on forces that control the body biology at different times of the day or month or year. The most obvious effects are those involving night and day cycles: The rat, hamster, and beloved cockroach awaken and wander around during the night, while the squirrel, sparrow, chicken, and human come out during the day.

There are monthly cycles that can cause changes in feelings and moods. The best known of these is the female monthly cycle designed for reproduction, but females are not alone. While most males deny it, studies show that males also have a monthly cycle in which they become

Chronobiology
The study of forces that control the body at different times of the day, month, or year.

The screech owl silently hunts for food at night.

listless, slightly depressed, and "different from usual" for three or four days (Luce, 1971; Moore-Ede et al., 1982).

Finally, there are annual cycles in which people slow down and lose energy toward summer. And there are annual changes in weight as well as in the chemical content of the body (Pengelley & Asmundson, 1971).

The most obvious annual rhythm in nature is bird migration. Birds don't fly south to be home for Thanksgiving; they are responding to a change in the light-dark cycle of the earth as winter approaches. They perform this feat by using patterns of the stars as a guide during their flight. They are so accurate that some of them can go across country to the same 25-square-yard space they used the previous year. If the sky becomes overcast, built-in magnets in their brains, which contain small particles of the mineral *magnetite*, are used to orient them to the earth's magnetic field so they can stay on course (Keeton, 1974; Emlen, 1975). To date, no similar system has been found in the human, although some studies show that many people are able to orient themselves to north, south, east, and west.

Biological Clocks

All creatures are under the control of **biological clocks**. Biological clocks are internal chemical units that control parts of the body all by themselves and are programmed and regulated by nature. Even fetuses inside the mother have working biological clocks (Schwartz, 1984). Our internal temperature is run by one of these clocks, keeping us, when healthy, at plus or minus two degrees of the same temperature no matter what the weather outside us is (Mork, 1983). The kidneys also operate independently. Their clock has to ignore the outside world because they must get rid of poisonous materials at regular intervals in order to protect us. Those clocks that ignore the environment use what are called **free-running cycles** because they are under their own control.

Some clock systems can be changed, however. This is most obvious with sleep-wake cycles. Even here, though, some species are free-running. Dogs and cats, for instance, continue to free-run throughout the light-dark cycle. If you pay close attention to Fido and Kitty, you will find that they are quiet at night just to keep from getting into trouble with their owners. They do not follow the same pattern as humans; they fall asleep and wake up on and off throughout both day and night.

Even though the human is free-running at birth, we are able to change the sleep-wake cycle. Babies start off driving everyone crazy because they want to eat and sleep at odd times during the day and night. After about twenty exhausting weeks, parents have usually trained the babies to fit the adults' schedule. This process of altering the free-running cycle is called **entrainment** (as in "training"). The human body has a natural

Biological clocks
Internal chemical units that control parts of the body and are regulated by nature.

Free-running cycles
Cycles set up by biological clocks that are under their own control, ignoring the environment.

Entrainment
Altering the free-running cycle to fit a different rhythm.

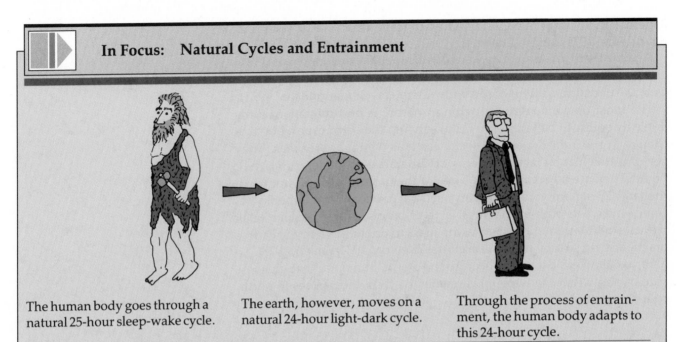

The human body goes through a natural 25-hour sleep-wake cycle.

The earth, however, moves on a natural 24-hour light-dark cycle.

Through the process of entrainment, the human body adapts to this 24-hour cycle.

Which is more natural: entrainment or the body's 25-hour cycle?

rhythm that free-runs on a cycle of 25 hours. If we lived in a cave (which some psychologists have done to prove the point), our body rhythms would go through a 25-hour cycle of sleep and wakefulness, of various chemical changes, and of the need for food or water. In other words, within 25 hours, each process has made a complete cycle of its own. Away from the cave, each of us has to entrain to the earth, which has a light-dark cycle of only 24 hours. The body can adjust to this one-hour change with little trouble, but some of you may spend the weekend doing everything you can to destroy this learned rhythm, putting it off by many hours. The result of changing your rhythm even by an hour or two can be a genuinely awful feeling come Monday morning—paying for one's fun as it were (Moore-Ede et al., 1982; Webb & Agnew, 1974).

You may have run across pamphlets, articles, and books that claim to be able to tell your personality and future based on "biorhythms." These have no scientific validity and are similar to fortune telling.

Circadian Rhythms   Every living thing on earth is controlled by the unseen forces that we call biological clocks. For example, there are plants that open up in the morning and close at night. Many think this happens so that the plants can get sunlight. Not so. If you take these plants into a lead-lined vault, they will open and close on schedule every 24 hours with no light at all. The plant is operating on what is called a **circadian rhythm**. *Circa* means "about" and *dian* means "a day," so the plant is changing its behavior twice in "about a day."

Circadian rhythm
Sequences of behavioral changes that occur every 24 hours.

The human circadian rhythm is based on an (entrained) 24-hour cycle. Within that cycle, we have a high point and a low point. For most people, the lowest point (low temperature, low blood pressure, weakness, and so forth) is between 3:00 and 5:00 A.M. That is why, if you wake up at that time, even on a hot summer's night, you will feel cold and shiver. Although everyone does not have the same rhythm, most of us come close. What happens if it is ignored?

Fighting the Clock   A Boeing 707 approached Los Angeles Airport. The pilots had slept the previous day, but their home city—and basic rhythm—were set for a time that made it 3:00 A.M. for them when they arrived in the Los Angeles area. The people in the control tower watched in horror as the plane stayed at 32,000 feet instead of landing. It flew on out over the ocean. The staff in the control tower made noises through the radio to awaken the crew, all three of whom had fallen asleep while the plane was on automatic pilot. They awoke with just enough fuel to get back to the airport and land (Coleman, 1986).

A study of 30 pilots for Airline X found that the pilots started to fall asleep while flying on an average of 32 times a month. Fortunately, rarely do they all fall asleep at the same time. Some pilots keep a kitchen timer in the cockpit, and they set it in order to keep themselves awake (Moore-Ede, 1986; Winfrey, 1987). These pilots are competent, but the airlines are asking them to fight nature, and that's hard to do at 3:00 A.M. with the steady sound and rocking of the aircraft. Thus, it is not so much the fact that you sleep as *when* you get your sleep that is important.

A person can change his or her basic rhythm so that the low point comes during the day, but this takes months to do, and airlines, hospitals, police departments, and factories rarely let it happen, since they keep changing the workers' hours.

Giving Up Sleep   What happens if we decide to give up sleep? It doesn't turn out too well, although most cases aren't as bad as the ones we describe here. A disc jockey set himself up in a phone booth on the street to do this. By the time he had been up for 200 hours, he saw things that were not there, and he thought people were trying to do him in. And, in a laboratory study, one man, after 168 hours without sleep, suddenly went berserk, sobbing and falling to the floor because he thought a gorilla was trying to get him.

Both the disc jockey and the subject in the laboratory had all the time in the world to rest. So rest alone will not do it. There is something special about sleep. It is clearly necessary. As you will find out, nature has set it up so that we sleep in order to do the most important thing: have dreams. If people are awakened whenever they are about to have a dream, thus stopping it, they feel as bad as if they had had no sleep at all. The importance of dreams is also shown by the fact that *all* creatures—except for one species of bird—have what appear to be dream periods.

Elephants, cows, rats, mice, cats, rabbits, and donkeys all have them. The donkey has to hurry up about it since it has only three hours of sleep per circadian cycle, while all the others sleep more than we do (Coleman, 1986).

The Nature of Sleep and Dreams

At first it seems that we simply get tired and go to sleep. But it's much more complicated than that. Sleep is far from a time of peacefulness and relaxation. Only the first hour could be viewed this way, since it contains the deepest period of sleep, and, during it, there is a dramatic fall in blood pressure, heart rate, and breathing. During the rest of the night, many unexpected events occur.

When we first lie down, electrical activity in the brain begins to slow. This is a period called the **twilight state**, with images and thoughts drifting in front of us, probably the one time during the day when we can totally relax and let the mind wander (Budzynski, 1979). And, before you know it, you are heading for your deepest sleep.

Twilight state
Time just before we fall into deep sleep.

There is no question that sleep helps restore the body. The making of new cells is at its maximum; chemicals the brain has used up during the day are restored. This is also the time when body hair grows most rapidly (Webb & Cartwright, 1978; Hartmann, 1973).

REM Sleep

The most important purpose of sleep is something of a surprise. But first let's look at what happens to each of us every single night—four or five times. The brain begins to fire furiously; blood pressure zooms upward; our eyes move rapidly from side to side and up and down; breathing and heartbeat are very rapid—all within a paralyzed body (Dement, 1979). This is called REM sleep.

So sleep is not a single state of consciousness involving only a single behavior. Instead, it can be divided roughly into two major types: The first is **REM sleep** (pronounced as one word: "rem"), and the second is NREM sleep, which we'll discuss in just a bit. REM stands for *rapid eye movement*, and REM sleep is that period when our eyes are moving about in all directions within the eye sockets. You can watch this in action with a dog or cat. They have an REM period every 30 minutes after they first fall asleep. Or you can watch your friends or members of your family. You can actually see the eyeballs rotating in the sockets. They will have an REM period every 90 minutes from the time they fall asleep until morning. If those you are watching are *really* in REM, you will not awaken them unless you call their name or make a *lot* of noise. In fact, as mentioned, they are paralyzed. The body does this to protect the person from the dangers of trying to act out a dream (Dement, 1979; Moore-Ede

REM sleep
Rapid eye movement sleep when we dream.

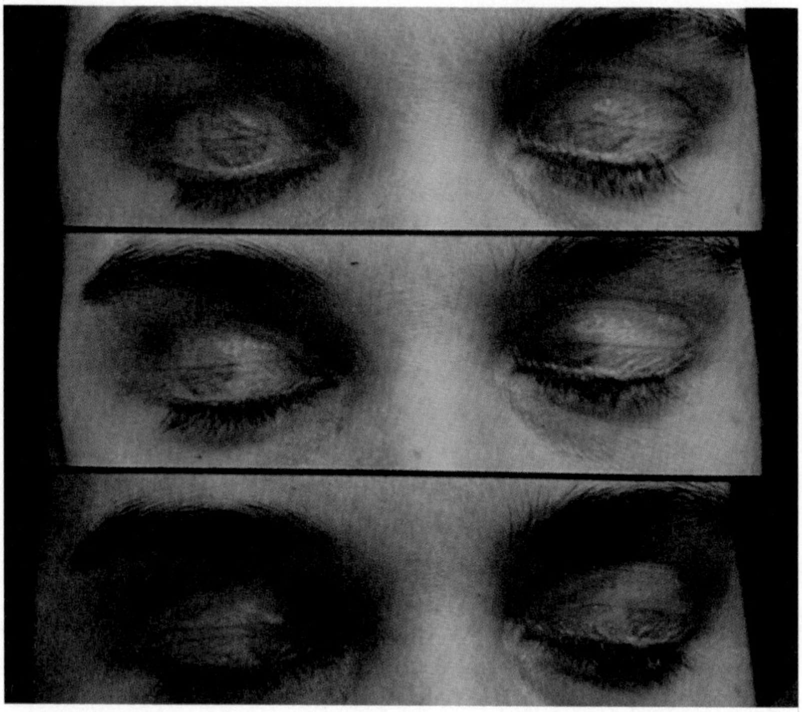

Time-lapse photography shows the movement of the eyes during REM sleep.

et al., 1982). Most likely you have had a number of dreams in which you were trying to get away from an attacker but were unable to move your legs to run. That's because you *couldn't* move your legs—literally. Sleep-walking, which we will discuss later, does not occur during REM.

How long do REMs or dreams last? You may have heard that dreams are over in about a second. That's not true. The actual dream lasts as long as it *seems* to take—roughly 5 to 40 minutes. Throughout the night, REM periods occur every 90 minutes with each REM lasting longer than the previous one. Figure 6.1 shows the typical pattern of a night's sleep. Note that REM periods come during times when we are *not* in deep sleep. Also notice that, as the night progresses, sleep gets lighter. The chances are that the dreams you remember are those coming closest to the morning since they are the longest, have occurred most recently, and you are the closest to being awake when you have them.

We need to pause here and give you an overview of the whole cycle of sleep, dreams, and the changes that occur during this time period.

Brain Changes During Sleep

In addition to the waking state, there are five other brain-wave patterns and corresponding stages of consciousness (REM and Stages 1 through 4). These are shown in Figure 6.1 on the right-hand side, with the typical brain-wave pattern shown next to each stage of sleep.

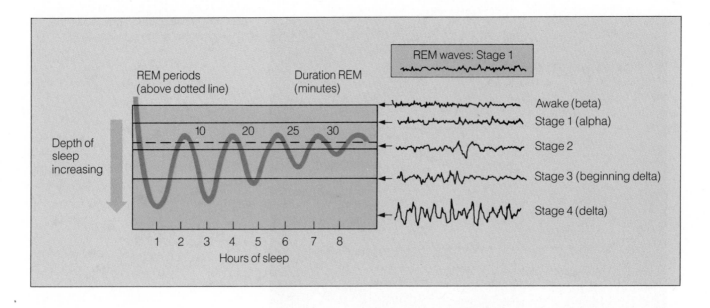

Figure 6.1
The sleep cycle

beta waves
Rapid brain waves; appear when a person is awake.

alpha waves
Stage 1, fairly alert brain waves occurring just before going to sleep; relaxed.

delta waves
Slow, lazy, deep-sleep brain waves.

Using the figure as a guide, first look at the brain waves running from the top to the bottom of the right-hand chart, comparing awake (**beta waves**) with Stage 1–relaxed, called **alpha waves**, and with the deepest sleep (Stage 4, **delta waves**). Notice that, the deeper the sleep is, the slower and "lazier" the brain-wave pattern is. In fact, the delta waves in Stage 4 are very slow and regular.

The chart on the left of the figure shows the typical pattern of a night's sleep, starting at the top. Before bed we are awake (beta). We get into bed and relax (Stage 1–alpha). As we begin to enter a twilight state, we are moving into Stage 2, and the alpha waves disappear. Stage 3 is next as we drift into deeper sleep, and finally we reach the deepest, delta-wave sleep (Stage 4). If you look to the left in Figure 6.1, you will note that, by the time you reach Stage 4, you are about one hour into sleep. At this point, you begin to go in reverse, heading from Stage 4 back toward Stage 1. Before the second hour, however, when you would be arriving back at the regular Stage 1–relaxed alpha, something unusual happens: Instead of going into the regular Stage 1, you enter Stage 1–REM; this is rapid eye movement, or dream, sleep. The first dream of the night occurs, lasting about 10 minutes. (Note: You will not enter the Stage 1–relaxed phase again until you awaken in the morning.) Thus, the rest of the night you will go from Stage 1–REM to Stage 4 and back again. Notice also that the length of dreams increases through the night, so that the last dream toward morning will be close to 30 minutes long.

Looking at the brain-wave patterns, you might assume that REMs are very close to the beta awake waves. The brain-wave pattern looks similar. But a person in Stage 1–REM is almost impossible to awaken. Not only that but, as mentioned, the person in this dream stage has periods of paralysis, and it is very difficult even to get a reflex from him or her. The similarity of brain waves between the two stages probably reflects

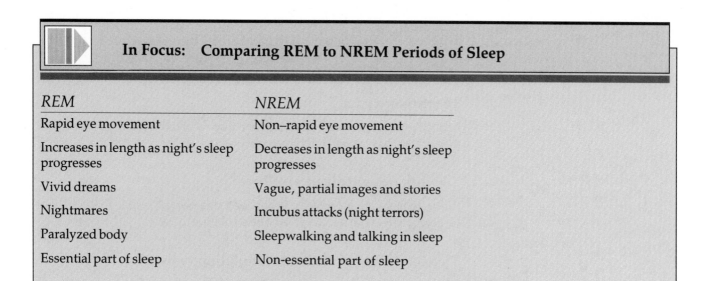

REM	NREM
Rapid eye movement	Non–rapid eye movement
Increases in length as night's sleep progresses	Decreases in length as night's sleep progresses
Vivid dreams	Vague, partial images and stories
Nightmares	Incubus attacks (night terrors)
Paralyzed body	Sleepwalking and talking in sleep
Essential part of sleep	Non-essential part of sleep

the fact that, during dreams, the brain is very active, just as it would be if we were awake and looking around (beta). In any case, we clearly are not part of the waking world during REM sleep (Webb & Cartwright, 1978).

NREM Sleep

The second type of sleep is called **NREM sleep**, which stands for *non–rapid eye movement sleep*. In Figure 6.1, all of the sleep below the dotted line is NREM sleep. During this "non-REM sleep," the brain is still active, providing partial thoughts, images, or stories. But these do not have the organization of the "stories" found during REM activity (R. M. Jones, 1970).

When you are not in REM, you are in NREM. NREM seems to be the time when the brain goes into "idle"; its operations are still going on, but they are neither at the level of wakefulness nor at that of REM dreaming. Some researchers feel that this is the time when the body rests. Remember, though, that you have to have REM sleep in order to feel halfway decent.

NREM sleep
Non–rapid eye movement sleep; sleep involving partial thoughts, images, or stories, poor organization.

The Purpose of Dreaming

There are three major hypotheses about why we dream. Evidence supports all of them, so they can sit side by side at this stage of our knowledge.

The first hypothesis is that dreams are used to get the brain reorganized after a day's work of thinking and dealing with problems. This makes sense because we know that brain chemicals are used up during

In Focus: Three Major Theories About Why We Dream

To reorganize the brain:

Brain chemicals are used up during the day. While the brain replenishes these chemicals, dreams organize the past day or week or more.

To work out unsolved problems:

We go to bed with a problem. When we wake up, the problem is solved (or forgotten—which in itself may be a solution).

To make sense of random stimulation to the brain

While we sleep, the brain flushes out the garbage we don't need. In the process, the brain is stimulated in a random or "crazy" way. So we dream to make sense of the random stimulation.

Rip Van Winkle trying to recover from a bout of 20 years' sleep.

the day. Notice how hard it is to study on nights when you have done a lot of mental work during the day. To restore the chemicals, we have to cut off the outside world in order to keep new problems—which would require more work—from getting in. The brain, however, cannot remain inactive. So dreams keep the brain busy with old material while it is being recharged, so to speak (Evans & Evans, 1983).

The second hypothesis is that dreams are designed to help work out unsolved problems left over from the day. You can find evidence for this in something that has happened to almost everyone. You go to bed with a problem of some sort that you haven't been able to solve—maybe in math or history, or maybe a personal problem. When you wake up the next morning, there's the solution, as obvious as can be (D. B. Cohen, 1980a; Webb & Cartwright, 1978). Further support comes from the fact that, when we are under stress or depressed, we sleep longer, and the amount of time spent in REM increases. This fact strongly suggests that we are working on the things that are worrying us while we dream (Hartmann & Brewer, 1976).

The third explanation comes from today's emphasis on the computer. It is possible that we get too much unnecessary material in our "files" from the day's tasks. Thus, dreams result from all the electrical realignments, revising, and updating going on in the brain. As various electrical circuits are being fired, different memory circuits are being triggered, and we have a dream (Crick, 1983; Evans & Evans, 1983). In other words, the brain is trying to make sense of the bits and pieces of information that are appearing while we are cleaning out the material, so it makes up a "story" to fit them. This would account for why we so often put odd things together in a dream.

There is one thing missing in our coverage to this point. What actually causes dreams, since there is no external stimulation? First, remember that all our memories, thoughts, and actions are controlled by electrical impulses within the brain. Add to this that we know there are electrical bursts that occur in cycles throughout the night. These bursts come from deep within the brain at regular intervals (90-minute cycles) and have special brain cells that turn them on and off. The electrical impulses move upward, hitting various portions of the upper brain, thus firing different memory circuits. The result is what we call dreams. These bursts also cause eye movements. We are not "watching" our dreams. Even people without sight from birth have rapid eye movements, but the content of their dreams centers on sound and touch (Coleman, 1986; Melnechuk, 1983).

Psychology of Dreams

Throughout history, dreams have been considered mystical and, in some cases, able to predict the future. There is no scientific evidence to support such claims. Since we know that dreams are made by electrical impulses causing the firing of our own memory circuits, it is obvious that the material is coming directly from us. If coming from us, then we should be able to tell the future just as much when we're awake as during a dream—if the future can be known. It also seems unlikely that dreams tell us much more about ourselves than we already know. A dream *can* trigger a memory that we have forgotten, or deal with something that we hadn't paid much attention to, but this is far different from receiving a special secret message.

Dream Content

Most dreams, most of the time, are about very ordinary events. We dream about things from a normal day: family, friends, and school. Dreams also contain a lot of material about worries, fears, or feeling inferior because these are concerns we all have. And often dreams involve an argument. The good part about these kinds of dreams is that, in them, we most always turn out to be right. That's not hard to understand since we're usually convinced we're right in the waking state. Still, it's nice to have our dreams agree with us (Webb & Cartwright, 1978).

While 70 percent of our dreams are about people we actually know, there are also other unexpected common images in dreams. For example, 40 percent of females dream about the sea or bodies of water, while only 27 percent of males do. Falling or being chased in a dream is very

The dreamer's world is not bound by time or space.

common and occurs about equally for males and females. Sex and romance are likewise typical. And the following themes occur with some frequency among completely normal males and females: violence, talking to dead friends or relatives, shoplifting, finding yourself naked in public, and discovering the "secret of the universe"—which unfortunately we forget by the time we wake up (Evans & Evans, 1983).

Bizarre dreams also occur. Usually the core of the dream is reasonable, but the story winds up happening in a strange place or with people you don't expect. Thus, ugly Uncle Harry is seen starring as the handsome leading man in a romantic movie. We suspect these strange combinations occur from the random nature of the electrical firing, putting things together we normally would not allow if we were awake and in control (Carrington, 1972). Strange dreams do *not* mean something is wrong with you. The only time you should be concerned is if the same dream occurs over and over and really is bothersome. Then it's time to sit down with a friend and try to figure out what it means. It will probably then disappear, as long as you don't let it worry you.

The concept that dreams are symbolic or represent deep, hidden impulses, needs, or desires has been around forever. Even many world leaders guide their movements by dreams. The story goes that Abraham Lincoln had dream warnings that it was dangerous for him to go to Ford's Theatre, where he was later assassinated. Most, but not all, researchers today believe that dream content of this sort is just a reflection of daytime, waking concerns that appear at night, rather than the result of some special message from another world or from our own unconscious world.

Finally, for something we don't understand at all: About 50 percent of our dreams are in color, and 50 percent are in black and white. Despite numerous experiments, we can't figure out why this is so. No, we don't even have a guess (Dement, 1974; Evans & Evans, 1983). It's not related either to the scenes in the dream or to the amount of color we see when awake. Researchers have even put colored filters over people's eyes for a week to see if that makes a difference, but it doesn't change the proportion of color in their dreams.

Nightmares

Nightmare
Frightening dream during REM.

There are two frightening experiences that can occur during sleep. The first happens during REM and is called the **nightmare**. Fortunately, nightmares are infrequent; only about 5 percent of the population has them as often as once a week. The odds that all of us will have a nightmare on occasion are very high since we all carry around bad memories that can be triggered. Nightmares also arrive in those who have missed REM periods for a day or so from drinking too much alcohol or not getting enough sleep (Hartmann, 1984; Coleman, 1986). The reason nightmares appear is that, if REM is blocked, **REM rebound** occurs. REM re-

REM rebound
Increase in the number of dreams after being deprived of them.

bound refers to the fact that, the first time we go to sleep after being deprived of REMs, both the length and the number of them increase (rebound) dramatically to make up for the loss. Hence, the chances of having unpleasant dreams increase. In general, however, we have no evidence that nightmares indicate something is wrong with the person. They seem to be just part of dreaming. And, despite the fact that you will hear the rumor frequently, nightmares do not come from something strange you have eaten.

Incubus Attacks

The second frightening experience during sleep is another kind of nightmare that you may have been lucky enough to avoid. It is called an **incubus attack** (IN-cue-bus), from the Latin meaning "to have a devil on your back." These are horrible dreams that are quite vivid and real.

The factor that makes them so awful is that the incubus attack occurs during NREM, not REM. The body knows that a regular dream is coming every 90 minutes and prepares for it, but the body gets caught completely unprepared by an unpleasant dream that appears to get triggered during NREM. The physical overload it causes sets off major bodily changes. Breathing rate zooms upward, the person feels choked, heart rate takes off to an unbelievable 170-plus beats a minute. These events create a feeling of panic and a fear of dying. The sleeper usually springs up in bed, sweating, nauseated, and afraid. Since to the body, which is unprepared, NREM is so much closer to reality than REM, we "know" it is "not" a dream, and it's too much to handle (Kahn et al., 1972).

The incubus attack, sometimes called a *night terror*, is fairly common in very young children. For some unknown reason, these dreams seem to be connected with a maturing brain. Thus, in general, night terrors should *not* be treated by a professional, since all that would do is to call attention to them and frighten the child even more (Dement, 1974; Coleman, 1986). The child will grow out of them. If incubus attacks occur with any frequency beyond middle adolescence, the chances are good that something physical is wrong, and this should not be ignored. A physical exam is clearly in order.

Incubus attack
Also called a night terror; a horrible nightmare occurring during NREM when the body is not prepared for it.

Practical Issues in Sleep

Patterns of sleep change as the years progress. Infants spend a good 75 percent of the time in REM sleep. The brain has so much building to do that chemicals are used up very quickly and need to be constantly restored. By adolescence, the brain is fully developed, but there are major physical and psychological changes going on during this period. As a result, regular sleep is important—at least in theory. Adolescents usually have so many "social obligations" that their sleeping schedule is chaotic (Carskadon et al., 1980). The male author of this text used to lean against things during adolescence; his father would sneer, tell him how disgusting it was he couldn't stand up straight, and claim if he got more sleep he wouldn't be just "leaning and hanging around doing nothing." (I still can't stand up straight when near a wall.) Finally, toward old age, people require much less deep sleep, probably from changes in the brain cells that control sleep. In this section, we deal with issues of sleep that apply to the teenage years through age 25.

Social Entrainment

Social entrainment
(of the sleep cycle) Fitting sleep and dreams to your social schedule.

Problems can arise from too much **social entrainment** of sleep cycles. This term means that, for social purposes, we alter our rhythms—because, for example, we are going to too many parties, visiting too much, or "hanging around" too much. Just getting eight hours of sleep is not enough. Sleep has to come at the right point in the circadian cycle. Otherwise the cycle gets off, which in turn makes the person feel terrible and also leads to errors on the job or to trouble solving problems. If there is not enough REM, the body craves more. The longer this goes on, the harder it becomes to get back to a reasonable rhythm (Weber et al., 1980).

Length of Sleep

People differ in the amount of sleep they need each night. For most of us, though, the body tends to seek about 8 hours' worth (Weber et al., 1980). Some people need a little more and some a little less. You actually have to experiment to find out what the correct amount is. Almost no one can get by for any length of time with less than 5 hours of sleep a night. There *is* a case of a man who suffered damage to the brain cells that control sleep, so he never sleeps. But he feels so terrible that he can't hold down a job, and he lives a life of misery (Coleman, 1986).

Although, on occasion, a normal person can sleep up to seventeen hours a night, too much sleep doesn't work either (Winfree, 1987). After eleven hours, the brain is "thick," and we do poorly on tasks requiring alertness (Taub & Berger, 1976). Long sleepers (10 hours plus) also tend to die earlier than short sleepers (6 hours). But this is probably not related to sleep itself. For one thing, long sleepers are less active. Another factor centers on something we discussed earlier: Those with problems need more REM, so they sleep more. If you worry a lot, your stress level is going to be much higher overall, and your body is more likely to give out earlier (Hartmann, 1984).

Walking and Talking in Your Sleep

A fair number of people sleepwalk or talk in their sleep. Neither indicates something is wrong with them. On the side of the brain, there are specific areas that control body movements and speech (Chapter 3).

When random electrical impulses hit these areas, they cause walking or talking (Guilleminault et al., 1977). Such behavior typically occurs during Stage 4 sleep, a deep NREM sleep period, so the person is not really awake or making much sense. Trying to communicate is fruitless. You may have heard it is dangerous to awaken a sleepwalker. That's not true at all. Sleepwalkers are just asleep. Wake them up so they don't wander off and hurt themselves.

Sleep Disturbance

About 30 million Americans have trouble sleeping. Most such problems are self-created. Dogs and cats, for example, don't have **insomnia** (in-SOM-nee-ah), the inability to get enough sleep.

Insomnia
The inability to get enough sleep.

The two most common causes of insomnia are getting out of the normal circadian cycle and taking drugs or alcohol, especially before going to sleep (Webb, 1982; Blum, 1984). The irony is that these drugs (including "relaxers" or "sleeping pills") tend to block REM sleep. As a result, over a week or so, we are losing more and more REM and feeling worse and less able to sleep. By that time, we are starting to feel depressed. The more depressed we are, the more we need REM, and so forth. Really heavy alcohol use for an extended period of time can cause such severe REM rebound that dreams appear while the person is still awake—in a form like the incubus attack. Bugs seem to be attacking, snakes crawling under the bed, and so forth. It is continued heavy use of drugs that results in this; on the other side, sometimes drugs can help bring on sleep for a very brief time after a trauma, such as a death in the family (Derryberry, 1983).

An infrequent problem that starts sometime between the teens and 20 years of age is **narcolepsy**. In this disorder, an individual can go into "instant" REM anywhere, anytime, even while driving a car or in the middle of talking to someone. Thus, although rare, it is extremely dangerous since the person immediately loses consciousness. Drugs are available that often help, so treatment is mandatory. We don't know the cause.

Narcolepsy
Disorder in which a person falls instantly into sleep no matter what is going on in the environment.

Another problem, usually with older people, is called **sleep apnea** (AP-nee-ah). The word *apnea* means to "stop breathing." Someone with this disorder literally stops breathing hundreds of times during sleep and keeps waking up. Normally the person doesn't know this is happening. Surgery that inserts an air tube is sometimes helpful.

Sleep apnea
Breathing stops while asleep, waking the person.

Hypnosis

Hypnosis has a colorful history. Before going on, it might help to give you a feel for why people think it is a strange and mysterious force. One of the words connected with "mystical" goings on that we still use is *mesmerize* (MEZ-mer-eyes), which means to put someone under your

Hypnosis
A state of suggestion in which attention is focused on certain objects, acts, or feelings.

Fashionable people attending Mesmer's "bath" in the 1700s.

power. This term comes from Anton Mesmer, who worked in the late 1700s "curing" people of their ailments. Mesmer claimed that he had special magnetic powers and that people who needed help could have their body magnetism "realigned" if they came to him. He had an enormous bathtub filled with iron filings, water, and ground glass. Iron rods stuck out from the side of the tub, and the "sick" visitors were told to hold onto them. Mesmer then entered the room wearing colorful, flowing robes and touched the tub, claiming he was mixing his magnetism with theirs. Mesmer was clearly a quack, since, for those who couldn't make it to his place, he sold bottles of his special magnetism for a "take-out" cure (Ellenberger, 1970).

The surprising thing is that many people were helped by this nonsense. We know today that such "cures" come from the power of suggestion. Suggestion is basic to hypnosis.

The Nature of Hypnosis

The formal definition of hypnosis is that it is a state that helps a person focus attention on certain objects, acts, or feelings. The best way to understand hypnosis is to think back to a time in the past few days when you were both studying and listening to music. You could not do both of them equally well and at the same time. If you focused on the music, what you were reading faded; or, if you focused on what you were reading, the music faded. So it is obvious that we have the power to control how much attention we give to different things in the environment (Hebb & Donderi, 1987; Hilgard, 1986). And, if we want, we can cut out some stimulation altogether. You have been doing that while reading this book. Here are some of the things you may have been blocking out: that you have shoes on your feet, that the room is light, that there is noise coming from an air conditioner or furnace, that your arms are connected to your body, that you are sitting on your rear, and so forth. Once you are aware of these things, they come into focus, one by one, demonstrating our point. Memories are cut off also. You have "forgotten," for example, the sights, smells, sounds, and feelings of your first day in high school—until reading this sentence.

The brain is like a mammoth stereo system with billions of speakers, switches, and filters so that you can turn on one, turn off another, blend them, mix them, or make most of them turn off completely. Some people get so good at controlling incoming stimulation that they can stick a knitting needle right through the arm and not feel a thing.

Depending on the goal, hypnotists use the power of suggestion to aid in focusing or blocking whatever system is desired. Thus, a person can be aided in forgetting something, remembering something, reducing pain, and so forth. All of us can do anything without hypnosis that we can do under hypnosis. Some people just don't have enough confidence in themselves to believe that this is the case, so they rely on an outsider to aid them—a hypnotist (Moss, 1965).

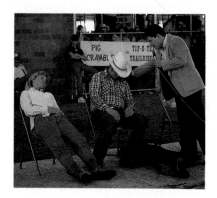

While hypnosis is real enough, much of the stage variety is mostly entertainment and questionable.

A Special State?

Some people think hypnosis is a form of sleep. This belief may have arisen because subjects can get so relaxed they are like rag dolls and they act semiconscious. Or it may be because some hypnotists say, "You are getting sleepy." But the hypnotic state is really not related to that of sleep. Hypnosis is an intense form of relaxation with the person fully conscious. Basic reflexes, such as the leg jerking if you tap the kneecap, are present in hypnosis but not in sleep.

Does the hypnotist really have control over the person? Only if the person wants to be under control, since he or she is still conscious (Spanos, 1986). If you tell someone in a deep **trance** to stay in the room and you'll be back in a couple of days, he or she may sit there for a while, relaxed, until what you said fully registers. The person will then get up and leave. "Trance" is just another word for the state of relaxation that the person is in. The deeper the trance, the more likely the subject will be relaxed and will cooperate with the hypnotist's suggestions.

Trance
Another word for the state of deep relaxation that can occur during hypnosis.

There is much arguing about whether someone can be made to do something "immoral" under hypnosis. This is very unlikely, unless the person really wants to do it and uses the hypnosis as an excuse. If, however, the subject is in a deep trance and is foggy, he or she may trust what the hypnotist says far more than normally; so that is a problem. In this sense, hypnosis *can* be dangerous, since the subject lets down defenses while putting faith in the hypnotist. Thus, hypnotized people can say or do things that would embarrass them later on. The actual physical dangers are few, but some subjects get a headache afterward or feel a little anxious or confused (Kline, 1972; Coe & Ryken, 1979).

Uses of Hypnosis

At one time or another, hypnosis has been claimed to cure almost everything. It *does* have some uses. It might help with reducing weight or with giving up smoking or drinking, but its effectiveness in these cases is only as great as the person's real *desire* to change (Wadden & Anderson, 1982). Hypnosis can help with minor pain, such as some dental work; it can help a person through a *normal* childbirth; it can help reduce some headaches. Hypnosis cannot improve memory, but it can help you focus better on such things as study assignments, so it has been useful in education (Schulman & London, 1963). While there is some disagreement about its use with major pain, most agree that, in Western society, it is usually not too effective (Hilgard, 1986, 1974; Barber, 1969). Those who can stick knitting needles through the arm are different because they have spent a lifetime practicing self-control or self-hypnosis, which are essentially the same thing.

A great deal of "hype" is given to the so-called posthypnotic suggestion, with people claiming that it causes someone to do something that they can't control. This is quite an exaggeration. Since a person is suggestible under hypnosis but still quite conscious, he or she may later do what was suggested, but doesn't *have* to do anything. The situation is roughly the same as the one in which you go to school and three people in a row say you don't look very well today. You don't have to believe them, but the repeated suggestion makes you wonder, and you actually start to feel not all that well, even if you were fine before they said anything. Or right now we can suggest that your right arm feels a little stiff. Aren't you moving it a little to check? No hypnosis involved, but you still check it because of the suggestion.

Meditation

Meditation is a form of self-control in which a person uses many of the "switches" and "filters" of the brain to cut off the outside world. He or she then focuses on some steady rhythm or sound, trying to put the brain more or less into "neutral" in order to feel peaceful and at ease (Ornstein, 1977). The steady sound can be a hum or a word or phrase that the person repeats, or even simply the ticking of a clock. Meditation can be very effective in lowering blood pressure or slowing heart rate (Wallace & Benson, 1972). The techniques of meditation are actually tools to help us relax. Some people can do it without going through any ritual. And some people cannot relax, no matter what. When some try to relax, it makes them nervous (Holmes, 1984; Heide, 1985)!

Meditation
A form of self-control in which the outside world is cut off from consciousness.

Meditation is basically a form of intense relaxation.

Wandering in the World of Consciousness

Here are some practical and, we hope, interesting applications of the material discussed in this chapter:

Try using the dream state for problem solving. This might be a little difficult because you may want to go ahead and solve a problem, especially if the answer is due the next day. But, if you can, look up a problem in a math book—a problem that you can solve but that will take some time. Look at it just before going to bed. You will probably have the solution by morning (or be very close) since your brain has been working on it.

Many people claim that the twilight state is the period when we are the most creative. Let your mind wander during this time and see if you don't come up with an unusual idea. If it sounds quite good, get up and write it down before you sink into deep sleep. Of course, it may not seem so hot in the morning—but who knows?

Try to *make* a dream. It can be done. Think about something very simple and not threatening, and tell yourself that you want it in the dream. It will probably appear in some form during the night. If you're lucky, it may occur late, toward morning, and you will remember it. Sometimes, though, it will not appear until the following night.

If you see a horror movie that really scares you, it also might appear in a dream—something you *don't* want. The computer

theory we discussed works pretty well in this case. Here's what you do: Just before getting into bed, go over the part that scared you and reassure yourself that it didn't—and won't—really happen. If you do this, the odds are great that you will have "cleared" that problem from your memory system, and it will not appear in a dream.

Find something you want to memorize. For example, pick a few lines of a poem or a saying. Read them over about five times while you sit on the bed. Then forget it and go to sleep. By morning, you will have most of the material stored, and it will require only a little more work for you to retain it permanently.

Night dreams are not the only dreams we have. Every 90 minutes during the day we have day-dreams, unless something is really distracting us. Now that you know this, think about a daydream *after* you've had one. (Don't try to "catch" it in midstream.) Notice how much more organized it is than a night dream. This is because you keep better control when you are awake.

Set your own internal alarm clock. You have one. Pick a time you want to wake up, but make it real; in other words, plan on doing something at that time. Your internal clock will time the number of 90-minute cycles and shorten the later dreams as you approach your wake-up time. The odds are that you will not hit the time exactly but that you will awaken

just before or after the REM closest to the time you set.

Notice how much easier it is to get to sleep if you go to bed an hour later than you did the night before, rather than an hour earlier. This is because, when you go to bed an hour later, you are actually moving toward the body's free-running cycle of 25 hours. On the other hand, if you go to bed an hour earlier, you are just adding another hour *against* your natural rhythm, which makes sleep more difficult to attain.

If you have been up very late over the weekend and not slept late the next morning, note that the following night you will feel like you had more dreams than usual. This is true. REM rebound will occur, especially after two such nights in a row.

Most of us know if we are "night" or "day" people. To "prove" it, take your temperature every hour for 18 hours or so. It will start to increase and reach its high point for the day (roughly 99.5 degrees) either in the evening or late morning. This increase tells you that you are entering your best time of day. If you're really interested, and if you are a day person, get up sometime at 3:00 or 4:00 A.M. and notice how low your temperature is.

Don't ever *try* to get to sleep, no matter how important it is that you do. The brain will decide you are trying to do something critical and will signal an "emergency." This will change your body chemistry so that you will never get to sleep. Instead, count something like imaginary horses jumping a fence. Such rhythmic thoughts will distract the brain and lull you to sleep.

Some animals, such as cows, sleep with their eyes open.

Observe your friends in a 2:00 P.M. class, and you will see behavior that resembles that of the cow. Chimpanzees, monkeys, and humans not only have a 3:00 A.M. dip in energy but also one at 2:00 P.M. This is a natural rhythm, not related to eating lunch. Recogniz-

ing this, many cultures allow for a nap in the early afternoon. Ours doesn't—hence, the condition of you and/or your classmates in that 2:00 class.

Summary

1. Consciousness is our awareness of events inside and outside ourselves. Consciousness seems to result from a series of scenes put together into a whole as we move about.

2. Chronobiology is the study of the effect of different rhythms on behavior. The rhythms are controlled by biological clocks that cause events to start or stop at certain times of the day, month, or year.

3. Sleep and waking follow a 24-hour cycle called the circadian rhythm. Each of us follows this rhythm and has a high and low point every 24 hours.

4. Sleep is divided into REM and NREM periods. The REM period contains most of the dreams.

5. Dreams occur every 90 minutes throughout the night, with each dream longer than the previous one. The basic purpose of dreams seems to be to keep the brain active while the outside world is shut off. It is during this time that the brain chemicals are restored.

6. Most dreams are about everyday events. Sometimes bizarre dreams can occur from random firing of the memory circuits. Likewise, sleepwalking and talking in one's sleep result if an electrical impulse hits the areas of the brain controlling these activities during NREM.

7. Hypnosis is the focusing of attention. People under hypnosis can control memories, bring them back, or make them disappear. Hypnosis is of some use in reducing pain, and can help a person lose weight or stop smoking—but only if the person already really wants to.

8. Meditation is a form of self-control in which outside stimulation is greatly reduced to create a peaceful state.

Key Words and Concepts

construct	twilight state	social entrainment
consciousness	REM sleep	insomnia
subconscious	beta waves	narcolepsy
unconscious	alpha waves	sleep apnea
chronobiology	delta waves	hypnosis
biological clocks	NREM sleep	trance
free-running cycles	nightmare	meditation
entrainment	REM rebound	
circadian rhythm	incubus attack	

Review Questions

Fill in the blank. Answer on a separate sheet of paper.

1. If someone is mad at his or her uncle but is completely unaware of this, the anger is probably hidden in his or her _____ .

2. _____ is the study of the body and the cycles that affect it.

3. A belief in something that can't be seen or touched is called a _____ .

4. The free-running daily cycle of most humans is
   _____ hours.

5. Most humans have altered their free-running cycle
   through _____ .

6. The human circadian rhythm is based on a
   _____-hour cycle.

7. Another name for knowing, or awareness, is _____ .

For each of the following states of consciousness, indicate A for alpha waves, B for beta waves, and D for delta waves.

8. Very relaxed   10. First ten minutes of sleep

9. Awake   11. Deep sleep

For each of the following, answer REM or NREM.

12. When the brain is idle

13. Associated with vivid dreams

14. Body is paralyzed

15. When incubus attacks occur

16. Gets longer as night progresses

17. Associated with narcolepsy

Matching

18. Episode of panic and fear   **a.** sleep apnea

19. Can be caused by drinking   **b.** narcolepsy
    alcohol
                                      c. insomnia
20. Breathing stops
                                      d. incubus attack
21. Falling suddenly into sleep

True–False

22. Hypnosis has been proved to improve memory.

23. Hypnosis is regarded as a special sleep stage.

24. It is unlikely that a person will do something immoral under hypnosis.

25. Most doctors in the U.S. agree that hypnosis can help reduce major pain.

26. Meditation helps us shut out the outside world.

Discussion Questions

1. Besides consciousness, can you think of any other constructs, or beliefs, that people have? List one. (Remember, a construct can't be seen or touched.) What evidence would suggest that this construct actually exists?

2. Consciousness is an awareness of what is going on inside and outside the organism. Do you think that people who are highly intelligent experience this awareness at a greater level than people who are less intelligent? Explain.

3. The unconscious contains thoughts and desires about which we have no knowledge. If you could suddenly become aware of these "hidden" thoughts by simply pushing a button, would you do it? Why or why not?

4. If you could completely give up sleep without many physical side effects, would you do it? Why or why not? Remember, no sleep means no dreaming.

5. Do you consider yourself a long sleeper or a short sleeper? If you're a long sleeper, how do you feel when you can only sleep a short time? Explain. If you're a short sleeper, how do you feel when you've had too much sleep? Explain.

6. Since dogs and cats have REM, it's probably safe to assume that they "dream." What would you guess makes up the content of their "dreams"? Explain.

7. With which of the three major theories that explain why we dream do you most agree? Explain.

8. If you could automatically remember and control all your dreams, would you want this ability? Why or why not?

9. In general, do you believe that you could be hypnotized? Why or why not?

Activities

1. Prepare a list of questions for an interview with your grandfather or grandmother or someone about the same age. Find out how sleep patterns generally change as a person gets older. Avoid too many questions that simply require a yes or no response. If you do receive a simple answer, ask the person to elaborate.

   Possible questions:

   a. How has the quality of sleep changed as you've grown older? Is it more satisfying now than 20 years ago, or less satisfying?

   b. Do you sleep more now than 20 years ago, or less? How does this affect your everyday routine?

   c. What kinds of events in your life forced you to alter your sleep-wake cycle?

   d. Are your dreams more vivid now than they were 20 years ago? Do you remember your dreams more today than you did then?

Write a detailed report of your interview. Be sure to include your questions. Also, include your general reactions to what you found out.

2. This chapter mentions that there seem to be some differences between long sleepers and short sleepers. Find out if the differences also involve personality. Use 20 subjects and ask each of them the following questions:

   a. Do you consider yourself to be (1) highly imaginative, (2) somewhat imaginative, or (3) not very imaginative?

   b. Are you (1) usually introverted or (2) usually extroverted?

   c. When you are given an assignment, are you generally (1) a highly motivated worker, (2) a somewhat motivated worker, (3) a somewhat unmotivated worker, or (4) a highly unmotivated worker?

   d. In general, do you consider yourself (1) a leader or (2) a follower?

   e. How long do you usually sleep? (1) six hours or less; (2) seven hours; (3) eight hours; (4) nine hours; (5) ten hours or more

   Analyze your results. Does there seem to be some correlation between personality and length of sleep?

3. Prepare a survey to find out about dreaming patterns and about people's beliefs in dreams. Avoid open-ended questions where the participant can fill in the blank with his or her opinions. These questions are hard to analyze. Instead, include objective questions that require yes or no responses or multiple choice. Hand out the survey to 30 high school students and analyze your results. In your analysis, include a discussion of averages and percentages (for example, "60 percent believed dreams are highly meaningful"); also include your own conclusions about why you got the results that you did.

   Possible questions:

   a. Do you think that dreams are (1) highly meaningful, (2) somewhat meaningful, or (3) not meaningful?

   b. What percent of your dreams are in color? (1) 0–30 percent; (2) 30–50 percent; (3) 50–70 percent; (4) over 70 percent

   c. Have you ever had a troubling dream that recurred over and over again? (1) yes; (2) no

   d. All of the following are common dream topics. Rank them from one to six. "One" would mean that the topic is most common in your dreams; "six" would mean least common: (supply your own list of common dream topics).

   e. Statement: "Dreams can predict the future." (1) I strongly agree; (2) I agree; (3) I disagree; (4) I strongly disagree.

4. If you decide to do this activity, you'll need to do number 3 as well. Hand out the same survey that you used for number 3 to 20 people who are 30 years old or older. Compare these results with the results from activity number 3. What conclusions can you draw?

5. Keep a dream journal for several nights. Write down each dream exactly as you remember it. After about a week of jotting down dreams, analyze them. Were there any common themes or common objects in many of them? Did you dream in color? Which colors? Did the dreams tend to be bizarre or somewhat orderly?

   What do the answers to all these questions say about your personality in general? Explain.

6. Write a report on Sigmund Freud's theory of dreams. Find out what Freud believed about the subconscious and the unconscious and what he said about how these concepts are revealed in our dreams.

7. Ask one of your close friends if he or she has had a vivid and bizarre dream lately. If so, give the friend a box of crayons and have him or her draw the dream. Then have the friend briefly and simply describe the scene, leaving out any possible interpretations about what the dream means. Finally, have the person write a paragraph analyzing and interpreting what he or she thinks the dream means.

   Before reading that paragraph, write your own paragraph about what you think the dream means. Take into account the colors used, the intensity of the lines drawn, and any details that stand out. Try also to relate the dream to your friend's life. For example, if your friend is extremely worried about a college entrance exam, maybe this (or some other worry) is reflected in the dream.

   Finally, compare and contrast the two paragraphs. How did they match up?

Unit Three

Cognitive Processes

What form of learning is this?

Chapter 7

Principles of Learning

Objectives

Be able to:

1. Explain the basic principles of classical and operant conditioning.

2. Explain the different schedules of reinforcement and give an example of each.

3. Describe social learning and explain how it differs from learning based on classical and operant conditioning.

4. Describe some of the complexities of learning unknown to Pavlov or Watson.

5. Explain the philosophy of the cognitive approach to learning and how this philosophy differs from other theories about how we learn.

Global Look at the Chapter

Most often when we think of learning, we think of the formal type that occurs in school. Learning, however, takes place continuously every day. In this chapter, we examine some of the mechanisms that aid in this process.

Conditioning
Making an association between an event and something positive or negative by repeated exposure.

Basic Conditioning

A nine-month-old baby lay in a hospital crib starving to death, his weight less than 12 pounds. The baby was so thin that his ribs stuck out and the skin hung from the bones of his arms. His eyes were wide and dull; he spent most of his time staring into space. Death seemed inevitable because, each time he swallowed food, it would reach a certain point in its downward movement and then his muscles would contract in the opposite direction, causing him to throw up.

Some central part of the child's brain was sending a signal to "throw it into reverse" when the food reached a certain spot. All available forms of medical and surgical treatment had been tried, and now there seemed to be no hope. But then someone hit on the idea of using a basic psychological principle—conditioning. In **conditioning**, an association is made between an event and something positive or something negative by repeatedly having the two occur close together in time.

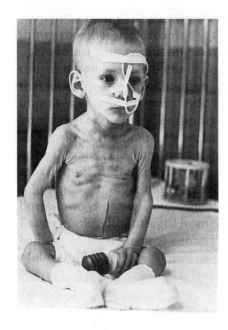 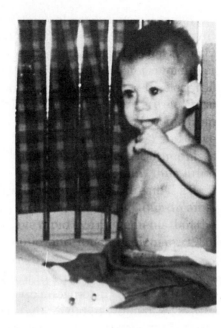

The power of conditioning is demonstrated in these two photos of the nine-month-old baby—before and after. *From "Case Report: Avoidance Conditioning Therapy of an Infant with Chronic Ruminative Vomiting" by P. J. Lang and B. G. Melamed, 1969,* Journal of Abnormal Psychology, © *by the American Psychological Association. Reprinted by permission.*

The next step was to find the exact location in the intestine at which the reversal of the food movement took place. This point was located with little trouble. Then the process of conditioning began. A wire that could carry an electric shock was attached to the infant's leg. Each time the food arrived at the "reversal spot," a shock was sent to the leg at one-second intervals until the vomiting was over. At first there seemed to be no significant change, but the doctors kept on with it. Treatment lasted for two weeks. By that time the food reversing had been thoroughly associated with something very unpleasant for the infant. His brain decided to stop the reversal process in order to avoid the shock. Soon afterward the infant began to gain significant weight, and he was discharged, well and happy (Lang & Melamed, 1969). Thus, it is possible to condition mental or physical behavior by a process of association.

Social Influence

This dramatic episode shows the value of conditioning, even at the most primitive level. However, conditioning can also be very subtle and complex. A good example is the concept of handsomeness, which is conditioned by each culture. Males in the Boloki tribe demonstrate their attractiveness and masculinity by chiseling their upper front teeth to V-shaped points, so they look rather like werewolves (Frumkin, 1961). Apparently the women in the tribe like it, but it is hard to imagine this technique attracting many among high society's "beautiful people" in New York or San Francisco.

Changes in style occur in every society over time, and we adapt to each change by constant association. The best example of this is the sheer panic each generation of parents feels over the music that is currently popular with their offspring. And the offspring, having learned to hear a different sound as pleasing, cannot fathom how the parents can actually listen to the "old-fashioned" music they enjoy.

Three Types of Learning

In this chapter, we will discuss three types of learning. The first involves unavoidable physical association, such as the shock to the boy's leg. This is called *classical conditioning*. The second involves learning caused by the actions we perform. For instance, we learn that pressing one's finger very hard on the edge of a knife is not a good idea. This is called *operant conditioning*. The third type of learning is the learning that results from observing others. If someone dives into a black lagoon and does not resurface, you know not to do that. This is called *social learning* (because it results from viewing other people).

Classical Conditioning

The most primitive learning is the kind we have just discussed in the example with the baby. It was first demonstrated by a physiologist and absentminded professor in the 1900s, **Ivan Pavlov** (PAV-lov). He was a man with an extreme temper who blew up at assistants for the slightest mistake. He fined them for being late to work, even though they had to walk through an ongoing Russian revolution to get there; when *he* was

The type of apparatus used by Pavlov in conditioning his dogs.

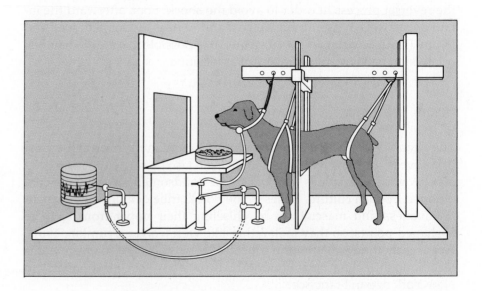

late, on the other hand, he did not dock his own pay (Miller, 1962; Windholz, 1987). Pavlov also became infuriated with the dogs used in his experiments because they were so bored with what was going on that they kept falling asleep. Despite these problems, his early discoveries led to major advances in understanding how people and animals learn.

Pavlov's original goal was to understand how the digestive system worked. He wanted to discover how salivation and gastric juices aided in digestion. By today's standards, the experiments were both basic and simple, but such was not the case in the early 1900s. Pavlov surgically separated the stomach from the esophagus (food transporter) in dogs. This operation meant that: (1) food taken by mouth would never reach the stomach and (2) food could be put directly into the stomach without having to travel through the mouth.

Importance of Association

Pavlov was quick to note three strange things. First, food put directly into the stomach did not generate all by itself enough gastric juices for digestion. Thus, salivation at the time of eating is critical to proper digestion. Second, even though *no* food was placed in the dog's mouth, the animal would still salivate copiously just at the *sight* of the food. But Pavlov's third finding was the most surprising and important one: The sight of the *experimenter* who fed the animal would cause the dog to salivate even if that person was not carrying any food. This meant that receiving food could be conditioned to (associated with) the mere presence of the (feeding) experimenter.

So far this is all clear and easy to understand, but, from this point on, students almost always get confused. This is because classical conditioning involves a specific terminology, not because there is anything really complicated about the ideas.

Outline of Classical Conditioning

A Model T Ford is one of the first cars that Henry Ford produced. This makes it an item of first importance—a classic. Since Pavlov's experiments were the first in the learning area, they also are considered classical. This is how we get the term **classical conditioning**.

The following steps are involved in classical conditioning. You start with a reflexive or "natural" stimulus-response pair. The word **stimulus** refers to anything that causes some kind of reaction. That reaction is termed the **response**. Thus, since meat makes a dog salivate, meat is the stimulus (S) for the response (R) of salivation. The behavior involved is completely automatic; the animal salivates when food is put into its mouth. Here is a diagram of this activity:

Receives food (S) → Salivates (R)

Classical conditioning
Ivan Pavlov's method of conditioning in which associations are made between a natural stimulus and a learned, neutral stimulus.

Unconditioned stimulus
A stimulus that automatically elicits a response, such as meat causing salivation.

Unconditioned response
An automatic response to a particular natural stimulus, such as salivation to meat.

Conditioned stimulus
A previously neutral stimulus that has been associated with a natural (or unconditioned) stimulus.

Conditioned response
A response to a stimulus that is brought about by learning—for example, salivating at the word "pickle."

So food is a stimulus (S) and salivation is a response (R) to that stimulus.

Note that no special *conditions* are needed for meat to cause salivation; it is natural and automatic. Hence, Pavlov called the food an **unconditioned stimulus** (UCS) and salivation an **unconditioned response** (UCR), because they occur without any special conditions needed. Replacing the diagram above with more accurate terminology, this is what we get:

Receives food (UCS) → Salivates (UCR), *unconditioned stimulus* and *unconditioned response*, respectively.

Since sight of an experimenter will not elicit salivation all by itself, some specific conditions are necessary—namely, the animal must associate the experimenter with food. When that association takes place over time, then "seeing the experimenter" becomes a **conditioned stimulus** (CS). In other words, the special condition of associating the experimenter with food has been met. So, the animal responds to the conditioned stimulus alone, by salivating, much as it did to the unconditioned stimulus of food. Salivation at the sight of the experimenter, since it is now triggered by a CS, with no food present, becomes the **conditioned response** (CR) (even though it's the same type salivation). The last step is:

Sight of experimenter (CS) → Salivation (CR)

Here is a quick review to help set the terms in your brain. You hear someone mention that he or she desperately wants a juicy dill pickle. Note that just reading this is causing you to salivate. How is this possible? In the past:

Eating pickle (UCS) → Salivation (UCR)

Each time you have eaten a pickle, you say to yourself, "Pickle." Over time, the word "pickle," which is only a sound and not a real object, becomes associated with a real pickle, which *does* cause salivation. So we now have:

Word "pickle" (CS) → Salivation (CR)

John Watson and Emotional Conditioning

Roughly twenty years after Pavlov's early experiments, psychologist **John Watson** appeared on the scene. While he was working his way through school, one of his jobs was to take care of laboratory rats. Gradually the rats became Watson's pets and friends. One of his favorite pastimes was to teach them all manner of tricks. The rats were able to find their way through elaborate mazes he built, to solve problems such as the need to dig through obstacles he had put in their path, to act as construction workers in tunnels he started for them, and so forth. Based on his observations, Watson eventually decided that what seemed to be the rats' complex behavior actually resulted from little more than a series of stimuli and responses, rather than from some exotic concept such as "intelligence." Watson went even further to suggest that, at the human level, "deep emotions" were also just the result of association and learning. One of his most famous experiments involved trying to get a human to spread (or generalize) the emotion of fear from one object to another; this, he thought, would demonstrate that emotions can be mechanically induced (Cohen, 1979).

Watson's work in this area has concerned many people because of the ethics involved in how he experimented with a child. His experiment would never be allowed today, but, since he did it, we might as well discuss it rather than let it go to waste. An employee who worked at the same clinic as Watson did would bring her child with her while she was working. Unknown to the mother, Watson started a series of conditioning experiments with the child. This eleven-month-old is now famous in psychology and is known as "Little Albert."

Watson put a white laboratory rat into the room with Albert. Albert loved the furry creature and played with it. While Albert played, Watson sneaked up behind him and smashed a steel bar with a hammer near the boy's ear, creating a horrible, startling noise. Albert fell forward, crying and burying his face in a mattress on the floor. The next time he reached for the rat, Watson repeated the crashing noise. Little Albert became terrified of the rat. Here is the situation:

Loud sound (UCS) → Fear (UCR)

which, after association, becomes:

Rat (CS) → Fear (CR)

Watson got Little Albert to show a mild negative stimulus generalization to a Santa Claus mask.

Stimulus generalization
A response spread from one specific
stimulus to other stimuli that resemble
the original.

Watson then went on to demonstrate what is called **stimulus generalization**, which means that a response can spread from one specific stimulus like the white rat to other stimuli resembling the original one in some way. To show this had occurred, Watson brought in a white rabbit, which also frightened Albert. Albert even showed some concern about a fur coat and a mild negative response to a Santa Claus mask, objects somewhat similar to the white rat.

Before the mother discovered these goings on and fled with Albert, Watson had shown two things: (1) Conditioning of emotions to neutral objects is possible; and (2) a conditioned emotion can generalize to other objects that have similar characteristics. All of this is helpful to know, but there still is a problem: Because no one ever located "Big" Albert after Watson's experiment and because no one since Watson has done a similar kind of experiment, we don't know how long such conditioned emotions last (Samelson, 1980). Most likely Albert's fear disappeared, since we do know from other studies (with adults) that, if you stop pairing something like a frightening noise with an object, the original association will begin to disappear. This disappearance is called **extinction**, as in the verb "to extinguish." Thus, after a while, Pavlov's dogs would extinguish (stop) their salivation at the presence of the experimenter unless the experimenter continued to feed them occasionally.

Extinction
The gradual loss of an association over
time.

Removal of Fears

One very important discovery was made as a result of Watson's experiments, and it came from a student who worked for Watson, **Mary Cover Jones**. Aware of the effect that Watson's experiments had had on Little Albert, she wondered if she could reverse the procedure and *cure* a child of a terrible fear. She found a three-year-old, "Peter," who panicked at the sight of a rabbit. In an experiment, she brought a rabbit into the room with Peter, close enough for him to see it. She then gave the child some food he liked. She moved the rabbit closer and gave more food, and she continued this process, associating the pleasure of food with the feared object. It worked: Peter lost his fear of rabbits. Jones had found the key to removing all manner of fears, called *phobias*, that can make people's lives miserable—fears of elevators, snakes, dogs, and the like. Associating something pleasant with a feared object is still used quite successfully today to reduce or stop such fears (Jones, 1924).

As a sort of footnote: Mary Jones was a close friend of Watson, so she never said anything negative about him. Even so, she does note that one day, when he was visiting her at home, she left him in a room with her child, who was about the age of Little Albert. From the other room she heard a very loud banging noise, but, when she hurried back, everything seemed normal (Jones, 1974). Was Watson trying to set up another "experiment"?

Operant Conditioning

Despite the importance of the above studies, most learning does not occur in a classical stimulus-response sequence. It usually is the result of some action taken by the learner. This type of learning is called **operant conditioning**, in which a behavior is learned or avoided as a result of its consequences.

Operant conditioning
Conditioning that results from one's actions and the consequences they cause.

Classical Versus Operant Conditioning

In classical conditioning, learning takes place without any choice; in other words, meat on the tongue (or something that has been associated with meat) will automatically cause salivation without any choice by the organism. In operant conditioning, the organism plays some role in what happens. This theory claims that humans and animals learn as an end product of performing certain actions (or *operations*).

The distinction between classical and operant conditioning is often hard to grasp when encountered for the first time. But the brain has a way of remembering unusual things better than it remembers the commonplace (we will discuss this in Chapter 8), and we want to take advantage of this fact now by giving you an example that is truly absurd, so you won't ever forget it. Here we go:

Someone in your household decides to classically condition you to hate a certain vegetable. At random times this person, carrying a handful of the cold vegetable, sneaks up behind you and shoves it into your mouth while talking into your ear about something disgusting. After a few of these encounters, you will find the thought of that vegetable quite unpleasant. You have now been *classically* conditioned to dislike the vegetable, since you had no control whatsoever over what was happening. Second scene: You find three different varieties of canned vegetables in the cupboard. You have never eaten any of them. You reach in, take one out, cook it, and eat it. You do the same thing with the other two later on. The one you like best you will probably reach for and cook again. In this case, you have been *operantly* conditioned by your actions (operations) to like one vegetable over another.

B. F. Skinner

Psychologist **B. F. Skinner** is best known for his work with the operant conditioning theory. He believed that how we turn out in life is the result of what we learn from all the operations we make over the years. If our actions result in people getting angry and disliking us, we are being operantly conditioned to believe that the world is a dangerous and threatening place. If the environment rewards us when we perform certain

Okay, I pushed the bar. Where's my food?

acts, then we tend to repeat them. Thus, if you study hard, do a good job on a paper, and get a note of praise, you will tend to study hard and do a good job again; if you get a nasty note on your paper even though you've done well, you will lose your desire to repeat these actions.

The seeds of Skinner's work were planted when he was a boy. He set up a pulley system in his bedroom closet that kept a large sign, "Hang up your pajamas," visible until he opened the door and placed the pajamas on a hook, at which point the sign moved out of view. He was operantly conditioning himself, and his action was probably reinforced by an absence of being screamed at for being sloppy (Fancher, 1979).

Later Skinner was so concerned about how our surroundings affect us that he reared his daughter in what he called an "air crib." In this crib, the environment—such as the temperature, humidity, and light—was carefully controlled at all times. The child was also not confined by diapers. The "diaper" consisted of a continuous roll of sheetlike material that was fed in one side of the air crib and pulled out the other. Skinner wanted the perfect environment for his little girl. She turned out just fine, but we'll never know whether she was really helped by the special crib.

Operant Conditioning Processes

Reinforcement
The strengthening of a tendency to do (or not do) something.

Reinforcement is an important ingredient in operant conditioning. It is a means of strengthening a tendency to do a certain thing. The word means the same thing in learning as it does in construction work: When something is reinforced, it is made stronger. For example, say that there is a bar inside an animal cage, and, each time the animal presses the bar, food appears. The behavior of bar pressing is reinforced by the arrival of the food. After a while, when the animal is hungry, it will walk right over to the bar and push it.

Primary reinforcement
Something necessary for psychological/physical survival that is used as a reward.

There are two types of reinforcement. The first is called **primary reinforcement**. The word "primary" means "of first and greatest importance." Thus, a primary reinforcer is something that is absolutely necessary for survival, such as food, water, or love. The possibility of obtaining one of these when you perform an action is the strongest incentive to learn.

Not all of our behavior involves primary reinforcers, however. For example, we engage in a truly weird activity that we take for granted: We work, struggle, fight, and wish for rectangular pieces of gray and green paper. People even commit crimes, lie, and cheat just to get these pieces of paper. Where's the reinforcement? We're talking about money, of course. Since you can't eat or drink it, it can't be a primary reinforcer, but it certainly does reinforce. Money has become a secondary reinforcer. A **secondary reinforcement** is anything that comes to *represent* a primary reinforcer. Because money can buy food and drink (if not love), it represents these primary reinforcers. All secondary reinforcers are related to

Secondary reinforcement
Anything that comes to represent a primary reinforcer, such as money bringing food.

In Focus: Classical and Operant Conditioning

Classical Conditioning:
How We Learn Involuntary Responses

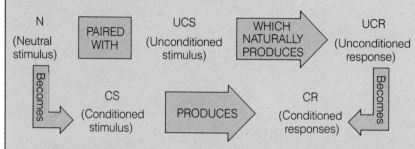

If we pair a neutral stimulus with an unconditioned stimulus, the neutral stimulus becomes a conditioned stimulus, and then produces the same response as the unconditioned stimulus. An example:

Bell (N) + Food (UCS) – – – – – ► Salivation (UCR)

Bell (CS) – – – – – ► Salivation (CR)

Operant Conditioning:
How We Learn Voluntary Responses

voluntary response FOLLOWED BY Reinforcement THEREFORE Same voluntary response is likely to occur again.

If we receive a reinforcement for a voluntary behavior, we'll probably perform the voluntary behavior again in the future. An example:

Study for test – – – – ► High grade – – – – ► Studying again for next test

In Focus: Positive and Negative Reinforcement

Positive Reinforcement

Tom drives conscientiously, courteously, and carefully so he can receive a safe-driving certificate and reduce his insurance rates.

Negative Reinforcement

Terri drives conscientiously, courteously, and carefully to avoid getting any more traffic tickets.

Positive reinforcement
Something pleasant occurs when an action is performed, increasing the tendency to repeat it.

Negative reinforcement
Something unpleasant is stopped if we do something; for example, nagging ceases if we do a chore.

some primary one. For example, you work for a high grade because it is a formal way of receiving praise, and this praise represents the physical love (primary reinforcement) in the form of hugs that you got from your parent(s) when you did a good job as a child.

We have been talking about **positive reinforcement** up to this point. Positive reinforcement occurs when something the organism wants (such as food) is added on (+, positive) after an action. There is also **negative reinforcement**. Negative reinforcement occurs when something is stopped or taken away (−, negative) if the organism does something. Don't confuse this with punishment. **Punishment** is designed to weaken, not increase, a creature's tendency to do something; hence, punishment is not a negative reinforcement. If the floor of a cage gives an animal a shock, the animal learns to push a bar in order to stop the electricity—this is negative reinforcement; it strengthens a response (pushing the bar). Say that someone wants you to take out the trash, which you keep forgetting to do. So the nagging starts, and it keeps on and on. You are being negatively reinforced: All you want to do is find a way to stop the endless whining about what a mess you are. You take out the trash and therefore are performing an act in order to stop something unpleasant.

In Focus: Generalization, Discrimination, and Extinction

As a child, Joey is beaten up every day by a loudmouthed bully with green eyes. Possible reactions:

Generalization

Joey becomes afraid of other loudmouths (or others with green eyes) and goes out of his way to avoid them.

Discrimination

Joey avoids loudmouths with green eyes, but he still talks to quiet people with green eyes.

Extinction

As he grows up, Joey encounters other loudmouths with green eyes who do not bully him, so he talks to them.

Generalization and Discrimination As mentioned earlier, a classically conditioned response can spread or generalize to similar stimuli. **Generalization** can also occur in operantly conditioned behavior. For instance, a boy who pats a dog and gets a wagging tail is likely to approach the next dog he sees in the same fashion. If that dog also wags its tail, the boy's action will generalize to all dogs, for the boy will assume they are all friendly. Suppose, however, that the third dog the boy pats bites him. In such a case, generalization has been instantly halted and replaced by **discrimination learning**. In other words, the child learns to tell the difference (discriminate) between dogs or between situations that are not all the same.

Babies often embarrass adults because of their generalizations. For instance, a baby girl hugs her father and says, "Dada." Daddy gets so excited about this that he praises her and runs to tell the mother that she has called him by name. The little girl generalizes the response, sensibly in her own mind, by calling every man she meets "Dada." When the other men don't give her the same positive reinforcement, she gradually discriminates between who is really "Dada" and who isn't—even though she doesn't really know what that sound means.

Shaping and Chaining Animals and people can be trained to perform certain acts by techniques called *shaping* and *chaining*. These are used to bring together a series of simple learned acts into a whole sequence of behavior by using reinforcement each step of the way.

Generalization
A behavior that spreads from one situation to a similar one.

Discrimination learning
Learning to tell the difference between one event or object and another. The reverse of generalization.

Shaping
The process of developing a part of a whole learning sequence.

Shaping refers to the process of developing, in an animal or a person, each part of a whole sequence. Thus, a lion that will have to jump through a hoop in a circus performance will first be reinforced by praise or food for approaching the hoop that lies on the ground. Next it is reinforced for walking through the hoop as it is held vertically touching the ground. Then the lion is shaped to jump through the hoop held a few inches off the ground, and so forth. Each act in the sequence is shaped or molded. The same process is gone through when someone is learning how to play a tune on the piano or how to swim; each part of the process is learned by reinforcement.

When it is time to get the complete sequence in order, each shaped act is connected to the others by reinforcing the connection with something rewarding. This process is called **chaining** as in "connecting together." Seeing-Eye dogs for the blind are highly intelligent and remarkable examples of what shaping and chaining can produce. They can read stoplights and traffic patterns, find curbs and doors, discover dangerous holes that might trip their owner, or find things the owner drops. The dogs are shaped to avoid or approach different objects in the environment; they are shaped to pull or stop when faced with various objects; they even will resist dangerous commands from the sightless person. All these behaviors are then chained into a smooth, ongoing process that looks completely effortless—and is, after being done hundreds and hundreds of times. Since these animals are capable of forming close psychological bonds, only occasionally during training is a reinforcer such as food used. The dog wants to please the trainer to such a degree

Chaining
Reinforcing the connection between different shaped acts.

The remarkable result of shaping and chaining.

that a pat on the head or some other form of approval or praise is more than enough and is generally even preferred.

The Coast Guard Search and Rescue teams have an unusual use for pigeons because a pigeon's vision is so much sharper than is a human's. The pigeons are shaped and chained to search for an orange disk and, when located, to push a button with their beaks as a signal. After training they go on helicopter rescue missions and watch for orange "disks"—life jackets attached to people in the water. Pilots have trouble seeing them, but the pigeons don't. Pigeons have a 90 percent success rate, whereas the pilots are stuck at 35 percent. The victims are endlessly thankful when the pigeon spots the life jacket and pecks a signal to the rescuers (Fox, 1980).

Schedules of Reinforcement

There are different methods of providing reinforcement during operant conditioning. So far we have focused on **continuous reinforcement**— that is, each time a desired behavior occurs, it is reinforced. In many cases this is not a good method because the creature gets used to having something and will quit if it doesn't show up every time. This problem can be avoided by using different **schedules of reinforcement**, which simply means different techniques. When the organism is not being continuously reinforced, it is on a **partial reinforcement schedule**, of which there are four. In partial reinforcement, the animal or person does not get a reward each time a desired act is performed.

Continuous reinforcement
Each time a behavior occurs, reinforcement is given.

Schedules of reinforcement
Different methods of reinforcing.

Partial reinforcement schedule
Reinforcement is not given each time an act is performed.

Variable Ratio A pigeon quickly learns to peck at a button for food. But, if you use continuous reinforcement, the pigeon will quit unless it is really hungry. On the other hand, if the pigeon gets food after five pecks, then after seven pecks, then three, or whatever variable number you want to use, once you stop the reinforcement, they will peck over 10,000 times before they give up on getting any food (Skinner, 1957). This is the **variable ratio schedule**; "ratio" refers to numbers. Thus, with the pigeons, you vary the number of pecks required before reinforcement occurs. Humans can really get hooked on this type of schedule, which is how slot machines work. Since players don't know exactly when the money will fall through the chute, they work hard at it, just like the pigeons. Usually the machines are set to give a few coins as reinforcement every now and then, but to give a jackpot only infrequently.

Variable ratio schedule
Reinforcement occurs each time a desired behavior occurs, but a different number of the desired acts is required each time.

Fixed Ratio What would happen if you kept the ratio the same, so there is one reinforcement every time the creature performs a *certain number* of acts? For example, what if the pigeon is rewarded after every five pecks? This is called **fixed ratio schedule** since the relationship between the number of pecks and the number of reinforcements is always the same.

Fixed ratio schedule
Reinforcement occurs after the desired act is performed a specific number of times.

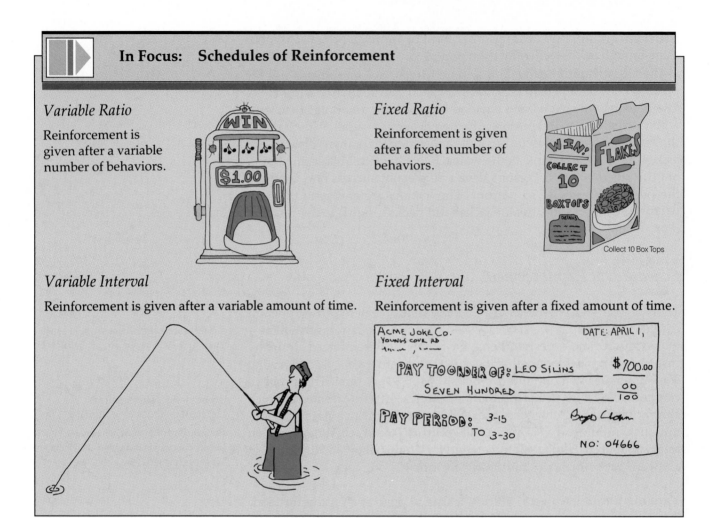

Variable Ratio

Reinforcement is given after a variable number of behaviors.

Fixed Ratio

Reinforcement is given after a fixed number of behaviors.

Collect 10 Box Tops

Variable Interval

Reinforcement is given after a variable amount of time.

Fixed Interval

Reinforcement is given after a fixed amount of time.

With this method, the pigeons will peck as rapidly as possible because they know that, the faster they go, the greater the number of reinforcements they will receive.

At first this seems like it might be a good way to squeeze every drop of work possible out of factory workers—but there are major pitfalls. Suppose that an auto company decides to put the workers on a fixed ratio schedule in which they are paid by the number of cars they produce. As workers are forced to speed up, they will put screws in halfway and leave out parts in order to save time and produce more cars. Even when this system looks like it might work—some workers may decide to try to out produce the others—pressure from the group as a whole will force a quick end to this competition. On occasion it may work, as with individual farmhands who are paid by the bushel.

Variable interval schedule
Reinforcement occurs after a varying amount of time if a desired act occurs.

Variable Interval   A third type of partial reinforcement is called **variable interval schedule**. Here the creature never knows (in terms of time, or "interval") when the reinforcement will arrive. It may come at the end of three minutes, then two minutes, then five minutes, and so forth. A real-life example can be found in that baffling activity called fishing, in which a person sits hour after hour holding a pole up in the air staring into space while apparently nothing happens. Actually, variable interval reinforcement is going on and keeps the person moving the boat or adjusting the line: The line is attached to a bobber that floats on the water, and at unpredictable intervals (from the current or a small wave most often, but on occasion from a fish), the bobber will disappear below water level, causing considerable excitement and keeping hope alive (Kary, 1984). With variable interval reinforcement, animals will keep working at a steady, sluggish pace, just to be sure they are performing the right act when the prize comes. But they don't overdo it in terms of speed.

Fixed Interval A fourth type of schedule, called **fixed interval schedule**, gives a reward when a specific, fixed amount of time has passed. It has an interesting effect on the behavior of animals. Pigeons that learn they are going to be rewarded every five minutes no matter how fast they peck become very casual about it all. They walk over to the pecking button, hit it once, saunter away for a while, and then return, hitting it again. They mope about until just before the five-minute interval is over. Then they move to the button and peck rapidly.

If you look at Figure 7.1, you will see that Congress behaves just like the pigeons. There is no particular reason why the production of bills (laws) should not be more or less continuous throughout a congressional

Fixed interval schedule
A reinforcement is received after a fixed amount of time has passed.

Figure 7.1
Cumulative number of bills passed during the Legislative Sessions of Congress from January 1947 to August 1954 (left) and cumulative number of responses of pigeons on the five-minute fixed interval reinforcement (right)

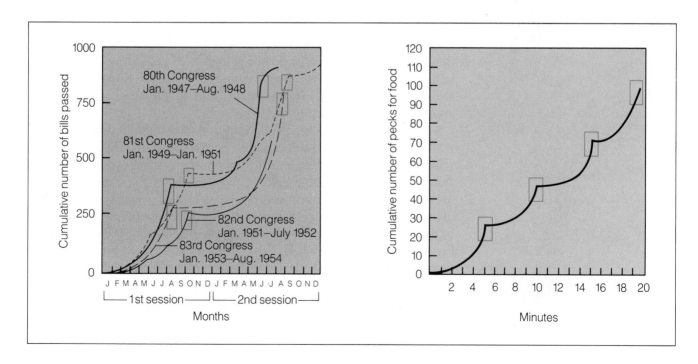

session, but, with the reinforcement of upcoming vacation time, there is always a sudden flurry of activity. Note how steep the curve becomes (meaning a dramatic increase in output) as the summer months—and adjournment—approach (Weisberg & Waldrop, 1972).

Social Learning

In present-day psychology, most of the research has moved away from classical and operant conditioning. While both play a role in learning, they fall short of explaining complex learning processes. One of the current theories about learning is called **social learning**, and its most prominent theorist is psychologist **Albert Bandura** (ban-DUR-ah). He claims that the most important aspect of learning was missed by Pavlov, Watson, and Skinner, for he feels that between the stimulus and the response is the complex "inner person" who is able to analyze events and make decisions before a response is given. (In case it slipped by you, the previous learning theorists we have discussed more or less ignored the individual and focused on robotlike patterns of stimulus and response or action and reinforcement.) Bandura feels that a more complex explanation for behavior is needed when analyzing group, or social, living. In order to survive, he says, we imitate directly the activities of those around us; "social learning" is the general term for this imitation.

Much of our behavior is acquired by **observational learning**, meaning that we learn patterns of behavior by watching others and deciding what to imitate. From the parent, a child learns speech patterns, personal habits, and how to react to other people. In other words, the child observes and then patterns behavior after that of the important people in his or her life (Bandura & Walters, 1963). Just in case you feel a little confused about the terminology: "social learning" refers to *all* learning in a social situation; "observational learning" is *one* of the processes used for social learning in which we (and many animals) watch events, persons, and situations for cues on how to behave.

In a now-famous experiment, Bandura demonstrated that children who observe aggressive adult models become aggressive themselves as a result. The children watched adults slugging plastic stand-up dolls. When the children were left alone, they imitated this behavior.

We once had a neighbor who was so afraid of germs that she would disinfect her house every 48 hours. She would not enter any neighbor's house, preferring to stay outside where she thought the air would be fresher and more germ-free. We were very surprised, however, when her daughter began to wear gloves while riding her tricycle—surprised, that is, until we were invited over to the woman's house for the first time; during the whole time we were there, the woman wore thin, latex, surgical gloves (true story).

Social learning
All learning that occurs in a social situation.

Observational learning
A form of social learning in which the organism observes and imitates the behavior of others.

Albert Bandura.

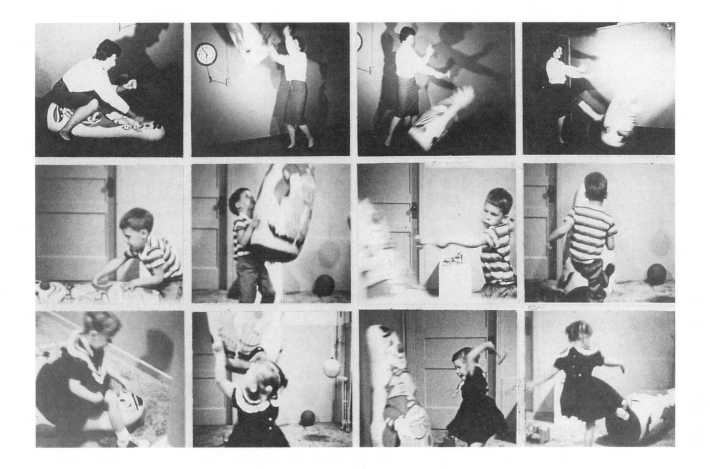

Don't miss the important point that Bandura is making: The child does not require a *specific* reinforcement such as food for learning to occur. Social learning can occur by exposure and imitation alone. Bandura felt that earlier explanations of learning were too simplified.

These laboratory film clips show children imitating aggression after seeing it.

Cognitive Psychology and Learning

Bandura's approach to learning is clearly more complex than earlier theories. Today psychologists are finding that even his version doesn't fully account for the elaborate task of learning. As a result, much of the present research looks at a means of learning called the **cognitive approach**. The word "cognitive" here means "knowledge-using," with "knowledge" meaning far more than just a stimulus and response or imitation. Using the cognitive approach, we are able to learn very abstract and subtle things that could not be learned simply through conditioning or social learning. For instance, some people have learned through the stories of others that it is very bad luck to walk under a ladder or to break a mirror: This kind of belief is very abstract and hence could not be

Cognitive approach
(to learning) A way of learning based on abstract mental processes and previous knowledge.

About as clear a case of observational learning as one would hope to find.

learned by any method other than the cognitive one. When psychologists study cognition, then, they focus on how complex knowledge is obtained, processed, and organized.

Complexities of Conditioning

Cognitive psychologists support their position by pointing out that even classical conditioning is not as simple as it first appears. For example, the type of cage an experimenter keeps an animal in will affect the animal's learning ability, as will the amount of time the animal has previously spent in the cage. If an animal is in unfamiliar surroundings, it gets preoccupied with its new environment and doesn't pay attention to the experiment (Hall, 1980). And, as in the case of Pavlov's dogs falling asleep, animals vary in the degree to which they are interested in the experiment. There are also strange individual preferences—for example, pigeons will tend to peck at lighted keys even without reinforcement, and they will peck differently if they are trying to get water as compared to food (Miller, 1983). Animals condition more easily to pictures of rats or spiders than they do to pictures of flowers and mushrooms (Marks, 1979). All of these findings make the animal far more complex than just a responder to stimuli. To see how complicated it can become, at the human level think about how the experimental results might have changed if Little Albert had been a bit older and had *known* that Watson was standing behind him banging the bar.

Under the cognitive theory, complexities Watson didn't know about take on a new light. For instance, at first it seems reasonable to assume that Watson's work with Albert can explain such human problems as phobias—in other words, that fears of closed spaces, heights, snakes, open places, or germs arise from straight association. But this is not necessarily the case. Psychologists have discovered a strange quirk about phobias: While many of them indeed may come from association, there is clearly a cognitive (or knowledge-based) aspect to them, because phobias only develop in relation to some kind of *natural* danger. Thus, if you are in a closed space, you really may be trapped; if you are up high, you may fall; some snakes are indeed poisonous; if you are out in the open, you may be more vulnerable; germs can kill you. All of these are known phobias; in contrast, there are no phobias for neutral or "unnatural" things, such as umbrellas, trees, light switches, or automobile tires (Seligman, 1971). As you can see, conditioning fears seems to be developing using a sophisticated cognitive process.

Cognitive Maps

In the 1930s, psychologist **E. C. Tolman** was already arguing that the mechanical stimulus-response view was too shallow an explanation for

A walk-through maze that requires a cognitive map to "solve."

all learning. But only with the emergence of cognitive psychology has his early claim been taken seriously and studied extensively. Tolman claimed that even rats in a maze were able to form what he called a **cognitive map**. This term refers to the human and animal ability to form a mental image of where he or she is located in the environment. Thus, when a maze is changed, a rat is able to visualize the change after going through it once and then can run the maze to seek food using the new mental image (Tolman et al., 1946).

We now know that Tolman was right, that there is no such thing as a simple organism. Rats in mazes, for example, not only form some kind of cognitive map but they also use **strategies** (techniques for solving problems) of their own to explore carefully the alleyways of a maze without going over the same territory more than once. Chimpanzees in a maze are remarkable. An experimenter can carry a baby chimp through a very complicated maze and deposit bananas in 18 different places in the alleyways while the chimp watches. When freed, the chimp can find an average of 12 of the 18 bananas quickly without duplicating any routes (Olton, 1979, 1978). Birds that store pine seeds in the ground for months at a time have the same excellent record; in fact, they even pass by storage places for other birds and pick up only their own seeds (Kamil & Roitblat, 1985).

The most enjoyable of such experiments involves bees who use a "scout" to find food (Gould, 1984, 1985). After finding the food, the scout flies back to the hive to tell the others where the food is. The location is indicated by an elaborate scout-bee "dance" that shows the direction and distance of the food location by the length of its up-down movement and the general pattern of its flying. One researcher took a scout bee out into the middle of a lake in a boat and exposed it to food. When it flew back to the hive, it dutifully reported direction and distance of the food to the others. Since the other bees also have cognitive maps, they presumably thought the scout was mentally disturbed (Food in the middle of the lake? He's got to be kidding!) because not a bee moved. In the next step of

Cognitive map
A mental image of where one is located in space.

Strategies
Methods for solving problems, usually involving cognitive maps.

the experiment, a scout bee was taken by boat to the shore at the other side of the lake, exposed to food, and let go. When it reported back to the same hive, all the bees came flying posthaste!

Here is an experiment for you to do; we will discuss the results below. Get a large piece of *unlined* paper. In the center, put where you live. Try to draw your map to scale, but don't use a ruler. Pick two places away from your home, one to the right and one to the left of it, approximately the same distance away. One should be a place you don't like for some reason, the other a place you have good feelings about. Draw a map of the streets from your home to each of these two places (Evans, 1980; Milgram, 1977).

The Map   Don't read this section if you haven't finished your cognitive map yet.

This experiment shows how psychological factors enter into a cognitive map. Note that you have made the distance to the unpleasant place greater than that to the pleasant place because you don't want to go to the unpleasant one. You have created a symbolic map that tries to move you closer to the pleasant place. In line with this symbolism, you have also straightened out the curves and bends in the road and generally altered the map to fit your own desires rather than strict reality. If the places are not actually equidistant from your home, you can still check with a ruler how much you "psychologically" changed the two distances.

Trying to Learn How to Try to Learn

There are courses as well as many excellent books on how to study. How far you want to go into the subject is a matter of personal choice. Here, however, are a handful of firmly established facts about studying that have stood the tests of time and of many experiments. We hope you will take them all to heart; at least the more of them you use, the better off you will be. Some of them require no pain whatsoever.

First, two "don'ts": There are many courses in speed reading, but speed reading doesn't work for studying. As your speed increases, comprehension decreases (Carver, 1971; Maxwell, 1969). If you are a very slow reader (less than 70 words per minute on a novel or newspaper article), you might benefit from extra training just to get your speed up to 100 or so words per minute. But speed reading reduces learning when you read faster than 250 words per minute. Learning "in your sleep," by using a tape recorder or other such device, also doesn't work. You learn only in proportion to how awake you are. All the machine will do is disturb your sleep (Evans & Evans, 1984; Oswald, 1966).

The single most effective thing you can do to help you learn is to write a synopsis in your own

words of every two or three paragraphs of the chapter you are studying. Stop when an idea seems to be completed and write it out in your own words. You should wind up with your own "minichapter" when you are done. Review your synopsis, note anything that isn't clear, and go back to the text to clarify that point, revising your notes. Keep your minichapters in a separate notebook so you can use them for review later.

Here is a technique you will like: The brain demands rest in order to bring together material properly. This explains why, when you have tried to solve a problem and have finally given up and gone to bed, the solution will suddenly be there when you wake up. The brain has

been working on the problem without all the clutter that normally distracts it during the day. While such a system won't work for regular studying, its principle can be applied. The maximum human attention span is about 30 minutes. So quit—eat or drink something, talk to someone, do anything that's different for about ten minutes. Then go back to studying for another 25 to 30 minutes.

The brain stores material on a specific subject in roughly the same location. History, for example, tends to be stored in one area. This means that an area can get overloaded and fatigued for a short while. Thus, you should change subject matters each study cycle (30-minute period), coming back later, if necessary, to the earlier ones. Keep away from similar material from one cycle to another. Put math between history and English, put English between math and chemistry, and so forth.

Finally, at the end of each subject studied, try to establish some principle that brings the material together. Ask yourself, "What exactly is the *issue* involved in what I've just studied?" Then review your summaries and leave them alone. If you have *really* studied, your brain will keep working on it.

Summary

1. Classical conditioning results from an involuntary association of a neutral stimulus with a natural stimulus until each brings the same response.

2. Operant conditioning requires some action on the part of the organism. These actions can be positively or negatively reinforced.

3. Social learning centers on observation of other people. We learn appropriate behaviors by watching others and imitating them.

4. Cognitive learning is the focus of a currently popular area of psychology that studies the meaning and use of knowledge. The methods by which knowledge is used, manipulated, processed, and organized are the subjects of cognitive research.

5. Classical conditioning is the least frequently used method of learning. Operant conditioning is basic to learned responses on a day-to-day basis. Social learning involves broad behaviors. Cognitive psychology studies processes of handling and integrating knowledge.

Key Words and Concepts

conditioning
Ivan Pavlov
classical conditioning
stimulus
response
unconditioned stimulus
unconditioned response
conditioned stimulus
conditioned response
John Watson
Little Albert
stimulus generalization
extinction
Mary Cover Jones and Peter
operant conditioning
B. F. Skinner
reinforcement
primary reinforcement
secondary reinforcement
positive reinforcement

negative reinforcement
punishment
generalization
discrimination learning
shaping
chaining
continuous reinforcement
schedules of reinforcement
partial reinforcement schedule
variable ratio schedule
fixed ratio schedule
variable interval schedule
fixed interval schedule
Albert Bandura
social learning
observational learning
cognitive approach
E. C. Tolman
cognitive map
strategies

Review Questions

For each of the following, indicate whether the capitalized behavior is learned primarily through classical conditioning (CC), operant conditioning (OP), or social learning (SL).

1. Nino *EATS* at Lou's Pizza for the first time. Since he enjoys the food, he returns there every Saturday for dinner.

2. The main reason that Nino *EATS* at Lou's Pizza is because all his friends eat there.

3. Every time Nino drives into Lou's parking lot, his *MOUTH WATERS* because he knows he will eat soon.

4. Little Lauren *WEARS* her mom's clothes simply because she wants to imitate her mom.

5. Little Lauren's *HEART RACES* every time she wears her mom's clothes.

6. Little Lauren *WEARS* her mom's clothes often because she knows she will always get a laugh.

Read the following example of a behavior learned through classical conditioning: "The first time that Sarah went to the DENTIST, he stuck a long NEEDLE in her mouth, which naturally caused her to experience FEAR. After a few visits, she experienced FEAR not only when the needle was stuck in her mouth but also when the DENTIST appeared to call her into the office." Using this example, identify the following concepts (possible answers are capitalized above):

7. The unconditioned stimulus (UCS)?

8. The unconditioned response (UCR)?

9. The conditioned stimulus (CS)?

10. The conditioned response (CR)?

11. The stimulus that started out as neutral (N)?

Which of the following are primary reinforcers, and which are secondary reinforcers?

12. Money

13. Food

14. Love

15. A promotion

Which of the following are examples of positive reinforcement, and which are examples of negative reinforcement?

16. Tom hangs up his coat in order to get a dollar.

17. Tom hangs up his coat in order to stop his mom's yelling.

18. Mary stays at home every weekend so she won't run into her old boyfriend.

19. Mary stays at home every weekend because her new boyfriend always comes over.

Matching

20. Phil loves to talk, but, when he discovers that no one really listens to him, he stops talking.

21. Phil learns that it's all right to talk during class discussions but not during tests.

22. Phil talks to a person in class wearing green shoes who actually listens to him. As a result, he tries talking to other people wearing green shoes in other classes.

    a. generalization

    b. extinction

    c. discrimination

Matching

23. Gamblers never know how many times they need to bet in order to win.

24. Factory workers get a break every three hours.

25. Whenever you kick a vending machine three times, candy bars fall out.

26. Every once in a while, candy bars fall out of the vending machine.

    a. fixed ratio

    b. variable ratio

    c. variable interval

    d. fixed interval

Discussion Questions

1. One day little Theodore is extremely startled when he hears the doorbell, and he begins to cry uncontrollably. In the days that follow, stimulus generalization occurs. Describe what might happen during the following days. How would you extinguish his fear?

2. Describe a fear that you once had that is pretty much extinguished today. Why or how was the fear extinguished?

3. Psychologist John Watson once said, "Give me a dozen healthy infants and allow me to control the environment, and I'll make them into anything I want." In other words, he could make them become priests, doctors, or even criminals. Do you agree with him? Explain why or why not.

4. According to operant conditioning, people continue to perform certain behaviors mainly because of the reinforcement they receive. This applies even to bad habits. Name one of your bad habits. What are several possible reinforcements that you receive for performing the habit? How would you remove or change some of these reinforcements and possibly extinguish the bad habit? Here's an example: Habit = biting nails; reinforcement = tastes good; changing reinforcement = apply bitter-tasting polish to nails.

5. Imagine a huge gorilla sitting stubbornly in the doorway of his cage, not allowing anyone to close the cage door. How would you use operant conditioning to get him to move? Explain.

6. If you were a teacher, would you use mainly positive reinforcement, negative reinforcement, or punishment? Explain. Provide specific, practical examples of how you would use the technique you choose.

7. Many animal trainers use the learning techniques outlined in this chapter to train their animals. If you have a pet, describe in your own words how you have trained the pet to perform certain behaviors. Do you see any similarities between your training techniques and the techniques described in the chapter? For example, did you use shaping and/or chaining? Explain.

8. If you wanted someone to become addicted to watching television, which schedule of reinforcement would be most effective? Explain. Which schedule would be least effective? Explain.

9. The end of the chapter discusses several techniques for studying. What strategies for studying have been effective for you? Explain.

Activities

1. Reread the map experiment described at the end of the chapter and try the same experiment on five friends to see if the results are consistent. In addition to telling them to draw a map, give them the following instructions:

   a. "On another sheet of paper, draw yourself in the center. On one side of you, draw someone you like and on the other side of you, draw someone you do not like."

   b. "On the same sheet of paper, draw a food that you like on one side of you and a food you do not like on the other side of you."

   Analyze the drawings: the map, the people, and the food. Is there any consistency in them? Are all the unpleasant items drawn farther away from the center than the pleasant items? Explain. Are all the unpleasant items drawn on the same side of the paper? Are there any other patterns that you notice?

2. Analyze a typical school day OR a typical athletic practice OR a typical day at work. Point out how reinforcement (both positive and negative) is used by your teachers, coaches, or bosses. Discuss whether these uses of reinforcement are effective in motivating performance or behavior—not only your behavior but also your friends'. Finally, discuss whether these uses of reinforcement should be increased. If so, how? If not, why not?

3. The following activity is for the lover of household pets. Take a cat or a dog and train the animal to perform a simple behavior like rolling over or pushing open a door. The best way to produce this simple behavior is through shaping: Every time the animal comes even close to performing the behavior you want, reinforce it with food. (Do the shaping when the animal is hungry.) Once the animal knows what it needs to do to get the food, put it on a fixed ratio schedule for a few days and then on a variable ratio schedule for a few days. (If it's at all possible, use two different animals and train each on a different schedule.)

   Which schedule seems to be most effective? Explain. Would it be more difficult to extinguish behavior learned through one schedule than through the other? Explain. Finally, jot down any general problems you have in training the animal(s).

4. B. F. Skinner has always been a controversial and fascinating psychologist. Write a brief report on his life. Focus particularly on how he applied the learning techniques he studied to his own life and to his family's life. Describe your reactions to his ideas.

5. Get a friend to participate in an experiment on shaping. Conduct the experiment where there will be few distractions. Sit across from the friend and read the following directions:

   "Imagine you're applying for a job and I'm the boss. I'm going to ask you a series of simple questions that will determine whether I'll hire you. My decision to hire will be based not so much on the content of your answers, but on other behaviors that you happen to perform in the next few minutes. So just pay attention and try to produce as many positive responses from me as possible after each question. The more positive responses you receive, the better your chances will be of getting hired."

   Have ready a list of twenty-five to thirty simple questions, such as name, address, and so on. Before you begin asking the questions, decide on a simple behavior you want to shape. For example, if you notice that your friend is slouching back in the chair, try to get him or her to lean forward and fold his or her hands.

   Slowly read the list of questions. The answers, of course, are meaningless. But, whenever the friend comes progressively closer to the behavior you want, nod and say, "OK." Your friend should interpret this as a positive response. If the friend continues to slouch, shake your head disapprovingly and say, "uh-oh" (or something similar). Note: Your first few responses will be negative since the friend has no idea what you're reinforcing. This whole process of shaping is similar to the "hot and cold" game that most of us played as kids. Whenever the person gets "hot," or close to doing what you want, you positively reinforce him or her; whenever he or she gets "cold," you offer no reinforcement.

   Repeat this entire procedure with two other friends and compare results. Discuss whether the shaping was generally successful. On the average, how long did it take for your friends to figure out the behavior you wanted? (Note: Even if your friends did not figure out the behavior but they still *did* the behavior by the end of your questioning, shaping can be considered successful.) Finally, what were some obstacles that interfered with the shaping process? Explain.

6. Find out who some of the top-ranked students in your school are. Interview two of them to find out about their study habits. Ask them this: "It's the night before an important test; what steps do you take to study? Be specific. How long do you study?"

Once you accumulate a list of specific studying behaviors, conduct an informal survey around the school, asking people whether they use any of the strategies on your list. Ask them to what extent they use the strategies: very often? once in a while? never? Finally, ask them their grade-point averages.

Compare the grade-point averages to the answers on your survey. Do you find that these are related in any way? Explain.

An alternative to a survey might be to convince two teachers to poll their classes about study habits. One class could be an advanced class, and the other could be a regular class.

A demonstration of some learning techniques.

Chapter 8

Acquiring, Processing, and Retaining Information

189

Be able to:

1. Compare learning curves when attention is high versus when it is normal.

2. Explain transfer of training.

3. Describe what a schema is.

4. List and describe special learning processes.

5. Explain how remembering differs when the task is recall versus when it is recognition.

6. Explain what it means to store memories in "code."

7. Explain the difference between short- and long-term memory.

Global Look at the Chapter

To acquire information, we must control what comes in and what is blocked out from the environment. Material that we retain is first sent through a short-term memory where it is processed and then moved to a permanent storage area where physical changes occur in the nerve cells.

Acquiring Information

All day long we talk, read, listen, discuss, fight, hope, believe, wish, despair, and analyze. All of these behaviors are taken for granted. But none of them is possible without learning and storing the information that we use in each case. We sit and mumble to ourselves, but we are mumbling *something*, and the something comes from things we have stored in memory. So, no issue is more critical than how we acquire and retain information.

To start off, we have listed here four passages for you to read. Read them only once, but, in order for us to make the points we need to make, *please* don't reread these passages until we refer to them later.

1. In 1925, lawyer William Jennings Bryan prosecuted the teaching of evolution and won the case. In 1920, many states were won to the cause of the Eighteenth Amendment for prohibition of liquor. Fourteen years later, the Twenty-First Amendment repealed the Eighteenth.

2. Raoult's Law states that the depression of the freezing points and the elevation of the vapor pressures of liquids that are dissolved are in proportion to the number of molecules of substance dissolved.

3. If you are attacked by a dog, hit its nose hard and fast. Put your forearm in front of you and jam it into the dog's open mouth. Bring your other arm around behind the dog and press it against the dog's neck. Force the dog's head backward and over your arm, snapping the neck.

4. The following is a poem about outlaw John Wesley Hardin, who roamed the West in the late 1800s (McMahon, 1987). He had killed five people by the time he was 15. Later he became a sheriff!

John Wesley Hardin, meanest outlaw of the West,
Killed over 40 men, and his reasons weren't the best.
From a hotel room next to his, a snoring man disturbed his rest.
So he simply fired through the wall and shot the man to death.

Learning Curves

Learning processes can be plotted out visually using graphs. For example, they can be used to study the influence of **attention** on learning. Attention refers to a person's alert focusing on the material to be retained.

Attention
Alert focusing on material to be retained.

Influence of Attention   When we attend to something, we become physically aroused, and this activates chemicals in the brain that aid our ability to learn (McGaugh, 1983). The item about John Hardin is a real attention grabber. Probably every one of you can repeat a good portion of its content without having to check back. A graphic view of learning the whole of John Hardin's poem would look something like Figure 8.1. In other words, Figure 8.1 shows that, on the first few trials, a person would probably make errors, but learning would take place rapidly until

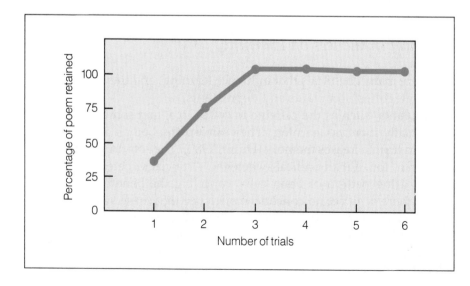

Figure 8.1
Learning curve for John Hardin poem

Figure 8.2
Conventional learning curve

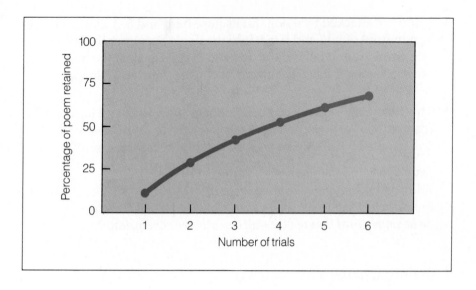

he or she reached 100 percent mastery. (A "trial" refers to each attempt to recite the material after a session of memorizing.)

Conventional Learning Compare John Hardin's poem with item number 2, Raoult's Law. Because the material is not an attention grabber for the average person, it involves a slower learning process. Motivation and attention are moderate, so learning is more of a struggle. Over a period of time and through a number of trials, the graph of learning this information will look like Figure 8.2. Note that here learning moves gradually upward with practice as the learning progresses, but the curve is nowhere close to the dramatic upward movement of learning the John Hardin poem. This curve (Figure 8.2) is the conventional (or usual) one that applies to most learning and is simply called the **learning curve**.

Learning curve
A gradual upward curve representing increased retention of material as the result of learning.

Chemical Influences on Learning

There are many chemicals that influence learning, and they fall into two broad categories: stimulants and depressants.

Stimulants, such as the caffeine in coffee, tea, and some soft drinks, can actually increase learning. They stir up the body's activity level, which in turn increases memory (Dunn, 1980). The soft drink must have sugar in it, too, not an artifical sweetener. Artificial sweeteners alter the normal firing pattern of brain cells, canceling the benefit of caffeine. (While there is as yet no conclusive evidence that these sweeteners do any direct damage, it would seem sensible to limit your intake of them or to avoid them altogether and take in a few extra calories from the sugar. This is especially true for very young children, since the cumulative effects of artificial sweeteners might not be desirable.) In any case, the stimulant is increasing the level of brain chemicals that allow for more rapid learning (Martinez et al., 1980). Strong stimulants, however, such as amphetamines (speed), overstimulate the brain and cause the reverse—loss of learning. Overall, the best of all worlds is to be naturally excited about what you are learning, because then your body will produce its own chemicals to assist in the task.

Anxiety about taking a test, at reasonable levels, acts just as caffeine does to stimulate the person, but some students "come apart" and drive the anxiety so high that it acts like the amphetamines, blocking learning.

Any depressant drug—such as a tranquilizer or alcohol—will block the firing of brain nerve cells and reduce learning. So will hot dogs or cold-cut meats. They contain a preservative that, in low concentrations, tends to depress learning ability (Martinez et al., 1979). But you have to eat three hot dogs or cold-cut sandwiches to get the effect, which is pretty hard to do without feeling horrible. Someone once said that "we are what we eat," which doesn't make much sense, but what we eat or drink *can* sometimes influence our behavior.

The fact is that taking in *any* chemical will alter a person's body condition or state. If someone learns something while in that altered state, the material learned will be easier to remember later on if the same state is reproduced. At the extreme, people who drink too much will not remember what happened once they are sober, but the odds are that the memory will return if they get in that condition again. The same principles apply to studying when someone has drunk three Cokes or three cups of coffee. And the same thing is true if a person smokes: He or she will remember better with the same level of nicotine in his or her body as when the material was first learned. This is called **state-dependent learning**, meaning that the learning and the reproduction of the material are reliant on (dependent on) the condition (state) of the body at the time of learning.

State-dependent learning
The fact that material learned in one chemical state is best reproduced when the same state occurs again.

Emotional Factors in Learning

The most important learning is that centering around survival. Animals whose existence depends on remembering who or what is bad are in an excited state when a crisis arises, and this excited state increases the brain chemicals for learning; hence, the animals have increased memory potential (McGaugh, 1983). Similarly, a place that provides food is a good place to remember, and animals' brains seem to become primed for learning at the discovery of such a source.

For humans, the principle is the same but more complicated. Here are the results of an experiment called "Nancy's Visit to the Doctor": Researchers gave subjects a long, tedious, and involved story about Nancy's visit. As you might have guessed, the subjects remembered little when they were tested later. In contrast, when the story was given to a different group and was altered to start off with the possibility of a

In the midst of this mess, all the person in the new manual-shift red sports car needs is to stall out from negative transfer.

major change or crisis in Nancy's life (an emotion generator), subjects remembered the details of the visit quite well (Owens et al., 1979).

So, emotional involvement increases learning. Another good example is the use of humor in the classroom. In moderation, it increases the level of brain activity. Too much humor, though, will wind up making humor itself the subject matter and will detract from learning. In some cases, the fact that a teacher is unpleasant can increase learning for a while because, even though the emotion created is negative, it still *is* an emotion. After a while, however, the teacher's nastiness or ridicule becomes the major focus of attention and learning decreases (Klatzky, 1980).

Transfer of Training

Transfer of training
A learning process in which learning is moved from one task to another based on similarities between the tasks.

One major learning process is called **transfer of training**. Its principle is relatively simple: Learning task A will carry over (transfer) to learning task B if there are possible similarities between them.

Positive transfer
A transfer of learning that results from similarities between two tasks.

Positive Transfer   Police officers who shoot on a range at targets that dart, hide, and suddenly reappear will be better able to shoot at real-life targets because of the similarity of the task. Hence, the material in one situation *transfers* to that of a similar situation. This is called a **positive transfer** because the two tasks are similar. The same technique is used by airlines when they have pilots fly in simulators that recreate precisely the feel and movement of a genuine aircraft. The pilots train on these simulators so that their good moves can transfer to the actual plane while any disastrous moves remain on the ground.

If you are interested in chemistry, you may have already been exposed to some of the elements found in Raoult's Law (item number 2 at the beginning of the chapter), and you probably remember at least part of what it said due to a transfer of training from your exposure to similar material. On the other hand, if you have never had any chemistry, chances are that Raoult's Law is already long gone from your memory storage area—or never even made it into your memory at all, as we'll discuss later.

So, positive transfer takes place when some useful similarity exists between what you have learned in the past and the new material. For example, a person who has taken courses in Latin will have an edge over others when taking Spanish, since many Spanish words are similar to Latin words.

Negative Transfer   There are occasions when transfer is not a useful thing, called **negative transfer**. If you learned to drive a car with an automatic transmission and then changed to a car that uses manual (hand) shifting, requiring a clutch, odds are that you stalled frequently, ground the gears a lot, and felt quite uncomfortable. If you learned how to drive with a manual transmission and then drove an automatic, you probably kept pushing an imaginary clutch to the floor and felt very foolish. The previously learned task is interfering with the present one.

Negative transfer
An interference with learning due to dissimilarities between two otherwise similar tasks.

Exercising the Mind?   Latin was picked merely as an example above. Still, for a while educators believed that, if you took very difficult and obscure courses like Latin, even if you didn't want or need to, somehow the pain and struggle involved in doing so "exercised" your mind so you would be smarter for most other courses. That has proved not to be the

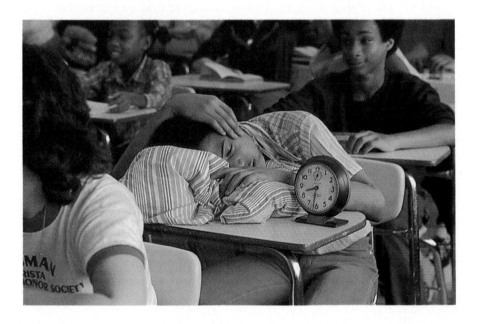

This is an example of either just plain sleep or consolidation of memory (p. 214) depending on your point of view.

case. Some courses are considered a necessity for a proper education, and for many people they are not easy; such courses include chemistry, physics, and advanced mathematics. But, although they are difficult, they don't "exercise the mind" in the sense of making it "stronger" for other courses. Chemistry and physics will transfer to one another because of some similarities, but there will be no transfer between, say, chemistry and history, physics and literature, or mathematics and Spanish.

Information Processing

Information processing
The methods by which we take in, analyze, store, and retrieve material in memory.

Learning and reproducing what we have learned is referred to as **information processing**. In other words, information processing is another term for the methods by which we take in, analyze, store, and bring back the various things we learn. Below we discuss studies of these various processes.

Using a Schema

Suppose we were to ask Little Red Riding Hood where Grandma lives. She would not come out with the answer automatically, but would have to go through a series of steps to figure it out. Various bits of stored mental information must be brought together in an ordered sequence before she can give an answer. Here are the steps: (1) Process words in the question asked. (2) Match the question to rough categories of information she knows in order to find the correct area where the information might be. (3) Within the area chosen, search to find a representation of Grandma in her house. (4) Hold that representation in her own consciousness while she locates the brain representation of where she herself is when the question is asked. (5) Find all the connections (streets and directions) between where she is now and where Grandma is located. (6) Answer the question step by step from where she is to Grandma's house, all the time blocking out incorrect connections that might appear (such as where Uncle Harry's house is) (Anderson, 1983). This process is diagrammed in Figure 8.3.

Schema
An organized and systematic approach to answering questions or solving problems.

This organized and systematic approach to answering questions or solving problems is called "making a **schema**" (SKEE-ma). The word *schema* comes from the Greek, meaning an "outline or pattern." So each of us has a built-in plan for solving problems (Horton & Mills, 1984).

An organized search is required because of the complexity and amount of material stored in the brain. In fact, it truly leaves one in awe to think that any of us can *ever* come up with an answer to any question, much less do so in a matter of a few hundreths of a second. Figure 8.3 shows only a small part of the schema used to find Grandma's house

(Craik, 1979; Klatzky, 1980). The original information given in the form of a question has to be processed through the correct sensory register (visual, auditory, smell, touch, taste)—in this case, auditory, since Little Red Riding Hood *heard* the question asked. Creating the answer requires, among other things, remembering how she got there (walking,

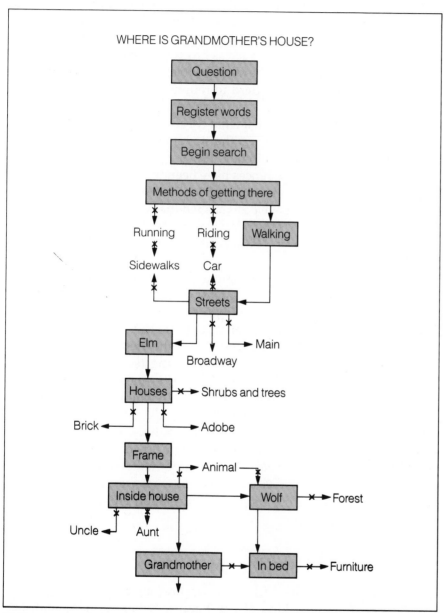

Figure 8.3
Finding grandmother's house

Make answer to where grandma lives: Wolf in bed in Grandmother's house on Elm reached by walking there.

Check answer: Match to question

Redo answer to match question: Grandmother's house is on Elm Street.

running, riding), deciding whose house she is going to (aunt's, uncle's, grandmother's), and analyzing the types of houses possible (wood, brick, adobe, or gingerbread).

Importance of Organizing Information

The importance of organization is demonstrated in the following experiment: Pictures of rooms were given to subjects to see how many objects in a room they could recall when the picture was removed. If the picture contained an unnatural scene, such as having a kitchen knife on the coffee table, pots and pans on the dining table, and flowers on the stove burner, the picture was very hard to remember. This experiment suggests that, in everyday activity, we form an organized, coherent, structured "map" of our world, and, if what we see doesn't "match" our existing memory (that pans belong on the stove), we have to stop and overcome confusion (Mandler & Ritchey, 1977).

Many of our memory sequences have been thoroughly learned. If the brain fires the information memory of "capital" for "United States," for example, the hookup is so well established that very quickly the answer will arrive: "Washington, D.C." (Anderson, 1983). Of course, there are always a few who will say, "Pitkinville, Montana," but that's the way life is!

You should note that an important aspect of learning is the ability to eliminate or block out the *incorrect* areas we run across during the search for an answer. As you can see in Figure 8.3, and if you remember the story, instead of meeting her Grandma, Little Red met a wolf with his snout sticking out over the bedcovers. So, as she tries to answer the question, she runs into a chain of information connected to wolves—forests, other animals, snouts, nose size, and so forth—most of which must be blocked out in order to get the right answer to where Grandma's house is. The X's in the diagram show some of the areas that must be blocked.

Finally, when we learn something new, it must be stored in the correct area. If information about a car is stored where flowers and bushes are located, the chances of ever retrieving that information are remote. There is some suspicion today that a fair part of what we call "intelligence" might be the ability to store and block information properly.

Special Learning Processes

Using a flashlight in the dark, you can find an octopus easier in an aquarium than another kind of fish because it has so many tentacles sticking out. If you find one of the tentacles, it is easy to locate the octopus's body. The same is true when trying to locate something we have learned. The more elaborate we make it, the greater the chance that one of the side branches will be spotted by a brain search and that we can then get to the main memory.

So now, the question is, do you remember item number 1 at the beginning of the chapter, about William Jennings Bryan and about Prohibition? No? There is a reason for this. First, you didn't give it your full attention because it wasn't that interesting. Second, it was too factual, meaning it had few associations or branches and no emotional color to help you hook onto the basics. Go back and read it again, then read this version:

1. In 1925, lawyer William Jennings Bryan prosecuted a young high school teacher who wanted to give students information about evolution. The trial took on the atmosphere of a circus; it became a free-for-all with shouting by "liberated" (for that time) college students and young reporters who reflected the antireligious feeling that was then erupting all over the country. The teacher was found guilty, so Bryan won the case, but he was mocked so much during the trial that some people believe that this led to his death five days later.

   In January 1920, a group of women, tired of having drunken, abusive husbands arrive home only after they had spent all of the family money at the local bars, organized the Anti-Saloon League to abolish alcohol. They rejoiced over the passage of the Eighteenth Amendment, which made the sale or possession of liquor illegal nationwide. Fourteen years later, it became clear that mobsters were reaping enormous profits from the sale of illegal alcohol and were using those profits in other crimes. Violations of the Eighteenth Amendment were rampant among all classes of people until Congress eventually gave in and passed the Twenty-First Amendment, which repealed the prohibition of alcohol.

The Elaboration Process   These revised passages should help you understand the process psychologists call **elaboration**. Elaboration is an effective method for storing learned material by using a maximum number of associations—as long as the associations make sense (Klatzky, 1984). Especially useful are colorful associations that grab your attention—such as the circus and the Anti-Saloon League women in the example just given—and help tie all the information together. The moral is that, if you have to read something dull, try associating it with something important in your life. Parts that are especially difficult to remember can be treated with the device for learning isolated facts that we will talk about in the next paragraph, but here's an example of it: The Twenty-First Amendment is for those *21* or older and not *for teens* (passed *fourteen* years after Prohibition started).

Elaboration
The process of attaching a maximum number of associations to a basic concept or other material to be learned so that it can be retrieved more easily.

Mnemonic Devices   Elaboration is somewhat similar to a method called **mnemonic devices** (nee-MON-ick), named after the Greek goddess of memory, Mnemosyne. She held an important position because memory

Mnemonic devices
Unusual associations in order to call attention to the memory when trying to retrieve it later.

In Focus: Elaboration

New material to be learned:	Associate this new material with "old" material:	The new material is effectively stored:
"Rapid eye movement (REM) is associated with vivid dreaming	New = REM Old = DREAM The new term, REM, is made up of nearly the same letters as DREAM, a word that's very familiar.	REM = DREAM
The cerebellum controls balance and coordination.	Associate the word CEREBELLUM with something else that represents balance or a lack of balance. Actually draw this in your notes:	An acrobat has excellent balance. An acrobat has a well-developed cerebellum.

CEREBELLUM

was vital in those days before books or photocopy machines existed. Even when a type of paper was developed in 3000 B.C., everything was written on long scrolls that had no pages, and, if they were unrolled a few times, the words on them would disappear. It is hard to imagine, but early English common law (part of the basis of our present legal system) was normally guided by memory, too, rather than by written record (Boorstin, 1983).

Mnemonics are not logical, but they can help you remember information. They can form the basis of unthinking, rote memorization, which is the most difficult learning process because it is so restricted in associa-

In Focus: Common Mnemonic Devices

Material to be learned:	Mnemonic device:	How information is stored:
Grocery list: milk, eggs, celery, and so on	**Method of Locations** Imagine a familiar location (like your house) and place the items to be remembered in various areas of that location. It's usually effective to enlarge the items in a bizarre way.	The sink is filled with milk that overflows onto the floor. Giant eggs roll along the tabletop. On the chairs, sitting at attention, are giant celery stalks; they prevent the eggs from falling.
Voluntary = Operant conditioning Involuntary = Classical conditioning	**Acronym** Take the first letter of each item on a list and make a word.	**V O I C E** V = voluntary O = operant I = involuntary C = classical "E" is thrown in to make a word.
A part of the brain: the cerebellum, which controls balance	**Narrative chaining** Tie together the material to be learned into a story.	He hit me in the cerebellum with a brick and I was thrown off balance. . . .

As you can see, some of these methods overlap one another. With practice, we all develop our own personal mnemonic devices.

tions with material you already know. If you can make sense of whatever you are trying to remember, don't ever use this kind of learning. Sometimes, though, it is unavoidable. For example, say you are at a party with mostly unfamiliar people. In the midst of them, you meet someone you like and want to remember, Harriet. You will have to make an association with her name that is sufficiently weird that you won't forget it. If you are lucky, she will have noticeably long hair, so you can keep saying to yourself "Hairy Harriet"; you have formed a mnemonic. Or, say that you are learning a foreign language, and you are trying to remember the French word for "dog" (*chien*). Associate it with a bulldog because the French word is sort of pronounced like "chin," and bulldogs have many of them.

There are serious limitations to this system if used excessively or with too bizarre images, because then you won't remember the associations much less the original word. Still, it is a useful technique for certain important things that you just keep forgetting. We hope you can see that mnemonics come down to little more than a type of elaboration in which you use the unusual to try to call attention later on to something during a mental search. One final note: Mnemonics will *not* work unless you use

New material to be learned:	Tie the new material to the general principle:
Infants sleep 12–22 hours a day and spend 20 percent of that time in REM.	The older you get, the less sleep you need and the less time you spend in REM.
Children sleep 10–12 hours a day and spend 15 percent of that time in REM.	
Young adults sleep 8–10 hours a day and spend 10–15 percent of that time in REM.	
Old people sleep 6–8 hours a day and spend about 5 percent of that time in REM.	

them from the beginning with whatever you are trying to remember. Attempting to attach them later won't help you remember (Rust & Black, 1972).

Principle learning
A method of learning in which an overall view (principle) of the material to be learned is developed so that the material is better organized.

Principle Learning   A very useful learning technique is called **principle learning**, which means you focus on the basic idea behind what is to be learned. See if you can't still recite the basic principle behind dog defense that you read about at the beginning of the chapter (item number 3). You should be able to; if not, one more reading and you won't forget it, because the method of defense is based on a principle of physics: Pressure exerted at one point and at a counterpoint will snap something.

   Another brief example: When learning a segment of history, tie it to a principle, and you can more easily make sense out of what the characters are doing. If you are studying the westward expansion of settlement in the United States, you can use a mental map as your principle. Then you will know that most of the Indians wound up to the left of the map, most of the stuffy people were to the far right, the gold rush was to the left, and so forth. While this is a rather primitive example, it should demonstrate the basics of forming some kind of principle to guide learning.

Chunking
Putting things into "chunks" so that items learned are in groups, rather than separate.

Chunking   It is not a good idea to treat items separately if they can be united in some sensible fashion. We learn better if things are clustered together. **Chunking**, at its simplest, means putting things into "chunks," such as organizing information by "either/or" descriptions

Without chunking	Number of items to be remembered	With chunking	Number of chunks to be remembered
Phone number:			
1234567	7	123–4567	2
Social security number:			
123456789	9	123–45–6789	3
Driver's license (in some states):			
A11001110111	12	A110–0111–0111	3
New zip codes:			
606060660	9	60606–0660	2

Don't you find it difficult to recite your phone number or social security number *without* chunking?

(good/bad; bright/dim; alive/not alive). On a more complex level, chunking relies on putting, say, all trees together as trees, even though they don't always resemble one another that well. In other words, when we call both oaks and evergreens "trees," we are *chunking* on the basis of bark, leaves (counting a pine needle as a leaf), trunk, and so forth in order to form the concept of "tree."

How confused the world would be without chunking! Every single item would have to be learned separately. In one study, children who were blind until about 12 years of age and who thus could not store information visually by chunking were extremely confused when finally able to see. For a while, their world was chaos. A rooster and a horse were confused because they both had tails. One boy who gained his sight at age 11 thought a fish was a camel because its fins looked like a hump (Delgado, 1969).

Both authors of textbooks and teachers have to have some basic organizational structure in the approach to their subject matter. This structure consists of units, or groupings within the whole subject. For example, in chemistry, first you learn basic principles about how molecules behave; later on you learn basic principles about how water molecules interact with acid (not necessarily very well). In each subject, you can use the teacher's or author's units to form your own chunks of information that will tie together the separate facts you need to learn.

Expert chess players chunk sets of moves to outwit their opponents.

Retaining Information

Learning material is not of much use unless we can hold onto it. In this section we will discuss the methods and systems by which we remember and the factors that go into causing us to forget that which we have learned.

Principles of Forgetting

Forgetting does not necessarily mean losing what we have learned. Often it involves only an inability to bring back certain material. In other words, a memory may still be in the brain, but, because other things interfere with it, it is hard to find. For example, if your home phone number that you have used for years is 434-2678, chances are you won't be able to retrieve easily a phone number of a recent acquaintance that is 434-2687 because the older learning will keep interfering. Viewed in this way, **forgetting** is an increase in errors while trying to bring material back (Isaacson & Pribram, 1975). But we are assuming here that there has been sufficient time to learn the material and that it has been stored. The next section shows what happens when there isn't time for enough practice.

The Forgetting Curve   Forgetting occurs very rapidly. If you look at Figure 8.4, you will see what happens if we learn something only to the point of being able to recite it one time and then we don't practice it. By the end of one hour, roughly 50 percent of a poem is gone. Retention falls to 35 percent by the end of two hours, and so forth.

The only way that we can permanently store something of average interest (unlike John Hardin's poem or the phone number of a special friend) is by **overlearning**. This term sounds strange at first, but, as you can see from the figure, if you just learn something to the point of one recitation, you aren't going to retain it. Hence, you have to *over*learn it, meaning that you rehearse it over and over beyond the one perfect recitation. After many rehearsals, the **forgetting curve** shown in Figure 8.4 will not apply. Such is the case with "I pledge allegiance to the ———— ————" and so forth. Note that your brain keeps going on and on for a while, filling in spaces because the material has been learned so well, or overlearned.

Recognition   In tests of how much we have forgotten (or the reverse, how well we can remember), psychologists classify memory into two types: **recall** and **recognition**. Both are tests of memory, but recognition is "easier" than recall. Recall involves a specialized memory that requires the bringing back and integrating of many specific learned details—as in an essay test, for example (Bower & Winzenz, 1969). Recognition, on the

Forgetting
An increase in errors when trying to bring material back from memory.

Overlearning
The process of learning something beyond one perfect recitation so that the forgetting curve will have no effect; the development of perfect retention.

Forgetting curve
Graphic representation of speed and amount of forgetting that occurs.

Recall
The ability to bring back and integrate many specific learned details.

Recognition
The ability to pick the correct object or event from a list containing the correct answer.

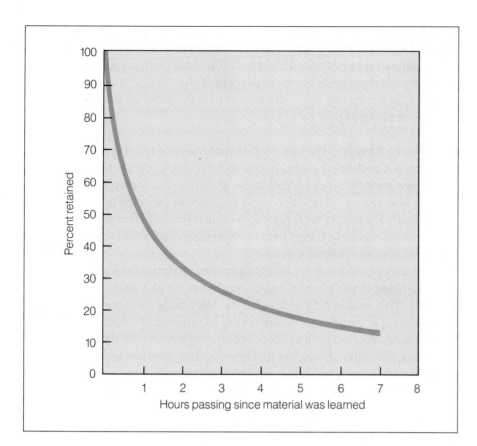

other hand, is used in the familiar multiple-choice tests ("Which one is correct? A, B, C, or D?") in which you must *recognize* the right answer.

Here is an example of the difference between the two. You see someone a couple of times a week who wears a uniform (at a burger place, a worker at the school cafeteria, someone who pumps gas, or the like). You don't know this person as a friend, but you see him or her regularly. Then one day you are shopping, and you see this person out of uniform. You know that you know his or her face from *somewhere*, but you can't quite get it. You are trying to *recall* who the person is, and you start a long search through all the possibilities, which can be innumerable. Eventually you might get it. If, however, you were given a *recognition* test, one of the items to choose from would be something like "Woman who works at the Taco Palace," and you would get it immediately. Why? Because a recognition test lists the memory storage areas for you to search; all you have to do is match the answer to your memory banks in the sense that you are already given the storage area; you need only to go to the memory store to see if there is a correct match.

How Little We Forget Here are some rather startling findings that show how much we actually store, how little we really forget. Subjects in one study had the capacity to recognize roughly 90 percent of 2,560 slides they had viewed. Two of the subjects who scored in this range had seen 1,280 slides in just one day (Haber, 1970). And persons 35 years out of high school can *recognize* about 90 percent of their classmates' faces in the yearbook, but they can recall the names of only about 25 percent of them (Bahrick et al., 1974).

Interference Theory   No one doubts that many of the things we start to learn are not practiced enough and merely disappear forever without being permanently stored. And some material that we do store just decays for one reason or another and is never to be seen again. But the major theory that explains forgetting is called the **interference theory**. Interference causes us to forget because there is a conflict between new and old material in the memory system.

The theory goes this way: Bringing in new material can cause processing difficulties if we already have somewhat similar material stored in that area. This would be the case for the telephone number example we gave earlier. Or, suppose you are trying to remember a sound, such as a musical note. You are in the process of storing tone A; the introduction of tone B shortly after A results in considerable interference, confusion, and difficulty in remembering A. The new tone, B, requires processing and will cause interference with remembering tone A, much more so than if there were a blank space of time after learning tone A (Massaro, 1970). The problem is that two memory systems for similar material operating at the same time cause confusion (Spear, 1978). Also, if new material is very much like old material, the brain has some trouble figuring out where it should go, since the two compete for the same space, so to speak, in the memory storage system. In either of these cases, the new material can fail to get stored properly or at all.

Mechanisms of Memory

People buy computers with a certain amount of storage capacity—for example, 3 million bits of information. Since you are familiar with this, it should help you to understand how much we can store in our own memory banks. For starters, a single bacterium can store 200 *billion* bits of information, using only thousands of nerve cells, which outdoes most computers (Benner, 1984). Compared to the very simple bacterium, humans have billions of nerve cells, each one with millions of connections, so our capacity is just about limitless. Suppose that you were to write out everything you have stored in your brain right this minute until the brain is empty. You would be writing a very long time, to put it mildly. If you are average, your present storage is the equivalent of 35 million pages the size of those in the book you are now reading! This is very hard to believe, but stop and think: You have stored almost everything that has

Interference theory
The belief that we forget because new and old material conflict (interfere) with one another.

ever happened to you—your first bed, your first room, the size and color of the seat on your first bicycle, the shape of the sidewalk in front of your home, and on and on (Sternberg, 1984). (As an aside, you will hear that people use only 10 percent of their "brain power". There is no evidence at all to support or disprove this claim. Someone just made it up decades ago, and it is still passed from one generation to another as a fact.)

When we remember something, it seems that we are "seeing" or "hearing" it. But that is not how the brain itself works. Memory is stored in some kind of physical chemical code, the nature of which we don't fully understand yet. We can grasp the principle, but not the physical details. An analogy would be the computer code of strings of numbers such as 0-1-1-0 or 1-0-1-0, each standing for something different. Thus, a long string of 0-1-1-0-1-0 and so forth might stand for "horse." We believe today that nerve cells fire in certain sequences, just like the combinations of 0's and 1's, and in this way they reproduce any memory desired. As they fire in sequence, they produce what we call "thought" (Farley & Alkon, 1985).

The brain contains about 100 billion nerve cells that are separated one from the other but that can communicate by electrical and chemical information going from one nerve cell to the other. Each of these nerve cell junctions is called a *synapse* (SIN-naps) (also discussed in Chapter 3).

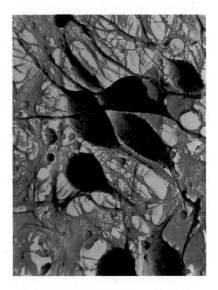

Some of the billions of nerve cells with synapses used to store information in the human brain.

One basic theory of memory suggests that, as we learn something, the physical structure of the synapses changes shape, a possibility suggested by microscopic studies of synapses after learning (Lynch & Baudry, 1984). These physical changes seem to alter which nerves will connect with which other nerves via synapses, how easy a set of synapses will fire, and what the sequence of firing will be. Thus, the memory becomes like a toy train with a series of switches turned on or off so that, as you learn something, you increase the chances of the same sequence of nerve firings occurring for each memory. The more often you repeat the material, the more solid becomes the "track" over which the memory train will travel. Similar theories suggest that the chemicals used to make the connections across the synapses increase with each learning, making certain connections faster and easier (McGaugh, 1983; Squire, 1987).

A second theory centers on the idea that the synapses grow, once a pattern is established. In other words, we make certain memories and, as they are stored, the synapses grow to hold them. Such growth is very obvious as a child develops. Learning, then, becomes a matter of using newly grown nerve cells in the synapses to form a map. If the memory is no longer useful, the growth slows down; later, a new growth starts for a new memory or for a modified memory (Rosenzweig, 1984). There is support for both this system and the one we just discussed. We don't know enough yet to bring it all together into a clear pattern.

While performing brain surgery, neurosurgeons have discovered that it is possible to touch parts of the brain with an electrically activated wire and the patient will relive, as if in a "movie" dream, a sequence from some earlier time in life, like a birthday party in childhood (Penfield, 1959). Such events certainly suggest that memories are stored in certain areas of the brain and that a whole sequence of nerve firings can occur from one stimulation.

Short- and Long-Term Memory

A common plot on television involves a man or woman who is struck on the head while witnessing a murder and forgets "everything." Fearful of exposure, the murderer follows this person around, waiting for a chance to do him or her in, not knowing that the memory of the murder is "gone."

Amnesia
The blocking of older memories and loss of new ones.

Although this situation is exaggerated (as usual), a good solid blow to the head, a major trauma, or an electric shock can produce **amnesia**, the blocking of older memories and loss of more recent ones. The term "blocked" is used because most of the material will return after a period, unless the person suffers a severe injury or the amnesia is from a disease (Graf et al., 1984). Strangely enough, the material that disappears is fairly selective. People rarely forget how to tie a shoe or brush their teeth. The most likely explanation for this is that these acts have been performed so often for so long that only massive brain damage would erase them, since they are so permanently fixed in memory. In many cases, however, once amnesia has started, people don't *want* to bring back certain memories, so they block them from returning even though physically they could be available.

Explaining Amnesia There are two possible explanations for the phenomenon of amnesia: (1) Amnesia could result from a temporary reduction of blood supply from an injury. This will disrupt the proper nourishment of the cells and reduce their chemicals, which, in turn, will alter the firing of the nerve cells to produce a memory (Dunn, 1980; Parkin, 1987; McGaugh, 1983). (2) A blow to the head will cause major electrical changes that will disrupt the transmission across the synapses and temporarily dislodge older memory systems, meanwhile just about wiping out most newer memories that haven't been thoroughly stored (Kinsbourne & Wood, 1975).

You may hear that, if a person has amnesia, another blow to the head will bring back the memories. As you can see, this is a ridiculous notion. The only possible results of another blow are further confusion and more disruption of the memory systems. It is truly hard to imagine how people can come up with such strange ideas.

Sequence of Memory Loss   Most people with amnesia can recall events from the distant past, but nothing recent. And, when memory returns, it always starts with older memories and moves up to the present. This was our first clue to the fact that we have both a **short-term** and a **long-term memory** system. Thus, the memories immediately preceding an accident are gone forever because they never made it from the short-term storage system to the permanent, long-term storage area.

The two memory storage systems seem to be at least partially independent. In cases of injury to different parts of the brain, some people can lose only short-term memory (STM), while others lose only large portions of long-term memory (LTM) (Kesner & Conner, 1972).

STM lasts from a few seconds to a few minutes. LTM can last from hours to days to a lifetime, depending on the amount of time a memory spends in the storage system where it becomes more and more solidified (Dunn, 1980). All incoming material goes first to the STM, where it is "processed"—that is, we make a decision about whether to keep it or not. Next, the material is either eliminated or moved to the LTM storage area where, over time, it is made permanent (Kellogg, 1980).

Under normal circumstances, the STM will hold only seven (on occasion up to nine) items before the material has to be moved on to the LTM (Miller, 1956). The only reason we can learn anything is because this memory system doesn't care how *long* each of the seven items is. This means we can group or chunk items together. Here are 13 items to learn:

Short-term memory
The memory system that retains information for a few seconds to a few minutes.

Long-term memory
The memory system that retains information for days, weeks, months, decades.

moon, cow, the, jumped, ate, over, the, hamburger, lunch, at, in, barn, the. The STM can't hold these 13 items. How do we do it? We chunk. The cow//jumped over moon//ate the hamburger at lunch//in the barn (Tulving & Partay, 1962). We now have only four items, which are easily put into STM.

In a very unusual case, a man called "S" had a defect of the STM system such that it *didn't* eliminate or block out any incoming material. His life became a private hell because he could not forget *anything* that arrived. When people talked, he could blank out nothing. Images came in, collided with one another, got mixed up, and triggered endless confusion. At times he felt that the word images were covered with smoke and fog. The more people talked, the less sense he could make of anything (Luria, 1968; Bruner, 1968).

We left out a slight technicality so you could understand the STM and LTM systems without any confusion. There *is* one additional system that comes just before STM, called the **sensory memory system**, which refers to direct receivers of information from the environment. The first set of receivers is called **iconic memory** (eye-KON-ick). The word *icon* means "image"; so we see and hold an image in front of us. The iconic system is probably just an electrical trace left over from firing the visual network, because it lasts only a few seconds. During that time, we make a decision about whether to send the image to the STM or eliminate it (Cowan, 1984). A quite similar system is the **acoustic memory** (ah-KOO-stik; sound) in which we can hold words for a few seconds while again we decide if we want to move them to STM or forget them (see Figure 8.5).

Unusual Types of Memory

You have no doubt heard stories of startling feats of memory. Usually these are tricks. When they are not, they may be caused by a defect in the memory system, such as occurred with the man called S.

Sensory memory system
Direct receivers of information from the environment—for example, iconic, acoustic.

Iconic memory
A very brief visual memory that can be sent to the STM.

Acoustic memory
A very brief sound memory that can be sent to the STM.

Figure 8.5
Diagram of the memory system

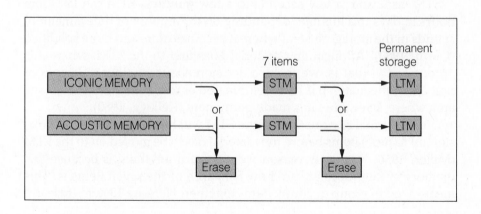

Figure 8.6
Study this picture for 30 seconds, then look at a blank wall and try to reproduce it in as much detail as possible.

If you really have the gift of eidetic imagery, you should even be able to tell how many trees there are.

Photographic Memory   One commonly-claimed feat is photographic memory, called **eidetic** (eye-DET-ick) **imagery**. Supposedly people can look at a picture of something like a chain, and then, when the picture is taken away, they can count the links in front of them even though the picture is gone. Some people *do* have longer iconic memories than others, possibly lasting a minute or so, and these are usually children (Furst, 1979). But, in all of the psychological literature, only one or two people might have had eidetic imagery. So, for all practical purposes, it doesn't exist. Try it out for yourself on Figure 8.6.

Eidetic imagery
An iconic memory lasting a minute or so that keeps images "in front of the person" so objects can be counted or analyzed; also called "photographic memory."

Eyewitness Memory   Memory is vitally important in "eyewitness" testimony, but unfortunately it is often wrong. For example, descriptions frequently fit a stereotypical image of a "bad guy" rather than the actual criminal. Further, under extreme stress, perception is faulty, and witnesses often use their LTM banks to fill in details that never existed (Loftus, 1984).

Eyewitness identification is usually quite inaccurate.

Eyewitness testimony is so bad because our brains are never content to let incoming information stand on its own. We process it, reprocess it, and keep working on it so that it makes *complete* sense in terms of everything we know, even though the facts in real life—what we actually saw—seldom fit together completely (Wells, 1984).

During class one day, a teacher staged a fake assault on himself. Later, during the "lineup," over 60 percent of the student eyewitnesses were wrong in their choice of who did it (Buckhout et al., 1972). In another (real) case, 17 eyewitnesses identified a man as the one who shot a police officer, but clear evidence later emerged that the man was not even near the scene at the time of the crime (McCloskey & Zaragoza, 1985).

Just to show you how easily memory can change, here is part of a laboratory study on eyewitness identification: In an accident case in which there was *no* broken headlight at all, two sets of witnesses were asked a slightly different question by the experimenter:

First group of witnesses: "Did you see *a* broken headlight?"
Second group of witnesses: "Did you see *the* broken headlight?"

The experimenter found that the use of the word "a" leaves the issue of whether or not there was a broken headlight in doubt. Only 7 percent answered "yes." On the other hand, when the word "a" was changed to "the," the witnesses assumed the presence of a broken headlight. The second group doubled the agreement based on just this one word change; 15 percent said they had seen one. Note how easily we are swayed by suggestion.

Hypnosis doesn't make eyewitness accounts more accurate because, under hypnosis, people are more suggestible than at almost any other time. Hence, identification can be even worse, depending on how the questions are formed (Laurence, 1983).

Identifying Faces and Seeing Through Disguises   Much of what we have been talking about in this chapter, if applied to identifying faces in a crisis, suggests that people would be very inaccurate in doing so. And this turns out to be the case. For example, there is very little opportunity for elaboration (developing associations) during the brief time of watching a crime being committed. Without time to make associations, an eyewitness has little chance of picking the right person later.

Even when warned in an experiment, subjects have problems remembering faces. One researcher gave subjects pictures of peoples' faces and told them that they were later going to identify one of these pictures as part of a second set. They were given a long time to analyze the first set. Later, one of the faces was put with a second set of pictures to see if it could be located. Most of the people failed the task, and there was none of the pressure in this experiment that would be involved in a real-life crisis (Harmon, 1973).

Our perception of others is quite faulty. This is clearly demonstrated by the effect of using disguises. If a person changes his or her hairstyle or adds a beard, accurate identification drops 25 percent. With both a hairstyle and a beard, or with a change of hair color for a woman, it drops 52 percent; and, if a person doesn't look straight at another but keeps a profile, he or she might look a little suspicious, but accuracy of identification falls a full 61 percent (Patterson & Baddeley, 1977).

Consolidation
The process of strengthening a memory and its parts over time until they are very solid.

Testing Your Memory

An established principle of learning and memory is called **consolidation**. Consolidation is a process by which over time a memory will solidify until it becomes permanent. The term itself refers to the fact that the memory is brought together (consolidated) into a clear and organized whole. Here's a chance for you to test this out. You will need a partner to do so.

The first experiment involves short-term memory, which allows for no consolidation. Take the "Yellow Pages" and put it on a table about 25 feet from the telephone. Have your partner stand by the phone book. Find a number at random and circle it. Read it once. Now, try to get to the phone to dial it. All the time you are on your way, your partner is to shout random numbers out loud to you (5, 29, 3, 12, 8, whatever . . .). You don't stand a chance of making it to the phone with the circled phone number intact in your brain, because each new number that your friend is calling out is fighting for a position among the magic quantity of seven items that can be stored in the STM. One "old" number is knocked out as a new one comes in. You can even try talking or humming to yourself as you run to the phone, but

even that won't work because now the STM is trying to store the words you are making or the humming sound (and you are still picking up some numbers from your shouting partner).

The second experiment centers on partial consolidation. This time put a pad and pencil next to the phone so, instead of dialing, you can write down what you would have dialed. That way you can see what we're talking about. First, remember that sleep is an excellent consolidator. All night the brain will be working on material you give it. The night before this experiment, pick a number from the phone book and write it down. As you sit on the side of the bed before going to sleep, rehearse it two or three times. Wait five minutes. Rehearse it again a few times. Then turn the piece of paper over so you can't see the number, and go to sleep. Next day: Don't look at that piece of paper next to your bed! When your partner arrives, do the same thing as before: Look at the piece of paper and review the number twice. Then head for the phone while your partner is shouting numbers. Write what you would have dialed on another pad. The odds are overwhelming that you will have most of the correct numbers, perhaps not yet in their exact sequence, but it is

obvious that they have been at least partially stored.

For the third part of the experiment, your partner—at random—picks a number you know very well and says it to you ("Amy's number"). You head for the phone as your partner keeps shouting numbers. This time you will be frustrated because you have to keep fighting STM storage as you bring back LTM (Amy's number), but you'll be able to do it because the number is permanently stored; it has been *consolidated*.

The final experiment involves being an "eyewitness." Somewhere in your home is a box of family photos. At least one photo you know very well, but you haven't seen it for a month or so. Tell your partner which one it is, and he or she can get it for you. Don't look at it. Next write out everything you think is going on in the photo—who is where, what they are wearing, and so forth. When you are done, compare what you have written down with the real photo, and note how many details you have added that are not in the actual photo—usually things that you wish were there or that you think would be logical to be there.

Summary

1. Learning takes place most rapidly with a high level of emotion and attention.

2. In positive transfer, material already learned is moved to a new task that is similar. Negative transfer causes interference when you are learning two tasks that are similar but that have some significant differences.

3. A schema is an organized pattern for analyzing information in the memory storage areas.

4. Memory is greatly aided by elaboration.

5. When material to be remembered is not easily organized, mnemonic devices can aid in retention. If items can be put together under a general principle, retention is greatly increased.

6. Recognition is easier than recall because it involves matching memories rather than a detailed searching

for one. Recognition demonstrates just how much we actually are able to retain.

7. Memory is the result of learning that has altered the chemistry and/or structure of the nerve cell endings, called synapses. Memory is divided into three parts: the very brief sensory memory system, the slightly longer short-term memory, and finally the long-term memory.

8. Photographic memory seems to exist in only a few people, and it is probably the result of an ability to hold images iconically longer than normal.

9. Eyewitness memory is quite defective because it is based on what people think and want rather than on what they actually observe.

Key Words and Concepts

attention
learning curve
state-dependent
  learning
transfer of training
positive transfer
negative transfer
information
  processing
schema
elaboration
mnemonic devices
principle learning
chunking
forgetting

overlearning
forgetting curve
recall
recognition
interference theory
amnesia
short-term memory
long-term memory
sensory memory
  system
iconic memory
acoustic memory
eidetic imagery
consolidation

Review Questions

Fill in the blank. Answer on a separate sheet of paper. (More than one word can be used.)

1. Tracy knows Italian, so learning Spanish is easy for her. This is called _____ transfer.

2. Stacy knows Italian, so learning Spanish is difficult because she confuses the two. This is called _____ _____ transfer.

3. A basketball player learns something at practice while sweating, forgets it at home, then remembers it again the next day at practice. This kind of learning is called _____ .

4. The mental outline we use to solve problems is called a _____ .

5. Taking in, storing, and bringing back the things we learn is called _____ .

6. _____ is the process of associating new material in some way with something important in your life.

7. Focusing on the basic idea behind a concept is called _____ .

True/False

8. Mnemonic devices often make use of weird images.

9. Chunking leads to negative transfer and should usually be avoided.

10. If we forget something from long-term memory, this usually means it is gone from the brain.

11. Overlearning will help to prevent forgetting.

12. The interference theory suggests that interference of ideas causes us to forget.

For each of the following, answer recall *or* recognition *or* both.

13. Essay tests

14. Matching tests

15. Fill-in-the-blank tests

16. True/false tests

Matching (Answers can be used more than once.)

17. Holds sounds for only a few seconds

18. Usually lasts for up to a few minutes

19. Visual electrical trace that lasts a few seconds

20. Photographic memory

21. Permanent memories stored here

22. Holds about seven to nine items

a. iconic memory

b. short-term memory

c. long-term memory

d. acoustic memory

e. eidetic imagery

Discussion Questions

1. Describe the kind of anxiety you experience before a big test. For example, what kinds of physical reactions do you have? What thoughts race through your head? Does this anxiety generally block or help learning? Explain.

2. The chapter explains that emotional involvement will usually increase learning. Describe a teacher you have now or have had in the past who "creates emotion" in class. What does the teacher do to "create" the emotion, and what is the effect? Explain.

3. In a few sentences, describe a time when you've experienced positive transfer and a time when you've experienced negative transfer.

4. Which schema would you guess would be more elaborate: (a) deciding to buy and actually buying a pair of shoes or (b) deciding to go to a party? Explain.

5. Teachers often use both recall and recognition in their tests. In your opinion, which method more accurately measures how much you actually know? (Be honest.) Explain.

6. The chapter explains that patient S's life became a private hell. This may be true, but S's ability might serve him well in certain occupations. Which ones? Explain. What problems would he have even in the occupations that you have listed? Explain.

7. Imagine someone having the opposite problem of S's—that is, he or she *does* eliminate *all* incoming information. Describe a typical experience this person might have.

8. Research has actually been done to find out which drugs will promote quick, solid consolidation and which drugs will tend to block consolidation. If these drugs were proved to be safe, what practical applications would each of these drugs have? In other words, when would you want quick consolidation, and when would you want to block consolidation? Explain.

Activities

1. Take a close look at the chart of a schema in Figure 8.3. Using this chart as a model, design your own schema. First, pick a possible question or problem that needs to be solved. For example, "Should I quit my job?" or "Should I date _____?" Second, jot down a rough draft of your schema. Be creative. Perhaps brainstorm with a friend or two. Third, decide on a final version of the schema and transfer it onto a poster. Use arrows, different colors, and boxes to clarify and highlight the entire process. Also include a "key" that will explain what your arrows and other symbols mean.

2. The chapter explains that we form organized "maps" of the world; furthermore, objects that don't "fit" on this map are more difficult to remember. Test whether this is true. Take a photograph of your kitchen. Include in this photograph common kitchen objects. Take another photograph of your kitchen. This time include objects that don't belong in a kitchen. Be subtle: For example, put a toothbrush on the table. Now repeat this procedure for your living room.

   With these four photographs, test six subjects, repeating the following procedure for each subject: (1) Present photo number 1; allow the subject 30 seconds to memorize it. (2) Have the subject start at 50 and count down aloud to 0 by fours (50, 46, 42, and so on). (3) Allow the subject as much time as necessary to write down as much information as he or she can remember from the photograph. (4) Repeat these three steps for the other photos.

   Analyze your results. Which objects were best remembered? Least remembered? Which photo(s) elicited the most mistakes? Are there any other conclusions that you can draw? Explain.

3. Test the effectiveness of mnemonic devices on ten subjects. Write up a typical 20-item grocery list and *slowly* read each item aloud to each subject, explaining first that he or she will have to memorize the list. Once

you finish, have each subject start at 50 and count down aloud to 0 by fours (50, 46, 42, and so on). Then have each subject write down as many words as possible without any time limit.

For half the subjects, teach them beforehand to use the following mnemonic device: Have them picture a room in their house. As each item is read, have the subject picture the item in some location in the room. In addition, have the person enlarge the item in a weird manner. For example, for "Milk," have the subject picture milk overflowing in the kitchen sink.

For the other half of the subjects, simply tell them to memorize the words.

Compare your results. Were the "mnemonic subjects" able to learn and use the mnemonic technique easily and effectively? (Ask them.) Why or why not? What conclusions can you draw in general? Explain. (An interesting side note: If the subjects using the mnemonic device did so effectively, they will often remember the list even a week or two later!)

4. The chapter points out that eyewitness testimony is not always reliable. See how well your friends do at picking out faces. Find an *old*, useless yearbook. Cut out 60 pictures (all males or all females) and put them into two equal piles. Have a friend study pile A for five minutes. Then, before giving him or her pile B, slip a picture from pile A into pile B. Tell your friend that he or she needs to identify the picture that you slipped in. Repeat this entire procedure on seven other friends.

How well did they do? If they did well, ask them what cues they used to help them. If they didn't do well, ask

them what interfered with their remembering the face. Explain their answers and any conclusions you can draw from the experiment.

5. Read activity number 4 and follow the same instructions, but, in this case, try the experiment on four male subjects and four female subjects.

Which group did better at remembering the faces? You were allowed to use all male photographs *or* all female photographs: Do you think that this had any effect on your results? Explain. If you were to use 2,000 subjects instead of just 8, do you think you would get the same results? Why or why not?

6. Conduct the experiment described in the "Psychology in Your Life" section at the end of the chapter. In this case, *you* become the experimenter and use two or three family members as subjects. Find an *old* photograph and briefly describe the photo to your "subject" just so he or she knows which one it is. Have the subject write down everything he or she can remember about the photo. During this time, ask a few leading questions, like "What color is my sweater in the picture?" or "What time is it on the clock?" Be as subtle as possible. In actuality, there will be no sweater or clock in the photo. You're simply testing whether they will fill in details or reconstruct the scene according to what they think *should* be there. Repeat this entire procedure for five other old photos.

How influential were the leading questions? Explain. Did subjects fill in other details that weren't there even before you started asking the questions? Explain your results.

We don't know what proportion of intelligence/creativity is needed to be able to do what this man is doing.

Be able to:

1. Explain Binet's four-part definition of intelligence.

2. Describe the original formula for IQ.

3. Explain why Wechsler developed a performance scale.

4. Give evidence for both views regarding the source of intelligence: environment versus heredity.

5. Describe the classifications of mental retardation.

6. Describe psychology's concept of creativity as "breaking set."

Global Look at the Chapter

While most of us can recognize the end product of intelligence or creativity, scientists are not certain what each one is. A number of tests have been devised, however, to try to measure these characteristics. This chapter looks at the nature of these tests as well as the pros and cons of using them.

Understanding Intelligence

In this chapter, we tackle one of the oldest and most researched areas of psychology: intelligence. In a way, though, it seems that the more we study the topic, the more complex it becomes. So we will deal with considerable controversy and disagreement as we proceed.

Defining Intelligence

Of all the words used by professionals, none seems so clear when we hear it but, on close examination, becomes so vague as does "intelligence." A formal definition might help a little: **Intelligence** is the ability to understand and adapt to the environment by using a combination of inherited abilities and learning experiences.

Psychologists first tried to measure intelligence in a mechanical way. In the late 1800s, researchers assumed that, since mind and body are so difficult to separate, it might be possible to measure intelligence by a series of physical tests. Some of these measures seem outlandish today. For instance, there was one test item in which a pointed rubber plug was pressed against the subject's forehead with increasing pressure until it

Intelligence
The ability to understand and adapt to the environment by using a combination of inherited abilities and learning experiences.

caused pain. The idea was to measure many supposedly "bright" and "dull" people, find out which group was better able to stand the pain, and then use these "test" results in order to measure other people with the plug and classify them as either dull or bright.

Another device that was part of this series of tests was what is called a *dynamometer*, which measures strength of grip. These devices are still around today at carnivals and amusement parks; they have a handle that a person grabs and squeezes as hard as possible. As this is done, a red arrow moves up a chart indicating strength, and the chart is usually labeled from "Superweakling" to "WOW! Superman!" As you might have guessed, these tests never did work very well for measuring intelligence.

The Binet Intelligence Test

The first workable intelligence test arrived in the early 1900s. In France, the minister of public instruction wanted to find some way of locating students who were not bright enough to be in the regular school system.

We now know that intelligence and creativity come in many forms—not necessarily directly related to school activity. (Beethoven at right.)

In Focus: Binet's Definition of Intelligence

Direction	—	Set goal
Adaptability	—	Adjust goal
Comprehension	—	Understand problem
Self-Evaluation	—	Assess solution

Mighty Stacy walks up to the plate. Annette, on the pitcher's mound, decides she's going to strike her out, but she can't give her any easy pitches (*direction*). She throws three pitches inside, and the count is now three balls and no strikes. She decides to give up speed for accuracy (*adaptability*) and throws the ball over the middle of the plate. Mighty Stacy swings and misses. Annette now understands the problem (*comprehension*): Mighty Stacy can't hit slow pitches. Annette throws another slow pitch over the middle. Stacy swings and misses. The count is three balls and two strikes. Annette winds up and lobs the ball over the plate. Mighty Stacy swings and launches the ball over the outfielders' heads. Annette sits on the mound and wonders whether slow pitches were the answer (*self-evaluation*). The coach sits down and wonders about Annette's intelligence.

Stanford-Binet test
The original intelligence test developed by Alfred Binet and perfected at Stanford University.

His goal was to provide them with special instruction. He appointed a psychologist, **Alfred Binet** (be-NAY), to solve the problem. An updated version of Binet's test is still used today, more than 80 years later. It is called the **Stanford-Binet test** because it was refined at Stanford University in California.

Binet was not sure what an intelligence test should include. At one point, he even tried handwriting analysis and palm reading—neither of which worked. He, like everyone else, had trouble defining the term, but eventually he came up with four elements that he believed were important for intelligence: (1) **Direction** is the ability to set up a goal and work toward it. (2) **Adaptability** means that, when faced with a problem, the person can make the adjustments needed to solve it. (3) **Comprehension** means having a basic understanding of exactly what the problem is. (4) Finally, the person working on the problem should have some idea of whether he or she has been able to solve it correctly. "Solving" the problem is worthless if the wrong solution is arrived at. Hence, Binet called the last item, **self-evaluation**.

Binet's ideas seem obvious today, but that is because we're used to them. At the time, they were very innovative. He developed test items that measured each of these areas; then these items were put in order of increasing difficulty. As the items got progressively more difficult, they applied to higher age groups; in this way he could test both older and younger students.

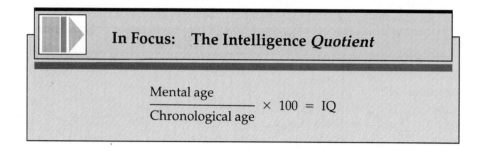

In Focus: The Intelligence *Quotient*

$$\frac{\text{Mental age}}{\text{Chronological age}} \times 100 = \text{IQ}$$

Test-Item Construction At the simplest level, typical Binet test items included naming major parts of the body (arms, legs, and so on) or finding specific objects from a pile (pick up the toy train; pick up the ball) when asked to do so by the examiner. More difficult items appeared for older children: "Indicate which number is not in its correct position: 12, 9, 6, 3, 15." At a higher level of abstraction, we have this one: "Bill Jones's feet are so big that he has to pull his trousers on over his head. What is foolish about that?"

Before the test was finished, each item was administered to a large group of children of varying ages. The items were then put in order of increasing difficulty. For example, if all five-year-old children could solve a particular item, it was considered too easy for that group, so it would be tried with four-year-olds. Or, if too hard for five-year-olds, it would be tried at the age-six level. The goal was to get items that most, but not all, of the children for a given age could answer. The final test was designed to measure mental ability from ages 3 to 15 years.

Mental Age We expect the average five-year-old to pass most items at the five-year-old level, since that is how the test was designed. Thus, the child who is chronologically five years old (age based on birthdays), if average, should also have a **mental age** of roughly five years. But, what if a certain five-year-old is brighter than the average five-year-old? This would mean that his or her mental age must be higher than that of the average five-year-old. Binet decided that the best way to handle this was to give to each test item a certain number of months' credit of mental age. For instance, if six test items are used at the five-year-old level, then each one counts two months each. That gives a full year of credit. Now, suppose this particular child answers all these items as well as a couple of items at the six-year-old level. When all the credits are counted, the child's mental age has gone beyond age five into the six-year area. So, his or her mental age would be six and chronological age would be five, showing that the child is brighter than most other children of his or her physical age.

A term you hear all the time is "IQ." The IQ, or **intelligence quotient,** is a measure of brightness obtained by comparing mental age with physical age. A "quotient" is a number obtained by dividing one number by another. To make calculation easy, the number 100 was chosen as the

Mental age
The level of intellectual functioning in years, which is compared with chronological age.

Intelligence quotient
A measure of brightness obtained by comparing mental age with physical age.

Table 9.1 Meaning of Intelligence Quotients

IQ	Category	Percent of People
130 or above	Very superior	2
120–129	Superior	6
110–119	High average	18
90–109	Average	48
80–89	Low average	17
70–79	Borderline	6
69 or below	Mentally retarded	3

center, or perfectly average, point of the test. An IQ of 100, then, is a perfectly average IQ.

Notice how we get this IQ of 100: Take the mental age, divide it by the chronological age, and multiply by 100 (to get rid of any decimals). Thus, the following would occur for our perfectly average five-year-old:

$$5/5 \times 100 = 100 \text{ IQ}$$

The child we've described as having mental age of six must have a higher IQ score. And that is the case:

$$6/5 \times 100 = 120 \text{ IQ}$$

Because this formula depends on the number of months' credit in mental age that the child gets on the test and on the physical age of the child, there is a wide range of possible IQs. Categories of IQs are shown in Table 9.1 along with the percentage of people falling into a given category as well as the label attached to each category. Note that most people do not have very high or very low intelligence quotients. The majority (48 percent) fall within the average range.

The Wechsler Intelligence Test

The Binet test certainly served its purpose of locating children who would have trouble in school, since the Binet test deals almost exclusively with words, and they are the core of schoolwork. Almost all the items require some kind of searching for a word answer, as in the question, "Brother is a boy; sister is a _____ ."

There were problems with the Binet test, though. One psychologist, **David Wechsler** (WEX-ler), worked at New York's Bellevue Hospital where he handled derelicts from skid row who were brought there by the police. Most of these people had had little formal education, and school-related material was not usually part of their life. Since Wechsler wanted to develop a program to help these people find jobs and get out of the mess they were in, he needed some measure of how bright they were in real-world intelligence rather than in schoolwork. The highly verbal

In Focus: The Wechsler Tests

Two frequently used intelligence tests are the Wechsler Intelligence Scale for Children, or WISC, and the Wechsler Adult Intelligence Scale, or WAIS (Wechsler, 1958). The Wechsler tests place more emphasis on performance tasks (such as doing puzzles) than does the Stanford-Binet. As a result, individuals who are not particularly skilled in the use of words will not be as likely to receive low IQ scores.

In addition to providing one overall score, the Wechsler tests yield percentile scores in several areas—vocabulary, information, arithmetic, picture arrangement, and so on. It is therefore possible to compute separate IQ scores for verbal and performance abilities. This type of scoring provides a more detailed picture of the individual's strengths and weaknesses than a single score does.

Below is a sampling of questions from five of the verbal subtests of the Wechsler. (Test items courtesy The Psychological Corporation, New York.)

General Information

1. How many wings does a bird have?
2. How many nickels make a dime?
3. What is steam made of?
4. Who wrote *Tom Sawyer*?
5. What is pepper?

General Comprehension

1. What should you do if you see someone forget his book when he leaves his seat in a restaurant?
2. What is the advantage of keeping money in a bank?
3. Why is copper often used in electrical wires?

Arithmetic

1. Sam had three pieces of candy and Joe gave him four more. How many pieces of candy did Sam have altogether?
2. Three men divided eighteen golf balls equally among themselves. How many golf balls did each man receive?
3. If two apples cost 15 cents, what will be the cost of a dozen apples?

Similarities

1. In what way are a lion and a tiger alike?
2. In what way are a saw and a hammer alike?
3. In what way are an hour and a week alike?
4. In what way are a circle and a triangle alike?

Vocabulary

1. "What is a puzzle?"
2. "What does 'addition' mean?"

Verbal scale
IQ test items that rely heavily on word comprehension and usage.

Performance scale
IQ test items that try to bypass verbal material and focus on problem solving without words.

Wechsler Adult Intelligence Scale (WAIS)
An intelligence test that provides three IQs: verbal, performance, and a combined (total) IQ.

The performance scale of the WISC.

Binet test just didn't do the job. Wechsler hit on the idea of a two-part intelligence test. The first part contained verbal items like the Binet (**verbal scale**), but a second part was a *non*verbal IQ test, called a **performance scale**.

Wechsler's performance scale relies minimally on the use of words, but it still requires the ability to reason. Here are a couple of the types of items he used when his test came out in the 1930s: In **picture completion**, the test taker was shown a series of pictures from which some important part had been removed. For example, at the simplest level, a picture of a pig with no tail was shown, and the taker was to indicate what was missing. In another type of item, the **object assembly**, a picture of a familiar figure or object (for instance, a picture of an elephant) was cut up like a jigsaw puzzle. The test taker first had to recognize what the parts made when they were fitted together; then the test taker was supposed to assemble them.

You can see that Wechsler was measuring reasoning ability and awareness of the environment with these types of test items, while they relied almost not at all on verbal material. As a result of his work, there are now Wechsler tests for children as well as for adults, the adult one running from 16 years through 74 years. (Since the Wechsler came out, IQ results are now based on statistical tables comparing people's scores. We no longer rely on months of credit in mental age. You can see the problem of trying to calculate such credit for a 74-year-old. The earlier discussion was designed to show you how the test originally was designed.) The **Wechsler Adult Intelligence Scale (WAIS)** gives three IQs. One is verbal, the other is performance. The third combines the two to give a total IQ.

Wechsler's idea worked reasonably well. The Wechsler and Stanford-Binet are both quite popular tests. Ironically, studies over the years have shown that even the Wechsler with its performance scale is measuring roughly the same thing as is measured by the verbal scale. This probably results from the fact that, to solve the performance items, a person must call on symbolic skills ("This is an elephant; an elephant has a trunk over here"). Symbolic skills are very much involved with verbal problems since words are symbols. So, all of our IQ tests are measuring the same general thing. This "same thing" may or may not be identical with a person's *real* intelligence, as you'll see in the next section.

What Is Intelligence?

Haven't we been spending all this time discussing intelligence? Actually, we have not, and this is very important: We have been discussing intelligence *testing*, which is quite a different matter.

Think about this for a few seconds: Since we are not certain exactly what intelligence is, but we do depend on intelligence tests, what we *call* intelligence is, in fact, whatever the intelligence tests measure. That sounds absurd at first, but note the predicament we are in. We have these tests that can tell the difference between people's school abilities in a general sort of way. We use the tests all the time to try to predict how bright a person is. Hence, we are constantly using the test results themselves as the equivalent of intelligence. There are some serious flaws in this system. For instance, all of us know people who score very high on these tests but who are blatantly stupid in most areas of life; we also know people who score low average but who are great problem solvers and really handle everyday life effectively (McClelland, 1973). Clearly the IQ test measures something important, but it certainly is not the final word on intelligence.

Influence of Society on Definition of Intelligence   Wechsler cautioned that definitions (and tests) always reflect the culture within which we live—in other words, they reflect whatever society at the moment views as worthwhile, meaningful, and valuable (Wechsler, 1975). In some times and places, for example, the skills needed to be an excellent farmer are far more important than the skills needed to be a lawyer.

One study compared the definition of intelligence used by the Australians with that used by the Malaysians and found that the latter group defines intelligence as the ability to get along well with other people and to do so in a socially efficient way. The Australians, on the other hand, are quite industrialized and emphasize academic skills, just as we do (Gill & Keats, 1980; Brislin, 1983).

While this situation makes the definition of intelligence that we use rather questionable in many cases, we can't throw the tests out just because they *do* reflect our culture. After all, we have to succeed somehow within the limits of our society. Also, some kind of test is better than none, and we don't know what to replace these tests with. Still, almost everyone knows that, if you just judge people's abilities based on the results of their IQ tests, you're going to miss some potentially very capable people who don't do all that well on the tests.

Is Intelligence Inherited?   Most of the evidence indicates that heredity plays an important part in basic intellectual potential. The majority of investigators in this area have concluded that roughly 50 percent of what we call intelligence is the result of some kind of hereditary influence, while the other 50 percent comes from all kinds of things—education, social class, environment, nutrition, amount of stimulation, and the like (Mackenzie, 1984; Plomin et al., 1980).

These conclusions have been reached after examining studies of the IQs of twins. Some twins come from the same egg in the mother. These *identical twins*, therefore, have exactly the same heredity. If they have the same heredity, and IQs are to some extent inherited, their IQs should be very close to one another, even if they are reared apart. And indeed that turns out to be the case.

Other twins are called *fraternal*. These twins will have the same environment inside the mother and will share many of the same characteristics, but they come from two separate eggs; hence, the heredity is not identical. Their IQs should be close, but not as close as those of the identical twins. Again, this turns out to be the case.

Finally, to round out the analysis, a comparison is made between the IQs for nontwins within the same family—that is, brothers and sisters. They share the same family environment but are not very close in terms of heredity. Hence, their IQs should be closer to one another than to the IQs of other children down the block, but not as close as the twins'. That also turns out to be true (Munsinger, 1975; Kamin, 1978). Still, environment *is* important: A brother and sister who live together are much closer in IQ than those who are reared apart.

Issues in Intelligence Testing

We want to discuss here some of the issues surrounding IQ scores. You will find that this area of study is far from peaceful and quiet.

Individual Versus Group Testing   Both the Binet and the Wechsler tests are administered individually. A psychologist sits at a table with a student, asking the test questions and demonstrating the problems contained in the test. These **individual intelligence tests** take an hour or so to administer, plus additional time for scoring. Such a lengthy process provides more opportunity for the test administrator to see the person in

Individual intelligence tests
IQ tests administered on a one-to-one basis—one examiner to one test taker.

action and to understand some of his or her reasoning behind the answers. The biggest problem, though, is the cost. An individual test administration costs about $150.

Other tests cost as little as 10 to 20 cents per person. These **group intelligence tests** are given to large numbers of people at the same time and scored by computer. Hence, they are done entirely on paper by marking the correct answer. Here are two group IQ test items:

Group intelligence tests
IQ tests administered to many people at one time; test is highly verbal and uses paper and pencil.

1. A hat is to: (a) smell (b) look through (c) wear (d) smoke.
2. *Ear* is to *hear* as *eye* is to: (a) tear (b) see (c) spectacles (d) eyelash.

Considering the amount of money and time involved, you would expect the individual test to give a much better picture of a person's abilities. It does, when dealing with a person who has serious problems or when used to help make a specific important decision. Overall, however, a number of group tests are reasonably accurate in predicting school potential, even though group tests present the problem of being completely verbal with no opportunity for performance scales (Anderson, 1970).

Uses and Limits of IQ Scores   In general, things like achievement in history, reading comprehension, and biology class are all closely related to how well one does on the IQ test (Bond, 1960).

But test results must be viewed cautiously, especially if school performance is better than IQ score. The test can be a poor predictor, most often failing to predict things like how well a person actually does a certain task in the real world (Lambert et al., 1976). And the IQ test *can* make errors, sometimes enormous ones, as great as 30 points. Errors are usually not that large, though, and on average vary about 7 points from what the correct IQ is supposed to be. Still, people should never be content to let one low IQ score stand as is. In such a case, it is very important to administer another IQ test to be certain the first one was not in error.

Court Cases   In recent years, federal and state courts have more and more been ruling that IQ test results cannot be used to make judgments about which classes or schools to place children in if the children haven't done well on the test (Opton, 1979). There are good reasons for many of these decisions. IQ tests are constructed by and contain material from the white middle-class group. As a result, these tests label six times more nonwhites than whites as "mentally retarded" (see the last section of this chapter). This difference is so high that the test immediately becomes suspect, rather than the basic abilities of the nonwhites.

The problem is that certain concepts, words, thoughts, phrases, and ideas vary from one subgroup to another in our mixed society. Chinese-Americans, Japanese-Americans, Hispanics, black Americans, Irish-Americans, and Italian-Americans all come from cultures that are not identical to middle-class white America. The differences are a valuable and important part of the American way of life; nonetheless, these differences can influence test results in an often subtle but unfair fashion. What seems like it should be an identical question for all groups can turn out not to be. Thus, for some reason, black children have trouble with the instruction, "Mark the apple that is whole." But they have no trouble with "Mark the apple that is still all there" (Wright & Isenstein, 1975). Since this is the same instruction, it becomes clear that how a question or instruction is worded—which is the result of the test maker's own race and social class—can alter test results.

Here is another example: In Brazil and some other Latin American countries, most people pay little attention to time. One study shows that almost all the clocks in Brazil (even the "official" ones) and the wristwatches are set incorrectly. If you arrive late for an appointment, nobody pays any attention (Levine et al., 1980). On the other hand, in the United States, people run around all the time clocking themselves to the vibrations of quartz watches, splitting the second down into little bits. A cultural difference of this sort can have a major impact on IQ test results when comparing someone from a Latin American culture with someone from a typical North American culture, since every item on an IQ test is carefully timed, and, if you run out of time, you lose IQ points!

Brain Size and Intelligence

A very strong relationship exists between the brain size of an animal species and the ability of that species to solve problems—as long as brain weight is compared to overall body weight. Elephants are intelligent and very sweet creatures, and, if their brain weight alone was used, they would be considered the brightest creatures on earth. Instead, brain weight has to be compared with total weight. This comparison makes the elephant brain only 1/1,000 of the animal's total weight. Comparing this with the human ratio, 1/60, makes the human brain weight exceptionally high in proportion to the human body (Jerison, 1976).

Brain capacity (how large physically) is important also. Chimpanzees have a capacity of 400 cubic centimeters, which accounts for their high intelligence. Human capacity is 1,375 cubic centimeters—much greater. Human brain capacity does vary from one person to another, but it is not important in intelligence as long as it stays above 800 cubic centimeters (Montagu, 1964).

The Effects of Mental Challenge

Inheritance clearly plays a role in what a person can become. But it only sets up certain limits. Within these limits, the environment plays its role. For instance, a person inherits a basic body structure, a certain lung capacity, and a specific leg structure. What the person does with these inherited traits is the result of effort and environment if, say, he or she wants to become a runner. His or her parents may or may not have provided, through heredity, the equipment for this person to become an Olympic candidate. But what they have given are the physical limits for a maximum and minimum running ability; this is what their child has to work with.

In the intelligence area, intriguing studies show that brain changes can occur in animals depending on the type of environment in which they are reared. Rats who live in a stimulating, enriched environment with plenty of activities to perform *literally* grow a thicker, heavier brain than other rats. The brain nerve cells actually branch out and weigh more if the rats have developed in a stimulating environment (Rosenzweig et al., 1972). Other studies show that, if an animal's visual system is given very high levels of stimulation—rather than, say, its hearing or smell—the visual portion of the brain becomes much heavier than these other parts (Greenough, 1985).

Researchers believe that exactly the same types of changes take place in the human brain. Figure 9.1 is very interesting in this regard. It shows the brain cell development of the normal child from 3 to 24 months of age (Pribram, 1971). What these studies demonstrate is the importance of en-

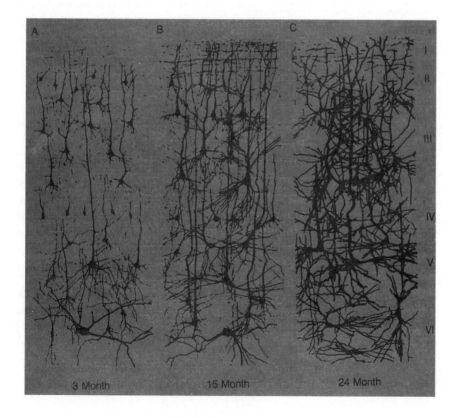

Figure 9.1
Sections from the cerebral cortex of children 3, 15, and 24 months old (Note increased branching and thickening of dendrites.) From the work of Conel (A) 1947; (B) 1955; (C) 1959. From *Language of the Brain* by K. Pribram, Prentice-Hall, Inc., 1971. Reprinted by permission.

vironment. They do not suggest that a child can progress faster than nature allows. As we discuss in Chapter 10 on child development, nature has built in a sequence of mental development that the child follows, with one stage leading into another. In one stage, for instance, a child cannot understand two different dimensions of an object at the same time. A pencil is seen as fat or long, *not* both at the same time. Only with physical brain changes can the child see a pencil as both fat and long at the same time. Training or stimulation *cannot* speed up the sequence of development. But it is critical that the child be given at each stage a very stimulating environment within which to develop. In other words, as the brain develops, it can take more and more from the environment; so the environment must contain stimulating objects and events.

Creativity

While intelligence tests have been the focus of much interest for generations, many psychologists have pointed out that these tests do not detect the "spark" that motivates a person to do an exceptional job in finding new and better ways of handling problems or in inventing something new—in other words, in being "creative." As a result, there is now a great deal of interest in trying to find a way to measure this dimension of the person. The IQ test doesn't tap whatever it takes to produce original, workable ideas; that is, it doesn't measure **creativity** (Getzels & Jackson, 1962).

Creativity
The mental processes that result in original, workable ideas.

Tests of Creativity

Suppose two people are shown a picture of a man sitting in an airplane and are to write a story about what he is doing:

1. Mr. Jones is flying home after a week away from the family. He will be happy to see his family again. The plane is only about an hour away from landing. He is hoping that soon he will have some good news about a promotion that he and his family have been waiting for. He decides to take a nap and dream about how well things have been going.

2. Mr. Jones is sitting in an aisle seat, looking toward the closed door leading to the cockpit at the far end of the plane. He wants to put on a leather flight jacket and goggles, burst into the cockpit, his scarf hanging from his neck and shimmering in the light as he takes over. He opens the windows and feels the cold air hit his face, invigorating him. He is going to show the pilots how a *real* aviator can do the job. He will take them all for a sightseeing trip over the North Pole.

Based on the same stimulus—a picture of a man in an airplane—these two stories show a striking difference. The first one is a standard, straightforward, dull account of a businessman flying home. The second is unexpected, novel, and humorous, showing a flair for the unusual—what some psychologists call "creativity," or at least an important aspect of it. They feel that a person must deviate from the expected in order to come up with creative products; invention is the result of unusual thinking. How many times have we all said, after seeing the solution to a problem, "Why didn't I think of that?" The answer was right before our eyes, but we didn't see it. Instead, we kept trying to solve problems in the old way. We were too conventional. We had what is called a **set**, a tendency to try to use the same old solution over and over again—even when it doesn't work.

Invention—and, we assume, creativity—is an ever-present necessity. Take the movie scene in a wild West saloon where a man breaks off the neck of a whiskey bottle and pours himself (and the bar-lady) a drink. In real life this procedure was often an actual necessity, rather than just a dramatic gesture, since sometimes a cork could be wedged so tightly into a bottle that 300 pounds of pressure would have been needed to remove it. The problem persisted until someone took a piece of metal, twisted it into a spiral, put a sharp point on it, added a handle to push down on the top—and there it was, the corkscrew.

Set
A tendency to solve problems in the same old way over and over.

Breaking Set

Creativity is in all of us. When we (your authors) were young, there was no such thing as a "flip-top" soft-drink can. A special pointed can opener was needed to open a can of soda. (Our generation was convinced, when the flip-top was first introduced, that it would not work and it wouldn't be around for long. This is standard practice for every generation when something new arrives.) In any case, if the opener was lost on a picnic, our ability to **break set**—think imaginatively with different objects—was remarkable. We used rocks, nails, fingernail clippers, hairpins (a failure), and tire irons to try to open the cans.

Psychologists, then, have come up with a definition of creativity as the ability to break set—to get out of the traditional mold and find a novel solution to a problem. But breaking set must be in the direction of something that works properly. An architect can break set and produce a bridge like no bridge anyone has ever seen before. But, if it falls into the river, that wasn't creativity. Truly creative people can move away from the expected but still keep enough of a hold on reality to make the solution workable (Barron & Harrington, 1981).

Tests of creativity, then, try to measure originality. One creativity test asks the test taker to give some uses for everyday objects such as a tin can

Break set
To come up with unusual, unexpected ideas; to use something in a different way than it is normally used.

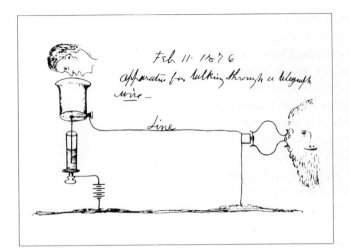 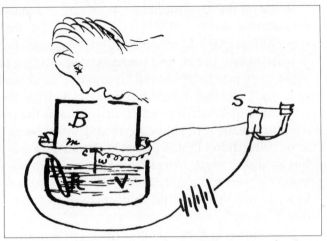

Great inventions tend to occur to more than one person at the same time. This happened with the telephone: at the left the idea of Elise Gray; at right Alexander Graham Bell.

or a brick. Creativity is measured by the kinds of responses given. If they deviate from the expected, then this counts toward a higher score. Answering "You can eat a brick" is original, but not creative, since it is not tied to reality and shows no cleverness of thought. On the other hand, "Grind it up and put it in an enemy's red-pepper jar" has some merit in the creative sense. So creativity tests try to measure the unexpected.

Creative Students

Evidence continues to mount that those who are creative are often different from the "very bright" as defined by the IQ test. Creative students are frequently unpredictable, and at times they may even seem bizarre (Torrance, 1979). Often they have trouble fitting well into the standard educational system, which focuses most often on straight academic achievement (Merz & Rutherford, 1972).

But truly creative students actually do learn the material in the classroom. They seem to be on some side road to accomplishment that is parallel but not identical to that of the "bright" students. While they do well on standard achievement tests, they don't score at the top in the IQ area. Most often their IQs are in the 125–130 range instead of 150–155 (Getzels & Jackson, 1962). So, the IQ test is measuring something different from the potential of the creative students. If we look just at the top 20 percent of students on IQ tests, we miss 70 percent of the creative students (Barron & Harrington, 1981; Torrance, 1980). Still, before creativity is possible, a basic IQ is needed on which to build ideas, so IQ can't be too low. Finally, some students do get a high score on IQ and creativity tests, but they are not the norm.

Mental Retardation

Mental retardation is usually present at birth, discovered at a young age, and affects quite a large number of people. There are about 5 million people with notable retardation in the United States. **Mental retardation** is defined as subaverage intellectual functioning in which an individual is unable to handle tasks appropriate to his or her physical age. Learning ability and social adjustment are impaired. The basic classifications for this problem follow, listing some of the things the people can and cannot do.

Mental retardation
Subaverage intellectual functioning so that such a person is not able to perform at the level appropriate for his or her age.

Basic Classifications

IQ 70–79: Borderline Mental Retardation Those labeled borderline score just below the "low average" group in IQ (see Table 9.1). They are slow learners, and most fail to complete high school. Generally, these people are employed in "nonintellectual" occupations and are not legally retarded in the sense that they would be entitled to disability benefits. (This is the classification of individuals about whom the courts are concerned when they restrict the use of the IQ test, as discussed earlier.)

IQ 52–69: Mild Mental Retardation Most people legally termed "retarded" fall into this category, and most attend special schools. The behavior of people in this group varies considerably depending on whether an individual's IQ is toward the higher or lower end of the range. Someone with a 69 IQ can function pretty well on his or her own, can usually marry, and can maintain a family. At the lower end of the range, some supervision is required, since these people have trouble with abstract reasoning and problem solving.

IQ 36–51: Moderate Mental Retardation People in this group have physical problems, often stemming from a serious disease. They are trained in how to take care of themselves and can live at home, but with supervision. When fully grown, most have the skills of a four- to seven-year-old and can read, write, and speak at that age level.

IQ 20–35: Severe Mental Retardation People in this group usually require constant supervision. About 75 percent have had a major disease or physical defect and cannot benefit from school (Cleland et al., 1980).

IQ 19 or Below: Profound Mental Retardation The smallest group, about 1 percent of the total population, fall into this category. Rarely do they mature mentally beyond age two, and, even as adults, they can engage in only limited communication. They are unable to dress or care for themselves without considerable training (Robinson & Robinson, 1970).

Many retarded people are not only able to work, but enjoy doing so.

Stanford-Binet	Measures mainly verbal skills
Wechsler	Measures verbal and performance skills
Multiple Intelligences	Identifies special skills and talents that define intelligence for each individual

Physical Defects

Only about 20 percent of those labeled retarded suffer from a known physical defect. Most of this 20 percent fall into the categories of severe or profound retardation, although a few are in the moderate group. The physical problems usually come from an injury or disease that has affected brain growth and development. The more common causes are lack of oxygen at birth, very poor nutrition, or exposure to toxic chemicals. Defects can also be inherited from the parents.

Most of the mentally retarded, then, do not have any obvious brain problem. You might expect, however, that, if an autopsy was performed on the brains of a very bright person, an average person, and a mentally retarded person, there would be a clear difference among these brains. That is not the case. All three brains will look approximately the same. It is true that there are differences in the way the brains *work*, but with our present state of knowledge, we can't *see* whatever those differences might be.

Environmental Factors

Is it possible that some factors in the environment can lead to retardation? One thing we do know is that proper nutrition is absolutely critical to brain development. This is one of the reasons school lunch programs are so important. If the nutrients are absent during critical periods of brain growth, development is permanently slowed. Poor health and infection can have similar effects. Finally, a lack of stimulation, as discussed earlier, won't actually damage the brain, but it can slow the growth of vital nerve cells. Any or all of these factors can be involved in mental retardation. Since the majority of people with this problem come from areas of poverty, we suspect that in many cases the environment is a major factor.

We have a lot to learn about mental retardation. There are puzzling cases in which the parents have done everything possible, the environment is reasonable, there is no *apparent* physical defect, yet the child still is retarded.

Methods of Treatment

For the mentally handicapped with physical defects, medicine is making great strides. For those suffering environmental problems, many programs are available to provide intellectual stimulation.

There are also programs that include training in motor coordination, practical social skills, and self-care. So, even though we don't all the way understand the cause, large numbers of those who a few years ago would have been left in an institution are now able at least partly to take care of themselves. One of the more effective treatments has been to place retarded people in "halfway houses" in which the retarded are supervised part of the time and encouraged to be on their own the rest of the time, with someone always available to help.

Theory of multiple intelligences
The assumption that, besides an "IQ," each of us has special skills—music, carpentry, design, and so forth—at which we are proficient.

Coping with IQ and Creativity

It seems that almost every time we turn around there is some new standard or test cropping up to make us worry about how well we measure up. Often we're not certain what it is that we are competing with; we just know that "here comes another challenge."

IQ is clearly a case in point. By now you probably have become aware of some kind of number regarding your intelligence. If not, you will someday. It is a distressing event, no matter what the number is. There is always someone above you. You don't care all that much who is below you, since the fact that someone is above you supposedly means that he or she is "better" than you. What gets lost in this game is the clear fact that an IQ score is nothing more or less than a *number*. Students often have a hard time accepting this fact, because society puts so much emphasis on this number and what it is supposed to mean. Think back to the beginning of this chapter. As we said there, we don't know, for starters, what the number really means. It is not as if you have 110 apples if your IQ is 110. You have 110 what? Scientists don't know what you have 110 of. And, if you have an IQ of 120 and your friend has an IQ of 105, then you have 15 more . . . what?

This may sound flippant, but it isn't intended to be. The notion of

Albert Einstein and Sherlock Holmes

IQ causes a lot of heartache and needless worry. The original intent of the Binet test had nothing to do with measuring how bright the person was. Its goal was to determine how *low* the student's abilities were in order to give

special attention to those needing help. As a result, neither the Binet nor the Wechsler test really measures much that is clear at the upper levels. But they can locate handicaps at the low levels—the original purpose of the Binet, and something Wechsler couldn't avoid.

One well-known and respected psychologist recently came out with a theory that is better for analyzing abilities, called the **theory of multiple intelligences** (Gardner, 1983). This theory claims that all of us have different skills, almost none of which is measured by the IQ test. Some people are good at music, others at math, some can design things. Some have special physical skills: The beauty and skill of the gymnast is a case in point, since communication in that area is not verbal but instead is carried out by the body and its motion. The multiple-intelligences approach is probably the "IQ test" of the future. Almost every person in your class has a special talent that few others have, and that is what needs to be developed and recognized. And, within that special area, most of us add our own stamp to it, our own creativity, if you will, which makes our job and our life more worthwhile (Weisberg, 1986).

Summary

1. The Binet Intelligence Test was designed to locate students who were not very bright so they could receive special training. Direction, adaptability, comprehension, and self-evaluation were the aspects of intelligence for which Binet developed test items.

2. Originally, IQ scores came from comparing mental age with physical age and multiplying the result by 100 to remove decimals.

3. Since the Binet test is so verbal, the WAIS test was developed. It has a performance scale. Although an improvement, the performance scale is still measuring approximately the same thing as the verbal scales do (whatever that is). We do know, however, that different societies define intelligence in different ways.

4. Roughly 50 percent of intelligence is inherited; 50 percent is environmental. The inheritance sets certain limits, and the environment fills in within these limits.

5. IQ scores can be as much as 30 points in error, but normally test error will stay within a range of 7 points.

6. Given a minimum brain capacity of 800 cubic centimeters, human intelligence is not affected by actual brain size. In proportion to body size, the human has the largest known brain.

7. Mental stimulation can increase size and thickness of brain nerve cells.

8. So many nonwhites score low on IQ tests compared to whites that the court system often forbids use of the test results in making decisions about nonwhites.

9. Creativity is defined as the ability to break set. Those who do well on creativity tests tend not to have extremely high IQ scores, so we believe this ability is a dimension of the person not tapped by the IQ test.

10. Most retarded people are not physically impaired. Those who are usually occupy the categories of the most severe retardation. Many environmental factors potentially influence retardation, especially poor nutrition and lack of stimulation.

Key Words and Concepts

intelligence
Alfred Binet
Stanford-Binet test
direction
adaptability
comprehension
self-evaluation
mental age
intelligence
   quotient
David Wechsler
verbal scale
performance scale
picture completion
object assembly
Wechsler Adult
   Intelligence Scale
   (WAIS)
individual
   intelligence tests
group intelligence
   tests
creativity
set
break set
mental retardation
theory of multiple
   intelligences

Review Questions

Matching (Answers can be used more than once.)

1. Deals mainly with verbal skills
2. Includes both verbal and performance scales
3. Uses picture completion
4. Takes into account special individual talents
5. One of the first intelligence tests ever used
6. The IQ test of the future, perhaps

a. Wechsler Adult Intelligence Scale
b. Stanford-Binet (or Binet)
c. Theory of multiple intelligences

7. The original purpose of the Binet intelligence test was to pinpoint:
   a. above-average students
   b. below-average students
   c. students with brain damage
   d. hyperactive students.

8. Which of the following best describes what Binet meant by "self-evaluation"?
   a. Relating an IQ score to your personality
   b. Feeling good about your IQ score
   c. Knowing that a solution to an IQ problem is correct
   d. Adding up your IQ score

9. Little Alfred is given a jigsaw puzzle, but he isn't able even to begin putting it together until he turns all the pieces over. This needed mental adjustment is what Binet called:
   a. adaptability   b. comprehension
   c. direction   d. self-evaluation.

10. Mental age refers to a person's
    a. chronological age
    b. attitude toward problem solving
    c. intellectual ability level
    d. performance ability.

11. The Stanford-Binet intelligence quotient compares:
    a. School grades with mental age
    b. School grades with chronological age
    c. Performance with chronological age
    d. Mental age with chronological age.

True/False

12. Wechsler's performance scale measures basically the same thing as his verbal scale.

13. All countries define intelligence in basically the same way.

14. Heredity seems to play some role in intelligence.

15. The Binet and Wechsler tests are usually given to groups.

16. The human brain weighs more than the elephant brain.

17. A stimulating environment may cause the brain actually to grow thicker and heavier.

18. An IQ score may be influenced by race and social factors.

19. Creativity is often increased through:
    a. set   b. breaking set   c. heredity.

20. Set refers to:
    a. Brainstorming and putting similar ideas together
    b. The first step in problem solving
    c. Looking at a problem in one way and only one way
    d. Flexibility in thinking.

21. Which of the following is *not* a possible cause of mental retardation?
    a. Lack of oxygen at birth   b. Heredity
    c. Disease   d. Cold parents

22. The theory of multiple intelligences takes into account:
    a. Each individual's creativity
    b. Special skills
    c. Unique talents
    d. All of the above.

Discussion Questions

1. Your friend, Jorge, believes that studying intelligence is a waste of time. All it does is allow others to discriminate against people who have low "intelligence." Besides, you can never measure it accurately anyway. Your other friend, Maureen, disagrees. She believes that intelligence testing can single out people of low intelligence and help those people through special programs. With whom do you tend to agree? Why? Explain.

2. Imagine that IQ tests made virtually no errors whatsoever. Should grade levels in school then be determined by IQ or by the traditional chronological method? Explain.

3. Imagine you're the boss of a computer programming firm. You're aware of the potential problems with IQ tests (they can make errors), but the courts recently decided that using the tests for hiring was legal. Would you administer IQ tests to potential employees? Why or why not?

4. Fascinating research is currently being conducted on ways to increase the efficiency of the brain (despite its already remarkable efficiency). If you were a parent and you could increase the "intelligence" of your future children by taking certain "safe" drugs, would

you do it? Why? (This may seem like an incredible possibility today, but it may not seem that incredible by the time you're a grandparent.)

5. See how creative you can be: Write down "tin can" at the top of a sheet of paper and make a list of 20 original uses for the can. Since creativity is being highlighted here, don't feel restricted by the "tin can" suggestion. Choose a different everyday object if you like.

6. Do you think that school in general tends to promote or block creativity? List several examples to support your opinion.

7. In the book *Flowers for Algernon*, the main character, Charly, is retarded but seemingly happy, in spite of others' ridiculing him. He sees the ridicule as friendship. Later, he is the subject of an experiment that increases his intelligence dramatically. His happiness, however, is threatened because now he understands the ridicule. Which extreme would you find preferable: to know and to be usually miserable *or* to not know and to be happy? Explain.

8. If you were tested for "intelligence," on which test do you think you would score highest: Stanford-Binet, Wechsler, or Multiple Intelligences? Explain.

Activities

1. It should be obvious that Binet and Wechsler are not the only ones ever to devise intelligence tests. Conduct research on other types of intelligence tests. Compare and contrast the criteria used for measuring intelligence on these tests to Binet's and Wechsler's criteria. Out of all the tests, which one seems closest to your own personal definition of intelligence? Explain.

2. The chances are great that the person in your school who knows the most about intelligence testing is your school psychologist. Prepare a list of questions beforehand, and then interview this person. Possible questions: What kinds of intelligence tests do you use? How do these tests differ from one another? How have recent intelligence tests overcome the possibility of cultural bias? Do you ever encounter students who purposely do poorly on the tests so they won't be moved out of a special program?

   Write a report on the interview and your reactions to what you learned.

3. Many people argue that the creative process is intuitive, and, if people are pressured into being creative,

creativity will decrease. Find out if this is true. Take a sheet of paper and write down these four objects across the top of it: paper clip, can of hairspray, automobile tire, scissors. Find six friends to participate in your experiment. Tell three of them (one at a time) the following: "You have to help me with this experiment. You see these four objects? You need to think of as many uses as possible for these objects. And you only get five minutes. This is really important to me—I need to get a good grade—so concentrate." You can use your own words, of course, but the idea is to create pressure. Tell the remaining three friends something like this: "Could you help me with an experiment? It's fun. You get five minutes to write down as many uses as possible for these four objects. Just do your best."

Once you get all six lists, go through each use that is listed and circle the ones that you think break set. Breaking set will be your way of defining creativity. The more items you circle, the more creative the person will be (according to this limited definition). How will you know which ones to circle? A good guide to use is this: If someone writes that scissors can be used to poke a hole in paper, and in your lifetime you have actually seen someone doing this, then this is *not* an example of breaking set. On the other hand, if the person writes that scissors can be eaten, this also should not be circled since it is entirely unrealistic. If someone suggests that scissors can be used as a paperweight, this probably would be accepted as creative.

Compare your results of the "pressured" group to the results of the "nonpressured" group. Who performed more creatively? Was pressure a factor? Were there any other factors that may have influenced your results?

4. Read activity number 3 and repeat the same experiment. This time, however, don't put pressure on any of the six subjects. This time, *you* are the one who will need to be creative. (Feel any pressure?) Once you get the six lists, it will be your job to develop a system that will measure creativity. In other words, you will need to decide on three or four criteria for measuring creativity. In the experiment in number 4, breaking set was one criterion. You may still use that one, but think of three other original criteria. *Hint*: Keep your eyes and ears open while your subjects fill out the lists; they may give you ideas for criteria.

According to your system, which friends were highly creative, moderately creative, uncreative? Explain.

5. Find a copy of the book *Flowers for Algernon* and read (or reread) it. It's fast and fascinating reading. Write a report comparing and contrasting the main character's happiness level with his intelligence level. When does he seem happiest? Saddest? Why? Is Charly, the main character, the same at the end of the novel as he was at the beginning, or has he grown in any way? Explain.

6. Contact a local college or university and ask about organizations that require special academic achievements or special "intelligence" to join. Once you find out, contact a member of the organization and interview the person. Possible questions: What criteria are used in choosing and rejecting members? Are there special privileges that members enjoy over other organizations? How would you define intelligence?

Another possibility is to contact a member of Mensa, an organization that claims outright that its members are highly intelligent. You can probably find the organization in the phone book, or try contacting the American Psychological Association (APA) for information. You should be able to find the APA or a local psychological association in the phone book.

Write a report on the interview and your reactions to what you learned.

Unit Four

Human Development

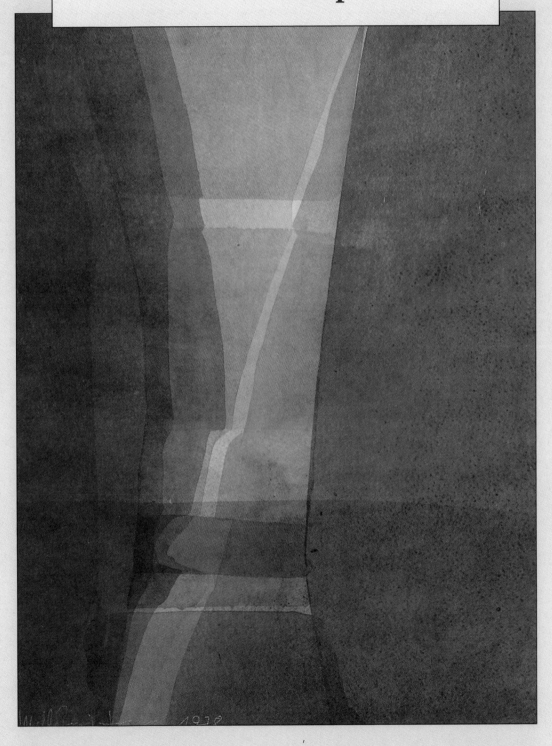

Fun to explore; nightmare to clean up.

Chapter 10

Infancy and Childhood

Objectives

Be able to:

1. Explain the importance of heredity and environment in human development.

2. Describe the way maturational processes work.

3. Explain growth cycles, critical periods, and imprinting.

4. Describe the role of the mother and the father in family life.

5. Explain the causes of child abuse.

6. List and explain Jean Piaget's four stages of child development.

7. List and explain Lawrence Kohlberg's three stages of moral development.

8. Describe what is meant by children's rules of language.

Global Look at the Chapter

Throughout childhood, everything that happens to us arises from and is controlled by maturational processes that follow a fixed plan or sequence. Mental, moral, and physical growth must evolve at their own speed with the aid of a suitable environment.

The World of the Child

Here is a conversation between a researcher and a four-year-old boy (Phillips, 1969):

"Do you have a brother?"
"Yes."
"What's his name?"
"Jim."
"Does Jim have a brother?"
"No."

Is there something wrong with this child? No. As we start this chapter, we enter a foreign world—that of the developing child. While children partially resemble the rest of us, their thought processes can be quite foreign to our everyday thinking. The "problem" Jim's brother has is that he is not able to look at something from any point of view but his own—not yet. We will discuss a possible explanation for this a little later.

Heredity versus Environment

For as long as scientists have studied animals and people, they have asked questions about what is caused by **heredity**—that is, what is actually contained in the genes themselves—and what is caused by the **environment**—which is what goes on in the world around us. The issue of which is responsible is called the **nature/nurture** controversy. Things that do not depend primarily on learning are due to physical factors, or *nature*; things that are learned are due to the environment, or *nurture*. Before we can understand how children develop, we need to know which abilities and characteristics are mostly due to our physical nature. We already know that the environment, or nurture, plays a large part in the development of most skills, but, almost all the time, the source of these skills is some combination of nature and nurture.

Until only recently, most people, including so-called "experts", claimed that the world of the infant was chaos and confusion. How very wrong this view turned out to be. The interaction between environment and heredity can be seen clearly in some recent experiments that show just how alert and intelligent the seemingly mindless infant really is. To look at a study in this area you have to know first of all that infants vary their sucking patterns on nipples or pacifiers. Specially constructed nipples that would register when the baby sucked were put in their mouths, and earphones were put over their ears so they could hear voices. The infants had a choice of hearing their own mother's voice or that of a different mother. In order to hear their own mother's voice, the babies had to learn to slow down their sucking and to leave a fixed amount of time between suckings. If they speeded up, they got a different mother's voice.

Amazingly, these infants were able to vary their sucking so they could hear their mother's voice, and that became their favored way of sucking. This means that infants are able to learn from the environment, that they can make discriminations among different voices, that they have a memory system that can hold the voices, and that they can understand something as complex as an association between sucking and hearing a voice. This is a beautiful example of the importance of the environment and the use of already inherited skills on that environment (Stillings, et al., 1987; DeCasper & Fifer, 1980). Oh yes, we forgot to tell you—all the infants were under 72 hours old!

Focus on Heredity

While the environment is critical to proper development, psychology in recent years has focused more and more on the influence that heredity

Heredity
Characteristics obtained directly from the genes.

Environment
A person's surroundings, which have an influence on a person's characteristics and development.

Nature/nurture
Contrasting views of how we gain certain characteristics: The first word refers to heredity, the second to environment.

has on many of our abilities and behaviors. The influence of heredity on intelligence is considerable, as we discussed in Chapter 9. And genes can clearly influence a child's activity level, how easily soothed an infant is, his or her emotional responsiveness, and such things as how a child reacts to new or novel things in the environment (Schwartz, 1979b).

Psychologists used to focus exclusively on how parents influence the child; today we believe that the child also influences the parents. There are even indications that tolerance for alcohol may well have a genetic background. Note, though, that, if something is inherited, this doesn't mean it can't be changed by the environment. A person may inherit the potential to be a great runner, but only with environmental training will he or she actually perfect this skill.

Twin Studies

Identical twins come from the same fertilized egg; thus, they have the same (identical) heredity. Psychologists study them thoroughly to see how they are alike—especially when they have not been reared together but have grown up in different homes. If they are reared apart and have similar characteristics, the environment probably has had little influence on this fact, while heredity has played a major role.

A careful study of 15 pairs of grown identical twins separated from birth has shown some startling similarities. For instance, these twins' basic temperament, occupational interests, hobbies, preferences for art and music, and athletic interests were quite similar, even though they had never actually met one another. At approximately the same age, the

Identical twins
Two people who come from the same egg in the mother; hence, they have the same heredity.

These triplets have identical heredity.

twins developed the same fears and nightmares, stuttering, bed-wetting, and bouts of depression. In one case, one twin was raised as a German Nazi while the other was raised as a Jew in the Caribbean. When they were first united in their late 40s, they both sported the same type of mustache, wore the same type of wire-rimmed glasses, liked the same foods, liked to scare people by sneezing loudly, stored rubber bands on their wrists, read magazines from back to front, and enjoyed eating alone in restaurants—something few men like to do (Bouchard, 1983; Holden, 1980).

While not all identical twins are this much alike, we now know that heredity plays a far more important role in development than we ever suspected. Most researchers today estimate that roughly 50 percent of personality traits and intelligence are the result of genetic factors (Bouchard, 1983).

Developmental Patterns

An early study in psychology took a very unusual look at the process of development. A husband-and-wife team adopted a chimpanzee, a lovable seven-month-old female. They decided to rear this chimp along with their other new (human) child to see what happened.

Both were treated identically, or as identically as possible, taking their physical differences into account. At first, this "experiment" looked like a disaster. In fact, the parents felt some panic for a while when the chimpanzee progressed faster than their son. For example, the chimp learned to feed herself, drink from a cup, and obey her "parents" much earlier and faster than the boy did. By the time both "children" reached the age of two, however, the boy had overtaken and passed the chimpanzee in every respect except physical strength and amount of body hair (Kellogg & Kellogg, 1933).

This dramatic study makes a point of major importance: Development within a species (people, elephants, dogs, and so forth) is orderly and specific; it has its own timetable and pattern. The pattern is related to how complex the mature organism ultimately will be. At first, the boy living with the chimp developed slowly in comparison, but later he went beyond the chimp's abilities because human beings reach a higher level of intelligence and other skills. The human has the longest developmental period of all creatures. This state of weakness and helplessness that lasts for such an extended time is probably the reason we have an elaborate social structure of closely knit families who can protect and care for the helpless young ones.

Much of our development is a process of integrating our extraordinary brains with our bodies. Thus, the baby starts out with a series of reflexes or automatic reactions. These reflexes will occur with the proper stimulation, and the baby does not have any control over them—not at first. For instance, if you touch a baby's cheek, it will turn its head and start sucking. If you place your finger in the palm of an infant's hand, it will grasp it tightly—just as a chimp does, incidentally. And, if a baby is startled, its arms and legs suddenly shoot out, away from its body. The sucking, grasping, and startle reflexes are some of the building blocks for later, more complicated behavior. With age, most of these reflexes disappear and can be regulated by the higher brain. In other words, they stop happening automatically and can be controlled; they become actions that we choose to do or not do. There are cases in which adults have suffered certain kinds of damage to the brain, which result in the reappearance of these sucking and grasping reflexes. Such people find themselves automatically and unwillingly sucking when the cheek is touched and unable to let go of objects placed in their hands. For these people, the higher brain has, for want of a better term, been "disconnected" (Brown, 1976).

Maturation Processes

A child is already preprogrammed for certain activities, such as walking, a natural skill that begins to develop sometime between 9 and 15 months after birth. To the casual observer, this process seems to be "learned," but it is not. As stumbling and uncoordinated as babies seem to be during the process of starting to walk, they will be able to walk on their own with no training at all. Some parents work and work with their children, thinking that somehow they are *teaching* the child to walk. All this training does, at best, is to help the child walk about one month earlier than he or she normally would have, at roughly 15 months, which is an average. Walking at an earlier or later age (within the normal range) is *not* a sign of future intelligence or of being "slow," but is just a reflection of individual differences. Nature must take its course.

For some reason, many people have trouble believing that developing the ability to walk is automatic. But some Indian cultures, especially in the past, strapped an infant to its mother's back so she could go about her chores, thus preventing the baby from "practicing" walking. When these children were finally freed, they very quickly walked quite well on their own. This kind of skill, which develops automatically as the child becomes more mature, is part of the process called **maturation**—the automatic, orderly, and sequential process of physical (and mental) development (Zelazo et al., 1972).

The same rules apply to other skills, such as speech and reasoning, which we will discuss shortly. Sequencing and timing are clearly part of the development of general "intelligence." Many toys on the market claim to increase a child's intelligence more rapidly, but these claims

Although bound, this infant will start to walk at the same age as children from other cultures.

Maturation
An automatic, orderly, sequential process of physical and mental development.

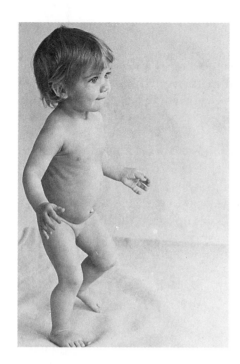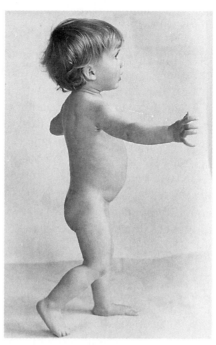

First steps.

should not be taken too seriously. There is no question that children need stimulation from their surroundings, and play is one of the best ways for that to occur. It is important for parents to spend time playing and "talking" with their babies, because this is a good way to stimulate the infants' brains. But it simply takes time for all the nerve cells to grow, develop, and branch out. No toy in the world can make that happen any earlier than it normally would. The child needs good nutrition, stimulation, and safety. A good environment is necessary for proper development, but it won't *speed up* the process. What we're saying here may require a moment's careful thought in order to be grasped: Without a stimulating environment, the child's mental growth can be slowed; with a stimulating environment, it will proceed at its own internal pace, not exceed it. Many parents are too impatient; they can't accept what nature dictates (Rust, 1984; Kagan, 1975).

Patterns (sequences) of maturation are essentially the same for all children. The *timing* of development, however, will vary from one child to another. Only notable extremes are important. A child who develops very, very slowly and walks, for instance, at a much later age than the average child may have something wrong physically. The timing of a child's development would have to be quite a bit slower than the average, though, before parents should be concerned.

Growth Cycles

All of our parts do not develop at the same rate. There are **growth cycles** for different aspects of human development; in other words, some areas develop more rapidly, some more slowly, and some develop in spurts or increase dramatically all in a short time. For instance, at age eight, 95 percent of the basic structure of the brain has been completed, but the body has 55 percent left to go, and the reproductive system more than 90 percent.

There are also differences between the sexes in these cycles. Girls are more orderly and stable in their growth cycles. From infancy, they show a continuous movement forward in babbling, word making, and bone and muscle development. Boys grow in spurts and mature more slowly, although eventually they reach the same level (Kagan, 1984).

Critical Periods

We can get insight into the human by studying animal behavior. Ducks and some other birds, for example, are programmed to accept a mother at a specific time in development. If there is no "real" mother around, some strange things can happen. One male researcher found that, shortly after ducks had hatched—somewhere around 16 hours—if the mother was not there, the ducklings would follow *him* around if he quacked and walked in a squatting position (Lorenz, 1952). They assumed that he was their mother.

As it turns out, ducklings are programmed to accept almost anything as a "mother" at this time. The term for this attachment is **imprinting**, which means that the animal's brain is ready to be engraved (or imprinted) with a mother image. The "mother figure" must move around for imprinting to occur. One of the most unusual studies of this sort involved imprinting ducklings on a beer can that was pulled around a pond in circles.

Imprinting occurs during a **critical period**. A critical period is a specific time period in an animal's maturation when a particular skill may be learned or an association made, but the learning or the associating can occur *only* during this period if it is to occur at all. Notice how, in Figure 10.1, the duck's acceptance of the fake mother peaks at about 16 hours after birth. Imprinting seems to be the result of a chemical released by the body at a certain time. If an animal's chemistry is deliberately altered, the critical period can be extended or even eliminated (Colombo, 1982).

Critical periods must be part of all species because they show up in so many places. Dogs, for instance, form solid human attachments only up to 12 weeks of age. After that time, they can be unpredictable. Because of this, you want to get a dog that has been around humans quite a bit before that 12-week period is over, especially if the dog is a large and possi-

Walking and swimming together—Konrad Lorenz and his imprinted "children."

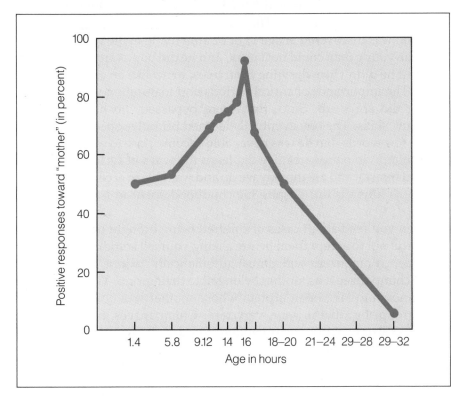

Figure 10.1
Ducks' response to imprinting. Note the critical period at 16 hours.

bly dangerous one. Dogs from pet stores should always be bought before the end of 12 weeks because they are frequently isolated behind glass and have limited social experience.

Just as a dog automatically wags its tail, a baby will start to smile during its first month, even if no one is around. By the second month, smiling occurs in response to a pleasant sound or a caress. This happens with blind infants as well, so it can't be a matter of imitation. Smiling becomes associated with certain events through learning at about four months (Kagan, 1984). Both animals and humans need frequent touching, holding, and rubbing from birth onward, or the results are disastrous (the case of Genie, discussed later, provides more details about this). Finally, a most intriguing critical period occurs for humans: If you want to learn a foreign language with a correct and natural accent, you must start learning it before the age of 12 years. After that age, you can learn the language, but you will never have speech sounds that match those of the "natives." There is one exception, though. A few people have a special ability to imitate sounds; the people are said to have an "ear" for languages. They will be able to get much closer to matching the correct accent, but the rule still applies for most of us.

Feral children
Wild, untamed children.

You probably have heard tales about children who supposedly have been reared by animals. They are called **feral** (FER-al) **children**, the term *feral* meaning "wild, untamed." Such children supposedly walk on all fours and swing from trees. There has been one documented case of a boy who was discovered at age 11 or 12 after living in the woods by himself. The young man could not speak, and he did bite as any human child will, but he didn't growl, swing from trees, or act like an animal in other ways. The importance of critical periods and maturation within a social setting did show up. Since they were bypassed, he had almost no "human" skills. The boy eventually learned primitive speech and could print a few words, but he was never able to come close to what others his age could do in either area. He did learn the ways of society, in that he cleaned himself and ate the way we do and was able to accept and give affection as humans do, despite his childhood spent in isolation (Itard, 1932).

When you read about cases of children being brought up by animals, be careful not to accept them before asking yourself some questions. For instance, chimpanzees will almost automatically "adopt" an orphaned infant chimpanzee if its mother belonged to their group. They have even been known to take in an orphan whose mother was not a member of their group, but that is very, very rare. Chimpanzees are more likely either to kill or to ignore such an infant (Goodall, 1971). If they are this reluctant to take in a "foreign" baby of their own species, wouldn't they be much more reluctant to care for a human baby? Also, remember how long human infants are almost completely helpless, unable to do much of anything for themselves, including eating. Unless an adult human is around to take care of them for at least the first year of life, and probably longer, they will die. Without that kind of care, abandoned infants could not survive long enough to be taken in by animals (Graber, 1988). As for stories about children reared by packs of wolves, human babies would probably be considered food by the wolves, not welcome additions to their group.

The Family and Child Development

Most children in our society grow up in a **nuclear family**, made up only of parents and their children living in the same house. An **extended family** includes other relatives, such as aunts, uncles, or grandparents all living under one roof. Most people think that the majority of Americans lived in extended families until very recent times. This is not actually true. On farms, grandparents and other relatives often lived on the family's land, but they usually had separate houses some distance apart. One estimate is that, since our nation began, no more than one-fifth of the American people has ever lived in extended-family households (Degler, 1980).

The typical American family of today, however, is different in some important ways from the family of 20 or 30 years ago. For one thing, the divorce rate has steadily increased since the 1950s. By the 1980s, half of all marriages ended in divorce. This means that, before children reach the age of 18, about half of them will spend some time in a single-parent family. When a single parent gets married again, the children usually are not sure what the "new" parent means to their life. Often, children resent stepparents and are afraid that they will try to take the place of the absent parent. When other children also come into the picture, confusion and jealousy are bound to occur. The best thing stepparents can do is go slowly. It takes time for everyone to get used to this new arrangement, and rushing things makes it worse. It is also important for the parent-couple to talk about these problems ahead of time and agree to back each other up. To do that, they must have similar ideas about what children should and should not be allowed to do. When the adults are prepared for confusion and are careful to treat everyone fairly, the family has a much better chance of making it work (Davis, 1972; Spain & Blanchi, 1983).

Another recent change has to do with the roles family members play. Most families today need more than one income in order to have a decent standard of living, and two-thirds of all mothers now have jobs outside the home (Graham, 1984). While it is true that household chores are shared more among parents and children, such changes are not as big as you might think. Women still do almost all of the housework, especially the cooking and shopping (90 percent) and most of the childrearing, too (Burros, 1988).

Mothers Working Outside the Home

Mothers play an important part in their children's lives and are typically the first person babies become attached to. Many people today have

Nuclear family
Parents and children living in the same home.

Extended family
Nuclear family plus other relatives living in the same home.

asked what happens to children when their mothers work outside the home. Two important issues are: (1) whether the amount of time children spend with their parents decreases and (2) whether the children's attachment to the mother is weaker.

Mothers who work outside the home obviously don't have as much time for their children as full-time homemakers do. In fact, full-time homemakers spend twice as much time with their children, playing with them, taking care of them, disciplining them, and so on. The issue is whether this difference in amount of time has a negative effect on the children of mothers who work outside the home. So far, the answer seems to be "Not really." The most important thing is not the amount of time itself, but whether the children feel loved and cared for. Apparently, this is possible, regardless of the amount of time spent, by giving children warm affection and by enforcing guidelines about which behaviors are acceptable and which are unacceptable (Bell, 1979).

Children's attachment to the employed mother seems to be the same as to the homemaker mother, given a general sense from the mother of love and acceptance. Children who spend half their time in day-care centers develop just as strong an attachment to their mothers as the children of full-time homemakers (Kagan, 1979). Whether the mother is satisfied with what she is doing and whether she has her husband's support seem to be more important for everyone's welfare than whether she works outside the home or not.

The Father

While mothers do more of the childrearing, fathers are still important to a child's development. They spend less time with their children, but they do the same kinds of things as mothers do—playing with the children, taking care of them, disciplining and teaching them. Having a warm, affectionate father around provides a complete family unit and helps children become independent and better able to do things for themselves. Fathers also help children develop **self-esteem**, which is a feeling that one is worthwhile and useful (Lamb, 1979; Parke, 1983).

When there is no father in the home, however, the effects are not always as bad as you might expect. Many problems found in homes where only the mother is present are caused by too little money and too much stress on the mother, rather than by the father's absence in itself. Boys from such homes are usually just as masculine as other boys, and neither girls nor boys necessarily get into more trouble at school (Lamb, 1979; Shinn, 1978). The important point is for children to feel loved and cared for. This is easier to do when two parents share the load, but it is not impossible with only one.

Self-esteem
The feeling that you are worthwhile and useful.

While not critical, having a warm father around helps children develop self-esteem.

Other Influences

Before leaving this topic, a few points should be made. Parents are not all-powerful. They can and do have a lot of influence, but they are not completely responsible for everything a child does or fails to do. To make any sense of this complicated matter, you have to look at the importance of other children, brothers and sisters, school, teachers, and the rest of the outside world. Also, children are born individuals. A parental approach that works well with one child may fail with another child.

Today you hear a lot about parents "teaching" foreign languages or an appreciation of classical music to their child before it is even born, while it is still in the womb! (No, it doesn't work.) And some parents are so worried about their child's success that they spend day after day trying to find the right prekindergarten preschool. Many psychologists are seriously concerned that the expectations placed on parents have gone too far. Psychologists are afraid that this pressure to be perfect parents may work against children, not for them. For example, when we put too much emphasis on parents' mistakes, we end up making them so insecure that they actually do a worse job, not a better one (Bell, 1979; Bell, 1983). Love, affection, guidelines, listening, encouragement—these are the most important things for a child's healthy development, and they are what most parents try hard to provide.

Child Abuse

We have mentioned discipline or guidelines as helping a child to grow psychologically. But the type of disciplining techniques or punishment that parents use is equally important. Physical punishment, like hitting, slapping, and so on, is not a good way to handle problems. It doesn't help the child learn very much about right and wrong, and it can also get out of control fairly easily. When physical punishment is too harsh, it becomes child abuse. Clearly, a child can be abused psychologically, too. But, because that problem is much harder to define, most of the information we have focuses on physical abuse.

In this country, there are about 160,000 cases of child abuse each year in which the authorities become involved. Such cases include broken bones, bruises all over the body, serious burns, and, for about 1,000 children, death. But these figures are much lower than the actual occurrences of child abuse, since most cases are never reported. When a large number of parents were asked whether they had been violent enough with their children that they could have injured them, the number of people who said yes jumped to at least 1.5 million. But that figure is probably low, too, since it only includes parents who were willing to admit to such violent punishment (Starr, 1979).

Whether a parent will abuse a child depends on a lot of different things. We don't know them all, but we do know some conditions that make abuse more likely to happen. For example, most child abusers don't know much about children. They don't know how old a baby must be before it can be toilet trained or before it will sleep through the night and so on. Such parents are usually not very mature themselves and often are looking for love *from* a baby, rather than understanding how much work and responsibility are involved in being a parent. Often, these parents come from a violent background themselves. While abused children run a higher risk of becoming child abusers themselves, the majority of child abusers don't fit this mold (Starr, 1979). Other factors that lead to child abuse are financial problems, unemployment, too much stress on the parents, and isolation or being far away from friends and family (Wolfe, 1985). For many of these reasons, teenaged parents are more likely to abuse their children than people who become parents at a later age.

Sequences of Development

One of the most important advances in understanding children has been the discovery that we develop in the physical, moral, and intellectual areas in a sequential fashion. This finding is important to both parent and child. Nature requires that the brain and nervous system grow and mature before certain events occur. Thus, until about 9 to 12 months after birth, most babies are happy to go from person to person and even to be left alone with a stranger. But, from 9 months on, the brain has developed enough that the child is very much aware of the mother or father and is just beginning to grasp the fact that parents can disappear and that in their place appears a "foreigner," the baby-sitter. So, from this time until about 18 months, the child completely panics when left with someone else; this is a normal phenomenon called **separation anxiety** (Kagan, 1984). Separation anxiety can be seen in every culture and every normal baby. Obviously, then, it does not mean the parents are doing a bad job or that there is something wrong with the baby. All it does mean is that the brain has reached a certain level of development. Just as separation anxiety seems to appear out of nowhere, it will eventually disappear, and it has nothing to do with how the parents are rearing the child.

Separation anxiety
The baby's fear of being away from the parent; the desire to avoid strangers; appears from approximately 9 to 18 months after birth.

By about the child's fourth year, the brain is mature enough to grasp the concept of monsters and the possibility that they are sitting there in the dark next to the child. Comedian Bill Cosby does a routine in which a child smears Jello on the floor so the monster will slip on its way in. While this is clever and funny to us, it certainly isn't to the youngster. It is helpful to know that the child is not a "sissy," that a fear of the dark and of monsters is normal, and that the child shouldn't be punished because he or she is afraid. Often it helps to get children to say over and over, "I am brave—I can take care of myself," as they are exposed to longer periods of time in the dark (Kanfer et al., 1975). Some children simply can't adjust to the dark. All the commotion about letting them have a night-light is not sensible. What possible harm is it going to do? (None.) Fears and nightmares about creatures disappear by about age eight when the brain begins to deal with more complex concerns, such as bodily injury and physical danger (Bauer, 1976).

Because understanding these patterns of development is so important, the next two sections will cover the core theories about how we develop mentally and morally.

Piaget's Theory of Cognitive Development

Jean Piaget (Pea-ah-ZHAY) studied **cognitive development**, the ways in which a child's thinking and reasoning change and grow (the word *cognitive*, remember, refers to thought processes). Piaget divided this development into four basic stages. While not everyone agrees with every detail of his theory, it clearly has stood the test of time, and, in its outline, it seems to apply to most children and to explain why they see the world the way they do. The stages and ages listed can overlap, and not all children follow the *exact* pattern, but, in general, the system is valid (Piaget, 1929).

Cognitive development
The ways in which thinking and reasoning grow and change.

Sensorimotor Stage (Birth to Two Years) During the **sensorimotor stage**, the child spends time on two activities: sensation (sensory) and movement (motor responses; meaning arm, leg, and trunk of the body movements). Thus, the baby sees, studies, and grasps a bottle, the milk providing a pleasurable sensation. So, learning requires the motor response and a connection with sensation. The two will later be tied together by symbols (the word "bottle"). The child also reaches for other objects that bring either pleasure or pain. A connection is made between these objects and the effects they create, and words are eventually attached to each.

These objects are not "permanent" during this learning process. From about three to five months of age, if an experiment is set up in which the child is playing with a toy and the toy disappears through a trap door, the child doesn't show any concern—doesn't even look for the toy. How could this be? Apparently children this age are so self-centered that they view everything in the world from their own reference point. Thus, since the toy is no longer in their line of vision, it no longer exists. The concept of things moving somewhere else is not possible yet (Bower & Karlin, 1974).

Children can see quite well. In the very beginning, their eyes focus most comfortably at a distance of somewhat less than a foot so they can focus on the breast for feeding. But their vision is sharp from the first few weeks. Even as adults, we are all programmed to respond to movement anywhere in our line of vision because it may signal danger. Since the child is still in training, so to speak, he or she will be most interested in the movement itself, not associating it yet with anything else (like danger). Thus, if you move a small white elephant toy along, pass it behind a screen, and bring out on the other side a red lion, a child younger than five months old will show no concern about the strange thing that has happened but will be fascinated by the movement alone.

In other words, the child has not as yet formed what is called **object permanence**; that is, specific objects are not a part of their world. An elephant is not an elephant or a lion a lion. The concept of permanent objects first appears at about ten months. Note that this is just about the time that separation anxiety appears; probably the presence and absence of the parent helps the child form this concept since, when the parent leaves, an "object" of great importance is gone (Coates et al., 1972). Toward the end of the sensorimotor period, the child begins to name real things in a real world. Thus, there are endless requests for a "bottle." The brain has replaced reaching for a bottle (mother) and getting it (sensation) with a symbol—that is, the word representing that object. The sensorimotor stage is over.

Preoperational Stage (Two to Seven Years) In the **preoperational stage**, children know that things can be permanent. The child is not yet able (pre) to operate effectively on and within the world because he or she is so completely self-involved. Children at this age think that rocks have the same feelings they do, and they have long discussions with them. In fact, they have long discussions with just about everything and everyone. Language develops at an extremely fast rate during this stage, and the child's vocabulary expands enormously. Many symbols, or words, are used to represent actions and objects. The child's point of reference, however, is still the child: The world only exists in terms of himself or herself. The conversation we quoted at the beginning of this chapter illustrated a child who could not imagine that his brother had a world different from his. During this stage, the child is unable to change places with someone else and see things from another point of view. The child cannot understand the principle of **reversibility**, which means that, if a relationship goes in one direction, it can be turned around and go the opposite direction, too. Thus, the little boy at the beginning of this chapter could only understand the relationship he had to his brother but not the reverse, the relationship his brother had to him.

Another interesting point is that children at this age cannot grasp something called **conservation**, the idea that you can change some of an object's characteristics while keeping others the same, or *conserving* them. For instance, the mass of an object stays the same (is conserved) no matter what you do to its shape. A ball of clay is the same mass (amount) if you stretch it out to look like a hot dog. A five-year-old will watch you take a glass of Kool-Aid and pour it into a taller, thinner glass (so the column of the drink is higher). If you ask the child which glass holds more Kool-Aid, he or she will insist that the taller one does, even though the pouring took place right there. By six years of age, a child will go back and forth and say that possibly the taller one has the same amount, but will not be certain.

The important point is that, even though the child is so self-centered, he or she is beginning to notice differences between people and objects in the environment; these will finally become clear in the next stage.

Concrete Operations Stage (Seven to Eleven Years) The third stage of the Piaget system is called the **concrete operations stage**. The world has become fixed and real (that is, concrete), with separate objects being different and lying outside the child in the world. The idea of reversibility, or seeing things from someone else's viewpoint, is no longer a problem. Thus, the child's ability to reason in a logical way has gone up a rung on the ladder.

Children at this stage are still limited, however. While they can see objects as permanent and complete, they have some trouble seeing objects as having more than one dimension at the same time. So, a child at the beginning of this period will say about some pencils: "This pencil is long; this one is thin; this one is fat." By the end of the seventh year, they can compare pencils: "This pencil is longer and thinner than that one."

Conservation is much less of a problem, too. By age eight, children

Even though these beakers contain the same amount, this boy is convinced the taller one has more in it.

Reversibility
Piaget's term for the idea that a relationship that goes in one direction can go in the other direction also.

Conservation
Piaget's term for the idea that some of an object's characteristics can be changed while others remain the same. Changing shape does not change volume.

Concrete operations stage
Piaget's third stage of child development in which the child understands that there is a real world with real objects, which exist apart from the child and which can be manipulated.

In Focus: Piaget's Stages of Cognitive Development

Approximate Age	Stages and Related Abilities
	Sensorimotor (birth to 2 years)
Birth	Raw sensation! lights . . . sounds . . . smells . . . tastes
3 months	Significant movement! Reaches for objects
5–8 months	No object permanence yet—if object leaves vision, it no longer exists
10 months	Object permanence appears
	Separation anxiety!
2 years	Begins to move from world of all sensations and movements to world of thought.
	Preoperational (2 to 7 years)
2 years	Object permanence well established
	No reversibility or conservation skills
	Self-involved—unable to view world from another's point of view
3–7 years	Growing awareness of reversibility and conservation
	Concrete operations (7 to 11 years)
7 years	Reversibility well established
8 years	Some conservation skills well established
9–11 years	Able to view world more and more from another's point of view
	Formal operations (11 and on)
11 and on	Growing ability to think abstractly and symbolically

have no trouble at all insisting that the two glasses of different shapes hold the same amount of Kool-Aid. From ages eight through eleven, the child seems to be bringing together all the principles we have just discussed. While doing this, however, he or she is forming rules and regulations that must be followed to the letter. It is hard for children at this stage to look at things in any other way than either black or white—gray areas are still a little too difficult to understand.

Formal operations stage
Piaget's fourth stage of child development in which the ability to deal with the highly symbolic thoughts found in logic, math, philosophy, and ethics begins to appear.

Formal Operations Stage (Eleven Years On) Piaget's fourth stage of development, called the **formal operations stage**, appears sometime after eleven years of age and can become more elaborate and complex into young adulthood. The term *formal operations* refers to the ability to deal with highly symbolic thoughts, such as those found in mathematics, logic, and philosophy. While some people never make it to this stage no matter what, you can spot it developing in those who suddenly become concerned about issues such as truth and justice, fairness and right (Elkind, 1978; Lyell, 1984). Such concerns are at their peak for most adolescents, but unfortunately too many people become calloused and begin to lose them along the way into adulthood. According to Piaget, then, the formal operations stage is the highest level of cognitive development.

Kohlberg's Theory of Moral Development

Moral development, the development of ideas about right and wrong, also seems to follow a maturational sequence, or series of stages. Like Piaget's system, there is not necessarily a fixed pattern of this development for every single person, and there can at times be a mixture of stages (Snarey, 1985). But a major difference between this theory of moral reasoning and Piaget's cognitive system is that a person may be at a high level of moral reasoning but still not be inclined to "be good." In other words, we have a choice regarding moral issues but not so with mental development. This moral system was developed by psychologist **Lawrence Kohlberg** and has many subcategories. For our purposes, however, the three main levels or stages should be enough to give you the general principle.

Preconventional Level (Younger Than Age Six) At the early **preconventional level**, morality is determined by the sheer power of outside authority. Adults impose their own wills on the children. At these ages, it is impossible for the child to grasp the complexities of right and wrong; instead, the child focuses on whether he or she is being punished or rewarded. If punished, you are "bad." If not punished, or praised, you must be doing "good."

 Toward the end of this stage, children do begin to grasp that, if people do something for you, you should do something for them. But the resulting behavior is not all that related to "morals": Children are in it for what they can get at this time because they are still so self-centered.

Preconventional level
Kohlberg's early stage of moral development in which morality is determined by the sheer power of outside authority.

Conventional Level (Seven to Eleven Years) The **conventional level** of moral reasoning focuses on the expectations of others as the major motivation for doing what is right or wrong. At first, children are seeking the approval of others. But gradually there emerges the idea of social order, or behaving in a certain way because society expects it. In time, the *intentions* of a person's actions become an important consideration in whether the child judges these actions to be right or wrong. In other words, whether or not someone meant to do something is taken into account,

Conventional level
Kohlberg's middle stage of moral development in which moral reasoning is based on the expectations of others regarding what is right or wrong.

just as the legal system makes a distinction between involuntary manslaughter and murder.

The majority of older people, adolescents or adults, don't go much beyond this conventional level of moral reasoning. But some do make it to the final stage.

Postconventional Level (Eleven Years On)   A relatively small proportion of the population reaches what is called the **postconventional level** of moral reasoning. If this development occurs, it does so at about age eleven or twelve. Now that the brain and experience have primed the person for dealing with them, issues like personal ethics and human rights come to the foreground (Snarey, 1985; Kohlberg, 1963). Here is a comparison of answers given by people at the earlier preconventional level compared with those given by people at the postconventional level:

Problem: After a shipwreck, eleven men are in a lifeboat, one wealthy and powerful, ten poor. You can save either the one rich man or the ten poor men. Which should you save?

Preconventional answer: The rich man because he will give you a big reward.

Postconventional answer: The ten poor men because human life has value regardless of wealth or status.

You probably will take the second answer for granted, but that took quite a bit of maturing. When you were very young, you probably would have given the first answer.

A complication with this system of moral development is that behavior differs depending on what kind of situation you are caught up in. Sometimes we let morality go out the window for our own convenience. With the intellectual development discussed by Piaget, we can't go backward, but, with morality, sometimes we "know better" and we still don't care (Blasi, 1980). Even so, some psychologists believe that establishing right and wrong might actually arise from biological changes in the brain, despite the fact that the rules vary from one culture to another (Kagan, 1984).

The Development of Language Skills

Psychologists study communication in any form, even among and by animals. Some claims have been outlandish, though. In 1852, it was said that a captain captured a pirate ship and found a dog that could sing and dance. In 1600, supposedly there was a beautiful white horse who could dance and count and one day just climbed straight up the side of a church steeple to talk to the people (Thomas, 1983). Despite these claims, we do know that dogs, cats, birds, and most other animals can communicate by

In Focus: Kohlberg's Dilemmas

Kohlberg compiled much of his information about morality through interviews with hundreds and hundreds of subjects. He would present these subjects with numerous moral dilemmas, similar to this one:

"Every day at the end of class, your teacher tells you to take down the attendance slip. One day a good friend runs into you before you reach the attendance office and begs you to take his name off the sheet. He says he can't tell you the reason why he cut class, but that it was important. Would *you* scratch off the name?"

For this example, Kohlberg would not be concerned so much with whether you would or would not remove the name from the attendance sheet. He was more concerned with the *reasoning* behind the decision. Kohlberg believed that this reasoning would reveal your level of moral development.

Typical Preconventional Reasoning

"It's all right to scratch the name off. There's no way I'll get caught."
"I'm *not* going to do it. I might get caught."
"I'm going to do it. Maybe someday I'll need a favor."
"No way. It's wrong. Besides, he wouldn't do it for me."

Typical Conventional Reasoning

"I better do it—what would my friend think of me if I didn't?"
"I'm not going to do it. What if the teacher found out? What would she think?"
"I'm not going to do it—you can't just break the rules whenever you want."
"I'm going to do it. One rule of friendship is that friends help each other out."

Typical Postconventional Reasoning

"I'm going to do it—the attendance system doesn't protect students' rights."
"I'm not going to do it. It's against my principles."

sound or action. So, before getting into the issue of human language, we want to set the stage with some other types of "language."

Chimpanzees can be taught to communicate symbolically using sign language somewhat similar to that used by the deaf, and some chimps have learned as many as 1,000 different sign-language words. The ability to use sign language clearly shows that they can engage in a form of

You can imagine the kitten's initial reaction, but the new "mother" turned out to be patient, kind, and loving.

speech. They don't, however, have the necessary vocal apparatus actually to talk, nor do they show the same level of language skills found in the human. After all, how well would we do on tests of tree-swinging and mutual chimp maintenance (such as cleaning and grooming one another)—tasks they do with great expertise? The point is that we are asking them to perform unnatural acts, and they do themselves proud even though they are not destined to become as proficient in word language as we are (Premack & Woodruff, 1978; Schwartz, 1980).

Despite the chimpanzees' remarkable feats, it appears that only humans are destined to speak, to communicate through a verbal language. We are the only creatures who have both the physical structures needed to make all the sounds and the brains to make rules of grammar and invent new words.

Processes of Language

Babbling is a natural activity for babies, even deaf ones who cannot hear their own or others' voices. Buried in all this noisemaking are the sounds used in *any* human language. A basic blueprint of all speech sounds is programmed in the infant from birth. The environment, by providing examples to imitate, then guides the infant to the correct speech pattern for the society within which the infant lives. From this vast array of sounds, children pick and choose the ones that fit the language of those around them. This is why older foreigners have trouble learning new languages. For instance, we use a *th* sound frequently, but it doesn't appear in German, so German children early on drop it from their supply of sounds unless they are also learning English.

Psychologists believe that language patterns develop because certain sounds are reinforced or rewarded whenever they occur. Thus, the sounds for "da-da" and "ma-ma" are among the first to be learned because they bring such joy to the parents.

Rules of Language

In the process of learning to speak, children follow rigid, fixed rules. For example, a child in an early Kohlberg stage will say that someone who breaks three cups accidentally is "badder" than someone who breaks one cup on purpose. Adding the "er" is a "rule" they learn and apply to almost any word to indicate a greater degree of something (Chomsky, 1980). Words like *doggie* are made plural by adding "s," so the rule is followed for all other words: "Those mans feeding corns to the sheeps." Correcting children does not affect their loyalty to these rules. They keep right on making the same mistakes, even though no one else speaks this way (Brown, 1973).

The most important thing at this stage is the location of the word. A child knows the difference between "Doggie eat" and "Eat doggie." Thus, grammar involving plurals and other rules are artificial and only learned from reinforcement at a later stage of development. Communication is the child's goal at the beginning.

Genie

In 1970, authorities in Los Angeles found a 13-year-old, Genie, who had been strapped to a bed or chair for the previous 11 years. Her father never spoke, nor was there any television or radio. Hence, Genie heard a few sounds only when her blind (!) mother, separated from the father, visited her. Of real interest from this sad case is the fact that, after rescue, Genie learned to speak by following the exact principles of children, moving from selected sounds through the rigid rules to making finer discriminations about grammar (Curtiss, 1977). Hence, there is a maturational process and fixed sequence involved when learning language. Sadly, though, Genie had missed so many critical periods in language learning that her speech level did not move much beyond that of a child aged four or five.

Since the sounds, words, word arrangements, and accents all vary from one culture to another and even from one section of a country to another, it is obvious that environment plays a critical role in speech de-

Although we might not find what these boys are saying all that funny, this type of interaction is critical to social development.

velopment. There is a general feeling, however, that many basic ideas or concepts might be inherited rather than learned. This might explain why all known societies have a concept of something being "in here" or "out there" or of something being "big" or "little." The belief is that there is a biological program that is in us from the beginning, but that needs an environment for fine-tuning (Bickerton, 1984; Chomsky, 1980). While controversy about inheriting "ideas" still exists, almost everyone now agrees that we do inherit the *potential* for speech sounds and that this is not environmental. It also seems obvious that sounds and words have to be stored over time, and this process in the normal child depends on brain development. By age two, the average child knows about 300 words, by age three roughly 1,000 words, and by age six can correctly use 5,000 words and understand almost twice that number. The average adult has a vocabulary of about 10,000 words, but can grasp the meaning of at least 50,000 words, probably partly from context. There seems to be no doubt about it: Humans are born to talk, and we will spend most of our lives in the world of words.

How Much of You Is Still a Child?

In the early days, it was believed that a child was a miniature adult. As a result, there were few, if any, provisions made for the child's need to develop and mature. Assumptions were made that children could handle almost any problem and were fully accountable for their actions. Today we know that the world of the child is a unique one in which thoughts, actions, and beliefs do not necessarily match or even come close to those of adults for many years.

Some philosophers and psychologists went to the other extreme of claiming that children could be made into anything adults desired. In other words, children were like empty blackboards on which nearly anything could be written and it would last a lifetime. One psychologist, John Watson (discussed in Chapter 7), said that the best way to handle children was never to hug or kiss them(!), but, instead, shake hands with them just before they went to bed each night. He also maintained that he could take any healthy infant and turn him or her into any kind of person he desired.

Sigmund Freud, the founder of psychoanalysis (Chapter 14), had tremendous influence on the whole course of beliefs about what makes people abnormal. He insisted that the first five years of life were the critical ones and that, by the end of the fifth year, we had become what we were going to be—at least in terms of our

We rarely forget events that cause us to feel this way.

abnormalities. It is hard, even today, to avoid hearing that someone who acts strangely probably does so as the result of something that happened in childhood. Few psychologists embrace this point of view any longer, but it continues nonetheless. Similarly, as we mentioned in this chapter, we hear what a terrible disservice mothers who work outside the home are doing to their children—another belief that is not supported by the evidence.

While it is possible that what we write here today will not bear the scrutiny of time, at least today's views are far more balanced, have

quite a bit of experimental support, and *seem* to make sense. A few very important discoveries have been that: (1) the child influences the parent by his or her behavior, rather than just the parent controlling whatever happens to the child; (2) childhood friends have a striking influence on how we develop, oftentimes outstripping the influence of the parents; and (3) there are very strong genetic influences on what we are. Most of us tend to remain the same basic type of person from middle childhood on—at least in the most general sense. For instance, if we were very dependent on others as a child, the likelihood is great that we are still this way today—only we are now dependent on some person other than our parent. If we were very independent children, the same holds true today. This is different from the Freudian belief, because we are dealing with inherited characteristics on which we are free to build with all kinds of experiences throughout our whole life, not just during the first five years.

The evidence is very strong that we have within our power the ability to determine much of our fate. Very few children who were abused or who grew up under horrible circumstances become delinquent, criminal, horrible people. We only hear and read about a selected few.

You might want to try a little private research on yourself to see what you come up with. Sit down sometime and just think for a while about the course of your own development. For example, what childhood memories are the strongest? List a few. Did they or did they not have a major impact on what you are today? What interactions with your parents when you were a child do you remember? The same question: How much influence did they have on what you are today? Or, how much similarity is there in your basic personality (dependent, independent, adventuresome,

shy, and so forth—don't lie to yourself) between what you were like as a child and what you are like today? What was the worst thing that ever happened to you, and did it really influence the course of your life up to the present? How similar or dissimilar are your real views on morality, the world, your friends, and so forth to those you think your parents had when you were growing up? And how much influence did your very good (or bad) childhood friends have on you?

It is very hard to come to any

final conclusion from such an exercise, but it will shed a great deal of light on your course of development, and a picture of yourself should emerge. There is no reason why your conclusions should be any less accurate than those of the "experts." In all probability, you will be *more* accurate, if you're being honest with yourself, since it has been your life, after all.

Summary

1. The nature/nurture controversy assumes that both heredity and environment are important, but one side emphasizes the genes (nature) and the other side emphasizes the world (nurture) in which the child lives. Identical twins play a major role in studying heredity and its effects.

2. Developmental patterns show that each species has a fixed rate at which development proceeds. The speed with which it occurs seems to be related to the final potential and complexity of the particular species.

3. Maturation is an automatic, orderly, and sequential process of physical and mental development. Training has little effect on the speed or outcome of the process, although growth cycles are involved that vary the speed and timing of a child's development.

4. The nuclear family is the most common family unit in the United States and always has been. An extended family is a rarity. Evidence is that the mother's working outside the home does little damage as long as she and the child spend warm, affectionate time together and as long as there is little family friction over her outside employment.

5. Child abuse results from two major factors: (1) pressure on a parent from unemployment, financial problems, and the like and (2) a lack of knowledge regarding developmental sequences, causing the parent to have unrealistic expectations of the child.

6. Separation anxiety occurs at about nine months of age and is a fear of being away from the parent.

7. Jean Piaget has a four-stage system of mental development that follows a sequence based on age and brain maturation. Lawrence Kohlberg has a similar three-stage system for the development of moral reasoning.

8. Language is a maturational process that starts off with a fixed set of rules for speech. Over time the child learns to conform more and more with his or her society's grammatical system.

Key Words and Concepts

heredity
environment
nature/nurture
identical twins
maturation
growth cycles
imprinting
critical period
feral children
nuclear family
extended family
self-esteem
separation anxiety
Jean Piaget
cognitive
   development

sensorimotor stage
object permanence
preoperational
   stage
reversibility
conservation
concrete operations
   stage
formal operations
   stage
Lawrence Kohlberg
preconventional
   level
conventional level
postconventional
   level

Review Questions

Multiple Choice

1. If we agree that violence is caused mainly by nurture, this means that:
   a. Violence is mainly inborn
   b. Violence is mainly learned
   c. Violence cannot be studied
   d. Violence is hereditary.

2. If violence is caused mainly by nature, this means that:
   a. Violence is mainly inborn
   b. Violence is mainly learned
   c. Violence is learned in nature
   d. Humans are as violent as other animals.

3. Once an ability is inherited, the environment
   a. cannot affect that ability.
   b. can affect that ability.

4. Which of the following statements about developmental patterns is *not* true?
   a. Development within a species is orderly.
   b. The human has a longer developmental period than other animals.
   c. It's usually possible through training to speed up a species' developmental timetable by quite a bit.
   d. The development process integrates the brain and the body.

5. Which of the following statements about growth cycles is *not* true?
   a. There are differences between the sexes.
   b. The brain develops sooner than the body.
   c. Girls develop in a more orderly and stable way than boys do.
   d. The reproductive system develops faster than the brain.

True/False

6. Imprinting is affected by chemical changes in the body.

7. Critical periods apply to all animals but humans.

8. In time, a feral child will usually catch up to the ability level of others his or her age.

9. Extended families are more common today than in the past.

10. Studies show that mothers who work outside the home form just as strong an attachment to their children as mothers who don't work outside the home.

11. One cause of child abuse is the abuser's lack of knowledge about children.

12. Separation anxiety seems to have more to do with nurture than nature.

Matching (Answers can be used more than once.)

13. Conservation skills are not quite established.
14. World becomes fixed.
15. Objects are not permanent.
16. Highest level of cognitive development
17. Sensation and movement are particularly important.
18. Object permanence becomes well established.
19. Conservation becomes easier.
20. Reversibility is difficult, if not impossible.
21. Logical and philosophical thinking

a. sensorimotor stage
b. preoperational stage
c. concrete operations stage
d. formal operations stage

Matching (Answers can be used more than once.)

22. Others' approval helps us determine right and wrong.

23. Society's expectations help us determine right and wrong.

24. People's rights are given great consideration.

25. Extremely self-centered

26. Highest level of moral development

27. Outside authority determines right and wrong for us.

a. preconventional

b. conventional

c. postconventional

Discussion Questions

1. Some communities from time to time pass ordinances that ban the sale of toy guns, the implication being that violence is provoked in large part by what we learn in the environment. Do you agree or disagree with this type of ordinance? Why? Explain.

2. A similar controversy to that described in number 1 involves the portrayal of violence in television programs. In your opinion, do children learn to be violent themselves through these programs? Should the violence be censored in any way? Explain. Note: Many cartoons include vivid violence.

3. Describe several aspects of your personality that are clearly influenced mainly by heredity, and describe several aspects that are clearly influenced mainly by the environment.

4. Alisha is a mother who works outside the home. She argues that she spends at least two to three hours of quality time with her child every evening. Her friend, Tonya, is a mother who is not employed outside the house. She argues that these two to three hours may be quality time for Alisha, but not necessarily for her child; maybe two to three hours of morning time (or afternoon time) would be the time when the *child* is most open to quality interaction. In other words, *maybe* the two to three hours in the evening are a "crabby" time for the child, and the child benefits little from the interaction. With whom do you tend to agree? Explain.

5. The chapter mentions that all normal children will eventually experience separation anxiety. Not all parents, however, deal with the anxiety in the same way.

For example, let's say that a "stranger" picks up the child, and the child begins to cry. Some parents will tend to take the baby away almost immediately to soothe the child; they let the child gradually decide when he or she is ready to approach the stranger. Other parents will let the stranger hold the child, hoping that the child will get used to the stranger, despite the child's continuing anxiety. In your opinion, which approach would promote a stronger and longer-lasting sense of security for the child? Explain.

6. In your opinion, what level of moral development best describes each of the following situations? (a) A courtroom judge addressing a jury (b) a teacher who rigidly enforces the rules of the school (c) an automobile driver when a cop is around. More than one answer may be possible for each of these situations, but defend your answer. For example, if one of the situations were "a politician addressing a crowd," you might answer *preconventional level*, arguing that politicians will grant us favors perhaps, but only if we vote for them.

7. If a person is at the postconventional level of *moral* development, this same person will probably also be at the formal operations level of *cognitive* development. Why? In other words, why would a person need to be advanced in his or her cognitive ability in order to be advanced in his or her moral development? Explain.

8. Imagine a very hypothetical situation where a child, for the first two years of his or her life, does little but watch educational programs like "Sesame Street" every hour, every day. Further, imagine that this child experiences almost no interaction with real people. Why would this child develop few, if any, language skills? Explain. (*Hint*: Refer back to the principles of learning discussed in Chapter 7.)

Activities

1. As suggested in the chapter, one of the best ways to learn about the effects of heredity and environment is to study identical twins. Try it. You can do it in one of two ways: (1) Find an article or two and write a report; emphasize the role of heredity and environment in the lives of the twins. (2) Prepare a list of questions and actually interview a set of identical twins. Ask around and you'll be surprised how easy it is to locate and contact a set of twins. Possible questions: What are some of your common personality traits? Interests? Values? Which of these similarities do you think are influenced more by heredity and which are influenced more by the environment? Do other people sometimes have

difficulty recognizing your individual uniqueness? In other words, do they look at you as *completely* identical?

Write a report on your interview and your reaction to what you learned.

2. This activity may help you discover how much your personality is influenced by your heredity and/or by your environment. Make a list of 20 characteristics that you have in common with your parents. The characteristics can be physical, mental, behavioral—just about any similarity that you can think of. After each item, write down whether the characteristic, in your opinion, is influenced mainly through heredity or mainly through the environment. The characteristics are most likely influenced by both, but choose the influence that you perceive to be slightly more dominant.

Next, have one of your parents make the same list, following the same instructions—but don't let him or her see your list.

Compare the two lists. Were the characteristics listed pretty much the same? Were your conclusions about heredity and environment about the same? What general conclusions can you draw from this? For example, which kinds of characteristics (physical, mental, behavioral, and so forth) seemed to be most influenced by heredity? Least influenced by heredity? Explain.

3. We can all think of memorable childhood experiences that have helped to shape our personalities. Pick one of these memorable experiences and describe it in a couple of pages. Include all the rich and vivid detail that made the experience memorable for you. Write the description not as an essay but as if you were telling a story to a good friend.

4. Probably one of the most successful educational television programs for children is "Sesame Street." Watch about an hour of the program and take notes on the various teaching techniques used: length of "skits," music, repetition, and any other techniques that you notice.

Next, watch about 10 to 15 television commercials (don't rely on memory) and take notes on techniques that advertisers use to sell their products: length of commercials, music, repetition, and so on.

Notice any similarities? Write a detailed report comparing and contrasting "Sesame Street" to the television commercials. If possible, talk to parents whose children watch "Sesame Street" and ask them about the effectiveness of the techniques used.

5. Contact three teachers: One should be a first- or second-grade teacher (whose students will probably be preoperational); another should be a third- or fourth-grade teacher (whose students will probably be concrete operational); the third should be a fifth- or sixth-grade teacher (whose students will probably be formal operational). Ask the teachers if they would be willing to participate in a 15- to 20-minute experiment. All they'll have to do is allow their students to draw pictures, reading to their students beforehand the following instructions: "Draw a picture of a typical day at your home." Try to get all the teachers to use the same size paper and the same writing utensils—crayons, for example.

Analyze the three groups of drawings. You might look at some of the following aspects of the drawings: the size and proportions of objects drawn; the colors used; the number of people drawn versus the number of objects. (Note: Artistic ability should probably not be given much weight in your analyses.) Try to relate these observations to Piaget's theory. Do the drawings reveal in any way the artists' stages of cognitive development? Explain.

Don't feel limited by these suggestions about your analysis. Although many therapists are trained in analyzing such pictures, most agree that there are no pat or set answers. They admit that their analyses depend on intuition and creativity to some extent. So be creative. Perhaps get a friend or two to help you brainstorm.

6. The chapter explains that maturation processes for the most part progress at one's own pace, that there's little that other people can do to speed up the process. Apparently, many preschool programs tend to disagree with this assertion. Some of these programs attempt to teach reading, writing, and spelling to children at a very young age. Conduct research on one of these programs and write a report. What is the school's philosophy about education? What teaching techniques does the school use? According to your research, how "successful" is the school? Do you agree with the school's philosophy and techniques? Is the school, in *your* opinion, successful?

You can probably get this information through library research, but, if you know of one of these programs in your area, it may be more informative actually to call up the school and interview one of the directors there.

Sharing with another and a sense of belonging are keys to feeling worth-while.

Chapter 11

Adolescence

Global Look at the Chapter

Throughout adolescence, significant growth and changes occur. Adolescents are different from other age groups in their physical, psychological, social, intellectual, and moral concerns and processes.

Defining Adolescence

The years between childhood and adulthood make up the period of development called adolescence. This period starts at age 11 or 12 and generally is considered over by 18 or 19. Pinpointing exactly when adolescence ends and adulthood begins, though, is not possible in our society. People can vote or join the military at 18. In most states, they can marry without their parents' permission at that age. On the other hand, a person must be 21 to have all the legal rights that adults enjoy. But even reaching that age does not automatically grant full adult status. Many people 21 and older are still single, still in school, and still dependent on their parents for financial support. They are adults in the eyes of the law, but are not yet self-sufficient or living on their own. In any case, since the physical and psychological changes of adolescence are fairly complete by age 19, that is a reasonable end point.

The range of ages from 11 to 19 is further divided, based on physical and psychological similarities within these smaller age groups. **Early adolescence** goes from 11 to 14. **Middle adolescence** runs from 14 to 16. **Late adolescence** ranges from 16 to 19. As we discuss these periods in greater detail, differences among the age groups will become clear.

Physical Changes

Throughout adolescence, the most startling developments are physical. Sudden changes take place in sexual maturation and physical growth. Changes in height and weight are dramatic and troublesome. The biggest problem, however, is that, while these changes in physiology remove from adolescents the label "child," they are not yet adults, and so they may feel for a while that they are "nowhere," neither adult nor child.

Sexual Development

Puberty, or the period of sexual maturation, is a notable feature of adolescence. **Hormones**, chemicals that control body growth, emotional responses, and physical changes, are responsible for sexual maturation. Several hormones are extremely active in adolescence. The **pituitary gland** (pi-TUE-i-ter-ee) secretes growth hormones and increases the production in other glands of other hormones. Two systems under the pituitary's control are the **adrenal glands** (ah-DREE-nal) and the **gonads** (GO-nads) or sex glands. Adrenaline from the adrenal glands and sex hormones from the gonads work with the pituitary to bring about sexual maturation.

Puberty is the time of breast development and the start of menstruation in females. Noticeable voice changes and the development of facial hair and thicker body hair occur in males. Both sexes begin the process of sex-organ maturation, which is accompanied by the growth of pubic hair (the word *pubic* means "downy" or "hairy"). Most people think sexual development is gradual over the years, but not so. Amazingly, 90 percent of sexual maturity occurs after puberty starts, which accounts for the concern and preoccupation with sexuality common for people in this period of their lives (Money, 1974). Other effects of hormones include skin problems, like acne, and increased sweating. While these are a natural outcome of the bodily changes taking place, they are also a source of embarrassment and concern for many adolescents.

Early adolescence
The period from 11 to 14 years of age.

Middle adolescence
14 to 16 years of age.

Late adolescence
16 to 19 years of age.

Puberty
The time of sexual maturation.

Hormones
The body chemicals that control body growth, emotional responses, and physical changes.

Pituitary gland
The gland that secretes growth hormones and increases the production in other glands of other hormones.

Adrenal glands
The gland that produces adrenaline, the stimulating hormone; helps sexual maturation, along with gonads.

Gonads
The sex glands.

Physical Growth

Growth spurt
The rapid increase in growth during puberty.

Nothing seems to feel right at times during adolescence because the body is moving upward and outward so rapidly in what is called the **growth spurt**. When growth spurts occur, development is not orderly. Arms and hands may grow at a different rate from legs, for instance, while other parts of the body develop at yet another rate.

Although they may look gangly, teenagers have exceptionally good coordination. It is because growth is so rapid and uneven that adolescents may *feel* awkward and "not quite right." Most teenagers, however, handle puberty much better than people think. In fact, only a small number of adolescents, roughly 15 percent, have any real trouble adjusting to these dramatic changes (Petersen, 1987).

Growth spurts come earlier for girls than boys, but, for both sexes, early adolescence is the time of maximum physical development. Between the ages of 9 and 12, girls may grow as much as three inches taller in one year. For boys, this growth occurs between 11 and 15, when they may gain as much as four inches in height in a year. The exact time when this growth will occur for any individual, male or female, is unpredictable.

Rates of Maturation

Differences between boys and girls in level of physical maturation are greatest and most obvious in early adolescence. By age 14, most girls have matured fairly completely, while most boys lag behind by two to three years. This difference between the sexes creates problems in relating to one another, especially where dating and dancing are involved. Most males are still shorter than females their own age, making the situation even more awkward. When girls start dating, many go out with older boys, largely because of these differences. By middle adolescence, the maturity gap between the sexes has narrowed considerably, and, for most, by late adolescence it has disappeared altogether.

Besides overall gender differences in the rate and timing of physical maturation, individual differences exist as well. Small differences do not have much impact on the individual. When physical development occurs substantially earlier or later than average, however, there are psychological effects as well. What kinds of effects occur depends on two factors: (1) whether the adolescent is an **early maturer** (one and a half years or more ahead of the average) or a **late maturer** (one and a half years or more behind the average) and (2) whether the individual is male or female.

Early maturation is more of an advantage for boys than girls. Boys who develop ahead of schedule have higher self-esteem and feel better about

Early maturer
Someone who develops one and a half years or more ahead of average growth.

Late maturer
Someone who develops one and a half years or more behind average growth.

Early Maturers		Late Maturers	
Boys	**Girls**	**Boys**	**Girls**
High self-esteem	Generally low self-esteem	Generally low self-esteem	High self-esteem
Satisfied with physical appearance	Dissatisfied with physical appearance	Dissatisfied with overall appearance	Satisfied with physical appearance
	Highly self-conscious	Highly self-conscious	

how they look. Early maturing girls feel awkward about being different from their friends. They are more self-conscious and dissatisfied with their weight and general appearance (Peskin, 1973).

Development that starts later than average is worse for boys than girls. Boys who are late maturers, like early maturing girls, feel awkward about their bodies. They are more self-conscious, less self-confident, and express greater dissatisfaction with their overall appearance than other adolescent males. Late maturing girls, however, do not seem to suffer many negative effects. Generally, they have high self-esteem and are satisfied with their physical appearance. They also have the advantage of being similar to boys their own age in height and overall maturation (Clausen, 1975; Peskin, 1973).

While pluses or minuses are created when maturation occurs later or earlier than average, their greatest impact is felt during adolescence itself. For most early or late maturers, neither the problems nor the advantages last into adult life.

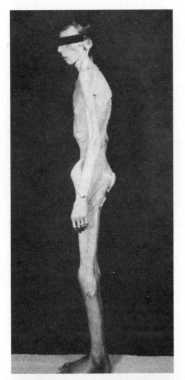

(Photographs at left) Two examples of *anorexia nervosa*, a disorder in which people diet excessively.

Weight: Too Much or Too Little?

Along with rapid growth and sexual maturation come weight changes. Concerns about weight are a common problem for adolescents. Being underweight or overweight can result from hormonal imbalances, psychological difficulties, or a combination of the two. Some males try to compensate for a temporary "stringbean look" by eating too much. In addition, food can act like a sedative to relieve loneliness—a feeling that arises very easily during this period.

But being overweight is nowhere near as risky as the attempt to become too thin. In this area, the victim is almost always the female, who lives under tremendous pressure to be slimmer than is either reasonable or healthy. As we discussed in Chapter 5, "Motivation and Emotion," the female adolescent often gets involved in unhealthy dieting. Excessive dieting can lead to **anorexia nervosa**, a condition with severe physical effects. It is a potentially fatal disorder in which food intake decreases to the point of starvation.

Patience on the part of adolescents is probably called for, as difficult as that may be. Physical changes *are* drastic during this period, but people in their early 20s are the leanest of all age groups.

Psychological Issues

Adolescence is often painted as a time of great difficulty and confusion. While the trials of this period vary from one culture to another, there is little indication that it is actually that bad for most adolescents. But many problems leave a number of teenagers in a type of limbo. One of the hardest issues to deal with is trying to find an identity. Until adolescence, there is no pressure to find out about yourself. Now it becomes necessary to try out different roles to see which ones fit. The problem of trying to find an identity is made worse in our society because the adolescent is normally not expected to take on adult responsibilities but, at the same time, *is* expected to show more maturity and a sense of commitment.

Other societies, especially primitive ones, handle the transition from childhood to adulthood more simply. This transition is made through some kind of initiation or **rite of passage**, meaning that a change in status is recognized by a formal ritual. Adulthood rituals often involve cutting oneself, being decorated in some specific way, or drinking a foul-tasting potion as part of an elaborate ceremony. After the ceremony is over, the whole community is aware of the person's official adult status.

We have no such ceremonies, so adolescents by and large find themselves isolated from the mainstream of society, and they need to form their own subculture in order to avoid complete isolation. Subcultures invariably have all kinds of rules, regulations, and dress codes so that members can take pride in belonging and can be distinguished from "outsiders." Forming groups and achieving a sense of identity are two crucial psychological issues during adolescence. And they are related to each other in some interesting ways.

Conformity

Because adolescents are left to fend for themselves socially, they evolve small "exclusive" groups, which are used as a form of self-protection. In this way, they don't have to cope with the world all alone. When adolescents identify themselves as belonging to a particular group, they take on its dress code, use its slang, and engage in the group's "approved" activities. All these behaviors add to a sense of belonging. They also help separate adolescents from adults, sometimes by shocking the adults. Thus, adolescents may shave their heads, wear their hair long and shaggy, curl it into points atop the head, dye it green or purple, wear deliberately scuffed boots, or leave the laces untied on their tennis shoes—whatever happens to be in vogue at any given time. For example, when we were adolescents, anyone who wore green on Thursday was considered "weird" and was in for a very rough day, and this "rule" controlled adolescents from coast to coast for several years! Such conformity to the group is understandable: Nobody wants to be alone.

Groups differ in terms of their size, how strictly defined they are, and how closely their rules must be followed. Fairly large groups, with loose rules and relatively changeable memberships are called **crowds**. Crowds usually have shared interests, and the members dress similarly, but their structure is looser than more clearly differentiated groups. Both the **clique** (kleek) and the **gang** are very tightly knit, have a limited membership, and strict rules for admission and proper behavior (Conger and Peterson, 1984). Major differences between the two are that cliques are usually made up of adolescents based on common school-related interests, such as athletics or other types of activities. Gangs, on the other hand, have a rebellious or antisocial outlook and are based on out-of-school activities.

The need to conform to the group in dress and language is strongest in early adolescence, between ages 11 and 14. Toward the end of middle adolescence, around age 16, it has begun a sharp decline. This rapid decline continues through late adolescence so that rigid conformity has almost disappeared by age 18 (Landsbaum and Willis, 1971).

Anorexia nervosa
An eating disorder that involves severe loss of weight from excessive dieting or use of laxatives.

Rite of passage
The socially recognized movement from adolescence into adulthood; requires some ritual.

Crowds
Large groups with loose rules and changeable memberships.

Clique
A very tightly knit group with limited membership and strict rules of behavior; normally tied in with school activities.

Gang
A rebellious, antisocial group with strict rules but not connected with accepted social organizations such as a school.

Most people feel comfortable with the Guardian Angels (left); outsiders aren't sure what to expect from the Savage Nomads.

Group Identity

Group identity versus alienation
Erikson's idea that early adolescents either belong to a group or feel lost (alienated).

An expert in personality development, **Erik Erikson**, sees this support from social groups as necessary for exploring individual identity (Erikson, 1968). Others have expanded on his idea by referring to early adolescence as a time of **group identity versus alienation**. In other words, an adolescent who fails to get a sense of belonging by identifying with a group will feel like a foreigner, alienated from others of his or her age. This adolescent will also have more trouble forming a sense of individual identity toward the end of middle adolescence and through late adolescence (Newman & Newman, 1984).

Individual Identity and Erik Erikson

Personal background often plays a key role in determining what a person emphasizes in both personal and professional life. Such is the case with personality theorist Erik H. Erikson. He never met his Danish biological father, who deserted his mother before Erikson was born; he never even knew his name. His mother was Jewish and married a Jewish physician named Homburger when Erikson was a very small boy. For years, Erikson thought Dr. Homburger was his biological father, and, until he was an adult, he used that last name. (His middle initial, "H," stands for Homburger.)

To protect young Erik from being confused and hurt, his mother and stepfather decided not to tell him about his father's abandonment. From a fairly young age, however, Erik felt that something wasn't right. For instance, his mother and stepfather were rather small, with dark hair and eyes, but he was tall, blond, and blue-eyed—obviously Scandinavian. He also felt out of place with his schoolmates. Those who were Jewish did not accept him because of his physical appearance. Those who were Christian considered him Jewish because of his parents' religious beliefs.

From childhood on, he was confused about his own identity, unsure where he fit in the scheme of things. Eventually he learned the truth about his father, which added to his feelings of insecurity. When he graduated from high school, he had no idea what to do or be. For several years, he wandered around Europe as an artist, painting and sketching, but with no real goals. In fact, he was 25 years old before he decided what he wanted to do with his life. It was then that he met Anna Freud, Sigmund Freud's daughter, and began to study psychoanalysis and child development. As if to free himself completely from his crisis of identity, he took Erikson as his last name, reducing his stepfather's name to an initial.

Due to Erikson's circumstances of birth and to his experiences in childhood and adolescence through young adulthood, his sense of self was poorly defined. It took many years and a lot of trial and error before he understood who he was and knew which roads he wished to travel (Hall et al., 1985).

It should come as no surprise, then, that Erik Erikson emphasizes the importance of forming an individual identity in his theory of personality development. From approximately age 12 until at least the end of the teenage years, accurately defining the "self" is our major psychological task. Belonging to a group is the first step. The next step is seeing how you are different from that group, how you are a unique person. Developing a sense of yourself as an individual means achieving **identity**. Never reaching this goal results in **identity confusion**—uncertainty about who you are and what direction you should take.

For Erikson, adolescence represents a crossroads, a time of upheaval, of selecting from many possibilities the ones that fit. This is not easy to do. As a result, adolescence is not an easy time. Too many decisions are forced on the adolescent too quickly. He or she must not only define the self and learn how to relate to the other sex but also make plans about occupations to pursue (Erikson, 1968). Because these decisions have long-range consequences, they create a lot of anxiety and insecurity.

It is natural for youth to flounder around, going back and forth before completing this task. Most adolescents experiment with a variety of roles, discarding one to try out another. In their search, some will identify with a public figure, perhaps an actor, actress, or rock star, taking on his or her mannerisms and style of dress, at least for a while.

Identity
A sense of oneself as a unique person.

Identity confusion
Erikson's term for an uncertainty about who one is or where he or she is going.

Quiet moments, deep thoughts—trying to sort it all out.

Moratorium
A term used by both Erikson and Marcia to describe the adolescent's delay in making the commitments normally expected of adults.

Delaying the usual commitments of adulthood to find one's identity is called a **moratorium** (meaning a period of "time out"). In our society, this means that adolescents can engage in behaviors that are not allowed for adults; an obvious example is that teenagers are not expected to marry, start a family, or support themselves. On the other hand, think of how your community would react to a group of adults who dressed like teenagers and drove around the local hamburger place hanging out the car windows, shouting and waving at people they know, and you can see that moratorium is definitely reserved for adolescence.

Because achieving an identity takes so long, some youths try to make decisions about their identity too soon. By not giving themselves enough time to sort everything out, they decide on an identity that does not really fit. Such adolescents may end up living a life that is not right for them. They may also marry the wrong person. During adolescence, falling in love is part of the identity process. Adolescents help confirm their own identity by gaining someone else's acceptance. As far as Erikson (1968) is concerned, real love between two people cannot exist until each knows who he or she is first.

Gaining a sense of identity carries with it a number of specific characteristics. The first is a clear and unique definition of self, plus acceptance of that self-concept. Other characteristics are: a commitment to goals and values; active planning for or working toward those goals; and confidence in the future, in the ability to achieve these goals.

When people have a sense of identity, they also have an understanding of **fidelity**. Fidelity is Erikson's term for being faithful to one's ideals and values as well as being loyal to others we care about, even if they don't always live up to our expectations.

Fidelity
Erikson's term for being faithful to one's ideals and values; loyalty.

Individual Identity and James Marcia

Researcher **James Marcia** (1980) expanded on Erikson's work and divided the identity crisis into four states. These are not stages, but rather processes that adolescents go through. All adolescents will occupy one (or more) of these states, at least temporarily. But, because these are not stages, people do not progress from one step to the next in a fixed sequence, nor must everyone go through each and every state.

Identity Foreclosure   Adolescents who simply accept the identity and values they were given in childhood are in a state of **foreclosure** (not giving themselves a chance to explore alternatives). They have not experimented with other possibilities before deciding who they are. Instead, their self-concept has been defined by other people. For some adolescents, a **negative identity** results from foreclosure. These are the kids who were labeled "bad" or "troublemakers" in childhood and who have come to accept that label. Whether the identity is negative or not, foreclosure means blocking off certain possibilities for growth and individuality.

Foreclosure
Marcia's term for the state of accepting the identity and values an adolescent was given in childhood.

Negative identity
Marcia's term for those who are bad or are troublemakers as a result of blocking growth using foreclosure.

Identity Diffusion   Adolescents who don't have a clear idea of their identity *and* who are not trying to find one are in a state of **diffusion**. These adolescents may have struggled with the issue of identity in the past, but they never resolved it, and they seem to have stopped trying. The outcome is a lack of self-identity and no real commitment to values or personal goals.

Diffusion
Marcia's term for the state of having no clear idea of one's identity nor attempting to find that identity.

Moratorium   Adolescents who are trying to achieve an identity through experimentation and trial and error are in a state of *moratorium*, discussed earlier. Adolescents remaining in moratorium or time out may or may not achieve a sense of identity. Some give up the struggle and wind up in a state of diffusion.

Identity Achievement   Adolescents who have gone through the identity crisis and come out with a well-defined self-concept, who are committed to a set of personal values, beliefs, and goals, have reached the state of **identity achievement**. Their identities may well be expanded and further defined in adulthood, but the basics are there, and such adolescents are well prepared to make meaningful lives for themselves.

Identity achievement
Marcia's term for the state of having developed well-defined personal values and self-concepts.

In Focus: James Marcia's Identity States

Foreclosure	Diffusion	Moratorium	Achievement
Individual makes *definite* commitment . . .	Individual makes *no* commitment . . .	Individual *delays* commitment . . .	Individual makes a *firm* commitment . . .
but commitment is *not* based on any internal "soul searching" . . .	and does *no "soul searching"* . . .	and struggles a great deal with internal "soul searching" . . .	after experiencing meaningful "soul searching" . . .
thus, individual *conforms*:	thus, individual *wanders*:	thus, individual *searches*:	thus, individual *finds* identity:
"I think I'm going to be a plumber because my dad and his dad were plumbers."	"I think I'll do some traveling after graduation . . . or maybe I'll get a job . . . or . . ."	"I don't know what I want to do, but I don't want to rush into anything either. I want to find something that's right for me."	"It took me a while to find what I want out of life, but now I think I have a good idea."
In summary . . . Commitment: Yes Searching: No	In summary . . . Commitment: No Searching: No	In summary . . . Commitment: No Searching: Yes	In summary . . . Commitment: Yes Searching: Yes

Intellectual and Moral Changes

Since adolescents must deal with such a staggering number of issues, it is fortunate that their thought processes and moral reasoning have reached their highest level. Agreement that general reasoning abilities reach their peak in adolescence is easily demonstrated. The most popular individual intelligence test for adults starts at age 16 (Wechsler, 1981). The last stage in Piaget's theory of cognitive development—formal operations—begins at age 11 or 12, and postconventional moral reasoning (discussed below), the highest level in Kohlberg's theory, also starts in adolescence.

Jean Piaget's Formal Operations Stage of Cognitive Development

Formal operations
Piaget's term for the ability to reason in abstract ways; complex thought processes.

Formal operations in cognitive (mental) development include the ability to reason in abstract ways—to consider the possibilities instead of being stuck with concrete realities. Adolescents are capable of logical thought, of testing hypotheses. When asked such questions as "*If* such-and-such takes place, *then* what will happen?," most adolescents think through the outcomes in systematic, logical ways that were not possible before. The ability to think abstractly helps the future become more real. Something that potentially exists is just as likely to be true as something that already does exist. Without formal operations, one is limited to the concrete, to the existing order of things. With formal operations, we can deal with what might be, what could be, *if* certain things took place.

Prior to this level of abstract thinking, the world was seen in concrete terms. Thus, if Mary got some extra money, so should Max—period. At the formal operations stage, however, the situation is seen differently. Say that Mary had been deprived while Max had had certain advantages earlier. Making up for past inequalities between the two is fair, the adolescent realizes; Max does not need any money because justice demands that their situations be made more equal.

This high level of reasoning ability helps adolescents consider how the world could be a better place or why personal principles are sometimes more important than external rules and laws. Consequently, it is almost impossible to separate general cognitive abilities or thought processes from moral reasoning.

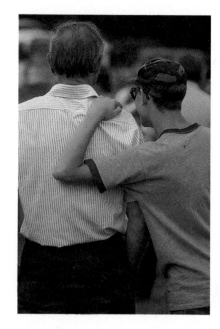

In the midst of difficult developmental crises, special moments stand out.

Lawrence Kohlberg's Postconventional Level of Moral Reasoning

Individuals who have reached the **postconventional level** of moral reasoning make decisions about right and wrong according to basic principles. This holds true even if their actions must go beyond society's laws or authority's rules and regulations. Generally, this level of moral reasoning is not reached before middle or late adolescence.

Postconventional moral reasoning is subdivided into two stages. The first emphasizes **social contracts**. When people agree to something because they believe it is best for everyone involved, they are bound by this mutual agreement, or social contract.

The second stage operates according to **universal ethical principles**; concepts like justice and honor are guidelines for right and wrong. This stage is the most complex and also the one least often reached by most people (Lloyd, 1985).

Lawrence Kohlberg tested his theory by presenting moral dilemmas to people and asking them not only what they would do in the situation but why they would do it. It is the "why" that shows one's level of moral reasoning, not the "what." For instance, in the example in Chapter 10, a person could either save the one rich man in a lifeboat or the ten poor men, but not both. The postconventional answer given was to save the ten poor men because human life has value regardless of wealth. It would be possible, though, to give a different answer from the postcon-

Postconventional level
Kohlberg's term for the level of moral reasoning that uses basic principles.

Social contracts
Kohlberg's term for agreements based on the concept of what's "best for everyone."

Universal ethical principles
Kohlberg's term for concepts such as justice and honor.

ventional viewpoint. Suppose a person said the one rich man should be saved because this one rich man could do more to improve the world through the proper use of his wealth than all ten poor men put together. Thus, the final justification for this choice is that human life has value beyond the people in the lifeboat. This answer is also an example of post-conventional moral reasoning. The same principle is involved in both answers—the value of human life. It is the interpretation of how to apply the principle that differs. But the fact that complex interpretation is going on is the key to this level of moral development.

The Family's Influence on Adolescence

We tend to take the existence of a serious "generation gap" for granted in this country. But does such a gap actually exist? And, if so, is it as serious as we are led to believe? The topic of how parents and teenagers relate to one another raises a number of questions. As before, the answers are slightly different for early, middle, and late adolescence.

Adolescents have been said to live in an "intense present." As a result, death seems quite foreign, and it is not a part of their thoughts very often. The distant future is also excluded from this daily living process. These feelings can be explained by the fact that the majority of adolescents are not tied to major lifelong responsibilities. Without these concerns, only the immediate past and present remain in focus most of the time, particularly in early and middle adolescence. By late adolescence, the future takes on greater importance as high school graduation nears.

But, as you know personally, adolescents are not a vague, wandering group with no sense of reality. Close scrutiny of the adolescent value system shows that what has been absorbed to this point is thoroughly locked in. Goals, such as trying to make life more moral, saner, and more humane—all improvements badly needed—reflect basically the same ideals that are held by most adults. More often than not, parents and teenagers are on the same wavelength. Most parents, at one point in their own past, were aiming for the same thing, and those ideals are still there, but, for many adults, actually working toward those goals has become less of a focus over time.

It is almost a tradition for the press to play up disagreements between children and parents. Despite this, teenagers and parents are in close agreement on almost every issue of importance. A survey of 986 people aged 13 to 18 indicates that youth tend to agree with their parents on the importance of education and the necessity of work, and they have similar views about drugs and politics. The amount of agreement is high, ranging from 78 percent to 83 percent. Interestingly, these percentages reflect agreement with the mother. Across the board, teenagers and fathers don't see eye to eye as much, though the figures are still high: 69–76 percent. The lowest areas of agreement are about sexual matters

Teenaged couple on a date—as perceived by the girl's father. *The Museum of Modern Art/Film Stills Archive*

In general, the "generation gap" is exaggerated by the press.

(with the mother: 69 percent; with the father: 62 percent) and clothing styles (mother: 65 percent; father: 53 percent) (White & John, 1984).

Most adolescents have a good and loving relationship with their parents. They share feelings of closeness and generally get along well together (Conger & Peterson, 1984). As both parents and adolescents know, however, things do not always run smoothly at home. Research has shown that, when children become teenagers, their parents, especially their mothers, experience greater stress, unhappiness, and dissatisfaction than at any other time (Emery, 1982; Degler, 1980).

Although the press has exaggerated the "generation gap," it is true that increased conflicts (arguing, nagging, and so forth) occur during a child's teenage years. This squabbling and bickering is at its worst in early adolescence—roughly between ages 11 and 14. During middle adolescence, it starts to decrease and usually is over, for the most part, by age 16. Late adolescence brings with it greater harmony with parents.

The distress is real even when teenagers and parents love each other and get along most of the time. Why, then, is there so much arguing and bickering between them? Some researchers see conflicts between parents and their teenage children as both unavoidable and *necessary*.

Adolescence as a separate time given special emphasis is a fairly new idea. Many experts believe that it has only existed since the 1920s at the earliest. A century ago, children left home when they hit puberty, and they began to work as apprentices for adults other than their parents; this was particularly true for boys. Among girls, sexual maturity occurred several years later than it does today. For most girls, sexual maturity meant marriage. And marriage meant leaving home (Degler, 1980).

It is only in the recent past that adolescents have remained at home, financially dependent on their parents, for several years beyond puberty. Many agree this is an economic necessity. Others suggest this situation may be an unnatural or artificial arrangement. Those who take this position point to animal behavior for support: Among chimpanzees and other primates who live in groups, the offspring leave their group when they start their own families. If they don't, they are forced out by the adults. A similar situation occurs even among solitary animals like the cougar. Cougars are "loners"; adult cougars stay together long enough to reproduce, and then they go their separate ways. The female rears her young alone. When they start to mature, she makes them go out on their own. A young cougar who doesn't want to leave home will be attacked by its own mother until it finally gives up and goes away.

There is clearly a connection for various animals between sexual maturity, or puberty, and a "natural" desire to become independent of the family unit. Is there a similar connection for humans? Quite possibly there is. It has been noted, for instance, that tension between parents and teenagers is highest during puberty. If the child is an early maturer, conflicts are worse at this earlier stage. If puberty comes later, so does the time of greatest conflict. It is to the advantage of the species for its youth to establish homes and families of their own. Consequently, it may be that puberty in some way triggers conflicts in order to make the separation easier for both sides (Steinberg, 1987).

Because our society as a whole does not have formal puberty–adulthood rituals as the Apaches do, the exact time of adulthood is not clear for most adolescents.

To see how this might work, consider one more example from animals that live in groups, like wolves and chimpanzees. The increase in strength and size plus the additional adrenaline and sex hormones of puberty give both young male wolves and chimpanzees a push to challenge the older, more senior males. By winning such a fight, a younger male can improve his standing in the group. "Adolescent" female chimpanzees seem to provoke irritation in their mothers and are competitors for the males' attentions. In other words, the physical changes of puberty create different attitudes in young animals *and* differences in how they are perceived by their elders (Goodall, 1971). If this is true for chimpanzees, could it also be true for humans?

Primitive cultures with rituals that mark one's entrance into adulthood (the rite of passage discussed earlier) are very clear about this issue. Once puberty starts, the children leave home. In some, even before puberty, older children no longer sleep in their family home. They see their family during the day, but at night they are with other adults or in "dormitories" constructed just for this age group. When they reach puberty, they marry and establish their own households. The separation from their original family is complete.

These studies suggest that making children and parents live together beyond the point of "natural" separation means that conflicts are bound to occur. In the words of one expert: "If teenagers didn't argue with their parents, they might never leave home at all" (Steinberg, 1987, p. 39).

Adolescent Activities and Concerns

A survey of 18,000 high school seniors completed by the Institute for Social Research at the University of Michigan gives an account of the current adolescent world. Driving around, as always, is still one of the favorite pastimes, 66 percent of the seniors having done it in the week previous to the survey. Most time was spent watching TV, visiting with friends, or doing something around the house; the percentage of seniors who had engaged in these activities in the previous week were: 96 percent, 86 percent, and 81 percent, respectively. Thirty percent of those in the survey worried about nuclear war, which is a considerably lower figure than we frequently hear is the case. School attendance was good; in the previous month, 70 percent had missed no school (Institute for Social Research, 1984).

There were two troubling statistics. Thirteen percent had gotten drunk on a binge—that is, had had five or more drinks in a row at some time during the previous two weeks—a very high figure. And, within the past year—a statistic that never seems to get any better—22 percent had been involved in an automobile accident.

Can We Talk?

The level of tension and conflict in any home comes from many different factors. One major source of trouble, though, is poor communication between teenagers and their parents. Most parents will never see this book, so we cannot deal directly with them. But, since adolescents can change the way discussions take place, too, a few rules of good communication follow. Some of them may seem too obvious to bother with, yet very few people follow them, which causes no end of unnecessary problems.

1. Pick a convenient time and place to talk for *both* parties. An example of *not* following this rule is: "Bob, get in here right now! I want to talk to you!" A different example: Bob tells his father he wants to talk to him; his father says, "Sure, I'll be finished with this in a couple of minutes"; Bob gets mad and shouts, "Oh, never mind! You're always too busy to talk to me anyway, so just forget it, okay?" A better approach is: "When you have a few minutes, there's something I want to talk about. How's right after dinner in the living room?" Be sure to set a specific time and place instead of leaving it open.
2. Be direct and clear when you speak, but also be polite rather than rude. If you're too subtle, your message won't get through; most people can't read minds. On the other hand, insults slam the door on communication. Amy tells

Genuine parent/child conflict increases notably with age. The complexities of modern society can require parents and children to live together too long.

her mother, "Your hair looks awful like that!" Laura says to her mother, "I saw a hairstyle the other day that would look great on you. Here, take a look at this picture I cut out of a magazine. Isn't that terrific? It's made for you, I can tell." Which one would you rather listen to and maybe even cooperate with?
3. Take responsibility for your own feelings and accept what the other person feels. Saying, "*You* make me so mad when . . ." puts the responsibility for your anger on the other person. Saying, "*I* get so mad when . . ." puts the responsibility where it belongs. An

example of acceptance is: "My doing that really bothers you, huh?" Nonacceptance is shown by: "Well, I don't see why you're upset! What's the matter with you, anyway?"; or "It's dumb to get so mad when it's not that big a deal." Try to understand that not everyone responds the same way to the same situation.
4. Stick to the subject. This rule sounds so easy, but it is broken all the time. For instance: "Oh, yeah? Well, what about the time you . . .?"; or "I just knew that's what you'd say. You always say that. You've been saying that for so long I'm sick and tired of hearing it"; or "I don't see why I can't have my friends over when I want to. What about Aunt Esther? You let *her* stay here three weeks, *in my bedroom!*" It's impossible to avoid emotional reactions to a sensitive subject completely. The goal is be alert and get the discussion back on track as soon as possible.
5. Don't play the "blame game." Trying to decide who's at fault is very tempting. But it usually doesn't solve anything. Eventually, it may be important to figure out how (not how much) each person contributes to the problem, so changes can be made. For the most part, though, it really doesn't matter who is more to blame. (Trust us!) The real point is that a problem needs to be solved. Looking at what needs changing rather than who is more responsible brings you closer to finding a workable solution.

6. Listen to what is being said. There are several parts to this rule. First, wait until the other person has finished speaking before you start thinking about your own reply. Second, never interrupt unless you honestly don't understand; if you don't understand, ask direct questions. Third, try to rephrase in your own mind what the other person is saying. Fourth, open your mind to the possibility that you may not have "heard it all before."

It is important to remember that following these rules will not solve every problem. Sometimes, even with excellent communication, people still find themselves on opposite sides of the fence.

After you have a basic understanding of these rules, try them out with a couple of friends or classmates, in a group of three. Everyone takes a turn at playing each of three parts: the speaker, the listener, and the referee or "official" who decides when a rule has been broken. The subject you choose to talk about is up to you. However, the more strongly you feel about a topic, the more likely you are to break the rules of good communication.

Summary

1. Adolescence starts at age 11 or 12 and ends at about age 19. Early adolescence runs from age 11 to 14, middle adolescence from 14 to 16, and late adolescence from 16 to 19.

2. Physical growth in adolescence includes sexual development during puberty, which is controlled by the pituitary gland and hormones from the adrenal glands and gonads. Changes during puberty include: maturation of the reproductive system, voice changes, breast development, and changes in facial and body hair.

3. Growth spurts happen earlier in girls, who may grow as much as three inches in one year; boys may later add four inches to their height in a year. In general, early maturation is an advantage for boys, but not for girls, while late maturation is a problem for boys, but not for girls.

4. Belonging to a group helps adolescents feel less alone and is a first step toward developing a sense of identity. Conformity to groups is highest in early adolescence, then falls rapidly from the end of middle adolescence on.

5. Crowds are fairly loose in structure and membership. Cliques are small, rigidly defined groups made up of adolescents with shared school-related interests. Gangs are small, rigidly defined groups with a rebellious or antisocial outlook, whose members share similar out-of-school interests. Those who do not have a group identity feel alienated from others.

6. Erik Erikson views adolescence as a time for developing a sense of identity. This means not only deciding who you are but also becoming committed to personal goals and values. During identity formation, a moratorium occurs, delaying adult commitments so that adolescents have the opportunity to experiment with different roles. Achieving an identity includes developing fidelity, or loyalty to one's values and beliefs as well as to people one cares about. Failure to achieve an identity results in identity confusion, or uncertainty.

7. James Marcia discusses four identity states. Foreclosure occurs when adolescents make identity decisions based on the identity and values given them in childhood by other people. Identity diffusion exists when adolescents have an unclear sense of self and have stopped trying to find themselves. Moratorium means trying out a number of possibilities. Identity achievement includes a clear definition of self and a commitment to the future.

8. During the formal operations stage, abstract thinking and logic are developed. Reasoning is systematic, and possibilities as well as realities can be carefully considered. Moral reasoning involves the application of social contracts or universal ethical principles to determine right and wrong.

9. Adolescents and their parents agree on most important issues, such as the value of education and work, their political views, and attitudes toward drugs.

Mothers' opinions are somewhat closer to adolescents' than are fathers' viewpoints.

10. On the other hand, tension and conflict between parents and children are highest when the children are adolescents. Some researchers believe this is part of a natural separation process that occurs among animals and in more primitive cultures. The greatest conflict arises when the adolescent reaches puberty, regardless of the specific age at which puberty occurs.

11. Adolescents of the 1980s enjoy visiting with friends, driving, watching television, and doing things around the house. Their school attendance is good. A fair number, however, drink too much on occasion and are involved in automobile accidents.

Key Words and Concepts

early adolescence
middle adolescence
late adolescence
puberty
hormones
pituitary gland
adrenal glands
gonads
growth spurt
early maturer
late maturer
anorexia nervosa
rite of passage
crowds
clique
gang
Erik Erikson
group identity
　versus alienation

identity
identity confusion
moratorium
fidelity
James Marcia
foreclosure
negative identity
diffusion
identity
　achievement
formal operations
postconventional
　level
social contracts
universal ethical
　principles

Review Questions

For each of the following, answer E for early adolescence, M for middle adolescence, and L for late adolescence.

1. What others wear is not that important
2. Highest level of arguing with parents
3. Females much more mature than males
4. A 15-year-old
5. Females slightly more mature than males
6. Rather than fighting, parents and adolescents develop greater harmony.

True/False

7. Nearly 10 percent of our sexual maturity occurs during puberty.
8. Less than 20 percent of adolescents have a difficult time coping with biological changes such as growth spurts.

9. Early adolescence is a time of maximum physical growth for females, but not for males.
10. An early-maturing boy generally has a higher self-concept than an early-maturing girl.
11. Both the clique and the gang have strict rules for how to behave.

Fill in the blank. Answer on a separate sheet of paper. (More than one word can be used.)

12. An adulthood ceremony or ritual is called a

＿＿＿＿＿＿＿＿＿＿ .

13. According to some psychologists, the main conflict in early adolescence is group identity versus

＿＿＿＿＿＿＿＿＿＿ .

14. Erik Erikson sees the main conflict in adolescence as identity versus ＿＿＿＿＿＿＿＿ .

15. Sticking to your beliefs is called ＿＿＿＿＿＿ .

16. Delaying commitments about beliefs and values is called ＿＿＿＿＿＿＿ .

Matching (Answers can be used more than once.)

17. No identity and has stopped trying to find one
18. Makes decisions about identity too soon
19. Trial-and-error period
20. Tends to wander
21. Well-defined self-concept
22. Delays making a commitment, but still trying
23. Has made a commitment through searching within
24. Forms an identity based on others' expectations

a. foreclosure
b. identity achievement
c. diffusion
d. moratorium

Discussion Questions

1. The chapter explains that, in our society, it's difficult to determine when exactly adolescence ends. Do you think you'd rather have the end of adolescence more clearly defined, or do you prefer it loosely defined as it is now? Why?

2. If you could be considered, as of this moment, a full-fledged, 100 percent, certified adult, would you want that? Discuss.

3. Consider a 15-year-old from a primitive society who becomes an adult after an elaborate ceremony or ritual (rite of passage). Does this 15-year-old, since he or she is considered an adult and since he or she considers himself or herself an adult, experience some of the same conflicts and frustrations that most adolescents in modern society experience? Explain.

4. Most of us at one time or another have been a part of a clique, whether we realized it or not. Why do people form cliques? Explain. Also, do cliques serve any positive or worthwhile functions? Explain.

5. Compare the ranges of adolescence (early, middle, late) to Marcia's theory of identity states. *When* would an adolescent most likely be foreclosed, diffused, in moratorium, and achieved? Explain. (In answering this question, you may be guilty of generalizing, but go ahead.)

6. Marcia acknowledges that parts of an individual may be foreclosed, another achieved, and so on. For example, an individual may make a firm and personally meaningful commitment to career and be achieved in this area, but this same individual may wander and be diffused in matters of religion, for example. Pick three of the four identity states and explain how you might fit into each category at this stage in your life.

7. As mentioned in the chapter, surveys show that teenagers and adults agree on important issues: education, work, politics, drugs. If you and your parents were surveyed on these four areas, what would the results be? Would the agreement be high? Explain.

8. No matter how well we get along with our parents as adolescents, there comes a point when we need to break away and begin to assert our own independence. There are several ways in which we do this, some of them deliberate and intentional and some of them not so intentional. For example, someone might join an activity at school for the enjoyment of it, which also causes this person to spend less time at home; as a result (but without really *trying* for this result), this person probably becomes more independent. Describe several ways, intentional or not intentional, that you use or have used to break away from your parents. Also, briefly describe your parents' past or present reactions to these ways.

9. Read through the rules of communication listed at the end of the chapter. Which one seems to be the hardest one for you to follow? Offer examples.

Activities

1. As discussed in the chapter, our society does not always make it clear when adolescence ends—we have no formal rites of passage. Often, this leads to confusion and frustration. Here's your chance to eliminate that confusion. Think of an appropriate rite of passage into adulthood for our society today. Make the plan as specific as possible. How old would the person have to be? What exactly would the person have to do? And so on. Feel free to use humor if it helps you to get your point across.

   Once you have an appropriate rite of passage in mind, pretend that you're about to go through it yourself, and describe the experience and your feelings in detail. It may help to imagine that you're writing a journal or diary entry.

2. Often, cliques acquire stereotypical names: jocks, burnouts, brains, and so on. List the names of ten cliques at your school and copy this list onto five other sheets of paper. Next, find five "strangers" or acquaintances at school (not close friends), and show each of them your list. After each clique, have them write down the following: (a) what a person needs to do in order to be admitted to the clique and (b) what is considered proper behavior within the clique. Without looking at their answers, follow the same procedure yourself.

   Finally, compare the lists. We don't want you to use friends for this activity since your friends will most likely have a similar perception of the cliques as yourself. We want you to discover whether "strangers" have the same perception of certain cliques as you do. Do they? Explain.

   If you want to be bold, show your list to one of the clique members you described on your sheet. Does this person feel your perceptions are accurate?

3. Find an article or two on *one* of the following topics and write a report: teenage alcoholism, teenage suicide, teenage depression, teenage pregnancy.

Part of your report will probably be a summary of the articles that you use. In addition to this, however, be sure to include your own reactions to your research: (a) compare and contrast your research findings with what actually occurs at your school; (b) discuss your agreement or disagreement with what the articles state as *causes* of these problems; (c) propose a possible solution to these problems.

4. This activity will give your parents a chance to reminisce about their own adolescence. (If your parents are unavailable, find someone that would be about the same age as your parents.) Have your parents think back on their adolescent years, and have them make a list of things that an adolescent needed to do in order to be "cool" (or what it meant to be "uncool"). Ask them to include at least 10 to 15 items. Without looking at their list, write your own list of things an adolescent needs to do today in order to be "cool." Again, try to think of at least 10 to 15 items.

Compare and contrast the two lists. What are some similarities and differences? Based on the lists, would you say that the period called adolescence has changed much in the past 20 or 30 years? Explain. Finally, show the two lists to your parents and discuss their reactions to the lists.

5. Erik Erikson's idea of identity versus identity confusion is just a small part of his overall theory on lifelong stages of growth. Conduct research on the rest of Erikson's theory and write a report. Focus particularly on Erikson's fourth, fifth, and sixth stages (late childhood through early adulthood).

Do these stages accurately describe what you've experienced and what you're going through now? Explain.

6. Review the information on Marcia's four identity states. Then sift through your music collection (or a friend's) and find four songs that seem to correspond well to the four identity states. For example, if a song describes a young man arguing with his father about

the future, you might conclude that the young man is in a state of moratorium and that the father is trying to foreclose his son's identity.

Once you find the four songs (one for each identity state), write down the lyrics. Underline the words or phrases that seem to indicate that the individual in the song is actively *searching* for an identity, and circle the words or phrases that seem to indicate a *commitment* of some sort. Note: Even your "identity diffusion" song may have words that you can underline or circle; the person in this song, however, probably turns his or her back on these experiences.

Finally, in your own words, explain which song represents which identity state and why. Your answers, of course, will depend on *your* interpretations of the songs, so be sure to *explain* your interpretations.

7. Marcia insists that an active searching for values, beliefs, and goals is essential to forming a meaningful identity. We want you to do some of your own searching. To do this, we want you to answer three main questions:

   a. "Who am I?"
      What are some of your major beliefs and values today? What are some of your strengths and weaknesses?

   b. "Where do I come from?"
      Describe several experiences from your past that have helped shape your personality. Describe the important people who have had an impact on your life.

   c. "Where am I going?"
      What are some of your career goals? Personal growth goals? What are some of your fears about the future?

The subquestions listed are merely suggestions; you need not address every one of them. This is one of those assignments, if taken seriously, that you can refer back to in years to come and really appreciate. (Trust us!)

Moving from adolescence to adulthood brings many joyful moments, many heavy burdens.

Global Look at the Chapter

The mental and social skills developed during childhood and adolescence have been more or less a training ground for what is to follow. Many problems have not been fully resolved, and, in adulthood, the time comes to try to bring everything together into a whole.

Finding Adulthood

No one knows when adolescence ends. Some definitions have it lasting all the way to age 21. To us that seems far too long. To many psychologists, even though society doesn't officially recognize it, a clear landmark in life (and probably the movement into adulthood) occurs at graduation from high school. If nothing else, this is certainly a major turning point in life. One of the biggest shocks comes when a person must break up with high school friends and is separated from the close-knit groups that were so important in the past. Although many try to hold onto the old group, the general rule is that, at graduation, the person is clearly set adrift on his or her own. Something has to be done—job, college, marriage. There is no turning back, so, along with the elation of finally being free, the young adult faces the need to aim in some direction. Even when a person has support from family or friends, the journey is clearly in his or her own hands for the most part.

Officially, though, there is no agreement regarding when late adolescence, adulthood, or aging occur. For convenience, we will break the periods up this way: Late adolescence/early adulthood runs from age 19 to the mid 30s; the midlife transition goes from 40 to 45; middle adulthood is the period from 45 through the 50s, and late adulthood begins at 60. As we discuss age ranges, remember that these are arbitrary. The problems and activities that belong to one age group or another are only generalizations, and not everyone will fit into these neat categories. This is especially true in our present society, since people live longer and healthier lives. As time goes on, the categories of "middle age" or "old age" apply to later and later periods of life.

Late Adolescence/Early Adulthood: 19–35

Despite the confusion regarding when adolescence ends, most people are accepted as adults once they have left home and are establishing themselves in the outside world. Although some start earlier and some later, sometime during their 20s many people take on the adult responsibilities of marriage, career, and children. Regardless of the exact age, in contrast with the uncertainty of adolescence, a sense of identity is gained through these duties, and this makes young adults more stable and less insecure (Baltes et al., 1980). These young adults feel better able than adolescents to share more deeply with others and to make stronger, longer-lasting commitments. They are more emotionally invested in the welfare of other people, particularly their mates and children, they take responsibility seriously, and they can make personal decisions about their own lives—something they have wanted to do for years. Along with all this commitment and responsibility, however, comes a certain feeling of disappointment that the ideals they had in earlier adolescence—a fully satisfactory job, an emotional relationship, or similar hopes—were not as realistic as they had wished. Nonetheless, despite some disillusionment during this period, it is usually overridden by the importance of getting on with the career and doing what the family needs (Gould, 1975).

For many adolescents, graduation marks the start of adult life.

Mid 20s

While careers are very important, most women in their mid 20s, according to statistics, focus on childbearing and caring for the family. Thus, most women carry extra burdens because so many have outside employment as well (Kamerman, 1986; Glick, 1977). Women also make more personal adjustments to the needs of their husbands than vice versa (Livson, 1976). In other words, society still views "man's work" as more sig-

In general, the woman winds up doing the child "maintenance" in the family.

nificant, even if the woman is doing exactly the same job. As a result, at least in theory, the males in their mid 20s are devoting most of their time to occupation and career.

Nothing indicates that women who work outside the home are actually *happier* than those who do not. As a group, however, women working outside the home are well adjusted (Kaluger & Kaluger, 1984). Their feelings about life depend a great deal on their mate's acceptance of their desire to work outside. Some males, though, are still threatened by having a working partner because they are afraid of losing the traditional female emotional support (Bell, 1983).

Many psychological variables interact during this time period. For example, a woman who is married and has a child has finally "made it" in the eyes of society and can relax about her role. But the way things are set up at present, she still *does* require the male's acceptance of her, or her self-esteem goes to the bottom (Lyell, 1984). (This will change later in life, as you will discover, when the woman goes off on her own, not seeking male acceptance.) Meanwhile, the man feels that he has to prove himself and that he is being tested in the areas of independence, occupational competence, and the ability to provide for others. Thus, men try to project the "super male" image and don't like to give away their feelings of fear and anxiety about their new roles—even to their wives (Gutmann, 1975).

While the man is trying to handle his role, the woman faces the prospect of depression. Depression hits in direct proportion to the number and ages of the children, whether she is employed outside the home or not (Pearlin, 1975). Even though this period can bring incredible rewards, it is, if truth be told, at the same time very difficult for both partners. All the wonders of adult life that the couple expected just don't happen, and they begin to blame one another when, in fact, the responsibility lies in most cases with both of them or is just part of life. While people may find that marriage is much better than being lonely, research suggests that no one makes it through this early period without all kinds of difficulties and frustration. At times, "nothing" seems to be working out right: the marriage, the children, the sex life, the job, the financial situation, and so on. If the partners understood that this was the norm, it would be much easier on them because they could fight "fate" together instead of fighting one another. In fact, the difficulties here offer a perfect opportunity for developing a very deep love and mutual respect.

30 to 35 Years

From ages 30 to 35, careers tend to become set and the family is more or less settled, but things are not fully satisfactory because the "sameness" causes worry and doubt for many. Are you doing everything with your life that you could or should be doing? Now that 30 has arrived, should life be reevaluated? Is it what you thought it would be? And, most of all, 30 sounds so much older than 20-something. Stress and a sense of urgency arise. From the 30s on, people begin to count how many years are left rather than how many have passed (Traxler & Linksvayer, 1973). In other words, with a little less struggle and more time for reflection, people in this age group begin to feel that maybe they haven't quite done enough, maybe they should somehow hurry up and set better priorities before it is too late.

In most cases, such feelings are primarily psychological reactions to realizing that age is creeping up rather than a reflection of major problems with the goals or activities established so far. Men in this age group tend to become somewhat more withdrawn and detached, less relaxed and sensitive. Sense of humor and playfulness tend to decline, and energies are turned even more toward careers rather than companionship. Women typically become more anxious, guilty, and full of conflicts, while still investing themselves primarily in their families (Gould, 1975). Such feelings arise in part from the fact that society gives very mixed messages to women: On the one hand, it does not recognize how important and difficult raising a family is; on the other hand, it urges women to do it, saying it is a wonderful thing.

The feelings typical of this period are prime examples of how psychological influences can be self-defeating. The sense of urgency, for instance, tends to drain the fun out of life. In a way, the adult at this stage is making the same mistake that many adolescents make, assuming that some undefined but amazing miracle—fame, fortune, who knows what—should be occurring. People moving into this 30–35 age bracket, who had expected the (nonexistent) miracle to happen sometime in the future, now are looking back and wondering whatever happened to it, or why it didn't occur. To some extent, this unrealistic attitude accounts for the rather humorless behavior of a number of people in this age group. The use of alcohol is sometimes the crutch people lean on to bring out at least a semblance of "fun."

The period from age 35 to 40 is not a clearly defined stage, but instead is a buffer zone to the next one.

Midlife Transition: 40–45

This time period involves real soul searching to decide whether or not things have turned out at least partially as planned. The end of life seems even closer as the person begins to focus on signs of physical decline and an awareness of age (Lerner & Hultsch, 1983).

Midlife crisis
A time of upheaval and loss of purpose that occurs to some people around the age of 40 years.

There is a widespread belief in our society in the existence of a **midlife crisis**. Is it real? For many people, yes, but it is not *inevitable*. In the United States, the age of 40 signals the true beginning of "middle age." But not everyone becomes depressed about it. For some people, this is a time for reassessing their life's goals and refocusing their energies on things that they consider important. For others, though, it is a time of terrible upheaval and loss of purpose, when nothing seems to make any sense. These people seriously question many of the values by which they have previously lived.

Most people do go through some confusion, uncertainty, and dissatisfaction during this period (Neugarten, 1980), which can make them feel

To most young people—to this man at the moment—life seems just about over at age 40. Studies show the opposite is really the case: he has taken the first step toward the "mellow" period of life.

Somewhere in the minds of males in their 40s sits a dread of the heart attack. Health concerns show up at the slightest ache or pain.

that they have moved "backward" psychologically to a more insecure time. Signs of death are all around people in this age group. There is no wide-open future ahead. Their own parents for the first time look really aged. A few friends have even had heart attacks. Their children are almost grown. All of these facts contribute to their feelings of vulnerability and uncertainty.

While people in midlife have the potential for enjoying greater freedom, it is also true that this period can seriously rock a marriage. This is most noticeable for couples whose children are now teenagers (Emery, 1982). Marital satisfaction is at an all-time low; fights over the "children" are frequent. The man especially has trouble since he typically views the grown "children" as obnoxious and demanding, challenging him and his authority while still remaining financially dependent on him and relatively free of responsibilities (Scarf, 1977). Since the "children" are theoretically grown, many women who had never before worked outside the home now go forth, and this often creates a further wedge between the husband and wife.

Strangely enough, the divorce rate does not increase dramatically during this period. Instead, the partners may withdraw into their shells, often attacking each other when they do come out but still staying together. Most divorces actually occur during the first few years of marriage (Degler, 1980).

Middle Adulthood: 45–60

Up to this point in time, most women have been involved with their families and most men with their careers. During middle adulthood, however, priorities seem to shift, and both men and women reverse their

In Focus: Adult Development: "Common" Tasks and Experiences of Men and Women

	"Typical" Man	"Typical" Woman
Mid 20s	Career becomes important Needs to prove himself as a provider—causes anxiety and fear Hides his feelings of anxiety and fear Experiences the common frustrations of marriage	Childbearing becomes important Makes adjustments to needs of husband—wants husband's acceptance of her role Depression is likely—which is usually related to children and work issues Experiences the common frustrations of marriage
30–35 years	Career set Routine—Being 30 seems old Stress and urgency—hasn't done enough Withdrawn, detached, less relaxed	Family settled Routine—Being 30 seems old Stress and urgency—wonders if role of raising family is significant enough Anxious and guilty
40–45 years	Possible midlife crisis May refocus energies—or feel loss of purpose Insecurity—wide-open future Marital satisfaction at all-time low	Possible midlife crisis May refocus energies—or feel loss of purpose Insecurity—wide-open future Marital satisfaction at all-time low
45–50 years	Becomes more feminine Becomes more emotionally expressive, warm, giving	Becomes more masculine Becomes more assertive and independent
50–60 years	Mellowing occurs	Mellowing occurs

focus. Perhaps because midlife is a time of reassessment and taking stock, they discover aspects of themselves that have been neglected, and they seek to give these aspects expression. This is potentially one of the best times of life. In general, men begin to appreciate their more "feminine" characteristics and women their more "masculine" ones (Levinson, 1978).

Beginning sometime in their mid 40s, men become more emotionally expressive and warm, more giving of themselves than before (Scarf, 1977). Relationships begin to be more important than job or money. At the same time, women are becoming more independent and assertive, more determined to go out on their own and do what they want to do instead of making so many compromises for the family. For a while, this situation can create conflicts. As the husband turns to his family to develop his more tender side, the wife has had enough of taking care of people and is vigorously, even aggressively, pursuing her own interests. The children, nearly grown, have little need or desire for closer contact. Thus, the man may feel betrayed and unnecessary. The woman, on the other hand, may bitterly resent his demands when she is finally free to accomplish and achieve on her own (McGill, 1980).

But, finally, there comes a breather, so to speak. The conflict doesn't last. The late 40s and early 50s are a time of mellowing, a time when people become calmer, more accepting both of the changes in their lives and of each other. In fact, men in their 50s accept women as more powerful and dominant than men, a reversal of what was true in their youth (Gutmann, 1975). So, even though on a collision course for a while, men and women settle down considerably once the children leave home.

The Empty-Nest Period

At the beginning of this century, most women were widowed within two years of the marriage of their last child; thus, virtually all of their married life had been spent rearing children. Now, most women who are finished with active motherhood still have 40 percent of their lives left to live, and most couples will be together about 15 to 20 years after the last child leaves (Degler, 1980).

The **empty-nest period** is the time of life after the children leave home. It has been suggested that, for some parents, mothers especially, when the children leave and the "nest" is empty, they feel useless and depressed. While this period does bring major changes, the concept that such feelings are inevitable has been discarded. Most studies now show that the majority of women bypass these feelings (Neugarten, 1976).

Nonetheless, there are still some women who suffer from the problem. Most often, they are people who have led rather restricted lives, lack intimate contacts outside the home, and have few interests or activities of their own. In addition, their marriages tend to be not all that great, so they have little to fall back on (McGill, 1980).

Empty-nest period
The time of life when the children are grown and leave; for some people, this event leads to feelings of uselessness and depression.

Menopause

At some time in their late 40s to early 50s, women go through a period commonly called the "change of life," or **menopause**. Menstruation and ovulation gradually stop as the result of a dramatic decline in the production of female hormones. Since both men and women have both male

Menopause
The "change of life" period for women when menstruation and ovulation stop; some women experience major physical symptoms, such as dizziness and "hot flashes."

and female hormones, this means that, as the female hormone decreases, the male hormone becomes more dominant. Hence, there is a slight lowering of the voice, and facial hair becomes more prominent. Physical symptoms include "hot flashes," dizziness, perspiring, and occasional heart palpitations (Neugarten, 1976).

Much has been made of the psychological problems of this time, but again they are somewhat exaggerated. Only a small number find it necessary to seek medical help (Neugarten, 1980). Still, difficulties can arise, and, for some women, the combination of the empty nest and menopause can lead to alcoholism or drug problems, deep depression, and, on occasion, even suicide (Lyell, 1984).

The Mellow 50s

Once past the mid 40s, some adults feel almost as if they are entering old age. Actually, though, things tend to get much better for most people. There are physical aches and creaks here and there, but there is almost a sense of relief that the struggle to "achieve" is slowing down, and people during this period tend to become more satisfied with life. They accept what they have in the way of money, their marriages become more settled, and they begin to feel a greater mastery of their personal world. Feelings of greater freedom and self-worth are common.

Friends and earlier values become more important, the dreams and goals of earlier years mellow into more realistic hopes, and life becomes a time of sharing with others. For most people, life now doesn't seem all that bad. In fact, this period even has been called the "mellow 50s," the prime of life (Levinson et al., 1975).

Late Adulthood: Over 60

As we grow older, we become more philosophical. We attempt to bring the pieces of our lives together, to reflect on all that we have done, and to see ourselves as part of the cycle of life on earth. Some of the major tasks we face at this stage of life include adjusting to an increased number of deaths among friends, accepting what we have not been able to do, and preparing for our own eventual death. Most older people take comfort in what they have done and relish the fact that at least they will leave something of themselves behind that will continue to live when they are gone.

There are approximately 35 million people over the age of 62 in this country, and the percentage of the population in that age range is increasing steadily. For the first time, the elderly outnumber the teenagers (Bureau of Census, 1984). By the year 2020, one in five people will be over 65 years of age (Eisdorfer, 1983). Average life expectancy is about 72.5 years, or 25 years longer than it was in the early 1900s. Women live roughly six years longer than men, and the majority of women over 65 are widows.

Along with the great increase in the number of older people has come a major expansion in a branch of psychology called **gerontology** (jer-un-TOL-uh-jee), which is the study of older people. Gerontologists study the aging process and the psychological difficulties that go along with it.

Gerontology
The branch of psychology that studies the aging process and the problems of those who are older.

The Aging Process

Aging in our country is a real challenge because, as a culture, we put a premium on youthfulness—to a ridiculous degree. We tend to spend a lot of money on products designed to help us deny or hide the fact that we are getting older. While ours is not the first civilization to struggle with the facts of aging, we may deserve an award for being the most blatant about it. People in other countries fight aging, but most recognize that older people may have grown wiser from their vast experience and should be valued and sought out for this wisdom, while Americans usually do not.

Cellular Time Clocks

The life span for different species is preprogrammed. Within a given species—horse, elephant, human, mosquito—each creature seems to have a fixed length of time on earth (Jarvik, 1975). Today, individual people are not really living *longer* than people in the past did, but *more* people are living into old age. In other words, if you were able to avoid serious disease in the 1800s, your chances of living to about 70 were roughly the same as they are today. The big difference is that today fewer people are wiped out by disease and childbirth at young ages. Unless we can figure out a method for controlling age by some manipulation of genes, humans would still die sometime around 110 years old, even if all diseases were removed (Rosenfeld, 1985).

As we age, our bodily functions slow down, problems with vision and hearing are likely to get worse, and we are more prone to disease and injury. Indications are that this occurs because body cells have internal "time clocks" which dictate how long each particular type of cell will continue to function and replace itself. Toward the end of the life span of a member of any species, the cells have notably deteriorated. In a fascinating study, researchers found that individual cells have a strict limit as to the number of times they will divide through the course of a creature's life. In fact, if cells are allowed to divide a few times and then are frozen for a period, when they are thawed, they will continue the doubling process up to the same fixed number of times—no more, no less (Hayflick, 1979).

Mental Ability of the Aged

Just as bodily processes slow down with age, there seems also to be a slight slowing of certain mental processes. But we have to be careful about assuming that all older people automatically become forgetful and absentminded. The bulk of evidence suggests that this is not the case. In animals and human beings, substantial memory deficits occur only in a minority (Jensen et al., 1980). The decline is most evident in tasks that are learned under pressure within a certain time limit and in things recently learned; long-term memory tends to remain intact. Further, the decline generally does not begin to appear until about age 70 (Hulicka, 1978).

Health and Mental Ability   Health is an important factor in mental ability. Old people in good health do about as well on learning tasks as younger people, as long as no time limit is imposed. Disease or accident, rather than aging itself, is responsible for most of the serious memory problems.

When older people *do* experience trouble with memory, it is very distressing and frustrating for them, it has a strong negative effect on their self-concept, and it causes anxiety and depression (Hulicka, 1978). There are hints that in time we may be able to correct many memory problems of this sort. We know that the number of nerve cells in the brain decreases with age, but this may not be the real source of the trouble, since we have so many of them to begin with. In fact, for the typical elderly person, the brain has shrunk only about 8 percent of its original size by the age of 75. Instead, studies with aged animals and humans show the more important loss is of chemicals that are used to communicate from one cell to another (Smith, 1984). The first "brain transplants" performed involved taking tissue from the adrenal glands, which produce this nerve cell chemical, and placing it inside the brain. While this is probably not the final answer, a number of people gained improved memory from the process. On the other hand, when enough of these chemicals are lost, it can cause senility, as we'll discuss a little later.

One often-neglected consideration is nutrition. Many older people get so fed up with fixing meals for three-quarters of a century or so that they don't eat as well as they should in their later years. In other chapters of the book, we have mentioned how disastrous this is for the mental development of children and adolescents. The same is true for the elderly, only here we are not dealing with development as much as with preservation of the brain cells (Goodwin et al., 1984).

Intelligence and Aging   Old age does not *automatically* indicate a decline in intellectual ability or achievement (Bromley, 1974). In many

Given adequate health and finances, age provides the freedom to do different—even weird—things.

cases, when standard IQ tests are used, older people do not score as high as younger people do, but the reasons do not have to do with intelligence itself. For one thing, those who take such tests may be trying too hard to succeed and may be highly anxious. For another, the test items are usually too small for many of the elderly to see and to handle with comfort. The test is not supposed to be a measure of a person's vision. But most of all, the IQ test is designed to measure school potential, and that clearly is not relevant to older people.

Most experiments aimed specifically at the elderly show it is incorrect to assume that intelligence declines with age (Schaie, 1983). As we've already mentioned, an older person's memory for the most part is intact. Individuals who were bright and active in youth tend to be the same in old age. Most of the time, when you run into an older person who is irritable, stubborn, and rigid, you will find that they were also this way when they were young. Such behavior is usually not the result of aging itself (James, 1985).

Senility Many older people are labeled **senile**, a term that is not very flattering and that refers to a deterioration of mental processes as the result of an aging brain. This term has become so common that many believe senility is inevitable with age. This is not the case. You will also hear that, as people get older and older, they eventually lose so many brain cells that they become mentally impaired. This is also not true. Only disease can result in a loss sufficiently dramatic to have such an effect. *Genuine* senility occurs in only 23 percent of the aged population. Of that 23 percent, only 3 percent are senile by age 70! The additional 20 percent get that way by age 100 (Reedy, 1983).

But substantial brain changes can and do result from a blockage of the blood vessels going to the brain—a condition called **cerebral arteriosclerosis** (ar-teer-ee-oh-skluh-ROH-sis). The major cause of senility, however, is **Alzheimer's disease** (ALTS-high-mers). Alzheimer's results from a loss of the chemicals used to fire the brain cells, as we discussed earlier. It most often seems to arise due to a genetic defect, and over time it leads to a disruption of speech, personality, and body control (Wurtman, 1985).

There is a tendency in too many cases to label the elderly person as senile even when there is no evidence of brain damage (Jarvik & Cohen, 1973). Brain damage is *very* hard to diagnose without evidence of disease or injury. The tragic aspect of all this is that a number of quite treatable ailments can produce symptoms of senility. Somewhere between 15 and 30 percent of those diagnosed as suffering from senility in reality are suffering from depression, alcoholism, or drug addiction (Sloane, 1983). Far too often, when the patient is old, no one bothers to make a thorough examination (Traxler, 1979). This may well be partly a reflection of our youth-oriented culture.

Senile
A broad, often misused, term referring to a loss of mental faculties as a result of aging.

Cerebral arteriosclerosis
A blockage of blood vessels, especially to the brain, that results in the loss of mental faculties.

Alzheimer's disease
The loss of chemical nerve cell transmitters and other damage to nerve transmission that result in mental deterioration.

Concerns of the Aged

Survival in old age is clearly related to having minimal physical and economic dependence on others. In other words, complete reliance on others is the worst thing that can happen to old people. When this occurs, they feel trapped because they no longer can make the changes they want; they no longer have *choice*. Most elderly desire self-sufficiency along with some degree of freedom and activity (Jarvik, 1975). These needs are clearly tied to the most basic fears they have: (1) poor health; (2) social isolation; and (3) having no social meaningfulness (Brody, 1974).

Retirement

Retirement has taken on a very negative image in our society, even though many people look forward to it. For a long time, it was believed that those who retired were indeed a very miserable lot. Some clearly are. For example, some men seem so lost that they follow their wives around the house, driving them crazy. They wind up putting all the soup and canned goods in the cupboard in alphabetical order. After that, they don't know what to do with themselves. So few women have been in the work force for most of their lives and then retired that, at this point in time, we have little data on them. One suspects they will have much less trouble than men, however, since men have been attached most of their lives to a "formal" job and had little time alone, while women are usually already adept at taking care of themselves. In any case, many studies are showing that retirement can be a good thing—particularly if one has prepared for it beforehand. Statistically, most people who are retired are pleased with their status.

You may think that the older someone is, the less active that person will be after retiring but, actually, age is not a very good predictor. Those people who have emphasized independence and personal involvement in life tend to stay active and to look forward to almost every day, regardless of how old they are (Skinner, 1983; Birren, 1983).

Isolation and Bereavement

Social isolation is a fear that the aged have, but it is a fear rather than a reality, for most older people, at least, according to the statistics. Those most vulnerable to isolation are in poor health or without a reasonable amount of money. Although overall our society leaves a great deal to be desired in terms of its approach to the aging, individual families do a pretty good job: The majority of old people are not isolated, withdrawn, or lonesome (Traxler, 1988).

Most old people are not lonely, but the possibility of loneliness is there and can be devastating.

But there are exceptions to this generalization. The death of a close friend or spouse at any time changes life considerably, but it is often more difficult for an older person than for a younger one because of the length of time the two have been together and the reduced chances of finding someone else. An older person whose spouse dies is very prone to developing both psychological and physical illnesses. Severe depression is a strong possibility. Women tend to survive this trauma better than men do, perhaps because men are expected to (and usually do) die first; when something is expected, even if unconsciously, it is always easier to deal with than if it is unexpected (Neugarten, 1977).

Attitudes Toward Old Age

The negative attitude toward aging that exists in this country has a very sad side effect: Many old people themselves have accepted it, and they wind up viewing themselves as a burden (Collette-Pratt, 1976). This can lead to a sense of "giving up," which is very destructive. In fact, surveys show that old people themselves devalue old age *more* than younger ones do (Perry & Slemp, 1980). Even though most elderly are not in institutions (see the next subsection), those that are may be encouraged to remain dependent. Institutional staff frequently do too much for the elderly, keeping them in a subservient role. While their intentions are good, they are making the older people feel even more helpless (Barton et al., 1980).

But positive changes are occurring. Young people are viewing aging in a more positive light, probably because older people today are so much more active for longer periods of time than they used to be. If the shift in attitudes is real and continues in the same direction, we can predict that future generations of old people will have a more positive view of themselves. When that happens, we will have achieved a reasonable view of the life cycle as a whole.

Institutionalization

Everywhere we look, we get an image of the old person in an institution. But only about 5 percent of the elderly live in nursing homes (Bureau of Census, 1983). Most older people still have active ties with their family and friends, which is very good for them and for the family.

Even so, being in an institution is not *necessarily* a bad thing. Whether it is good or bad depends on whether institutionalization is intended to "remove" a person from society and on what the quality of life in the institution is. If institutional life includes the opportunity to visit with family and friends or to take part in such activities as study groups, field trips, or even camping trips, then life can be quite pleasant. If the institution is not well run, however, its elderly residents risk experiencing isolation because they have no meaningful activities, no chance to be around children, and no opportunity to use any of their remaining skills. Depression, giving up, serious physical illness, and death can all quickly result under these circumstances (Bromley, 1974).

Thanatology

Thanatology
The study of death and of methods for coping with it.

Thanatology (than-uh-TALL-uh-gee—*thanatos*, death, + *logy*, study of) is a relatively new area of study that came into its own in the 1970s. Until that time, the general attitude of psychology was that death was a "nonproblem," a "nontopic"—something to be ignored. This has changed noticeably.

Hiding from Death

One of the most common complaints from thanatologists is that our society refuses to admit that death exists. We do everything in our power to hide from it and to shield others from its existence. The reality of death is denied by the sentimental or sensational deaths so often seen in the movies or on television. The portrayal of death as glorious and uplifting or at least sudden and dramatic ignores the reality of it all. We even hide the grossness and agony of killing in wartime by making it the action of patriots and heroes. While patriotism and heroism are not bad in themselves, in this case they are part of an attempt to escape from the basic fact of a person's death and the decomposition of the body.

Check out sympathy cards sometime: There will actually be *no* reference to the fact that a life has ended. Mentioning death in such a card is taboo. Although flowers are the most popular picture on the cards, these flowers are not alive and growing, nor are they ever shown in some kind of container, like a vase (McGee, 1980). Apparently, the card manufacturers don't want to suggest anything resembling an urn.

Issues Regarding Death

One theme occurs continually in recent studies about those who are dying, and it is so basic that we usually don't pay any attention to it: Death has never happened to any of us before. We may have read about it, come close to it, or seen someone else's death, but we ourselves have never experienced it. Thus, we face the ultimate unknown, and the fact that our society refuses to admit that it is a natural process gives the unknown an added dimension of terror (Kübler-Ross, 1975).

We must be careful about assuming that every normal person is afraid to die. In cases of terminal illness, a number of studies have shown that most old or dying people eventually come to accept death as a natural process, and they are more concerned about making preparations for the end than about the end itself. They may well have periods of being anxious and scared, but they benefit greatly from a chance to talk about their feelings (Kastenbaum & Costa, 1977).

What are terminally ill people most afraid of? They have three basic fears: (1) loss of mastery over oneself; (2) separation from loved ones;

The meeting of two lifestyles. It's fascinating to look carefully at this encounter for a few minutes and try to imagine what each person is thinking.

and (3) the gnawing fear of being replaced by another (Kavanaugh, 1974). Their major concern is about being left alone in an unpredictable situation where they are also faced with the frustration of not being able to do anything about it. Those who suffer most are unable to risk the unknown, which comes only with the realization that they are indeed important and that they have had a significant life. People need to leave life with a sense of having accomplished something—not necessarily something earthshaking, but important things like having done their best in many circumstances or having helped another person who may then in turn have helped someone else. In other words, the biggest struggle is to understand that we did become "heroes" and "heroines" in our own right during our lifetime (Imara, 1975). Those who work with the dying, then, must concentrate on demonstrating that the life these people have led was important. The dying person needs reduced conflict, time to assemble inner resources, and a continued relationship with a loved one up to the end.

Stages of Dying

A researcher on death, Elisabeth Kübler-Ross, proposed that people who are terminally ill go through a series of stages as they approach death. She suggested that first they *deny* that they are dying. This is then followed by *anger* or resentment that it is happening to them. Third, people try to *bargain* with God for a little more time. Fourth, they become *depressed*, and finally they adopt a more or less *peaceful* attitude toward the whole event, trying to *tie up* loose ends for themselves and their loved ones (Kübler-Ross, 1969).

In many ways, Kübler-Ross created a double-edged sword with her suggestion. On the one hand, her system holds up in a general sort of way and helps explain many of the behaviors of people who are terminally ill. On the other hand, critics of her system feel that it takes away from the individuality and personal responses each of us may have if we face this crisis, so it may rob the dying person of respect for his or her personal feelings. Thus, if someone in this situation is angry about something, he or she may indeed have a legitimate cause other than the illness, but too many people will say, "Oh, he's going through the anger stage; that's all" (Kastenbaum & Costa, 1977). Today there is a movement toward acceptance that, although the emotions of the dying person may well follow a rough pattern, he or she should be recognized as an individual all the way up to the end.

Help for the Dying

While you may not agree with all the conclusions of the thanatologists, it can be interesting to look at some of the other things they believe.

In Focus: Kübler-Ross's Stages of Dying

The Monologue of the Terminally Ill . . .

Denial "There must be some mistake with the test results. Are you sure you're looking at *my* results? This is nonsense. I'll just have to get another opinion—from a doctor who knows what he or she is talking about."

Anger "Why me? I exercise every day. I don't smoke. I do all those crazy things you're supposed to do to live longer. It's not fair."

Bargaining "Please, God, let me live another year and I promise I'll go to church every Sunday. It's just that there are a couple of things I want to accomplish. Just another year."

Depression "I become sad thinking about all the friends I'll miss. I grieve when I think of losing my family."

Peaceful Acceptance "I'm not afraid to die anymore. I know now that death is part of life. I still feel sad at times, but I've come to accept death, and I'm at peace about it."

For one thing, they point to the fact that dying away from home is a relatively new thing and is primarily an outgrowth of our mechanized society. In many parts of the world, death is prepared for by the family unit, with everyone participating, including the person who is dying. One of the most frightening experiences is being alone when dying. If at home, the person feels considerably less alone. In fact, most present funeral rituals started out as something done within the home. Thus, washing and preparing the body were previously done by the family. The "wake"—in which family and friends stay with the body—was common before mortuaries existed. The body was kept outside, and members of the family stayed up during the night to keep animals away from it in order to preserve it until the funeral. No one is suggesting that this last part be done today, but many point out how death used to be part of a natural, ongoing process of life itself.

The Amish (AH-mish) society has managed to hold onto its traditions separate from the hectic modern world and is a model for handling death. These people still make a living by farming, using horses instead of tractors, and in general have resisted so-called scientific advances. When someone dies, the immediate family is relieved of all work except for making a list of people to be notified. The family assumes responsibility for dressing the body in special funeral clothing. (Each person in the community has his or her own set of white garments to wear only when

Our society has real trouble accepting death as part of an ongoing process. This is a funeral for a 16-year-old whose heart was used for another person. In a way, from the death, life goes on.

Hospices
Places where terminally ill people can live out their lives in comfort and away from a hospital.

he or she dies.) Everyone is prepared for death, and the attitude is one of acceptance. Most Amish people die at home in the presence of their families. This is in stark contrast to the rest of our country in which three-quarters of the deaths take place in institutions (Bryer, 1979).

One emerging trend is the use of **hospices** (HOS-pis-es), places where terminally ill people can live out the remainder of their lives in relative comfort and away from the coldness of a hospital. Most hospices are "open" 24 hours a day for visits by family, friends, and pets. The goal is to provide a warm setting in which death is accepted. They are more like homes than hospitals, and they provide almost any activity desired as well as the opportunity to talk about feelings and concerns with others who are in the same situation (Melzack & Wall, 1982).

Trying to Look to the Future

Of all the chapters in this book, this one probably seems the most unrelated to you at this point in your life. This might be a good place, therefore, to try to bring together some of the overall issues discussed and to offer a little speculation that may give some order to the subject matter.

First of all, you may have noticed that many of the descriptions of the concerns of different age groups had a somewhat negative tone to them. This is not because, from your age onward, everything is a disaster or something close to a disaster. Instead, it merely reflects the fact that, if all is going well, there's hardly anything to say about it—in other words, there's not much research to report. Psychologists rarely are involved when life is moving along wonderfully; we just wish the people well and hope for their continued success.

There is one problem, however: Parents and other older people tend to wrap a cocoon around their children, but, when the children are older, as you are, the adults never draw the line and say "*Now* let's tell the truth in its entirety." One of the best examples of this is the information you get about marriage. Despite all the research, the truth of the matter is that we don't know how to predict a good marriage. While it is obvious that, if two people can't get along before marriage, they are not going to get along after marriage, the rest is vague. Love is one of the most

powerful emotions in the world, and the old question "Is this *true* love?" is a rather silly one. All love is true love—for as long as it lasts. The real question is how long and enduring it will be. Nobody knows the answer to that—no psychologist, no test can accurately predict it. The truth is that you find out if your marriage is a good one only if and when it continues to make you and your partner happy and allows you to grow, all the time while putting a lot of hard work into the relationship. The point is that the tinge of negativity in some places is but to keep you from feeling too abnormal later if things start to go wrong with marriage, job, or family. People still tell their children that marriage is the most wonderful thing in the world. That is too sweeping a statement. With luck and work, it will be wonderful. You won't know beforehand—the 50 percent divorce rate shows that.

Most older people you are around will act as if they know a big secret that you are not privy to yet. This "secret" is almost always hinted at in the phrase "Wait until you . . ." whatever. All this means is that you have not yet experienced the trouble or difficulties that the older people have had. There is no real secret, but it makes the adults feel a little more important to have survived the crises you still face.

For example, the period of middle age has extreme ups and downs, just as you have at times.

True stability is hard to hold onto at any age. All the love of the parent for you is still basically there, but friction is going to develop until you, too, have gone through the ritual of things being badly messed up—bills, health problems, job threats, threats to family integrity, feeling inadequate, and so forth. It is sort of an initiation, so everybody gets back together again after you have spent some years with your share of unpleasantness. This may seem weird, but it is very common. In many ways, the whole thing is like a tribal rite.

To state the obvious, death is something we all try to avoid. But that is a shallow statement. The majority of old people are not sitting around waiting for and fearing dying. While it is sometimes hard for many of us to separate the fact that the body is deteriorating from wanting to avoid being close to death, they are two entirely separate things. There are so many stories about old people being "senile" and long-winded that many young people avoid them. This is a sad situation, since most old people have cast off their prejudices and are quite interested in younger people, in what they think and do. Those who are boring were boring when they were in high school and on through adulthood. A friendly relationship with an interesting older person can bring incredible rewards to both of you.

Summary

1. During late adolescence and early adulthood, most people start their families and careers. In very general terms, the male devotes most of his time to career and the female to family, even if the woman works outside the home.

2. From age 30 to 35, people begin to feel that they are growing older; this is a time for reevaluating their lifestyle.

3. In the 40s, some people experience a midlife crisis. This shows up most clearly between the mid 40s and 50s with the empty-nest period and menopause.

4. The 50s and late adulthood are a time of mellowing and peace for most.

5. Aging results from a slowing down of cellular growth. Mental ability for most people is quite good, although a little slower than before. Senility occurs in a minority of the elderly. The symptoms of Alzheimer's disease result from nerve cell chemicals being depleted by the disease.

6. While isolation or institutionalization are feared, neither is the common lot of the elderly person.

7. Thanatology is the study of death; it emphasizes making death a natural part of the life cycle. Dying people should be an active part of the family as much as possible. There is much opposition to how we handle death in this country.

Key Words and Concepts

midlife crisis
empty-next period
menopause
gerontology
senile

cerebral
  arteriosclerosis
Alzheimer's
  disease
thanatology
hospice

Review Questions

True/False

1. Studies show that women who work outside the home are generally well adjusted.

2. A sense of humor tends to decline for many people during the period from age 30 to 35.

3. The midlife crisis, though not as tragic as everyone used to think, is inevitable.

4. Marital satisfaction is typically at a low point during the midlife period.

5. The divorce rate increases dramatically during the midlife period.

6. Men and women tend to reverse their focus—or adopt the others' characteristics—during middle adulthood.

7. Studies show that the majority of women never experience the empty-nest period.

8. The onset of menopause tends to create significant psychological problems for the majority of women.

9. Studies show that the majority of old people are isolated, withdrawn, and lonesome.

Fill in the blank. Answer on a separate sheet of paper. (More than one word can be used.)

10. The study of death is called _____ .

11. The study of older people is called

_____ .

12. Women live roughly _____ years longer than men.

13. The blockage of blood vessels going to the brain is called _____ .

14. Older people are often called _____ if their mental processes seem to deteriorate.

Multiple Choice

15. Alzheimer's disease disrupts:
    a. speech
    b. body control
    c. personality
    d. all of the above
    e. a & b only.

16. Which of the following is *not* a myth about senility but is true?
    a. Senility is caused by disease.
    b. Senility occurs to a majority of older people by the age of 70.
    c. The brain cells lost during aging lead to mental impairment.
    d. Senility is inevitable with age.

17. Those people who were highly active in youth usually:
    a. Slow down in old age
    b. Remain active in old age
    c. Live very long lives
    d. Experience fewer worries about old age.

18. If a person living in the 1800s avoided disease, the chances of that person living to 70 were:
    a. Still worse than today
    b. About the same as today
    c. Better than today.

Discussion Questions

1. As noted in the chapter, society still views "man's work" as more significant than woman's. If you're a male, would it bother you if your wife's career was more "significant" than yours and if she made much more money than you? Why or why not? Be honest. If you're a female, would it bother you if you made more money than your husband? Why or why not?

2. When you hear about research on manipulation of genes to prolong the life span, do you tend to become excited about the prospect, or do you think the life span is something that really shouldn't be toyed with and manipulated by science? Argue for one of these points of view.

3. The chapter explains that the number of people over 65 has increased dramatically and will probably continue to increase. Let's assume that many of these people choose *not* to retire; consequently, the unemployment rate among young people rises sharply. Should the older people be forced to retire? Why or why not? Explain.

4. If you were about 75 years old and were unable to live independently, do you think you'd prefer to live in a well-run nursing home so you could associate with others your age, *or* do you think you'd rather live with your own children (assuming they welcome you!)? Explain.

5. The chapter describes several ways in which our society tends to ignore the reality of death. For example, even sympathy cards avoid mentioning words like "death" and "dying." What are some other ways in which we ignore it? Explain. Consider language, hospital procedures, and funeral rituals.

6. If you found out that you had only a year to live, would you be likely to continue to live life as usual, or would you drastically alter your life-style? Explain. If you *were* to change your life drastically, what would you do differently? Be specific.

7. Imagine that you're a parent and your 18-year-old son announces that he wants to marry the 16-year-old girl-friend he has been dating for the past two years. Would you try to talk him out of it? Why or why not? Would your answer be different if the situation were somewhat reversed, and your 18-year-old daughter announced that she wanted to marry her 16-year-old boyfriend? Explain.

Activities

1. The chapter mentions that graduating from high school and breaking off with friends can often be a shock to young people. In fact, college students seem to be one of the groups hardest hit by depression. Contact someone who graduated from high school within the past year or two and interview the person. Possible questions: (1) Do you still see many friends from high school? Why or why not? (2) What's the biggest adjustment you had to make after high school? What kinds of things get you down? (4) What worries you most about the future?

2. For this activity, we want you to consider your future—not only what you'll be doing but also how you'll feel about yourself. Imagine yourself at the ages of 30, 40, 50, and 60. Then write four journal entries (one for each age) in which you assume the point of view of one of your future selves each time. Note: The ages are approximate. If it makes more sense to you, for example, to use the age 33 instead of 30 go ahead. You might save this journal for the future to see how accurate your predictions turn out to be.

3. If we summarize some of the findings discussed in the chapter, we might say that adults in early adulthood (19–35) tend to be stressed and anxious, while adults in middle adulthood (45–60) tend to become more compassionate and mellow. This is obviously a generalization and not true for everyone, but we want you to use this as a basis for this next activity. Conduct an experiment to determine whether "middle" adults, being more relaxed, will be more likely than "early" adults to help a stranger.

General Procedure: Walk through a mall with a shopping bag that has a ripped bottom. Stuff the bag with merchandise and some papers. As you approach someone in the mall, allow the contents of the bag to slip through the bottom of the bag and then record if the person helps. Repeat this procedure 20 times, half the time on "early" adults, half the time on "middle" adults. (You'll have to use your own judgment here as to ages.)

Specific Points: (1) The reason you want to include papers in the bag is that papers will tend to cause a mess and will create a *need* for help. If you simply dropped an item or two, others may not feel that you need any help from them. (2) You probably want to conduct this experiment with a friend. One person can drop; the other can record. (3) Record not only if the person bent down to help you but also what the person said or didn't say, and so on. In other words, record as much information as possible about each subject. (4) If possible, test only subjects who are alone. If they're with others, this may be a factor that influences their helping behavior, and this is not what you're testing in this case. (5) If possible, divide your subjects equally between men and women. If this is not possible, try to use all men or all women. Again, gender is not a factor that you're studying either, and this will be one way of partially eliminating this factor.

Discuss your results. Can you draw any conclusions? Was our hypothesis about the characteristics of the two age groups supported by your findings? Explain. Be sure to include the specific reactions of each subject.

4. As mentioned in the chapter, our society is obsessed with youth, and many products on the market today reflect this obsession. In fact, many products seem to be designed to stall or deny the aging process. Collect several advertisements that promote these kinds of products and organize them in a creative way for a collage. Note: Some products may not be specifically designed to stall or deny the aging process, but perhaps you can somehow display these products to show how they reinforce the obsession with youth.

5. Write a dialogue between a husband and wife arguing about whether they should invite one of their parents to live with them. The parent in question is not always able to move around easily. One person in the dialogue should support housing the parent; the other should be against it. End the dialogue with some kind of resolution. The dialogue will certainly be influenced by several factors: if the husband and wife have children living at home; if the husband and wife both work; and so on. You can fill in these details in any way you like.

You don't need to use quotation marks, but make it clear when a new speaker is talking—maybe by using different colored pens or skipping lines or introducing each speaker with *H* and *W* (for "husband" and "wife") or giving names to your characters.

6. Conduct research on Alzheimer's disease and organize your information into a report. Be sure to include your own reactions to the material—not reactions like "Oh, it's horrible," since no one would disagree with that, but more along the lines of what should be done to help these people or to increase public awareness, and so forth. Also answer some of the following questions: (1) What are the stages of the disease that an Alzheimer's patient experiences? (2) What are the possible causes? (3) What research is being conducted on "cures"? (4) Is there anything one can do to reduce the risks of getting Alzheimer's disease?

7. Visit one of the following three sites and write a report from the point of view of whether you would ever want to be a "customer" at the place—assuming you *needed* the services. Explain in detail why you would or would not want to be a customer.

   a. Nursing home: Talk to someone in charge who can inform you of the services and activities that the facility provides. Also, find out the costs of the care. If possible, visit with a few of the residents to get their feedback on the facility.

   b. Funeral home: This may sound a bit morbid, but visiting such a place when you don't really *need* to can be fascinating. Again, find out about services and costs. Ask the director about the main functions of funeral homes in our society.

   c. Hospice: More and more hospitals are developing hospice programs as an option for terminally ill patients. The chances are good that you can find a hospice in your area. Find out about the services provided, how a hospice is different from a normal hospital setting, and the functions that hospices serve.

We automatically assume that the boy will stop the girl in this game, but is there no doubt at all about it?

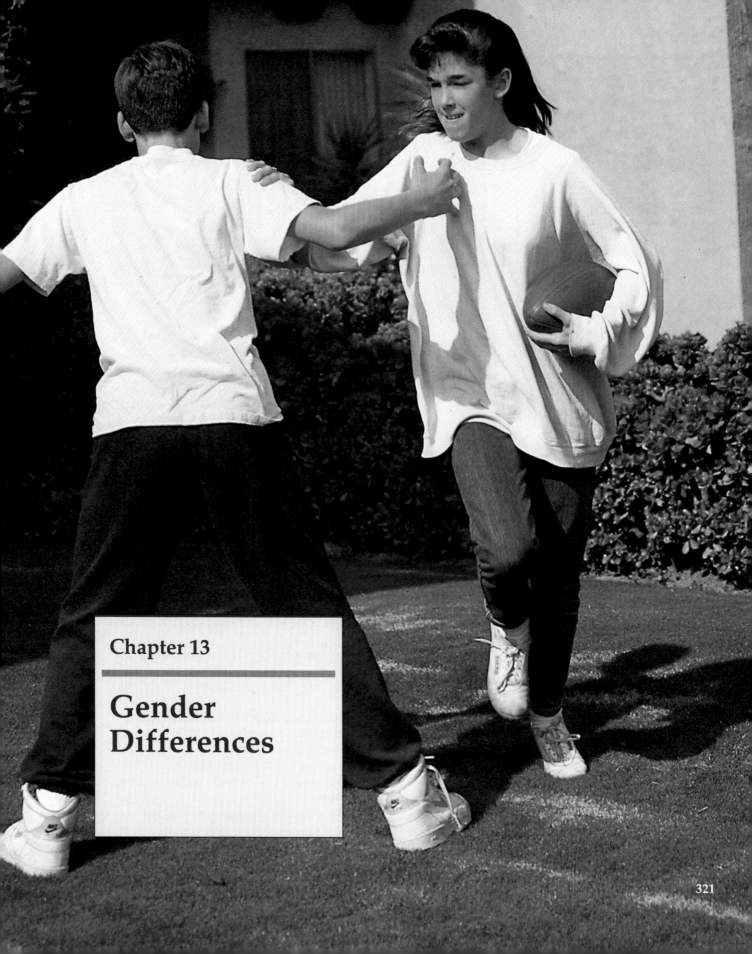

Chapter 13

Gender Differences

Objectives

Be able to:

1. Explain the role of hormones in gender development.

2. List and describe the areas of mental ability in which males and females show differences.

3. Explain why in each of these areas we cannot come to a firm conclusion about the results.

4. Explain if the evidence is clear women have strong maternal drives.

5. Explain the process of identification.

6. Describe androgyny and the positive and negative aspects of pursuing it.

Global Look at the Chapter

There are all kinds of myths about differences between the sexes. In this chapter, we explore what science has learned about the differences between males and females. In general, the two sexes are quite similar. A few differences have been found, but most of them have social rather than biological sources.

In Focus: Gender Quiz

Complete this true/false quiz before reading the chapter. (See Activity number 5 for answers to the quiz.)

1. Females have fewer genetic defects and have greater endurance than men.
2. The front part of the brain is more developed in males than in females.
3. Males have a natural ability to handle mathematics better than females.
4. Males are more oriented toward achievement than females.
5. Women seem to have a special, natural ability to take care of children—some might call it a "maternal instinct."
6. Only females experience monthly hormonal changes.
7. Studies show that the happiness level of mothers rises automatically after the birth of their children.
8. If parents are extremely strict, the children will tend to develop more masculine traits.

Male and Female—A Brief History of Myths

The word **gender** refers to the sex of an individual, either male or female. Studying the similarities and differences between the sexes, as you might imagine, has had a rather colorful history. In the old days, the males' desire for domination led to some bizarre "scientific" attempts to show that the male is smarter than the female. We might look at a few of them.

One of the claims by males 100 years or so ago concerned brain size. Since women have smaller heads than men, their brains must be smaller, so the male scientists said that females were not as bright. This idea was finally given up when it was discovered that physical brain size is not related to intelligence. Then the scientists decided that the front part of the brain was better developed in the male. So that must be the area showing that men were smarter! But they found this, too, to be false since it was eventually shown that the female was as developed in this part of the brain as the male was. These disputes became stranger when it was claimed that the male hormones kept men's minds cool and "dry," leading them to have a clever, "dry" wit. Then it was said that females should not be educated because this drained vital fluids from their bodies. And so forth. The point is that male/female relationships have been dominated even in science by mud slinging rather than by research. Today, the studies are much more scientific and accurate, and we hope we can shed some light on what differences, if any, really exist between the two sexes.

A distinctly unfeminine lady, old West outlaw Belle Starr and her husband "Blue Duck." Note handcuffs.

The Role of Hormones

Each of us, male or female, has both male and female hormones, regardless of gender. **Hormones** are chemical agents that cause physical changes in the body. There are two types of sex hormones, **androgen** and **estrogen**. Males have more androgen, and females more estrogen. Whether a person becomes male or female results from which hormone is present in the fetus in greater quantities. Until the second month of development, male and female fetuses are exactly the same. Basically, it is a matter of one hormone being dominant in each individual. Thus, which sex we become depends on inheritance, which causes certain mechanisms to increase the amount of one hormone over the other.

Hormones have some interesting effects on male/female behavior. For instance, injection of androgen into a pregnant monkey can produce an offspring that by nature should be female but that also has some physical male characteristics. Androgen injected into a human adult female can increase her aggressiveness. And male monkeys with too little androgen will show many patterns of behavior normally found in female monkeys.

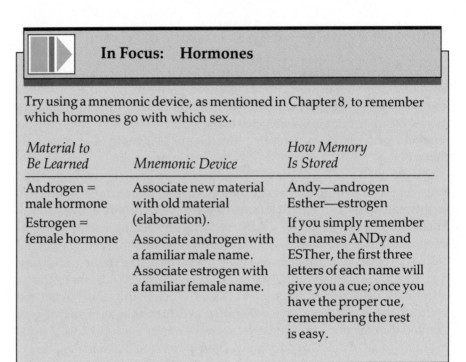

Try using a mnemonic device, as mentioned in Chapter 8, to remember which hormones go with which sex.

Material to Be Learned	Mnemonic Device	How Memory Is Stored
Androgen = male hormone Estrogen = female hormone	Associate new material with old material (elaboration). Associate androgen with a familiar male name. Associate estrogen with a familiar female name.	Andy—androgen Esther—estrogen If you simply remember the names ANDy and ESTher, the first three letters of each name will give you a cue; once you have the proper cue, remembering the rest is easy.

A Tierra del Fuego native. In times of famine they ate older women to spare the dogs. But the question is, "What sex is this person?" (We don't know.)

Levels of sex hormones can be off slightly without producing serious abnormalities, yet they can result in slight changes in behavior. For example, some years ago a number of pregnant women were given medication that had the side effect of making their bodies produce more androgen than normal. Their female offspring tended to be somewhat "tomboyish." On the other hand, males who before birth had their androgen production reduced were a bit less rough and aggressive. In both cases, though, it is important to remember that the children were not abnormal; they were behaving within the normal range for their sex (Ehrhardt, 1979). When the levels of hormones are genuinely defective, children with characteristics of both sexes can be born. For instance, some can have the internal equipment of males but the external parts of females, or vice versa.

Despite these findings, hormones play a lesser role in humans than they do in other animals. For the most part, we are able to limit their effect on our behavior and on how masculine or feminine we feel.

Male/Female Differences

Males are bulkier and stronger as a group compared to females, but females have fewer genetic defects, live longer, and have greater physical endurance. The other obvious, major male/female difference is that the female bears the offspring and provides the nourishment for the infant, which creates a very strong bond between the two.

Childbearing—The Only Absolute Difference

The only activities, then, that clearly and absolutely belong to one sex are those involved in reproduction. Only a woman can bear a child and make milk to feed that child. All other differences are simply a matter of degree or frequency of occurrence. In other words, there are certain trends for one gender versus the other, but no rule holds hard and fast. For example, the average male would hesitate to come up against a female wrestler in an alley. The average female wouldn't want to compete with a male hairstylist in that field.

You may have heard that men can get pregnant. While this is quite an exaggeration, there is some truth to it, as long as we put quotation marks around "pregnant." There have been cases of men with serious psychological problems who begin to believe they are pregnant. They go through all the symptoms of pregnancy, including morning sickness. Remarkably, their bellies begin to enlarge so that, as time progresses, it indeed appears that they have a baby in there. At the end of nine months, though, no baby is there, just a great deal of body fluids that have accumulated. This is a remarkable demonstration of the power our minds have over our bodies, but it certainly doesn't contradict the fact that childbearing is the exclusive province of females.

Activity and Aggression

We usually see aggression as primarily a masculine characteristic, and males do indeed generally show more aggression than females (Deaux, 1985). Does this mean, then, that females are not aggressive? Absolutely not. Given the right circumstances, females may not only equal males in aggressive behavior but may also exceed them (DeBold, 1983). What it does mean is that more males than females are more likely to behave this way in more situations. For instance, when packed together in a big crowd, men tend to get aggressive while women tend to get nervous (Schettino & Borden, 1976).

This is important: Researchers note that attention is rarely given to gender similarities. And yet the sexes are far more alike than they are different. In other words, gender differences are the exception; gender similarities are commonplace (Money, 1980). We can discuss what differences do appear, but we are always faced with the additional problem of sorting out which differences are biological and which are learned—a formidable task.

Gender differences in *activity level* appear in infants as early as 45 hours after birth, with males more active. When asleep, male children twitch and jump, use their muscles more; females smile more. Male children engage in more physical activity than females. This difference also shows up in monkeys, suggesting a biological origin. From infancy, male monkeys are wrestling, pushing, and shoving one another, while females are relatively quiet (Caplan, 1984). Such findings have, in the past, been interpreted to mean that the female wants to be dominated. *Very few people now agree with that suggestion.* In fact, when a male monkey gets a little too heavy-handed, the female will clobber him one; this has been known to happen among humans too.

The best-documented difference between males and females, then, is in the area of rough physical play, probably the result of different hormone levels. If male hormones are given to a pregnant monkey and the offspring is female, she will engage in rough play just as the males do (Maccoby & jacklin, 1974). Similar results appear among humans if the mother has had an accidental excess of male hormone before the female infant's birth.

Intelligence

In infancy, the basic intellectual processes of the male and female seem the same. Over time, however, each sex develops more elaborate skills in a given area than the other sex does. Despite this, scientists suspect that males and females are very close in overall intellectual abilities (Feingold, 1988).

Spatial Skills

Spatial skills
The ability to imagine how an object would look if it was moved about in space.

At about 11 years of age, boys begin to score better on tasks involving mathematics and spatial skills. **Spatial skills** refer to the ability to imagine how something would look in space—for example, getting a three-dimensional image of the parking lot if the cars were parked at right angles to the curb and then mentally rotating them so that they are parked parallel to the curb. Video games involve considerable spatial skills. In general, boys are better at these games than girls, but there is a "trick" here in that girls don't get involved with these machines very often. When they do, they learn the skills quite well. (See Chapter 2, where we discuss a study comparing males and females on video games.) There also are unexplained research findings such as this one: A study of 3,000 junior and senior high school students found that 13-year-old girls scored better on spatial skills than boys the same age (Meece et al., 1982). Whatever differences in spatial skills exist are best explained at the moment as resulting from differences in social role, social class, ethnic background, and the type of test given, rather than from differences between the sexes.

Some people have suggested that there might be physical differences in the brains of males versus those of females. Indeed, the brains do differ: Certain areas in the brains of one sex will have more cells than the same areas in the brains of the other sex and vice versa, but to date we have not been able to relate these facts to any differences in mental abilities (Swaab & Fliers, 1984). In fact, such findings can lead to the same type of claims cited at the beginning of the chapter with men trying to show that women are not as bright. This would be hard to prove because school-age girls take an early lead in verbal skills (word problems, reading, and the like), for example, and continue to hold a slight edge in this area through the years.

Mathematical Ability

A study of 40,000 seventh-grade students showed that by age 13 males did better than females on the Scholastic Aptitude Test (SAT) that measured mathematical reasoning. There were 13 boys to every 1 girl scoring over 700 (95 percent) on the math portion of the test. Boys *seem* to have a wide lead in the area of mathematics (Benbow & Stanley, 1983). This difference is real, but explaining it is a whole other issue.

A few have argued that, because girls can have the same formal training as boys in mathematics if they want to, these tests must indicate some innate, basic difference between the sexes (Benbow & Stanley, 1985). But evidence for this claim is at best quite mixed.

Problems that contradict a theory of male superiority in math show up in other studies using the same group that took the Scholastic Aptitude Tests. These show that girls did better than boys in math courses and in advanced placement math tests. It seems unlikely that the SAT would measure math skills while the math courses wouldn't (Beckwith & Woodruff, 1984). Other studies show no difference at all between girls and boys on tests of high-level reasoning, such as geometry proofs (Senk & Usiskin, 1984). Possibly the answer lies in the fact that, without even knowing it, many people have a bias against girls being involved in math, which has traditionally been part of the male domain. For example, some studies show that a number of teachers give more attention to boys than girls in math classes (Sadker & Sadker, 1985).

So, at present we can only come to this conclusion: Taken as a whole, the studies do not show that there is some basic difference between the sexes in the ability to handle mathematics. A great number of things would have to be cleared away first before we could conclude that there *is* a difference. Here are some: (1) The test results would have to be more consistent from one study to another. (2) We would have to compensate for the fact that teachers and parents expect males to do better than females in this area. (3) We would have to look at the fact that more boys than girls claim they "enjoy" math. If it's really true that boys tend to like math more, then we have a serious problem comparing the sexes in math abilities (Meece et al., 1982). (4) In general, a lot of people don't want to struggle with math. It may well be that females take advantage of the social forces claiming they are not that skilled in this area in order merely to bypass it and avoid the hassle.

Much of the difficulty in drawing conclusions about male/female abilities can be demonstrated by the fact that, statistically speaking, most girls do not know how to insert a battery properly into a flashlight. This has got to be the result of environmental pressure on girls "not to know," since it is such a simple task that certainly anyone can learn it (Jacobson & Doran, 1985).

The fact that no conclusion can be reached is in itself very important, since this leaves the question wide open, and this is certainly a critical area that should not be closed without very hard evidence.

Environmental Influences

There is no way to remove environmental influences from the development of either spatial or mathematical abilities. For example, research has shown that more mathematical toys are given to boys. Also, boys play with toys such as footballs, which require spatial orientation in order to catch and throw them (Mossip, 1977).

The real clincher has both its humorous and sad sides: Right at junior high school age, females as a group take a sudden and dramatic drop in grades and in intelligence test scores. Does female intelligence suddenly plummet like a rock at this age so that they know hardly anything anymore? Naturally that is ridiculous. Females have been convinced by the

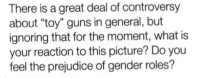

There is a great deal of controversy about "toy" guns in general, but ignoring that for the moment, what is your reaction to this picture? Do you feel the prejudice of gender roles?

"system" that they are supposed to be dumb to be appealing to males. Interestingly, females who refuse to go along with all this and assert themselves show no decline in intellectual ability (Maccoby & Jacklin, 1974). Also, when females are past that "dumb" period, they really soar, especially in college where their grades are almost always better than those of males. Finally, we must not forget that there are many women who can leave men in a cloud of mental confusion just from watching their mathematical and spatial skills in operation.

At this point, then, there do seem to be a few differences between the male and female, but, except for size, weight, endurance, and genetically caused diseases, the differences *do not* mean we are dealing with innate, biological factors. Environment plays a major role. Thus, we would probably find differences in knowledge about how an elevator works if we compared the explanations given by a group of people from Chicago with those given by a group from an island out in the Pacific Ocean. Such differences would not be biological.

Social Skills

Social factors play an important part in how we view the sexes. As a result, much of what you will hear is myth about sex differences.

Self-Confidence

Females are not more influenced by others' suggestions than males; in fact, surprisingly, studies show males are more likely than females are to go along with the group (Eagly, 1978). Females consistently rate themselves as high on self-confidence as males do, at least through childhood and adolescence. Both have about an equal tendency to explore novel environments, engage in unusual activities, and refuse to be stepped on by others. Also, girls feel as important as boys—at least until the middle of high school.

In some studies, girls *claim* that, in their daily lives, they are more anxious and fearful than boys. But we can't put scientific faith in this finding either, because girls may be feigning weakness as part of a social role. When faced with something frightening, boys sweat and swallow a lot and girls screech, but privately they admit to being equally terrified. So, what conclusion can be reached about self-confidence? No notable difference exists.

Drive for Success

Achievement is often described as a masculine goal. But research indicates that females are, in fact, just as oriented toward achievement as males. Large numbers of studies find no overall sex differences in the desire to achieve (Zuckerman & Wheeler, 1975). Why, then, do people have this image of men being more driven to achieve? The evidence points to societal beliefs that suggest that there is something wrong with a woman who seeks success. Girls are told not to be "too important" or they won't appeal to boys. Stop and think for a minute: Isn't there at least a hint of this belief even in your own group?

The causes are all around us. Watch the TV ads carefully sometime, and note how the women are almost always connected somehow with ads for soap or for food products that need cooking. The men tend to be the focus in any ad involving something mechanical, such as a product that would be used with a car or lawnmower. In this way, then, both sexes are subtly indoctrinated. That this has happened shows up even more in females who are presently in college and hence have been exposed to even more of this propaganda, because they were young longer ago when sexism prevailed to a greater extent. When they get higher grades than males—which is the norm—they still anticipate doing poorly in the future; the males, including those who have not done well in school, expect success in the future (Dweck et al., 1980). The good part about all this is that females who are presently in high school by and large are aware that they don't have to restrict themselves any longer to "female" occupations but can become involved in the wide spectrum of occupations available to all (Zuckerman et al., 1980).

Maternal Instincts

Do women *really* have a special empathy with, concern for, and ability to take care of children? Besides the ability to conceive and bear children, is there really something that makes women different in regard to kids? The answer seems to be "no" (Eisenberg & Lennon, 1983). One way to determine this is to search the animal world, where creatures are not guided by social forces to the same extent we are. There are exceptions to the rule we're about to describe, and the male lion is one of them. He is a genuine slob (there just doesn't seem to be a word that will fit better). He demands that the female go get food for him. He won't take care of the offspring; in fact, he will eat them when they are very small unless the mother lion keeps constant vigil. He doesn't even bother with personal hygiene as much as he should. So, we can give up on him. But, in the animal world as a whole, the story is different if the male is forced to take care of the infants. For instance, male rhesus monkeys typically respond to their babies with either hostility or indifference. The close bond is between mother and infant. Yet, in a series of studies, researchers have taken away the mother, forcing the male in the family to be left alone with the infant. At first the father complains and objects violently, as most human males would, but, within a short time, he begins to groom, care for, and show strong attachment toward his infant. And there are male rats who also act awful about being left alone with their offspring. Within a day or so, they "suddenly" manage to find their own version of the maternal instinct and begin to care for the infants in the same way the mother did.

The human mother with her first baby has not the faintest idea what to do with this creature she suddenly faces. For one thing, the baby's head looks like it is going to twirl and wobble itself off at any moment. The task of caretaking seems absolutely hopeless. Mothers must, of necessity, call on other women with experience or frantically read baby-care books to find out "what to do." Taking care of the new baby is hardly "instinctive."

The evidence, then, is that "maternal" behavior is a matter of convenience for nature. Since the female animal gives birth to the infant, she must be programmed to take care of it, which *is* what happens. This "instinct," however, must also exist in the male animal. There is no evidence that any difference in ability or knowledge exists. Apparently, nature has made the female animal (in most species) more involved while allowing the male to hide from the task as ingeniously as he can—behavior we can sometimes see reflected among humans (Suomi, 1983; Berman, 1980; Degler, 1980).

Menstrual cycles
Monthly cycles that revolve around the elimination of the lining of the female uterus because it has not been fertilized.

Hormonal Cycles

With large numbers of women now employed in very responsible positions, some discussion has focused on what effect **menstrual cycles** have on their behavior. Menstruation occurs approximately once a month when the lining of the woman's uterus, which could have been used to hold a fertilized egg, is eliminated because it is not needed. The lining comes out as a harmless bloody fluid. It will build anew the following month to complete the cycle. Because there are so many hormonal changes that go along with this process, many females have physical discomfort and moderate changes in mood. From these facts arises the male belief that females will act strangely once a month. This belief has sparked comments from the more inept male legislators concerning whether a woman, in light of these hormonal changes, would be able to handle the office of president of the United States.

Much of this is nonsense. In the 1870s, advertising headlines screamed "A FEARFUL TRAGEDY" over the story of a clergyman murdered by his wife, who "had become insane from 16 years of suffering with female complaints." Supposedly she would have been all right if she had taken Lydia Pinkham's Vegetable Compound, a liquid mixture of exotic ingredients, including a notable amount of alcohol, that was popular at the time (Jackson, 1984). In the 1950s, women were expected to come apart during "that time of the month"; they literally would not swim, play

The thrust of this ad is to suggest that any woman using the product will remain as blemish-free as a little girl.

games, or go to work, and it was considered dangerous to take a bath. In the 1980s, female defendants have claimed they were under the influence of menstrual symptoms when they murdered their husbands. This defense has been used fairly successfully in England.

As usual, we must try to get a little perspective on the issue. Just as there are some men and women with a disease that is made much worse by something like alcohol, in extreme cases there is something physically and psychologically wrong with a handful of women, and, for them, the major hormonal changes of the menstrual cycle can trigger deviant behavior. But this happens so very rarely that it is not something to worry about for the average female.

On the other hand, just from the point of view of physical discomfort, there is the aspect of the hormonal change called **premenstrual syndrome (PMS)**, which is extremely uncomfortable for about 10 percent of women (Helas, 1984). PMS usually occurs three to seven days prior to menstruation itself and causes anxiety, irritability, and mental confusion (Turkington, 1984). Most women do not have severe symptoms, but, when they do occur, they are very unpleasant (although rarely leading to murder!). Medical treatment to reduce the severity of the symptoms is available (Muse, 1985).

As we discussed in Chapter 6, all of us are controlled by unseen forces, especially bodily rhythms. The female's monthly cycle is one of these. And, as we mentioned earlier, males also follow a monthly cycle, although they will deny it—loudly. Males have a monthly hormonal change that is not as major as the female one, but it does cause mild depression, lethargy, and moodiness once about every 28 to 30 days (Luce, 1971). And, when a husband and wife live together for a long time, their cycles tend to become synchronized—that is, they happen at the same time, which is not necessarily a blessing (Nicholson, 1984).

Premenstrual syndrome (PMS)
Anxiety, irritability, and mental confusion resulting from monthly female hormonal changes.

Marriage

Marriage is supposed to be a wonderful institution, and society says it is close to ideal. Such claims contain certain stereotypes that keep society going. At the extreme, there was a book called *Fascinating Womanhood*, which suggested that a woman should shop in the children's department for clothing ideas in order to be like a little girl for her husband. She was to express her anger by stamping her feet and beating her "little fists" against his chest. The book sold more than 700,000 copies. A companion book also did well. It was called *Man of Steel and Velvet* and suggested that the man should be sure his wife did the family bookkeeping, cooking, and other chores in order to keep his image intact (Farr, 1975).

So, what about *real* marriage? Well, it doesn't quite work this way as you have probably observed. When all married people are lumped to-

Statistically speaking, this is the happiest time for a marriage. Later stress increases until the children are grown, at which time the happiness increases beyond that of the first year.

gether, we find that, as a group, they are more satisfied than those who remain unmarried. But there are some interesting findings that go beyond this surface generalization.

Married women up to the age of 35 stand a high probability of seeking professional help for problems; this is not true for married men. Single women in the same age group do a lot of fretting about not being married, but they show less disturbance (Nicholson, 1984). Divorced women, as a group, are much more miserable than divorced men, probably because these women are typically left with the children to care for and support. On the other hand, single women beyond the age of 35 seem to be thriving, apparently finding out that there is hope for a happy life outside of marriage. Most males of all ages are not happy when they are single (Campbell, 1975).

New brides, statistically speaking, are the happiest people on earth. But, with the arrival of children, satisfaction drops to an average level for most women. They have to wait until the children grow up, at which point their happiness moves upward again. In fact, the parents of grown children are even happier together than they were as newlyweds. We suspect this is the case because the couple has matured together, no longer has the same level of responsibility for others, and usually is relatively secure financially.

Marrying but having no children, marrying later in life, and not marrying at all are fairly frequent scenarios today. The statistics do not bear out the belief that late or childless marriages are necessarily happier or longer lasting (Falbo & Peplau, 1980).

Gender Role Behavior

Many of our ideas about sex role behavior come from society, and we start picking up these ideas at a very young age. For instance, the color blue is used for baby boys; this comes from an old superstition that evil spirits threatened boys in the nursery and that blue, borrowed from the "heavenly blue" of the sky, would ward off these spirits. Later, legend suggested that baby boys were often found under cabbages (which are often blue in Europe). Girls were supposedly born inside pink roses, so that is their color (Brasch, 1967).

Identification and Gender Role

Gender role behavior
Acts that reflect society's view of what is appropriate for males versus what is appropriate for females.

Identification
The process of modeling behavior patterns after (usually) a member of the same sex.

Gender role behavior involves acts that reflect society's view of what is appropriate for males versus what is appropriate for females. A simple example is society's idea of who should play with dolls versus who should play with soldiers. Gender role behavior is thought to arise from **identification**. Identification is the process of modeling one's behavior after the behavior patterns of another person of the same sex. Even though the mother tends to have more influence than the father on children of both sexes, a child will most often actually *imitate* the parent (or another person) of the same sex (Green, 1974). But it is a little more complicated than that. Fathers who are very warm and affectionate toward their daughters tend to "masculinize" them, producing a *mild* tomboyishness (Sears et al., 1966). On the other hand, extreme strictness, severe control of the child, or unusual physical punishment tend to "feminize" both male and female children. These children become docile, at least externally, and they submit to others (Block, 1973). This submissiveness can be deceptive, though, because a time may come when such a child will "explode."

Boys whose fathers were not present during preschool years—that is, up to the age of five—tend to be less aggressive and not quite as active in sports (Biller, 1970). This finding, even though it is only a statistic and does not apply to all males, deserves a little elaboration. The assumption that males should be football players and females powder puffs in order to be "normal" turns out to be just the opposite of what is actually the case. The most normal people in terms of mental health are those who lean slightly away from excessive masculinity or femininity. This is an important finding because many single mothers panic unnecessarily, afraid that something is going to go wrong with their fatherless children (Lebovitz, 1972). Most boys in such a position tend to find a role model outside the home very quickly and imitate a male teacher or an uncle or someone.

Identification can be complicated. In families where either the mother or the father is unusually dominant, the children tend to identify with

that dominant parent, even across sex lines (Hetherington, 1965). If there is no striking dominance, some daughters identify with the father, some sons with the mothers, and some identify with both. In addition, children can identify with brothers and sisters. Boys who have only brothers and girls who have only sisters tend to adopt the more traditional gender roles than those in families with a mixture. And girls who grow up without an older brother are more competitive than those who grow up with one (Stewart & Winter, 1974). (Remember in all this discussion that we are not trying to say that one kind of behavior is "better" than another; instead, we're just trying to demonstrate how complicated identification can be.)

Psychologically Generated Gender Roles

As far as we can tell, animals of all kinds are very aware of gender. Monkey mothers carefully examine their newborn babies' genitals and treat them differently depending on their gender. For instance, they do not allow as much fighting and bickering between females (Money, 1980). Among humans, as mentioned, playthings for boys contrast notably with those for girls. There is no reason at all why boys would not want to play with doll furniture, since they usually spend considerable time with miniature soldiers and tanks. In fact, when families send their children to nontraditional nursery schools where fixed gender roles are not taught, the children do not show the usual tools-only-for-boys and teacups-only-for-girls interest (Selcer & Hilton, 1972). So, we know that much of gender role behavior is the result of social training.

Adults will treat a baby differently, depending on whether they think they are dealing with a boy or a girl. Even with a baby only a few months old, if adults are told it is a boy, they will have some kind of male toy ready and vice versa for a girl. In one study, subjects were introduced to a baby (who was actually a boy) and later asked to describe the infant's characteristics. Those who were told that the baby was a girl described him in female terms as being soft and smiling (Sidorowicz & Lunney, 1980).

Mixing Gender Roles   By strictly defining gender roles and emphasizing differences when they don't exist, we tend to restrict the full range of possibilities for both men and women. "Masculine" men, for instance, have difficulty enjoying and showing affection toward babies, playing with small animals, or even listening to the personal problems someone has. "Feminine" females often can't assert themselves or make independent judgments. Thus, it would seem that a mixture of so-called feminine and masculine behaviors makes for the richest life, and we restrict this potential when we stress gender differences (Bem, 1975).

It is difficult to describe what is strictly masculine or strictly feminine. Masculinity tends to be associated with dominance, assertiveness, achievement, and leadership, while femininity is associated with compassion, sociability, and tenderness. For example, if someone is upset, men are more likely to try to solve the person's problem, while women are more likely to express concern and put themselves in the other's place emotionally (Hoffman, 1977).

The problem is that people who fall into the more extreme gender roles are more rigid and have fewer options open to them in different situations. Nothing says that people can't be in between. For this reason, psychologist Sandra Bem (1975) developed a concept she called **androgyny** (an-DRAH-ja-nee), a term that means that a person is relatively high in both masculine (andro) and feminine (gyn) characteristics. The ideal androgynous person would be both an achiever and a social creature, capable of expressing emotion and of taking action.

Bem found that androgynous people are in better psychological health than those with very strong gender identities. This makes sense when you think about it, because the broader the base of one's activities, the

Androgyny
The quality of having both masculine and feminine characteristics.

more varied and exciting life can be. There are serious pitfalls, though. A woman who adopts what society considers to be too many masculine characteristics is not going to fit in very well. Worse in society's mind, however, is the man who adopts too many feminine traits—he's in for even more trouble. To complicate Bem's proposal, society values masculine traits more highly than feminine ones, so both men and women are better off, according to society, with masculine traits (Bernard, 1980).

Despite these problems, Bem's work is important because it focuses on the extremes that too many people adopt. Her basic idea about androgyny is useful because it leads the way to more flexibility and a greater willingness to share the characteristics of members of the opposite sex. Even changing one's view moderately and realizing that every boy doesn't have to play ball or every girl play with dolls can make life more rewarding for both groups (Taylor & Hall, 1982).

Advantages of Changing Gender Roles It would appear that the more completely a man defines himself as the traditional provider, the more difficulty he will have in abandoning the old ways. But things are changing in this area, and men are gradually loosening their hold on trying to be the symbolic "lord of the manor." Once they have done that, they can find new areas of interest open to them and greater opportunities for self-expression. Surprisingly, many of the changes taking place today in terms of the integration of gender roles is a step backward in time toward the frontier days. Then, things were so rough, especially on the frontier of the early West, that the man and woman had to share almost every responsibility or they were doomed not only to failure but also to death from harsh winters, lack of food, and the like (Bernard, 1981).

A female who sticks to the traditional role is also in for a distorted life. Women who fight the mold become more independent, more self-confident when making decisions, and have a more varied life-style. Also, there is some irony in the finding that women who do not stick strictly to the ultrafeminine role in a marriage can handle marital problems and the related stress much better than "traditional" women. The evidence suggests that society's old version of the ideal woman and the ideal man, well separated from one another in behavior, is a prescription for awkwardness and loneliness rather than a workable arrangement (Krasnoff, 1981; Richardson et al., 1980).

Searching for Gender Differences

We want to look here at some differences in the behaviors of the sexes. As far as we know, there have been no formal psychological studies of any of them, but they do seem to be real differences—at least in the sense that society apparently encourages them. Observe them for yourself, and see if we aren't correct. You might want to try to figure out why they occur. We have our own ideas for each, but they're just guesses, so try your own.

Note the difference in how males and females talk to members of their own sex when they are close friends. Males are very rude and aggressive to those they like best ("Hi there, ugly!"). Apparently the ruder the men are to one another, the closer the relationship. No matter how close females get, they don't ever express affection in this fashion.

Note that females will hug one another, put an arm around the other's shoulders, and touch one another's hands. Males, on the other hand, will hit the other in the shoulder with a fist, shove the other person, or, in sports, pat one another on the posterior.

When a group goes out to a restaurant, note how females tend to get up and go to the restroom together. Men go to the restroom separately, usually not getting up en masse to exit as the females do.

The male readers may have balked at an earlier statement about females doing better in school than males do. Try this out:

Ask ten males and ten females their grade point averages. Take the numbers, add them up for each sex, divide by the number of people you asked, and you have the average. Note that the female grade point average is higher than the male one.

In the next paragraphs, we have constructed a "quiz" of sorts, which might be fun to try out the next time a group is together. You'll be surprised at the major differences in responses between the sexes, and we hope it helps you gain some insight into the opposite one. If you actually reach the point where you can explain the opposite sex, you will have done something nobody has done before.

1. (a) Think about the pluses and minuses of being a male in America today; of being a female. In your opinion, do males or females have it better? Why?

(b) Imagine that you are a member of the opposite sex. How would you be better off? What would the problems be?

2. (a) If you were married, would you want your mate's income to be above, below, or equal to yours? (Think about it, and answer truthfully!) How important is this to you, and why? Ask yourself the same questions about intelligence and looks.

(b) Suppose you had to choose between your mate's having a job with more prestige and status than yours and your mate's having a job that pays more than yours. (It must

be one or the other; it can't be both or neither one.) Which would you choose and why? Compare your answers with those of the opposite sex.

3. If you could decide your baby's sex, would you? If so, would you prefer a boy or a girl? Would your answer change if you already had a child of that sex? If you could decide what your baby would become as an adult, including talents, personality, and occupation, would you? If not, why not? If so, what would your decision be? Is there a difference between the kinds of answers given by males versus females to these questions?

4. (a) A millionaire will give you, absolutely free, a brand-new car of your choosing if you agree not to speak to any of your friends for a month. During that time, if you tell anyone why you are doing this, the deal is off. Would you accept the offer?

(b) The same millionaire will give you $25,000 if you agree not to take a bath or shower, not to change your clothes, and not to wash your hair or comb it for two months, while keeping the reason secret. Would you accept this offer? (Do more males or females answer "yes" to either offer?)

5. If you had all the money you wanted to spend on entertainment, what would you plan for one 24-hour period for yourself and no more than three friends of the same sex? (No dates allowed, please.) How do males versus females differ in their answers?

Summary

1. Hormones control the basics of physical gender development. Both sexes have both male and female hormones, but, in each sex, one kind of hormone dominates over the other.

2. The major difference between males and females is the fact that females bear children. Another difference that shows up in humans and animals is that the male tends to be more aggressive more often and to have a higher activity level.

3. When taken together, studies show no clear-cut differences between the sexes on: intelligence, self-confidence, drive for success, or "maternal instincts." When such differences exist, they can be explained as coming from social training.

4. Menstrual cycles can cause emotional upset and physical distress, but normally these changes are at a reasonable level, not exaggerated as they have been by the press.

5. People who are married seem to be happier overall for a longer time than those who are not married, especially males. The high points in a marriage are when the couple is first married and then again when the children leave home.

6. Identification can be quite complex, and a person can identify with a brother or sister as well as with either parent or another adult. But, in general, males identify with older males and females with older females—usually the parents, if they are available.

7. Androgyny seems to be a goal worth working for, but we also discussed the risk of social disapproval if a person goes too far in mixing gender role behavior.

Key Words and Concepts

gender
hormones
androgen
estrogen
spatial skills
menstrual cycles
premenstrual
  syndrome (PMS)
gender role
  behavior
identification
androgyny

Review Questions

Multiple Choice

1. Injecting an animal with androgen would probably increase:
   a. breast size
   b. brain size
   c. moodiness
   d. aggressiveness.

2. The female hormone is called:
   a. estrogen   b. androgen   c. androgyny.

3. Which of the following characteristics apply to females?
   a. Greater endurance
   b. Live longer than men
   c. Fewer genetic defects
   d. All of the above

4. Evidence indicates that males are naturally:
   a. More physical than females
   b. Less physical than females
   c. Equally as physical as females.

5. Which gender *performs* better on tests of spatial skills?
   a. Males   b. Females   c. Neither

True/False

6. The brains of males are different from the brains of females.

7. Evidence indicates that males are naturally better than females at math.

8. Surveys consistently show that males have higher self-confidence than females.

9. Females are as oriented toward achievement as males are.

10. Studying animal behavior helps us realize that the maternal "instinct" is present only in females.

11. Premenstrual syndrome afflicts a majority of women.

12. Males experience their own hormonal cycles that start and end every three months.

13. Women's happiness level is average with the arrival of children and increases as the children grow up.

14. Overly strict parents will tend to feminize their children.

15. Children tend to identify with the dominant parent.

16. Androgynous people on the average are:
    a. Less healthy than people with strong gender identities
    b. More healthy than people with strong gender identities
    c. Just as healthy as people with strong gender identities.

17. Which of the following reasons might discourage a person from becoming androgynous?
    a. Society values masculine traits over feminine traits—so why be feminine?
    b. Women who are masculine may not be accepted by society.
    c. Men who are feminine may not be accepted by society.
    d. All of the above

18. A woman who is *not* traditional or strictly feminine in a marriage:
    a. Handles stress worse than the traditionally feminine woman
    b. Handles stress better than the traditionally feminine woman
    c. Handles stress about the same as the traditionally feminine woman.

Discussion Questions

1. If you were a parent, would you ever consider buying your daughter a toy machine gun or toy soldiers? Why or why not?

2. If you were a parent, would you ever consider buying your son a doll or a toy kitchen set? Why or why not?

3. If you took a survey, you'd probably find that despite a leveling of gender role differences today, males still are primarily responsible for asking females out for a first date. In your opinion, why do a majority of females usually refrain from initiating dates? Explain.

4. Many people advocate passage of an Equal Rights Amendment (ERA) that would ban sex discrimination. Others argue that laws already exist to stop this discrimination. Furthermore, passage of the ERA would mean that women could be drafted in the event of a war. Do you think that the ERA should still be passed? Why or why not?

5. All of us are androgynous to some extent. Describe several of your own characteristics that reveal your an-

drogyny. In other words, describe some of your "masculine" traits and some of your "feminine" traits.

6. This part of the question is for the males: Describe the advantages of being a female. This part is for the females: Describe the advantages of being a male.

Activities

1. Neatly print the following information onto two index cards:

"The reason I want to be an engineer is because I've always done well in math and I enjoy it. For example, in third grade, I won first place in a math test in the area, and, ever since, I've always been excited about math classes. I know that my other grades are just average, but I've always gotten an A or B in math."

At the top of one of the cards, print "Georgia Roanoke"; at the top of the other, print "George Roanoke." Take another index card and print the following information onto it:

"How would you rate the chances of this person succeeding in a career in math?

0	1	2	3	4	5	6	7	8
DISMAL	VERY POOR	POOR	BELOW AVER-AGE	AVER-AGE	ABOVE AVER-AGE	HIGH	VERY HIGH	OUT-STAND-ING"

Are you beginning to get the idea? Find 32 high school subjects, 16 males and 16 females. Eight of the males and 8 of the females will see the "Georgia" card; the other 8 males and 8 females will see the "George" card. Record their ratings onto some kind of data sheet.

In order to get accurate and honest ratings, you must make sure that your subjects don't find out the purpose of the experiment—which is to see if the male, with his supposedly "superior" math skills, will be rated higher, despite *identical* qualifications. To make sure your subjects don't know your purpose, you might say something like this: "In English class, we're learning about how to write résumés and how to fill out job applications. We all had to write a paragraph, exchange the paragraph with someone in class, and then that person goes around and collects ratings. We thought the ratings would be more accurate if we exchanged paragraphs rather than collecting our own ratings. So be completely honest."

Analyze your results. What was the overall average rating for Georgia? For George? What was the female average rating for both cards? What was the male average rating for both cards?

Draw a simple chart and list all these ratings. Discuss your results. Did our hypothesis seem to be supported by your findings: *Is* there a sex bias against females involved in math? Were you surprised by your results? Why or why not?

2. This next activity is a variation of the previous one. Follow the same procedure, except this time you'll use middle-aged adults as your subjects to see if people with more traditional backgrounds will, in fact, be "traditional" with their ratings. Discuss your results in detail. (Try to choose subjects whom you consider to have "traditional" backgrounds.)

If you're conducting this experiment *and* the previous

If you're conducting this experiment *and* the previous one, compare and contrast the results—*or* maybe you can conduct one activity while a friend conducts the other, and then you can compare and contrast each other's results.

3. Most libraries save back issues of the most popular magazines for years and years. Sift through several magazine ads from 1955, 1965, 1975, 1985, and the present. As you look through these ads, jot down information about the ones that seem to promote traditional gender role behavior and the ones that seem to defy traditional gender role behaviors.

Organize your notes into a report. Which products and brand names are most commonly linked to gender roles? How has the nature of the ads changed from 1955 to the present? Do you notice any patterns? Be specific. Finally, are ads today still sexist? Explain.

4. Follow the same directions as in activity number 3, but instead of doing a written report, hand in a visual report. For example, you might take several poster-boards and create charts to *show* how ads have changed. Include headings and captions. Or you might want to put together a magazine of ads, including some from the past up to the present. You can include your own explanatory captions for the ads. Or, if you're ambitious, you might even put together a slide show (or videotape) with appropriate music and narration.

5. Take another look at the gender quiz at the beginning of the chapter (see In Focus). As you found out while reading the chapter, all but question number 1 are gender myths. Show the quiz to eight males and eight females and record their answers. Then go back to the

person who got the highest score and the one who got the lowest score, and interview these two people. If there is a tie for highest or lowest, randomly pick one of the people who tied. For your interview, you can use the questions listed in Psychology in Your Life at the end of the chapter, or you can write your own—as long as both people are asked identical questions.

This will be your hypothesis: The person who scored lowest on the quiz probably has less knowledge about gender differences and similarities than the person who scored highest. The person who scored lowest then would also tend to exhibit more traditional attitudes about sex roles—simply because this person doesn't know any better. In other words, you're testing whether ignorance breeds sexist attitudes.

Analyze and compare the two interviews in detail to determine if this hypothesis seems to be true. The most difficult part of this analysis is trying to decide objectively whether the answers are, in fact, traditional and sexist—or not so traditional. You'll have to use your judgment. Just make sure you can support your judgment in some way. Also, try to be fair. The answers to questions numbers 1, 2, and 3 in the Psychology in Your Life "quiz" will probably be the most revealing.

6. Interview a woman who was 16 sometime between 1955 and 1965, a time when traditional sex roles prevailed for the most part but were beginning to be seriously questioned. Possible questions: (1) What were the main career opportunities open to women in 1960? Were women limited in their choices? How? Were these limitations real, or were they just women's perceptions at the time? (2) In dating, what role were females supposed to play? What about males? What was the attitude about marriage in 1960? (3) How did you feel about the women's liberation movement when you were young? How do you feel about it today? Also, how do you feel about the changes in attitudes since 1960? Write a report of your interview and include your reactions.

7. The effects of hormones on behavior can be fascinating and enlightening. New discoveries are made every day. Conduct research on the role of hormones on behavior, focusing particular attention on male and female hormones. *Warning*: Books on the subject may already be dated; try using recent magazine articles. And, of course, organize your research into an enlightening report.

Unit Five

Personality, Adjustment, and Conflict

Under normal circumstances, our buttons, stickers, or labels reflect who we are and what we stand for. This person would present problems in this area.

Chapter 14

Theories of Personality

Global Look at the Chapter

Personality is a term referring to long-lasting patterns of behavior. This chapter discusses different theories, each one of which views human beings as motivated by different forces. Some suggest we are the product of unconscious forces, some that we are what we learn, and some that we inherit our personalities.

Difficulties in Understanding Personality

In this chapter we try to get a handle on personality. And what a difficult task that is. People aren't always what they seem. For instance, the majority of professional comedians are very quiet at home, and some of the better ones suffer from heavy bouts of depression. Classmates and teachers often misunderstand what you are really like and what you really feel. They may think you are aggressive when you are really shy; they may think you are outgoing when in fact you look forward to being alone. They may see you as a loner but you actually need company. And, as if this isn't complicated enough, we all assume different personalities at different times. When we are eating alone at home, our manners may be disgusting; when we are out for dinner, no one would suspect how sloppy we can be.

You can see, then, that trying to pin down personality is going to be a rough task. And we won't succeed all the way. Still, it is worthwhile going over some of the theories that psychologists have about how our personalities develop. These theories attempt to bring together in an organized, coherent way a set of beliefs about how we become who we are.

The Usefulness of Theories

What is the purpose of having theories? There are a couple of answers to this. First, part of a theory may turn out to be correct. Thus, eventually we might be able to explain how we got the way we are by combining the most workable parts of a number of theories. Second, theories give us a framework in which to study people; then we can either accept or reject the claims of the theory based on what studies show to be the case. For instance, at one point it was said that those who abuse and beat their children had parents who beat *them* when they were children. As it turns out, in reality this is more often *not* the case than it is. But the theory was useful because it gave us something to study, to either accept or reject. While some abusive parents may themselves have been abused, this is not the major cause, so we have to look elsewhere to explain it.

Defining Personality

Some people are cheats and liars on one day and super-religious on the next. But most of us most of the time respond roughly the same way in many situations. In fact, this is the definition of "personality." **Personality** consists of broad and long-lasting patterns of behavior. These patterns are fairly consistent from one day to the next. Thus, the odds are that a person who is afraid of canoe trips, hiking, swimming, and heights will also be afraid of a roller coaster. On the other hand, those who constantly take chances, drive like fools, and will bet on anything will ride a roller coaster that has all the support bolts loosened. Once we assume that some aspects of personality are fairly stable, we can look at theories that try to explain their origin.

Personality
A person's broad, long-lasting patterns of behavior.

Psychoanalysis

Psychoanalysis is a personality theory based on the assumption that how we develop and behave is the result of impulses or needs that are unknown to us. In other words, what we are comes from hidden forces. The theory arose from a belief that people with psychological problems were unable to see the origin of their difficulties. To view these forces requires a trained professional who will *analyze* one's thoughts, feelings, and history to reveal what is going on beneath the surface. That's how we got the term psycho*analysis*.

Psychoanalysis
A theory that personality is based on impulses and needs in the unconscious.

Sigmund Freud

Sigmund Freud, the founder of psychoanalysis.

The most famous psychoanalyst was **Sigmund Freud** (FROID). His theory of how we develop and what controls us dominated psychology from the early 1900s through the late 1940s. Freud believed that the core of one's personality appeared within the first five or six years of life and was more or less fixed by that age. For him, individual development had its source in the family and the conflicts that every family has. Our feelings about ourselves come from jealousies, anxieties, and guilt regarding how we relate to other family members and about how they view us.

This emphasis is not hard to understand since Freud's own family life was chaotic. His father was 20 years older than his mother and had a couple of children by a previous marriage before he married Freud's mother, and he had a mistress as well. Freud's mother then had eight children. At one point, there were the eight children, a half-brother the age of Freud's mother, the father, and a nephew all living in the same cramped 30-foot-by-30-foot room (Clark, 1980). It makes sense that the family friction and unwanted intimacy this brought about would lead to many of Freud's beliefs.

Freud studied to become a physician and for a while actually practiced medicine in the traditional sense. But two things changed the course of his life: (1) As he listened to patients, he became more and more convinced that the problems they were having were coming from psychological forces rather than physical ones, and (2) he couldn't stand the sight of blood. Freud often tried to treat his patients by giving them cocaine. Eventually he became addicted himself and just about ruined a very meaningful career before overcoming the problem (Reisman, 1966).

One of Freud's early patients was a woman who couldn't drink water but who stayed alive by eating only fruit such as melons. This clearly wasn't a "normal" sickness, and Freud couldn't make sense of it at first. A physician friend of Freud's told him that he had been successful in using hypnosis with patients who had bizarre symptoms in order to find out what was going on. So, Freud thought he would try it. Under hypnosis, the woman recalled that, when she was a child, she one day found a hated servant's dog drinking out of a water glass in the kitchen. Thus, it seemed that hypnosis helped Freud get to parts of the patient's mind that were unknown to her normally (Freud, 1938). Another colleague of Freud's had a truly bizarre case: He was treating a female patient for dizziness, fainting, and coughing spells. Before long, the woman had what is called an "hysterical childbirth." The word *hysteria* refers to physical symptoms that come from a psychological problem. In hysterical childbirth, the patient has all the symptoms, pains, and even a major swelling of the abdomen (from body water) that goes on for nine months, so you expect a baby when it is all over. But there is no baby in there (Schultz,

1969). A few such cases still occur every year, even on occasion to males, as we mentioned in the previous chapter.

You can see how Freud began to believe that we are guided by impulses and needs that don't show up on the surface. From this belief arose his famous concept, the unconscious.

The Unconscious

Freud believed that childhood conflicts within the family are removed from conscious memory but are still "in us." These events are held in the **unconscious**, the part of us we are not aware of. Our true feelings sometimes might appear in dreams or in mistakes we make when speaking. Freud claimed that, if he talked to a patient long enough, he found some of the material causing the trouble that was buried below the surface. So, he gave up hypnosis as not needed, and used his "talking cure." Freud reached the unconscious by using **free association**, a process in which the patient says *everything* that appears in the mind, even if seemingly not connected. In other words, no "censoring" is allowed. The basis for this method of treatment was Freud's assumption that the unconscious was always trying to seek expression in one way or another, and, if the patient talked long enough, more and more of the unconscious would appear in what was being said. The analyst could then put it all together into a coherent picture and thus explain problem-causing behavior. For example, if you have a deep-seated anger toward a friend, the more you talk about this person the more likely it is that some unconscious material about what caused the anger will appear.

Freud was quite taken by the theory and writings of Charles Darwin. Darwin's work suggested that the human was basically an animal, even though we have higher mental abilities as well as the ability to make moral decisions. As a result, Freud focused on our behavior as mostly animal-like. In other words, he focused on our very strong drives to satisfy bodily needs—food, comfort, sex, self-preservation. Since all human societies in one way or another try to block expression of too much animal-like behavior, we can't always satisfy these needs—or even admit we have them. Since they won't go away, we try to hide from them by putting them into our unconscious. If everything we wanted to do was good, there would be no problem. But all of us have desires that we would just as soon no one else knew about, so we make them "disappear." This disappearance is called **repression**. According to Freud's theory, from childhood on, needs and desires that are forbidden cause guilt. As a result, they are pushed out of consciousness (repressed) into the unconscious where they live. They do not remain quiet, however, but reappear as conflicts and anxieties that interfere with daily life and normal functioning.

Unconscious
According to psychoanalytic belief, this portion of us contains hidden material that controls our behavior.

Free association
Freudian process in which the person says everything that appears in the mind, even if the ideas or images seem unconnected.

Repression
The process of pushing the needs and desires that cause guilt into the unconscious.

When we bury forbidden impulses, we bury them alive. These buried impulses then are forgotten, but they will be expressed in other forms—such as anxiety or conflict.

REPRESSION

Hmm . . . I can't remember why I was so angry last week . . . oh, well. It must not have been that important.

The Libido

Freud's theory focuses on an interaction between these conscious and unconscious forces. Because Freud developed his theory during a time of great scientific discovery in the fields of chemistry and physics about electricity, magnetism, and energy forces, he absorbed some of these ideas and assumed that the human had *real* (biological, not symbolic) energy inside, which controlled behavior. This energy he called **libido** (la-BEE-dough). The libidinal energy constantly seeks some kind of discharge, just as lightning will when it finds a high tree and discharges into the ground. In the process of seeking discharge, this energy creates a

Libido
Freudian term for internal energy forces that continuously seek discharge.

tension that needs release. If release is not found in real life, the desires appear as dreams or fantasies. An attempt at release can also appear as psychological disturbance.

Freud's Map of the Mind

Freud divided the individual's inner world into three parts. One is responsible for survival needs, another for society's rules of behavior. The third part deals with the real world and tries to keep the demands of the other two in balance.

Id   All of our basic needs and drives make up the **id**. Therefore, it contains our major energy force (libido), which is constantly seeking expression. We cannot know, directly, what goes on in the id because it is unconscious. It is also completely unconcerned about any reality except its own desires. The id can cause many psychological problems. Without it, however, we would not eat when hungry or defend ourselves if attacked. Without it, we could not survive.

Id
Freudian unit containing our animal impulses.

Superego   Although the id is necessary, if we acted out any impulse we had at any time, society would fall apart. To hold the id in check, we each have, according to Freud, a **superego**, a term that is an approximate synonym for conscience. The superego causes guilt for being bad and pride for doing the right things. It develops out of the punishments and rewards we get from our parents, the first representatives of society's laws and customs. We need a superego, but, like the id, it exists only for what it wants. If allowed to operate unchecked, it would block all our drives and instincts, letting us die rather than break a rule.

Superego
Freudian unit roughly synonymous with conscience.

Ego   The third portion of the individual is called the **ego**. The ego is roughly the same as the *self*. The job of the ego is really to allow the id to express itself in some safety. In other words, the ego pays attention to reality and monitors what is going on in the environment as well as listening to what the superego has to say. If the id wants to steal wallets at a police station, the ego will listen to the superego and examine reality, saying, "That's not a very clever idea." So the ego acts as a controller attempting to moderate between our desires and reality.

Ego
The "self" that allows controlled id expression within the boundaries of the superego.

Our personalities show how good a balancing act we have developed. For instance, if the id takes over because the superego is not strong enough, we will develop personalities that are more and more demanding of animal needs. If the ego loses its ability to strike a balance, we become pouty, whining individuals who are never satisfied. On the other hand, if the superego dominates as the result of endless control of our every desire, we become guilt-ridden, shy, fearful, and withdrawn.

Stages of Development

Freud's five stages of personality development go from birth through adolescence. As mentioned earlier, Freud believed that personality is basically formed by age five or six. Consequently, all the major conflicts and psychological tasks we must deal with take place in the first three of his stages. The two later stages are necessary for completeness, and they expand on what has happened earlier, but neither one presents any important new crises or demands.

According to Freud, adults' psychological problems have their roots in early childhood and can be traced to unresolved conflicts during that time. In fact, many of the behaviors that indicate that there was trouble in one of Freud's first three stages usually appear only later on in life, not in childhood. Examples of this include such problems as alcoholism, eating disorders, and severe depression. We give more examples of these behaviors in each of the following paragraphs.

Oral Stage: Birth to Age One and a Half   In the *oral stage* of development, feeding is the main source of infants' pleasure, and weaning is the task to be dealt with. When a child is weaned too early or too late, personality problems develop. Examples of oral-stage behaviors are too much dependency on other people, rejection of others or being very sarcastic, drinking problems, and either overeating or self-starvation.

Anal Stage: Ages One and a Half to Two and a Half   The psychological task during the *anal stage* is toilet training. Toilet training that is either too lenient or too harsh will cause psychological problems. Anal-stage behaviors include such things as being excessively stingy or overly generous as well as sticking very rigidly to rules and regulations or being irresponsible and rebellious.

Phallic Stage: Ages Two and a Half to Five or Six   During the *phallic stage*, children experience the "Oedipus complex" (conflict), named for a character in a Greek play who killed his father and married his mother—without knowing it at the time. The Oedipus conflict, then, involves a desire to marry the opposite-sexed parent along with jealous and hostile feelings for the same-sexed parent. Because parents are bigger and more powerful than children, there is also a fear of punishment involved. In turn, the possibility of being punished causes guilt because, in the child's mind, one is only punished for being bad. A complicated set of emotions must be dealt with during this stage.

The only way to cope with all of these romantic, jealous, aggressive, anxious, and guilty feelings is to "identify" with the parent of the same sex, which means taking on as many of his or her characteristics as possible. Failure to resolve this conflict through identification can result in a wide range of psychological disorders. Freud believed that unreasonable anxiety, extreme guilt, phobias, and depression, for example, originate in the phallic stage of development.

Latency Stage: Ages Six to Early Adolescence   When something is latent, it is below the surface, hidden, not obvious. In the *latency stage*, conflicts and problems from the earlier stages remain subdued or latent. No new ones arrive on the scene during this period.

Genital Stage: Adolescence Onward   As people seek an appropriate marriage partner and prepare for adult life, the conflicts of early childhood reappear. No new conflicts arise during this *genital stage*, but all of the old resolved ones resurface. Although the ways in which they are expressed may have changed, their content is left over from the first five years of life.

Assessment of Freud

Sigmund Freud's organized theory of human development, the conscious, and the unconscious, revolutionized how the human was viewed. His beliefs and ideas filtered down into everyday language as well as influencing how people with problems were viewed—all the way up to the present. But, by and large, today's psychology deemphasizes the influence of an unconscious and focuses far more on a person's ability to control current, ongoing behavior rather than dwell on childhood influences and unconscious impulses. There are reasons for this change in thinking.

As much as we hear about and use the term "unconscious," the truth of the matter is that we have no *direct* evidence it exists (Balay and Shevrin, 1988). We all know about things that we want to do that we shouldn't, but the mere fact that we *do* know about them makes them conscious, rather than unconscious. We certainly have things stored in us that we can't remember for the time being, and often we do things that we shouldn't that are obvious to others but that we deny. But none of this proves an active unconscious that controls us against our will.

As for the three-part system of the person, there is little evidence it exists. Freud had hoped that someday it would be found, showing the ego, superego, and id as having a biological basis. This has not happened.

As you will find out shortly, many have objected to the idea that we are little more than animals. But, in fact, that might have been Freud's greatest contribution—not that we are animals, but the fact that sometimes we do indeed lose control and behave in a fashion that is completely unac-

A mandala, Jung's symbol for the collective nature or oneness of human experience.

ceptable. In other words, his theory focused on the fact that humans are not completely rational and in control, something we often lose sight of.

Carl Jung

Carl Jung (YOONG) was a friend and follower of Freud. The two men had grown quite close, so that, when their relationship got rocky, strange things happened. For example, Jung one day told Freud that he (Jung) had had a dream about corpses in coffins. Freud thought this meant Jung wanted him dead, and as a result he fell over in a faint. Then they started calling one another names fitting to their profession—crazy or neurotic (Brome, 1967). In any case, Jung began to doubt the Freudian theory's emphasis on animal functions and eventually went off on his own, emphasizing what he really believed: The unconscious is a well of mystical and religious beliefs that controls our behavior.

Pursuing his belief, Jung studied very old paintings, statues, relics, and books about myths and religion. The more he read, the more it became clear to him: No matter what civilization he studied—ancient, old, or new—he kept finding stories about and pictures of great heroes and concepts of "mothers" as strong and supportive, especially "Mother Earth" as something that provides us with food and care. And the concept of God in one form or another kept repeating itself (Jung, 1933, 1958). If such concepts are everywhere throughout history in separate civilizations that have had no contact with one another, Jung figured that they must be part of all humans from the very beginning of each life.

Instead of being guided by an unconscious that seeks bodily pleasure, then, all humans must be controlled by certain beliefs we inherit. People in every civilization from the earliest times on must be guided by myths that make up a **collective unconscious**. It is called collective (meaning "everyone together") because the ideas are shared by the entire human race. Jung felt that it was "unconscious" since we are not fully aware we are part of these forces.

Collective unconscious
Jung's term for the portion of a person that contains ideas (such as hero, mother, and so on) shared by the whole human race.

So, each generation inherits beliefs in certain ideas or roles that are connected with certain behaviors—for instance, all civilizations have beliefs about mother, hero, wise man or wise woman, and so forth. Without even knowing it, we imitate the fixed beliefs about these concepts and develop personalities to fit them. Thus, despite the fact that a new mother has absolutely no idea what to do with a newborn—and at times might fear that its head could come off because it wobbles so much—she nonetheless *pretends* to know all and be all for the child. A skinny, weak, and hopelessly shy male will actually feel guilty if he doesn't stand up to another male who is six-foot-four and weighs 240 pounds. The man feels he should be a "hero." While both the man and woman are being unrealistic, it would seem they are trying to fit into the myths of this collective unconscious.

At least one part of Jung's theory certainly is true of all of us. He claimed that, in the process of trying to become like these mythical people, we hide our real feelings and our real personalities. This fake personality is called a **persona** (per-SONE-ah), which comes from Latin and refers to the frowning or smiling masks that were worn by players in Greek and Roman stage plays. We use psychological masks to fit what we think we are supposed to be, rather than let ourselves be what we actually are. How many times, for instance, have you smiled and been pleasant around someone who is irritating you?

Persona
Jung's term for a "mask" people wear to hide what they really are or feel.

Assessment of Carl Jung

Jung's personality theory is not discussed in psychology very much anymore. Still, it was worth considering here because it adds quite a dimension to the possibilities of how we might get at least part of our personalities. There is no proof for it. On the other hand, we know animals of all kinds inherit certain broad rules of behavior. Try building a bird's nest sometime, and you'll realize just how incredibly complicated it is. Somehow this behavior is programmed in the bird. So, very complex and elaborate things can be passed on. Why not some of Jung's concepts, many of which do indeed seem to be universal?

Social Psychoanalytic Theories

Both Freud and Jung dealt with an unconscious that was thought to be biological. In other words, they thought that needs or mythological beliefs control people, with little influence from what happens in the environment. A number of psychoanalysts agreed with the concept of an unconscious but objected to the fact that the early theories ignored the impact of social forces. These psychoanalysts believed that the unconscious also holds all the worries and concerns about how well we get along with others. Think about how sweaty and anxious you got the last time you met someone of the opposite sex you wanted very much to like you. While the desire to associate with that person might start off biologically, it quickly became a social issue. Given this different focus, this splinter group of psychoanalysts came to be known as social psychoanalysts or **neo-Freudians**, the latter term meaning "new" (revised) Freudians.

Neo-Freudians
Those psychoanalysts who broke away from Freud to emphasize social forces in the unconscious.

Karen Horney

Psychoanalyst **Karen Horney** (HORN-eye) was outspoken about breaking with the Freudian tradition. She strongly disagreed with Freud's focus on biological drives (Murphy & Kovach, 1972). Horney felt that dealing with impulses from an id was less important for personality than coping with the stress of social needs. Hence, she was a neo-Freudian. She claimed that the human feels most helpless, anxious, and lost in life around the issues of getting enough love. All of us need love badly, so we are constantly afraid that important people (like our parents when we are very young) will not like us. This is so threatening that we build our personalities around fighting rejection. As a result, we go along with people when we don't want to. A person without love is one who is ever anxious and afraid (Horney, 1950). Rather than Freudian id impulses, the unconscious gradually gets a buildup of social anxiety from confused or inadequate social relationships. The person's behavior will then be dominated by social concerns because of the constant pressure from the unconscious.

Alfred Adler

Alfred Adler was a follower of Freud who also had trouble with the heavy emphasis on biological needs. He believed, like Horney, that social interaction was the key to proper development. He said that one of the biggest problems people face is trying to feel important and worthwhile around others. Those who are insecure struggle to make themselves look better. They spend their lives trying to dominate and control others in order to avoid their own inner feelings of inferiority. School bullies are perfect examples of this type of behavior. When one gets beneath the surface to the unconscious, one finds that these people doubt themselves, are afraid and weak; hence, they take off after those physically weaker in order to try to make themselves feel important and strong.

Erik Erikson

As mentioned, Freud felt that personality is pretty well set in the early years. Very few psychologists believe this anymore. As we'll talk about later, some aspects of personality tend to remain the same, but there are many things about us that change throughout life.

One theorist who supports the idea of change is **Erik Erikson**. His theory divides life up into eight stages. Like Horney and Adler, Erikson believes that social forces are most important, so it is the type of relationships a person has during each of the stages that forms his or her personality. Erikson's theory is appealing because it implies that we can "rescue" ourselves from problems almost anytime in life, all the way up to old age.

Stage one is in infancy. Erikson stresses the importance of warm relationships with the mother during feeding. Depending on how the mother and child get along, the child either relaxes and feels trusting, or is tense and mistrusting of others. Erikson, therefore, called this stage *trust versus mistrust*.

Stage two comes at year two of the child's life. During this time, the child tries to become an individual—of sorts. Clearly he or she is pretty helpless but nonetheless is seeking a feeling of being a separate person. If the parents don't allow this, the ego is injured and the child feels shame. If the parents allow some freedom, a feeling of independence occurs, called autonomy (aw-TON-oh-mee). Erikson called stage two *autonomy versus shame*.

Even in *stage three*, from ages three through five, children are still very dependent on the parents. But this is the time when children try to take control of their environment—within limits. Thus, making a pile of rocks of their own design is important. Pretending to be a teacher or police officer or parent begins, and children make up their own rules about how these tasks are performed. They are taking the initiative in developing the behavior and rules of their pretend work. If not allowed this chance, the child begins to feel bad and guilty for having failed. This stage is called *initiative versus guilt*.

By *stage four* (ages six to 12 years), children begin to get rewards for what they do. These can range from stars pasted on the forehead (for the younger ones, we hope) to extra TV privileges. These are rewards for a job well done. The children are being molded to do more and better things (that is, to be "industrious"). If the rewards are not forthcoming, they feel inadequate. This stage, then, is called *industry versus inferiority*.

Erikson sees *stage five*, adolescence (also discussed in Chapter 11), as the most important stage. This is the time when one is old enough to accept the past with its good parts and to try to repair the bad things. One

Erik Erikson, a socially oriented psychologist.

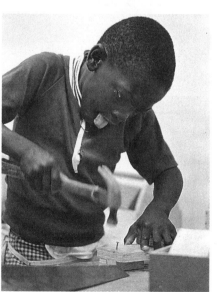

Erikson's Industry Stage: Does it require that the tongue be out?

In Focus: Erikson's Eight Stages

Trust	versus	**Mistrust (Birth to 2 years)**
Infant is totally dependent on others—learns to trust these others		or learns to distrust them.
Autonomy	versus	**Shame (Ages 2–3 years)**
Child tries to become a separate individual		or, if not allowed, feels shame.
Initiative	versus	**Guilt (Ages 3–5 years)**
Child tries to take control of environment		or, if not allowed, child feels guilty for having failed.
Industry	versus	**Inferiority (Ages 6–12 years)**
Child wants to do more and better things—to be industrious		or, if child does *not* do better, child feels inferior.
Identity	versus	**Role Confusion (Ages 13–18 years)**
Adolescent searches for role or identity in life		and feels confusion if no role is found.
Intimacy	versus	**Isolation (Ages 18–30 years)**
Young adult shares special or intimate feelings with one special person		or, without the sharing, loneliness and isolation prevail.
Generativity	versus	**Stagnation (Middle adulthood)**
Adult feels need to generate or contribute something important to the world		or, if nothing important is contributed, the adult deteriorates or stagnates
Ego Integrity	versus	**Ego Despair (Late adulthood)**
Person looks to past and feels a sense of accomplishment or integrity		or person looks back and feels no sense of accomplishment and feels empty and despairing.

tries to get a hold on an inner self by seeking an answer to "Who am I?" Finding self-identity requires the safety of a group. For this reason, adolescents form tightly knit groups to keep the self free from adult or "outsider" influence. The groups even have uniforms of sorts, which adults can't seem to handle without coming unglued. Certain types of shoes, clothing, special language, hairdos, and the like all help to keep the group together for this important process and exclude older or younger people. This is also the time for falling in love so the person can find out the answer to "Will someone love who I am?" (Muuss, 1975). (Fortunately, for almost all of us, there usually is *someone* somewhere who will see us as a little more than adequate.) Finally, this is the time when young people start a search for solutions to religious, vocational, and personal issues (finding a "role" in life) (Erikson, 1968). Stage five is called *identity versus role confusion*.

Stage six occurs during young adulthood, starting in the late teens and running until about age 30. This is a time of forming permanent relationships and sharing on an intimate level, usually with a member of the opposite sex. This intimacy provides a true feeling of satisfaction because you are important to at least one special person. There is a sharing of a special closeness with another, a true process of give and take. Without it, there is loneliness. Hence, this stage is called *intimacy versus isolation*.

Middle adulthood is *stage seven*, from age 30 to 65. During this time, a person must either expand and give (generate) something important to the world in the way of a family or job, or they psychologically stand still and produce nothing (stagnate). This stage is called *generativity versus stagnation*.

In late adulthood, *stage eight*, from age 65 on, that which has gone before should, with a little luck, make some sense. One should be able to accept that the end is coming and find that life has been a worthwhile event, that something good was accomplished from living. The self (ego) should feel reasonably complete when viewing what has happened, despite all the problems along the way. If a person doesn't feel this, he or she despairs, feeling life has been meaningless. Thus, this stage is called *ego integrity versus ego despair*. (*Integrity* means a feeling of wholeness or completion in this context.)

Assessment of the Neo-Freudians

The neo-Freudians brought an important new dimension to psychoanalysis: the influence of social forces. Clearly they provided more to work with in analysis than simply biological drives. Erikson's theory was especially helpful in allowing the possibility that we all have a chance to "repair" ourselves as we go along in life and are not stuck with something from childhood. Despite these alterations, however, the problem of whether we have an unconscious or not still exists.

Behaviorism

Not all personality theories deal with the unconscious. In fact, in **behaviorism**, the unconscious is ignored altogether. Early theories in this

Behaviorism
A personality theory that focuses on acts or behaviors rather than on consciousness or unconsciousness; Skinner and Bandura are examples of behavioral psychologists.

area focused on our acts or behaviors as if we were robots. Our personalities evolve from a series of rewards or punishments without concern about any deep motives. For example, those who drop out of school to work will, in the long run, lose a great deal of money. But, for the short term, each week or so they get a lot more money than their friends who are still in school. Thus, they are getting a continued series of rewards that are more important than the pleas of their parents to stay in school. They are developing shallow personalities based on short-term benefits. Note that the psychoanalysts would claim that these people have a deep-seated fear of failing in school or that they feel unimportant. As a result they use the fact that they are making more money than their peers to feel superior. The Freudians, then, approach personality with much greater depth and complexity than the behaviorists.

Burrhus Frederic Skinner

The best known of the behaviorists is **B. F. Skinner**. We mentioned in Chapter 1 that Skinner had a very strict religious upbringing; his grandmother used to hold his face over a stove of hot coals to show him "what hell was like." Later, when he was in school, he chose to withdraw from social activities, and he spent his time reading science books instead of going to movies, hanging around, or dating much (Skinner, 1967). If we were using the psychoanalytic method, we might come up with the idea that these early events in his life were part of what led him to see people in mechanical terms: The negative associations he had with religion and social activities may have developed his later picture of people as mechanical rather than as thinking, reasoning creatures. (Of some interest, as he has entered Erilson's Stage Eight he has mellowed quite a bit and views the human in much less mechanical terms.)

In any case, for the early Skinner, everything we do is the result of a mechanical association of events. For example, if you plan to go over to a friend's house tonight but then later in the day you decide to find a different friend with whom to go get something to eat, this was *not* a voluntary decision on your part, according to Skinner. Instead, you added up the number of pleasant experiences you have had with friend number one and the number of ones you have had going to get something to eat with friend number two, and you chose the second friend because you had more positive associations with that person. While you *think* you had a choice, you really didn't. In the months to come, the number of positive experiences with different people might change so that you will choose friend number three. Thus, all our behaviors are the result of a series of **reinforcements**. Those who make clothing know that there are certain parts of the shirt that take more of a beating than others. If you haven't bought something really cheap, the manufacturer will have used extra stitches or material to *reinforce* these parts—make them stronger. A similar thing happens to humans, according to Skinner's system. Each time

Reinforcement
Events that strengthen a behavior by bringing the results desired by the organism; this was primarily Skinner's term but is in general use now.

Just looking at these three pictures for a short period, note how many personality characteristics and traits you give the people just on the basis of appearance.

you laugh or share with friend A versus friend B, you reinforce the odds that you'll want to see that friend again. The same thing applies throughout all personality development: If studying is reinforced by good grades, you will study more often; if skipping school offers more reinforcement than it creates guilt, you will continue to skip school.

Albert Bandura

Note again the last sentence. A person might base behavior on feelings of guilt. Guilt obviously is a broad, internal concept that doesn't fit all that well with Skinner's mechanical view of behaviorism. Skinner's system is flawed because it doesn't give a person enough credit for being a thinking creature.

This was the complaint of **Albert Bandura**, a behaviorist who elaborated on Skinner's system. He did not deny that we learn a great number of things just by straight association. If you're bitten by a dog, a cat, a raccoon, and a snake when you are growing up, there's no question that your personality will include a clear-cut fear of animals. On the other hand, we learn many things by using our ability to think, analyze, and interpret. Bandura felt that much of our personality comes from observing others and **modeling** ourselves after them. This process can be very complex, rather than just mechanical: If you observe an alcoholic uncle in the family who is very friendly and outgoing and an aunt who is a teetotaler but nasty and aggressive, your feelings for or against alcohol are going to be very complex—something Skinner's system doesn't allow for. Bandura still is behavioristic, though, because he believes learning is a process of association, but the organism interprets and chooses between associations rather than just "counting" them and responding automatically to the one that for the moment has the most positive reinforcements. In other words, the organism performs an internal analysis.

Modeling
Bandura's term for learning by imitating others.

Bandura's studies on modeling have been very important. They have shown that, if children observe someone beating up a plastic doll, these children will become aggressive themselves. More important, perhaps, Bandura showed that, if someone is really, seriously afraid of snakes, for instance, he or she can lose that fear over time by seeing another person handling snakes comfortably. The person with the fear of snakes can model his or her behavior on that of others who handle snakes with little fear and with nothing happening to them. The important point is that we can relearn or retrain ourselves by deliberately developing a new set of associations (snakes are harmless) to replace the old.

Assessment of Behaviorism

We have mentioned most of the problems with behaviorism as we've gone along. The biggest one, especially for Skinner, is that it shortchanges the human's ability to think. On the positive side, though, the theory does show that we learn many behaviors just because they have been reinforced by positive associations.

Humanistic Theories

As you might have guessed, some people soon objected to what they saw as a rather depressing picture of us either as a bubbling id trying to express itself or as a robot. These people considered Freud's unconscious filled with id impulses unacceptable and the behaviorists' failure to acknowledge the importance of personal experience unworkable. In reaction to these theories, some psychologists developed **humanism**, which emphasized the whole person with his or her positive potential and which accepted the person as an individual human with all kinds of good

Humanism
A personality theory that places emphasis on the positive potential of the person; Rogers and Maslow were humanistic psychologists.

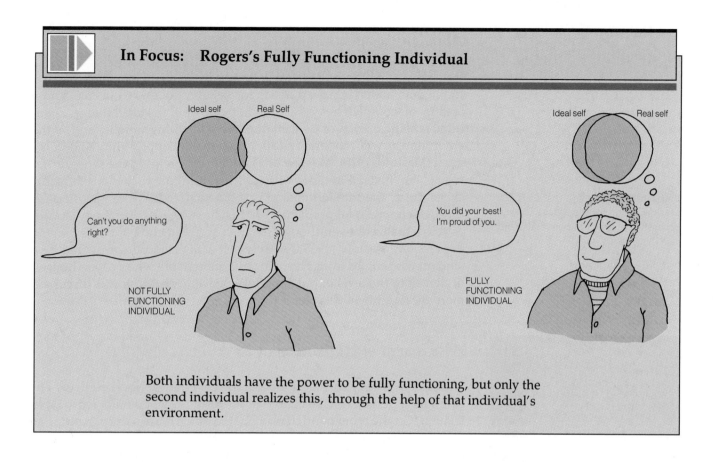

Both individuals have the power to be fully functioning, but only the second individual realizes this, through the help of that individual's environment.

qualities. So the focus is on *human* qualities, which explains how the name of this theory came about.

Carl Rogers

The leading humanist, **Carl Rogers**, was a minister for a while, but he had trouble with the idea that people are sinful and bad. Instead, he believed that we are basically good. The biggest problem we have, he said, is living up to what he called the **ideal self**. The ideal self is as close to perfection as one can get. We come into the world ready to become this ideal self, but at times we fall by the wayside while trying to get there. We are like a flower in our potential. If the environment is halfway decent, we will grow into a human who can be proud and internally beautiful. This can be accomplished by almost anyone who has the acceptance and warmth of love from parents in the early stages, from friends in the next stage, and from an intimate, personal relationship with someone as an adult. When we have united what we *should* be with what we *are*, we have become what he called a **fully functioning individual** (Rogers, 1951).

Ideal self
Rogers's term for the goal of each person's development; perfection.

Fully functioning individual
Rogers's term for someone who has become what he or she should be.

Abraham Maslow

Psychologist **Abraham Maslow** followed in Rogers's footsteps. He saw the human as having deep needs for beauty, goodness, justice, and a feeling of completeness—all the hopeful and positive things about human beings. Each of us has inherited something unique, and, *if* the environment will cooperate a little, we have the opportunity to become great (Maslow, 1970). Maslow does not mean "great" in the sense of "famous," but instead in terms of *actualizing* (bringing to life) our personal skills. Thus, the fulfilled person is **self-actualized**. We can accomplish this despite personal problems. For instance, he saw Abraham Lincoln as self-actualized, even though the man suffered endless bouts of deep depression (Maslow, 1968). A truly self-actualized person would be a student who comes from a terrible environment but who propels himself or herself to the level of outstanding achievement (Maslow is discussed more thoroughly in Chapter 5.)

Assessment of Humanism

Humanism is very upbeat; it makes us feel good. It also positively encourages a person to take charge of his or her own fate in a reasonable fashion. On the other hand, it may put too much faith in the person; after all, each of us wants to avoid the more difficult parts of life at times. For example, in the 1960s, humanism took over in the high schools. Students were allowed to take whatever courses they wanted, based on the assumption that they would choose the right thing. This became a disaster, since so many skipped all math, chemistry, literature, physics, and composition. An embarrassing number of graduates left school not able to solve the most basic math problems, to spell, or to write a coherent sentence. So, while humanism is a good theory for offsetting the negative focus of the other theories, it probably goes too far in its own positive direction.

Examining Personality Traits

The more or less permanent characteristics each of us has are sometimes called **personality traits**. In this section, we cover recent studies on traits, discussing what is known about them and where they might come from. A great deal has been learned from major research being conducted at the University of Minnesota, where 350 pairs of twins are being studied. Since identical twins have exactly the same heredity (they come from the same egg in the mother), they can be compared with fraternal twins (who do not have as much heredity in common since they are from different eggs) or with just brothers and sisters (least amount of common

Self-actualized
Maslow's term for the state of having brought to life the full potential of our skills.

Is this behavior the result of inherited characteristics or the environment? Do people who engage in activities like this have certain personality traits in common?

Personality traits
The more or less permanent personality characteristics that an individual has.

In Focus: The Big Picture: Major Personality Theories

	Early Psychoanalysis	Social Psychoanalysis	Behaviorism	Humanism
Major Theorists	Freud Jung	Horney Adler Erikson	Skinner Bandura	Rogers Maslow
Main Beliefs	Personality and behavior are determined by hidden, or unconscious forces.	Personality is influenced by the unconscious, but this unconscious is not all biological—social factors help shape the unconscious.	Personality is shaped by rewards and punishments and by modeling—forget the unconscious.	Personality is influenced by the unique potential within each of us.
Role of the Environment	Plays big role during first five years of life—but, after this, inner forces are more important	Plays big role in supplying love and making person feel important	Environment is all-important—it makes us who we are.	Decent environment needed to nurture inner potential
Definition of Healthy Personality	One that adequately balances conflicts between conscious and unconscious forces	One that recognizes the social forces of the unconscious and that tries to repair itself by resolving conflicts	One that receives effective rewards and punishments—the individual has little choice in this	One that is fully functioning and self-actualized

heredity). If the same trait shows up in the identical twins but not in the other pairs, then the odds are very good that it is an inherited trait.

Major Permanent Traits

The most recent evidence from these twin studies suggests that there are three traits that seem to be inherited or at least that appear from an early age (Lykken et al., 1987). The first one is how well people get along in social situations. The second is how traditional the person is—that is, will he or she follow the rules most of the time or be rebellious? The third is how comfortable a person feels. In other words, is the person relaxed and confident, or instead does he or she feel alone and not quite with it?

A different type of study followed 10,000 people—ages 25 to 74—for nine years to see how they changed over this period. Again, three characteristics tended to remain the same regardless of age. These three are very close to the ones just mentioned: (1) degree of friendliness; (2) how eager people are to do different or novel things; and (3) how anxious or comfortable they feel (Lykken et al., 1985; Costa & McCrae, 1986; Costa et al., 1987). (Since you have to remember this material, just learn the second list; it is the clearest, and it is close enough to the first one that you'll be safe.)

People *do* change throughout life in terms of how satisfied they feel, how high their morale is, and how active they are. To this point in time, only the three traits mentioned in the last paragraph seem pretty well set, maybe in "plaster," by the early 20s. Remember, though, that these three traits appear from birth and only later are they reinforced or not as other people respond to them. Thus, learning does have an influence, but only after certain tendencies have already been inherited. We all know of families in which two children were very different from birth; one was aggressive and cried a lot while the other was quiet and smiled. Parents and others respond in a certain way to these differences, and thus they continue to add to whatever inherited tendencies are already there.

Effects of the Environment

Most scientists who study personality today feel that roughly 50 percent of the total personality is controlled by heredity. Obviously, the environment will have an effect, but we seem to lean toward certain types of behavior from birth, as we've just discussed.

An environment, however, is not simply "good" or "bad." One of the more interesting recent findings is that even what seems to be exactly the same environment for the children in the family is, in fact, different for each child since each has a different personality from the beginning. So, they react differently to the same thing. If two children in a family are taken to a movie together, for example, it will have a different effect on each child. Such findings suggest that parents cannot control how children will respond; parents can only provide the best possible environment for their kids.

You will sometimes hear that birth order (whether one is the first, second, or third child, for example) is very important in how a child turns out. But, after thousands of studies in this area, there seems to be very little support for any lasting effect. Parents in normal families tend to treat the children as equally as possible, and, for the most part, they succeed. But each child sees what is going on from a different point of view. Finally, current studies are showing that interaction with a brother or sister or with playmates or school groups carries far heavier weight over time than do the parents. Of course, this assumes that the parents are not causing the children to live in a house of horrors but are giving them an acceptable environment (Plomin and Daniels, 1987; Daniels, 1986).

Finding Yourself in Personality Theories

As we mentioned at the beginning of this chapter, we don't have enough information yet on how accurate different personality theories are. Still, it might be interesting for you to explore some things about yourself, and see if you can find support for the theories discussed. Don't take it all too seriously; we're just doing an "experiment," so to speak.

Start with the Freudian theory. Go back in your mind to the last time you had a secret desire to do something you didn't think proper or moral. Note that you didn't merely go out and do it without caring. Instead, what probably happened was that you felt a very strong internal "push" to go ahead and do it. Next you began to feel concerned and guilty, and you had a sinking feeling in your stomach that you might actually do it. Then you weighed the pros and cons, the rights and wrongs of the situation. Finally, you did or didn't do it. Note how very close this comes to your ego (your *self*) trying to let the id have its way, but also balancing the reality and morality of the situation by listening to the superego. It certainly seems like Freud might have been partly right, doesn't it?

Now the behavioral theory. Pick a couple of habits you have that you're not necessarily happy with:

biting your fingernails, smoking, doing funny things with your fingers, tugging at your socks, or who knows what. Go back in your mind to the last couple of times you did this behavior. You didn't want to do it, but it came automatically. Such habits are very hard to trace in some cases, but here is how they likely get started: Sometime in the past you felt a lot of stress and strain. The way the body is constructed, when stress occurs, we prepare to take some kind of action, like running away. That's natural. But we can't actually run away—society won't allow it. So, rather than run, you started doing something—anything—with your body to relieve the tension. Having done *something*, your body relaxed a little; this made you feel better, which reinforced the behavior (even though what you did wasn't *really* helpful). Thus, you tend to repeat this something—smoking, nail biting, and so on—year after year; each time, the reinforcement adds up so that the drive to do it gets stronger and stronger. The behavior becomes part of you. As you can see, this is the behavioral explanation for how we gradually develop patterns of activities that come to represent our personalities.

For the third example, the

humanistic theories, you have to use your "Freudian superego" and not cheat. At a certain point, we will tell you not to read any further. Please don't, or you'll spoil the experiment. Don't even peek a line ahead. Here we go: In privacy, write down the three things that you most admire about yourself. Beneath that, write the three things about yourself that you find obnoxious, gross, or unpleasant. Be *very* honest. Don't read any further until you have finished the writing.

Now you need to examine your inner feelings very carefully. Notice how much stress and strain you felt, how physically uncomfortable you were, when you wrote the bad part. Note how you avoided and wanted to get away from it. Why? Could it be that you are basically a good person seeking self-actualization and fulfillment and that you are destined to be good? That these negative things just don't seem to belong to you and should go away? That's what the humanists would say. (Don't forget to destroy what you wrote! And remember that defects are part of all of us, and you're not alone at all in feeling bad about certain aspects of yourself).

Summary

1. Freud's system focuses on unconscious impulses that are constantly seeking expression. The id contains our animal needs and tries to do what it wants. It is controlled by the ego or self, which balances the desires of the id with the restraints and judgments of the superego, or conscience.

2. Carl Jung felt we were guided by a collective unconscious, which holds all the myths about personality types (such as "mother" or "hero") and passes them on from one generation to another. He believed we also make up "fake" personalities or masks, called personas.

3. Karen Horney thought that social influences were most important in personality development. We live from birth with a dread that we will not be accepted by others, and this concern colors our personalities. Alfred Adler agreed about the importance of social factors and stressed that we feel inadequate and spend our energies trying to be important to offset such feelings.

4. Erik Erikson developed an elaborate theory in which life is divided up into a series of eight stages. In each of these stages, we have to deal with others; how we turn out depends on how good these relationships are during each stage.

5. Behaviorism sees personality as arising from learning and association. B. F. Skinner claimed that we act strictly in terms of the kinds of reinforcements we get, rather than in terms of conscious choices. Bandura focused on learning also, but claimed that we were more than just robots, that we could accept or reject certain kinds of behavior that we have learned by a process called modeling.

6. Humanistic theories stress that we are basically good and are aiming to fulfill our potential if the environment cooperates even a little bit. Carl Rogers saw us as destined to become fully functioning individuals. Abraham Maslow called people who found a place in life and did their jobs with excellence "self-actualized."

7. The three personality traits that seem to be inherited (or, at least, that are with us from a very early age) are degree of friendliness, conformity or novel behavior, and how anxious or comfortable we feel.

8. The most important influences from the environment on our personalities seem to come from brothers, sisters, playmates, and school groups.

Key Words and Concepts

personality
psychoanalysis
Sigmund Freud
unconscious
free association
repression
libido
id
superego
ego
oral stage
anal stage
phallic stage
latency stage
genital stage
Carl Jung
collective
    unconscious

persona
neo-Freudians
Karen Horney
Alfred Adler
Erik Erikson
behaviorism
B. F. Skinner
reinforcements
Albert Bandura
modeling
humanism
Carl Rogers
ideal self
fully functioning
    individual
Abraham Maslow
self-actualized
personality traits

Review Questions

Matching (Answers can be used more than once.)

1. The unconscious is biological and remains basically unaffected by the environment.

2. Anxiety and fear stem from a lack of love.

3. Free will does not really exist.

4. Sigmund Freud

5. Observing others helps shape our personalities.

6. Critics argue that it reduces humans to little more than animals.

7. Carl Rogers

a. humanism

b. behaviorism

c. early psychoanalysis

d. social psychoanalysis (neo-Freudians)

8. B. F. Skinner

9. Emphasizes the whole person

10. Conflicts exist throughout life that need to be resolved in order to feel worthwhile.

11. Humans have a powerful potential for good.

12. The unconscious is concerned about how we get along with others.

Fill in the blank. Answer on a separate sheet of paper. (More than one word can be used.)

13. According to Freud, the part of the personality that makes us feel guilty is called the _____ .

14. Freud's method for studying the unconscious is called _____ .

15. One's psychological mask, or _____ , hides one's real personality.

16. Those psychologists who broke away from Freud to emphasize social forces are sometimes referred to as

    _____ .

17. _____ argued that love is an essential ingredient for a healthy personality.

18. Erikson's term for sharing a special closeness with another is called _____ .

19. According to Maslow, a person who strives to fulfill his or her potential is becoming _____ .

True/False

20. Evidence suggests that friendliness may be partly inherited.

21. Studies consistently show that birth order has a significant effect on personality.

22. Evidence suggests that a tendency to feel anxious may be partly inherited.

23. The willingness to try new things may be partly inherited.

Discussion Questions

1. There was a time when it was very fashionable to be psychoanalyzed. Why do you suppose it was popular? Also, do you think you would ever want to be psychoanalyzed? Why or why not?

2. Sharon suffers from a severe bout of depression. How would Horney's explanation of her depression differ from Adler's?

3. Freud was probably correct to some extent in saying that much of our personality remains the same as we grow. Erikson was also probably correct to some extent in saying that much of our personality *does* change. Think back on your junior high school years. Describe aspects of your personality that have changed and aspects that have remained essentially the same.

4. If you were suffering from depression over the breakup of a relationship and you decided you wanted to see a therapist, would you prefer to talk with a behaviorist or with a humanist? Why?

5. As noted in the chapter, implementing humanism in the classroom in the 1960s turned out to be a disaster. Despite this, some people might argue that there's nothing wrong with applying humanistic ideas in the classroom, as long as certain guidelines are set. Propose a humanistic change you'd like to see adopted at your school. Make the proposal practical and somewhat detailed. (A "humanistic" change would be one that would encourage students to handle their own fates.)

6. If you could magically change one aspect of your personality—right now—would you choose to change something? If so, what would you change and why? If not, why not? Also, what is one aspect of your personality that you would never change? Explain.

7. The chapter explains that three personality traits seem to be inherited: friendliness, trying new things, and anxiety. Does this conclusion accurately describe your own life? Why or why not? Describe in detail several of your traits and compare these traits with other members of your family.

8. Out of all the theories presented in the chapter, which one seems best suited to understanding someone with a severe mental disorder, and which one is best suited to understanding someone who is relatively healthy? Explain.

Activities

1. Write five unemotional statements on an index card. For example, one statement might be, "My middle name is Inga." But make one of these statements a complete lie. Write the statements before reading any further.

Next, find 15 males and 15 females who would not know whether these statements are true or false. Tell each subject that one of the statements is a lie and to try to pick out the lie. Record their responses. Also, record their reasons for their choices.

As the chapter mentions, there is no clear scientific evidence for the existence of the unconscious, but this activity might be an informal way of testing its existence. According to Freud, even though we're unaware of our unconscious, it reveals itself in many subtle ways—handwriting, for example. So you may have unconsciously given yourself away when you wrote down the lie—maybe by the size of your lying words as compared to the size of your truthful words or by the way you phrased the lying sentence, and so on.

Analyze your results. How many picked the lie? Which gender did better? Can you draw any conclusions from this? Is one gender more sensitive to the unconscious, perhaps? What conclusions can you draw about the unconscious or about studying the unconscious? Explain in detail.

2. The chapter introduces two topics, unrelated to one another, that lend themselves well to library research:

   a. Child abuse—Many myths surround this issue. Try to find several recent articles that dispel these myths. Also, relate your research to personality. Is it possible to develop a personality "profile" of an abuser—where you can say that one personality is more likely than another to become an abuser? Why or why not?

   b. Famous psychologists—Pick one of the psychologists discussed in the chapter who caught your interest. Focus particularly on the psychologist's personality and how this personality may have led to the formulation of his or her theory.

   Pick *one* of these topics and write a report. Be sure to include your own reactions.

3. When we think of modeling, we usually think of the long-term effects that our parents as models have had on us. It might be fun to examine if modeling is a factor at all between strangers. You'll need to go to a mall (or a similar setting) with a friend to conduct this experiment. The hypothesis will be this: People are more likely to be influenced by a model who resembles them than by a model who is vastly different.

   General Procedure: Either you or your friend should dress in a "traditional" manner. *You* decide what might be considered traditional for your area. The other person should dress in a more "radical" manner. Again, you decide what radical means. Your task will be to find 20 people who fit your "traditional" definition.

   Specific Procedure: The traditionally dressed person, or the *model* in this case, will sit next to a subject. After about a minute or so, the radically dressed person will approach the model and say, "I'm doing a report for school on shoppers in malls. Would you mind filling out a survey?" Repeat this procedure ten times. Half the time, the model will say, "Yes, I love filling out surveys"; the other half of the time, the model will say something like this: "Nothing personal—but it seems that every time I come here I fill out ten surveys. I'd rather not right now." After each "yes" or "no" from the model, the survey person will then ask the subject, who has been overhearing all this, the same question. Record whether the subjects agree to take the survey and if the subjects' responses match the model's. Finally, repeat this entire procedure, using the "radical" person as the model this time.

   The survey mentioned is mainly camouflage, but, if the subject agrees to take the survey, you need to have something ready. So just write a quick survey with questions like, "How often do you shop?" and "Do you usually shop with friends or by yourself?"—and make 20 copies of the survey. If you want, you can include one or two "meaningful" questions that you *will* analyze, which might relate to your modeling hypothesis. For example, "Should male store clerks be required to wear ties? Should female store clerks be required to wear dresses?"

   Analyze your results. It might be helpful to draw a simple chart summarizing your results for each model. *Did* the traditional model have a greater effect on responses than the radical model? Make several guesses as to why or why not. What other conclusions can you draw from your results? Discuss. Finally, describe some of the memorable reactions you received from your subjects.

4. This next activity is a variation on the previous one. Follow the same procedure, but this time both experimenters should dress "traditionally" (since dress will not be a factor examined this time). This time you will examine what *kinds* of subjects are most likely to be affected by modeling. To find out, use *one* of the following three categories for your subjects: (a) ten "young"

versus ten "old" subjects; (b) ten females versus ten males; (c) ten people alone versus ten people in a group. Analyze your results, draw a chart, discuss your conclusions, and describe memorable reactions, just as in the previous activity.

5. As explained in the chapter, we all have some notion of our ideal selves, how we would ideally like to be. Pretend that you have, at this moment, become this ideal self. Don't make this ideal so perfect that you could never possibly achieve it. Simply envision how you would like to be in the near future. With this notion of your ideal self in mind, consider the following categories and describe your attitudes toward these categories from the point of view of your ideal self.

(a) school   (b) money   (c) gender roles
(d) family   (e) friends

Remember, you should describe your ideal attitudes—not your material ambitions. For example, for the money category, you wouldn't describe how much money you'll make as your ideal self, but your attitude toward money in general. Here's a sample (remember, the ideal self is writing): "I used to think that I wanted to be rich, but it's not that important to me now." You might write something like this, for example, if you presently seem too preoccupied with money. Write approximately a paragraph for each category. (If writing from the ideal point of view is awkward, write it in any way you like, as long as you still describe your ideal attitudes.) Write your descriptions before reading further.

Write the five categories listed above on four separate sheets of paper. Hand two of the sheets to two friends and the other two sheets to two family members. In-

struct them to write about what they perceive to be your *real* attitude today toward these categories. Have them write about a paragraph on each category. In other words, these four people will describe your *real* self, as they see you. Tell them to be as specific as possible.

Compare your *ideal* descriptions with others' *real* descriptions in detail. Are they very similar or dissimilar? Explain. According to your comparison, would you say that you're a "fully functioning individual"? Explain.

6. Not only do we have notions about our own ideal selves but we also have notions about ideal relationships. Survey five males and five females at random, and have them describe, in order, the top three *ideal* personality traits of someone they'd like to date.

Next, survey five males and five females (not the same people as before) who have been dating the same person for over a month. Ask them to describe, in order, the top three (*real*) personality traits of their dating partners.

Compare the *ideal* traits with the *real* traits in detail. Are they very similar or dissimilar? Explain. What conclusions can you draw about dating from all this? Explain. Finally, answer this discussion question:

According to Rogers, if a person feels a big discrepancy between his or her real and ideal self, that person can work to bridge the "gap." What if a person's conception of an ideal dating partner doesn't match the real traits of his or her partner? Can the person who feels this discrepancy do anything to bridge *that* gap (besides breaking up or trying to *change* the other person)? Explain.

An unusual job for which we have no
aptitude test.

Chapter 15

Measuring Personality and Personal Abilities

Global Look at the Chapter

Psychological tests are designed to measure facts about the individual objectively. The goals are to avoid bias of the type found in an interview and to compare individuals as factually as possible. The major tests are for personality, aptitude, achievement, and vocational interest. So far, such tests are the most accurate method we have to evaluate people in these areas.

Why Tests Are Used

The first thing we want to do is find out how many criminals and dangerous characters there are in your class. We can do this by using a book from 1911. According to its author, the really evil ones have the following four characteristics: (1) very low forehead; (2) strangely shaped head and jaw; (3) eyebrows growing together over the bridge of the nose; and (4) very protruding ears (like Mickey Mouse?) (Lombroso-Ferrero, 1911). You may find it hard to believe—or maybe not—but, after the book came out, police frequently held people who looked this way on suspicion.

Next, let's divide up your classmates by body type. The very heavy ones are smiling, happy people, really good-natured. Those with muscular bodies love adventure and athletics and have muscles in the brain. Those who are skinny are extra sensitive to pain and read books all the time (Sheldon, 1936).

What do you think? The first theory you probably don't believe because it never became part of our culture. The second one, however, is a little harder to fight since so many people accept it, even though studies over the years have shown it to be false. While there are happy heavy people and brainy thin people, overall the body does not reflect a specific type of personality.

To try to find out what a person is really like and to avoid such wild speculation, psychologists use **psychological tests**. A psychological test is an objective measure of what people know; how they act, think, or feel; or what their goals are or should be. A psychological test can be one that measures personality, intelligence, occupational needs, or job skills. These tests try to be as factual and unbiased as possible and provide a picture of personality or personal skills.

Psychological tests
Objective measures of what people know, how they act, think, and feel, and what their goals are.

Making a Personality Test

Suppose you wanted to make a test to find out what Sally X is really like. One of the first things you might do is pick test items that could reflect personality. Here are some: Did you have nightmares about monsters when a child? Do you sometimes hate school more than anything else in the world? Did you ever wet your bed? Do you ever have trouble getting to sleep?

These sound like they might give us some useful information for exploring Sally's inner workings. But, if you take these items and ask Sally to reply and she says "yes" to all of them, does she have a personality problem? The answer is *no*. Everyone will answer "yes" to all these questions, if they are being truthful. So, we have a problem: if everyone answers "yes," we have no way of focusing on an individual personality.

Establishing Norms

How, then, can we make up a test that will work? First, you have to use many items covering many areas. Once you do that, you must give the items to a large number of different people—older, younger, male, female, and so forth. You do this to find out how most people in each group answer the questions. The answers will vary, depending on the group. You want to know what are the *norm*al, expected, responses for most people in a specific group. By doing this, you are finding what are called **norms**. Norms show you the pattern of answers for different types of people. Since, in a personality test, we are trying to find something *individual* about the person, we will focus on the answers that are *not* common to those of her group to get a clue about Sally. If she answers questions like "I feel very happy most of the time" or "I never lie down when I'm studying" differently from her norm group, we believe we are picking up something special about her. In this way, we try to form a personality picture of her as compared to others. (Note that, for purposes of testing, we assume that, if most people feel a certain thing, it must be "normal." While this is not necessarily a good idea, it's the only way we can do it.)

Norms
Patterns of test answers from different types of people.

Establishing Validity

The test has been given to enough different types of people to establish some norms. Can we now give the test to Sally X? Suppose her answers differ from the norm group in that she finds things upsetting that others do not, she has trouble getting along with teachers, and she can't seem to accept the standards of society. Can we tell her she has a personality problem and needs help? If we do, based on these findings, we are making the same error as the developer of the "criminal test" mentioned in the first paragraph. Just because something sounds good and we *think* it is the case doesn't make it so. As a matter of fact, if these are Sally's "problems," they match the answers of a group of highly creative students who also deviate from the norm about as much as those who have serious personal difficulties.

So, how do we ever make certain a test is measuring what it is supposed to? For example, apart from personality, if we want to develop a test that will predict how good an accountant you would be, what do we do? Once the items are chosen, the test can be given to a group of students about to enter an accounting class. We would score this test, wait until they finished the class, and compare the scores they made with how well they did in the course. If the high scorers did well in the course and the low scorers did poorly, we know the test works. This is called test **validity**. If a test is valid, it measures what it is supposed to measure. Thus, before we can give the test to Sally, we have first to establish the validity of the test items we are using. This could be done by giving the personality items to large numbers of students and then finding out if those who answer certain items deviating from the norms drop out of school, are sent to the principal, get into fights, and so forth. If these people have all kinds of trouble, we have established validity; if not, the test is not valid—it doesn't measure what it is supposed to be measuring.

Establishing Reliability

One final thing must be done before we can have confidence in the test Sally will get. Test items can always be affected by what is going on around us. Most personality tests contain items such as "I feel depressed" or "I feel left out and don't have many friends" and so forth. Suppose that Sally goes to a movie the night before the test. To her it is a very sad, depressing movie that makes everything seem hopeless. But her companion doesn't agree and hence cannot share Sally's emotions regarding the film. If Sally takes the test the next day, the odds that she will say she feels depressed and left out by her friends are very high—even though this may not be her typical state. So, answers to test questions should not be too influenced by temporary changes. In other words, the test must have **reliability**.

Although at times defective, the aptitude or achievement tests are still the best measure of what has been learned.

Validity
Whether a test measures what it is supposed to measure.

Reliability
Whether what a test measures is influenced by temporary changes.

Reliability means that the answers must be reasonably consistent over time. A friend who shows up one time for a date 20 minutes late, one time 3 minutes late, one time 50 minutes late, and so forth is clearly unreliable. So, too, with the test. It is unreliable if it is inconsistent. One way to measure reliability is to give a test to group A on a given day. Then you give the same test to the same group, A, two weeks later. If their answers are mostly the same, then the test is reliable. If many answers have changed, the test is unreliable. You can see what would happen with the accounting test if one week you got 98 percent and the next you got 34 percent on the same test. Obviously, the test would not be measuring with any accuracy and couldn't be used to measure a person's accounting abilities or anything else.

In summary: A test must have a large number of items. It must be normed so that we know how different groups of people tend to answer the questions. It must be valid and measure what it claims to measure. And, finally, it must measure reliably.

Personality Inventories

A **personality inventory** is a list of items about beliefs, habits, hopes, needs, and desires. The test is given using a test booklet and answer sheet. The questions are very similar to the ones we've been talking about: "I believe people like me." "When I get bored, I stir things up." "I have a happy home." And so forth.

Personality inventory
A list of items about a person's beliefs, habits, hopes, needs, and desires.

The test used most often in schools is the **California Psychological Inventory**. It has 480 items, which are scored in terms of categories like feelings of self-acceptance, self-control, desire to achieve, how you get along with others, and the like (Gough, 1960). The test is one of the best of this type, but, even given that, it is only *fairly* valid and reliable. Thus, it can be faulty for any given person, even though overall it is useful for locating quickly some people with difficulties. The trouble with these tests is that they too often pick out those who *don't* have problems. Still, they are useful for general screening in order to locate those who might need help. A score that indicates a problem must always be followed up by a face-to-face discussion with a counselor or psychologist to avoid serious error (Anastasi, 1982).

A word of caution is in order: If not already, then sometime in the future, you probably will be given a series of tests as part of a job interview. They may include a test similar to the California inventory but more personal (and offensive). These tests are designed to search for abnormality. Sometimes, after taking these tests, you are turned down for a job. This can be very upsetting and make you feel that something might be wrong with you. The validity of these personality tests is so poor that they make many errors. The ethics of using them is highly questionable. But, the

Figure 15.1
Example of a projective test

Projective tests
Tests measuring inner feelings projected onto a vague stimulus, such as an ink blot or unclear picture.

Rorschach test
Ink blot projective test developed by Hermann Rorschach.

Figure 15.2
Ink blot test similar to the Rorschach

important point is: Don't go off thinking the test found a deep, secret defect that cost you the job. It didn't.

Projective Tests

It is not too hard to "fool" a personality inventory by merely checking items to reflect the way you *wish* to be or the way you see yourself (which might not be that accurate). The inventories do have built-in lie scales to catch those who are not telling the truth. For example, one of them has a question, "I read every editorial in the newspaper every day." Nobody does that, so it trips up those who are faking. Also, personality inventories seem to deal pretty much with the surface, rather than getting down to the nitty-gritty of our deeper personalities.

To try to offset these problems, **projective tests** were designed. (You have to pay close attention here to get the logic of how these operate.) *Projection* here means the same thing that it does for a singer. A singer must project (throw) the voice outward until it lands on the audience. The same is true of the projective test. The test taker projects his or her innermost self onto the stimulus provided. For example, look at Figure 15.1. What is it? Some will say a cactus, some a fork, some a flower, and so forth. The answer will vary, depending on the person's experiences in life. Such an example is simple, but it shows the principle of the projective test. If the stimulus is more complex and the test taker is told to list a number of things it looks like, psychologists assume that some of the answers are coming from deeper in the personality.

The Ink Blot Test

The most famous projective test is the "ink blot," called the **Rorschach test** (ROAR-shock) after the designer, a Swiss psychiatrist named Hermann Rorschach. (Incredible as it seems, his nickname in school, "Klex," meant "ink blot.") Rorschach spent much time in his basement splashing ink onto the middle of pieces of paper and then folding them together to get designs similar to that shown in Figure 15.2. After going through hundreds, he finally settled on ten of them, some in color, which were printed on cards. He believed that those who look at the card and see something moving in the blot (projection) have a lot of emotion and a good fantasy life. Those seeing color are explosive people. Those seeing lots of white space are negative people. What Rorschach based his conclusions on has never been clear, and the validity of the Rorschach is terrible. So is its reliability, because the second time around most people see entirely different things.

The Principle of Projection

Our goal here is to discuss the principle of projection. You see a vague stimulus, you have to give responses. The more responses given, the more likely you are to dig into your deeper self. Even if this works, though, it is still hard to know what the responses given really mean.

If you look at Figure 15.3, you will see another projective test item, this one a picture of two women. The picture is vague, and the test taker is asked to make up a "story" about what is happening. One person might say, for instance, that the woman in front is listening to the evil part of herself, telling her to do something. Such an answer might indicate a conflict in the test taker. Or it might just be a theme from a television show or novel. But, if the test taker sees enough cards and tells enough similar stories about personal problems of the same type, the tester can get a rough idea of some of the core problems that might exist. Again, validity and reliability are low, but they are better here than with the Rorschach.

Are projective tests of any use? Probably some, but not as much as you might think. They do offer the counselor or psychologist a chance to talk to the test taker, and they give some idea of how the test taker approaches problems. If the test taker is very disturbed, he or she might see bizarre, strange, objects and events in the pictures (Anastasi, 1982). Some psychologists ignore the poor validity and claim the tests help them understand the person. While they are entitled to their views, in general high validity is much preferred.

Aptitude and Achievement Tests

The major goal of any kind of testing is to sort out individual skills or characteristics when dealing with large numbers of people. An attempt is made not only to understand people but also to aim them in the right direction. For instance, a person whose eyes widen and who secretly begins to feel terrified (like one of the authors of this book) and wants to scratch the floor on an airplane in an attempt to escape should avoid working toward being a flight attendant or pilot. On the other hand, people who love small detail and are precise should check out their skills in bookkeeping or accounting to see if these might be the fields for them to pursue.

We will discuss some of the tests available in these areas, but first we have to sort out some confusing terminology. *Intelligence*, which was discussed at length in Chapter 9, is supposed to be a measure of our overall ability to handle general mental problems. The word "general" is used because intelligence is not thought to be specific. The two types of tests we will cover here *are* specific; they deal with specific, not general, abilities.

Figure 15.3
Thematic Apperception Test projective test item

Aptitude Tests

Aptitude
One's special skills as measured by an aptitude test.

Aptitude tests
Tests that measure one's special skills (in carpentry, medicine, and so forth).

The word **aptitude** is part of our everyday vocabulary. We say so-and-so has an aptitude for medicine, or for law, or carpentry, or engineering. We mean that this person seems to have special skills in that area.

Aptitudes are hard to measure with tests. But there are some **aptitude tests** available. These tests are usually grouped together, in the sense that the person takes all of them to see in which categories he or she scores highest. Here are some examples:

Figure 15.4
A mechanical aptitude test item: If the gear on the right turns in the direction of the arrow, what direction does the gear on the left turn?

Mechanical Comprehension This test attempts to predict success in fields involving repair of autos, refrigerators, air-conditioning equipment, and the like. A typical item is shown in Figure 15.4. If gear X is moving in the direction of the arrow, will gear Y move: (a) clockwise or (b) counterclockwise? This item and many *very* complex ones are used to measure a person's understanding of mechanical devices. The scores are compared with the scores of people who are already in these fields to see how well the test taker does. (Remember norm groups and validity?)

Verbal Skills This test measures a person's interest in and knowledge about words. We assume that someone who scores poorly in this area will not do well in occupations requiring a great deal of reading or writing. An example of a simple test item in this area is: Which word is spelled incorrectly? (a) horse (b) house (c) humit (d) hanger.

Clerical Speed and Accuracy Attempts to measure some of the skills necessary in clerical and office jobs fall into this category. This particular test is a timed, speed test because, even though you might be able to get the answers, if it takes you forever to do so, you won't be much use on the job. A typical item is: As quickly as you can, find the underlined test items and mark them on your answer sheet.

Test Item	Answer Sheet
MS MQ <u>MP</u> MF	A. MF MQ MP MX
A7 B2 AB <u>C3</u>	B. C3 B3 B2 A7

This sampling should give you an idea of the kinds of aptitude tests available. None is accurate enough to predict success in a field. But they can give clues to areas in which you might do well or that you should avoid. Their validities and reliabilities are good, but they measure only a small part of what would be involved in any given occupation (Cronbach, 1980).

Achievement Tests

Another kind of test is given in elementary school and high school to measure student progress. These tests are often used to determine how well a school system or class is doing, but they can also be useful when counseling an individual student. They resemble the exams given in history, English, or math courses, but they are usually normed for the whole country or for certain segments of it. Sometimes they are used to give advanced placement in a certain course to a student. Such tests are called **achievement tests** because they contain specific content that was (or should have been) learned in the classroom. Those who do best in class achieve the most in a certain area. The tests are not designed to predict future performance or skills, as is the case with an aptitude test—even though we assume that, if you do well now in a particular area on the test, you will do so in the future.

Achievement tests
Tests that measure the amount of specific material remembered from the classroom.

Most students who plan to go to college will run head on into one of life's more dreaded experiences: taking the Scholastic Aptitude Test, called the SAT for short. We saved this test for last in this section because it is a controversial mess, and it is likely to remain so as long as it continues to exist, inflicting mental agony on high school students and their parents.

The SAT is made up of advanced verbal and mathematical problems. You have to be able to define the meaning of words as they fit into certain sentences, solve word puzzles, and deal with fairly complex logic and mathematics problems.

But there are some difficulties. The SAT is supposed to be a *predictor* of college work, not an achievement test. Is that even possible? Doesn't the test require that you have learned specific math techniques in order to answer the questions? Or that you have had a course in social science in order to deal with verbal social science problems? That certainly seems to be the case. For example, let's take this:

Columbus discovered America in: (a) 1492 (b) 1700 (c) 1859 (d) 1950.

This item is a good *achievement* test item for a history test in fourth grade. We would expect it to be part of a course in basic American history. It is assumed that, by high school, everyone has already learned the answer and remembers it. We certainly hope you do (it's not 1950). So, this same item can become part of an *aptitude* test for high school students. How is this possible? Aptitude tests use such items based on the assumption that, as one goes through school life, those who absorb and retain the most material are also going to be the best in that area in the future because by then they will know even more. You see how complicated this is? There seems to be no way to write an aptitude test item without getting involved in how well you've done in school and how much you remember from school. Thus, the SAT should probably be called the Scholastic *Achievement* Test.

The biggest problem with the SAT is that environments differ so much from one person to another. We knew a psychologist who had never before been out of New York City itself and had never seen a live horse, cow, or pig. He was giving a talk to some grade-schoolers in a rural part of West Virginia. The children couldn't believe it when he asked them if any of them had the task of milking the cows that were in a pen next to the school. The problem was that the "cows" were pigs.

It is, then, impossible to measure aptitude without at the same time measuring achievement, which makes the SAT somewhat questionable (Green, 1978; Owen, 1983). Since schools vary as much as does the overall environment, the test leans toward those from well-to-do schools. There are other problems: A low score can damage a person's self-esteem, and the test *can* err as much as 30 points in either direction just by chance. Expensive coaching for the test beforehand can help some students, again giving an advantage to those with money. But, on the average, coaching doesn't help to an extent that matches the cost. Some people claim that the test is biased against minorities, and there is support for this (Morgan, 1984).

On the positive side, the test has good validity and reliability for enough students to make it worthwhile. And it does a much better job of predicting college success than an interview or letters of recommendation (Kaplan, 1982). While high school grade averages are better predictors of college success than the SAT, the test can add a little bit to predicting a person's chances for success (Weiss & Davidsom, 1981). (Note, though, that college success is only about 50 percent predictable, no matter how many or what measures are used.)

Vocational Interest Tests

Probably one of the most important decisions any of us ever makes is the one involving occupation. If things turn out well, most of us stay in the same general field throughout life, even though we may change where we work a number of times.

Areas of interest keep changing for most students until their junior or senior year in high school. Then they begin to become focused—at least in a general sort of way.

Vocational interest test
A test that attempts to predict a good occupational area for an individual.

One of the most useful tests a student can take is the **vocational interest test**. Fortunately, the major tests in this area have some of the highest validities in psychological testing. Hence, their ability to predict is exceptional compared to the other tests we have discussed. Over 50 percent of people in some studies have been checked up on for more than 20 years after taking the test and are still reasonably happy in the selected occupation (Walsh & Betz, 1985).

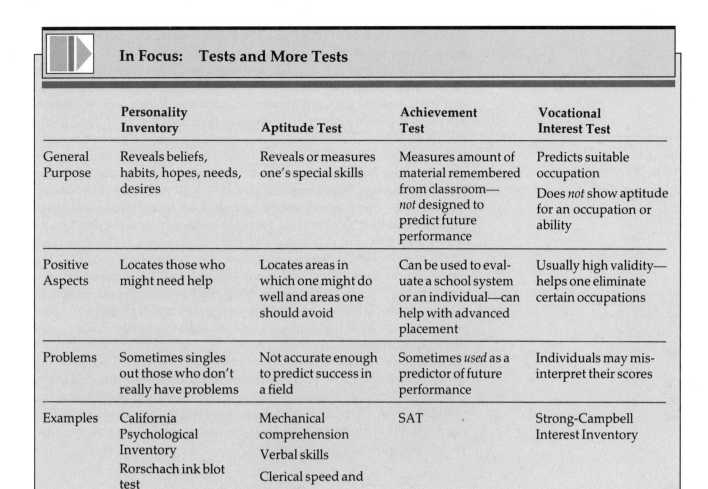

	Personality Inventory	Aptitude Test	Achievement Test	Vocational Interest Test
General Purpose	Reveals beliefs, habits, hopes, needs, desires	Reveals or measures one's special skills	Measures amount of material remembered from classroom—*not* designed to predict future performance	Predicts suitable occupation Does *not* show aptitude for an occupation or ability
Positive Aspects	Locates those who might need help	Locates areas in which one might do well and areas one should avoid	Can be used to evaluate a school system or an individual—can help with advanced placement	Usually high validity—helps one eliminate certain occupations
Problems	Sometimes singles out those who don't really have problems	Not accurate enough to predict success in a field	Sometimes *used* as a predictor of future performance	Individuals may misinterpret their scores
Examples	California Psychological Inventory Rorschach ink blot test	Mechanical comprehension Verbal skills Clerical speed and accuracy	SAT	Strong-Campbell Interest Inventory

The Strong-Campbell Interest Inventory

The most used interest test is called the **Strong-Campbell Interest Inventory**. It is named after the two developers of the test. The test taker is provided with a test booklet and answer sheet. The test contains hundreds of statements and choices to which the test taker responds with "like" or "dislike," "agree" or "disagree." Or the person is asked to choose among such things as being an actor, being an artist, or being a botanist. This is simple enough, but the test is actually more clever than it seems at first. Most people starting out, when faced with a choice of occupations, aren't sure at all what they want to be. Hence, it might do no good to ask these questions; if you already knew the answers, you wouldn't need the test. So the test's authors took thousands of people reasonably successful in all kinds of occupations and gave these occupational questions to them. Also included in the test were all kinds of questions not related directly to

Strong-Campbell Interest Inventory
The most used interest test; based on answers of people successful in certain fields.

occupation, such as "Would you like to drive along the side of a mountain, discuss the purpose of life, or go fishing?" and so forth.

Next, all the test answers (occupational and otherwise) for all these people were divided up according to what occupation they were in, *not* according to how they answered the questions. When new test takers answer questions, a computer compares their answers with those of the people in each of hundreds of occupations and points out the occupational groups with which the test taker has the most in common. The content of the item is *not* important, which might well be the key to the success of the test. For example, if you agree that you would like to be an "auctioneer," this carries a *negative* weight for a score high on engineering since real-life engineers don't want to be auctioneers. We don't know why—they just don't. It turns out that, as a group, real-life lawyers might prefer to be skydivers—at least on paper—and so, if you check the same answer they do on that item, you are credited a plus toward a career in law. Hence, the test is showing you how similar you are in hobbies, activities, interests, and the like to people already in different occupations. If you have that much in common with them, you will probably like that occupation (Cronbach, 1980).

The results from the test are reported on a computer printout showing many occupations that fall into such categories as working outdoors, working in science, engaging in artistic tasks, helping people directly, working in sales or politics, and doing business or clerical work (see Figure 15.5). How high you score in these areas is shown as you are compared with others in the various fields.

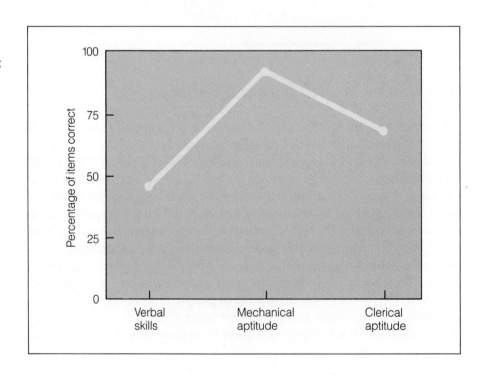

Called a "profile," this is a visual representation of scores on three tests used to compare skills in three different areas (see page 380).

One of the biggest problems faced in using these tests is a misunderstanding about how they work. Students might score high on an occupation like "funeral director" and come away from the test saying, "Oh, ick, I don't want to deal with dead bodies." But none of the occupations is to be taken at face value in that way. A funeral director is interested in running a small business, dealing with the public, helping people who are in need, and the like. He or she doesn't like dead bodies any more than anybody else does. If used in the right spirit, the test can be enormously helpful. Finally, the test is very good at helping you to eliminate certain occupations. If you score low in most occupations within a certain area, the chances that you will like any of those occupations are quite remote (Walsh & Betz, 1985).

Cautions About Interest Tests

It is critical to understand that the interest test does not show that you have the aptitude or ability for an occupation in which you score high. So, try not to set your sights on jobs that, deep in your heart, you know you are not qualified for. But we all can adapt goals to a different type of work in a field we like. For example, in real life, the pilots think they are the most important part of an airline, the mechanics feel *they're* the most important, the flight attendants feel the airline would fail without their aid and public relations work, and the executives think they are really keeping it all together. The point is that a person with clear-cut aviation interests will fit into one (or more) of these subcategories better than into the others and can still be in his or her desired field.

A Second Look at Test Validity

Tests of all kinds have a way of seeming more powerful and accurate than they really are. This is a lot like the idea that, if you read something in print, it *must* be true. Stop and think about all the dummies you know. Someday many of them will be writing things that find their way into print. Would you believe something you read, if you knew they had written it? The same principle applies to tests.

This is a good place to look again and a little more closely at *validity*. We will use completely imaginary numbers just to help you grasp the point. Suppose you had a tub filled with 100 red marbles and 100 white marbles, mixed. We will blindfold you and have you pull out 100 marbles. White means no error; red, an error. We will call perfect validity 100 white marbles. You pull out 53 white and 47 red ones. That means you made an "error" 47 times. Such is the case with validity—which is never perfect. In fact, in real life, tests that produce results like this would be considered to have good validity. Why? Because, as you'll see in the next section, many methods, such as interviewing, will produce maybe only

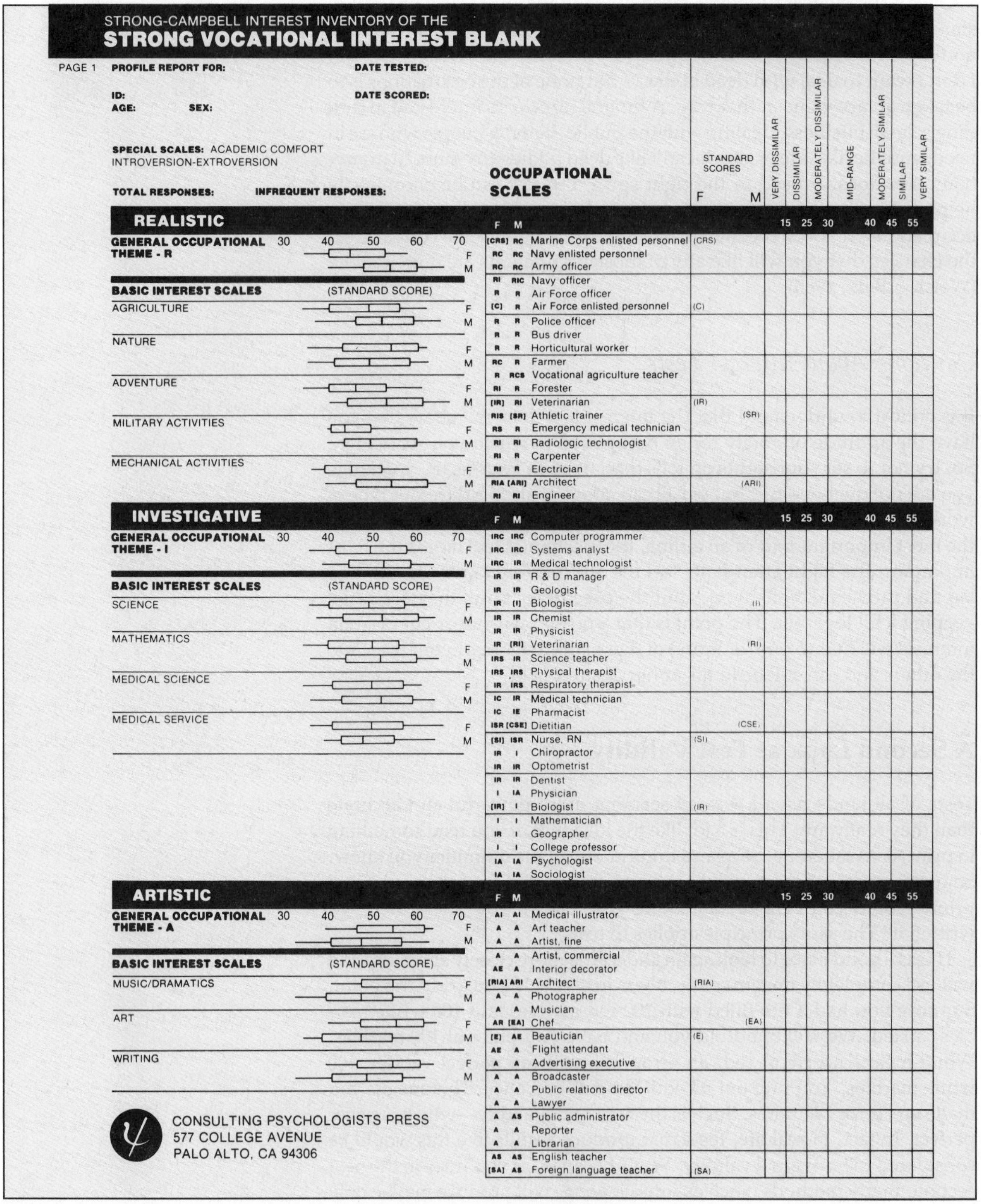

STRONG-CAMPBELL INTEREST INVENTORY OF THE
STRONG VOCATIONAL INTEREST BLANK

PAGE 1 **PROFILE REPORT FOR:** **DATE TESTED:**
ID: **DATE SCORED:**
AGE: **SEX:**

SPECIAL SCALES: ACADEMIC COMFORT
INTROVERSION-EXTROVERSION

TOTAL RESPONSES: **INFREQUENT RESPONSES:**

OCCUPATIONAL SCALES — STANDARD SCORES F M — VERY DISSIMILAR, DISSIMILAR, MODERATELY DISSIMILAR, MID-RANGE, MODERATELY SIMILAR, SIMILAR, VERY SIMILAR — 15 25 30 40 45 55

REALISTIC

GENERAL OCCUPATIONAL THEME - R 30 40 50 60 70 F M

BASIC INTEREST SCALES (STANDARD SCORE)
AGRICULTURE F M
NATURE F M
ADVENTURE F M
MILITARY ACTIVITIES F M
MECHANICAL ACTIVITIES F M

F	M	Occupational Scale	Standard Score F	Standard Score M
(CRS)	RC	Marine Corps enlisted personnel	(CRS)	
RC	RC	Navy enlisted personnel		
RC	RC	Army officer		
RI	RIC	Navy officer		
R	R	Air Force officer		
(C)	R	Air Force enlisted personnel	(C)	
R	R	Police officer		
R	R	Bus driver		
R	R	Horticultural worker		
RC	R	Farmer		
R	RCS	Vocational agriculture teacher		
RI	R	Forester		
(IR)	RI	Veterinarian	(IR)	
RIS	(SR)	Athletic trainer		(SR)
RS	R	Emergency medical technician		
RI	RI	Radiologic technologist		
RI	R	Carpenter		
RI	R	Electrician		
RIA	(ARI)	Architect		(ARI)
RI	RI	Engineer		

INVESTIGATIVE

GENERAL OCCUPATIONAL THEME - I 30 40 50 60 70 F M

BASIC INTEREST SCALES (STANDARD SCORE)
SCIENCE F M
MATHEMATICS F M
MEDICAL SCIENCE F M
MEDICAL SERVICE F M

F	M	Occupational Scale	Standard Score F	Standard Score M
IRC	IRC	Computer programmer		
IRC	IRC	Systems analyst		
IRC	IR	Medical technologist		
IR	IR	R & D manager		
IR	IR	Geologist		
IR	(I)	Biologist		(I)
IR	IR	Chemist		
IR	IR	Physicist		
IR	(RI)	Veterinarian		(RI)
IRS	IR	Science teacher		
IRS	IRS	Physical therapist		
IR	IRS	Respiratory therapist		
IC	IR	Medical technician		
IC	IE	Pharmacist		
ISR	(CSE)	Dietitian		(CSE)
(SI)	ISR	Nurse, RN	(SI)	
IR	I	Chiropractor		
IR	IR	Optometrist		
IR	IR	Dentist		
I	IA	Physician		
(IR)	I	Biologist	(IR)	
I	I	Mathematician		
IR	I	Geographer		
I	I	College professor		
IA	IA	Psychologist		
IA	IA	Sociologist		

ARTISTIC

GENERAL OCCUPATIONAL THEME - A 30 40 50 60 70 F M

BASIC INTEREST SCALES (STANDARD SCORE)
MUSIC/DRAMATICS F M
ART F M
WRITING F M

F	M	Occupational Scale	Standard Score F	Standard Score M
AI	AI	Medical illustrator		
A	A	Art teacher		
A	A	Artist, fine		
A	A	Artist, commercial		
AE	A	Interior decorator		
(RIA)	ARI	Architect	(RIA)	
A	A	Photographer		
A	A	Musician		
AR	(EA)	Chef		(EA)
(E)	AE	Beautician	(E)	
AE	A	Flight attendant		
A	A	Advertising executive		
A	A	Broadcaster		
A	A	Public relations director		
A	A	Lawyer		
A	AS	Public administrator		
A	A	Reporter		
A	A	Librarian		
AS	AS	English teacher		
(SA)	AS	Foreign language teacher	(SA)	

CONSULTING PSYCHOLOGISTS PRESS
577 COLLEGE AVENUE
PALO ALTO, CA 94306

Figure 15.5 Strong-Campbell Interest Inventory of the Strong Vocational Interest Blank

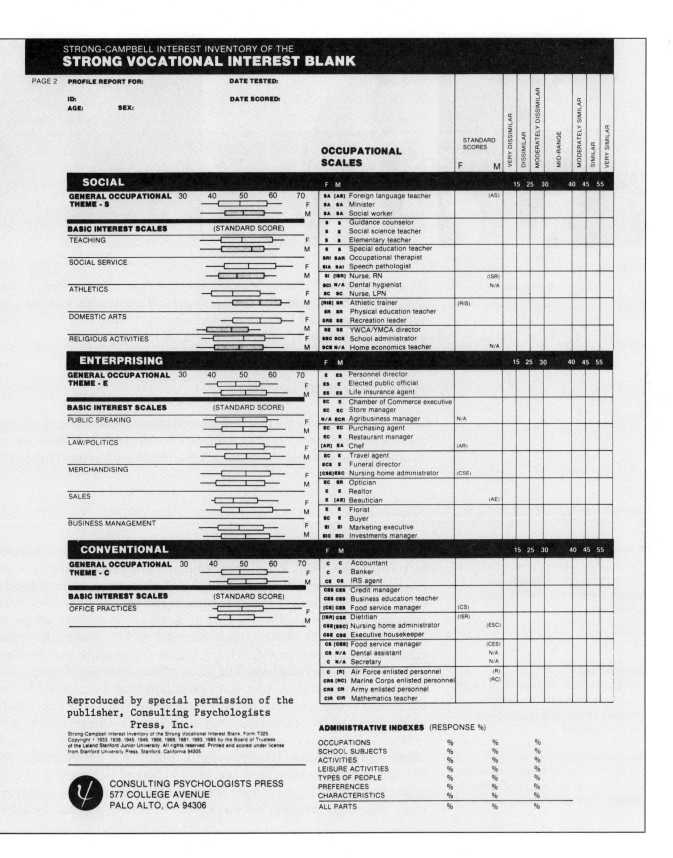

STRONG-CAMPBELL INTEREST INVENTORY OF THE
STRONG VOCATIONAL INTEREST BLANK

PAGE 2   PROFILE REPORT FOR: DATE TESTED:

ID: DATE SCORED:
AGE: SEX:

OCCUPATIONAL SCALES

	STANDARD SCORES							
	F	M	VERY DISSIMILAR	DISSIMILAR	MODERATELY DISSIMILAR	MID-RANGE	MODERATELY SIMILAR	SIMILAR	VERY SIMILAR

SOCIAL

GENERAL OCCUPATIONAL THEME - S   30 40 50 60 70   F / M

F M   15 25 30   40 45 55

			F	M
SA [AS]	Foreign language teacher			(AS)
SA SA	Minister			
SA SA	Social worker			
S S	Guidance counselor			
S S	Social science teacher			
S S	Elementary teacher			
S S	Special education teacher			
SRI SAR	Occupational therapist			
SIA SAI	Speech pathologist			
SI [ISR]	Nurse, RN			(ISR)
SCI N/A	Dental hygienist			N/A
SC SC	Nurse, LPN			
[RIS] SR	Athletic trainer		(RIS)	
SR SR	Physical education teacher			
SRE SE	Recreation leader			
SE SE	YWCA/YMCA director			
SEC SCE	School administrator			
SCE N/A	Home economics teacher			N/A

BASIC INTEREST SCALES   (STANDARD SCORE)

TEACHING — F / M
SOCIAL SERVICE — F / M
ATHLETICS — F / M
DOMESTIC ARTS — F / M
RELIGIOUS ACTIVITIES — F / M

ENTERPRISING

GENERAL OCCUPATIONAL THEME - E   30 40 50 60 70   F / M

F M   15 25 30   40 45 55

			F	M
E ES	Personnel director			
ES E	Elected public official			
ES ES	Life insurance agent			
EC E	Chamber of Commerce executive			
EC EC	Store manager			
N/A ECR	Agribusiness manager		N/A	
EC EC	Purchasing agent			
EC E	Restaurant manager			
[AR] EA	Chef		(AR)	
EC E	Travel agent			
ECS E	Funeral director			
[CSE] ESC	Nursing home administrator		(CSE)	
EC ER	Optician			
E E	Realtor			
E [AE]	Beautician			(AE)
E E	Florist			
EC E	Buyer			
EI EI	Marketing executive			
EIC ECI	Investments manager			

BASIC INTEREST SCALES   (STANDARD SCORE)

PUBLIC SPEAKING — F / M
LAW/POLITICS — F / M
MERCHANDISING — F / M
SALES — F / M
BUSINESS MANAGEMENT — F / M

CONVENTIONAL

GENERAL OCCUPATIONAL THEME - C   30 40 50 60 70   F / M

F M   15 25 30   40 45 55

			F	M
C C	Accountant			
C C	Banker			
CE CE	IRS agent			
CES CES	Credit manager			
CES CES	Business education teacher			
[CS] CES	Food service manager		(CS)	
[ISR] CSE	Dietitian		(ISR)	
CSE [ESC]	Nursing home administrator			(ESC)
CSE CSE	Executive housekeeper			
CS [CES]	Food service manager			(CES)
CS N/A	Dental assistant			N/A
C N/A	Secretary			N/A
C [R]	Air Force enlisted personnel			(R)
CRS [RC]	Marine Corps enlisted personnel			(RC)
CRS CR	Army enlisted personnel			
CIR CIR	Mathematics teacher			

BASIC INTEREST SCALES   (STANDARD SCORE)

OFFICE PRACTICES — F / M

Reproduced by special permission of the publisher, Consulting Psychologists Press, Inc.

CONSULTING PSYCHOLOGISTS PRESS
577 COLLEGE AVENUE
PALO ALTO, CA 94306

ADMINISTRATIVE INDEXES (RESPONSE %)

OCCUPATIONS	%	%	%
SCHOOL SUBJECTS	%	%	%
ACTIVITIES	%	%	%
LEISURE ACTIVITIES	%	%	%
TYPES OF PEOPLE	%	%	%
PREFERENCES	%	%	%
CHARACTERISTICS	%	%	%
ALL PARTS	%	%	%

Which job are you best suited for?

20 white marbles. Hence, tests work better than interviewing. In any case, always check with a counselor about any test results, and then, assuming you are being truly honest and reasonable with yourself, go with your instincts about whether the results are right or not.

Alternatives to Testing

Despite the problems we have mentioned, a test remains the most valid and reliable method for getting information. All of us like to think we are as objective as the tests if we are called on to be so, but that apparently isn't the case.

Interviews

Halo effect
The situation where a person comes off well in class or in an interview, even though this is not his or her "real" personality.

Reverse halo
The situation where a person has skills but covers them over, or distracts others from seeing them, by doing unacceptable things.

Standoutishness
Doing something or wearing something at an interview that is so startling that it detracts from the person's real abilities.

One of the worst problems in interviewing someone is called the **halo effect** (Thorndike, 1920). We all know students who keep playing up to the teacher so that they seem to have a "halo" glowing above their heads. Often these students get special treatment and recommendations when everyone in the class knows they are unpleasant and devious people. In almost any kind of interview, they will come off well, making the interviewer think they are bright, helpful, useful—all of which may be false. There is also the **reverse halo**. The student who does dumb things, like throwing things in class, may have great potential, but it is hidden by this insecure behavior. So, in this case also the teacher or interviewer tends not to see the real person; they are taken in by the reverse halo.

Since the interview takes place in person, there is another pitfall, called **standoutishness** (Hollingsworth, 1922). In a job interview, for example, a male wearing a red and yellow checked jacket and a tie with bright flowers on it or a female wearing stockings with small playing cards and dice embossed on them will completely distract the interviewer from whatever qualities he or she possesses that are appropriate to the job. This description is deliberately exaggerated to get across a point. While such things shouldn't have any effect on how your intelligence or skills are viewed, they clearly do, and there's no way to get around it. A test measures the relevant qualities better because it doesn't know what you look like or how you act.

Should the interview be skipped? No, it can add important information if well done, but it must always be viewed with caution (Kaplan, 1982).

Situational Assessments

Another alternative to testing is secret observation of people in action. Especially for research purposes, people are watched to see how they act when they think they are alone. For example, researchers wanted to understand what might lead people to help others in trouble. One study used stooges who faked a "flat tire" at the side of the road. Few people stopped to help. *But*, if, a few blocks before this, another scene was set up in which stooges were obviously helping someone who had a flat tire, then when the people being observed arrived on the scene of the second "flat tire" they tended to stop and help. Clearly, this results from a form of imitation, but it also shows that the specific situation alters behavior (Bryan & Test, 1969). The researchers in this study were engaging in what is called **situational assessment**.

Situational assessment
The process of looking at how the circumstances surrounding an event influence people responding to that event.

The biggest difference between testing and the situational approach is that, with the latter, the researcher is observing and can't interfere or ask questions. Hence, we can never know what is going on in the minds of those whose behavior is changing. The moment we start to ask questions, we are testing, not observing.

Ethics of Testing

When you take a test in math, history, English, psychology, or what have you, the worst outcome is that it will show that you haven't studied or that you have trouble with that subject. It is not a personal threat to you. Such is not the case with the personality tests we have been discussing. They almost always require answers to things that many of us prefer not to talk about. Hence, they can be extremely threatening. As a result, certain ethical standards exist to protect the test taker. Here are some of the core ones:

1. Depending on your age and state or federal law, someone—either you or your parent(s)—must give permission for you to take personality tests. And the reason why such a test is being given should be spelled out.

2. Your privacy must be respected. Remember, however, that somehow law enforcement people can always find a way to see just about anything. So, be careful when you take a personality test. You might be merely joking when you agree to answers that are strange, but they could become part of your permanent record. If you are truly deeply worried about personality problems, which can happen to almost anyone at some point, it is worth taking the test if you have a counselor in whom other students have faith. Often these counselors can help a great deal.

3. When personality tests are being given for research, you always have the right to refuse to take them. That's standard practice.

And here are some general tips on testing that might be of use:

1. Whether or not you have to take an intelligence test is controlled by many state and federal laws. Court battles are going on in this area all the time. Your counselor can inform you of your rights.

2. If you *do* take an intelligence test for some reason, a record will be made of the score. If you have any reason to doubt its accuracy, you should request a reexamination before you leave high school. This is important because these tests can make major errors at times, and you might carry along on your permanent record a lifetime score that does not reflect your real ability.

3. It is to your benefit to take a vocational interest test. We know of none that is a disguised personality test. Not taking the SAT will likewise hurt you. Some colleges require it for admission. You can always take it again or go to some school that doesn't require it if you don't like your scores. Most colleges *do* look at your high school records, so, if the SAT scores are terrible and your grades have been good, the grades tend to carry more weight with most admission committees. Remember that the SAT, at its best, *only* measures school potential and has nothing to do with the possibility of great success in thousands of occupations.

4. As mentioned, anyone who takes a personality test may feel exposed and vulnerable. The worst part about this is that you might begin to feel that there *really* is something wrong with you just from the types of questions on the test. The chances that you are sane and about as normal or abnormal as most of the rest of us are overwhelming. The test has not made you the victim of some all-seeing, all-knowing psychologist. To illustrate this last point, we have developed the "Learned Pig Personality Test." Maybe it will help you rest easier.

Barnum effect
Stating the obvious as if it comes from special knowledge.

The Learned Pig Personality Test

Please answer each of the following eight questions either true or false as it applies to you. At the end, we will tell you how to score your answers, and we will discuss the test.

1. I worry more often than I wish I did about the future. While sometimes the future seems reasonably clear, at other times it's too unknown. True   False

2. I have had a recent upsetting experience that it is hard for me to forget. Sometimes it will pop into my mind at the strangest times. True   False

3. I worry about my body. It doesn't seem to be all that it should be, especially when I compare it with some other people's. True   False

4. I worry that I don't have enough really close friends. Many of my relationships seem too superficial. True   False

5. I'm not all the way sure who I *really* am. Sometimes I feel like my personality is pretty good, but it doesn't feel all the way right at other times. True   False

6. I'm uncomfortable about sex matters. Lots of other people seem to know what's going on, but sometimes it makes me uncomfortable, and most of all it doesn't always make a lot of sense. Also, it seems to be out of proportion—but I'd never tell anyone that because they'd think there was something wrong with me. True   False

7. Being in love feels so good, and it's supposed to be a natural state. But I worry because sometimes

Figure 15.6
The remarkable Toby: a glimpse of his act, an ad for his book, circa 1817

things are so very messed up about it that I wish it would go away. True   False

8. People always say that adolescence is the time when you don't really have any worries or burdens. There must be something wrong with me because that sure doesn't seem to be what my life is like. True   False

Scoring Key: Count the number of "true" responses you made. If you checked seven to eight "true," you

are normal. If five or six, you're either awfully lucky or fooling yourself. If you checked four or fewer, you're either lying or not human.

There are a number of goals behind this little experiment. First, it should make you feel a little more at ease about your personality. Everyone is worried more often than they wish they were, and things don't go smoothly no matter what area of life you're dealing with. Second, you can see that a test can be made up in such a way that persons can be made to *appear* abnormal when, in fact, they are not so. And third, it should show you that many of the things that seem to be deep, all-knowing questions from psychologists are often just a statement of the obvious made to look like there is special knowledge behind them.

Around the turn of the century a famous circus called "Barnum and Bailey's" thrived. P. T. Barnum, one of the founders, said there was a "sucker born every minute." He was referring to the fact that you can fool people with great ease. Such fooling is still done today through palm reading and horoscopes, and the few remaining circuses usually have a "fortune teller." All these people merely state the obvious or the common in such a way that it seems they know the deep, inner recesses of our minds. This is called the **Barnum effect**, and it is a serious problem because so many of the things these people say seem to be mysteriously probing us when they aren't (Meehl, 1956).

We called our test the "Learned Pig" test because, for about 100 years, starting in the late 1700s, pigs became the "in" thing in touring acts and stage performances. The pigs were supposed to have incredible abilities: They supposedly could sing, dance,

spell, tell time, tell your age, and speak in many languages. In those days, people sometimes believed that women were very frail and would "swoon" (fall into a faint) if they weren't dealt with very carefully. As a result, the promoters had to promise that ladies who attended the performance would not have their personalities revealed by the Learned Pig—thus,

no one would know the ladies' secrets (Jay, 1987). The point is that the personality test we made up is similar to the one used by the pigs (on men only). The pigs would stick their snouts toward certain items on a big card that listed personality characteristics—in that way, they "told the future." An advertising leaflet for a "learned pig" is shown in Figure 15.6.

Summary

1. Personality tests are of two general types. The first is objective and uses factual questions to which the person responds. An attempt is made to build a picture of the person's personality using these statements.

2. Because personality inventories don't seem to reach "deep" enough and are subject to problems like faking, projective tests like the ink blot are sometimes used. These tests are designed to get material from the test taker that is more hidden, since the stimulus he or she is responding to is so vague.

3. An achievement test is designed to measure what has already been learned. An aptitude test is intended to predict how well a person will do in the future, but these tests still have to use the person's current knowledge.

4. Vocational interest tests are used to predict a person's satisfaction in certain job areas. These tests measure interest only, not aptitude.

5. All of the above tests must have good validity and reliability to work. Norms must be established by using different groups. The best validities and reliabilities are found with interest and aptitude tests. Next lower are the personality inventories. At the bottom sit the projective tests and personal interviews, both of which can be very inaccurate.

6. Situational assessments are used primarily for research purposes. They involve observation of how people behave when they think they are alone. They do cast light on behavior, but they don't provide an opportunity to find out why the people are doing what they are doing.

Key Words and Concepts

psychological tests	California	aptitude tests	Strong-Campbell	situational
norms	Psychological	Scholastic	Interest	assessment
validity	Inventory	Aptitude Test	Inventory	Barnum effect
reliability	projective tests	achievement tests	halo effect	
personality	Rorschach test	vocational interest	reverse halo	
inventory	aptitude	test	standoutishness	

Review Questions

Matching (Answers can be used more than once.)

1. Some are projective in nature
2. Can include clerical speed tests
3. Measures how much one has learned in the past
4. Helps one to eliminate certain career choices
5. Helpful in singling out people who need help
6. Designed to predict future performance, but sometimes not accurate enough
7. Not specifically designed to predict future academic performance—but often misused in this way
8. Useful for placing advanced students
9. Strong and Campbell developed a widely used one
10. At times, identifies abnormalities that don't exist
11. Reveals special abilities
12. Its ability to predict is very high

   a. aptitude test
   b. personality test or inventory
   c. achievement test
   d. vocational interest test

Fill in the blank. Answer on a separate sheet of paper. (More than one word can be used.)

13. If we take a test in April and score high and take the same test in May and score low, the test may not be highly _____ .
14. Teachers' pets often benefit from the
15. If 98 percent of the population answers a question in a similar way, they are establishing a pattern, or a _____ .
16. Test "A" is supposed to measure intelligence, and it *does!* The test, therefore, has a high degree of _____ .
17. Gathering information by observing people in different settings and situations is called _____ .

True/False

18. A personality test can usually be administered to someone without permission.
19. A personality test need not be taken too seriously since the score will probably not be recorded on your permanent record.
20. You have the right to refuse to take a personality test used for research.
21. Certain laws exist that control whether you have to take an intelligence test.
22. Vocational interest tests are usually disguised personality tests.

Discussion Questions

1. You may have filled out a personality inventory or two in your lifetime, but you were probably never made aware of your score. Why do you suppose scores are not made more readily available? Explain.
2. Should personality information be made more easily available? For example, should personality inventory scores be routinely sent out in the mail? Why or why not? Explain.
3. A reliable personality inventory should paint a somewhat accurate picture of various personality traits. What trait would a personality inventory have an easier time identifying: honesty or shyness? In other words, Joe fills out a personality inventory; if you (as an expert) were to analyze his answers, would it be easier to draw conclusions about whether he is honest or whether he is shy. Explain.
4. In your opinion, do students attempt to achieve a halo effect more often during junior high school or high school? Why? Does it have anything to do with peers?
5. Describe several experimental situations where researchers would want to use situational assessment rather than interviews. Remember that the problem with interviewing or asking questions is that the answers may not be truthful or accurate; also, once someone knows that he or she is being tested, that person's behavior automatically tends to become less natural.

Activities

1. Your school counselor probably has a great deal of knowledge about the purposes and uses of various aptitude, achievement, and vocational interest tests. Pre-

pare a list of questions and interview your counselor. Include questions about: (a) the differences and similarities among the three types of tests; (b) the general strengths and weaknesses of each type of test; (c) the main kinds of tests your counselor uses and why—and whether these tests are "valid" and/or "reliable"; (d) students' rights in regard to testing—especially intelligence testing.

Write a report of the interview and include your reactions.

2. As you may have gathered from reading the chapter, many of the personality and achievement tests commonly used often inspire controversy. Collect several articles that clarify and explain these controversies. Then design a detailed chart that presents the pros and cons of using these tests. Finally, in about a page, argue either for or against using these tests.

3. Conduct an experiment to see if a halo and a reverse halo effect can be created through brief positive and negative descriptions. Print the following information on two index cards:

"Denise Smith.
Sixteen years old.
Job objective: Computer programmer.
Job experience: On the weekends, Denise is a frequent volunteer at a nursing home in the area. She enjoys working with the residents and feels she is contributing something important. Denise had a regular job for a few months as a waitress, but she quit because she didn't have enough time to study."

At the top of one of the index cards, right after "computer programmer," print: "Grade point average = 2.1 (or C−)." At the top of the other index card, list the grade point average as "4.1 (or A−)."

Take another index card and print the following rating scale:

1	2	3	4	5
POOR	BELOW AVERAGE	AVERAGE	ABOVE AVERAGE	EXCELLENT

Finally, print the following information onto yet another index card:

"Based on the description of Denise, how would you rate her:

a. Friendliness
b. Honesty
c. Generosity
d. Confidence level
e. Chances of succeeding as a computer programmer?"

Present the good-grade card, the five-part question, and the rating scale to ten subjects. Record their five ratings on a separate sheet of paper. Repeat all of the above steps for the low-grade description (but use ten different subjects).

Analyze your results. The information about Denise's job experience may, in itself, have created a halo effect, but did the good and bad grades have any effect on this? What was the average rating for the good-grade card? The poor-grade card? Which of the five categories got the highest and/or lowest ratings? Why do you think you got the results that you did? Explain. Do you think that teachers are often guilty of this halo and reverse halo effect when dealing with students due to grades? Provide examples, but do not include names.

4. Visit your school counselor and tell him or her that you'd like to take a vocational interest test. (The counselor will be thrilled!) Fill out the test and take a look at the three occupations in which you scored highest. Pick any one of these occupations and interview someone who is currently employed in that occupation.

The main purpose of the interview will be to discover the similarities and differences between you and the interviewee. You might want to make a list of activities that you enjoy and have the interviewee rate each activity—perhaps like this:

Activity = Fishing
Rating: (a) enjoy very much (b) enjoy (c) do not enjoy at all

Briefly summarize your similarities and differences. Would you say that the vocational interest test that you took is highly valid, valid, or not valid? Why?

Coffee, cigarettes, stresssss.

Chapter 16

Frustration, Conflict, Stress, and Drugs

Objectives

Be able to:

1. Explain the four types of conflict.

2. Discuss the differences between good and bad stress.

3. Describe the physical changes that take place during stress.

4. Describe the general adaptation syndrome.

5. Explain the principle of how drugs affect the body, and describe the effects each drug has.

6. Describe suicidal feelings and how best to help someone with them.

Global Look at the Chapter

Frustration, conflict, and stress are basic parts of life. They are most destructive when bottled up and turned into an inner anger or rage. Those who take change and problems in stride can often use the stress as motivation to greater things. Those not able or willing to cope can quickly be beaten by drugs or even suicide.

Frustration

If you plan on wearing something that matches your blue sweater, this item is bound to be either lost or all rolled up in a ball. If you are really in a hurry to get somewhere, the traffic will be unbelievable, and all the stoplights will turn red just as you finally get up to each of them. If there is a tape sale and one tape you want badly, there are two possibilities: (1) You don't have any money at present, or (2) you have the money, get the tape, but your stereo picks this time to break down.

These are the frustrations of daily life, which do take their toll. While none of these problems may be earthshaking in and of themselves, they gradually wear us down, since each of them causes tightening of the muscles, clenching of teeth, and a desire to run screaming down the street. This frustration can't be good for us—and it isn't.

Frustration
The blocking or hindering of goals we are seeking.

Frustration is defined as the blocking or hindering of goals we are seeking. Most frustrations are relatively minor, if we can keep them in perspective. The problem is that, since there are so many of them, we can get buried and lose that sense of perspective. Some minor frustrations are still hard to handle for almost anyone—try those irritating busy signals seven calls in a row. And frustrations can be serious, as when someone doesn't have the skills to play a particular sport or lacks some other talent in an activity that is special to him or her.

Conflict

Conflicts are particularly difficult to deal with because they demand a decision. A **conflict**, then, is a situation in which we must decide between two or more alternatives (to do one thing or another, or to do or not to do something). They are not going to go away by themselves. There are four types of conflict.

Conflict
A problem that demands a choice between alternatives in order to be resolved.

Approach-Approach Conflict

The **approach-approach conflict** is not all that bad. It involves two attractive alternatives. We have to choose between two things we want to do (approach). There are two movies you want to see, for example, but have money for only one. You have to choose.

Approach-approach conflict
A choice between two attractive alternatives.

Approach-Avoidance Conflict

The **approach-avoidance conflict** can be distressing. One part of the situation makes it attractive, but the other part makes you want to run away. You want to go out with someone, say, but are afraid you won't really be liked. The process of trying to decide what to do can leave you drained and feeling hopeless for the moment.

Approach-avoidance conflict
One part of the situation is attractive, but the other part is not; the choice is whether to do or not do something.

Avoidance-Avoidance Conflict

You can't win with the **avoidance-avoidance conflict**, the worst of the three because it involves two unattractive alternatives. If you don't go to the dentist, your mouth will rot (bad), but, if you do go, he or she will bring out the whirling monster that sends bits of teeth and water flying all over the room while you squirm in agony (also bad).

Avoidance-avoidance conflict
A choice between two unattractive alternatives.

Double Approach-Avoidance

The **double approach-avoidance conflict** is the one we face most often. It is called "double" because there are both good and bad parts no matter which way we go. For example, if you have a vote on moving to another city, the school might be better, but you aren't used to it; special new friends could be there, but you have to leave those you already know and care about.

Double approach-avoidance conflict
A choice between alternatives, both of which have good and bad parts.

Approach-Approach

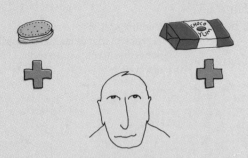

Two attractive alternatives, but you can only choose one

"Should I eat a hamburger or candy bar? I only have enough money for one."

Avoidance-Avoidance

Two unattractive alternatives; avoiding one brings you closer to another

"I hate liver, but, if I don't finish it, Mom will never let me hear the end of it."

Approach-Avoidance

One goal or choice that is both attractive and unattractive; the person reaches for the positive feature of the goal, but the goal includes both positive and negative features.

"I want to have a candy bar, but I don't want to gain any more weight."

Double-Approach-Avoidance

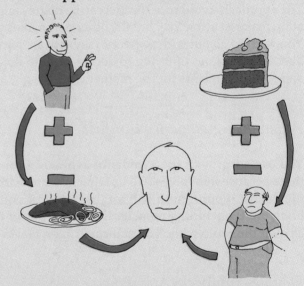

Both alternatives include attractive and unattractive features

"Should I eat liver, which is not very tasty but is nutritious, or should I have the dessert, which is rich in calories but makes my mouth water just thinking about it?"

All of these types of conflicts are normal. They can't be avoided. Still, a steady diet of painful conflicts, especially when one feels alone and not supported, can result in true feelings of hopelessness. After a while, the person begins to make incorrect decisions or is unable to make any decision, and eventually he or she can develop psychological and physical symptoms from the steady drain on the body and psyche (Wolpe & Lazarus, 1966).

Anxiety

Conflict and frustration lead to **anxiety**, the dreaded feeling that something is seriously wrong and that disaster sits right around the corner. Anxiety results when we cannot resolve a conflict or when frustration builds too high. If anxiety goes on for a long time, it will eventually do a person in. Severe attacks of anxiety can cause a rapid heartbeat, fatigue, breathlessness, chest pains, dizziness, fainting, feelings of doom, and headaches, to name but a few things. The anxiety comes from a feeling of helplessness when we are trying to solve problems, and it spreads to a general feeling that we can't cope.

Anxiety
The feeling that something is wrong and disaster is imminent.

Stress

Stress is defined as the *physical* pressure and strain that result from demands or changes in the environment (Mandler, 1984). Stress arises whenever there is a change in the body that requires us to readjust. Conflict, frustration, and anxiety can all lead to stress. But *any* kind of change, even a positive one, causes stress, because we have to adapt to a new environment. We'll talk more about that in a few paragraphs.

Stress
The physical strain that results from demands or changes in the environment.

Good Stress

Stress is not necessarily a bad thing in and of itself. It is relative to the individual: What is terribly difficult for one person can make another person feel interested and alive. For example, meeting new people can be a very stressful situation. Most of us are uncomfortable and on the verge of an anxiety attack if the person we are meeting is someone whom we want to like us or who might be important to us. But, since never making any new friends or getting a job or leaving home is much worse than stress, we have to go ahead and do these things (Kobasa et al., 1979). In fact, in these cases, stress turns out to be a good thing because it keeps the body going, and this, in turn, keeps us moving toward a new goal. Similarly, at least in theory, stress from doing homework is good in the long run because one learns. When stress is "good," leading to something desirable, it is called **eustress**.

Eustress
The stress that motivates us to do something worthwhile.

In a stress reaction such as this, the firefighters can actually "do something"; so their adrenaline will be used up. For the victims and family, the stress will go on quite a while.

Bad Stress

On the other side of the coin, the negative effects of stress are great. These include confusion, inability to make decisions, avoidance of people, as well as, eventually, physical or psychological illness (S. Cohen, 1980). It would seem that whether stress is bad or good has a lot to do with how we view a particular problem. Moving to another city, for instance, can be seen as a chance to make a new and better life for ourselves, or it can be seen as a hassle and a loss (Pittner & Houston, 1980). Making up your mind to make the best of what you have to do can produce wonders—even though this is often easier to say than to do. When stress is "bad," it is called **distress**.

Distress
The stress that is nonproductive and that causes physical problems.

Physical Changes with Stress

The effects of stress come from the physical responses that occur whenever we are facing a change, a conflict, or frustration. To understand this, we need to look for a moment at the lower animal world where things are a little simpler to grasp.

Fight or Flight In the wild, animals are designed to deal first of all with physical safety. The key to safety for them is an environment that remains the same. For example, an animal will sleep as long as everything around it is steady. Any change in the environment, such as an unusual sound followed by some type of movement, immediately signals the possibility of danger. Some life-threatening event could be about to happen, and the sound and movement are warning signs: There might be a predator creeping up. As a result, the vision and hearing systems of all animals (including humans) are physically designed to detect immediately *any* change in the surroundings. (How about when you are at home alone some night, especially after seeing a horror movie recently? You are sitting there and it is completely quiet, when all of a sudden you hear scratching, creaking sounds, and you see some kind of movement outside the window. Your body goes into full alert.) Thus, any kind of change triggers a physical alarm. That is nature's design.

Assume that the animal is correct about coming to alert status: There is a creature on its way to attack. The animal's body is fully mobilized to do one of two things—fight or flee. There is no third choice. Thus begins what is called the **fight or flight reaction**. In nature, the animal either wins, loses, or escapes. If the battle is won or the animal runs away, special chemicals are then sent through the body to cancel out the ones that were triggered in order to handle the emergency.

Fight or flight reaction
The body's reaction to a crisis; these are the only two possibilities for action.

The Human Response   The major parts of the human that respond to emotional stress are: the higher brain, the part we do our thinking with; the lower brain, the animal part that controls all the basic bodily functions; and the **adrenal** (ah-DREE-nal) **glands** that sit to the right and left and above the kidneys and that stir up the body's activity level. Here are three examples of the kinds of things that can trigger an emotional response: having an operation; going out on a first date with a new person; having to accept the fact that a loved one has died. Notice that all three of these human problems involve a *psychological* change because they deal with *mental* issues. This does not reduce their potential for distressing us; instead, it makes them harder to handle than real life-and-death physical struggles.

Adrenal glands
The glands that secrete chemicals that activate or energize the body.

In each case, the higher brain assumes that threat and danger exist. It signals the lower brain about the emergency. The lower brain secretes a special chemical called the **stress hormone**, which signals the adrenal glands to send to the body *adrenaline* (a-DREN-a-lin); this, in turn, causes the muscles to tense, the heart to beat faster, the liver to send out more sugar to be used by the muscles when we either fight or flee (Axelrod & Reisine, 1984). Thus, the body can't tell the difference between a physiological and a psychological threat and will respond in the same way to either kind of "danger."

Stress hormone
A special chemical that signals the adrenal glands to activate the body.

If we were able to solve these problems immediately, the human body would go back to normal quickly, as it does with animals. But, because our concerns are more abstract than physical, it is tough to find an end to them. Hence, the stress lasts a long time, and eventually it can cause physical problems because we are running (on the inside) at full alert too much of the time (G. E. Schwartz, 1979).

Examining Stress

Some stress results from change, whether the change is good or bad. In this regard, Table 16.1 might be of some interest. Two stress researchers estimated the amount of change involved in certain life events and called them *life change units* (Holmes & Rahe, 1967). This table is interesting because it shows how upsetting certain events can be. For example, serving a jail term and getting married are not that far apart as stressors. But one would hope that the changes involved in getting married would quickly pass from a stressful event to one of a warm, happy relationship. Hence, one cannot add up these scores and predict how much damage will occur. Those who are subjected to major stressors, however—such as the death of a spouse, loss of a family member, getting fired, and the like—are more likely to develop disease or sickness later on, especially if a couple of these stressors happen at about the same time (Krantz & Manuck, 1985).

Stress research also focuses on things that do not cause an actual change in one's life. For example, a continued beating from all of life's little annoyances, such as we discussed at the beginning of the chapter, if

Table 16.1   Social Readjustment Rating Scale

Rank	Life Event	Mean Value	Rank	Life Event	Mean Value
1	Death of spouse	100	23	Son or daughter leaving home	29
2	Divorce	73	24	Trouble with in-laws	29
3	Marital separation	65	25	Outstanding personal achievement	28
4	Jail term	63	26	Wife begin or stop work	26
5	Death of close family member	63	27	Begin or end school	26
6	Personal injury or illness	53	28	Change in living conditions	25
7	Marriage	50	29	Revision of personal habits	24
8	Fired at work	47	30	Trouble with boss	23
9	Marital reconciliation	45	31	Change in work hours or conditions	20
10	Retirement	45	32	Change in residence	20
11	Change in health of family member	44	33	Change in schools	20
12	Pregnancy	40	34	Change in recreation	19
13	Sex difficulties	39	35	Change in church activities	19
14	Gain of new family member	39	36	Change in social activities	18
15	Business readjustment	39	37	Mortgage or loans less than $10,000	17
16	Change in financial state	38	38	Change in sleeping habits	16
17	Death of close friend	37	39	Change in number of family get-togethers	15
18	Change to different line of work	36	40	Change in eating habits	15
19	Change in number of arguments with spouse	35	41	Vacation	13
20	Mortgage over $10,000	31	42	Christmas	12
21	Foreclosure of mortgage or loan	30	43	Minor violations of the law	11
22	Change in responsibilities at work	29			

Reprinted with permission from T. H. Holmes and R. H. Rahe, "The Social Readjustment Rating Scale," *Journal of Psychosomatic Research*, 1967, Table 3, p. 216. © 1967, Pergamon Press Ltd.

added to an environment of poverty, overcrowding, poor health, or the like, weakens a person's defenses to illness. In fact, some researchers feel that the accumulation of many moderately stressful problems might well be the real cause of early sickness or death (Lazarus & Folkman, 1984).

Pushing Too Hard   Excessive, continued, and unnecessary stress leads to trouble (Kobasa et al., 1980). One study that supports this belief examined 32 sets of male identical twins. In each pair, only one had heart problems. When the researchers looked into the history of each set of twins, they found that the ones whose hearts weren't working well had much more trouble with their marriages, took little time off, drove themselves too hard at work, and overall were less satisfied with their lives (Liljefors & Rahe, 1970). The last item seems more important than the others: We can overcome or avoid all kinds of problems if we can find some satisfaction within ourselves and some meaning in our lives.

Personal Attitude   In fact, personal meaning or attitude is a key factor in how well we survive. While it can be extremely hard to do, it is probably worth it to convince ourselves that, if so-and-so doesn't like us or if so-and-so is better at something than we are, who cares—that's the way it is. If we can find alternatives to what we think we want or need, or if we can even take a break from life's responsibilities for a *short* while, we will dramatically reduce the effects of stress (Grant et al., 1981).

Stress and Personality

The higher brain, as mentioned, makes our problems abstract. How many animals do you know who fret and worry about a history exam? Our concerns are certainly real enough, but we make life so complicated. People in groups—that is, society—do the same thing. For instance, there are rules against punching a rude salesperson. We couldn't survive as a group without such restrictions. On the other hand, these restraints *do* cost us something. The more angry we get without being able to do something about it, the more the walls of the stomach engorge (fill up) with blood, putting pressure on that organ; the more our muscles tighten up; the higher our blood pressure gets, until we make ourselves sick (Krantz & Manuck, 1985).

Unrelieved Tension   In one study, researchers deliberately frustrated the subjects. Then the researchers allowed half of the group a chance to get back at them verbally (no injuries allowed). The other half wasn't allowed to do that. The blood pressure and heart rate of those who were able to pay the researchers back dropped noticeably, while those of the other subjects did not. So, bottling up your feelings *too much* isn't good for you (Case, 1985). There's a limit to this, however. None of us wants to be around those who have no control over themselves. The point seems to be that a person needs to learn to pass off most things and to take a stand only on things that really seem to matter. In actuality, there aren't that many things that matter deeply, if we are really truthful.

Personality Types   Much research has focused on what is called the **type A personality**. Type A's are always running full speed ahead. They can make people uncomfortable because, even if you get them to sit down, they don't really seem to be with you in a conversation. They are impatient, thinking of other things, and can't be corralled long enough to share anything (Friedman & Rosenman, 1974; Yarnold & Grimm, 1982). They keep comparing how they are doing with how others do. But all type A's don't seem to suffer major problems. The ones who do are those who distrust others and are angry most of the time (Case, 1985). The type A's who see others as a threat, who misinterpret events, and who refuse to accept that they are acting the way they do are the ones most prone to physical disorders such as heart problems (Friedman, 1984).

The **type B personality** is the opposite of type A. These are people who are open to change and are flexible, who enjoy life because they don't put competition first, and who like a variety of activities (Weinberger et al., 1979).

One study compared over 150 male executives from the same company. Roughly half the group had become physically ill following some stressful life events, and the other half had not. Both groups had experienced roughly the same kinds of stress with the same severity, so they didn't differ in that respect. Analysis of the men showed that those who didn't get sick were type B's—those more open to change and who viewed problems more as a challenge than as a threat. They felt that they were in control and could do something to improve themselves and their environment (Kobasa et al., 1981). These studies suggest how critical it is to be a little more flexible and to try out a few new things, while accepting upsets without letting them eat up your insides. Doing this should not require a complete personality change, just a little loosening up and giving things a chance. The hardest part is figuring out what is important and what isn't, and then forgetting those things that aren't.

The General Adaptation Syndrome   Any creature put under major stress for long periods of time will eventually collapse. The events that occur under such stress have been outlined in what is called the **general adaptation syndrome**. Translated, this term refers to "the overall (general) process by which the creature adjusts (adapts) to various levels of stress." The word *syndrome* means a fixed sequence of events, one following the other, so this system assumes that the same pattern is followed each time stress is heavy. As with all things, we can't make a rule that fits every case, but the following three-part sequence that makes up

Type A personality
People who are always operating at full speed, are impatient, and are filled with distress.

Type B personality
People who are open to change, are flexible, enjoy life, and have low levels of stress.

General adaptation syndrome
The sequence of behavior that occurs in reaction to prolonged stress. It is divided into stages: **alarm reaction**, preparation for an attack; **stage of resistance**, trying to restore balance; and **exhaustion**, giving up the battle.

Type A Personality

Someone with a type A personality is like a SPRINTER who needs to reach the finish line before everyone else.

Type B Personality

Someone with a type B personality is like a JOGGER who is willing to try different routes every day.

the general adaptation syndrome seems to occur frequently (Selye, 1956).

The first stage is called an **alarm reaction**. The body sends out emergency signals that stir it up in preparation for an attack—either psychological or physical.

Next, the **stage of resistance** occurs. This means that the organism tries to fight back against the attack. The organism wants to restore psychological and physical balance. If the threat is removed at this point, the body and psyche begin to restore themselves to their normal chemical and emotional balance.

If the stress doesn't let up, continuous fighting becomes impossible. This third stage, **exhaustion**, means the battle is over, and we have lost or, at least, have quit.

The three-stage sequence is easiest to see in an accident, such as when you break your leg. When the limb is broken, the first response is one of panic or alarm, and the body starts the heart beating rapidly, increases the breathing rate, and so forth. Next comes an attempt to see if the leg will move despite the pain, trying to offset it somehow, to make it all go away (resistance). Finally, when the pain is too much and the break is obvious, you give in and lie there helpless. Note that this would be the case if the break happens around others. But, if it occurs when you are alone, then the stage of resistance is seen very clearly because you struggle, fight, and drag yourself toward help before collapsing.

One thing might be bothering you: Stress, frustration, conflict, and anxiety have each been defined. They are each slightly different, but they all interact. Stress can cause anxiety; anxiety can cause stress; conflict can cause frustration; frustration can cause stress. So, just learn the differences among them in a formal sense, and don't be too concerned about the fact that they seem to get mixed together when we talk about them.

There are many ways of handling stress, conflict, and frustration—some reasonable, some disastrous. In the next two sections, we will cover the two worst methods for handling problems: substance abuse and suicide. The reasonable ways are discussed in the next chapter.

Substance Abuse

Substance abuse
The use of drugs to excess in order to alter consciousness.

Chemical dependence
The same as substance abuse.

Misuse of drugs is formally called either **substance abuse** or **chemical dependence**. Using drugs to alter consciousness is not just a human activity. Reindeer, cattle, and rabbits eat intoxicating mushrooms; tobacco plants are preferred by baboons; elephants in the wild seek out fermented grain such as would be found in beer. There is some indication that stress is a factor in these behaviors because, when elephants are restricted in the amount of space they have, they increase dramatically their consumption of the grain (Siegel, 1983). For humans, most scientists agree that stress, conflict, and frustration are major factors in drug use. The taker is trying to alter the world enough to make it more tolerable. Also important is peer pressure: Some who get started on drugs do so because others are doing it and they don't want to feel left out of the group.

One of the biggest problems we face in writing this section is that people have been lied to so often and in such exaggerated terms that it is hard to get anyone to listen to what the scientific findings are. A classic in this regard was the poster (Figure 16.1) put out by the government in the 1930s about marijuana, which warned that the drug caused murder, insanity, and death.

On the other hand, there *are* problems with telling the truth about drugs. Many people have the ability to read what they want to, regardless of what something really says. For example, bypassing the fact that some believe that drinking alcohol in any form is wrong, we can report that the scientific evidence does not support the claim that alcohol is dangerous in and of itself. A glass of wine or a beer with dinner can be enjoyable and relaxing. But some will read this as saying that, if one or two beers is safe every now and then, so are three or four—or more. That is not true. The chances of becoming an alcoholic are very high as one increases the amount and frequency of drinking.

Beware! **Young and Old — People in All Walks of Life!**

This may be handed you by the **friendly stranger.** It contains the Killer Drug "Marihuana"-- a powerful narcotic in which lurks *Murder! Insanity! Death!*

WARNING!

Dope peddlers are shrewd! They may put some of this drug in the or in the or in the tobacco cigarette.

WRITE FOR DETAILED INFORMATION, ENCLOSING 12 CENTS IN POSTAGE — MAILING COST

Address: **THE INTER-STATE NARCOTIC ASSOCIATION**
(Incorporated not for profit)
53 W. Jackson Blvd.   Chicago, Illinois, U. S. A.

Another point is that over the years roughly half the population has used alcohol in one way or another on a fairly regular basis. To avoid the stigma attached to "drug" use, people often discuss alcohol as if it were not a drug. This is false. Alcohol works exactly the same way other drugs do, as we will describe in a moment. In fact, its general method of action is about the same as the popular tranquilizer, Valium.

The final point that should be made is that, once a drug habit really gets started, it takes heroism to get rid of it. This does not mean that, having taken a drug a few times, a person can never stop or is already damaged. On the other hand, no matter what "they" say, no one can have a steady intake of a drug and not eventually wind up in a very messy and painful situation. This is just common sense. The user becomes too attached to the sensations the drug produces to give it up. Such users keep saying, "I'll give it up tomorrow," but it doesn't work that way. If tomorrow ever *really* comes, a terrible battle must take place before the person can win.

How Drugs Work

It is hard to grasp some of the issues about drugs without at least a rough idea of how they work. So that's what we want to do now. Drugs all operate on the same general principle. If you look at Figure 16.2, you will see a nerve junction. The brain has billions of nerve cells, connected one to the other using these junctions. The space between the junctions

Figure 16.2
Nerve junction

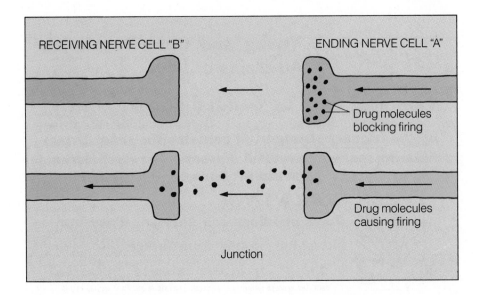

helps keep different thoughts and feelings separate from one another. If certain nerve cells have to connect in order to complete a feeling or thought, chemical messages are sent across the junction to the next nerve and then, if needed, on to the next nerve, and so forth until the whole thought or feeling is complete. So, at the end of each nerve cell there are chemicals that either send a message across or block one from crossing the junction.

Drugs have a molecular structure that physically resembles the different chemicals already in the nerve cells. Hence, when we take in a drug, it lodges in the endings of specific nerve cells designed to receive certain types of chemical molecules. The body will do what these drug molecules say because it thinks they are coming from inside, not outside. For instance, alcohol and tranquilizers have a structure similar to the chemicals that tell the nerve cells *not* to fire. When these drugs arrive in the brain, they hook onto certain nerve cell endings and give a message to stop firing. As more and more cells are stopped, the person becomes thicker, more dazed, and eventually can lose consciousness. Drugs that speed up the body are molecularly similar to the nerve cell chemicals that make the cells fire faster. Hence, as a person takes in greater quantities of these drugs, more and more cells begin to fire, and the person becomes more and more agitated. A third kind of drug causes its effect because normally the nerve cells are designed to keep different parts of the brain separate—hearing, seeing, smelling, and so on. So, drugs like LSD lodge in different systems of the brain and cause the circuits in more than one of these areas to start firing together (Jacobs, 1987). As a result, people who take such drugs feel like they are "hearing colors" and "seeing sounds" and often wind up in a world so strange that it is terrifying.

Alcohol

Certain drugs tend to become fads for a while. For instance, in colonial America, alcoholism was twice as prevalent as it is today. Not unusual was the party given by the governor of New York for 120 guests: They consumed 120 bottles of Madeira, 36 bottles of port, 60 bottles of beer, and 30 bowls of rum punch (Rorabaugh, 1979). Twenty years ago, LSD was very popular; marijuana was very popular about 15 years ago, but the number of current users among 12- to 17-year-olds has dropped from 40–50 percent to a little over 20 percent (*Statistical Abstracts . . .*, 1986). Cocaine use by this same age group is roughly 10 percent, having increased about a percentage point in the last five years. Through all the years and all the fads, though, alcohol has remained the most used drug. Roughly 70 percent of all teenagers have used alcohol, but not all of them necessarily to excess.

Obviously, not everyone who uses alcohol is an alcoholic, but there are more than 11 million known alcoholics across all age groups, and many more we don't know about (Blum, 1984).

Chemical Effects   Because many of those who seem halfway reasonable when sober do wild things when they drink too much, many believe that alcohol is a stimulant. What actually happens is that the first few drinks remove a person's inhibitions about making a fool of himself or herself. This creates an impression of freedom. Alcohol is really a *depressant*, which is why country and western songs have so many drinkers crying in their beer. As the amount of alcohol in the body increases, more and more cells are shut off. Eventually this leads to unconsciousness.

Alcohol is absorbed by the body in two to six hours, depending on how much is taken in, how much the person weighs, and, to a large extent, how much has been eaten. Eating prior to or during drinking helps to reduce the effects of alcohol notably, if we're talking about a reasonable amount of the drink (Blum, 1984).

Physical Effects   Repeated heavy drinking causes serious damage, but it takes a while to show up. About 10 percent of alcoholics develop permanent liver damage, and about the same percentage develop irreversible brain damage. Alcohol over time can directly destroy the liver. On the other hand, you will hear that every time someone takes a drink they destroy large numbers of brain cells. There is no real support for this claim (Blum, 1988). Hundreds of brain cells do die every day all by themselves. We have so many of them (100 billion) that most people can get to over 100 years of age and still function quite well. The real trouble comes from the fact that alcohol is basically a food product: It fills you up and is high in calories, but very low in nutrients. Hence, as people continue

Alcoholic withdrawal delirium
The "horrors" that can result from
severe alcoholism; includes weakness,
anxiety, cramps, hallucinations.

Hallucinations
Seeing or hearing things that are not
physically present.

Synergistic effect
The result of taking two drugs in
combination, which makes each more
potent than either one by itself.

drinking over time, they gradually reduce their regular food intake, causing a vitamin loss. Vitamin loss is one of the few things that directly and permanently damages the brain cells.

Severe cases of alcoholism can lead to nightmarish experiences. When alcoholics can't get to a drink, they can experience what are called the "horrors," or an **alcholic withdrawal delirium**. It starts off as weakness, anxiety, and severe stomach cramps. These are followed by gross and terrifying **hallucinations**—that is, seeing or hearing things that are not really there. Typically, the person is being attacked and eaten up by bugs, snakes, and other crawling things. The progression of the delirium is from confusion to disorientation, to stupor, and often to death. Ironically, one translation of the word *alcohol* is "the water of life" (Blum, 1984).

The Synergistic Effect   The liver gets rid of foreign substances in the body. But it cannot handle two chemicals of slightly different structure at the same time. In fact, when two drugs are present in the liver, each of them *increases* in its potency. This is called a **synergistic effect** (sin-er-JIS-tic) (Gold, 1985). Hence, people run a notable risk when they take both barbiturates, or tranquilizers, and alcohol in the same period of time, since the effect of each will increase and can be fatal.

Causes of Alcoholism   You will hear that body chemistry, allergies, brain waves, and who knows what have been discovered as the cause of alcoholism. We obviously assume that the alcoholic is or has been under some kind of stress, but are there other factors that lead to alcoholism? We don't know for certain. While many studies find some common problem in one group of alcoholics, the problem doesn't show up in the next group that is studied. Thus, there is no known "cause."

Heredity is sometimes cited as the origin. We don't know that, either. We do know that, if one's parents and other relatives are alcoholic, then the chances are good that the offspring will be also. But this type of finding does not separate out the influence of environment. Someone living in an alcoholic family is clearly exposed to an alcoholic environment. To show you how difficult studies of heredity are—even with rats—here is a typical finding: Some types of rats prefer alcohol as a drink while other kinds of rats don't. This certainly would suggest that some rats have an inherited desire or need for alcohol. But, other studies of rats show that some groups of them like to drink alcohol in one type of laboratory setting but not in another kind. Hence, it could be environmental as well. Other studies of humans show possible genetic defects in that certain abnormalities appear in alcoholic parents and in their offspring who also become alcoholic, but again this finding does not appear consistently. For the moment, we are stuck with the possibility of a genetic (inherited) factor but not enough evidence to prove it (Waller et al., 1984; Tabakoff et al., 1984; Vaillant & Milofsky, 1982; Schuckit, 1980).

A bar can be a comforting, friendly place, but for some it is a dangerous refuge from life through alcoholism.

An indication of the importance of social factors in drinking is the consistent finding that Orthodox Jewish people have almost a zero rate of alcoholism. This is probably because alcohol is used as a basic part of that religious tradition and is frequently part of family celebrations at home during religious holidays. Since it is, excessive drinking is not considered clever or funny, which is certainly at least one factor that influences many people to start drinking. From their early years, Jewish children drink small amounts of wine and other beverages; as a result, alcohol becomes just another "thing" in their environment, not something to be sought after because it is forbidden—which is another reason people start drinking (Blum, 1984).

Indicators of Alcoholism   A person clearly has a serious problem with alcohol if any of the following signs show up: (1) frequent drinking sprees—"frequent" is a little vague, but drunkenness once a week suggests real trouble; (2) a steady increase over time in the amount of alcohol drunk at one sitting; (3) morning drinking—to almost everyone, alcohol in the morning is nauseating, so if the day starts off with a drink, then alcohol has become a crutch the person needs to get started; (4) going to school or work drunk—this shows that the alcohol has taken over life to the point that *it* has become the major goal rather than anything else; (5) blackouts—rather than periods of unconsciousness, this term refers to memory loss for events that occurred while the person was drinking; (6) drinking whenever faced with a crisis—most people drink on occasion to "relax," but, if drinking goes along with facing most problems, it's serious.

Concerns About Alcoholism as a "Disease"   Of late, many scientists have expressed concern about calling alcoholism a "disease." Over time, alcohol can certainly devastate the body, but that alone does not qualify it as a disease. Being beaten up repeatedly can have similar effects, but no one would put that in the same category as something like cancer. Excessive use of alcohol seems to be an individual behavior that people engage in for almost as many reasons as there are people who drink. Normally, what we're saying here would seem to be little more than an argument about which words to use, but, as you will see, the issue is far more important than that. In most cases, a disease is something that continues on its own course with very little chance for the victim to control it. If medicine can't help, people are at the mercy of the disease, and that can make them just give up trying to fight it.

By assuming that alcoholism is this kind of disease, we become its victims, unable to do anything about it. The evidence to date, however, is pretty strong that anyone can stop the heavy use of alcohol. The keys to ending the problem are (1) really wanting to stop and (2) stabilizing one's psychological well-being enough to do so. The major problem with calling alcoholism a "disease," then, is that it tends to make the alcoholic feel hopeless. Another problem is that younger people overall feel quite good (at least compared to the rest of us), and the suggestion that they are suffering from a disease is usually seen as ridiculous, so it is ignored.

Since there is almost no evidence that alcoholism is indeed a disease in the formal sense, a leading researcher in the field of alcohol use and abuse has suggested merely calling the problem "heavy drinking" (Fingarette, 1988). At first, this seems to be a simple-minded distinction. But not so. A heavy drinker is headed for trouble—physically, legally, financially, what have you. Too many people who are heavy drinkers talk themselves into thinking that they are not "alcoholics" and thus they do not have a problem. But, if society sees "heavy drinking" itself as the problem, then these people will have to look at what they are doing. For example, if certain people get drunk at most parties, it may mean any number of things, but most clearly it means that they are unable or unwilling to be themselves. They can't trust who they are when they're sober; they can't relate well to others unless they are in a fog. They are afraid. By avoiding the label "alcoholic," they can also avoid the obvious fact that they need to stop depending on alcohol and gain the strength simply to be whoever they really are. Since there is no question that they are drinking to excess, it would be much harder for them to avoid the label "heavy drinker," which would let them know they need to get help.

One final point should be mentioned. Alcoholics Anonymous has had considerable success with a number of heavy drinkers and considers alcoholism a disease. None of the current researchers desires to take anything away from their fine work; on the other hand, the AA does not contain anything close to all the heavy drinkers and these researchers feel that the term "heavy drinker" is more appropriate than "disease" for general use, experimentation, and understanding.

Marijuana

The proportion of adolescents steadily using marijuana is roughly 20 percent. This is one-half the percentage of the 18- to 25-year-olds who used marijuana when it was more popular in the 1960s and '70s (*Statistical Abstracts . . .*, 1986). There are no obvious personality defects among those who use the drug on occasion (Loftus, 1980). But the heavier smokers—those who use the drug once or more a day—seem to have more than their share of personal problems. The drug is also influenced by social surroundings. Thus, those taking it alone tend to be quiet and depressed; those using it in groups are more talkative and outgoing (Blum, 1984).

Marijuana is a **psychedelic** (sigh-kuh-DEL-ik) drug, which means it distorts or confuses the user's perception of the world. Especially notable effects are that time seems to stretch out longer than usual; the person becomes sleepy and has a floating feeling (Grinspoon, 1969). While alcohol causes more problems with coordination and makes people more aggressive than marijuana, it still is not safe to perform any task involving coordination when taking this drug. When experienced pilots took marijuana and then were studied in flight simulators, the pilots made all kinds of serious errors (Blum, 1984; Zeichner & Pihl, 1979).

Some studies suggest that marijuana reduces the level of male sex hormone in the user. Not all studies agree with this, however. The major concern here would be the danger involved in a pregnant woman using marijuana. During the first three months of pregnancy, the male fetus's sex characteristics are developed by this hormone. Hence, if the studies turn out to be right, damage to the developing male fetus is possible from using marijuana (Kolodny et al., 1974; Blum, 1984).

The most serious clear-cut effect of marijuana is on the memory system. People have short- and long-term memories, as we discussed in Chapter 8. Everything we learn must first go into the short-term system and then be transferred to the long-term, permanent storage. While the drug does not affect long-term memory, it does wipe out the short-term storage for a few hours after being taken, so newly learned material is never transferred and hence not retained. The result is that frequent use of marijuana typically leads to very poor school achievement (Lipton & Marel, 1980; Miller & Berman, 1983).

Psychedelic
A drug that distorts or confuses the user's perception of the world.

Amphetamines

Tolerance
The need to take larger and larger dosages of a drug while still only getting the same effect as from the original dose.

Stimulants, called amphetamines, are very dangerous. They do create a feeling of excitement, freedom, and energy, but they also create a heavy **tolerance** in the user. Tolerance refers to the fact that, if on day one the person takes, say, one tablet, then two tablets will be needed on day two in order to produce the same effect as one tablet did the day before. By day three, three tablets are needed, and so forth. Hence, tolerance means that the body adapts to each dosage. In a short time, the user is taking a dosage hundreds of times greater than the original one in order to get the same effect (Seevers, 1968). Heavy dosages, in turn, result in bizarre mental images, trembling, convulsions, and notable **paranoia** (pair-uh-NOI-ya), the belief that others are out to get you (Kokkinidis & Anisman, 1980).

Paranoia
The belief that others are out to get you.

Such drugs should never be used for weight loss; they do a poor job, and tolerance will build up quickly. Continued use to stay awake for studying will backfire, too, not only because of the buildup of tolerance but also because of the temporary memory loss that begins to occur.

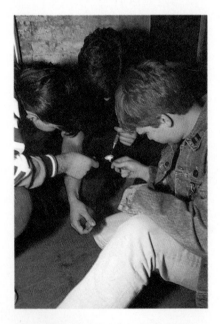

No matter what the drug, if it is being injected, the person is in very serious trouble.

Cocaine

Cocaine, which comes from cocoa leaves, is also a stimulant producing many of the same sensations as amphetamines. Some cultures use it to get, for lack of a better term, "revelations." The first soda fountain in the 1800s United States served Coca-Cola or "Coke," which contained cocaine. It was quite a success, as you may have guessed, until some of its dangers were noted. Today's Coca-Cola uses caffeine to provide stimulation (Blum, 1984). (You may hear that Coca-Cola mixed with aspirin acts like cocaine. It doesn't.)

Sniffing (snorting) is the most popular way to take the drug. It creates a warm "rush," which radiates through the body for about ten minutes. Cocaine in any form leads to severe hallucinations, mental confusion, and paranoia after a time (Siegel, 1985). *Crack* is very dangerous because it is a highly purified form of cocaine with great potency. It is a cocaine in paste form, normally smoked, which means that within a very brief time it is absorbed by the lungs and quickly enters the brain through the blood, causing an intense "high."

Psychological dependence
A craving by the psyche for a drug, although the body doesn't demand it.

Cocaine produces a very strong **psychological dependence**, which means that, although the body doesn't demand it, the user wants it so much that life becomes empty and intolerable without it. Most people who use cocaine do not die from it. Nonetheless, it can cause an instant heart attack and death in young and apparently healthy people who are using only a normal dose. The exact cause of the heart spasms is not

clear, but there is no way to know beforehand who or when it will kill (Isner, 1987).

Opiates

Heroin, morphine, and opium are all **opiates**—that is, sedatives—that dramatically depress nerve operation in the brain. At first, they make people feel very good and on top of the world, but suddenly the person comes crashing down into a deep depression. Opiates not only cause psychological dependence and create a drug tolerance but they also cause **physical dependence**, which means that the body itself, not just the psyche, begins to crave the drug. Most people are killed by these drugs from the additives put into them and from unsterile equipment (Ruttenber & Luke, 1984). These drugs can make those addicted to them so desperate that some have been known to cut open a vein in order to pour the drug in if they can't find a syringe (Stephens & Cottrell, 1972).

Opiates
Sedatives; drugs that reduce body functioning.

Physical dependence
A craving by the body itself for a drug.

LSD

Hallucinogen
A drug that produces major hallucinations.

LSD is a very potent psychedelic drug called an **hallucinogen** (ha-LOOSE-en-uh-jen) because it produces major hallucinations. Doses as small as ½₂₅₀,₀₀₀th of an ounce can cause marked changes in behavior. It makes the brain cells from different areas fire at random and mixes the senses, as we discussed earlier. Most of the danger from this drug comes from panic by users who can't cope with the sensations, often running around or mutilating themselves.

Steroids

Steroids
Artificially produced male sex hormones.

Steroids are artificially made male sex hormones that are used by many athletes, mostly male but also a few females. Since the (normal) male sex hormone helps build muscles, these people are hoping to increase their body size and strength with the drug. While this works, roughly a third of the users experience severe problems. They lose control of their emotions, often going way up and then way down. They begin to feel an unrealistic sense of power. For example, some have thought they could jump out a window three or four stories high without hurting themselves (they couldn't). One deliberately drove a car into a tree at 40 miles an hour while his friend made a videotape of the scene. The symptoms end when intake of the drug is stopped, but, while on it, the individual is quite unpredictable (Pope & Katz, 1987).

Table 16.2 summarizes some of the effects of common drugs.

Suicide

For the population as a whole, roughly 12 people per 100,000 kill themselves every year. Approximately double that number *try* to commit suicide. Among those aged 25 to 74 years, roughly 16 per 100,000 kill themselves, and, for ages 65 to 84, the figure jumps to 20 per 100,000 (*Statistical Abstracts* . . ., 1986). More males than females *actually* kill themselves, while females attempt it more often. The reason for this difference seems to be that males don't consider it "manly" to take drugs or use methods such as inhaling carbon monoxide from the car exhaust. Hence, they have less of a chance of being rescued. Males most often use a gun; females most often take drugs.

Common Stresses

Some of the most common stressors leading up to suicide are the loss of important friends, drinking problems, serious conflicts within the fam-

Table 16.2   Effects of Common Drugs

Drug	Psychological Dependence	Physical Dependence	Physical Withdrawal Effects	Development of Tolerance
Depressants				
Alcohol Barbiturates	Mild to very strong Develops slowly	Very strong Develops slowly	Severe/dangerous Death possible	Minimal
Narcotics				
Opiates (heroin, morphine)	*Very* strong Develops rapidly	Rapid/increases with dosage	Frightening symptoms but not dangerous	Very high Goes down quickly after withdrawal (Danger if user returns to original dose)
Stimulants				
Amphetamines	Strong	Strong	Mild	Extremely high
Cocaine Crack	*Very* strong	Not in formal sense but body seeks "rush"*	None	None (Can cause heart spasms and instant death even in healthy)
Psychedelics				
LSD	Unpredictable	None	None	Extremely high
Marijuana	Mild to strong	Some to high doses	None	None (Some to high doses)
PCP, called "angel dust"	This drug is so potent that we have no real information on it. Those who take it become dangerous and lose all contact with reality within a matter of hours. Should never be taken under any circumstances.			

*Researchers in the late 1980s developed serious doubts about cocaine not creating physical dependence. They now believe that this drug forms physical memory patterns which store the desire for a "rush" and create a physical need for it. Hence, a distinction is being made between the "brain" craving a drug like cocaine as opposed to bodily effects which are more common with other drugs.

ily, and severe trouble at school or work. Usually added to these specific problems is a feeling that everything is meaningless and boring and that there is no point in trying to make things better (McMahon & McMahon, 1983).

Teenage Suicide

The suicide rate for people ages 15 to 19 is about .012 percent. This rate stays roughly the same year after year, varying only a fraction of a percentage point. So, the number of suicides for this age group of 19 million people is 2,280 people a year. That is not very high, despite the pain and

Suicide hotlines have become a point of contact for thousands throughout the country.

anguish each suicide causes. The media's claim that adolescent suicide is taking over like the plague is clearly false. The press also distorts the facts by using percentages: A small group of communities will have, say, one adolescent suicide during a year. If, for whatever reason, this happens to change to three people the following year, what we read is that suicide among teenagers in that area is up 200 percent!

Here is an example of the point we are making: About a month before we wrote this section, there were a couple of "shoot-outs" between motorists on California highways. The press kept playing this up in article after article. With each article, another couple of shootings would occur, illustrating the effects of stress and press exaggeration. By the time you read this, the shooting will have stopped, we hope—or possibly bulletproof cars will be common. But, in all such cases, suggestible people are involved. The same thing results from the media's focus on the occasional teen suicide. There is an increase in suicides by a few cases every time these events are reported. The facts are that adolescents are not on a suicidal rampage. The leading cause of teenage death is accidents—about 10,000 per year.

Dealing with Suicide

Regardless of the number, suicide in any age group is so traumatic to all of us that the issue deserves some space. Not only that, but most of us have had either a relative or a friend contemplate or commit suicide, so it touches many lives. Also, most normal people have thought about suicide at least in passing at some point in their lives. Finally, depression is part of the problem, and this discussion applies to that as well.

Suicide has been called the "disease of hope," meaning that it is a last-ditch effort to get someone to care or pay attention to what must be horrible distress (Farber, 1968). Since people who feel suicidal are so desperate, almost always they will give clues to others, saying things like "No point in getting this watch fixed, I won't need it," or "We'll do so-and-so, if I'm around." In this regard, it is a myth that people who threaten suicide won't do it. If they say it, chances are good that they will try.

Other myths: (1) Once suicidal, always suicidal. (2) Suicides aren't likely among those with money and good health. (3) Suicides happen only to the mentally disturbed. (4) Most people who commit suicide are better off. The last item isn't true because almost all those who have been rescued from a suicide attempt say they are thankful that they didn't succeed.

Here are some suggestions for handling someone who is thinking of suicide. First, don't hide from it. If suicide is suggested as a possibility, the worst thing to do is panic and say something like "You certainly aren't thinking of that, are you?" This makes the person feel very wrong, unaccepted, and completely alone. Deal with it directly: "Are you thinking of killing yourself?" In other words, don't treat it as a taboo topic, or the person will withdraw from you. Next, accept the feelings that the person is expressing. Don't say that he or she doesn't really want to commit suicide, and don't

protest that everything is or can be wonderful. Those responses can make the person feel more alone. Try to understand what the person is saying, so he or she feels that someone cares and understands.

A good way to handle these discussions is called "reflecting." For example, if a male friend says he wants to die because his family doesn't like him, all you have to say is basically what he has just said, "You feel your family doesn't care," sincerely reflecting a basic interest in him. This gives him an ally for a while. This can be done without ever agreeing that suicide is the right thing to do. So, the best way to provide a person with a chance to think about it all and with some hope is by showing acceptance of the feelings but not of the suicide itself (Lester, 1971). Finally, if the person goes through with the suicide, in no way is this your fault. One tragedy is enough; don't add your own guilt to it.

Summary

1. Frustration results from the blocking of goals. Conflict occurs when a choice must be made between alternatives. Stress and anxiety are brought about by frustration, conflict, and change.

2. With stress, the body prepares for an emergency just as animals do. But, for humans, social restrictions make it more difficult to discharge through either fighting or fleeing. Our higher brains tend to see abstract crises that are much harder to handle.

3. Any kind of change can trigger a stress response. Being under stress for too long can lead to physical problems such as heart disease. The type A personality—the opposite of type B—drives too hard for too long and is in serious trouble if the person is also angry most of the time. Fighting off stress involves a three-part sequence called the general adaptation syndrome.

4. Drugs affect the brain by blocking the firing of nerve cells, increasing their firing, or by disturbing one's

normal ability to keep hearing, seeing, or smelling apart as different sensations. Depending on which drug is used, drug tolerance, physical dependence, and/or psychological dependence make them very hard to stop taking.

5. Suicide results from feelings of loneliness and loss. The frequency of teenage suicide is grossly exaggerated, but those who are suggestible are influenced by press reports of other suicides to attempt it.

Key Words and Concepts

frustration
conflict
approach-approach
  conflict
approach-
  avoidance
  conflict
avoidance-
  avoidance
  conflict
double approach-
  avoidance
  conflict
anxiety
stress
eustress
distress
fight or flight
  reaction
adrenal glands
stress hormone
life change units
type A personality
type B personality

general adaptation
  syndrome
alarm reaction
stage of resistance
exhaustion
substance abuse
chemical
  dependence
alcoholic
  withdrawal
  delirium
hallucinations
synergistic effect
psychedelic
tolerance
paranoia
psychological
  dependence
opiates
physical
  dependence
hallucinogen
steroids

Review Questions

Matching (Answers can be used more than once.)

1. "Should I go to Europe or Florida for vacation?"

2. "Should I quit my job? If I do, I can spend time with my friends, but I won't have much money. If I don't quit, I can buy a new stereo, but I won't have much time to listen to it with my friends."

3. "I don't want to do my homework, but I don't want to fail."

a. avoidance-
   avoidance
   conflict

b. double
   approach-
   avoidance
   conflict

c. approach-
   approach
   conflict

d. approach-
   avoidance
   conflict

4. "I want to stay home from school, but I know my dad will find out and punish me."

5. "Should I go out with Gail who has a good sense of humor but can never be serious or with Terri who is a good friend and a good listener but doesn't laugh much?"

6. "Should I crash into the oncoming car, or should I swerve and perhaps injure a pedestrian?"

7. "Should I watch TV? If I do, I won't have time to finish my homework."

8. "Should I treat myself to dessert or have a snack later? I know I can't have both."

Multiple Choice

9. Eustress is "good" because:
   a. It helps us to live longer
   b. It helps push us toward new goals
   c. It blocks out "bad" stress
   d. It causes us less pain than "bad" stress.

10. Stress can be good or bad depending primarily on:
   a. The body's initial reaction to a problem
   b. The number of problems a person encounters
   c. The type of problem
   d. How a person views a problem.

11. If an animal experiences a fight or flight reaction and then no longer needs to fight:
   a. Chemicals will be released to balance or calm the body
   b. Chemicals will be released to further intensify the body's reaction
   c. The animal will then run away
   d. The animal will probably fight the next animal to come along.

12. The purpose of the Social Readjustment Rating Scale is to show that changes in life:
    a. Will cause sickness
    b. Can cause an early death
    c. Can result in stress
    d. Should be avoided.

True/False

13. Evidence indicates that extreme type A personalities often develop heart problems.
14. According to the general adaptation syndrome, we respond to stress in an established sequence.
15. There is clear evidence that heredity is the sole cause for alcoholism in an individual.
16. Drug users often become dazed because drugs may stop nerve cells from firing.
17. Alcohol acts as a stimulant to the body.
18. Marijuana use seems to have an effect on short-term memory.
19. Studies clearly reveal that even occasional marijuana use reduces the level of male sex hormones.
20. Steroids operate as male sex hormones.

Discussion Questions

1. If you had to create a chart similar to the Social Readjustment Rating Scale, which would you rank as more stressful: moving to a new school or breaking up with a boyfriend or girlfriend whom you have been dating for two months? Explain.
2. If someone followed you around with a video camera from the beginning of this school year to the present—and only filmed you at school—what conclusions would a person viewing the video draw about your personality? Would your behavior indicate a type A or a type B personality? Explain. *Note*: Conclusions should be based only on your behavior, not on your thoughts.
3. Answer the question in number 2, but this time, imagine someone is reading only your thoughts and not seeing any behavior. What conclusions would be drawn in this case? Explain.
4. As noted in the chapter, the general adaptation syndrome isn't going to apply to every stressful situation. We have all experienced, at one time or another, however, each of these stages. If you found out that you had to get a tooth pulled in three hours, which stage would you probably experience more intensely in the next three hours, the alarm stage or the stage of resistance? Explain.
5. You are probably familiar with the theory that one of the reasons young people drink alcohol is that it is illegal or forbidden. Do you think this reason applies to the young drinkers in your area? Why or why not? Explain.
6. It should be fairly obvious to you how advertisers glorify alcohol use. Some people claim that this type of glorification has little effect on nondrinkers, that it will not significantly alter drinking habits. Furthermore, the purpose of the ads is to promote or highlight a particular brand name, not drinking in general. Others argue that the constant barrage of alcohol ads certainly does affect drinking habits. The ads send the message that it is perfectly acceptable to drink. With which argument do you tend to agree and why? Explain.
7. As stated in the previous question, advertisers explicitly condone alcohol consumption. Some would argue that not only do advertisers promote this drug use but also our society as a whole condones the use of alcohol and other kinds of drugs. What are some of the subtle ways in which our society says it is all right to use drugs? Explain.
8. As noted in the chapter, the press often plays up suicide. Should there be restrictions on what the press can report when a suicide occurs? Why or why not? Explain.

Activities

1. The chapter includes a chart that awards a stress ranking for various kinds of life changes (Table 16.1). We want you to adapt this chart to your school by making a list, not of *life* change units, but of "school change units" that may cause stress. The following are possibilities: an upcoming test, being called down to the principal's office, getting caught for cheating, getting expelled, being asked to deliver a speech because of your high grades. *Note*: Include both positive and negative changes. You can probably come up with at least 20 or 30 of these changes that potentially cause stress.

   Next, assign a ranking to each of these changes—a ranking of 100 would be most stressful; a ranking of five or ten would be least stressful. This ranking process will, of course, be subjective, but try to be fair. Before deciding on a final ranking, you might consult with several friends and teachers to get their input.

Once you've decided on your final rankings, place the items in order and include the numerical rank next to each item (just like in Table 16.1).

Next, either photocopy the chart so that each person in your psychology class can have a copy, or transfer the chart onto a poster so that everyone in class can see it. Ask your understanding psychology teacher for about five minutes of class time. Have everyone in class check the changes that they have experienced in the past month. Then have them add up the rankings for these changes. Finally, have them write down all the "illnesses" they have had in the past month—including sore throats, minor pains, and so on.

Collect their scores and their descriptions of their illnesses, and compare the two. Is there any relationship? Explain. Draw several possible conclusions from your results.

2. When we think of stress, we usually regard it as negative, as "distress." Conduct a simple experiment to see if a moderate amount of stress will actually improve performance. *Procedure*: Write out ten multiplication problems, all involving three-digit numbers multiplied by two-digit numbers: 336×75, for example. Find 20 subjects to solve the problems. Put 10 of the subjects under moderate stress, and the remaining subjects under no stress. The stressed subjects should be told that they have only a minute to complete as many problems as they can and as accurately as they can. The remaining subjects should simply be told to do their best, that it is just an assignment *you* need to complete. Don't tell them they are being timed. In other words, all 20 subjects will be allowed just one minute to solve the problems, but only half of them will know that they will be stopped at the end of a minute.

Compare the results of your two groups. Which group solved more problems? Which group answered more problems correctly? Based on your results, would you say that moderate stress increases performance? Explain.

3. Sift through several magazines and cut out ads that clearly glorify alcohol or any other kind of drug use. Next, find several pictures that show the possibly ugly realities of alcohol and other drug use. For example, you might use a picture of a vagrant sleeping on a bench with a pint of whiskey at his or her feet. Arrange both sets of pictures into a creative collage in which the message is clear that alcohol and drug use are often *not* glamorous activities. Your collage doesn't have to preach against anything; it should simply present two sides of an issue. It may be helpful to give a title to your collage or to include captions.

4. One of the most successful groups to deal with alcohol and drug abuse is Alcoholics Anonymous (AA). Contact an AA center in your area and interview someone there. Possible questions: (1) What are some indicators that might reveal whether a person has an alcohol or drug problem? (2) How common is it for a person to deny these indicators, to deny that a problem exists? (3) In what ways does this denial often express itself? (4) What steps need to be taken in order for a person to recover? (5) Is there such a thing as a cure for alcoholism?

Write a report on your interview and include your reactions.

5. Conduct research on one of the following drug-related topics: (a) Korsakoff's syndrome; (b) steroids; (c) how various drugs affect the body.

You will probably gather most of your information from books in the library. But write your report in a question and answer form, as if you were interviewing an expert.

6. Find the nonemergency phone number of a suicide hotline center and give the center a call. Interview either a director there or someone who handles the incoming emergency phone calls. Find out: (a) the techniques used by the operators; (b) how the telephone operators are trained; (c) the various reasons why people call; (d) the number of calls the center receives; (e) how successful the hotline seems to be. Also, prepare a list of your own questions that you would like to have answered.

Write a report of your interview and include your specific reactions. If you were extremely troubled and needed help, would you call this particular center? Why or why not?

In theory at least, this is the state of health and happiness we all seek.

Chapter 17

Toward a Healthy Personality

423

Global Look at the Chapter

The healthy personality is one that is able to reduce or cope with stress, frustration, pain, or illness. As you will discover, the evidence is overwhelming that we are able to gain control of all these problems by the use of mental powers.

Body-Mind Interactions

In one East African tribe, during the wife's first month of pregnancy, the husband suffers along with her, supposedly "feels the growth of the embryo in his own body, and develops great thirst." And, in a study at a Boston maternity ward, 41 percent of the husbands showed physical health problems—nausea, faintness, leg cramps—that were not present before the woman's pregnancy (Munroe & Munroe, 1971). No matter how one views these situations, two facts are clear: (1) The man is not pregnant, and (2) the man's symptoms have to be connected with the woman's symptoms by the power of suggestion.

In similar fashion, study after study shows that there is a strong connection between mind and body. For example, if we are told about a butcher slicing off a finger, we can actually feel a real discomfort, possibly nausea, just from hearing about it. And we all know people who have used a headache or stomachache as an excuse so often that by now the pain has become real and the person doesn't even know how it got started.

And the reverse is true: Giving the brain important information can reduce physical problems. For instance, "rehearsing" people who are scheduled for medical treatment—either by letting them observe someone getting the same treatment or by putting them through a dry run—reduces the pain they feel during the actual treatment compared to those who have not been rehearsed (Neufeld & Davidson, 1971). Patients told before an operation exactly what kind and how much pain they will feel after it is over have much less trouble coping with the pain, and they actually get out of the hospital earlier than those not briefed because fear of the unknown is reduced. So, the connection between the **cognitive** ("mind," "brain") and the physical is very strong.

If you want literally to feel the power of suggestion in operation—actual nerve impulses "moving," so to speak—think right now about your right foot, especially the big toe and the second toe that is touching it. Maybe you should wiggle the big toe a little. Doesn't it feel a little large? Doesn't that make you want to wiggle your second toe? Now, are they both going or at least trying to? Note that you weren't even thinking about them before we gave you a mental suggestion.

An Extreme Case: Voodoo

Dramatic cases of death illustrate the effects of cognitive control over the body. There is a form of "religious magic" called *voodoo* in which believers might wind up with a hex put on them. A *hex* is a "spell" in which victims may be told the day and time they will die. Some scientists followed up these cases to see if such voodoo "works." Indeed it does. Most believers will die right on schedule. The scientists even paid off a few corrupt "witch doctors" to remove the hex, and the victims survived *as long as they knew the hex had been removed*. In a few cases, the word didn't get to them in time, and they died (Cannon, 1942). Autopsies show that what is going on in this **sudden death phenomenon** is that, as the "time of death" arrives, people panic so badly that they send major electrical impulses through the critical nerve controlling the heart, causing it to get out of rhythm and stop (Lachman, 1983).

Sudden death phenomenon
A death resulting from panic and overload of the major nerve going to the heart.

Issue of Control

It is obvious, from the previous discussion, that we can affect our health by the way we view life. Those who see themselves as worthless and who are anxious, depressed, angry, or hostile increase stress dramatically and set themselves up for heart problems and a generally weakened body.

One of the more important factors leading to a damaged body and psyche seems to be the degree to which we feel we have lost control of our lives. In an experiment using a pair of rats, each of them was placed in a separate cage with a wire attached to the rat's tail. Both were then subjected to a series of shocks. One of the rats was an "executive." It was able to stop the shock by turning a wheel with its paws. This ended the shock for the other rat also—but the other rat had no control over what was happening. Hence, both rats got the same amount of shock, but only one of them was "in charge," so to speak, because it could turn the wheel. The health of the rat controlling the wheel remained good, while

In Focus: Locus of Control Scale

Instructions

Answer the following questions the way you feel. There are no right or wrong answers. Don't take too much time answering any one question, but do try to answer them all. One of your concerns during the test may be, "What should I do if I can answer both yes and no to a question?" It's not unusual for that to happen. If it does, think about whether your answer is just a little more one way than the other. For example, if you'd assign a weighting of 51 percent to "yes" and assign 49 percent to "no," mark the answer "yes." Try to pick one or the other response for all questions and not leave any blank. Mark your response to the question in the space provided on the left.

The Scale

____ 1. Do you believe that most problems will solve themselves if you just don't fool with them?

____ 2. Do you believe that you can stop yourself from catching a cold?

____ 3. Are some people just born lucky?

____ 4. Most of the time do you feel that getting good grades means a great deal to you?

____ 5. Are you often blamed for things that just aren't your fault?

____ 6. Do you believe that if somebody studies hard enough he or she can pass any subject?

____ 7. Do you feel that most of the time it doesn't pay to try hard because things never turn out right anyway?

____ 8. Do you feel that if things start out well in the morning that it's going to be a good day no matter what you do?

____ 9. Do you feel that most of the time parents listen to what their children have to say?

____ 10. Do you believe that wishing can make good things happen?

____ 11. When you get punished does it usually seem it's for no good reason at all?

____ 12. Most of the time do you find it hard to change a friend's (mind) opinion?

____ 13. Do you think that cheering more than luck helps a team to win?

____ 14. Do you feel that it is nearly impossible to change your parent's mind about anything?

____ 15. Do you believe that parents should allow children to make most of their own decisions?

____ 16. Do you feel that when you do something wrong there's very little you can do to make it right?

____ 17. Do you believe that most people are just born good at sports?

____ 18. Are most of the other people your age stronger than you are?

____ 19. Do you feel that one of the best ways to handle most problems is just not to think about them?

____ 20. Do you feel that you have a lot of choice in deciding whom your friends are?

____ 21. If you find a four leaf clover, do you believe that it might bring you good luck?

____ 22. Do you often feel that whether or not you did your homework has much to do with what kind of grades you get?

____ 23. Do you feel that when a person your age is angry at you, there's little you can do to stop him or her?

_____ 24. Have you ever had a good luck charm?

_____ 25. Do you believe that whether or not people like you depends on how you act?

_____ 26. Do your parents usually help you if you ask them to?

_____ 27. Have you felt that when people were angry with you it was usually for no reason at all?

_____ 28. Most of the time, do you feel that you can change what might happen tomorrow by what you do today?

_____ 29. Do you believe that when bad things are going to happen they just are going to happen no matter what you try to do to stop them?

_____ 30. Do you think that people can get their own way if they just keep trying?

_____ 31. Most of the time do you find it useless to try to get your own way at home?

_____ 32. Do you feel that when good things happen they happen because of hard work?

_____ 33. Do you feel that when somebody your age wants to be your enemy there's little you can do to change matters?

_____ 34. Do you feel that it's easy to get friends to do what you want them to do?

_____ 35. Do you usually feel that you have little to say about what you get to eat at home?

_____ 36. Do you feel that when someone doesn't like you there's little you can do about it?

_____ 37. Do you usually feel that it is almost useless to try in school because most other students are just plain smarter than you are?

_____ 38. Are you the kind of person who believes that planning ahead makes things turn out better?

_____ 39. Most of the time do you feel that you have little to say about what your family decides to do?

_____ 40. Do you think it's better to be smart than to be lucky?

Scoring the Scale

The scoring key is reproduced below. You should circle your yes or no response each time it corresponds to the keyed response below. Add up the number of responses you circle, and this total is your score on the Locus of Control Scale. Record your score below.

1. Yes	9. No	17. Yes	25. No	33. Yes
2. No	10. Yes	18. Yes	26. No	34. No
3. Yes	11. Yes	19. Yes	27. Yes	35. Yes
4. No	12. Yes	20. No	28. No	36. Yes
5. Yes	13. No	21. Yes	29. Yes	37. Yes
6. No	14. Yes	22. No	30. No	38. No
7. Yes	15. No	23. Yes	31. Yes	39. Yes
8. Yes	16. Yes	24. Yes	32. No	40. No

My Score _____

Reprinted by permission of Stephen Nowicki. From the Instructor's Manual prepared by Wayne Weitan for _Psychology Applied to Modern Life_, Second Edition, by Nowicki and Duke, published in 1986 by Brooks/Cole Publishing Company.

What the Scale Measures

Locus of control is a personality dimension originally described by Julian Rotter (1966). According to Rotter, people vary in regard to how responsible they feel for their own fate. Individuals with an *internal* locus of control tend to believe that we are responsible for our own successes and failures. Conversely, people with a relatively *external* locus of control tend to attribute successes and failures to luck, chance, or fate. The scale you just responded to was developed by Stephen Nowicki and Marshall Duke (1974) in order to remedy some technical problems that were characteristic of the original Rotter (1966) scale. Like the original, it measures one's belief about whether events are controlled internally or externally.

Interpreting Your Score

Norms

External Score:	16–40
Intermediate Score:	7–15
Internal Score:	0–6

External Scorers: A score above 15 suggests that you have a fairly strong belief that events are beyond your control. In other words, you do not feel that there is much of a connection between your behavior and your outcomes. This means that you are relatively less likely than others to take credit for your successes or to take the blame for your failures. Instead, you tend to believe that success and failure are primarily a matter of luck and chance breaks.

Intermediate Scorers: A score in this range means that you have inconsistent views about the degree to which you control your own fate. You probably believe that you do control your own fate in some areas of your life, while believing that you have little control in other areas.

Internal Scorers: A score below 7 indicates that you have a firm belief in your ability to influence your outcomes. Your relatively internal score means that you generally do not attribute your successes and failures to good and bad luck or chance factors. Instead, you feel that you can influence the course of what happens to you. An internal locus of control is often associated with relatively great stress tolerance.

the other one suffered ulcers and sickness—despite exactly the same level of shock (Weiss, 1972). The key here seems to be the ability to *feel* in control of a stressful situation, even though the stress must still be faced. Also important, in cases where control isn't really possible, is whether or not there is a sense of *complete* helplessness. If an event can be predicted, or at least partially controlled, the negative effects are reduced dramatically (Burger & Arkin, 1980). Many studies on many different types of creatures, including the human, support these claims.

Such studies are important because they show that we are able to handle our fate in far more instances than first suspected. You may believe that there are too many cases where we can't do anything about it, but that is not completely true. Suppose, for instance, that you have a teacher or boss who makes life miserable. Since you can't quit school or work, what is going on seems impossible to deal with. It isn't, though.

Control often comes from *inside* us. Thus, you take a good, objective look at this person causing you all the trouble. Is he or she really a nice person compared to you? Probably not. Are they more important than you? Again, probably not. They merely claim to be. And usually people who act like that haven't done much that is very meaningful with their lives, and that isn't the way you want to be. So, you have got the situation under control: You see it for what it is, and you have things in perspective. You do have to put up with the nastiness, but, if you accept it within reason for what it is (the *other* person's problem), you can come out actually reducing your stress and anger greatly. You triumph despite some unpleasant moments.

It should also be noted that some people can find strength through strong spiritual or religious beliefs. In this case, they believe that the control starts from outside them, but they still benefit because they believe (inside) that there *is* some control somewhere on their behalf over what is happening.

Coping with Bodily Stresses

If you get a splinter in your finger and leave it, some intriguing changes take place. The area surrounding it will first become reddened, but after a while a yellowish circular mound will form around the splinter. What has happened is that the body's defensive system has gone into action. It has dispatched special cells to that area to surround the foreign object, swallow it up, and kill any bacteria that have gotten into the wound. The result of the battle is the yellowish fluid of dead invader cells that comes out if you squeeze the splinter area.

This reaction is part of what is called the **immune system**. The immune system is our body's method for fighting off injury, disease, or illness, ranging from the splinter all the way through pneumonia. There are a number of types of these fighting cells, called **antibodies**, that are sent to various locations to ward off the invaders.

The chemicals that are triggered by stress actually slow down the immune system. While this doesn't "make sense," we didn't design the body—that's just the way it is. When people are depressed or anxious, the immune system is very low, and these people are easily infected. The antibody secretions of students during exam time are decreased because of the stress, leading to an increase in the number of sick students. And evidence is pretty clear that a psychological catastrophe, such as a death in the family, can cause the immune system to be weakened to a point that some of the survivors are in life-threatening danger (Ornstein & Sobel, 1987; Schleifer, 1985; Jemmott, 1984). And the reverse is true to a more limited degree; optimism can increase the number of immune cells (Rugg, 1985). Thus, we play an active mental role in our health. You will read that even diseases like cancer can result from a "poor" attitude. That

Immune system
The body's method for fighting disease or injury.

Antibodies
Cells that fight off invading foreign bodies that might prove injurious; part of the immune system.

sult from a "poor" attitude. That is quite exaggerated, but it has a *grain* of truth. What it refers to is that people who are beaten down by life have a weakened immune system, which can allow any incoming disease microorganisms to take over with greater ease. It doesn't mean that we can completely fight off cancer by having a healthy outlook.

The same principles apply to the illnesses discussed next. The evidence is again present that physical problems such as ulcers, asthma, and headaches can get worse as the result of psychological factors, but certainly psychological factors are not the "cause" of these difficulties (Friedman & Booth-Kewley, 1987).

Ulcers

Ulcer
Wound in the intestine or stomach resulting from severe irritation.

Many medical people have tried to relate stomach **ulcers** to psychological stress. An ulcer is a severe irritation of the stomach lining that can become an open wound inside. Some ulcers probably result from an excess of acid in the stomach. When people are under stress, the amount of acid increases dramatically. We in the United States spend about $8 million a year on antacids, so our stomachs must not be in very good shape. The easiest way to get an ulcer is to drink alcohol and take aspirin. The chemical combination of the two breaks down the protective lining of the stomach (Davenport, 1982). Overall, the origin of most ulcers is not well understood. Nonetheless, the studies on control that we've already discussed do support the likelihood that people who feel helpless and who feel they lack control over their environments will get ulcers more often than people who feel a sense of control and who are relaxed and easygoing.

Asthma

Asthma
Muscle spasms and tissue swelling in the air tubes of the lungs.

In bronchial (BRON-kee-al) **asthma**, the muscles spasm and the tissues swell in the bronchial (air) tubes entering the lungs. This makes it very difficult to breathe. Physicians often claim that this is a psychological disorder, but it more likely is related to allergies or defects in the immune system (Friedman & Booth-Kewley, 1987). One would expect a person having trouble breathing to panic at times, so there also is a psychological component. Stress can make asthma worse, but it is probably not the origin of the problem.

Headaches

It may be hard to believe, but the brain itself has no pain receptors at all. Hence, it cannot hurt. Because of the thick, sturdy skull, nature considered pain receptors inside unnecessary. Your brain can be touched,

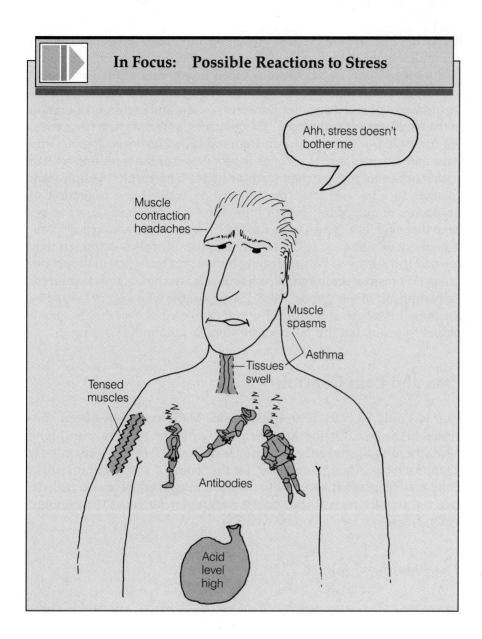

squeezed, and pinched, and you will feel nothing. Even so, we spend about $1.8 *billion* a year on headache remedies, so there is a problem somewhere. Actually, the "head" ache is coming from the muscles and blood vessels pushing against nerve endings that surround the neck and forehead.

There are two types of headaches. The first type is called a **muscle contraction headache**. It comes from stress or from spending long periods of time holding oneself in a certain position. These headaches can develop from driving long distances without getting out of the car and moving about or from those (rare) cases when one studies too long. Muscular

Muscle contraction headaches
Headaches from holding oneself in a fixed position, causing the muscles to spasm and putting pressure on the nerves.

Migraine headache
A headache resulting from an insufficient supply of the brain chemical serotonin.

headaches also appear because, when we are under stress, we tighten our muscles and hold ourselves in rigid positions for extended periods.

The second type of headache is called a **migraine headache**. People with migraine headaches have trouble with sleep and digestion, have disturbances of mood and emotional responses, and improper operation of the blood vessels in the head. These factors, as well as pain responses, are controlled in part by a brain chemical called *serotonin*. People who have migraine headaches seem to have a defect of the serotonin system so that not enough of the chemical is available. This results in unpleasant changes in all these areas of behavior as well as the triggering of headaches of staggering proportions. While professionals used to believe that such headaches were caused by stress or psychological problems these do not seem to be the origin of the difficulty—although they can add to the effects. We are dealing here with a biological malfunction; drugs that restore serotonin to proper levels are showing great promise in treating migraines (Brody, 1988). Some people who are not helped by the drugs have been able to develop sufficient control over their bodies to reduce the pain, but this takes a considerable amount of training.

Pain and Pain Control

Pain has only recently been understood. Many cures have been suggested in the past. On the American frontier in the 1800s, a "cure" for a headache was to shake the rattles of a rattlesnake by the person's ear (Dunlop, 1965). A late 1800s "cure" for the "bends," a very painful and at times fatal illness that happens to divers or miners who come to the surface too rapidly, was to put onion rings over the ears (McCullough, 1982). Neither of these worked well.

The Phantom Limb

Today we understand pain mechanisms much better. All pain is registered and controlled by the brain. This is shown most clearly by what is called **phantom-limb pain**. People who have had to have an arm or leg amputated can still feel the missing part. To add to their problem, on occasion the *missing* limb is felt to be in a certain position and causing an extreme, burning pain. This can happen because not only the sensation of limbs but also pain itself is stored and registered in the brain, not in the arm or leg.

Phantom-limb pain
Severe pain that feels as if it is coming from a missing limb.

Subjective Pain

Pain is subjective. By this we mean that each of us, depending on our personality, interprets the amount and severity of pain differently.

Thus, a cut or scrape you get playing a game will hurt less than one you get when someone hurts you deliberately. You can see this in operation by asking someone (you trust!) to scratch you *gently* on the arm with something like a nail file. If you are like most people, you could do this to yourself all day and have little reaction. But, if someone else does it, you will make a sucking sound, taking in your breath through clenched teeth, and you will pull your arm away before the scratch even gets started. If you go through with it, you will actually feel greater "pain" than if you did it to yourself.

Chemical Relief

Morphine is a heavy sedative that comes from opium. When radioactive morphine was injected into the body and then viewed by X-ray, researchers found that some nerve cell endings had absorbed and held onto the opiate. This was a puzzle until the nerve cells were examined more closely. It seems that some of them naturally and normally contain a substance that is almost identical to morphine, only it is produced by the body itself. At this point, scientists discovered that the body has built-in stress and pain reducers, called **endorphins** (en-DORF-ens). Endorphin, then, is a mor*phine*-like substance produced naturally within (*endo*) the body. The level of endorphins increases from sports activities because these activities put a strain on the body. This is why you feel so awful the next day after strenuous exercise—the extra endorphins you

Endorphins
Morphine-like substances produced naturally within the body.

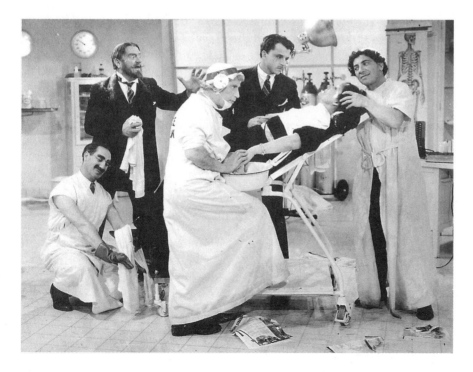

A notable amount of surgical pain comes from expectations. But, with this group one would expect the worst.

had while doing it and for a time afterward have been used up. No more extra "painkiller" has been made since you stopped the exercise, and now you ache all over.

Endorphins in the average person are heavily concentrated in the part of the brain that brings us pleasure (Romagnano & Hamill, 1984). From this arrangement, we can guess that they contribute to a feeling of well-being and help block pain. The reverse is true also: If we inject a chemical that stops the operation of endorphins, the person feels fatigued and out of sorts, loses some sense of well-being, and gets depressed. But, when someone thinks positively and relaxes, this increases the level of endorphins in the body (Levine & Gordon, 1985).

Endorphins cause pleasurable feelings that are not the same as drug addiction; unlike external drugs, endorphins are naturally pleasurable and rewarding because the body produces them and they are a perfect match to our pleasure receptors (Bozarth & Wise, 1984). But the discovery of the endorphin mechanism seems to explain drug addiction to illegal opium products. As opium, morphine, or heroin (all three are similar in structure) is taken in, it replaces the "natural opium" of the body, the endorphins, at the nerve endings and within the brain. The body, thinking it has all the "drug" it needs, will stop manufacturing natural endorphin. As a result, if the person withdraws from the drug, the body is without both the artificial drug *and* the natural opiates, which leads to discomfort and a craving for the drug.

The Placebo Effect

Placebo effect
Physical reaction to the power of suggestion.

Probably the best way to understand how the mind or brain and body interact is to examine what is called the **placebo effect** (pla-SEE-bo). Physicians discovered years ago that, if they couldn't figure out what was wrong with a patient, so-called "sugar pills" could be given and would often work as a "cure." Such pills contain no active medical ingredient; they work by the power of suggestion. The word *placebo* comes from the Latin for "I shall please," meaning that the patient is being pacified by getting *something* for the problem, even though it is not a real medicine. Scientists now know that the placebo actually changes the body chemistry and can start a healing process just because the individual believes that it will work. In fact, in a few cases, patients have become "addicted" to placebos in the sense that they have come to "need" them or else the symptoms return (Levine & Gordon, 1985). Since pain or stress gets worse as we tense up and worry, the pill, by this power of suggestion, can also help us feel more in control and, hence, more relaxed, which will reduce the stress, anxiety, and pain (Rachlin, 1985; Hilgard & Hilgard, 1975).

We might mention two remarkable events in the history of placebos. First, there is a medicine given to those who take poison that causes them to throw up immediately. In one study, it was used as a placebo by telling a group of people with *upset stomachs* that it was a cure for their illness. It worked (Wolf, 1950). Second, in ancient China, a useful drug for curing many ills was ground-up "dragon bones." What the dragon bones were really composed of is unclear. In any case, if the "pharmacist" was out of this concoction, records show that he would simply write the name of the drug on a piece of pharmacy paper, and the patients would carry this paper around with them to obtain the needed relief (Howells, 1962). So that is the power of the placebo.

Pain and Mental Processes

One indication that pain is a matter of interpretation comes from the finding that it seems to be learned, at least in part. Cases demonstrating this are rare, but in a few instances children who were reared in isolation (that is, with almost no human contacts, love, or stimulation) showed little or no response to a cut or minor injury. This doesn't mean that no pain is felt, but rather that reactions to moderate injuries are learned, probably within the social environment of getting attention from the parent (Freedman & Brown, 1968).

Some children are taught to be "brave" or "tough." Many have taken the lesson to heart: They show little or no response to minor pain. Others, who have gotten a lot of attention for crying over every little scrape, often show an exaggerated reaction to minor pain. Even in the animal world, when dogs are reared in complete isolation, they seem to have no concept of pain. They are quite willing to stick their noses into a candle flame with little reaction. This is seen as evidence that responses to some pain must be learned from others at a specific time early in development (Fox, 1968).

The physical setting and social surroundings where pain occurs also affect a person's reaction to it (Rachlin, 1985). Living in a group that tends to remain unemotional about pain guides an individual's reaction to pain, just as does living in a group that gets very upset. Interestingly, there are no sex differences in pain reaction, except that men have to complain more than women do before someone will give them a pill (Weisenberg, 1977). So, the environment, our upbringing, as well as what our friends do, all influence what we feel. The classic study in this regard comes from comparing soldiers' behavior on the battlefield with that of civilians having the same basic wounds. Only 25 percent of the soldiers asked for a painkiller, while 80 percent of the civilians did (Beecher, 1956). This is explained by the fact that the soldiers had a differ-

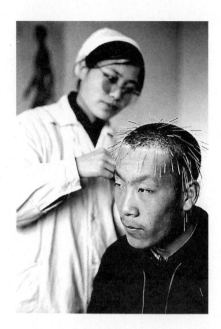

The man clearly is having his pain impulses rerouted by acupuncture.

ent interpretation of the wounds than the civilians. To the soldiers, the injury meant they had survived and were going home. Hence, that message from the brain was far more important than the wound itself and made the soldiers feel relaxed and hopeful compared to the civilians. Thus, the brain diverted or canceled most of the pain impulses, considering them insignificant (Melzack, 1987).

Rerouting Nerve Impulses

Our brains, then, have the ability to switch or reroute the meaning of incoming impulses or even neutralize them, depending on how we interpret the situation (Young, 1978). For instance, suppose you go to a restaurant and have a fantastic meal. The next time you go into that restaurant, before you are even served, you will salivate (politely) at the sight of the decorations inside—from association. The second time around, however, you are served rotten bits of liver in a cream sauce over spaghetti. This is sufficiently dreadful that, if you should ever go to that restaurant again and see the decorations, you will get queasy; you may even panic and run out. But note that the decorations are exactly the same all three times you go to the restaurant. Your brain has reinterpreted what they mean.

Acupuncture

Acupuncture
A system of pain relief that involves inserting needles into the skin.

A good way to bring together some of the concepts in this section might be a brief discussion of **acupuncture** (AK-yu-punk-chur). This is a 5,000-year-old technique for pain relief used originally by the Chinese and somewhat popular in the West today. It involves the insertion of needles into the skin. They are twirled, vibrated, or even activated electrically. In many cases, the technique seems to reduce pain.

One explanation for how acupuncture works is that the needles "confuse" the pain impulses already going through the body that are causing the person trouble. The needles also cause a release of endorphins, which further reduces pain. We also suspect a large part of the relief comes from the power of suggestion. For instance, from childhood, the Chinese expect little pain from medical work, with the result that Chinese children have their tonsils removed by lining up, getting an anesthetic sprayed down their throats, climbing on a table, and having the tonsils snipped out. The children get up smiling and leave the table with little obvious discomfort (Chaves & Barber, 1974). To some extent, then, pain is a matter of expectation. It should be noted, though, that, despite all the fantastic claims for acupuncture, the Chinese "cheat," in that there is heavy use of narcotics and anesthetics during most surgery.

Thus, in acupuncture, we have cognitive (mental) control, suggestion, distraction, and endorphins all working together. Many Chinese believe that acupuncture works because two supposed energy forces within us—the *yin* and the *yang*—get out of balance, and using the needles puts them back in balance again.

Controlling Thoughts

The key to handling pain, stress, anxiety, or worry is to learn to control one's thoughts. While this may sound simpleminded, it actually works.

Cognitive Strategies

A **cognitive strategy** is a mental technique in which we try to convince our brains to feel something different from what the incoming impulses say is going on. In the area of pain relief, there are two cognitive strategies: (1) **distraction**, in which we think of something else during pain and (2) **redefinition**, in which we talk ourselves into believing that the incoming stimulation is something other than pain (that is, we define the sensations over again).

Distraction works best with minor pain. You think of something like a beautiful sunset or some pleasant experience while being stuck with a needle. Redefinition works best with chronic (unending) pain. In the latter case, the task is to accept the incoming impulses, rather than distract them, but to reinterpret what they mean. Thus, you tell yourself that the impulse coming from an injured ankle is a warm, soothing one that will make you feel good. Or, if you are out camping and starting to get cold, you imagine how warm the air is getting. If the dentist is getting ready to drill, you concentrate on something pleasant happening. Developing these opposite cognitive messages actually does a reasonable job of reducing pain, and it requires little practice (McCaul & Malott, 1984; Brown & Chaves, 1980).

Cognitive strategies work for two basic reasons: (1) They reduce the stress and anxiety aspects of pain, which are really a large part of it, and (2) they put into operation the brain's ability to alter incoming messages from "pain" to "no pain" or "little pain." If you approach a situation with the attitude of catastrophe, the stress and pain will be much greater. Those about to be operated on who think about the horrors that have existed in their lives make it much worse than those who concentrate on some very warm, happy memories.

Preparing the brain beforehand also works. Providing detailed information about and methods for coping with childbirth consistently reduces the pain for those who take such courses. Whether or not this suggests that one should use "natural childbirth" (no direct medical control) is another question entirely. While there may be less pain using psychological methods, women still rate the pain as severe and usually

Cognitive strategy
An organized mental task designed to convince the brain that all is well.

Distraction
The cognitive strategy that consists of thinking of something else during pain.

Redefinition
The cognitive strategy that consists of talking ourselves into believing that an incoming stimulation is different from what it is.

Pharmacist's placebo prescription. (Have a Chinese friend translate for you.)

request medical pain reduction in the late stages of labor (Melzack, 1987). This brings up the important point that mental control really won't work well for a major operation or for stopping major pain, even though it may reduce it somewhat.

A practical hint: If some medical or dental procedure is being done to you, *don't* close your eyes. By doing so, you cut off all distracting stimulation from the environment and cause the body to focus only on the cut, stick, or drill.

Biofeedback

Biofeedback
A method of mental control in which a machine attached to the body records events going on (for example, high blood pressure) so that the individual can change them.

A popular method for developing control is called **biofeedback**. In biofeedback, a machine is attached to some part of the body and records its condition. The machine doesn't change anything—it merely gives information. Thus, it is useful for measuring stress (as recorded by muscle tension), anxiety (as recorded by amount of sweat), and high blood pressure (Miller, 1985). Information about the body's condition is given to the conscious mind by the machine. We take this information into account and try to achieve conscious control over the body. For example, if anxiety is too high, we try to relax until the machine says we are successful.

We don't know exactly how people are able to control themselves using biofeedback, but there are a few clues. First of all, using this technique causes us to *expect* benefits. Expectation is a large part of "cure." Second, merely going through the procedure of biofeedback gives us *something* to do rather than remain helpless. Third, when we focus on any object—in this case, a machine—attention gets locked in, and we typically go into a state of relaxation. Overall, relaxation is the most important aspect of the training.

As this woman views different scenes, changes in brain wave patterns are reported to her. She will then try to duplicate them on her own.

Hypnosis, which we discussed at length in Chapter 6, is similar to biofeedback, since hypnosis also involves expectations and distraction. As mentioned, hypnosis is just the focusing of attention on some idea or object. So, hypnosis, like all other methods we have discussed, will only work if you really want it to. There is no way to reduce weight, stop smoking or drinking, be relaxed, and the like unless you genuinely want to make a change. Some people don't want to give up certain styles of life; nothing is going to change them, other than themselves. This can apply to biofeedback, too.

Psychological Defense Mechanisms

Defense mechanisms
Techniques used to remain psychologically stable, or in balance.

When threatened, everyone does their best to keep some kind of balance. We protect our inner selves from too much attack by using **defense mechanisms**, psychological methods designed to keep us stable. If someone says you are a slimy, rotten worm of a person, these defenses go into action instantly, and you either think of how terrible that person is or you try to make yourself look better to offset the comment. Therefore, we use defense mechanisms to reduce threat to ourselves and to feel like a decent person. Defenses are normal in and of themselves, but they can be used too often. When that happens, we are refusing to face reality, and this is not adaptive. In the next subsections, we cover several different defense mechanisms. Usually these are not fully conscious because we use them to protect ourselves. If we fully admit that we are using a defense mechanism, it loses its effectiveness; we have to believe at least partially in what we are saying to and about ourselves while we are saying it.

Repression

With **repression**, we do not allow ourselves to remain aware of painful material; we push it out of consciousness. If we hate a relative and want to do him or her in, we force these feelings and impulses to remain out of consciousness (repress them).

    Repression can be unhealthy. For example, those who repress the feeling that someone like a parent doesn't love them ask for trouble. Pushing it away can interfere with the ability to give and receive love. Better to find out where this belief comes from and resolve it. But repression—or, at least, partial repression—can also be healthy. Someone cheated you and there is nothing that can be done about it. To keep the anger active and alive for a long time is destructive. The healthiest response is, over time, to focus on something else and repress the incident as if it didn't ever exist.

Repression
The process of pushing a painful event or thought out of consciousness.

Rationalization

With **rationalization**, we explain what we do in such a way that we avoid any responsibility for a bad outcome. For example, say we take some money that is needed for something important and spend it on something frivolous. We could rationalize this behavior by saying that we are all entitled to *some* enjoyment in life. On the other hand, rationalization can be used to our benefit to get rid of something we can't do anything about anyway. If someone we have loved very much tells us to shove off, we could rationalize by thinking of some defect that he or she has (terrible breath? strange smile? who knows what?). So we are "tricking" ourselves into believing we didn't want the other person anyway.

Rationalization
The process of explaining away a problem so that we don't have to accept the blame.

Projection

Projection refers to the process of mentally giving to someone else our own thoughts or feelings. For example, if a person is fired from a job for genuinely poor performance, he or she might claim that it is the super-

Projection
The process of attributing our thoughts to someone else.

visor who is incompetent. In this way, the responsibility is shifted onto someone else. All of us, at times, have a few bad days in a row. We decide that those around us are acting strangely and making life difficult for us on purpose. For a while this is all right, but a continued pattern of this type is self-destructive, since it doesn't help us face up to how *we* might be causing the problems.

Regression

Regression
The process of going backward in behavior and thought to a period when we were taken care of as a child; childish behavior.

This behavior probably should be called a "tennis tantrum," but its formal name is regression.

Denial
The process of refusing to admit that there is a problem.

With **regression**, we defend ourselves by "moving backward" and behaving like children. This defense is a reaction to the extreme frustration of having to be an adult and take responsibility. We regress (move backward) to a time when we were helpless children and someone had to take care of us. What we want when we are on the firing line is to be home in bed with someone bringing us chicken noodle soup. Regression is sometimes seen in sports events when the player lies down on the ground and has a temper tantrum, just as a child would. It is also seen in general behaviors such as pouting, sulking, and name calling. If we can find someone willing on occasion to take care of us, regression might offer some comfort, but usually it tends to make others reject us, since anyone acting this way appears ridiculous. It is not a very useful defense in the long run.

Denial

In some ways, **denial** is similar to repression. With denial, we *refuse* to admit that anything bad has even happened. Faced with a major decision, we simply deny that a problem exists. Some authors try to make a distinction between denial and repression, but it's a very fine one. With repression, we are at least partly aware of the problem, and then we push it out of consciousness. With denial, we don't let the problem come into consciousness at any time. But the point is that either of them puts distance between ourselves and what we should be facing. Beyond that, it is hard to keep them apart.

Why We Use Defense Mechanisms

The list of defense mechanisms can be expanded beyond the ones covered here, but making lists is not the important thing. The point is that we all are threatened, which makes us anxious. Anxiety brings a desire to get back in balance. We use the defense mechanism to establish

In Focus: Defense Mechanisms

equilibrium. Once in balance, the problem seems to be "gone." This often can be an illusion, however. The real world is still out there, and eventually we must cope with our problems or lose the battle. These mechanisms work in small doses to reduce anxiety. That makes them rewarding; hence, we want to use them more often. The more we use them, though, the more we are losing control of the situation.

Dealing with Stress

Who knows how many books and articles have been written about handling stress? As with many things, the issue is addressed over and over based on the idea that we can and should be "perfectly" free of stress. But none of us has ever achieved perfection, whether in freedom from stress, in health, in intellectual skills, what have you. And no one has a formula for dealing with stress that works all the time.

All of us know that too much stress and worry is not a good thing. But none of us can get away from them. Thus, it becomes a matter of how best to handle and modify our world so that we are reasonably content. The key to much of the problem is so simple and obvious that it is often ignored. What is needed is some kind of meaningful dialogue or discussion with *ourselves*. The problem is that there are so many people giving so much advice so endlessly that most of us reasonably shut them *all* out. But, in the process, we tend to shut off our own inner controller, which is actually quite smart. For example, the evidence accumulated over the years is strong that we have within us the ability, in many cases, to choose some of the proper foods we need to survive (Logue, 1986). This is why every now and then we have a craving that is very strong for a certain food. Sometimes we would give anything to have a piece of fruit or a tomato or a tortilla or a pizza. On occasion, there is some reason for this; the body is signaling us. But, on most occasions, we yield primarily to social pressure and don't listen to our bodies or minds, so we get into a pattern of eating the same thing over and over.

The point is that, if you eat nothing but pizza all the time, you're not listening to your inner self. And, if you go around all the time thinking your life is a failure, or you will never amount to anything, or you'll never get things done fast enough, you're not listening to the level of tension in your body, the level of frustration, or to common sense. This generalized criticism of yourself is sometimes called "shadowboxing" (a nonscientific term) because, no matter how hard you swing, you'll never connect with your shadow.

The first thing to do is genuinely to relax. This can be very hard. Few of us can accomplish it well. To deal with stress or a specific problem, you must be alone and you must relax. Relaxation is best accomplished by lying down and first tensing all your muscles, breathing deeply, and then gradually relaxing every part of your body until you can lie there, breathing gently and not fidgeting. Then, *really* talk to yourself. Analyze the issues. Be honest about yourself (very hard to do). There are things you have that no one else has if you look for them. Decide what is truly important for you in the long run. Try to get a perspective on how you are spinning your wheels on many things that don't matter in the long run. Get your own priorities in order. With relaxation and concentration, you can think things through into the future. For instance, how important in the long run is it to get good grades, participate in certain activities, have certain friends, and so forth?

There are other things to do, of course: Eat right, exercise, get enough sleep, don't this and that. But, if you practice this technique of listening to yourself, it should be a great help. You have to listen, really listen, and then you'll know how to set your priorities. Still, the stress is not all going to go away. For instance, just yesterday one of us was driving to work and someone very slow was in front of us. Result? Hit the accelerator; swear; slam on the brake; hit the accelerator; swear; slam on the brake. What's going on? Sometimes we don't stop and listen. In this case, the inner self was saying, "Stupid fool."

Summary

1. There is a very strong connection between mind and body. Everyone can fall prey to the power of suggestion. Voodoo is an extreme example of this.

2. The key to handling many of life's problems seems to be either actual control of various situations or at least the belief that one is in control. Helplessness can be the most destructive of attitudes or feelings.

3. The immune system is critical to survival. It is active or inactive as a function of our state of mind as well as of our physical health. Stress reduces the effect of this protecting system.

4. Pain is controlled by both mental and physical factors. The reaction to pain is subjective, and there is evidence that we learn at least part of how we react to pain. The body does have chemicals, such as endorphins, that automatically reduce pain and increase the feeling of well-being. The brain can also "reroute" (reinterpret) pain or other types of nerve impulses so that they do not have as great an effect on us.

5. Cognitive strategies are methods of using thoughts to reduce pain. The same principles probably apply to stress or frustration.

6. Psychological defense mechanisms are used to keep the psyche in balance. By using them in moderation, we are able to protect our sense of well-being enough to recover from personality defects, mistakes, or problems. But using them often is not a healthy system for surviving.

Key Words and Concepts

cognitive
sudden death
   phenomenon
immune system
antibodies
ulcers
asthma
muscle contraction
   headache
migraine
   headaches
serotonin
phantom-limb pain
endorphins

placebo effect
acupuncture
cognitive strategy
distraction
redefinition
biofeedback
defense
   mechanisms
repression
rationalization
projection
regression
denial

Review Questions

Fill in the blank. Answer on a separate sheet of paper. (More than one word can be used.)

1. The _____ system helps the body fight off disease.

2. The actual cells that fight disease are called _____ .

3. The nerve that controls the beating of the heart can sometimes trigger _____ .

4. Sitting in the same position for a long time can cause _____ .

5. Defects of the brain chemical system controlling serotonin may cause _____ .

True/False

6. Studying people with lost limbs reveals that pain is stored in the brain.

7. A placebo may ultimately change a person's body chemistry.

8. A placebo contains no medical ingredients that might alter the body's chemistry.

9. The level of endorphins decreases dramatically during exercise.

10. Evidence indicates that responses to pain are partially learned.

Multiple Choice

11. Acupuncture reduces pain by:
    a. Creating expectations of reduced pain
    b. Causing endorphins to be released
    c. Distracting pain impulses
    d. All of the above.

12. When would "redefinition" of pain be most effective?
    a. When the pain is a long-lasting one
    b. When the pain is brief
    c. When the pain is experienced suddenly
    d. None of the above.

13. Cognitive strategies work because:
    a. They completely block out pain messages
    b. They increase stress, which helps the body deal with pain
    c. They tend to reduce anxiety
    d. Of all of the above.

14. Biofeedback works because:
    a. It fools the body just as drugs fool the body
    b. It gives the user information about the body
    c. It puts the user in an hypnotic trance.
    d. Of all of the above.

15. Defense mechanisms are usually used:
    a. Unconsciously
    b. To reduce threatening thoughts
    c. To protect ourselves
    d. For all of the above.

Matching (Answers can be used more than once.)

16. Will is unable to remember an accident he witnessed 24 hours ago because the accident was too traumatic.

    a. rationalization
    b. regression
    c. projection
    d. repression

17. Jill claims she flunked her math course because the teacher didn't like her.

18. Bill hates his teacher, but he won't admit it. Instead, he claims that the teacher hates him.

19. Phil runs to his dad for advice whenever problems become too intense.

Discussion Questions

1. Imagine you are locked for an hour in a room in which a virus has been released into the atmosphere. Do you believe that there are any mental strategies you could use to prevent the virus from entering your body? If so, what kinds of strategies would you use? If not, why not? Explain.

2. The chapter explains that sudden death phenomenon occurs because of a person's cognitive outlook: The person *believes* he or she will die. Do you think that a person can literally kill himself or herself, not only because of beliefs but also because of a *desire* to die? In other words, can a person wish to die and, simply through wishing, actually die? Explain.

3. We all experience times when we feel that we have little control over circumstances. Do you tend to feel this way more often at school or at home? Explain.

4. If you found out today that: (1) many people who get ulcers feel helpless and lack control over their environment and (2) that you had an ulcer, would you change anything about your life-style? If so, what specifically would you change? If not, why not? Explain.

5. If you suffered from migraine headaches and you could eliminate these headaches either by taking medication for the rest of your life or by undergoing an *intensive* five-days-a-week, yearlong training program in biofeedback, which would you choose and why?

6. Let's say that five years ago you suffered from severe headaches. Your doctor, however, prescribed pills that virtually eliminated these headaches. If the pills that the doctor prescribed were, in fact, placebos, would you now want to know this? Why or why not? Explain.

7. If it is true that responses to some pain must be learned, what have you learned about pain and from whom have you learned it? Discuss.

8. The chapter mentions that the success of acupuncture depends, to some extent, on the patient's expectations. With this in mind, would acupuncture ever work on you? Why or why not? Explain.

Activities

1. There are numerous "self-help" books on the market today that are indeed helpful and very interesting. Books alone are obviously not going to make someone's personality healthy, but they often supply needed inspiration. Have your psychology teacher recommend several of these worthwhile self-help books, or simply go to a bookstore or library and choose your own (you will be surprised at the wide selection); then read any twenty pages out of one of them. Write a review of the pages and include the following information: (a) a summary of the pages; (b) your personal reactions to the pages; (c) whether the information seems practical and helpful; (d) whether you would recommend the book to a friend and why.

2. When we hear of programs that train people to integrate the powers of the mind and body, we often dismiss these programs as impractical and too mystical. We want you to unveil a bit of that mysticism by visit-

ing a center in your area that emphasizes, in one way or another, the integration of mind and body. Before you dismiss this activity as impractical, please read on. Some organizations will outwardly claim that their goal is to integrate mind and body. Examples include yoga centers, meditation programs, and acupuncture centers. These kinds of places are probably the places you would visit. If none of these is available in your area, then you need to be a bit more creative. For example, some organizations may not outwardly claim to integrate mind and body, but this, in fact, is their goal. For example, pregnant women often take Lamaze classes to learn how to "relax" (as much as that is possible under the circumstances) and to minimize pain during labor and delivery. Or people with high blood pressure often become involved in biofeedback programs. Where do you find these kinds of programs? Your best bet is to contact a local hospital and ask about the special programs that the hospital provides.

Once you contact one of these centers, interview one of the directors or trainers there. Find out: (a) the goals and philosophies of the training program; (b) specifically *how* the program achieves its goals; (c) what a typical training session is like; (d) how long it usually takes before a person realizes any benefits from the program; (e) costs, if any.

Finally, include your specific reactions to the program. If you had a desire to enroll in such a program, would you enroll in this particular one? Why or why not?

3. You will need to get permission from your psychology teacher to do this next activity. Why? A certain degree of secrecy needs to be maintained; therefore, the number of students allowed to conduct this activity must be limited. Read on and you'll see why.

You will need the help of three teachers who have freshman classes. (In all likelihood, freshmen are not allowed to take psychology and will not be familiar with this experiment.) One teacher should be a science teacher, another can be a math teacher, and the third should be a nonscience or nonmath teacher.

Procedure: Have each teacher bring a jar of water (with the lid on) into one of their freshman classes. The teachers will announce that they want to conduct an experiment on sensation. They should *suggest* that the jar contains a cleaning agent that has a powerful odor and that they want to test how long it takes for the smell to reach the back of the room. They should then

remove the lid and have students raise their hands (no talking) when they smell something unusual. What the students won't know is that, beforehand, the teacher secretly told four students in the front of the room to raise their hands, one by one, after about 30 seconds or so. So not only will the teacher suggest a smell but so will the four students, in a sense.

What you will be testing, in this case, with the three different kinds of teachers, is whether *setting* has any effect on the power of suggestion. Your hypothesis will be this: If someone offers a suggestion in a setting where you would *expect* the particular suggestion, others will be more likely to follow the suggestion. In this case, students *expect* science teachers to conduct these kinds of sensation experiments, and, therefore, these students should be highly suggestible. Furthermore, students don't really expect a math teacher to conduct sensation experiments (although they *may* be able to justify it in their minds a little), and therefore, they should be less suggestible. Finally, students least expect a nonscience or nonmath teacher to conduct a sensation experiment, and therefore, they should be the least suggestible.

The three teachers should pretend to time the responses of the students, but, in actuality, they will simply count the number of students who raise their hands—other than the four "spies." Also, you might get them to write down the gender of the students in order to see if this seems to be a factor. Collect the data from each teacher and compare results. Also, have each teacher describe specific reactions and include these descriptions in your report. Was the hypothesis supported? Explain.

4. The following is an alternative to the previous activity. Follow the same procedure, except this time contact three science teachers but from varying grade levels: fourth grade, sixth grade, and eighth grade. The hypothesis this time will be that younger students will be more suggestible than older students. Again, compare data and draw conclusions. (Since setting is not a factor being studied this time, it's important to keep this factor constant by using three science teachers.)

5. Collect several recent articles on headaches and write a report on the discoveries currently being made. Focus on the following areas: types of headaches, causes, prevention, and various cures and therapies. Include your reactions: If you had severe headaches, which kinds of therapies would you prefer?

6. Pick any four of the five defense mechanisms described in the chapter and find four songs that seem to correspond well to each. For example, if a singer sings about not admitting his or her feelings for another, you might use this as an example of *denial*. Then write out the lyrics of each song and underline key words and phrases that reveal the defense mechanisms at work in the song. Finally, write about a paragraph on each song, explaining why the song appropriately illustrates the defense mechanism.

7. Take a look at the cartoons used in the In Focus on defense mechanisms. Pick any four of the five defense mechanisms described and create your own visual for each. Feel free to deviate from the kinds of visuals used in the In Focus. Be creative. For example, instead of using a single cartoon, you might want to use a comic strip. Make the visuals large enough so that they can be displayed in class.

Psychological Disorders

In this situation, it looks very much as if the counterman is about to become a helpful therapist.

Chapter 18

Behavior Disorders

Global Look at the Chapter

Behavior disorders in most cases involve an exaggeration of certain behavior patterns that are found in all of us. The people with such disorders have buckled under to the stress in their lives and can no longer cope. There is another, different, group of people, called psychotics, who suffer from severe psychological disturbances most likely induced by chemical malfunctions as well as by psychological problems.

The Nature of Behavior Disorders

There are about 1.5 million people presently hospitalized in the United States for mental disturbances. An additional 4 million people annually seek psychological help of one sort or another. Despite these facts, it is surprising how incredibly difficult it is to define a behavior disorder. It is obvious that those people who think they are someone famous like the president (but are not) or those who carry on loud conversations in public with themselves have something very amiss in their lives. But very few people with psychological problems are anything like that. Television depictions of those with severe problems are almost always inaccurate. The ax murderer who goes from house to house on Halloween chopping people up because of some early childhood experience shows little grasp of reality—on the part of the person who wrote the script. While there are a handful of the disturbed who are dangerous, the average mental patient is confused and withdrawn, bothering no one. Statistically, mental patients are less violent than those making up the "normal" general public.

In Focus: Mental Health: It's All a Matter of Degree

| "ABNORMAL" | SEVERE DISORDER | MILD DISORDER | RELATIVELY HEALTHY | "NORMAL" | "SUPER-NORMAL" OR SELF-ACTUALIZING |

All of us fall somewhere on this scale. Furthermore, we all fluctuate from week to week or month to month from one point to another. The further left we fluctuate, the more likely it is that we will need outside help. The two end points are theoretical, of course—no one is either completely "abnormal" or "super-normal." (The psychotic goes at the far left and overlaps the left side of "severe disorder"; the nonpsychotic, or neurotic, would fit "mild disorder" and overlap the right side of "severe disorder.")

If you pick an emotionally disturbed person at random, the odds are that he or she will not be that much different from you or your friends in most areas, except for an exaggeration of certain behaviors. In other words, the person distorts or exaggerates behaviors that are shared by all of us. It comes down to a matter of degree.

Definitions of Behavior Disorders

It's important to note that there is something "abnormal" in all "normal" people. Have you ever done anything "strange" that you don't want others to know about? We have. By itself this is not significant. One very workable definition of those who *do* need help has three parts to it: (1) The person suffers from *discomfort* more or less continuously. The discomfort shows up as extreme anxiety, endless worry, or long periods of depression. In addition, the person feels that something is wrong with his or her life far more so than the average person does. (2) Another possibility is that the person is behaving in a *bizarre* fashion. He or she constantly misinterprets what is going on and what others are doing or saying. For instance, this person could be afraid to go to work or school. He or she frequently comes completely apart over minor things or sinks into a depression about them. (3) Finally, people who need help can be very *inefficient*. This means that they are unable to perform their life roles properly. Examples would be: an alcoholic who refuses to accept that there is a problem; a person who does nothing while his or her family life is falling apart; a mother at home with the children who cannot cope with the dishes, allowing foreign things to begin growing on the plates; a student who reads no assignments, doesn't attend class, and has nothing but trouble with most of the teachers.

Any one of these symptoms or a combination can indicate trouble. In addition, just as the degree of disturbance will vary, so will the degree of the symptoms. For example, the student just mentioned is in far worse shape if we add that he or she has no friends, locks himself or herself in a room most nights, and doesn't talk to family members (Buss, 1966).

Nonpsychotic Versus Psychotic Disorders

Psychotic disorders
Disorders that involve a serious inability to think rationally and to perceive the world accurately.

Psychotic disorders (sigh-COT-ik) involve a serious inability to think rationally and to perceive the world correctly. This is the most serious type of mental disturbance. While the symptoms vary, people who see things that are not there, hear voices, or cannot think and speak without confusion would fit into this category.

Nonpsychotic disorders
Disorders characterized by severe discomfort or inefficiency from which the person seeks relief.

Nonpsychotic disorders are characterized by severe discomfort or inefficiency from which the person seeks relief. On occasion there is some bizarreness, but never to the degree found in a psychosis. Nonpsychotic symptoms can take many forms: exaggerated fears, long periods of anxiety, temporary loss of memory, endless tension, or shyness to the point of hiding from everybody. Most nonpsychotic disorders used to be referred to as *neuroses* (new-ROW-seize).

Nonpsychotic disorders can be distinguished from the more severe psychotic disturbances in the following way: The world in reality can be upside down and threatening, and the nonpsychotic person is still able to see it more or less for what it is without *grossly* distorting or misrepresenting what is going on. Unlike the psychotic, nonpsychotic people are fairly well oriented to reality as most of us view it—they simply find it intolerable much of the time. Although nonpsychotic people are free of the major thinking problems found in psychotics, they still are at cross-purposes with themselves and get little accomplished. The nonpsychotic person, for instance, gets the feeling that nothing ever goes right, that things are too much to handle, and that people are not very nice. On the other hand, psychotic people can think that there is an organized plot against them that is causing things to go wrong.

At least on the surface, one would suspect marital problems, but sometimes it is difficult to tell if a person is just eccentric or is seriously disturbed.

Characteristics of Nonpsychotic Disorders

Although there are a few categories of problems that do not exactly fit the material we are about to discuss, we want to give you here a *general* idea of behaviors that are typical of the nonpsychotic. (Those that do not fit will be called to your attention as the chapter progresses.)

Most nonpsychotics have trouble getting along with others and are typically *inflexible*. This means they can't go with the flow of life but instead plow ahead with a fixed set of responses to almost everything. Thus, a shy, withdrawn male goes to a party and a few people are nice to him. This should help his self-image, but instead he misinterprets, just as he always does, and thinks they are only "feeling sorry" for him. Or a person who cannot tolerate elevators never accepts that they are reasonably safe, even after hundreds of forced trips. So, feelings, thoughts, and actions won't vary much for the nonpsychotic. They establish self-defeating boundaries around themselves that won't budge (Bower, 1981).

Another characteristic is that these people constantly see a *threatening environment*. A number of studies suggest that the world of most nonpsychotics is colored a gloomy gray because the worst is always expected or seen. Their thoughts and feelings are hardly ever warm and outgoing but instead are tinged with fear. They see danger, rejection, and failure around every corner (Hearn & Seeman, 1971).

A good example of nonpsychotic behavior was a woman we ran across a number of years ago. This person was a secretary whose job it was to type letters for the manager. This was during the days before self-correcting typewriters. She tried to turn out a *perfect* letter every time with no corrections. When this didn't work, she would become irritable toward others, type some of the letters 10 or 12 times, finally getting depressed. You can see what a mess her life had become. Nonetheless, she was not psychotic because she knew what was going on in the world. Rather than being unreal, her personal world was just extremely unpleasant.

Classifying Disorders—The DSM-III

In the next sections, we discuss several classifications of nonpsychotic disorders. These are part of a system in the mental health field that categorizes people according to the types of symptoms they have. There are hundreds of different sets of symptoms, all of which fit into a certain classification. These are contained in a book called the *Diagnostic and Statistical Manual of Mental Disorders III* (1980) (DSM-III), which is

Diagnostic and Statistical Manual of Mental Disorders III
A book that classifies the symptoms of mental problems into formal categories.

used by mental health workers to determine what classification a particular person belongs in. The classifications we will use are accurate, but we have taken some liberties with them just for the sake of clarity, since you are being exposed to them for the first time. In any case, remember that, even though these categories have names and symptoms, no person really fits into any one category perfectly, and symptoms overlap with one another. The DSM system is used only to provide some degree of order when trying to decide the kind of problem the patient has. To keep you from getting lost, please refer to Table 18.1 as the chapter progresses. It contains the basic information you will need and will keep you from losing your way in all the details.

Table 18.1 Behavior Disorders

"Neurotic" or Nonpsychotic Disorders	Psychotic Disorders

I. Anxiety disorders
  A. Panic disorder
  B. Phobic disorders
    1. Simple phobia
    2. Agoraphobia
  C. Obsession/compulsion
	I. Major affective disorders
	  A. Major depression
	  B. Mania
	  C. Bipolar disorder (mood swings)

II. Dissociative disorders
  A. Psychogenic amnesia
  B. Multiple personality
	II. Schizophrenia

III. Dysthymic disorder	
[Fear, anxiety, memory loss, tension, shyness, inflexibility, and a sense of the environment as threatening can be part of *any* neurotic disorders.]	[Thought disorders, word salad, delusions, hallucinations, clang associations, and psychotic episodes can be part of the behavior of *any* psychotic disorder.]

Discomfort, inefficiency, and bizarreness can be symptoms of either group. It becomes a matter of degree. Discomfort is most likely in the nonpsychotic; bizarreness most likely in the psychotic.

Personality Disorder

The antisocial personality (sociopath) fits into neither of the above groups and is discussed separately at the end of the chapter.

Anxiety Disorders

The three categories of problems we are about to cover—panic, phobia, and obsessive-compulsives—have in common one thing: The person suffering from them also suffers from severe anxiety. Hence these are called **anxiety disorders**.

Anxiety is a generalized feeling of apprehension that includes many bodily upsets. The palms sweat, the throat closes up, breathing is erratic, the heart pounds, hands tremble, and the armpits become a perspiration disaster. The feeling is a great deal like the one you get in a public speaking course when your turn comes to talk. All of us experience anxiety, but people with anxiety disorders have these anxiety attacks a few times a day, and in between they are restless, sleep poorly, don't eat well, and are not capable of calming down.

Anxiety disorder
Living in a continued, destructive state of anxiety.

Anxiety
A generalized feeling of apprehension and pending disaster.

Panic Disorder

The person with a **panic disorder** cannot relax—ever. He or she is afflicted by frequent and overwhelming attacks of anxiety. Sometimes a panic disorder originates in the person's psyche, probably developing from years of feeling insecure and helpless. But often such a disorder starts because something is physically or chemically wrong with the person. Once occurring, these panic attacks tend to repeat themselves whenever the person is under stress. In other words, the anxiety at first is not really connected to anything specific; it is just a physical occurrence. Soon, however, the panic begins to spread, as the fear of dying or making a fool of oneself is associated with more and more objects, events, or people. For instance, a person may be afraid to go for a walk because of a fear of rain, afraid to go shopping because of a fear of crowds. Eventually, the person may reach a point where he or she is afraid to leave home at all. When that happens, the problem is no longer simply physical but is psychological as well. Still, many who suffer can be treated with drugs that will reduce the symptoms (Fishman & Sheehan, 1985). Psychotherapy is also very effective and is discussed in the next chapter.

Panic disorder
A type of anxiety disorder in which one cannot relax and is plagued by frequent and overwhelming attacks of anxiety.

Phobic Disorders

In a **phobic disorder**, the person becomes disabled and overwhelmed by fear in the presence of certain objects or events. Anxiety is still extraordinarily high but usually only in the presence of the problem, instead of all the time as is the case with a panic disorder. The word *phobia* means "fear of," and there are two types of phobic disorders.

Phobic disorder
A type of anxiety disorder in which a person becomes disabled and overwhelmed by fear in the presence of certain objects or events. Two kinds were discussed: simple phobia and agoraphobia.

In Focus: Phobias

Achlophobia: Fear of crowds
Acrophobia: Fear of heights
Aerophobia: Fear of high objects
Agoraphobia: Fear of open spaces
Ailurophobia: Fear of cats
Algophobia: Fear of pain
Androphobia: Fear of men
Ankhophobia: Fear of flowers
Anthrophobia: Fear of people
Apiphobia: Fear of bees
Aquaphobia: Fear of water
Arachnephobia: Fear of spiders
Astraphobia: Fear of storms
Aviophobia: Fear of flying
Baccilophobia: Fear of microbes
Bacteriophobia: Fear of germs
Ballistophobia: Fear of bullets
Bathophobia: Fear of depth
Belonephobia: Fear of pins and needles
Botanophobia: Fear of plants
Brontophobia: Fear of thunder
Chromophobia: Fear of certain colors
Claustrophobia: Fear of enclosed places
Clinophobia: Fear of beds
Cynophobia: Fear of dogs

Decidophobia: Fear of making decisions
Demonophobia: Fear of demons
Domatophobia: Fear of being confined in a house
Entomophobia: Fear of insects
Equinophobia: Fear of horses
Ergophobia: Fear of work
Gephydrophobia: Fear of crossing bridges
Gynephobia: Fear of women
Hematophobia: Fear of blood
Herpetophobia: Fear of reptiles
Hydrophobia: Fear of water
Iatrophobia: Fear of doctors
Monophobia: Fear of being alone
Mysophobia: Fear of dirt
Necrophobia: Fear of dead bodies
Nosophobia: Fear of disease
Nucleomitiphobia: Fear of nuclear bombs
Numerophobia: Fear of numbers
Nyctophobia: Fear of night
Ombrophobia: Fear of rain
Ophidiophobia: Fear of snakes
Optophobia: Fear of opening your eyes
Pathophobia: Fear of disease

Peccatophobia: Fear of sinning
Pediphobia: Fear of children or dolls
Phobophobia: Fear of your own fears
Psychrophobia: Fear of cold
Pyrophobia: Fear of fire
Sitophobia: Fear of food
Sophophobia: Fear of learning
Stenophobia: Fear of open places
Syphilophobia: Fear of syphilis
Taphephobia: Fear of being buried alive
Technophobia: Fear of technology
Thalassophobia: Fear of the ocean
Thanatophobia: Fear of death
Topophobia: Fear of performing on stage
Trichophobia: Fear of hair
Triskaidekaphobia: Fear of the number 13
Tropophobia: Fear of moving
Verbophobia: Fear of words
Vestiophobia: Fear of clothing
Xenophobia: Fear of strangers
Zoophobia: Fear of animals

Simple phobia
A major anxiety that arises when faced with a specific object, such as a snake, dog, elevator, and so on.

A **simple phobia** centers on simple objects in the environment: cats, dogs, snakes, tall buildings, elevators, water, even knives. Faced with the object, the person has an anxiety attack. (Note the difference here: A panic attack is not attached to a *specific* object, as the phobia is.)

The most common explanation for phobias today is that they result from association or learning. If a little boy cut himself and the parent began screaming, crying, and running around shouting, "You're bleeding! You're bleeding!" the child, with repeated such incidents, could easily develop hematophobia, a fear of blood (*hema*).

All of us have mild phobias. Many people fear that they will jump off high buildings; others are hesitant to use public restrooms for fear of getting germs. But, for true phobics, the danger is so real that they live in mortal fear of being anywhere near the object. Caution: Trying to get real phobics to overcome their fears by deliberately forcing them into the feared situation can be very dangerous. Phobics have been known to die from an overload on the system. The problem can be treated by a professional in a matter of a month or so both efficiently and safely.

A second type of phobia is called **agoraphobia** (ah-GORE-uh-pho-bee-a), meaning the fear of leaving a familiar environment. Agoraphobics are so fearful of the world outside that they become virtual prisoners in their own homes. The following case (McMahon & Mc-Mahon, 1983) is interesting because it shows how an accidental event such as an ear infection, can trigger a mammoth psychological event—the agoraphobia—that will go on and on.

> A 42-year-old married salesman had been in traveling sales work for ten years. One night when on the road at a motel, he developed an infection which spread to the inner ear making him feel very dizzy. He decided to go to the bar and get a drink to "pick himself up." While sitting at the bar, things began to whirl around and the next thing he knew, he was lying on the floor, looking up at strangers all peering down at him as in a nightmare. He was certain he was dying because his heart was racing and people were saying things about a heart attack. He felt desperately alone, frightened, and embarrassed. The infection cleared up and everything seemed to be all right. But a week or so later, when driving down the highway, he started to feel "funny," weak, dizzy. He pulled off to the side of the road and waited the attack out. Instead of going on, he turned around and went back home where he felt safe. Within a matter of a month, he began to have anxiety attacks every time he left the house, and called in sick more and more often so he wouldn't have to leave home.

The word *agoraphobia* literally means a fear of open places. *Agora* is from the Greek for "marketplace" (an ancient shopping mall). We label the poor salesman as agoraphobic because his basic fear is one of being

Agoraphobia
The fear of leaving a familiar environment, especially home.

If you have acrophobia (fear of heights), this picture should be enough to get you started.

away from the closed, secure atmosphere of his home and out in public. Some believe such trouble starts in childhood when a child is accidentally lost in a place such as a department store. But many agoraphobics are women, especially homemakers without an outside job, in which case we suspect that the frequent isolation of this occupation makes them feel threatened about relating to other people in the "outside" world, and the fear grows and grows over time.

One oddity of agoraphobics might be of interest. Most of them have a specific boundary beyond which they cannot go. It varies from person to person. Thus, some people can go up to three blocks, some ten, some another number, from home. If they go even a few feet beyond, they come apart, but, if they stay within the boundary, they are all right.

Obsessions and Compulsions

Obsession
An endless preoccupation with an urge or thought.

An **obsession** refers to an endless preoccupation with some type of urge or thought. Each of us has experienced this to a limited degree when we can't get a popular tune out of our minds. Eventually it disappears, but magnify this many hundredfold and you have the concerns of the person suffering from this disorder. The thoughts simply will not leave them alone.

Compulsion
A symbolic, ritualized behavior that a person must keep acting out in order to avoid anxiety.

A **compulsion** is a symbolic, ritualized behavior that a person must repeatedly act out. Each time they do so, whatever anxiety they feel is decreased, so the behavior becomes self-rewarding and is repeated. Most people have minor compulsions, such as a desire to step on every crack on the sidewalk. Genuine compulsions are different because the people *must* carry out the act or they get more and more anxious. Some, for instance, wind up checking dozens of times to be certain the front door is locked before going to bed each night. That's not normal.

Obsessive compulsive disorder
Having continued thoughts (obsession) about performing a certain act over and over (compulsion).

The two words, **obsessive-compulsive**, are generally used together, even though it is possible for a person to be only one type. Most compulsive people, however, are obsessed with their compulsion; for instance, the compulsive hand washer is obsessed with the thought that he or she is "dirty." And being obsessed with cleanliness leads to compulsive washing.

The stranglehold that this disorder can exert is remarkable. Compulsive gamblers are examples. (These people are actually listed in the DSM-III slightly differently, but they serve our purposes well here.) They are constantly obsessed with the desire to keep on gambling no matter what. Thousands every year wipe out all the family finances, certain that the next hand of cards will change their luck. The strength of the problem is illustrated by a patient who entered a program in which he wanted to learn *not* to play a slot machine by having the act associated with something unpleasant, a shock. A slot machine was put in his hospital room, and he was wired up to receive a 70-volt shock to the forearm each time he pulled the lever. Over a period of time, he received 672 shocks. Only then did he decide to stop gambling. But his "cure" lasted only 18 months, at which point he started again and had to go back to the hospital for a series of "booster shocks" (Barker & Miller, 1969).

Obsessive-compulsive behavior seems to result from faulty attempts to resolve guilt, anxiety, or insecurity. For instance, insecurity and anxiety can result in someone *having to* get up and check the front door dozens of times before finally going to sleep.

Some behavior in this classification is quite symbolic. For example, many children are told that something they did was "dirty." This makes them associate cleanliness with goodness. Over time, whenever they feel "dirty" (guilty), they will wash their hands—up to hundreds of times a day. Just the act of doing *something* (even though it doesn't work) reduces their anxiety and guilt (Turner et al., 1985). Hence, they come to repeat it, rather than seeking a more sensible solution. On the other hand, recent research has found that there is a defect in the amount of some brain chemicals for many people with this problem. The result is the triggering of circuits in the brain over and over to repeat endlessly things that are reasonably normal for most of us. There are new drugs that help people begin to get it under control, at which point most can handle the problem effectively and understand themselves better (Rapoport, 1989).

Believe it or not, this is an enormous ball of tin foil. Hobby or obsessive compulsive behavior?

Dissociative Disorders

Dissociative disorders (dis-SO-see-ah-tiv) are best known from soap operas on television. The major character develops amnesia and forgets she is married to a prominent attorney. She falls in love with a wealthy physician at the local hospital where she is treated for the flu. The physician is married to the head nurse, who is really a multiple personality who got the woman-of-the-year award but steals drugs, which she sells on the street. Meanwhile . . .

If one paid any attention to television, it would seem that this sort of thing goes on all the time. Actually, dissociative disorders—amnesia and multiple personality—are extremely rare. The word *dissociative* refers to the fact that people with these disorders can disconnect or "disassociate" certain events or behaviors from one another. There is a bit of this ability in all of us. We have things we want to forget, and we can do a good job of getting rid of them. It is a rare individual who doesn't "absentmindedly" miss a doctor's appointment, for example. We have a bit of multiple personality also, which we carry out all the time—without getting confused as to which part we are playing. For instance, no one uses the same language or discusses the same (sometimes crude) thoughts at a family dinner as he or she does when alone with close

Dissociative disorders
Nonpsychotic disorders in which a part of one's life becomes disconnected from other parts; amnesia, multiple personality.

friends. So, dissociative disorders are very elaborate behaviors that have seeds in our everyday activities (Bower, 1981). Most of us can change our behavior in different circumstances and rebound to whatever our "core" personality might be. The multiple personalities, however, are different because they have an aspect of themselves that causes such guilt (for example, a repeated tendency to violate the law) that they cannot face this aspect and thus block it off. Since this part won't disappear, for these people it grows and grows until eventually they form a separate personality that can do these acts and not be responsible and guilty for them when they return to their "good" personality.

Psychogenic Amnesia

Psychogenic amnesia
A dissociative disorder in which traumatic events "disappear" from memory.

In **psychogenic amnesia**, a dissociative disorder, memories related to a terrible trauma "disappear." They are still "in" the person, but they are cut off from consciousness. While some amnesias can be caused by a high fever or a blow to the head, the term "psychogenic" means the problem is psychologically (*psycho*) caused (*genic*). In fact, people with this problem often show little concern that parts of their past seem to be gone. Hence, there must be a psychological benefit involved, or they would indeed be alarmed at losing some of their memories.

Selective forgetting
"Forgetting" only things that are very traumatic.

A common and easily understood type of psychogenic amnesia is a soldier's loss of memory for nightmarish events that happened in battle. In such cases of amnesia, **selective forgetting** is involved, which means that only the traumatic portion of the memories disappear. For example, a soldier may completely blot out the part of his identity connected with his fighting battalion and the friends there, and everything in the more recent past leading back to a horrible war experience. The terror and guilt these memories produce therefore disappear, occasionally reappearing in nightmares (Hartmann, 1984). But only certain events are gone: The soldier doesn't forget how to tie a shoe, childhood friends, old memories, and so forth. In fact, amnesia in all these cases is selective.

Multiple Personality

Multiple personality
A person who divides himself or herself into two (possibly more) separate personalities that can act independently.

Another dissociative disorder is the **multiple personality**, which, in basic form, is similar to amnesia. Instead of forgetting specific events, though, such individuals, as we've mentioned, "forget" a portion of themselves, and that portion begins to live a life of its own. Although multiple personalities are all over television and are usually called schizophrenics, which they AREN'T (!), they are extremely rare; there are only about a dozen or so *scientifically* and *carefully* documented cases in the last 50 years (McMahon & McMahon, 1983; Horton & Miller, 1972).

Again, all of us have secret fantasy lives that we don't want others to know about. In a fashion similar to the true multiple personality, we make a division that is usually based on a "good" person and a "bad" person. But for the true multiple personality, the dissociative behaviors are exaggerated to the point of becoming at least partly independent of each other.

Multiple personality is probably so rare because a number of conditions must align themselves in just the right way in order to produce it. Such conditions typically include a haunted, confused personality, some kind of very upsetting experience, and a long-term habit of escaping from almost any problem. Usually these people have very strong, conflicting desires and needs in their life-styles. For example, a withdrawn and righteous man (call him A) who desperately wants to give vent to animal impulses develops mammoth guilt over these desires. To distance himself from this pain, another personality gradually creeps into the picture containing these unacceptable desires. This is evil personality "B." He can then go about doing whatever he wants as long as he is B. When A returns, he becomes very self-righteous, even prim, prissy, and obnoxiously good. Complete amnesia can be involved, with A not knowing about B and vice versa. Sometimes, however, the dominant or stronger personality knows about the weaker; the weaker rarely knows about the stronger one (Gruenewald, 1971).

The multiple personality disorder is not a psychosis; hence, it can't be schizophrenia. There is really only one person involved with two or more sides that tend to live independently. But the basic core personality is the same, and this core is well aware of general reality as we know it, does not have trouble thinking or communicating, and does not believe things that don't exist. These facts are the opposite of what happens in a psychosis, discussed in detail later.

Before leaving the subject, we should mention one more thing. The articles, stories, and books you will see about people who have 20 or so personalities are sheer hocus-pocus. The authors are exaggerating the way things are; typically the patient in such cases, loving the attention he or she gets, goes along with it and keeps making up new "personalities." It comes down to a situation that is somewhat similar to this: You have a habit of humming when you wash your hair in the morning, but at no other time. Hence, if you wanted to, you could say that you have a "shower personality."

Dysthymic Disorder

The term **dysthymic disorder** (dis-THIGH-mic) comes from the Greek word for "low spirits." Hence, it is a moderate, nonpsychotic depression. It is so frequent—5 to 12 percent of the population has had it—that

Dysthymic disorder
A moderate, nonpsychotic depression.

it is referred to as the common cold of mental health (Weissman, 1985). Typical symptoms are lack of energy, unhappiness, loss of interest in activities and people, loss of sense of humor, sadness, and rock-bottom feelings of self-worth (Beck, 1967). All of these feelings can occur in the normal person who, for instance, loses a loved one.

The best way to know whether depression of this sort is normal is to see if it has served its "function" or instead has taken on a life of its own that just keeps on going. Loss of a friend, for instance, would trigger these problems in any normal person, but, if they go on and on with the same degree of severity, something else is probably wrong. Or, if they appear "out of nowhere" or arise following an insignificant event, again something is present that may lead to an emotional problem.

A dysthymic disorder is a neurotic depression rather than a psychotic depression. Hence, although very distressing, it is much milder in symptoms and quite common. In the section coming up titled "Major Affective Disorders," we discuss psychotic depression. Since the causes of both are similar in many respects—except that the psychotic probably has a physiological defect also—we will save further discussion of depression for that section.

Characteristics of Psychotic Disorders

A psychosis involves a major disorganization of thought processes, confused and extreme emotional responses, and distorted perceptions of the world. There is a loss of contact with and difficulty in recognizing reality. Thus, it is a very serious mental disturbance. Most researchers do not think that it is an extension or outgrowth of neurosis, but a separate problem that arises all by itself.

There are four major symptoms that can appear in a psychosis. All four may not be present in one individual, but typically at least two are. (1) The first symptom is a serious distortion of mental processes. Often it is hard to understand exactly what psychotic people are trying to say or to grasp what they are thinking. This behavior comes and goes so that they are lucid for a while, then very confused. This symptom is called **thought disorder**. (2) The second symptom involves seeing and hearing things that are not present. Again, this comes and goes. It is not unusual for psychotics to hear voices or see objects that are not present. This behavior is called **hallucinating**. (3) Next, many psychotics hold grossly inaccurate beliefs, such as thinking of themselves as avenging angels or as victims of persecution by some secret organization. Such a belief is called a **delusion**. (4) Finally, psychotics have a great deal of trouble with emotional responses. The emotions shown are quite inappropriate; they might show no response at all when something interesting happens, for example, or they might laugh at a tragic event. We seriously doubt that

Thought disorder
A serious distortion of the ability to think or speak.

Hallucinating
Seeing or hearing something that is not present.

Delusion
A belief in something (for example, that you are a king or queen) that is not true.

they really think it is funny; instead, we think that they are quite confused and dominated by a malfunctioning brain.

The man who is squatting down is suffering from a major depression. The man sitting alone is probably an example of dysthymic disorder.

Major Affective Disorders

The *affect* (AF-fect) of an individual is his or her emotional status—elated, depressed, angry, neutral, and so forth. Thus, mental disturbances involving a depressed mood, an exaggerated "up" mood, or an alternation between up and down are called **major affective disorders**. The dysthymic disorder discussed earlier is an affective disorder, but mild compared to this psychotic problem. Compared to the dysthymic, the major affective disorder is far more severe and completely disables the person. At one time it was (and sometimes still is) called a *manic-depressive disorder*.

Major affective disorders
Serious disturbances of affect, or emotion; person's moods go *very* high or *very* low.

Major Depression

The most common symptom of this psychosis is the **major depression**. Typical symptoms are very slow speech (if the person speaks at all), deep ongoing depression, a severe loss of appetite, a sense of hopelessness, extreme feelings of worthlessness, and continuous thoughts of death or suicide. It is not unusual to have hallucinations involving monsters, gore, death, or "evil" eating up the soul (Miller & Orr, 1980; Beck, 1967).

Major depression
A psychotic effective disorder involving mammoth depression, loss of appetite, hopelessness, thoughts of death.

Most patients in this category have trouble moving or even carrying out simple tasks. They often lie motionless in a rolled-up fetal position for hours at a time.

Mania

Mania
A affective psychotic disorder involving extreme agitation and restlessness.

Since the word *affective* refers to any kind of emotional disturbance, there are some psychotic affective patients who go in the opposite direction from depression and have extreme *up* moods. This might sound at first like something that wouldn't be all that bad, but unfortunately that is not the case. This behavior, called **mania** (MAIN-ee-ah) from the Greek for "mad excitement," involves agitation, restlessness, inability to concentrate, and extremely rapid speech. The speech problem is the most notable part of the behavior. The patients' thoughts are moving so quickly through their minds that they literally collide with one another into a mass of confused speech, making comprehension almost impossible. This problem is called a **flight of ideas**, meaning that thoughts are running so fast they are flying in all directions. Here is a brief example: "I went to the store where I kept the containers of milk which all babies should have in order to survive which not everybody can do because of the threat of nuclear war between countries which are divisions of various parts of the land which is filled normally with rock and dirt." These patients often get so excited that they begin to have delusions that they have special powers or great influence, so they make plans for controlling the world or some such project (Depue et al., 1981).

Flight of ideas
A confused psychotic speech in which thoughts and speech go in all directions with no unifying idea.

Bipolar Disorders

On occasion, a few psychotic affective patients go on swings between the ups of mania and the downs of a major depression. The official term for this problem—which you might have heard of as "manic depression"—might confuse you at first, but it is logical. First, remember that the earth has two poles, north and south. The word *pole*, in this sense, means "one of the two most extreme possibilities"—one pole is at the top, the other at the bottom. They couldn't get farther from one another. Next you need to understand the word *bi*. *Bi* means "two" of something. So, patients who have these wild swings from up to down and back are categorized as having a **bipolar disorder**. Here is a case history of such a disorder (McMahon & McMahon, 1983):

Bipolar disorder
A major affective disorder with up and down swings of moods from "high" to "low."

> The patient, a 25-year-old woman, was admitted to the hospital for observation after the fire department was called by a neighbor who saw smoke. The patient was dressed in a grass skirt she had purchased in Hawaii during her honeymoon. She had built a "bonfire" in the middle of the living room floor and was dancing around the fire, leaping, jumping, and singing what seemed to be college football cheers.

Mania

Mania
(serotonin
too high)

Depression
(serotonin level too low)

At the hospital she was placed in restraints because she was not only danc-ing, but trying to throw touchdown passes at the same time, mixing obscenities and quarterback play calls in a continuous outpouring. She seemed only partially aware of her surroundings, making such comments as "Sing along with me! Statue of Liberty on three, you son of a bitch! Okay, here we go!"

The same patient was readmitted to the hospital 17 years later at the age of 42 with a diagnosis of bipolar disorder. Her husband brought her to the hospital because she had refused to eat for three days, slept only two or three hours a night, and spent long hours staring off into space. She would speak to others, but only after more or less continuous coaxing. In very slow, monotonous speech, she commented that she was talking to her dead sister who was wearing a white gown, but her face was eaten up by worms and part of her eye socket was missing. This hallucination was intermixed with a conversation with God, a combination of pleading with Him to do something about her sister and blaming Him for her hospitalization.

In the years between her first hospitalization and her present admission, she had been treated on several occasions in the outpatient clinic for depressive episodes, but there had been one additional manic episode.

We don't understand the origin of psychotic affective disorders very well. In fact, strangely enough, they disappear all by themselves (at least 80 to 90 percent of them) within about six months, although they tend to recur in many people (Rennie, 1972). Just as the dysthymic disorder may be caused by the loss of a loved one, major affective disorders, we suspect, may come from a lifetime of many separations, losses, and unpleasant setbacks (Benjaminsen, 1981; Strauss, 1979). Again, like the dysthymic but at a more severe level, these people have a very poor self-image. They see themselves as responsible for many bad events and don't even struggle to put up a defense against such an unrealistic burden (Lewinsohn et al., 1980; Beck, 1972).

The problems are so bizarre and severe and they appear (and disappear) so rapidly in the psychotic affective disorders that we suspect some chemical imbalance is involved. Probably psychological components then help send the person over the edge, so to speak. Studies show a pretty clear pattern of chemical defect in the brain. One brain chemical that helps keep the brain active in normal people, called **serotonin** (ser-un-TONE-in), is very high—much higher than normal—in many manics; the same chemical is very low in depressives (Snyder, 1984).

Could this defect be inherited? It is possible, but we can't be certain. Here is the problem: There is typically a family history of depression when you interview the patient. *But* depression is psychologically "contagious," so it may well be that being around depressed family members could be the cause rather than a specific gene (Kidd, 1985). We'll have to wait, but for the moment a combination of psychological factors with a physical or chemical defect seems a good bet as the source of psychotic affective disorders.

Schizophrenic Disorders

Schizophrenia (skitz-oh-FREN-ee-ah), a psychosis, is the most serious of all mental disturbances. Obvious symptoms of this problem are disorganized thoughts and garbled speech, as well as hallucinations and delusions. Researchers doubt that schizophrenia is a single disorder, but in-

Serotonin
The brain chemical that in excess, leads to mania; in too low concentrations, to depression.

Schizophrenia
The most serious mental disturbance, involving loss of contact with reality, thought disorders, hallucinations, and delusions.

stead feel that there are different causes and degrees of severity. For example, about a third of such patients have one episode and get better, never to have it happen again; a third have very severe symptoms and respond to no treatment at all; the final third are in and out of institutions most of their lives (Restak, 1984). We suspect that schizophrenia results in part from some physical or chemical problem because it appears in late adolescence or early adulthood, almost never earlier. This fact would tend to rule out the suggestion that it is mostly psychological, because psychological causes should result in the problem appearing at almost any age.

Schizophrenics do differ from one another. A common type, however, is the person who is in a stupor and shows little evidence that anything going on around him or her is registering. This person is *not* depressed or sad but instead seems not to care at all. When you meet this kind of schizophrenic, the general impression you get is that he or she is operating like a mechanical toy whose batteries are about to give out—dimly perceiving and sluggish. The person speaks in a monotone: "I started with a sense that justice was next to the nebulous thing which no one can describe but which dissolves all other relationships in its vapor" (Lorenz, 1961).

In some cases, schizophrenics will speak what is called **word salad**. Like the ingredients of a tossed salad, the words are all mixed together: "The house burnt the cow horrendously always" (Vetter, 1969). Or there are what we call **clang associations**, which refers to the fact that the speech has a rhythm like a bell: "You wear clothes and how much does this watch cost? Have you a sister? I have three and they are all fine girls, curls, furls, isn't that funny?" (Sherman, 1938). The clang comes with "girls, curls, furls."

Word salad
Speech in which words are mixed together incoherently.

Clang associations
Psychotic speech in which words are rhymed.

Psychotic Episodes

Schizophrenics are not out of touch with reality all the time. Their unusual behavior (called **psychotic episodes**) comes in cycles, and in between the person is reasonably lucid. But often even those who seem unaware of their surroundings are not really as completely lost as they may appear.

One story about this involves a loud and obnoxious student nurse who frequently made unflattering remarks about the patients. One day she leaned over to make a bed next to the one on which a schizophrenic patient had been sitting immobile for many hours. She commented on how stupid she thought his behavior was and suddenly received a good solid kick in the rear. By the time she had whirled around, the patient had "resumed his 'poker face' expression and former posture" (O'Kelly & Muckler, 1955).

Psychotic episodes
Periods of psychotic behavior that can alternate with periods of relative coherence and calm.

Incidence of Schizophrenia

The estimate is that about one-half of 1 percent of the population has this disturbance. At any given time, there are about 200,000 hospitalized schizophrenics (Dohrenwend et al., 1979). Here is a case study of a schizophrenic named Michael (McMahon & McMahon, 1983):

Michael W., a 29-year-old married male, was brought to the hospital emergency room after refusing to eat or speak and staring out the window for four days. An interview with family members revealed that Mr. W. had had such episodes before, but they had never lasted this long. In addition, he had periods in which he was suspicious of everyone in his family and claimed they were trying to poison him. During these periods, he accused his wife of infidelity and became extremely agitated and hostile towards her. He had never been physically abusive, but his behavior was so irrational and out of control that she was quite fearful of him at those times.

Following high school graduation and vocational training, Mr. W. had been regularly employed in television repair until two years ago when economic conditions forced his employer to lay him off. Since that time, he worked occasionally at different jobs, the last one delivering for a local pizza parlor. He was fired from that job six months ago. Apparently, he would leave the parlor to make his deliveries, but would then become confused, park his truck, and sit for hours before returning with no deliveries made. Lately he had stopped seeking employment.

According to the older brother, he and Mr. W. had been reared by an unmarried aunt who was in her 50s when they came to live with her as small children. Their mother was killed in an automobile accident shortly after Mr. W.'s birth, and their father afterwards developed a drinking problem, eventually becoming totally unable to care for them. The brother described his aunt as an emotionally cold woman who resented caring for her nephews, but he stated they were well fed and clothed and their physical needs generally attended to. Visits from their father were rare, and usually resulted in bitter arguments

This series of paintings was made by the same artist over a period of time. Unfortunately, he was becoming schizophrenic, and it is possible to see the progression of the disease in his work.

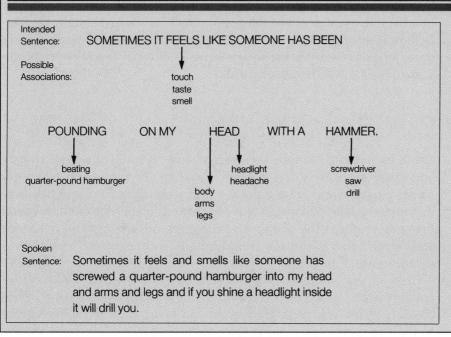

Intended Sentence: SOMETIMES IT FEELS LIKE SOMEONE HAS BEEN

Possible Associations:

touch
taste
smell

POUNDING   ON MY   HEAD   WITH A   HAMMER.

beating
quarter-pound hamburger

headlight
headache

body
arms
legs

screwdriver
saw
drill

Spoken Sentence: Sometimes it feels and smells like someone has screwed a quarter-pound hamburger into my head and arms and legs and if you shine a headlight inside it will drill you.

The speech of the schizophrenic often sounds jumbled and senseless. A closer analysis of this speech, however, may reveal that it is not as senseless as it appears. Read the sentence at left and note the possible associations that the schizophrenic may make while mentally constructing the sentence.

with their aunt, after which the boys were denied supper and confined to their room for the remainder of the day. Neither had seen or heard from their father for over 10 years, and the aunt died 6 years ago.

During the interview, Mr. W. answered no questions, but merely stared at the opposite wall. Every now and then he would jerk his head sideways and inhale sharply. He sat in a very peculiar posture, his right hand and arm held rigidly at a 45° angle, the left stiffly at his side. When he walked, his knees bent only slightly with each step, giving him a robotlike appearance. He was admitted to the hospital and given antipsychotic drugs.

After several days of observation and drug treatment, Mr. W. began to respond to direct questions, but did so in a monotone. He revealed that he believed himself to be controlled by magnetic fields beamed at him by the communists, and that he thought his wife and brother were working with them. Because of his severe motor problems, the diagnosis given was schizophrenia, catatonic type, with paranoid elements. (*Motor* refers to awkward and strange arm and leg movements. *Catatonic* means taking "frozen" positions with arms, legs, or body and holding them for hours and hours.)

As you can see from the case study of Michael, the home life of the schizophrenic is often very disturbed. We suspect that a bizarre family may be enough to tip the balance for people who are already potentially schizophrenic. But there are many, many cases in which the family is quite normal, things are very pleasant, other children seem to be fine, but still one of them will develop the psychosis. The odds of getting schizophrenia if close family members have it are moderately high. The studies of direct inheritance, however, are fairly confusing. When we look at identical twins, if one has the disorder, the odds are fairly high that the other will, too. For the population as a whole, though, the suggestion is strong that heredity is not the key factor since 90 percent of those who develop it do *not* have parents or other close relatives who are schizophrenic (Mosher et al., 1973).

Chemical Factors in Schizophrenia

Think back to the last time you were at a party with some good friends and everyone was sitting in a circle. When the discussion really got going, people were talking rapidly and were agitated; thoughts were moving *very fast*. When that was happening, one of the chemicals that fires nerve cells in the brain was quite high, causing a speed of speech and thought that eventually would exhaust most people. This chemical is called **dopamine** (DOUGH-pa-mean) (Wong, 1985).

A major discovery about many schizophrenics is that they have incredibly high, abnormal levels of dopamine in the brain (Bower, 1985; Snyder, 1980). This certainly can explain many of their thought problems. If thoughts are running through their heads at maximum speed hour after hour, day after day, this would cause confusion and eventually stupor from fatigue—which is just the way many schizophrenics act. Studies with animals show that drugs that increase the levels of dopamine far beyond normal produce bizarre behavior in the form of strange posturing and robotlike movements—again symptoms often seen with schizophrenics (Kokkinidis & Anisman, 1980). Finally, some schizophrenics get much better when they are given drugs that reduce dopamine levels. The only problem is that these same drugs can cause all kinds of side effects in some patients, including uncontrollable tremors and death (Breggin, 1983). Of importance here, though, is that scientists are on the right track. But they have not been able to refine the medication enough so that it works safely for most patients. We should add that some researchers feel that psychological problems can also cause the body to manufacture too much dopamine, so we are not limited only to a physical problem that can be cured by merely chemical means. Still, we are on our way toward solving one of life's most destructive disturbances.

Two additional points: (1) The rapidity of thought with the schizophrenic does not ever resemble that of the manic discussed earlier. Schizophrenics speak and act thickly as if exhausted from too much thought. (2) The chemical defect in major affective disorders does not involve dopamine. That chemical, as mentioned, is serotonin. There is some very subtle difference in these chemicals that we don't completely understand as yet.

Dopamine
The brain chemical present in excess in schizophrenics, which causes nerve cells to fire too rapidly and leads to thought and speech confusion.

Personality Disorders

To avoid hopeless confusion, we have limited the previous discussion to disorders involving anxiety, guilt, conflicts, depression, and the like. Just for completeness, you should be aware of one additional category of people with problems, a group that has nothing in common with the others discussed so far. These individuals do not fit into the categories we have mentioned. They are not out of touch with reality, so they are not psychotic, and they do not show the guilt or anxiety so common in the nonpsychotic "neurotic" disorders. Instead, they seem to have formed peculiar and unpleasant personality patterns. For example, some are very secretive, some very self-centered and selfish, some suspicious all the time. Hence, we use the term **personality disorder** because their personalities are off center, so to speak. There are many personality disorders, but one in particular causes serious problems for society: the **antisocial personality disorder**.

Originally, people with an antisocial personality were called *psychopaths*, a term you will still sometimes hear used. The label was given to those who committed crimes ranging from beating up little old ladies to committing ax murders. Such behavior is not typical of neurotics or psychotics.

A lack of conscience is central to this disorder. It is for this reason that the more recent term **sociopath** is used, meaning that the behavior of these people toward society is clearly abnormal (*path* from "pathology," abnormal).

These people repeatedly come into conflict with the law and show little or no concern, guilt, or anxiety. Nothing in the way of drug or psychological treatment works to help them. They are very smooth and agreeable on the outside and will go along with almost any treatment that is suggested. They will cooperate, tell you they are getting better, thank you, and seem to be well. But, as soon as they are released, they go right back to whatever their favorite crime happened to be.

In truth, we don't understand how these people got the way they are or what to do with them. For many, there is a family history of neglect and rough treatment. The parents are often alcoholic and abusive, but there must be millions of people over the years who have had such a background and didn't act this way. Sociopaths don't even abide by the rules usually followed by criminals. Most criminals have at least some standards. (Even the Mafia doesn't work on Mother's Day—true!) Measures of body chemistry and studies of genetic patterns have yielded nothing of any real significance regarding the origin of the sociopath's behavior.

Personality disorder
A disorder in which the person is neither neurotic nor psychotic, but the personality is clearly disturbed.

Antisocial personality disorder
The name of the disorder that the sociopath has.

Sociopath
Someone with a personality disorder who is in constant conflict with the law and seems to have no conscience.

Do You Need Help?

This question, as it stands, is simple enough to answer. Of course you do. So does everybody. The standards of perfection set up for all of us are something to work toward, but they cannot be attained. The closer the better, but you're still not perfectly normal. The important point, though, is that, after reading a chapter like this, most people begin to worry that something might really be wrong with them. Since we don't know you personally, only you can get some kind of fix on how reasonable your problems are. What we *can* do, however, after years and years of experience, is go through some of the thoughts and feelings of adolescents that are so common that you should be able to relax a little about most of them.

For example, your body has by no means stabilized. All kinds of changes are going on, which may seem simple at first but which actually are major. Growth, for instance, involves a major hormonal upheaval. As a result, you will not feel quite right physically. Even if you are in good shape, follow all the rules, and have good coordination, your body doesn't seem to "fit" completely. The feeling is something like a key that works in a lock but doesn't do so smoothly. You probably are not able to look in the mirror and see what you really want.

It is extremely hard for anyone to get social relationships and friendships to work out perfectly and smoothly. Add to this the fact that emotional chemistry and physical changes are running rampant during your age period, and you start to understand how friendships can appear and disappear in a matter of minutes no matter how intense or perfect they seemed to be. If you have one or two good friends for a reasonable amount of time, you're doing well.

The chances of feeling lonely, lost, or depressed for brief periods of time are very high. On the other hand, if you are subject to bouts of depression for two or three days at a time fairly often and can't even relate to a few friends, then you do have a problem and need someone to help. But, when you try to analyze whether you have a serious problem, don't exaggerate. If you do have one, it can be handled, but the odds are that you don't. There is no way you can completely get away from feeling some loneliness and feeling not quite in step.

Odds are that adults are not going to feel comfortable around you. Many adults may not be able to get their lives together either, and they resent the lost years that you still have ahead of you. But whatever worries or concerns you have about relating to adults will simply disappear with physical age. And you belong to a different (not better) generation from your parents. Toleration in both directions is necessary; friction is at times inevitable.

Sexuality means trouble for every single person you will ever meet of any age beyond 12 or 13. There is a heavy toll carried by the pleasure it gives. For everyone—no matter whom—it also provides anxiety, confusion, awkwardness, guilt, feelings of emptiness, short depressions, and loneliness. If this is bothering you, trust us: It bothers everybody. It's part of the human condition.

Finally, in terms of being lost about where you are heading, try to compare yourself and your goals objectively with those of others. Don't just focus on the handful of students who seem to have their act together. Look around. More than half the students you see don't know where they are or where they are going for the time being.

If, after reading this, you are still convinced that something serious is wrong, you may be right. But it's not the end of the world. In fact, it is good to know it so early. We will discuss treatment and therapies in the next chapter.

Summary

1. The person with a behavior disorder exaggerates the problem behaviors that all of us have. The symptoms of a behavior disorder include discomfort, bizarreness, and inefficiency.

2. A psychotic disorder results in very confused thinking and an unreal perception of the environment. A neurosis or a nonpsychotic disorder does not have the same degree of bizarreness and confusion found in a psychosis.

3. Most people with nonpsychotic disorders are inflexible and find the environment threatening. In the panic disorder, anxiety dominates. In the simple phobia, there is incredible fear of specific objects in the environment. Agoraphobics are more complex in that much of their problem is not related to an object, but is symbolic.

4. An obsession involves thinking constantly about a certain object, urge, or event. A compulsion is the ritualized behavior of carrying out some act usually related to an obsession.

5. In a dissociative disorder, one part of the person's memory system is separated from the remainder. In amnesia, the person forgets things that are upsetting. With a multiple personality, the person acts out conflicting desires, usually to be good and bad, independently of one another.

6. The dysthymic disorder is a moderate depression. It is usually the result of the loss of a job, friend, or a series of small setbacks.

7. Psychotics can hallucinate—that is, see or hear things that are not there. They also develop false beliefs, called delusions.

8. Major affective disorders involve severe, disabling depression or mania, or a bipolar swing between the two. We suspect that they also have a physical or chemical basis in addition to their psychological aspects.

9. Schizophrenia involves severely disabled thought processes and bizarre speech patterns. Since it usually appears at a certain age period, late adolescence/early adulthood, we suspect that it has a chemical or physical basis aside from the psychological causes.

Key Words and Concepts

psychotic disorders
nonpsychotic disorders
Diagnostic and Statistical Manual of Mental Disorders III
anxiety disorders
anxiety
panic disorder
phobic disorder
simple phobia
agoraphobia
obsession
compulsion
obsessive-compulsive disorder
dissociative disorders
psychogenic amnesia
selective forgetting
multiple personality

dysthymic disorder
thought disorder
hallucination
delusion
major affective disorders
major depression
mania
flight of ideas
bipolar disorder
serotonin
schizophrenia
word salad
clang associations
psychotic episodes
dopamine
personality disorders
antisocial personality disorder
sociopath

Review Questions

Match the symptoms below with the appropriate anxiety disorder on the right.

1. An anxiety attack—but not directed at a specific object

2. A dog causes extreme anxiety

3. Thoughts that won't go away

4. One is unable to leave an unfamiliar environment

5. Repeated actions

a. obsession

b. agoraphobia

c. compulsion

d. simple phobia

e. panic disorder

True/False

6. A dissociative disorder can be referred to as the common cold of mental illness.

7. Psychogenic amnesia refers to a biological inability to remember.

8. Someone suffering from selective forgetting still retains abilities and skills learned before the onset of the amnesia.

9. A person who suffers from multiple personality disorder can also be labeled schizophrenic.

10. In a multiple personality case, it is possible for one personality to be aware of another.

Fill in the blank. Answer on a separate sheet of paper. (More than one word can be used.)

11. Someone who thinks he is Napoleon is having _____ .

12. Schizophrenics often mix words together, which is called _____ .

13. Schizophrenics also seem to chant in a rhythmic pattern; these patterns often include _____ .

14. The "up" part of an extreme mood swing would be called _____ .

15. A person suffering from wild up and down mood swings would be suffering from a _____ disorder.

Multiple Choice

16. A high level of serotonin might cause a person to become:
    a. manic
    b. depressive
    c. withdrawn
    d. dissociative.

17. The fact that the onset of schizophrenia usually occurs during late adolescence suggests that the cause of schizophrenia may be:
    a. psychological
    b. biological
    c. learned
    d. easily prevented

18. High levels of dopamine may trigger:
    a. an affective disorder
    b. schizophrenia
    c. a bipolar disorder
    d. all of the above
    e. a and b only.

19. A sociopath would most likely have:
    a. a high level of serotonin
    b. a high level of dopamine
    c. abusive parents
    d. all of the above.

20. Someone with a personality disorder would probably exhibit high levels of:
    a. depression
    b. guilt
    c. anxiety
    d. none of the above.

Discussion Questions

1. Other than violent behaviors, list five behaviors that our society would consider abnormal. Then, for each of the five behaviors, describe a situation where the abnormal behavior *might* be considered normal. For example, eating another human is certainly regarded as abnormal, but, if this happened three weeks after a plane crash in which the person had died and the survivors were stranded, the behavior *could* be construed by many as normal.

2. If a high school student has been drinking alcohol for a year and has gotten drunk *every* weekend—but only on weekends—should this person get help from a professional? Yes? No? Depends? Explain.

3. Courts today still sometimes use the verdict of "not guilty by reason of insanity." The logic here is that the person was unaware of his or her actions and should not be held responsible. Most likely, the person who is awarded this verdict will be committed to a mental institution until psychiatrists determine that the person is "sane"—at which time, the person will be released. Do you agree that this type of verdict should be allowed, or should "insane" criminals be treated just like any other criminals? Explain.

4. Why would it be unlikely that a person suffering from a personality disorder would be awarded a verdict of "not guilty by reason of insanity"? Explain.

5. If someone had an intense fear of water, which of the following "solutions" would be most effective in reducing the fear: letting the person gradually get used to the water *or* throwing the person into the water and letting him or her confront the fear all at one time? Explain. Which method would you prefer and why?

6. Describe a simple phobia that you have. As noted in the chapter, this simple phobia is probably the result of learning. You may not have ever thought about it, but make several guesses as to how you learned this simple phobia.

7. If a person supposedly suffering from multiple personality committed a felony and his or her lawyer pleaded not guilty by reason of insanity, what are several ways that you might be able to determine whether the alleged criminal is truly suffering from the disorder or faking it? Explain.

8. We have all suffered mild bouts of depression from time to time, but we usually snap out of it in a relatively short time. Let's say that you had a friend who was more than mildly depressed. What kind of advice would you give this person to help him or her snap out of the depression (not that we necessarily recommend you actually offer this advice)?

Activities

1. If you think back to elementary school, your classes were probably divided into different reading groups: the top readers, the average readers, and the slow readers. The groups were often given cute names like the "blue jay" group or the "robin" group, but everyone knew which group was the top and which was the bottom. One of the reasons for using these cute names was probably to avoid placing the stigma of being "dumb" or "smart" on the members of the groups. A stigma is a mark or a spot, usually negative, that sticks with a person for a long time.

   This problem of acquiring a stigma is especially dangerous when it involves a mental illness. For example, if a person is labeled a "manic depressive" when he or she is 20, that label may influence others' perceptions of him or her years later. Conduct an experiment to see how true this is. Write the following information on an index card:

   "Read the following description and rate the chances of this person being elected president of the United States.

   George Johnson. Age 54. OFFICES HELD: governor, 12 yrs., congressman, 10 yrs., lieutenant governor, 4 yrs. BACKGROUND: graduated from Yale Law School in top 10 percent of class; married at age 22; at 24, treated for depression with electroconvulsive therapy, but completely cured; practiced corporate law for 4 yrs.

1	2	3	4	5	6	7
DISMAL	VERY POOR	POOR	AVERAGE	HIGH	VERY HIGH	EXCELLENT

   Write the same information on another index card, except replace the entire depression sentence with this: "at 24, divorced—remarried at 29."

   Show the first card to 15 people; show the second card to 15 different people. Record their ratings. Compare your results. What was the average rating for each card? Did the "depression" card receive a lower average rating? Why do you think you got the results that you did? Explain. Regardless of your results, why do you think some people are stigmatized by mental illness in our society? What effect do you think the stigma has on the person who is labeled? Explain.

2. Back in the 1960s, legislators decided that they wanted to shift the emphasis from large state-run mental institutions to local mental health centers. As a result, thousands of hospitalized mentally ill patients were eventually let out into the community. One of the problems of this deinstitutionalization process was that communities were not prepared to handle all these patients. Do some research on: (a) the original intentions of this deinstitutionalization; (b) the problems that arose as a result; and (c) what solutions are being proposed today. After you organize this information into a report, discuss which solution you support and why.

3. One of the most controversial verdicts of "not guilty by reason of insanity" involved John Hinckley after he shot President Reagan on national television. Research the case. Find out: (a) the nature of Hinckley's mental illness; (b) the insanity defense used by his lawyers; (c) the changes that have occurred since then in the types of verdicts allowed—for example, the verdict of "guilty but insane." Also, include your reactions. Should Hinckley ever be allowed freedom, given his verdict? Do you agree with the changes in verdicts that have occurred? Explain.

4. Ask three of your teachers if you can use five minutes of class time to survey the classes about phobias. Copy the following onto a sheet of paper and photocopy enough copies for the three classes:

   Phobias Survey

   Use the scale below to rate how anxious you usually become around the following items.

1	2	3	4	5
NOT ANXIOUS	NOT VERY ANXIOUS	SOMEWHAT ANXIOUS	VERY ANXIOUS	EXTREMELY ANXIOUS

   On a separate sheet of paper, place a number from the scale next to each item.

____ 1. Spiders	____ 6. Snakes	____ 11. Giving speeches
____ 2. Heights	____ 7. Dogs	____ 12. Open spaces
____ 3. Elevators	____ 8. Tall buildings	____ 13. Tests
____ 4. Water	____ 9. Closed spaces	____ 14. Cats
____ 5. Knives	____ 10. Needles	____ 15. Crossing bridges

   (Notice that we didn't list just 13 items—fuel for another phobia.) Tally your results and create a table.

Place the phobia that received the highest average rating at the top, and work your way down to the phobia that received the lowest average rating. Transfer your table onto a poster and include appropriate captions—then put the poster up in class.

If you're ambitious, create another chart that shows the difference between males' and females' phobias. In this case, you would have each person mark "male" or "female" at the top of his or her rating sheet.

5. The following is a variation of the previous activity. Instead of using high school students as your sample, use at least 30 people who are over 20 years old. Again, create a chart. Compare this chart with the chart from the previous activity (either yours or a classmate's) to see if perhaps anxiety level toward these items decreases as one gets older. (Then again, if anxiety level *does* go down, maybe what you're really measuring is how well one lies as one gets older.)

6. Another category of disorders not mentioned in the chapter is called "childhood disorders." Do some research on one of the following childhood disorders and write a report: hyperactivity *or* infantile autism. Focus on: (a) common characteristics; (b) how commonly the disorder occurs; (c) symptoms; (d) possible causes; (e) effective treatments. Some of the treatments used, especially for autism, are controversial. Discuss your reactions toward these treatments.

In group therapy problems are aired to others. In return the group and therapist offer support and suggestions.

Objectives

Be able to:

1. Describe the different kinds of mental health workers.

2. Compare psychoanalysis with humanism as a therapy.

3. Describe how behavioristic methods differ from others.

4. Explain the advantages of group therapy.

5. Describe chemotherapy and psychosurgery; explain the benefits and problems involved in each.

Global Look at the Chapter

For those with emotional problems, therapy often helps. It involves the active intervention in the life of another by a professional to try to bring stability to the individual's life. This chapter discusses the various methods by which help is provided.

Mental Health Through the Years

People typically are afraid of anything odd or unknown. Historically, reactions have been most violent, however, to those with some kind of emotional disturbance because the origin of the problem is often unclear. Before the 1700s, mental problems were thought to be the result of influence by the devil or demons. Behavior such as hearing voices or speaking strangely usually led to gross torture and hanging. In some communities, such people were boiled alive, and their parts were hung on posts in the public square (Deutsch, 1946). When there were outbreaks of disease, such as the Black Death plague in the 1300s, mental patients were blamed and "extremities were jerked from the . . . sockets, feet were torn from limbs, thumbs were squashed, and skin was torn with red-hot pincers" (Anderson, 1970).

With the arrival of the age of science, a search began for some method of treating those with serious mental problems. This new atmosphere was triggered by the work of a French physician, **Philippe Pinel** (Phil-LEAP Pea-NELL), who was put in charge of a hospital for the insane during the early 1700s. With great fanfare he entered the hospital, which was really a dungeon, and freed the "patients" who were chained to the wall. Given their freedom, they did not go on a rampage and pillage the town, but showed signs of improvement. This was the beginning of humane treatment.

People in the town were very suspicious of Pinel as a result. When a cholera epidemic broke out later, they blamed him for poisoning the water supply, and an angry mob tried to kill him. The story has a romantic, but true, ending. Pinel was rescued from the mob by some of those he had freed (Reisman, 1966).

Even today, mental problems are still one of the most feared maladies for people to be around, but attitudes have changed a fair amount regarding therapy or treatment. It has become a more or less accepted part of our environment (Halpert, 1969). Therapy for those with such problems as phobias, moderate depression, and the like is so common that a person having treatment is no longer considered all that unusual (Garfield, 1981).

Types of Mental Health Workers

Many people use the terms *psychologist* and *psychiatrist* without being aware that these are different occupations. Before discussing therapies, we should make the differences clear.

Psychologists

Psychologists who work directly with people, seeking to assist them with their problems, are called either *counseling* or *clinical psychologists*. **Counseling psychologists** deal mostly with people who do not have formal classifications of mental disturbance. Typically, they work with people who have marital or family problems or general problems with living. **Clinical psychologists** perform all the tasks of the counseling psychologists, but some of them also work in mental hospitals and clinics with "classified" patients.

Counseling psychologists
Those who deal mostly with problems not fitting into the formal classifications of mental disturbance.

Clinical psychologists
Those who deal with emotional disturbances of any kind; may work with formal mental patients.

Although many counseling psychologists have a doctor of education (Ed.D.) degree, the typical clinical psychologist has a doctor of philosophy (Ph.D.) degree. After graduating from college, members of both groups continue in graduate school for an additional four to five years, studying psychology. Clinical psychologists must also have a year's internship in a mental health facility. Most states require an additional year of supervised training, so the total winds up to six or seven years before it is all over.

Psychiatrists

Psychiatrists are medical doctors who spend four years as students learning about physical medical problems rather than mental ones. After this general medical training, they can specialize in the mental health

Psychiatrists
Mental health workers with a degree in medicine.

field. Training in their specialization can include one to three years of hospital residency—which resembles an apprenticeship. The most striking difference between psychiatrists and psychologists is that the former can prescribe medicine. As a result, most psychologists downplay the role of medicine for the average person in treatment, and most psychiatrists do just the opposite. There probably is something to say for both sides. Your authors are psychologists, so, if you pick up any bias in how we cover the material, it is not intended—but we probably are right!

Other Mental Health Personnel

Psychiatric social workers
Mental health workers with a degree in social work; help patients and families deal with problems.

Psychiatric nurses
Registered nurses with special education in psychiatric medicine.

Other mental health personnel include **psychiatric social workers**, who usually hold advanced degrees in social work. They help patients find jobs or housing and assist families, among others, in dealing with problems. **Psychiatric nurses** are registered nurses with special education in psychiatric medicine.

In the early years, mental health workers were mostly physicians (medical doctors) or ministers. Ministers today are still active in the field, but we can't specify their education or training because it varies so much from one individual to another. Clinical psychology as an official field began in the late 1800s.

Psychotherapists—The Blanket Term

Psychotherapies
Broad term for any method used to try to help people with emotional and psychological problems.

In the next sections, we discuss the major methods used to try to help people with their problems. All these techniques are called **psychotherapies**, a term meaning that there is an attempt to relieve (therapy) problems of the *psyche* or mind. *Psychotherapist* is a broad term for any professional who tries to help others psychologically. Thus, a psychotherapist can be a psychologist, a psychiatrist, a social worker, a minister, or a psychiatric nurse. In each of the different methods (psychotherapies) used, the goal is for the therapist actively to help the person change his or her views that are causing trouble, to help reduce tension, to remove certain behavior patterns or habits that are causing trouble, or just to provide a source of support in a time of trouble.

Psychoanalytic Treatment

Psychoanalysis
Therapy practiced by followers of Freud, who analyze the psyche via the unconscious.

Psychoanalysis (analysis of the psyche or mind) is a very symbolic and complicated treatment. It usually involves from three to five hours of treatment per week over a period of years. Thus, it is reserved for those who have quite a bit of money. Its method is based on the theory of the psychiatrist Sigmund Freud.

The Freudian system focuses on *anxiety* as the main problem people face. According to this theory, as you may remember from Chapter 14, anxiety arises from deep-seated animal impulses that we all have. Thus, we have strong sexual and aggressive impulses that we want to act out, but, since such expression is taboo, we live in constant anxiety that our impulses will break loose. And we suffer guilt whenever we partially act out the desires. This guilt in turn produces more anxiety.

These desires operate at the unconscious level, causing endless battles within the self. The self is caught between the animal desires, which go all the way back to childhood, and the conscience, which has, over the years, developed to try to prevent these behaviors.

The animal desires are viewed as a physical force within the person. This physical force is trying to be heard, and its voice can get louder and more demanding as it seeks expression. But, since it is operating at the unconscious level, we are not aware of it. The psychoanalytic theory claims that some of the unconscious energy is released and can appear as symbolic dreams. On occasion, it is freed enough actually to express itself in the acts we perform. But most of the time it stays bottled up and building greater force, which increases anxiety. It is the task of the psychoanalyst to help the patient free some of this energy in a safe form.

The world's most famous couch—it was here that Sigmund Freud had his patients recline as they explored the unconscious.

Free Association

Free association is a major technique of psychoanalysis. The process involves the patient saying *whatever* comes to mind, no matter how disconnected or unimportant the material might seem. The theory behind this is that, since desires in the unconscious are seeking escape, they will often hook themselves onto what at first might seem innocent sentences. For instance, the male patient might claim that he wants to *tell* his parent something. Instead, he says, "I want to *kill* my parent." This "slip of the tongue" is the unconscious impulse escaping. Freudians believe that the longer the patient talks, the greater will be the amount of information coming from the unconscious. The therapist then points out to the patient the kinds of things that are being said, explains what they mean, and in this way puts the patient more in control of those impulses. In other words, the psychoanalysts believe they are allowing inner conflicts to come out, be explored in safety, and be resolved.

Free association
The process of saying whatever comes to mind; uncovers the unconscious in psychoanalysis.

Transference

Another important aspect of psychoanalytic treatment is called **transference**, meaning that the patients transfer their emotional conflicts of earlier years onto the therapist. Since the therapist is emotionally neutral and is not personally part of any of the patients' conflicts, the therapist

Transference
The process in which patient transfers emotional conflicts of earlier years onto therapist.

Traditional therapy involves support and reassurance as a key ingredient in the healing process.

has no ax to grind one way or the other; he or she is emotionally objective. So, here lies the crux of the treatment: Since the therapist is neutral, whatever the patient claims about the therapist is made up by the patient's unconscious trying to find expression. If patients can recognize this behavior for what it is, they will see that the therapist is being blamed for something he or she had no part in. As a result, the patient's inner conflicts become visible. Once they are visible, this provides an opportunity to deal with them "out in the open," so to speak, rather than hidden where they can cause us grief without our understanding the source. The following is a condensed excerpt that illustrates the basic principle of transference:

> **Patient:** I don't feel well today. I had a headache and I was going to stay in bed.
> **Analyst:** You really didn't want to come in.
> **Patient:** Yes, you might say that. I had a bad night, and I dreamed that I was falling and falling—off a building, you know—and I couldn't find anything to grab hold of.
> **Analyst:** You feel like you might be losing control of the situation?
> **Patient:** Well, of course. That's true. But I don't need a dream to tell me that. So I had a dream, so what?
> **Analyst:** [*silence*].
> **Patient:** No comment about that? You should say something, you know. [*silence*]. Well, why shouldn't you say something? You know I come here endlessly—for what? I feel anxious right now and you say nothing. I feel like I'm losing control, just like in the dream, and when I come in here it just gets worse. So, why should I come? You don't know what it's like.
> **Analyst:** You seem rather angry with me.
> **Patient:** [*silence*]. Well, shouldn't I be? Angry, I mean? I keep trying to get myself straightened out and you just sit there—like a lump. So know-it-all and pompous.
> **Analyst:** Do your feelings seem familiar? Do I remind you of someone?
> **Patient:** Now let's not start that crap.
> **Analyst:** [*silence*].
> **Patient:** Well, OK. Sure. Who cares? Yes—yes, you remind me of my father. Isn't that beautiful? But you really had a lot in common. Every time I started to do something, there he was, like some kind of god, ready to jump all over me.

Humanistic Therapy

You may have felt when you read the previous section that the psychoanalyst lives in a pretty gloomy world regarding the human condition. We can't say that this view of the human is incorrect. Still, there are other theories that take the opposite approach. These other therapies are based on the principle that people have within themselves the potential to know where they are heading. Eventually they will be able to reach this potential and blossom like a flower. Thus, there is not an unconscious filled with baser desires. It is the therapist's function to bring out the best in people, a "best" that is already in us from the beginning but that needs to be freed. These therapies are called **humanistic** because they emphasize the power within the individual human to control his or her own fate and movement toward fulfillment. We will cover below the major therapy in this area.

Client-Centered Therapy

The term **client-centered therapy** gives a clue to the orientation of this approach. To begin with, note the word *client*. This term means something very different from the term *patient*. Humanists have no patients, only clients, because to them the word *client* conveys a working relationship in which the two (therapist and client) are partners or coworkers working toward a common goal. *Patient* always has a one-above, one-below feeling to it. The client-centered approach, which is most closely associated with psychologist Carl Rogers, has also been called Rogerian therapy, or **nondirective therapy**. The word *nondirective* is designed to convey the idea that these therapists do not prod or push ("direct") the clients, but instead let them decide for themselves what is important to be talking about and in which direction the therapy should be going.

The technique of client-centered therapy rests on the assumption that each of us aims toward living a meaningful life. To reach that state, we must accept ourselves for what we are, not for what others may think we should be. Since we are basically good, the humanists feel this is safe to do. Disturbed behavior, then, arises from worrying too much about the mismatch between what our inner selves are telling us and what others claim things should be like. We cannot live by others. Therefore, the therapist helps clients to clarify and accept inner forces and directions.

What if these inner forces are wrong? This supposedly results from a distorted environment blocking the inner forces for good. So, according to the humanistic theory, disturbed people will be able, over time in therapy, to see for themselves that they are on the wrong track.

In the actual therapy, the therapist acts like a mirror that is held up to the client, a mirror that tries to reflect what the client is saying, *not* trying to put interpretations on the statements. Atmosphere is crucial: The therapist must provide a safe, nonjudgmental environment so the client can freely explore problems. So, the therapist reflects on and rephrases the client's own feelings and thoughts. You can see this in the small excerpt of dialogue that follows:

Client: I don't feel well today. I had a headache and I was going to stay in bed.
Therapist: You just didn't feel like coming in today?
Client: Yes, you might say that. I had a bad night and I dreamed that I was falling and falling—off a building, you know—and I couldn't find anything to grab hold of.
Therapist: It sounds like that dream really bothered you and you feel insecure or afraid.

Unconditional Positive Regard

Unconditional positive regard
A principle of humanistic therapy in which the client's feelings and thoughts are accepted for whatever they are; Carl Rogers's term.

One final point about this treatment method. The one critical thing that the therapist is to provide is called **unconditional positive regard**. This term means that the client's thoughts, feelings, hopes, and desires are to be accepted for what they are—a part of the growing person. The people themselves are not to be judged. Obviously, a client who wants to kill someone is not holding an acceptable belief, but the Rogerians maintain that the *feeling* can be accepted as part of the person, even though the idea itself must be rejected. So, there are no conditions on acceptance and the person is free to talk, to listen to themselves, and to grow (Meador & Rogers, 1973).

This method of treatment may still seem a little vague to you. Basically, the therapist sits and listens, then rewords and reflects what the client is saying. The client "hears" himself or herself through the therapist's words. Over time, then, the client is talking to his or her inner self through the therapist. And, since the client is basically good, eventually the right road will be discovered.

Behavioral Therapy

Behavioral therapy
Therapy that uses principles of learning to alter the person's behavior that is causing trouble.

Behavioral therapy involves techniques designed to bring about changes in people's behavior by using principles of learning. While the goals are the same as those of other therapies, its philosophy is different.

These photographs show models interacting with snakes. In an attempt to overcome their fears, people with snake phobias watch the models handling the snakes.

Behavioral therapists believe that most mental disorders are not complex problems, but instead are the result of unacceptable behaviors learned over a period of years. Both "normality" and "abnormality" are learned. Thus, whatever symptom the person has is not from some deep-seated problem, but is simply the result of learning poor habits or responses to problems. Behavioral therapists say basically that, if someone is afraid of elevators, it doesn't make any difference where the problem came from; instead, let's just get rid of the fear and ignore its origin, whatever that might be. No discussion about it. We will just bring about a relearning to reduce the fear.

This type of treatment is rapid (usually a matter of months) and highly effective for dealing with problems that center on some kind of specific fear or bad habit. It is not as useful with issues that are quite complex, such as friction between members of a family. In such a case, the behaviors involved are an interplay of so many factors that it is hard to focus on exactly what behavior one is trying to remove by using learning principles.

Systematic Desensitization

The goal of behaviorists is to weaken a habit that the person has and replace it with something else that is newly learned. The most elaborate method in this area is called **systematic desensitization**. The term refers to a process in which the therapist step by step (systematically) increases the anxiety the patient feels, but, each time it is increased, that level of anxiety is associated with something pleasant. In this way, the person becomes much less sensitive (desensitized) to the problem.

Here is a real case: A college student had a phobia (unreasonable fear) about dissection, to the point where she could not even enter a room where it took place. This meant that she was going to fail biology. First, the student was taught how to relax. The therapist then made up a list of items in order of increasing anxiety. The first item was presented to the student. Perhaps it was something like being on campus near the biology building. She was told to relax while thinking of this item. The next step was thinking about approaching the biology building. As anxiety built up at this thought, she was to relax once again. Then thoughts about the odors and atmosphere of the biology lab were introduced, creating greater anxiety. She again relaxed. Over time, she began to relax at the actual thought of cutting up a frog and hence was able to actually participate in such an activity if she found it acceptable to do (McGlynn & O'Brien, 1972).

This procedure sounds almost simpleminded. But, surprisingly, it works quite well with thousands of patients every year. Its only drawback is that it is not very effective with long-term, complex, symbolic issues, such as not being able to get along with other people. It does work

Systematic desensitization
A behavioral technique in which the therapist step by step increases the patient's anxiety and counters it by association with relaxation in a step by step sequence.

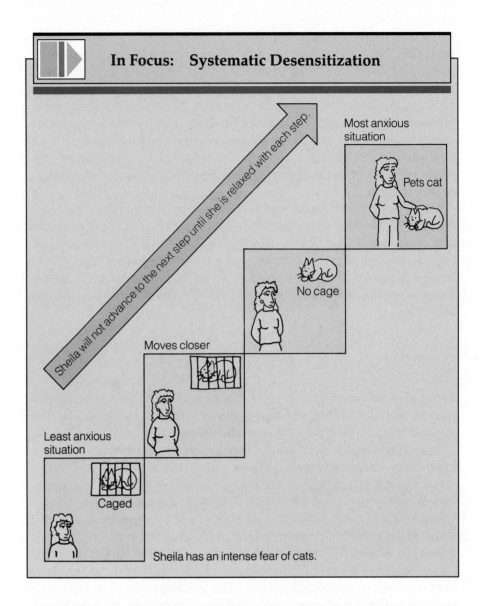

In Focus: Systematic Desensitization

Sheila will not advance to the next step until she is relaxed with each step.

Most anxious situation

Pets cat

No cage

Moves closer

Least anxious situation

Caged

Sheila has an intense fear of cats.

well with any kind of phobia, and it is the fastest, most efficient, cheapest method of treatment in such cases.

Aversive Conditioning

Aversive conditioning
A behavioral technique in which unpleasantness is associated with acts that are to be avoided.

In **aversive conditioning**, the goal is to make certain acts unpleasant so that they will be avoided. For example, alcoholics can be given a medication that will make them nauseated when they take alcohol. The relearning process involved is to try to associate the aversive (negative) feeling with taking the alcohol, and hence reduce its use. The rate of improvement for this method is about 50 percent, with the "cure" lasting about six months. Thus, it is not a solution as much as a good beginning for a number of alcoholics (Ullmann & Krasner, 1969; 1975).

The Token Economy

The **token economy**, a buying system (an economy) in which patients use tokens to purchase things, sounds again like something a little too simple. But it works quite well with mental patients on hospital wards. The tokens—paper slips, poker chips, or the like—are given for "good" behavior, such as making the bed, brushing teeth, or taking a shower. In day-to-day living in close quarters, doing these things vastly improves the comfort of the living conditions and reduces episodes of frustration and increased abnormality. The tokens give the patients something to do and a tangible reward. It is always a problem to figure out what the patients should be doing with their days, so here is a solution that solves it and gives a reward at the same time.

Major changes take place on wards using this method. Patients work for tokens to buy extra walks on the grounds, more television time, cigarettes, and the like. They become less withdrawn, have fewer confused thoughts, and improve their social relationships (Gripp & Magaro, 1971).

We need to add a word here about the term *behavioral*. Students almost always have trouble with the word, but you need to understand it for the material that follows, so here we go: There are three processes possible in therapy. These are mental (cognitive), verbal (talking), and behavioral (performing actions). In the systems just discussed, taking action (behavioral) was the most important aspect—going into the biology lab, not taking a drink, making a bed. The therapies did not involve the verbal (talking) aspects that the Rogerians or Freudians use. The treatment also downplayed the mental (cognitive). Now you should have some idea how the word is used and be prepared for the next section.

Token economy
A behavioral technique in which rewards for desired acts are accumulated through tokens, which represent a form of money.

Cognitive Behavioral Therapy

We mentioned the limitations of the straight behavioral therapy in terms of its inability to handle complex problems arising from mental, symbolic issues. Because of this failing, it wasn't long before a psychologist, **Albert Ellis**, came up with the idea of uniting behaviors with cognitions (thoughts) as a method for helping people. This therapy becomes one of actively working on the client's thought processes (cognitions) and hav-

Cognitive behavioral therapy
Therapy in which thoughts are used to control emotions and behaviors.

Rational emotive therapy
Treatment centering on getting emotions under control by using reason; Ellis's term.

Internalized sentences
The opinions we form of ourselves by listening to our own inner voice; Ellis's term.

Awfulize
To see things in the worst possible light; Ellis's term.

ing him or her change views and emotional responses to be more appropriate (behavioral) (Goldfried, 1980). Thus, this is called **cognitive behavioral therapy**.

Ellis's approach to problems is based on a belief that we humans are made up of two components: the rational (mental) and the emotional (emotive). Treatment focuses on getting emotions under control by using reason; thus, this technique is called **rational emotive therapy** (Ellis, 1980). Put another way, we are disturbed "not by things but by the view we take of them." External events can't do us in half as fast as how we think about them can. For instance: (1) A woman loses a job. She becomes depressed. (2) A woman loses a job and looks forward to greater opportunities at a *new* job. Two entirely different responses to exactly the same set of circumstances. This is the key to Ellis's system. Each woman's beliefs are based on what Ellis called **internalized sentences**. To understand what he means, stop and listen to yourself for a few minutes. Notice how you talk "inside" all day every day. How well you do in life depends on what kinds of sentences you are giving yourself. If they are "I'm doomed," "I'm hopeless," or the like, you've got trouble.

Someone who is important to us rejects us. We can **awfulize** (Ellis's term) the whole thing and say to ourselves, "This is just terrible. I'm no good, no good at all, and no one will ever like me again. I'm not worth anything. Doom. Doom." But we can change (behavioral) such internal sentences (cognitions) to read: "That's upsetting and disappointing. Maybe I'll have better luck next time." Sometimes this is very hard to do, but Ellis's ideas are well worth considering and trying to put into action for better mental health.

In therapy itself, Ellis and his followers assume people are straight thinkers and can be reached by reason to redo their internal sentences. Sometimes the therapy can get pretty rough, as the excerpt that follows shows, but the patient knows the therapist cares, which offsets the roughness.

> **Client:** I don't feel well today. I had a headache and was going to stay in bed.
> **Therapist:** Well, why didn't you?
> **Client:** Well, I . . . uh . . . well, I thought maybe I should come in because I was supposed to.
> **Therapist:** That's not much of a motivation. Why are you coming here at all? Out of some obligation to me?
> **Client:** No . . . I'm coming . . . well, you know, because . . .
> **Therapist:** You tell me.
> **Client:** Because . . . well, because I need some support. I need someone to talk to. I have some friends, but my parents . . . especially my father, don't *really* care about me. You know.
> **Therapist:** So your father doesn't really care about you? So what? If you think that's the end of the world, then that's just stupid. Do you really believe that all fathers care about their children? I mean, just because it says that you should love your child doesn't mean everyone does. Don't you have friends? Didn't you just say that?

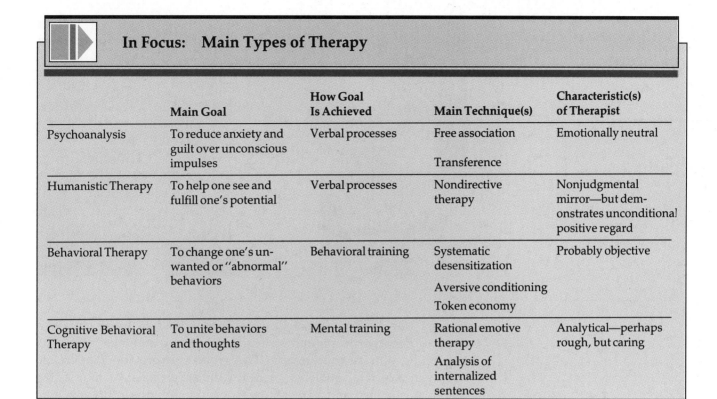

In Focus: Main Types of Therapy

	Main Goal	How Goal Is Achieved	Main Technique(s)	Characteristic(s) of Therapist
Psychoanalysis	To reduce anxiety and guilt over unconscious impulses	Verbal processes	Free association Transference	Emotionally neutral
Humanistic Therapy	To help one see and fulfill one's potential	Verbal processes	Nondirective therapy	Nonjudgmental mirror—but demonstrates unconditional positive regard
Behavioral Therapy	To change one's unwanted or "abnormal" behaviors	Behavioral training	Systematic desensitization Aversive conditioning Token economy	Probably objective
Cognitive Behavioral Therapy	To unite behaviors and thoughts	Mental training	Rational emotive therapy Analysis of internalized sentences	Analytical—perhaps rough, but caring

Client: Yes, but . . .

Therapist: No buts. If you've got friends you should stop saying to yourself, "I'm not cared for, I'm not loved." That's just not true, is it? No! It's not true. If your father doesn't like you, he doesn't like you.

Group Therapy

Group therapy has two purposes: (1) It is an attempt to treat more than one person at a time; this makes it cheaper for the patient and more efficient for both therapist and patient. (2) Patients can share their feelings and problems with one another and learn that they are not alone in their difficulties, a very important aspect of this method. Its usefulness is most noticeable when dealing with people suffering from grief or an addiction, not only because it offers companionship but also, if one or two can overcome the problem, it puts pressure on the rest to follow suit.

Group therapy
Therapy in which more than one person at a time is treated.

The Group Method

In group therapy, patients sit in a circle and talk to one another about problems under the guidance of a mental health worker. This type of

Closeness in encounter groups can help some people, but such groups frequently lead to dangerous personal over-exposure.

therapy provides a more realistic world than individual therapy in which there are only two people and very little of the "give-and-take" of interaction found outside the therapy. The group can provide support, go deeply into certain problems, or deal with social skills. As long as the therapist is skilled and knows how to handle the group, there is little danger to the patient. One of the things that makes mental patients what they are is an extreme sensitivity to the feelings of others in most cases. The odds of their being understanding and sympathetic are very high.

Group therapists don't really follow a particular system such as Freudian, behavioral, cognitive, what have you. The therapy usually involves a mixture of a little bit of all of them. On occasion, a given therapist sometimes prefers one approach to another.

Encounter Therapy

Encounter groups
Therapy in which normal people are brought together to become more sensitive to others' problems as well as to themselves.

You probably have heard about **encounter groups**. In such a group, "normal" people are brought together to share their sensitivities and problems. The label "encounter" is used because people are forced to reveal inner conflicts and to share secret emotions and feelings. The purpose behind this is supposedly to expose peoples' psyches in order to make them more aware and stronger.

Give this therapy wide berth. In regular group therapy with a professional, there are either implied or stated rules that prevent anyone from taking more psychological abuse than he or she can handle. In encounter groups, the goal is to expose oneself in order to get in touch with the "inner self." While some people survive and possibly even become better for the experience, the process is too dangerous for most to handle. Many wind up revealing inner feelings to others that they come to regret later. They feel exposed, betrayed, helpless, and too open to the world after it is all over and everyone has gone home (Yalom & Lieberman, 1971; Kuehn & Crinella, 1969).

Commonalities of Therapy

All therapies have certain factors in common that are important to note: (1) They are all designed to help the person resolve conflicts and problems, especially "Who am I, what do I want in life, and how do I get it?" (Orlinsky et al., 1970). (2) There is some direct relationship with a therapist for the purpose of trying to answer these questions. (3) There is the anticipation of some kind of positive change (Frank, 1971).

Patients benefit from therapy in a number of ways, usually: (1) they start some kind of program to find better methods for handling problems; (2) they learn new rules for understanding and correcting their behavior; (3) they feel better for having developed a relationship with someone who wants to help; and (4) they overcome present problems and are therefore better equipped to handle new ones that will arise later on (Harper, 1968).

Effectiveness of Therapy

You will sometimes hear that people with problems often get better all by themselves. While that is possible, it is unlikely. Certain factors work behind the scenes to help those who don't enter formal therapy. For example, those with a higher education will tend to do better in the long run because this usually reduces financial and environmental stresses. Those who are married tend to get better because they have a spouse who can care for and support them emotionally. And those who have a job get better more quickly because they have something that provides income and meaning to life. It doesn't seem to be the passage of time itself that cures people, but rather this "informal therapy" (Eisler & Williams, 1972; Jansen & Nickles, 1973).

In terms of formal treatment by a therapist, the evidence falls on the side of therapy being both helpful and useful (Nicholson & Berman, 1983). Millions claim they feel better and lead more useful lives after therapy.

Which therapy is best? The answer partly rests on the type of problem (Matarazzo, 1985). Behavioral therapy works very well with phobias, smoking, or overeating. With depression, a combination of drug therapy and cognitive behavior therapy seems to provide the best and longest-lasting improvement (Simons, 1984). The client-centered humanistic approach works very well with anxiety problems. Behavioral relaxation programs also help with anxiety (Phillips & Bierman, 1981). There is further evidence that it doesn't make much difference which therapy one is getting in the sense that feeling comfortable with and trusting the therapist carry such heavy weight. If a patient has a good therapist of any type who is trusted, the chances of getting better notably increase.

Certain principles of psychoanalysis have proved useful in other therapies. For example, other therapists often explore childhood in *brief* fashion, or assume that all is not as it appears on the surface. Even so, strict psychoanalysis is the most questionable of the therapies. There is no doubt about the fact that Freud laid the foundation for much of the treatment present today nor about the fact that he was a brilliant thinker. Even so, there are serious difficulties presented by his treatment method. For example, one study that followed up over 100 patients who had undergone an average of *600*(!) psychoanalytic sessions found that 60 percent showed substantial improvement (Brody, 1962). This is a fairly typical showing for any therapy, but, at today's rates, that would have cost between $80,000 and $100,000. But, in another study, 14 percent of the patients were worse off after therapy than before, and 26 percent showed no change at all (Kernberg et al., 1972; Garfield, 1981). One suspects that the problem with psychoanalysis is that it often involves continuous dwelling on problems dating all the way back to childhood, only partly dealing with the present. This may well increase the patient's feelings of being overwhelmed by the idea of a lifetime of problems. Given the speed and relatively inexpensive nature of other available treatments, we find it hard to recommend this one.

Chemotherapy

Chemotherapy
The use of drugs to relieve psychological disturbance.

Chemotherapy (KEE-mo-therapy) involves the use of drugs to relieve symptoms, so this treatment is handled only by a psychiatrist. The main drugs used are tranquilizers and energizers. The drugs alter the rate and pattern of firing of the brain nerve cells (Tosteson, 1981). Thus, if one is dealing with a depressed patient, the drug of choice would be one that *increases* the level of brain firing and thereby increases alertness. With someone very nervous and anxious whose nerve cells already are firing rapidly, a tranquilizer would be more appropriate. The reaction of a particular patient to a particular drug is unpredictable, however; so-called tranquilizers can act as energizers *or* tranquilizers, depending on the person and the dosage.

Given in moderation and with careful supervision, these drugs can be quite useful in lessening anxiety or depression and reducing psychotic symptoms. Many patients are able to function in life after taking the drugs when that was not the case before. Thus, there is no question about their usefulness. Still, as you will note in the next paragraph, the drugs don't work all that well with many patients and are used too often just to keep the patients quiet. While this benefits the staff trying to control them, it leaves many patients with serious problems unresolved. The general public and, to some extent, many professionals may think the problems of these patients are under control when they aren't. Finally, in too many cases, the patients are helped enough to be able to leave the hospital but not enough that they are able to function on their own, so the streets of every major city are filled with homeless and lost schizophrenics who don't know where to go or how to get help.

Most of us are accustomed to the idea that certain drugs treat certain diseases. This is not the case in the mental health area. The majority of the drugs currently used only make the patient more manageable and reduce symptoms somewhat. There is no drug that makes the person "well." So, a problem exists. Some workers in the field are concerned that the patient is only being "helped" by being made semiconscious. In some hospitals, for instance, the daily dosage of a tranquilizer for psychotics is the same one used by veterinarians to subdue a 400-pound lion. It is no wonder that these patients complain of their lives being filled with "empty feelings" (Breggin, 1983). And continued use of some psychotic medication can cause permanent disability in the form of involuntary arm, leg, and mouth movements (Bower, 1985).

Electroconvulsive Shock Therapy

In **electroconvulsive therapy (ECT)**, a shock is deliberately sent through the patient's brain to produce convulsions. The procedure is not painful, but it certainly is quite terrifying to many patients. The treatment is very controversial. A major objection to it is that no one knows what it does, why it works when it does, and whether the risks involved are worth it

Electroconvulsive therapy (ECT)
Therapy in which an electrical shock is sent through the brain to try to reduce symptoms of mental disturbance.

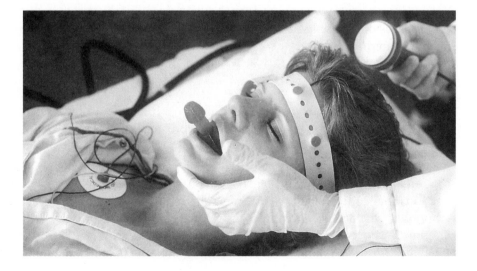

Patient is prepared for electroshock therapy.

(Weiner, 1984; Scovern & Kilmann, 1980). The actual physical changes that occur after ECT are best summed up as confusion and loss of memory, which disappear after a few hours. With continued shock treatments, however, the memory loss persists for longer and longer periods, and eventually ECT results in brain damage (Freeman, 1985; Squire, 1985; Breggin, 1984).

What also makes the treatment worrisome is the fact that it is so primitive. It resembles a treatment used in the very early days of mental hospitals around Pinel's era, called the "snake pit." Patients who were behaving strangely or depressed were thrown in a pit that contained dozens of nonpoisonous snakes. Patients were left there until they "quit acting strangely." But, from the previous chapter, you may remember that all psychotic patients have periods when the symptoms disappear. The hospital personnel were convinced that these patients were getting better as a result of the "treatment."

There are two final things to say about ECT that are important. First of all, it, like the snake pit, will jar a person out of a deep, suicidal depression, so *maybe* there is some justification for using it in such cases. Second, it doesn't work with any other category of mental disturbance and should not be administered to people who fall into those. For example, it makes schizophrenics worse, probably convincing some of them that their previously false belief that someone is trying to hurt them is true (Weiner, 1984; Scovern & Kilmann, 1980).

In a way, it may seem that we are being too harsh on this treatment. On the other hand, there is a real stigma attached to any person getting electroshock treatment. People think something really horrible is wrong with them. And most patients fear it. Since it *is* useful with some cases of *severe* depression, one could hardly fault its use in many of those cases. Nonetheless, the evidence is pretty clear that it does little good and sometimes harm with cases other than severe depression, yet it is still used for people with other disturbances. Some claim that this is the case because there is money to be made. We won't be cynical, but using something that is of little value and has so many negative aspects deserves to be questioned.

Psychosurgery

Psychosurgery
Surgery that destroys part of the brain to make the patient calmer, freer of symptoms.

Any technique that involves entering the brain to alter one's psychological state is called **psychosurgery**. The most common operation involves destruction of part of the front portion of the patient's brain, just behind the forehead. This part, the *frontal lobe*, contains most of the nerve connections that control what we call "personality," especially our complex emotional responses. Usually a laser is aimed at this portion, and enough tissue is damaged to try to slow down the patient. Unfortunately, brain tissue never restores itself, so the effects are permanent.

Another problem: If the wrong area is hit, the patient can get much *more* violent and unmanageable. This is a treatment that is very hard to justify. When it is used today, it is on the grounds that the patient is uncontrollable otherwise. That is often hard to believe, given our arsenal of tranquilizing drugs.

Controversy: Mental Illness

As discussed in the previous chapter, the evidence mounts that psychotics have a physical or chemical problem. They probably could, in the broad sense, be said to have an "illness," a term that implies a physical defect. But psychotics are a minority among those with mental problems.

For the rest of the people who have serious problems, the issue is whether they should be listed as having a mental *illness*. Once a person has an illness, they are either supposed to be "cured" or removed from society—a distressing idea (Woolfolk, 1985). If you say someone has a "disease," you are labeling him or her forever. Is that justified? What about Uncle Harrys and Aunt Marthas who spend a lot of their time in the attic chatting with imaginary friends? Are they really hurting anyone? Should they be removed from society just because they are a little "quirky"?

One psychiatrist has suggested that rather than "disease" or "illness," we should say a person has "problems in living" (Szasz, 1961). Look what a difference just a change in wording would make, and decide for yourself: A man you know slightly is behaving strangely and seems distracted, so you ask a mutual friend what's wrong with him. Answer: "He has some problems at work. His marriage is in trouble. It's all getting to him." Now, here's the second scenario: "Charlie has a mental illness and had to be hospitalized. They say he has some kind of severe neurosis."

Both describe the same person. See any difference in how you would respond to Charlie the next time you saw him, depending on which version you got?

Seeking Professional Help

There are so many television shows and movies that distort the reality of what those with problems are really like and what happens to them in therapy that we have our work cut out for us here. Having used the box at the end of the last chapter, you may have decided you have a serious problem. You could be right. But you do *not* have a serious mental disturbance or illness. There is an enormous difference! A serious mental disturbance involves seeing things that are not there, believing things that never have happened, and having extremely confused thought processes. If these applied to you, chances are close to zero that you would even be reading this.

As mentioned a number of times, everybody has problems. Quite a number of people cross the line from having day-to-day problems to being involved with one that has become so disruptive that it is hard to function. This still does not mean that you have a serious mental disturbance. It means that someone will have to help you get back on track. The odds of your doing it on your own are remote because the problem gets distorted when it fills up so much of your time and thinking. You need someone objective.

Only a handful of counselors or psychologists today are very interested in trying to uncover deep dark secrets. Most of them are interested in rapid, clear results. They want to work with you to get to the heart of the problem and get it over with for you, not delve into every nook and cranny of your personal life. Most therapies today are measured in months, not years, to completion.

One of the most important ingredients in getting yourself repaired, so to speak, is some degree of confidence in the therapist. School counselors are like people in every other profession. There are good ones and bad ones. You can get a feel for what one is like by discussing other areas, such as occupational choice, with him or her to see if you think he or she might be the kind of person who can help you deal with more personal issues. Go to your school counselor only if you feel good about doing so, but don't base your decision on bizarre rumors that crop up among students. Sort out what seems to be real from fiction.

From the outset, you can count on the fact that, for a counselor or a psychologist, the problem you have is not something new and startling. Lots of other people have had it—whatever it is. If you decide to go to the counselor, be certain to ask him or her what the rules are about confidentiality. Counselors will be happy to tell you. The rules vary, and you don't want to get yourself into a position in which your problems become part of a school record.

If you decide to go to an outside psychologist, you will need your parents' cooperation and help in most states—but not always. It is likely that your parents will be somewhat upset if you approach them about it. But that is not because you are so weird. It's because they endlessly worry that somehow they haven't done right by you. It's almost inevitable that they have done the best they can and that they have little to do with what is bothering you. When you talk to them about the problem, be direct, but don't exhaust them with details so they think you are worse off than you are. With or without parents, one of the best sources for finding help is to contact a "hot line," such as suicide prevention or "runaway" or anything like that. You don't have to have that particular problem to call them. All these organizations have endless sources of help available in almost any problem area.

Two things to trust us about: (1) You will find that "therapy," when conducted properly, is very close to just sitting down and talking with a friend. Nothing strange or really different goes on. (2) *Don't* stick with a therapist you are not comfortable with. If you do, you will wind up fighting two battles—first, your problem, and second, your negative feelings about the therapist. Change therapists. But, if you keep wanting to change, your expectations are probably too high.

Summary

1. A psychologist has an advanced degree in psychological principles and methods. A psychiatrist is a medical doctor who has added a number of years to his or her training during which mental abnormality is studied. Psychotherapist is a broad term applied to almost any professional working with psychological problems.

2. Psychoanalysis is based on a theory that assumes unconscious animal impulses are seeking expression. Treatment focuses on free association and transference to reveal the inner forces and to reduce their strength and the anxiety they cause.

3. Humanistic theory centers on the belief that the person is basically good. The therapist mirrors the thoughts of the client to bring out the potential that lies inside.

4. Behavioral therapy tries to change people's behavior or actions. Three methods used are systematic desensitization, aversive conditioning, and the token economy.

5. Cognitive behavioral therapy, using the rational emotive technique, tries to reorient internal sentences so the individual has better control over his or her emotions.

6. Group therapy benefits the patient because it is closer to real-life relationships than therapy involving just doctor and patient. This treatment is also cheaper because more than one patient is handled at a time.

7. There doesn't seem to be a "best" therapy. People benefit most from working with a therapist they can trust. Therapy in general is effective, but your return for the money with psychoanalysis is highly questionable.

8. Chemotherapy is drug treatment. Drugs in reasonable doses seem beneficial to many, but there are dangers. Electroconvulsive therapy is controversial. It does seem to help those who are severely depressed. Psychosurgery is a highly questionable method involving brain destruction in an attempt to make the patient more manageable.

Key Words and Concepts

Philippe Pinel
psychologists
counseling
   psychologists
clinical
   psychologists
psychiatrists
psychiatric social
   workers
psychiatric nurses
psychotherapies
psychoanalysis
free association
transference
humanistic therapy
client-centered
   therapy
nondirective
   therapy
unconditional
   positive regard

behavioral therapy
systematic
   desensitization
aversive
   conditioning
token economy
Albert Ellis
cognitive behavioral
   therapy
rational emotive
   therapy
internalized
   sentences
awfulize
group therapy
encounter groups
chemotherapy
electroconvulsive
   therapy (ECT)
psychosurgery

Review Questions

Matching (Answers can be used more than once.)

1. Treatment often lasts years.
2. Client essentially heals himself or herself
3. Treatment often works relatively quickly.
4. Therapy is based on Sigmund Freud's theory.
5. Client's thought processes are analyzed.
6. The therapist reflects what the client is saying.
7. Therapy based on Albert Ellis's theory.
8. Patient transfers emotional conflicts onto therapist.

a. behavioral therapy
b. humanistic therapy
c. psychoanalysis
d. cognitive behavioral therapy

9. Goal is to unite the mental or rational with the emotional.

10. The origin of the problem is essentially ignored.

11. The therapist remains completely nonjudgmental.

12. Disorders are the result of learned responses.

True/False

13. In group therapy, "normal" people get together to share feelings without the guidance of a mental health worker.

14. The goal of most encounter groups is to train group members to become therapists themselves.

15. Psychoanalysis often tends to become a very expensive method of treatment.

16. A common treatment used by psychologists is chemotherapy.

17. One or two treatments of electroconvulsive therapy will tend to cause long-lasting memory loss.

18. One reason why electroconvulsive therapy is still used today is that it seems to work well on deeply depressed individuals.

19. Psychosurgery is sometimes used on patients who are difficult to control.

Discussion Questions

1. What kinds of problems would be better dealt with using psychoanalysis, and which problems would be better dealt with using behavioral therapy? Explain.

2. Describe a person, in your past or present, who consistently has demonstrated unconditional positive regard toward you. What effect, if any, did (or does) this have on you? Explain.

3. If your principal wanted to incorporate a token economy system at your school, what are several ways in which to do this? Be specific. Do you think adopting your suggestions would realistically have any effect on students' behaviors? Explain.

4. Despite the many problems associated with chemotherapy, why would it be virtually impossible and even undesirable for a mental institution to eliminate chemotherapy completely? What kinds of problems would result? Explain.

5. Imagine that one of your parents has been severely depressed for several months, that he or she has been completely listless and uncommunicative. All kinds of treatments have been ineffective. The last resort seems to be ECT; however, the hospital needs your approval to administer it. Do you give your approval? Why or why not? Explain.

6. Do you think it would ever be justified to use psychosurgery as punishment for criminals in prison? Why or why not? Explain.

7. Of all the therapies and treatments discussed in the chapter, which one would you tend to prefer if you had a problem? Explain.

Activities

1. Take out a sheet of paper and write down the first ten things that come to mind when you think of a mental hospital. Your list needs to be somewhat detailed—not just a list of single words and phrases. Then contact a mental health hospital and interview someone there, focusing particularly on the accuracy or inaccuracy of the ten items on your list. Also, prepare beforehand a list of other questions to ask about the hospital. Write a report on the interview. Be sure to include a comparison between your original list and what you learned. Was your list accurate?

2. Contact someone who conducts therapy on a more or less daily basis and interview this person. Possible questions: (a) What are the most common kinds of problems that you treat? (b) Would your answer to question A have been the same five or ten years ago? (c) What are the typical kinds of treatments and therapies that you use? (d) What is the average length of treatment time for your clients? (e) What are your feelings about chemotherapy? (f) Do you ever get tired of listening to other people's problems? Write a report on your interview and include your specific reactions.

3. You will need to do this next activity with a classmate. Instead of being evaluated on any written work, you will be evaluated this time on three role-playing situations that you will present to the class. First, choose a hypothetical problem on which you want to focus: de-

pression over the breakup of a relationship, anxiety over a weight problem, frustration with parents, and so on. Second, select three of the four main types of therapists presented in the chapter and brainstorm how each would deal with the problem. You might refer back to Chapter 14 on personality theories for more insight into this. Next, write a dialogue between a patient (or client) and one type of therapist. Write two more dialogues for the other two types of therapists. Try to make each dialogue about two to three minutes long. Finally, rehearse your dialogues: One of you will be the therapist, the other will be the client. Then arrange with your teacher a time when you can present the dialogues in class. *Note:* Your dialogues do not have to be entirely serious—have some fun with them—but they should be informative and accurate. Also, as we mentioned, be sure the problem you choose is *hypothetical* (for instance, do not use a person with a weight problem to play the role of someone who has a weight problem); a classroom is not the ideal setting in which to discuss your own personal problems.

4. This next activity is similar to the previous one in that you and a classmate will present a skit to the class. You are probably familiar with therapists who conduct therapy on television or on the radio. As with anything, some of these therapists seem qualified and helpful, while others should seek therapy themselves. Regardless of the therapists' qualifications, this kind of "fast-food" therapy is a natural target for parody. We want you and a classmate to prepare a five- to six-minute skit in which one of you will be a new TV or radio therapist and the other a client. Again, arrange a time when you can present the skit in class. Definitely have fun with this one!

5. In the next couple of days, pay special attention to the problems of two of your close friends. "Friend" can be broadly defined: family member, boyfriend or girlfriend, and so on. What you will be looking for is a time when your friends seem to feel a need to talk about a problem. The problems can range anywhere from frustration over studying for a test to irritation over serious family problems. If in the next couple of days your friends don't seem to have any problems in mind, perhaps you can prompt them with a simple question about a past problem. If, on the other hand, you encounter five or six friends with problems, pick the two with the most serious ones.

As your two friends (one at a time) begin to discuss their problems, we want you to try to act as a mirror and simply rephrase your friends' own feelings and thoughts. In other words, you will be using Rogers's nondirective technique. Reread the sample dialogue from the chapter to get an idea of how to do this. Some pointers to keep in mind: (1) Don't give *any* advice; (2) simply put their words into your words; (3) be completely nonjudgmental—show unconditional positive regard. This entire experience may seem like a game at first, like you are simply repeating or mimicking what your friends say. But, if you are sincerely concerned with your friends' problems, you will probably find that the experience is worthwhile.

Once you've tried this on two friends, write a report describing your reactions. Include how you felt at the time, whether you thought the experience was worthwhile and effective, whether you would use the technique again—for real—not just for an assignment. Be specific about your reactions, but do NOT disclose the content of your conversation—which should remain confidential.

6. We want you to practice identifying negative internalized sentences and supplying the more rational response after each sentence. Situation A: You have to give a speech tomorrow in front of your entire psychology class. Situation B: You decide you are going to ask someone out for a date. Write down these situations on two separate sheets of paper. For each one, write down ten possible negative internalized sentences—leave plenty of room after each one. For example: "No one will like my speech; everyone will think I'm stupid." After each sentence, write down the more rational response. For example, after the sentence above, you might write: "It's probably an exaggeration to say that *no one* will like my speech. Even if the speech as a whole is not that good, there will be parts of it that will be OK—and there will be *some* people who will recognize this. And not *everyone* will think I'm stupid; people in class know how difficult it is to give a speech." Notice how the rational response is not just a single sentence: You will need to explain yourself. So, you will be writing a total of 20 sentences with rational responses after each. This is typical of the approach cognitive behavior therapists might use. (Sounds like homework, doesn't it?)

As mentioned, this whole exercise is just practice. If you'd rather use two real situations from your own life, go ahead. It will probably make the activity much more meaningful. Your answers will not be read aloud in class.

Once you complete your two lists and the rational responses, write down your reactions to the exercise.

How did you feel as you filled out the sentences and responses? Was it difficult? If you were to choose real situations and if you had more practice at this, do you think this kind of exercise would be helpful? Why or why not? Explain.

Self and Social Influences

Any group—even one this size—follows specific rules of dress, speech, and social interaction.

Chapter 20

Social Influences and Relationships

Be able to:

1. Describe attribution theory and how we use it.

2. Describe the role of physical attractiveness in falling in love.

3. Describe how it is possible for physical factors to start aggression.

4. Explain the evidence that psychological factors can cause aggression.

5. Give the evidence for both sides regarding whether TV causes violence.

6. Describe the key factors in whether people will help one another.

7. Explain the difference between density and crowding.

Global Look at the Chapter

This chapter focuses on the social factors that guide our feelings and actions toward one another. We will look at the external influences that interact with an individual's personality to create beliefs about and actions toward other people.

Hidden Influences in Behavior

The fact is we all do things that at times can surprise even us. The surprise is not necessarily pleasant, especially when we discover things about ourselves that we don't like. For example, say that you are walking down the sidewalk on a busy street. A person falls down in front of you, moaning, rolling up into a ball. Would you stop and help? You claim you would. But is that true? Since we don't know you personally, we can't say you won't, but statistically, in real life, the odds are staggering that you will walk on by. Later we will discuss why this happens so often. This behavior has caused the press to call our society cold and heartless. But that is a simplistic and inaccurate explanation. (Just to tantalize you to read further—we hope—if you are on a relatively dark street with only a handful of people around and the same thing happens, statistically the odds are very *high* that you *will* stop and help the person!) But first let's look at some of the details about how people think in their relationships with others and how they view the actions of others.

Attribution Theory

Much social interaction is colored by our own psychological makeup. A major factor in how we interpret the behavior of others is covered by **attribution theory** (at-tri-BYOO-shun), which concerns the process by which we form opinions about another. Attribution theory can be divided into three parts, each of which interacts with the others. (1) The first consists of **antecedents**, a word that means "things that come before"—that is, we rely on information, beliefs, and motivations we already have in forming our opinions. (2) The next part is the actual **attribution**, which refers to the causes that we come up with to explain why people do what they do. In other words, we "attribute" (give) reasons to them for their actions. (3) The final part involves **consequences**, such as our behavior (what we do about the situation), our emotional responses, and our expectations (what we think will happen in the future) (Weiner, 1985).

Here is an example of what we are talking about: You have a friend named Maria, a classmate you know casually in that the two of you speak when you meet at school. You are going home at 4:00 on a Tuesday afternoon, and you see Maria coming down the sidewalk. As usual, you say, "Hi." *Not* as usual, however, she replies, "Go away!" and stalks off. Maria is usually a friendly, pleasant person, has always seemed to like you, and you in turn value the acquaintance. Those beliefs are part of the *antecedents* (what existed before you were rejected). You had already formed a concept of what Maria was like, and now you must try to explain her behavior within this framework. There are two possibilities. Either something about the situation caused her to act this way, or there is something personal involved. Perhaps something happens on Tuesday afternoons, causing Maria to behave that way. Because you want to find out what is going on, you keep trying. So, the following day you say "Hi" to her again, and this time she says "Hi" back. The same thing happens the next day, and the next, and so on. The following Tuesday, however, at 4:00, when you say "Hi," she says "Go away!" and stalks off.

Now you have additional information, characteristics that can be noted and that are consistent. Only on Tuesday does she act this way. On further investigation, you find that Maria has a standing appointment at the dentist at 4:30 on that day, is having painful procedures done, and hates going there. Now you can make an *attribution*; that is, you make up a cause for her weird behavior. You perceive it as rooted in the fact that she has to go to the dentist.

Once an attribution is made, it leads to *consequences*: You then can explain her behavior and not take it personally. Had the antecedents been different—if you had viewed her as an unpredictable, explosive person, for instance—you might have attributed her actions to instability, not bothered to investigate, and avoided her in the future.

Thus, we are always seeking an explanation for why something happens, even if we unknowingly come to a false conclusion. Using such a

Attribution theory
A theory about the process by which we form opinions about another.

Antecedents
Information and beliefs we have beforehand about another.

Attribution
The causes we use to explain another's behavior.

Consequences
Out emotional responses and expectations regarding another.

In Focus: Attribution Theory

Situation: Ann sees her boyfriend talking with *her* best friend.

system can lead us to accept or reject others based on this information. For instance, if a Republican publicly praises another Republican, most people pay no attention to what is said since both politicians belong to the same political party and since politicians are not very high on people's lists of most trusted people. But, if we hear a Democrat praising a Republican, we are much more likely to attribute honesty to that person and tend to believe in him or her, even though that might not be sensible (Quattrone, 1985).

Now that you grasp attribution, note that its principles are used all the time. We use it to explain the behaviors of our friends, parents, and people we work with. For groups we don't like, we attribute all kinds of strange things to them—they don't bathe, the family has strange rituals it performs—and then look for clues that might support our beliefs. With groups we like, such as the ones we belong to, we see the members as having all kinds of positive characteristics, some of which don't really exist.

Attributions can be quite distorted. When it was discovered that the earth was round, many famous people of the time believed that there was a whole race of oddly acting creatures who got that way from living "upside down" at the bottom of the earth. They were called *Antipodes*. *Anti* means "opposite," and *podes* is another word for "feet." These Antipode people had their feet going the opposite direction, or upside down. They lived at the bottom of the earth where trees grew upside down and rain fell upward. They were not creatures at all like the rest of us. Some people did object to this strange idea, but they tried to fight it by claiming that the earth was a *square* (Boorstin, 1983). That wasn't much of a solution because, using the logic of the day, you would then have some people who grew sideways as well as some who grew upside down!

Attributions are a subtle part of any relationship. In the very early stages, however, the critical factor in people getting together is how they view one another emotionally. Hence, in the next section we will review the factors involved in what seems to attract one person to another.

Interpersonal Attraction

One of the more difficult subjects to handle scientifically is "love." Equally hard is trying to tell the exact differences between "like" and "love." We know what we feel, but we cannot define it very well. So, here are reported the valiant attempts by scientists to understand these feelings.

We can start with that overwhelming feeling we all have had at one time or another, "falling madly in love." There is no feeling quite like it since it can consume us one minute, make us feel wonderful the next, and miserable and lost the minute after that. The most obvious characteristics of this state are the physical responses: rapid heartbeat, stomach contractions, and general body chaos. Ironically, these "symptoms" are identical to those of fear and anxiety. The major difference is that the behaviors have become associated with someone we find physically attractive. When this association occurs, we know it isn't "fear" but "love" (Sherrod, 1982). So, we start off with a physical base, add emotional responses, and then top it all off by getting involved mentally with the person.

Importance of Associations

We also know that there is a considerable amount of high-level emotional association going on in this state, which is what makes it so special. For example, most people in love have a special song that belongs to

Studies suggest that love starts out as physical attraction but continues based on personality factors.

them. It was heard during a special moment together. Now the song is associated with them and the emotions they felt the first time they heard it. Thus, each time they hear it again, the emotions recur. There are also special places they have gone to; again, these places and the things connected with them get associated with this high level of emotional arousal. As a result, we build more and more associations to the core response we had at the beginning. The more connections we have, the more associations and the stronger the feeling gets. What starts off as a physical feeling takes on broad emotional and mental associations.

Ingredients in Liking and Loving

Creatures don't fall in love with just anyone. There is something special that occurs. Many species of birds pick a specific mate for life. The wolf is quite selective in choosing a mate, and the couple tends to stay together as a unit with the "family." A male peacock will spread out its beautiful plumage to attract a female. Some females will like what a particular male shows; others won't and will prefer a different male. Finally, as is also true for humans, the female peacock is far more selective than the male and will often reject a mate for reasons we don't understand.

Physical attractiveness is a large factor in interpersonal attraction when people first meet and get to know one another (Edinger & Paterson, 1983). At that point, there is little else on which to judge someone. The pitfall here is that we tend to see more attractive people in a generally more positive light, to see them as competent, confident, and so forth. In fact, just from appearance we attribute all kinds of good things to those who are more in line with society's expectations of attractiveness. Again, females are far more discriminating; they are more likely to view the whole person rather than just the body or hairstyle.

Less attractive people, by society's standards, are at a disadvantage—but only in the beginning. There is a saying that "beauty is in the eye of the beholder." Scientifically, this saying seems to be true because studies show that people tend to match up more or less with people who are roughly the same level of attractiveness (Reis et al., 1980; Cash & Janda, 1984; White, 1980). In any case, over time, personalities become more important to others than the physique. While physical looks can often get a first date, whether or not there will be a second one will usually rely heavily on personality. So, there is at least some hope for most of us.

Both liking and loving are based on *familiarity*. In other words, the more we see specific people, the more we like them (if there is something to them), since we tend to find that the familiar is less threatening. This principle holds true as long as the interactions are spaced over time (Myers, 1983). There is a lesson here: In beginning relationships as well as in long-standing ones, we can overdo ourselves and exhaust the other person no matter how wonderful we are. Too much closeness too fast often reduces attractiveness. It is better to be at least *slightly* aloof so that there is still psychological territory for the other person to explore and be fascinated by (Myers, 1983).

Revealing oneself to the other person has its place, time, and limits. While love seems to grow with mutual understanding and sharing of intimate feelings, endless exposure of the self turns the other person off, especially if it comes early in the relationship and involves ongoing baring of the soul (Myers, 1983). Believe it or not, our problems, shared in excess, are rather boring to others. Limited sharing, though, can deepen a relationship. At the very least, the partner needs a chance to let out some of his or her problems (Franzoi, 1985).

You will hear that those with opposite interests are best suited for a long-lasting relationship, but there is no evidence to support this claim. Hundreds of studies have explored this area, and most conclude that those who stay together the longest are more alike than they are different (Nias, 1979). Variation is interesting, but major differences are threatening.

While it is probably not applicable to your life at present, this is a good place to mention a few tips from seasoned marriage counselors. These ideas are too important to ignore: (1) Marrying someone with the intention of helping him or her get over a drug or alcohol problem almost never works. Things inevitably get worse. (2) A little jealousy goes a long way. Most experts agree that someone who is very, very jealous will make daily life miserable, and the odds against getting rid of this problem are staggeringly high. (3) Any kind of violence in a relationship is there to stay. The odds of the victim being able to avoid it are so low that the time to end the relationship seems to be immediately, before it gets a foothold. (4) Love in the best of circumstances is a *very* fragile mixture of self-esteem, self-importance, giving, taking, and trying to keep a balance (Davis, 1985).

Aggression and Violence

War and violence are as old as human records. Fossil remains from the Neanderthals (100,000 years ago) show wooden weapons and spear tips embedded in human bone (Stewart, 1969). As the result of such findings, many people claim that we are merely an advanced animal and that aggression appears among animals of any kind (Lorenz, 1963).

Indeed, there are societies in which daily activity centers on a chance to cheat and be as cutthroat as possible toward one another (Benedict, 1934). But other societies exist in which violence is absent and people live in basic harmony (Malinowski, 1929).

Most of the evidence suggests that humans began as hunter-gatherers—that is, we wandered the forests where food was usually available. In such groups, violence would be at a minimum. Similar groups still exist in remote forest lands and show little aggression (Montagu, 1974). This finding leads some to think that aggression may have arisen from some natural disaster that stripped the forest bare and left people fighting for food. Whether we are supposed to be carnivores (meat eaters) or not is still argued. The evidence is ambiguous. Our intestinal systems are long, winding mazes, the kind that are normally found in creatures that require a lengthy digestion process for vegetation, as opposed to the relatively short and direct intestine of a meat eater such as a dog.

Be all that as it may, though, violence does indeed erupt all around us, and, since most of us have more than enough to eat, we have to assume that at least part of such behavior is the result of imitation or social learning.

Influence of the Brain

Given our elaborate brains, we produce all kinds of variations on situations; we can be either peaceful or violent depending on how we *interpret* situations (Lazarus, 1974). For instance, people leaving a movie that had aggressive content who are "accidentally" pushed (by experimenters) are more likely to get aggressive than those who just saw a peaceful movie. The people are stirred up, but they don't know that it is from the movie; hence, they attribute (remember attribution?) the cause of their arousal to the person who jostled them (Rule & Nesdale, 1976). Thus, the current hypothesis for aggression focuses on mental activity rather than on the fulfillment of basic needs (such as getting food). At least once a week, we read about someone stabbing or shooting a family member to death because they lost the *TV Guide* or some equally absurd thing. A moment's reflection and it becomes obvious that this aggression is the end product of some kind of symbolic issue, rather than of deprivation, starvation, or a specific basic need that was not met.

Environment and Aggression

Human aggression also develops from environment and culture. The United States is a very violent country. Japan is relatively free of violence despite notable overcrowding. Although violence is on the rise in England, the rule still is that police officers do not carry firearms, even when they are capturing thieves, burglars, or petty criminals.

To get some perspective on how humans vary in their aggressive behavior, we might consider the frontier West, which is often thought to have had very high crime rates. This was not the case. Murder was very rare among ordinary citizens. In Bodie, California, from 1878 to 1882, bodies did pile up at a rate three times that of today's murder capital, Miami, Florida. But these were the bodies of young men who wanted to go around "shooting it out," not of everyday citizens. Only one woman was robbed during this whole period, and there were no rapes. Juvenile crimes were nonexistent (McGrath, 1985). In fact, even among the worst of criminals, it was strictly taboo *ever* to bother a woman in any way. That was the code of the West. Only an "insane" man would do such a thing; hence, such aggressive behavior was close to nonexistent.

Humans also seem to set up special places for aggression, such as football games and boxing matches. And bars. One psychological study focused on all the bars in one city—185 of them. Only a few accounted for the majority of the aggression that took place in bars. The psychologists found that those who entered these few bars *expected* either to attack or to be attacked before the evening was over. Such bars had certain characteristics in common: unclean and cheap surroundings, ill-kempt patrons, patrons drinking rapidly, people talking loudly to themselves, unfriendly bartenders, downtown location, and poor ventilation (Graham et al., 1980).

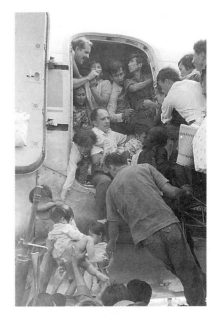

Victims of aggression in Indochina fighting for space on an aircraft to flee the scene.

Psychological Factors in Aggression

There is much more violence among men than women. While one could make a case for hormones causing this, social learning—that is, the childhood training received by males versus females—seems more important.

More often than not, aggressive behavior starts early in life and continues on through adolescence. Most of it seems to result from family upbringing focusing on "masculine" activities that are typically aggressive—such as fighting back and standing up to someone "like a man." This kind of training has to be tempered very early, many feel, or it is too late to do anything about it. Aggressive patterns apparently are somewhat set by middle childhood (Eron, 1980).

In addition to family influence, psychologists point to the anonymous nature of our society as a cause of aggressive behavior. When people are ignored as individuals this can lead to antisocial behavior. The term used for this is **deindividuation** (DE-in-di-vi-ju-AYE-shun), meaning a loss of one's sense of individuality (Diener, 1976). A study performed on Halloween supports this hypothesis. When children were given an opportunity to steal change from a money bowl about two feet from the candy bowl, they stole about 8 percent of the time if they were alone and if the person answering the door knew who they were, but they stole about 20 percent of the time under the same conditions if they were with a group and known—probably the result of group "bravado." The figure jumped to 57 percent, though, when the group was not known to the person answering the door. In one case, an experimenter answering the door told the children that she was going to leave the room, pointed to the smallest child, and said, if she found any money missing when she came

Deindividuation
A loss of one's sense of individuality and responsibility when in a group.

back, she was going to hold that child responsible. The stealing soared to 80 percent since the group then had someone to blame (Diener et al., 1976).

As you can see, individuals reduce the sense of their own responsibility when they are with other people. In other words, in a group, each person apparently feels less responsible for what happens. Also, the individual feels more powerful and less vulnerable when with other people. This situation has been called the **risky shift phenomenon**, meaning that, when in a group, the risk or danger for each individual is shifted (divided up) among all the group members (Wallach et al., 1962). Hence, group behavior fosters much more risk taking than individual members would engage in by themselves. The risky shift may help explain horrible events like lynch mobs, gang beatings, and mass riots.

Risky shift phenomenon
The situation where the danger of an act is split among the members of a group; hence, it is smaller for each person.

Biological Factors in Aggression

There is evidence that some aggressive behavior can have physical causes. We discussed in Chapter 3 the fact that, in the inner core of the brain, roughly midway between the nose and the back of the head sits a unit called the *hypothalamus*, which controls rage, anger, pleasure, and other behaviors. We believe that the rage portion of the hypothalamus might well be responsible for uncontrolled outbursts of violence.

Here are a few examples: Allergies to certain substances can cause dramatic changes in a person's behavior. There was a case of a child who was perfectly normal until he ate bananas. After doing so, he would try to tear up the room and destroy his toys. This only occurred after eating that fruit. Another child would bang his head against the wall whenever he ate wheat. And we personally knew about a very sweet, normally calm mother who every now and then at breakfast would throw dishes against the wall and stomp on the silverware. This behavior was restricted to breakfast time and lasted only about 20 minutes. Of course, very few people can witness small children in action at breakfast without feeling a little crazy, but this was truly out of the ordinary. After careful exploration, it was discovered that, just before these episodes, she would sample pancakes she was cooking. She normally didn't eat them. It turned out that she was allergic to the yellow dye some manufacturers use to make the pancakes look more "eggy." Normally, when people are allergic, they break out in hives, but, in the above cases, they were "breaking out" inside their heads, causing the brain tissue to swell and put pressure on the rage center in the hypothalamus. Thus erupted the woman's uncontrollable morning episodes (Moyer, 1975).

Amphetamines ("speed"), used over time, can cause brain cells to start firing at random and can make the world so confusing that the person feels threatened and begins striking out at others to protect himself or herself from being harmed—even though no one is really even paying attention to that person. The effects of alcohol are very much involved with changes in the psychology of the person. Alcohol reduces inhibitions and leads to violence in people who are insecure or obnoxious to begin with and who, when they drink, can no longer hold these traits in check.

Recent attention has focused on other factors as contributors to aggression, especially television and movies. We will take a look at that next.

Effects of Mass Media

It may seem hard to believe, but, for 50 years in colonial America, newspapers and books were considered a danger to the general public. Printing presses were carefully controlled, and what few things were published had to have government approval. The fear was that somehow freedom of publication might damage the morals of the general public. In the 1600s, a highly spiritual book (today considered a Christian classic), the *Imitation of Christ*, was banned because it might lead to differing views about religion. In Nathaniel Hawthorne's classic novel, *The Scarlet Letter*, a woman had to wear a large red letter "A" (for adulteress) on her clothing because she had a child outside of marriage. The book was banned in the 1850s. Later, in 1925, censors would not allow the movie based on the book to be shown unless the main character was married—which destroyed the whole point of the story (Tebbel, 1974).

Today, movies and television programs are at the center of attention in the same general way, with much concern expressed about violence and sex as part of their content. While there may well be important issues involved here, we have to move cautiously to keep from winding up with the same restrictions and censorship that existed in earlier centuries. There have been only a couple of studies on the issue of sex in movies and television, but roughly 100 or so on violence, so we will focus on the latter to try to get some perspective.

Basic Film Studies   An early core study on the influence of film violence involved showing part of a movie called *The Champion*, starring actor Kirk Douglas. In the part shown to subjects, Mr. Douglas received a grotesque beating. After seeing the movie, subjects were told to judge the merit of a drawing made by a young man whose outline could be seen behind a screen. If they didn't like his work, they were to administer shocks to him. The shocks were not real, but the subjects thought they were because the person would groan. Again unknown to the subjects, all the drawings used for different groups were identical.

In one variation of the experiment, the "artist" was introduced as "Kirk" to some subjects and by another name to other subjects. The intensity of shock administered to "Kirk" was much greater than that to the person with another name. These findings suggest that we can identify with violent behavior and carry the activity seen on the screen into real life (Berkowitz & Geen, 1967).

In a second version that used the same arrangement, some subjects were told before viewing the scene from the movie that a bad guy was receiving the beating. Another group was told that a good guy was getting the blows. In other words, for the first subjects, the beating was justified; for the second, it was unjustified. This study showed that *justified violence* bred greater violence (shocks) against the stooges than unjustified violence.

Some principles emerged from these studies. First, violence can breed violence. Second, justified violence is likely to breed greater violence than unjustified violence does. Thus, violence in the name of right, honor, and good in movies and television actually leads to more violence, at least in laboratory settings (Diener & Woody, 1981). In a way, society has condoned violence if it is "right." This is important because few of us ever feel that we are *not* justified in "paying someone back" (Collins & Zimmerman, 1975).

These studies are based on the principle that people imitate all kinds of behavior, including violence. What, then, are the effects on children of viewing television? First of all, in the laboratory, if children see a movie with violence, they tend to become violent themselves by a process called **imitation learning** (Bandura et al., 1963). Logic, then, suggests that TV can contribute to imitation and aggression (Roberts & Bachen, 1981). But the evidence is not all one-sided. "Good" (nonviolent) television leads to imitation for a short while, but children seem to lose interest in it. Instead, they actively seek out the novelty in strange and wild pro-

Imitation learning
The process of learning behaviors by viewing others and imitating them.

Watching violence on television may encourage children to be violent themselves. (Photograph © Michael Kagen, Monkmeyer.)

grams such as the "Three Stooges" series (Comstock et al., 1978). Some suspect the key to appropriate TV programming, for children at least, is plenty of nonviolent novelty.

There is only one clear finding. The short-term effect of violent TV and movies is a very high level of *physical* arousal, which could lead to aggression if the person is then provoked in some way. This arousal lasts only about 20 minutes, however (Doob & Climie, 1972). No one disputes this finding on the short-term effects, but some question the long-term effects.

Trying for Perspective   It is hard to get perspective on an issue once it "goes public" and becomes controversial. This is especially true in an area that involves something like TV, when the average child 2 to 11 years old watches 27.3 hours a week (Nielsen, 1985). But one psychologist has brought together all the research on TV and aggression and provided a detailed, careful analysis of the results (Freedman, 1984). We want to discuss that analysis here.

These are his basic findings: Government reports and newspaper accounts say that there are 2,500 or more studies on TV and aggression, but this number is misleading. The same studies are being reported over and over, only each time a little information is added to one of them. Actually, there are about 100 studies directly relating to the subject, most of them from the laboratory. That filmed or videotaped aggression leads to aggressive behavior in a laboratory may or may not reflect what happens in real life, so we want to focus on the nonlaboratory studies.

Some conclusions are possible. In *field studies*, behavior is directly observed in a natural, nonlaboratory setting; in this case, subjects are watched after they view violent and nonviolent TV. Taken as a whole, these studies give only weak support to the belief that TV aggression causes real-life aggression. In fact, some aggressive people are *less* aggressive after seeing violence, and some nonaggressive people are *more* aggressive. Why this happens is not clear. In any case, there is insufficient evidence in field studies to conclude that TV viewing leads to aggression. Some unclear, but important, difference exists between the laboratory study and the behavior of people outside the laboratory.

Correlational studies are studies in which TV viewing is compared (correlated) with self-reported aggression. This type of study uses questionnaires in which the person lists the amount and type of TV watched and the amount and type of aggressive acts occurring afterward. The frequency of each behavior is then compared. Most studies show a very weak relationship between TV and aggression. Thus, whatever aggression arises may be partly from TV, but other factors must play a greater role.

Examination of the overall behavior of children (not just their television viewing) does show something important. Children who are already aggressive and view a lot of TV get progressively worse. In addition, already aggressive children actively seek out aggressive television (Eron, 1983).

The final item is clearly ironic. The most popular programs on television over time are those that contain emotional conflicts and have little or no violence (Diener & Woody, 1981). Apparently, program makers are adding an ingredient (violence) that people don't care all that much about, and then everyone is getting upset about it.

Conclusions? (1) Studies to date show no strong relationship between TV and later violence in the average person. (2) Aggressive people seek out aggressive television and then become more aggressive (Eron & Huesman, 1985). Note: As mentioned, there are very few studies regarding sex and television. One cannot use these violence studies to draw any conclusion whatsoever about a behavior that is entirely different.

Catharsis
The supposed ability to get rid of aggressive energy by viewing others acting aggressively.

Catharsis   Before ending the discussion, we should make one more comment. You will hear that seeing violence might help us get rid of our aggressive impulses—that is, that it can "discharge" the energy connected with those impulses. The psychological term for this is **catharsis** (ca-THAR-sis), which comes from the Greek meaning "to cleanse or purify." The idea is that, by fantasy, we can purify ourselves of this need in real life. As much as one might like this theory to be true, the evidence over a number of years shows that it doesn't work. Instead, people merely get more agitated (Geen, 1977).

Violence obviously leads to victims who need help. As a result, social psychologists also study the other side: Under what circumstances will people come to the aid of someone in an emergency? The answer is surprising.

Helping Behavior

At 3:00 A.M. in New York City, a young woman by the name of Kitty Genovese was attacked on the street in front of her apartment house by a man bent on killing her. She let out endless bloodcurdling screams and broke away from him, only to be caught again and attacked once more. It took the man over half an hour to murder her, during which time 38 of her neighbors stood at their windows and watched. One of the neighbors was seen opening his door, going to the top of a stairwell, watching the attack going on down below him, and then returning to his apartment. Fifteen minutes later that man was the first person to call the police (Seedman & Hallman, 1974).

These events and others like them have been the topic of almost endless discussion in the news media. Have people lost all sense of right and wrong? Don't they care anymore?

Two experimenters decided to examine these issues using a series of elaborate psychological observations. They wanted to learn why people sometimes will not help others in obvious distress (Latané & Darley,

1970). The experimenters set up situations in which people were sitting in a room when one of the following events occurred: Smoke began to creep through one of the air vents, or a man was having an epileptic seizure (fake) in the other room, or a woman fell down in an adjacent room and was apparently seriously injured, indicated by all kinds of noise, moans, and groans coming from her. Each of these events was staged in such a way that the behavior of those who were "bystanders" to the event could be observed: (1) In the smoke experiment, different arrangements were tried: a student was placed alone in a room taking a test when it happened, then two students were in the room, three students, and so forth, all observed through a two-way mirror. (2) In the epileptic experiment, subjects were isolated from one another, but "found out" that one of the subjects was epileptic. The subjects were to carry on a discussion with one another via earphones and microphones, so they could hear but not see one another. They were told that this was to allow them more freedom of speech. When the "seizure" came, they could hear it going on and had access to help if they wanted it just by getting up and looking for the laboratory assistant. (3) The same basic setup as in number 1 was used for the "injured" woman, but the door to the testing room, where differing numbers of people were, was left open so that they could hear the woman.

Apparently very strict "rules" guide whether or not someone in need gets assistance.

After all these experiments, the subjects were interviewed. The findings are quite consistent and strong. First of all, though, no particular personality type responded to the need for help more than others. Second, all the subjects were quite concerned about the plight of the person in need, so there was no lack of feeling. Some came to the rescue; large numbers did not. What was the difference? The answer is so simple that it is startling, and at first unbelievable, but this type of study has been done so often over the years that there is no question about it.

The factor that controlled whether or not someone helped others was how many people the subject was with at the time the emergency arose. That makes sense, doesn't it? But there's a twist to it, because the *more* people present at the emergency, the *less* likely any one person was to give aid to the victim, and this held true for all the experiments. The results, part of which are shown in Table 20.1, are striking. In this table, the

Table 20.1 Effects of Group Size on Likelihood and Speed of Response to Epileptic Emergency (Letané & Darley, 1970)

Group Size	Percent Responding by End of Epileptic Seizure	Percent Ever Responding Before Experiment Ended
2 (subject and victim)	85	100
3 (subject, victim, and one other	62	85
6 (subject, victim, and 4 others	31	62

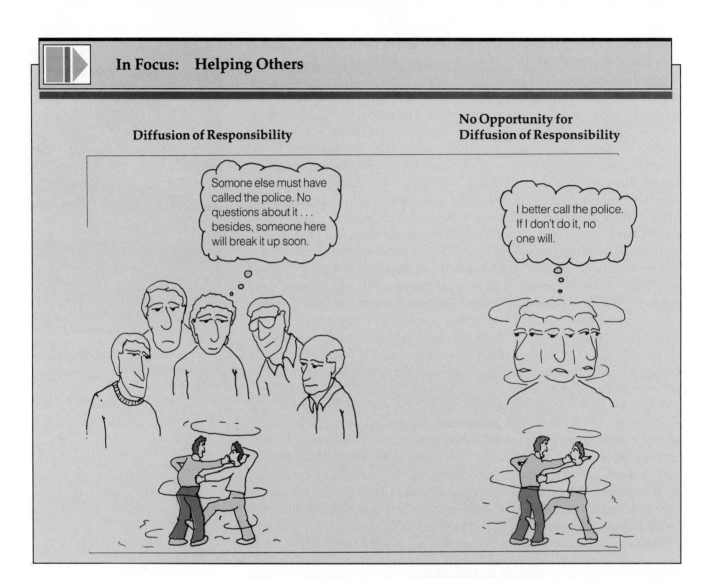

Diffusion of Responsibility

No Opportunity for Diffusion of Responsibility

subject is the person being observed to see if he or she will respond to the cry of the epileptic; the victim is the epileptic; "others" are just added people put into the situation by the experimenter.

How do the experimenters explain why this happens? Here are some of the conclusions that have been clearly demonstrated over time:

1. When others are present, we are inhibited from acting for fear we will make fools of ourselves in public.

2. If others are standing observing the emergency, we use them as a guide for how to act, just as, when we go to a party with people we don't know, we use others at the party as a guide for how to behave. If they don't help, we don't; if they do, we do.

3. Subjects who think or know that others are present are less likely to take personal responsibility because they will feel that it is someone

else's job. This is called **diffusion of responsibility**, meaning that the more people there are, the less responsibility each of us has to take (because responsibility is diffused, or spread out, among the members of the group).

Diffusion of responsibility
For an individual member of a group, responsibility for others is spread out among all group members.

4. But why don't people at least phone for help? Calling the police, in and of itself, admits that there is an emergency. If we admit that, then we get ourselves into a bind (Milgram, 1977): If it is indeed an emergency, we should do something more about the problem than just hang up the phone and wait for help to arrive!

5. We won't help in a strange environment where we don't know the rules. Here is a study that shows that: A well-dressed man on crutches fell down. Would someone help? He was a stooge for an experimenter and was not really injured. The first series of experiments was done in a subway, and 83 percent of passersby came to his aid. In a second set, he fell down at an airport. Only 41 percent tried to help. Is this some kind of social class difference? No. The people were interviewed, and here is the finding: Those familiar with the airport were more likely to respond to the need for help; those familiar with the subway were likewise more likely to help. The difference comes from the fact that an airport is less familiar to far more people; this was the deciding factor in whether or not help was forthcoming (Pearce, 1980).

The issue of familiarity is critical to behavior. We are always concerned about the proper behavior and what others will think about us. This feeling is called **evaluation apprehension**, which means that, without our even knowing it, we are apprehensive or concerned about how others will judge our performance. If we see someone helping someone, we tend to join in because that is expected; if not, we stand back (Schwartz & Gottlieb, 1980).

Evaluation apprehension
The concern about how others will judge us; we make our behavior conform to what we think they will approve of.

Finally, you may have thought that these studies might somehow seem "fake" to the subjects, but that was not the case. To prove the point, experimenters used experienced stuntmen to enact an apparently genuine violent situation with people fighting in public, beating each other up over an allegedly stolen item. The results were identical to the previous studies. So, we are without doubt influenced by those around us—especially by the number of them. But none of the subjects later interviewed ever was aware of this influence (Shotland, 1985).

Environmental Influences on Behavior

How we feel and how we interact with others can be strongly influenced by the physical environment. For example, a noisy environment can be distracting and nerveracking. Students from schools with a great

Notice how personal space and a sense of territory is maintained by facing away from one another.

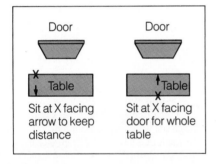

Figure 20.1
Methods for controlling where or if others sit near you.

Density
The actual number of people per square foot in a given space.

Crowding
A psychological feeling of too little space.

amount of noise are edgy, uncomfortable, and tend to have higher blood pressure than students from other schools (Russell & Ward, 1984).

Overcrowding is another problem. When animals are in crowded conditions, their behavior patterns become abnormal, some of them kill one another, they fail to breed, they develop brain defects, and many die from the stress of this situation (Calhoun, 1962; Fox, 1968).

Human reactions to space are highly psychological. Thus, ten people living in a 500-square-foot room for a couple of days will be overwhelmed by the feeling of closeness; the same number of people on a train for a day or so with approximately the same total square feet can feel lonely (Russell & Ward, 1984). Psychologists therefore divide lack of space into **density** and **crowding**. Density is the actual number of people per square foot, while crowding is the *feeling* of being too close. Density at a rock concert can be high, but crowding low; sitting at a restaurant counter with someone on your right and your left can be very crowded, but density compared to the rock concert is low (Stokols, 1978).

Much work has been done with prison density, since high density can create such serious problems as riots. One very workable system that is far cheaper than dealing with trouble in a prison is to give each prisoner an individual cell. Interestingly, it makes no difference how small the cell is (as long as the person can move!) or how cheap it looks (Cox et al., 1984).

Keeping Our Distance

All animals have a sense of **territoriality**, a fixed amount of space set aside for their use, and they will attack anything that comes within that space. The distances can vary from just a few millimeters for barnacles on a rock to several miles for a herd of buffalo (McFarland, 1981). It is even true that, if an apple is occupied by a worm, an intruder worm will hunt for another, empty apple (Andrewartha, 1961). Some gulls mark off a 25-yard-diameter space for themselves and migrate back to that same 25-yard circle each year, with the other birds respecting the "owners" of that area (Tinbergen, 1969).

Notice that your teacher has roughly 50 times more free space than you do and can walk around in it, because symbolically the teacher has greater authority. Note that, for the same reason, the principal has the largest office. It is intriguing that human territoriality can be "carried around" with us. This territoriality develops in us at about age 12 and is called our sense of **personal space** (Evans & Howard, 1973). Depending on

Territoriality
Attachment to a fixed amount of space set aside by and "belonging to" a member of a species.

Personal space
Human territoriality; amount of space we define as belonging to us.

how close you are (psychologically) to another person determines the exact distance you place yourself away from him or her. For someone you truly love, personal space can be close to zero most of the time. For a dreaded aunt, it can be a couple of yards, a space she always manages to violate when she hugs you during a visit. Males have a larger personal space than females. On the average, for strangers, our personal space is roughly two feet; if a stranger comes any closer, we feel very uncomfortable.

Try this one (but mix sexes so a fight doesn't break out!): Walk up to a stranger in the hallway and talk to him or her from about two feet away. As you do so, gradually move closer and closer. When you reach about a foot or so, the other person will begin backing away from you.

There are some "rules" of personal space that we don't fully understand. Here is an experiment to try: Use Figure 20.1. Go to the library at a time when it will not be completely full. Find an empty table near an entrance or doorway. Get to the table before anyone else. Then watch what happens. If you want to keep others who will sit at the same table as far away from you as possible, sit on an end chair and face away from the door. If you want the whole table all to yourself, sit in the middle chair, facing the entrance. As long as there is room in the library, you will be left alone (Sommer, 1969). In the latter case, the person facing the newcomer probably asserts dominance before the newcomer can get oriented; hence, the newcomer will stay away. As for the first case (people staying far away but at the same table), probably the first person there is entitled to the maximum amount of space, since he or she has established rights to that territory.

Summary

1. In attribution theory, we rely on what we already know, try to interpret and explain the present event, and then guide our beliefs and behavior by combining the two.

2. The emotions of love and like seem to start from a physical base. This base is typically related to how attractive the person seems to us. After that, closeness develops by a process of association of many events and actions with the other person, and the person is viewed in more ways than just the physical.

3. Aggression and violence may be natural to animals and humans when in dire physical need. But the evidence leans toward psychological causes for human violence in most cases. Some instances of violence develop from physical defects or allergies.

4. Despite what "common sense" seems to tell us, we do not have the evidence to demonstrate clearly that violence on television results in long-lasting imitation. Some people—those who are already aggressive—do seem to be negatively influenced by aggression they see on TV.

5. Whether or not we help other people in an emergency seems primarily related to the size of the group we are part of when the emergency arises.

6. Density and crowding can have a notable influence on behavior. Crowding is the more important psychological factor, since it represents how "closed in" we feel. Density is more a measure of the actual physical space the person has to work or live in.

7. Humans and animals have a sense of territoriality. Humans also have what is called personal space, which indicates the distance away from us that we desire people to stay when interacting with us.

Key Words and Concepts

attribution theory
antecedents
attribution
consequences
deindividuation
risky shift
    phenomenon
imitation learning
catharsis

diffusion of
    responsibility
evaluation
    apprehension
density
crowding
territoriality
personal space

Review Questions

Multiple Choice

1. According to the attribution theory, our opinions about others are influenced by:
   a. Our own motivations
   b. Our emotional responses
   c. Our beliefs
   d. All of the above.

2. An antecedent refers to the information we:
   a. Have before an event happens
   b. Receive while an event happens
   c. Conclude after an event happens
   d. Block out during all of the above.

3. Studies show that couples who stay together a long time are:
   a. More different than alike
   b. More alike than different
   c. Exactly the same
   d. None of the above.

4. The risky shift phenomenon suggests:
   a. That we will take fewer risks when in a group
   b. That we will take more risks when in a group
   c. That risk in a group is shifted to other group members
   d. None of the above
   e. Both b and c.

True/False

5. Studies show that we tend to form relationships with others who are at about the same level of attractiveness as we are.

6. Revealing personal information about ourselves is best done in small doses, especially at the beginning of a relationship.

7. Men tend to be more violent than women.

8. Deindividuation will lead to a stronger sense of personal identity.

9. People are more likely to be violent when they can justify that their violence is right.

10. Most people agree that exposure to violence on TV will have long-term effects on children.

11. Field studies clearly show that violence on TV causes real-life violence.

Multiple Choice

12. Which of the following is *not* a valid conclusion about TV and violence?
    a. The average person acquires no long-lasting violent tendencies after being exposed to violence on TV.
    b. Already aggressive people are most affected by violence on TV.
    c. Watching violence on TV will actually reduce the need to be violent in real life.
    d. None of the above—they are all valid conclusions.
    e. Both a and c.

13. Experiments on helping behavior tend to show:
    a. That people do not help because they do not care
    b. That people are more likely to help when there are a greater number of people around
    c. That some types of personalities are more likely to help than others
    d. None of the above.

14. The diffusion of responsibility theory suggests that, during an emergency, we:
    a. Assume less responsibility
    b. Assume more responsibility
    c. Assume others will be responsible
    d. Do none of the above
    e. Do both a and c.

Fill in the blank. Answer on a separate sheet of paper. (More than one word can be used.)

15. The feeling of being closed in is called _____ .

16. If there are three fans at a football game we can assume that the _____ is low.

17. Worrying about what others expect during an emergency is called _____ .

18. If we stand so close to someone that we can count his or her cavities, we would probably be violating that person's _____ .

19. Animals who have a strong sense of _____ will attack others who attempt to take their "space."

Discussion Questions

1. A nonhuman but intelligent being captures you and explains that the only way it will set you free is if you adequately define the concept of *love*. Define it.

2. Some people argue that love is a subject that should not be scrutinized under a microscope by psychologists. Do you tend to agree or disagree with this? Explain.

3. Imagine a high school where there was a real possibility for violence on a daily basis. You can probably assume that a certain amount of deindividuation exists at the school. Give several possible reasons for this deindividuation. For example, you might say, "The school is probably very large." Then describe several ways in which you might decrease this deindividuation.

4. As made clear in the chapter, psychologists have accumulated a great deal of information about why people help or do not help others. What should we do now with this information in order to increase helping behavior in our society? Explain. *Or* do you believe that nothing *can* be done to increase helping behavior? Explain.

5. How might diffusion of responsibility occur within a typical family situation? Describe several examples.

6. The chapter explains that evaluation apprehension during an emergency decreases the likelihood of someone helping. In what ways could evaluation apprehension help to *create* emergencies? Also, offer several real examples of emergencies perhaps caused by evaluation apprehension. For example, one could argue that those who saw problems with the space shuttle before it exploded did not voice their opinions loudly enough because of evaluation apprehension.

7. Describe a personal experience where density was low but crowding was high, and describe an experience where density was high but crowding low. Be specific.

Activities

1. Conduct an experiment to determine the role of antecedents in people's judgments. What you will do is to supply the antecedents and then measure "attributions" and "consequences." Write the following on an index card:

   "Read the description below and answer the two questions beneath it.

Melissa Weeber is 28 years old. She has been a high school counselor for six years. She enjoys the job, but feels that her role has been reduced simply to scheduling students for classes. She now wants to become a marriage counselor. When asked to describe her, her students commonly use the following adjectives: caring, dependable, and hardworking.

How would you rate this person's chances of becoming an effective marriage counselor?

1	2	3	4	5	6	7	8	9
EXTREMELY LOW	VERY LOW	LOW	BELOW AVERAGE	AVERAGE	ABOVE AVERAGE	HIGH	VERY HIGH	EXCELLENT

If you were responsible for hiring this person as a marriage counselor, what would be the likelihood that you would hire her?

1	2	3	4	5
VERY LOW	LOW	AVERAGE	HIGH	VERY HIGH

Write down the same information on another index card, but this time replace the adjective "caring" with "efficient." Show the first card to 20 people; show the second card to 20 other people. Record their ratings.

Analyze your results. The first question measures attribution; the second measures consequences. Were the subjects' answers to the first question similar to their answers to the second question? What were the average ratings for both questions on the first card? On the second card? Discuss why you think you got the results that you did.

2. As mentioned in the chapter, attractive people are initially perceived as more competent than others. Conduct a simple experiment to test this assertion. *Procedure*: (1) Find a paragraph or poem that you had to write for one of your classes, or use a poem or paragraph from a book. Neatly copy the material onto an index card. (2) Sift through an *old* yearbook and cut out four pictures: an "attractive" male, an "attractive" female, an "unattractive" male, an "unattractive" female. Your choice of photos will be subjective, so maybe a few classmates can help you with your final decision. Also, remember that the pictures should be *old* so that your subjects will not recognize the people. (3) Write the following information on another index card:

"How would you rate this person's writing skills?"

1	2	3	4	5	6	7
AWFUL	POOR	BELOW AVERAGE	AVERAGE	ABOVE AVERAGE	GOOD	EXCELLENT

(4) Show the paragraph (or poem), *one* of the pictures, and the rating scale to 20 males and 20 females. Here's how: (a) 5 males and 5 females will see the attractive male; (b) 5 males and 5 females will see the unattractive male; (c) 5 males and 5 females will see the attractive female; (d) 5 males and 5 females will see the unattractive female.

Record your subjects' ratings on a separate data sheet and analyze your results. Were the attractive pictures rated higher? Were female subjects less influenced by attractiveness, as suggested in the chapter? Half the time, subjects saw pictures of the opposite sex; were these ratings higher than the others? Discuss why you think you got the results that you did. Also, make a chart summarizing all your results.

3. Collect several articles on jealousy and write a report. This time, write your report using the format of an advice columnist for a newspaper. For example, you can list several questions written by a jealous husband or wife and then you can assume the role of an advice columnist and answer the questions. The answers should be informative, and they should be primarily based on the articles you collected, but you can also include several "creative" responses. Be sure to make up a name for your column.

4. The chapter mentions that about 100 studies have been done on the effects of filmed violence on real-life violence. Find an article that describes in detail the findings of one or two of these studies and present a brief summary of these findings. Then, write a paper from the point of view of a parent who wants to persuade other parents to act or *not* act on these findings. Notice that you are trying to convince other parents to *act*, not just agree. So make your suggestions practical and specific. For example, you might propose that young children should not be allowed to watch television after 6:00 P.M. or that young children and parents should watch TV together. Again, be specific and support your proposals with information found in the article that you summarized.

5. In order to do this activity, you will need to do the previous one as well. This time, you will write a complete rebuttal to your proposal in number 4. This is a good exercise in persuasion, and it may force you to think about a side of the issue you hadn't considered.

6. Conduct an experiment on helping behavior. The procedure will be simple: Fall down, stay on the ground for about 15 seconds, holding your ankle the whole time. Do this in exactly the same way 20 times.

This time *you* will supply the hypothesis. For example, half the time you can fall in an environment familiar to your subjects; the other half the time, the environment will be unfamiliar. Look back through the chapter for other ideas, or think of an original hypothesis. Be sure to have your teacher approve your hypothesis.

Also, you should probably get a friend to help record responses. A few remarks about responses. Devise a data sheet that will outline the degree of help that your subjects offer. The following is one example: Level 1 = "completely ignored"; Level 2 = "stopped, but did not help"; Level 3 = "offered help"; Level 4 = "helped immediately." In addition to recording these levels, write down as much information as possible about each subject. This information will give you something on which to base your conclusions.

As always, analyze your results in detail and draw conclusions. You might consider videotaping this experiment and showing it to the class—perhaps your teacher will give you extra credit for this.

One final option: If you do not think you are bold enough to fall in front of strangers, consider testing helping behavior in another way—maybe through dropping money or a wallet—and see who helps. Be creative.

7. Conduct *one* of the two experiments described in the Application at the end of the chapter. For the first experiment, if you are not bold enough to talk to a stranger, simply *stand* close to the person and gradually move closer. Or go to a shopping mall and sit close to customers who are resting on benches outside the stores. In this case, all you will have to do is sit close and read a newspaper or a book and then progressively move closer. Do this to 16 different people, 8 males and 8 females, and record their specific reactions: (a) Did they ignore you completely? (b) Did they look at you, then look away? (c) Did they move slightly or turn away? (d) Did they get up? (e) Did they swear at you? Notice that these questions are measuring the *degree* of your influence. Your data sheet should reflect these kinds of degrees.

For the other experiment, you will need to spend a morning or an afternoon at the library in order to give others ample opportunity to react to you. While you are collecting data, you can be doing other homework as well.

Whichever experiment you choose to do, write a report afterward analyzing your results and describing your reactions in detail.

Members of a group gain strength and
resolve by having slogans and by
enlisting new members for support.

Chapter 21

Attitudes and Beliefs

Be able to:

1. Explain how a reference group influences attitudes.

2. Describe the usefulness of stereotypes.

3. Explain how prejudice can be reduced.

4. Explain how cognitive dissonance changes attitudes.

5. Explain how much one can rely on polygraphs.

6. Explain the techniques of "brainwashing."

Global Look at the Chapter

Although it may seem that we arrive at attitudes and beliefs on our own, closer examination shows that we form many of them based on the behavior and actions of others. This chapter looks at the origin of many of the thoughts and feelings that people have.

Attitudes

The groups people belong to clearly influence how they think, feel, and behave. For example, normally the school principal is set apart from other teachers, the teachers form their own group, and the students are a third group. The principal and possibly a vice-principal are often symbolically alone, and they behave and dress as they believe all principals do. Teachers normally do not dress as formally as the principal. Students follow their own dress code, which is designed to resemble that of the other two groups as little as possible. Dress, eating habits, patterns of speech, hobbies, entertainment—these are all partly the result of the group we belong to. The more important a particular group is to us and the longer we have associated with it, the stronger its hold on us will be. In other words, the more we identify with a group, the more we **internalize** (take as part of ourselves) the attitudes, beliefs, and uniform of that group.

Internalize
To take as part of ourselves the attitudes or beliefs of others.

Reference Groups

Reference group
A group with which one identifies and that provides standards of behavior.

A **reference group** is a group with which a person identifies and that provides standards of behavior. A person can have more than one reference group—for example, family, church, workplace, and school groups. Reference groups often provide for us a particular way of seeing things in the world, and, in fact, they can sometimes actually control *what* we see.

Here is an example of that in terms of cultural reference groups. An experimenter used what is called a *stereoscope*, which can show two separate pictures to a subject, a different one to each eye. Quickly flashed to one eye was a picture of a baseball player and to the other, at the same time, a bullfighter. Mexican subjects almost always saw only the bullfighter, while United States subjects saw only the baseball player, if the viewing time was kept short (Bagby, 1968). In another study without the stereoscope, experimenters showed subjects obviously satirical cartoons making fun of prejudice. Prejudiced subjects saw the cartoons as *supporting* their distorted and biased ideas (Cooper & Tahoda, 1964).

One of these graduates clearly seems to be taken over by his own reference group.

Fitting Attitudes to the Group

As we've said, people with whom we associate help form our attitudes. Many of our beliefs begin very early in the family and tend to remain firmly implanted. But, when new reference groups come along, they can change the earlier values. A study of college students demonstrated this power. A group of conservative students entered a liberal college where they formed new reference groups. By the time the students graduated, they were quite liberal in their outlook, except for the ones who did not form strong ties to a new group but stayed close to the family. Twenty-five years later, these two groups (both those who had changed and those who hadn't) had held onto their college attitudes, showing the staying power of group influences (Newcomb, 1963).

The Prisoner-Guard Experiment One of the most dramatic—and frightening—examples of reference-group influence occurred in an experiment that took place in the basement at Stanford University in the 1970s. A psychologist set up a mock prison, complete with cells, "security" doors, and drab surroundings. He then hired 24 male students for a "live-in" experiment. Twelve of them were *randomly* assigned to the role of guards, and 12 were assigned to be prisoners. Each group was then given the proper attire—guard uniforms or prisoner garb, thus increasing identification with their new reference groups through these symbols.

At that point, the experimenter left the two groups living on their own. He acted as "warden" but did not intervene in the situation. The result was a nightmare that no one expected. By the end of six days, the "guards" had become genuinely brutal and vicious toward the "prisoners," who in turn had become docile and bitter. The experiment had to be stopped because it literally was getting out of control.

Most of the young men never lost the memory of how they had acted, whether they were guards or prisoners, and a number temporarily suf-

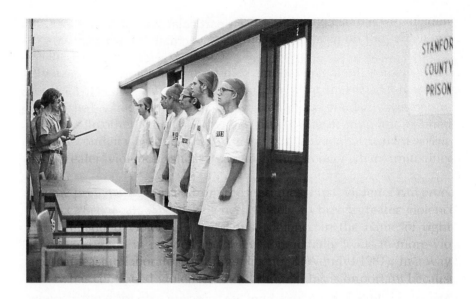

Photo from the actual "prison experiment" that turned so vicious.

fered emotional upset that had not been evident prior to the experiment. When there was an investigation, two consultants—a 16-year inmate of a real prison and a prison chaplain—commented on how closely the behavior of the students had come to resemble that of real prisoners and guards (Zimbardo, 1972).

How We View Others

We assume we judge others objectively, relying on their individual characteristics. But that generally is not the case.

Stereotypes

Stereotype
A fixed set of beliefs about a person or group that may or may not be accurate.

Stereotypes are printing plates used to reproduce printed material. When the word **stereotype** is used in the realm of human relations, it refers to one group's ability to turn out *identical* information about every member of another group. For instance, a group may believe that all members of group A sleep on the floor at night, or all people in group B have a bad character trait such as laziness. Stereotypes can become so broad and familiar that dozens of meanings are summarized by just one derogatory name; when using the name, all within hearing range are supposed to know the bad characteristics of the group being stereotyped.

The origin of stereotypes can be seen in studies in which subjects were given descriptions of a certain group of foreigners whom they never actually met. Most of the subjects preferred those people who were said to have characteristics similar to their own (Katz & Braley, 1958).

What purpose do stereotypes serve? They solidify the "in-group," thereby increasing that group's self-esteem by making the stereotyped group seem "worse" or inferior. Stereotypes also tend to ward off the possibility that different cultural ways will "take over" one's own group. In other words, the in-group wants things to stay the way they are; ridiculing the other group reduces that group's importance and influence.

Stereotypes can be very subtle. For example, group members do not pay as close attention to their own people as they do to outsiders. Thus, when evaluating job applicants, if the evaluator is female, far more attention is given to the small details (dress, speech, and so on) of a male applicant than of a female one; if the evaluator is white, then far more attention is given to the details of a black applicant. Such is not always negative, even though it may be unfair. For example, studies show that a white evaluator of black and white applicants with exactly the same credentials will rate the black higher. A female, rating two applicants, male and female, with the same credentials will rate the male higher. This probably results from the fact that, because of the careful scrutiny, the rater becomes more familiar with the "outsider" applicant and therefore more conscious of the fact that he or she fits the job qualifications (Linville & Jones, 1980).

"Doctor" and "Reverend" also generate stereotypes associated with those titles. Such titles are provided by society to assure the well-being of its members and to reassure them that they are in good hands.

What stereotypes do you form of this man?

Prejudice

Stereotypes are not, in and of themselves, bad. In fact, most evidence suggests that they cannot be avoided, since it is impossible for us to evaluate everything we see or hear on a case-by-case basis. If we think of a foreigner of a specific race, for instance, even though every single person looks different, we "take an average" so to speak and come up with a stereotype of what "those foreigners" look like. We do the same thing regarding what a teacher will look like, a mechanic, or a nurse. The nurse will be female and will always appear in white, even though many hospitals use different colored uniforms today, and many nurses are male.

We need a basis, then, for categorizing and analyzing our environment, and the stereotype helps us do this. The problem comes when stereotypes cause **prejudice**, a tendency in real life to treat people based on these general ideas rather than dealing with them based on what they are actually like individually.

Illusory Correlations   A stereotype will fight off incoming information that contradicts it. This is because we tend to form **illusory correlations** (il-LOOSE-uh-ree). That is, we see relationships that match our previously set beliefs, and we ignore others. Because these relationships match (correlate), we think we have seen the two together far more often than is really the case (illusion), thus making the stereotype even stronger. A simple experiment illustrates the principle: Subjects are shown several pairs of words an equal number of times; one of the pairs of words is *bacon-eggs*, a connection we already have. The number of times *bacon-eggs* appears is identical to that of other pairs that appear, but subjects think it has been seen far more frequently than it has. In the same way, if we have a stereotype that the fictitious "Slobvian" race is lazy, all we have to do to start the "bacon-egg" process is to see a couple of "Slobvians" on different occasions lying down under a tree instead of working. We will then be convinced they "all" act that way (Hamilton, 1979; Hamilton & Rose, 1980). Another example is that most males of a certain generation are convinced that females are bad drivers—at least compared to the males' incredible expertise! What happens to feed this illusory correlation is that the males store in their memories every incident in which they see a female doing something stupid in a car, all the while ignoring males who do the same thing or females who perform an excellent avoidance maneuver. Or, if these males do store positive events, they put them into the "chance happening" category.

Perception is clearly changed by these correlations. For instance, if you flash on a screen a picture of a well-dressed man holding a spoon while he stands on a subway train, adult viewers are puzzled because they see a spoon. But, if you show them a teenage male holding a spoon in the same situation, they more often than not see it as a knife.

Prejudice
A bias that leads to treating people unfairly, ignoring the real person involved.

Illusory correlations
Connections that seem very strong in one's mind but that don't really exist.

Overcoming Prejudice On the positive side, when students from a mixed-race class rate one another *individually* on personal characteristics, stereotypes do not show up, not even across social class or race (Sagar & Schofield, 1980). This suggests that stereotypes can exist for a group even though an individual member is viewed differently. Again on the positive side, the longer one lives around a different culture, the more the original negative beliefs toward that culture begin to fade (Smith et al., 1980).

In the same vein, the odds that someone will help another across races is affected by whether the helping behavior is face to face or "remote"; that is, in the latter case, the potential helper and helpee are not physically within one another's view. In face-to-face studies, experimenters set up a situation in which a black or a white man dropped a grocery bag at a market. There was no difference in helping regardless of the race of the helper or of the individual helped. The result was the same if a black or white man with a cane fell down in a subway car. But a difference does show up in the "remote" setup because illusory correlations are in control with no "real person" present—just a stereotype. In one study, different college applications *with pictures* were left in a phone booth at an airport, with a stamped, addressed envelope and a note to "Dad" to please mail (hence, "Dad" must have dropped it on the way to his plane). As compared with the face-to-face arrangement, the response was different. Those applications with an opposite-race picture were mailed less often (Lerner & Frank, 1974). So, even though prejudice is still around, the face-to-face type is decreasing noticeably (Crosby et al., 1980).

Prejudice can be reduced. For example, groups "at war" with one another, as in a sports competition, feel strongly toward their own group and "hate" the other group. In one experiment, when a truck taking two opposing teams back to town from a game broke down (courtesy of the experimenter), the two groups had to cooperate and thus became one group working toward a common goal. The rivalry disappeared (Sherif, 1982). If students in racially tense classes are given projects requiring every group member's help to complete them, racial barriers also go down (Aaronson, 1972).

Scapegoats

If things go wrong at school or at home, most of us tend to blame someone else. Even if we are fairly open-minded, we are likely to say, "Yes, it was partly my fault, but *he* (or *she*) was mostly responsible—at least, *he* (or *she*) started it," or some variation on this theme. Psychologically, we retain balance—keep ourselves safe—by not taking the full blame.

The same mechanism works with groups; others are blamed for whatever goes wrong. Prejudice is built on this process, called **scapegoating**, in which group A blames group B for its ills. The word *scapegoat* comes

Scapegoating
Blaming someone else for one's own problem.

The really bad side of group behavior: Looking for a scapegoat.

from the biblical reference to a sacrificial goal on which sins were symbolically laid before it was killed as an offering. A blatant example of scapegoating was the Nazi movement of the 1930s, which managed to incite people to the point of mass murder. Germany had been plunged into despair; in 1933, millions of Germans were unemployed. Adolf Hitler, a scrawny man who had been rejected by the army, came up with just the right formula: "We are the result of the stress *for which others [the Jews] are responsible,*" he shouted (Bullock, 1953). Things got so far out of control that eventually a group of 80,000 "technicians" (experts at efficient murder) exterminated approximately 6 million Jews. Assembly lines were set up in the camps, and each worker was assigned a gruesome specific task. One removed the clothing; another formed victims into lines; some took out gold fillings to get money for the Nazi cause; others worked on methods for increasing the heat to burn the bodies that were piling up. All of this resulted from Germany identifying a scapegoat to blame for its ills.

Removing Deviates

In less dramatic but still serious cases, group members will try to "drive out the demons" by ejecting those whom they feel threaten the group's integrity. In other words, they try to remove anyone who might make the group look different from the desired image. A group may also be threatened by the prospect of including people who compromise its goals or ideals. In group workshops, for example, where people explore ways to improve their lives, their business conditions, and so forth, the group will on occasion turn against "masculine" women who express anger or against "feminine" men who express supposedly nonmasculine emotions (Kahn, 1980). This behavior becomes quite cruel at school or in the workplace when someone is "boycotted" or kept out of a group because of certain characteristics that the group doesn't like, such as manner of speech, body size, appearance, or a physical defect.

Changing Attitudes

We join groups that believe the same things we do, and thus we strengthen our ideas by associating with those who agree with us. The more we think and talk about things that everybody around us agrees with, the more extreme our beliefs can become. Thus, people with strong opinions on, say, gun control typically join an official group and become even more fanatical in their positions. The more frequent the contact with the group, the greater the emotional investment, and the harder it is to alter one's opinion (Tesser, 1978).

How, then, do attitudes change? We have already seen the influence of new reference groups. The subjects in the prison experiment discussed earlier had no idea that they would adopt the attitudes they eventually did. So, playing a role, such as a guard, can be a powerful agent in attitude change. There is more than a grain of truth in the old saying that you will understand people better after you have walked a mile in their shoes. None of us can be certain how we will respond to certain circumstances until they occur.

Cognitive Dissonance

If we find that our beliefs (cognitions) are contradictory (dissonant), it makes us uncomfortable and puts us in a state called **cognitive dissonance** (DIS-o-nance) (Festinger, 1957). Suppose you fall madly in love with someone who later tells you that you are stupid and a bore. Since you can't reconcile the love and the insults, you are in a state of cognitive dissonance. (Cognitive dissonance, then, creates an imbalance of beliefs.) You must do something to relieve the discomfort this causes; you must find some way to justify what happened since it is not in harmony with what you feel about yourself or about the other person. Since you cannot change what happened, you change your beliefs, thus providing a justification and saving face. After the initial hurt, you will probably decide that your "loved one" wasn't that great a bargain after all.

Many experiments demonstrate cognitive dissonance in operation. For instance, psychologists have measured people's attitudes on a par-

Cognitive dissonance
A contradiction between actions or events and beliefs, which must be reconciled or justified.

Photographs taken during Asch's experiment on conformity. In the top photograph, Subject 6 (sixth person from left) listens to the others express identical (but wrong) answers that differ from his own. He has to make a choice: does he express the judgement he knows to be correct and risk being different from the group, or does he conform to the group's judgement? In the next two photos, Subject 6 shows the strain of being in repeated disagreement with the group, but he did stand by his own opinion, saying that "he has to call them as he sees them."

ticular subject and then had them take the *opposite* position by giving speeches and writing essays to get others to believe that point of view. Just completing this exercise has some effect. But, if the subjects were then led to believe that their arguments were successful and had changed other people's minds on the subject, the subjects became very uncomfortable indeed, especially if they knew the people they had affected. As a result, their own attitudes shifted in the direction of what they had been preaching (Cialdini et al., 1981).

Yielding to Others

Group pressure toward conformity can be very hard to fight off. In a classic experiment, subjects were asked to judge the length of different lines drawn on a piece of cardboard. Subjects were formed into groups, but only one member of each group was not "in" on the experiment. All the other members worked for the experimenter and had the task of exaggerating the length of the line shown to the group. The goal was to put pressure on the one subject to see whether or not he or she would yield and go along with a ridiculous claim that the line was much longer than it really was. So, it was a study on how much people will conform to pressure from those around them. Roughly 25 percent of the subjects consistently buckled under and agreed that the line was much longer than it really was. About the same proportion held on to their beliefs that the line was shorter than the group claimed, despite the pressure from the others to agree. The remaining subjects went back and forth in their judgments. This study showed just how strong is the need that most people have to "go along with the crowd."

Using basically the same experimental setup, researchers had just one of the stooges go over to the subject's side and agree that the line was shorter than everybody else said. With only one stooge on the person's side, what had been unanimous group pressure disappeared, and the subject's agreement with the exaggerated length of the line declined dramatically (Asch, 1952).

Compliance with Authority

Unquestioning obedience can be very dangerous. In a now-famous laboratory experiment, the subjects, young adults, were told that they were to be part of a "learning experiment." The task was simple. On the other side of a screen from the subject sat a person who was a "learner." Each time this person (a confederate of the experimenter, but the subject didn't know this) made an error, the subject's task was to increase progressively a shock going to the learner by turning a dial marked off in voltages. The dial was labeled from "mild shock" through "danger" all the

way to a setting of 450 volts. The final point was marked in red, suggesting that it might trigger a fatal charge of electricity. Even when the stooges cried out "in pain" (they were not really receiving shocks), many subjects obediently continued to give the erring "trainees" seemingly agonizing shocks.

In fact, a full 65 percent of the subjects obeyed instructions to give severe shocks as a penalty for failure to answer questions properly. Interviews after the experiment indicated that the subjects were genuinely concerned that they might be injuring the people (Milgram, 1971). Incidentally, there was no difference between male versus female behavior in this experiment.

Sometimes people are skeptical, thinking that the subjects had somehow caught on to the experiment and would not do this in "real life." But, in an identical experiment, with puppies right in view, subjects were willing to shock them at the command of the researcher as a "training" device. The shocks did cause the puppies to yelp and squirm uncomfortably, but the shocks were not great (again unknown to the subjects). As in the other experiment, the subjects had a dial in front of them that indicated increasing voltages (Sheridan & King, 1972).

Psychologist **Stanley Milgram** (1977), who pioneered these studies, was very distressed at how things turned out. He decided to try the experiment using direct physical contact with the victim, figuring *that* would make a difference. But the victim crying out, pleading heart trouble—nothing—seemed to stem the blind obedience of most subjects to go ahead with the punishment and torture on command. Naturally, at that point, Milgram began to worry about the "kind of character produced in American democratic society that can't be counted on to insulate its citizens from brutality." He said this after he found that subjects ordered to force the victim's hand onto a shock plate supposedly containing 150 volts were willing to drag the person over to it and place the hand on the plate. In one case, the subjects were dealing with a screaming 50-year-old man.

We are faced here with a frightening amount of obedience to authority. In fact, one experiment shows that it is possible to get these kinds of results using a telephone, so the "authority" is not even present in the room. This study was set up at a real hospital, and 22 nurses were *telephoned* by a "physician" unknown to them. They were told to administer a drug to a patient while the physician was en route to the hospital, so the drug would have started taking effect by the time he got there. The experimenters used the name of a fictitious drug and had already placed the bottle, clearly labeled with a maximum dosage in the nursing station drug locker. On the phone, the "physician" prescribed an administration of *double* the safe dosage. Twenty-one of the 22 nurses had to be stopped by the experimenters as they left the nurses' station, medicine in hand to give it to the patient as ordered (Hofling et al., 1966).

Is there any saving grace in this mess? A little, at least in terms of learning a lesson. As two social psychologists have summarized, the key to a lot of this destructive obedience may lie in the fact that people are often not given full responsibility for their own actions. When subjects are told that they are in charge and must account for what happens, obedience to these outlandish commands drops dramatically (Worchel & Cooper, 1983).

The machine and procedure used in the studies of obedience. Note in the photo at right that the man at the controls is forcefully holding down the arm of the "learner" who is screaming in agony. (Copyright © 1965 by Stanley Milgram. From the film OBEDIENCE, distributed by the New York University Film Division and the Pennsylvania State University, PCR.

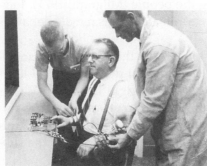

Verbal Persuasion

Verbal persuasion is all around us. It runs the gamut from a radio commercial to a defense attorney's plea to a jury. Persuasion by itself is neither good nor bad; each of us tries to convince others of our point of view. While none of us is totally immune to the effects of persuasion, how resistant we are to an appeal depends on a number of factors.

Defenses Against Persuasion

Psychologists have studied techniques for fighting off persuasion, called **immunization**. Can a subject be immunized against propaganda as if it were the measles? Results are inconsistent, but a few points do stand out. For one thing, a two-sided argument in which opposing viewpoints are stated and compared seems to be a more effective immunizer than merely giving the person a one-sided lecture. This technique helps prepare the listener before he or she hears the opposite point of view from the actual "persuader," so the propaganda loses some of its punch (McGuire, 1964). In the same way, lawyers gain an advantage by presenting some of the opponent's views in watered-down form or in a way that makes those views seem insignificant. Doing this unconsciously impresses judges and juries since the lawyer seems more "open" about the issues, less biased. As a result, when the opposing attorney gets up, everyone has "already heard that argument"—only they got it from the first attorney who probably slipped in his or her own bias (Cialdini et al., 1981).

A second point is that passively reading arguments is not as effective as having to work out one's own case against something. Actively working on arguments about things like nuclear disarmament or capital punishment results in our becoming more certain of the side we are taking, since we begin to think that this was our view all along (Eagly & Himmelfarb, 1978). Of some interest, if we hear a counterargument before this new argument is all the way settled in the brain, we tend to return to our original beliefs (Rogers & Thistlethwaite, 1969). As you can see, people *gradually* change beliefs so that their beliefs match what they are saying but it requires work on their part.

Thus, immunization works to some extent. Complete resistance to new points of view is impossible and a fiction. Nonetheless, long-standing beliefs can be very resistant to change.

Effect of Having an Expert

As a general rule, we are more likely to listen to a genuine expert on a subject (or one who seems to be!) than to an appealing but relatively unknowledgeable person. Advertisers should pay more attention to this

Immunization
An attempt to train a person beforehand to resist persuasion or propaganda.

fact, given their tendency to use movie or television personalities in ad campaigns. If a tennis star is advertising sports equipment, it works reasonably well, but having the same person push efficient soapsuds is a different matter, since the viewer knows full well that stars rarely do their own laundry.

In many cases, it doesn't make as much difference *what* the person is saying in a commercial or a persuasive argument as *how* it is said. If you make up lots of "impressive" statistics and claims, the true facts of the situation may be hidden and might not play a role in the opinion the listener forms.

Consciously or unconsciously, realistically or not, we are always evaluating the source of our information before we act on it. If we feel it is reliable, we tend to agree; if not, we don't. Consider the following experiment: Trying to determine the influence of source credibility on saving energy, experimenters sent out two batches of identical "Consumer Energy-Saving Tips." One was sent from the electric company and the other from a "public service group." Those who received the utility's letter did not cut their energy use, while those who thought it was from the service group reduced their use by 7 percent (Stern, 1984).

Social Persuasion: The Polygraph

Polygraph
A lie detector.

The lie detector or **polygraph** is an instrument that measures changes in heart rate, breathing, blood pressure, and perspiration. Hence, it is given the name *poly* (many) *graph*(s) because the machine prints out on paper the changes in these bodily responses. The polygraph does *not* determine whether or not a person is lying. There is no way it can do this. It is simply a record of physical changes that require interpretation. Therein lies the problem. In theory, a guilty person will show changes in all these physical responses, but there is no evidence that everyone does, and considerable evidence that some do not while others do so just because they are afraid.

The earliest form of "lie detector" used the fact that, when people are anxious, their mouths get very dry. So, potentially guilty people were lined up and told to swallow rice. Those with dry mouths would be unable to do so. As a result, many confessed and many more were deemed guilty. You will find that, although today's polygraph doesn't claim as many innocent people are guilty as the rice method did, it also has to rely very heavily on the power of suggestion.

Social Basis of the Lie Detector

The significance of the polygraph for our purposes here is that it is a social instrument. We all learn from an early age that it is best to confess to a parent what horrible thing we did and get it over with. Society as a whole encourages confession, and we come to believe that this is the only way we can live with ourselves—by "getting it off our chests."

The polygraph, being but a machine, is a double-edged sword. If one has a strong conscience, then guilt will cause an easily measurable physical change, even though these can get mixed up with changes from other causes. So, from the outset, the instrument presents problems because it doesn't measure all people the same. And there are people who can deliberately distort the results (Dean et al., 1968).

More important than the polygraph itself is the fact that it can lead to confession. Because of social pressure, confession offers an active and symbolic way to relieve guilt and to tell others that we will change in the future. In many cases, its accuracy is not the key to the types of results obtained, but social conscience is. Still, its accuracy is quite important, and highly questionable.

Accuracy of the Polygraph

The accuracy of the lie detector is argued back and forth for two additional reasons. First, subjects are able to change the results from the truth. In one study, they altered polygraph results from 75 percent accuracy to 10 percent just by tensing and thinking about their big toes (Honts et al., 1985). And blood pressure measures can be far off. In one study, the machine indicated that blood pressure was increasing (which would indicate guilt) when in fact it was decreasing (Geddes & Newberg, 1977). Second, the skills of the test administrator vary widely. In one study, the test giver caught only 14 of 76 lies, while another one found 63 out of 76 (Moroney & Zenhausern, 1972). It seems fair to say that the lie detector is, on the average, reliable only 70 percent of the time. The number of innocent people who might be convicted and the "bad" ones who might be missed at such a rate is staggering and makes use of the polygraph unethical (Lykken, 1981). Without a confession, one has to be *very* skeptical about results indicating guilt, since we are dealing with people's lives and welfare (Katkin, 1985).

Social Persuasion: Brainwashing

In war and terrorist activity, it is not unusual for a captive to "confess" to something that is untrue or even to defect to the "enemy." This is commonly called "brainwashing." Why this happens is very complex, but we do have clues that might help explain it.

Friendliness

Having a common enemy usually unites a group of prisoners around the prisoners' own ideals and goals. In World War II, torture was common in prison camps, thus bringing the prisoners closer together. In such situations, they did a good job of resisting exposing secrets or confessing. But in the Korean and Vietnam wars, prisoners dealt with a new situation: captors who at times were unusually friendly. This approach was unexpected and, as a result, caused prisoners confusion about resisting the enemy (Lifton, 1961). It was a calculated technique that weakened the prisoners' resolve to resist.

Sensory deprivation
A kind of torture that consists of removing all external sensations from the victim.

Sensory Deprivation

Other prisoner-of-war incidents have called attention to a phenomenon called **sensory deprivation**, a severe type of punishment that involves no physical torture, as such, but that deprives the person of the use of his or her senses. Sensory deprivation is accomplished by using gloves, earmuffs, and a blindfold, in some cases suspending the person in water set at body temperature. Because our bodies require stimulation, this treatment becomes intolerable very quickly.

Many a cocky college student have been taken down a peg or two by this procedure. In one study, students were asked to volunteer for a sensory-deprivation experiment in which they had to do absolutely nothing but wear some of the equipment mentioned above. They were paid the equivalent of $100 a day. Despite this, only the stoutest students could last a full three days. Deprivation induces a fear rather like that of being lost in a vast wasteland without a sight or sound around. Because there is no stimulation, the brain begins to call on its own inner resources to make things up. For instance, visual hallucinations—seeing things that are not there—are common (Heinemann, 1970). Thought confusion, worry, disorientation, regret, and panic are common symptoms (Zubek et al., 1971).

Blindfolded students who were wearing gloves and earmuffs and whose arms were wrapped and feet covered, were placed in an isolation chamber. This kind of sensory deprivation becomes intolerable for anyone after roughly three days maximum. Human beings cannot remain oriented without some sort of stimulation, and without it we will begin to see and hear things that are not really present.

One has to assume that the students' symptoms were moderate, since they knew they could quit at any time. Prisoners are left in a state of deprivation until they agree to whatever the captors want. As far as we know, everyone gives in to this psychological pressure.

You will hear about a "therapy" using isolation chambers. People lie in a capsule of water and meditate. This has helped some get more in touch with themselves, but it is completely voluntary, relatively brief, and not externally controlled. Hence, there is no comparison with psychological torture (Kammerman, 1977).

Reward System

Difficult to fight is a reward system in which prisoners are given, say, extra food for providing basically useless information about others. This technique is clever because, once a person has given in a little, each similar behavior is a bit easier to obtain. Along the same line, minor (but useful) confessions may be elicited for a reward (Schein et al., 1961). Larger confessions soon follow. Probably the most destructive aspect of this method is that it undermines the prisoners' group structure. Every person walking around with extra food is immediately suspected by the other prisoners, and they don't know exactly who is giving significant information to the enemy and to what extent. The same basic approach is often used by the police, and it rarely fails. They bring in two suspects who were working on a "job" together. They question each one separately. Neither knows what the other said, but the police officers make one of them think that the game is up by being very friendly, suggesting that a confession has already been obtained from the other suspect (Nizer, 1966).

Brainwashing and the Consumer

Brainwashing and other forms of control are often based on the principle of compliance with a small request, followed by a reward, followed by a larger request. This same system is used by advertisers who enter you in a contest if you simply write down the name of their product or send in a box top. Having gotten you to do one small act, they assume that you will probably engage in the larger behavior of buying their product.

Studies have been fairly consistent in showing that such small requests are a good method for getting people to comply with larger ones. In one study of such techniques, women were called on the phone and asked to answer a few questions about some household product such as soap. A few days later, the same women were called and asked if the experimenter could bring *five men* and take a two-hour inventory of the products in the home. Having given in to the small request, 52 percent of the women agreed to the larger request. To see if the first request had made a difference, another group was given only the large request. Only 22 percent of them agreed to allow the inventory (Freedman & Fraser, 1966). While there is a difference between giving in on soap and other products versus a major issue, the principle is fairly sound.

Finally, despite the commotion we hear on occasion about thought control and such, rarely does a person change deep-seated opinions. While we may be willing to "change" our beliefs for a short while, when the pressure is over, lifelong philosophies reappear.

Winning Over Attitudes and Beliefs

Getting a job involves a direct confrontation of the values, attitudes, and beliefs held by two different generations. The interviewer, unfortunately, is prejudiced and has a stereotype of you—sight unseen. It is a form of psychological war in which, more often than not, you have to "lose" for the moment in order to gain over a longer period of time. There are some tried-and-true psychological principles and details that deserve consideration. It may well sound like we are dictating what you must do. That's not our purpose. Sometimes to win you have to swallow your pride. None of the suggestions presented here should compromise your integrity; they are only nuisances that will eventually put you on top. Follow these ideas for a job interview, and you increase your odds of success dramatically.

1. There are important rules about eye contact. *Never* look down at the floor. In "body language," this indicates complete submission, guilt, and weakness. When someone is talking to you, look directly at them. If you are talking for a long time, look away for a brief period, but return your eyes again. When you are talking to the other person, look at them only for brief periods because the other person will be watching you. The goal here is to avoid the threat of continuous eye contact, which can be distressing, so most people automatically follow these rules.

2. Do not ever say "yeah," "sure," "okay," or "right." While these sound acceptable when with friends, to others they sound terrible and may, in and of themselves, be enough for you to lose the job. Don't kowtow or be too subservient, but saying "Mr. ____" or "Ms. ____" (Mrs.) on occasion sounds awfully nice.

3. Rules for clothing, males: Find the most boring thing you own and have it cleaned and pressed. Use solid colors—not too bright. Wear only regular shoes—no tennis shoes, boots, or sandals. Check your fingernails for cleanliness just before going in for the interview. Females: You should always wear a skirt. The more you accentuate your "good looks," the *less* the chances you have of getting the job. Watch out for too much makeup or eye shadow. Both male and female interviewers are highly prejudiced against a "flashy" woman because she is threatening to both. She is competition for the female, and males still believe the stereotype that the better-looking you are, the dumber. So, look reasonably plain, but attractive.

4. Look up something about the company with the help of your librarian and ask a few sensible questions during the interview so you appear interested in the company. Try also to ask a question or two about something that the interviewer tells you about the company—again to show interest.

5. Be sure to nod occasionally so you seem interested. But watch out for the "nodding-dog-on-a-spring" effect.

6. Write down beforehand the skills you have developed, no matter how trivial they might seem. Try to cover everything you have done. Then, if the issue of a certain skill comes up and you have done something using a similar skill sometime in the past, be prepared to say, "I had some related experience when I . . ."

7. Regarding apprehension and anxiety, both of which are natural: There is a useful, workable "trick" that psychologists suggest for clients who panic when they have to face other people. It sounds silly, but it really will help. Visualize the interviewer in underpants or some other awkward situation. This will make him or her seem more like a plain old human rather than some great authority figure, and it will help you feel more equal and less threatened by that person.

8. You must rehearse these things for a few days beforehand with a friend or parent. They are not natural and must be learned.

Summary

1. We identify with a reference group that helps form and continues to support a set of beliefs that we have internalized.

2. People form stereotypes because they bring organization to our world. They are not bad in and of themselves but can lead to prejudice. Once prejudice starts, it is kept going via illusory correlations. Scapegoats are people who are not responsible for but are blamed for our own problems.

3. Many of our attitudes are changed because cognitive dissonance causes us to feel uncomfortable, so we realign our beliefs. We also will often yield to pressure from others without even knowing it. Obedience studies show that any of us might yield too much to the pressure of authority.

4. The polygraph only measures physical changes. It can be accurate, but typically it misses on too many people to be a legitimate instrument. It is most effective as a social instrument in which it pressures the person into confessing.

5. Brainwashing is not a technique that normally has lasting effects. To change opinions for a limited time, friendliness and sensory deprivation are the most effective methods.

Key Words and Concepts

internalize
reference group
stereotype
prejudice
illusory correlations
scapegoating

cognitive dissonance
Stanley Milgram
immunization
polygraph
sensory deprivation

Review Questions

Fill in the blank. Answer on a separate sheet of paper. (More than one word can be used.)

1. The statement, "All Slobvians are lazy," is an example of a _____ .

2. Treating all members of an ethnic group the same way is a sign of _____ .

3. When we _____ a group's beliefs, we adopt them as our own.

4. We often perceive the world differently because of the various _____ with which we identify.

5. If we blame tall people for indirectly raising clothing prices, tall people then are _____ .

6. When we use _____ , we only see in others what we want to see and ignore other information.

7. Two-sided arguments often lead to _____ .

8. Contradictory beliefs lead to _____ .

True/False

9. Stereotypes often lead to prejudice.

10. Illusory correlations tend to weaken stereotypes.

11. Recent studies indicate that face-to-face prejudice seems to be decreasing.

12. When faced with cognitive dissonance, most people will change their beliefs.

13. Milgram's subjects delivered "high" voltages of shock because they suspected that no one was actually getting hurt.

14. Someone who will be held responsible for his or her actions is less likely to obey an authority.

15. A polygraph measures how often a person lies.

16. Without external stimulation, the brain creates its own stimulation.

Discussion Questions

1. Describe two of your most important reference groups. Discuss several similarities and differences between these two groups. Overall, are there more similarities or differences? Explain.

2. List several stereotypes of teachers and discuss (without using names) whether your teachers this year fit these stereotypes.

3. If you were dating someone for several months and then found out that this person was extremely prejudiced against a certain ethnic group, do you think you

might eventually stop dating this person for this reason? Yes? No? Depends? Explain.

4. Compare some of the attitudes you have today with those you had when you were in junior high school. Have they remained basically the same? If yes, do you *express* them differently? Explain. If your attitudes have changed, in what ways? Explain.

5. While Milgram's obedience studies are fascinating, they also put the subjects involved under a great deal of stress at times. Experimenters always need to strike a balance between *how* they get their results and *what* they find out. Some might argue that Milgram's studies do not achieve this balance, that it is not ethical to put subjects under this great stress, regardless of what is learned. Do you agree? Why or why not? Explain.

6. How do advertisers establish credibility for their products? Describe several real advertising examples to support your answer.

7. As noted in the chapter, sensory deprivation may cause hallucinations. What kinds of occupations would be most affected by this problem? Explain. Keep in mind that not all the senses need to be deprived at one time to cause problems.

8. One of the suggestions listed at the end of the chapter was to write a list of job skills that you have developed. You may not have an interview soon, but this will be good practice. So, go ahead and write down your skills now.

Activities

1. Pick two people who have helped to shape your attitudes and beliefs, and write a letter of appreciation to each of them. Be specific as to the kinds of things that the person did or said and what effect these things have had on your past and present values and beliefs. Something unexpected usually happens after writing these kinds of letters: You not only feel better about the people to whom you are writing but you also tend to feel better about yourself! No one will force you to do this, but once you receive credit for the letters from your teacher, why don't you mail them and spread some of the positive feelings you experience to others?

2. Conduct the illusory correlation (or "bacon-egg") experiment described near the beginning of the chapter. Think of five familiar word pairs: bacon-eggs, lion-roar, and so on. Think of five unfamiliar word pairs: night-fork, gamble-bed, and so on. Write *each* of these ten word pairs, both familiar and unfamiliar, onto five separate index cards. In other words, five cards will say "bacon-eggs," five will say "lion-roar," and so on. You will have a total of 50 index cards.

Procedure: Mix up the cards and hand them to your first subject. (*Note*: Do *not* mix them blindly as you would with playing cards; make sure the same word pair does not appear two times in a row.) The subject will look at the first card for three seconds (yes, time it), and then you will announce, "Next." The subject will then put the card face down onto the table or desk and look at the next card. Continue doing this until all the cards are used. Then have a separate sheet of paper with all the word pairs listed and ask the subject how many times the word pair appeared on the cards. This list should mix the familiar and unfamiliar word pairs evenly: Word pair number 1 would be familiar, number 2 would be unfamiliar, and so on. Record the subject's answers. Repeat this entire procedure on 20 subjects.

Of course, analyze your results in detail. By this point in the text, you should be an expert at this!

3. Do some research on extreme kinds of reference groups: cults. Find out: (a) the broad definition of a cult; (b) *how* new cult members internalize the beliefs and attitudes of the cult; (c) what the established members of the cult do to promote this internalization process; (d) why people join cults; (e) how and why people leave cults. Organize this information into a report and include your reactions.

You will probably acquire your information from books or magazines, but at least consider another source: a police station. Often there will be someone there who, through necessity, has become a sort of expert on the topic.

4. The chapter mentions that advertisers often use celebrities to promote products about which they probably know little. In other words, these ads do not seem highly credible. Flip through several magazines and find a bunch of ads that *do* strike you as credible for one reason or another, and also find ads that do *not* strike you as credible. Organize these ads into a creative collage. Be sure that the collage somehow presents the message about credibility versus incredibility. Perhaps you can do this by including appropriate captions. For example: "Would this man do his own laundry?" Once the collage is completed, display it in class.

5. Visit a local police station and interview someone there about interrogation techniques. If you have a police consultant at school, he or she may be able to help you or at least tell you whom to contact. You have probably seen enough TV shows and movies about the police to help you with your questions. Also, find out particularly about the polygraph. What exactly does it measure? How often is it used? How can one fool it? Why might one polygraph technician catch more lies than another? Write a report of your visit and include your specific reactions.

6. There are several valuable suggestions about job interviews listed at the end of the chapter. If you've already gone to an interview or two, these suggestions probably seem meaningful. If not, the suggestions will one day become meaningful—trust us. What we want you to do *now*, mainly so you will hear these kinds of suggestions from more than one source, is contact a personnel director or someone who does a lot of hiring and conduct an interview. It will be a nice switch for a personnel director to *answer* questions. Find out what kinds of qualities, behaviors, and clothes leave the best impression on a personnel director. Since this information will someday be of practical importance to everyone in your class, we don't want you to write a written report; instead, present what you have learned to the class in a five-minute informal speech. Be sure to practice what you preach when you *deliver* your speech: eye contact, language, and so on.

Statistical Measures: Reporting Experimental Findings

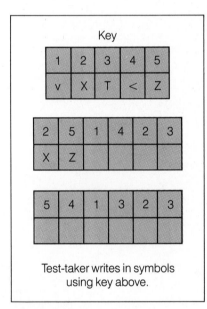

Key

Figure A.1
Digit-symbol task

Statistics are nothing more than a kind of shorthand, a way to collapse large groups of numbers into one or two, so comparisons can be made easily. **Statistics**, then, include any numerical process used to group, assemble, organize, or analyze information.

Graphical Analysis

In some studies, the experimenter has varied the instructions on a particular task in order to vary the amount of pressure put on the individual who has been asked to solve a problem. As pressure to solve the problem increases, anxiety increases, and, with high anxiety, efficiency decreases drastically.

One study shows the effect of anxiety on test performance. Discussing the results will show how graphs work and how they help to clarify the findings of a psychological study.

One experimenter administered a questionnaire to a large group of students (Sarason et al., 1952). From the information he obtained through the questionnaire about their feelings and responses to test situations, he was able to pick out two smaller groups. One group was what might be called "high-anxious"—or, in everyday terminology, high-strung, prone to nervousness, or quite jumpy in a tight situation. The other group was low on the anxiety rating, meaning these people were calm, not nervous or jumpy under pressure. The two groups were given a test in which each subject worked individually on the task of matching various symbols with numbers. The experimenter used a key that showed the subject a series of figures that were already numbered (see Figure A.1). The test was too long to be completed in the time allotted, yet the subjects were given the instructions that they were "expected to finish."

The subjects were given five chances to succeed at the task. In other words, they took the test five times in succession. In psychological terminology, these five chances are called five **trials**.

Here is a report of the results: The scores varied from 27 through 43 for the five trials for each of the groups. The low-anxious group scored consistently higher (better) for each of the five trials, and in every case did better on the task than the high-anxious group. Even on the fifth trial, the low-anxious group continued to score better than the high-anxious group.

Although this verbal report is accurate, the results of the experiment are difficult to visualize, no matter how well the report is organized or written. This problem comes up frequently in the reporting of psychological experiments. **Graphs** are used to clarify and organize facts visually. A graph of this experiment is shown in Figure A.2.

The horizontal line at the base of Figure A.2 is marked off to indicate the number of trials (1, 2, 3, 4, 5). The vertical line at the left indicates the scores obtained by the subjects. A legend, similar to one found on a road

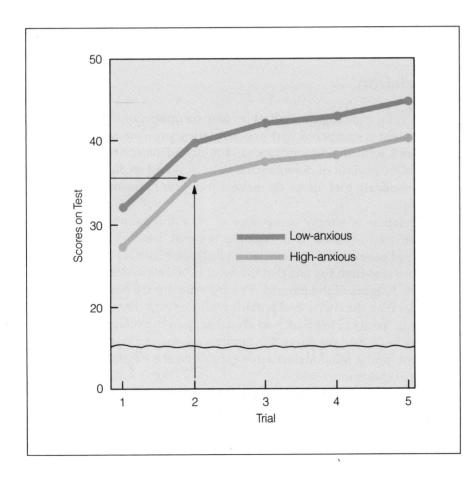

Figure A.2
Test performance of high- and low-anxious subjects

map, shows the reader which lines within the graph represent which group in the study. The lines themselves connect a series of dots. Each dot represents a point on the horizontal axis (trial line) and a point on the vertical axis (score line).

The two arrows you see in Figure A.2 do not appear in real graphs, but have been added here to explain how the position of the dots is determined. Assume that the experimental results show that, on trial 2, the average score of all the subjects in the high-anxious group was 35. An arrow moves from 35 on the score axis (vertical) over to the right until it meets an arrow coming up from trial 2 on the trial axis (horizontal). The point at which they meet is the point where the dot is placed. Put another way, the dot represents trial 2, for which the average score of high-anxious subjects equaled 35.

With that out of the way, notice how easy it is to see the results of the experiment just by looking at the graph. The dotted line (high-anxious) is consistently below the straight line (low-anxious); high anxiety, then, appears to keep the level of performance low through all five trials. If this explanation is not completely clear, go back to the paragraph in which the results of the experiment were described, and compare the verbal description with the graph in Figure A.2.

You will see hundreds of graphs in scientific reports. They all follow the *same* principle as the one we've just shown you.

Correlation

Almost all psychological studies involve comparisons. The intelligence of a student is compared with school grades; problems in the home are compared with delinquency rates; amount of narcotics taken is compared with amount of disorganized behavior; and so on. One statistical (mathematical) tool used to make these comparisons is called **correlation**.

Correlation is simply a measure of how things are related to one another, or co-related. For example, look at Table A.1 in which the heights of parents and their grown children are listed. Nothing could be more obvious than the fact that the heights of the children are correlated with the heights of the parents. Parents who are tall have children who are taller than the children of parents who are short. For example, the off-spring in family C (69.5 inches) are taller than the offspring of family E (68.2 inches). And the parents in family E are smaller than those in family C. Therefore, a relationship must exist between height of parents and height of children.

How do we go about putting these relationships into numbers?

Well, you can see by looking at the table of heights that the two variables are related, but the problem is to express this relationship

Table A.1 Average of Heights of Parents and Offspring (in inches)

Family	Parents	Offspring
A	72.5	72.2
B	71.5	69.9
C	70.5	69.5
D	69.5	68.9
E	68.5	68.2
F	67.5	67.6
G	66.5	67.2
H	65.5	66.7
I	64.5	65.8

mathematically. Mathematicians figured out that if you plot points representing the height of parents (vertical axis in Figure A.3) and the height of children (horizontal axis) and then draw a diagonal that comes as close as possible to all the points and still is a straight line, then the amount of distance *between the dots and the line* will indicate how close a relationship there is between the two different characteristics (height of parents and height of offspring).

For example, Figure A.4 (hypothetical) shows a perfect relationship; there is no difference between the points and the straight line. Figure A.5 (hypothetical) shows a weak relationship; there is a great difference between the points and the line of best fit. It is possible, with highly accurate graph paper, actually to measure the distances between points and the diagonal line and to place them in a formula to determine the degree of relationship. Rather than do all this measuring, however, we can obtain the same results by dealing with the numbers *directly* by means of a mathematical formula. The reason for using graphs here for correlations is to provide a visual image of what we are talking about.

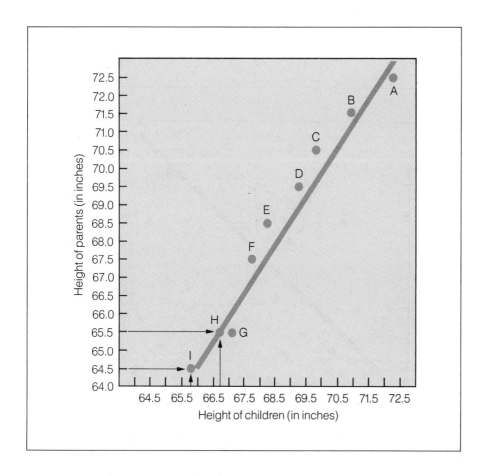

Figure A.3
Correlation of average heights of parents and children

Figure A.4
Perfect correlation

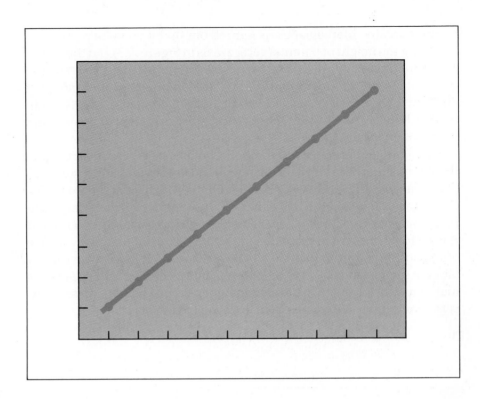

Figure A.5
Weak correlation

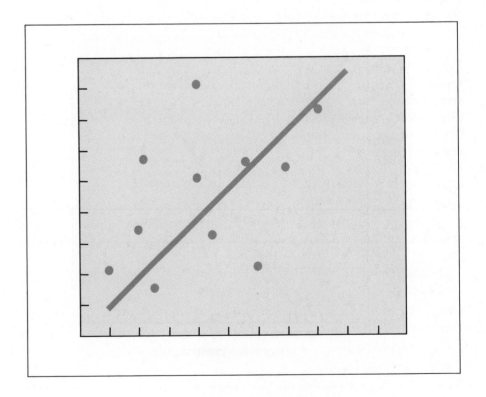

Reading, Interpreting, and Reporting Correlations

Correlation, then, is a measure of the apparent relationship between two different things. The numbers for correlation are called **correlation coefficients** and vary from 0 to 1. Zero means no relationship exists, while 1 means a perfect relationship exists.

Words of caution: It is a rare student who does not confuse correlation with percentages at the beginning. A correlation is not in any sense the same as a percentage. Correlational numbers *look like* percentages. They are *not*. Nonetheless, at least one similarity does exist—the higher the number, the more the two items seem to be related.

So, the size of the correlation indicates the strength of the relationship; the higher the number, the stronger the relationship:

Typical correlations:

.00   .15   .38   .59   .70   .89   .90   1.00

Relationship getting stronger   →   →   →

The number .00 means no correlation exists; 1.00 means perfect correlation exists. A correlation coefficient can be *any* number between 0 and 1.

Now, suppose we examine the relationship between bottle feeding and age. As age increases, bottle feeding will decrease. At age five, there are a few hangers-on, and maybe one by age seven. Look at Figure A.6, where this correlation is plotted. Something is different. For one thing, the line is running in a direction opposite from the ones seen previously. For another, even though the line fits pretty squarely between dots, if you report something like this—"Correlation between age (through age 7) and bottle feeding is .90"—you are saying that, as age *increases*, bottle feeding *increases*, which obviously is wrong. Yet we know there is a strong relationship between age and bottle feeding. To allow for this kind of situation, scientists use the correlation coefficients in the negative (minus) direction as well as the positive (plus) direction; both mean the *same thing* in terms of *degree* of relationship. A negative .90 correlation ($-.90$) is just as strong as a positive .90 correlation (.90). The negative correlation means that, as one variable (age) goes one way (increases), the other variable (bottle feeding) goes the other way (decreases). The positive correlation means that, as one variable goes one way, the other variable goes the same way (as height of parents goes up, that of the children goes up).

The following *rough* guides can be used to interpret correlation coefficients:

- From .00 to + or −.20 means an indifferent or negligible relationship exists.

- From + or −.20 to + or −.40 means a low correlation exists; a relationship is present but slight.

Figure A.6
Correlation of bottle feeding with age

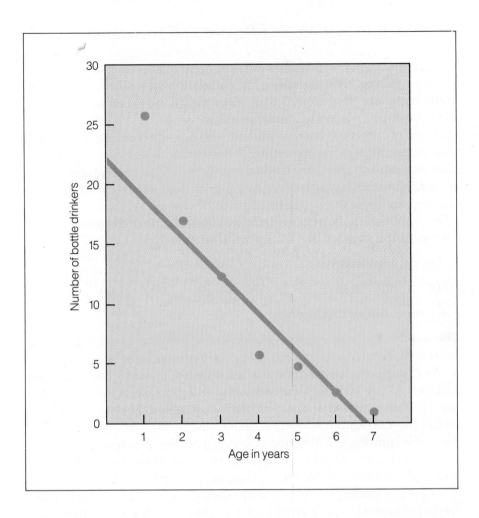

- From + or − .40 to + or − .70 means a substantial or marked correlation exists.
- From + or − .70 to + or − 1.00 means a high to perfect relationship exists

A Word of Caution

Correlation coefficients show the degree to which two things are related to each other. They do *not* necessarily show a cause-and-effect relationship. For instance, suppose we find that students with good grades in school tend to do well on achievement tests. Given these two numbers, grade point average and achievement-test performance, can we say that grades cause the test scores or vice versa? No. Instead, it is far more likely that both are caused by other things, like basic intellectual ability, study habits, quality of education, home atmosphere, motivation, and so on.

Similarly, the length of one's arms and legs are correlated with one another, but it is not very likely that one causes the other. Instead, both are probably caused by a "program" in the genes that directs the body's overall development, with nutrition and general health playing a role.

The Normal Curve: Fitting People into Groups

All sciences must bring order to a large number of facts. This holds true for psychology, also; somehow people and their characteristics have to be brought together in an orderly fashion. Otherwise, people can't be studied in a way that permits comparison.

The scientist putting things and people into categories often uses diagrams to represent these categories. Take the case of the investigator who, by the use of numbers, must show the difference in wealth among various groups in the United States. For example, how many families in the United States make under $6,000 a year? How many make between $12,000 and $15,000, and how many make more than $40,000? Grossly approximating for purposes of illustration, we could say that 3 million families fall into the first category, 15 million into the second, and about 3 million into the third.

Suppose that you draw a line to equal, in length, the number of families in each category:

	3 million
Under $6,000	—— ↓ 15 million
$12,000–$15,000	————————— ↓
Over $40,000	——

You have created a visual representation of income and families divided by categories. If you wanted to include more data, you could draw a line for each of a large number of income categories, making wealth appear to be a little more equally distributed than it actually is; you would obtain something approximating this diagram:

	Number of Families
1 Under $6,000	——
2 xxxxxx	———
3 xxxxxx	————
4 xxxxxx	—————
5 $12,000–$15,000	———————
6 xxxxxx	—————
7 xxxxxx	————
8 xxxxxx	———
9 Over $40,000	——

(The larger the number of families, the longer the line.)

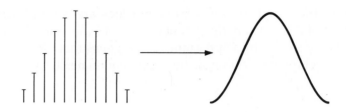

Now you can turn the diagram on its side, connect the highest points, and remove the lines, as shown in Figure A.7. The curve that results is called a bell-shaped or **normal curve**. This same curve represents the distribution (in a rough fashion) of such a large number of things in the world that psychologists use it frequently to illustrate characteristics of people as a whole or to categorize people along a certain dimension. It is used to represent visually how large numbers of people are distributed.

You can see how it works if you take a hypothetical curve of cleanliness. Most people (the norm, or normal—that is, what is to be expected) are going to be in the middle in the more-or-less clean group. Assuming that the soap operas get their messages across, there will be a large group of people right around the middle of the curve (see the rectangle in Figure A.8). Some groups of people are going to deviate from this norm, or normal position. At the far right of the curve in Figure A.8 might be the superclean, the bathtub dwellers. As we move along the curve toward the superclean, the number of individuals becomes smaller and smaller. Sliding to the left, we move away from the norm toward the superdirty, represented at the far left (and fortunately they also are in the minority). The technical name for this figure (A.8) is a *normal frequency distribution*. This means that, after having counted (determined frequency), we have a distribution (arrangement) that fits the normal (quite frequently found) arrangement of things: few superdirty, few superclean, most in the middle (Figure A.9).

Height of individuals is a characteristic that also fits this curve. Another is intelligence-test results, which would include the very bright

Figure A.8
Normal frequency distribution

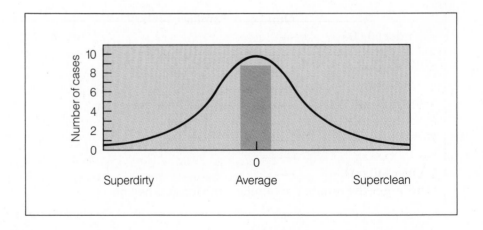

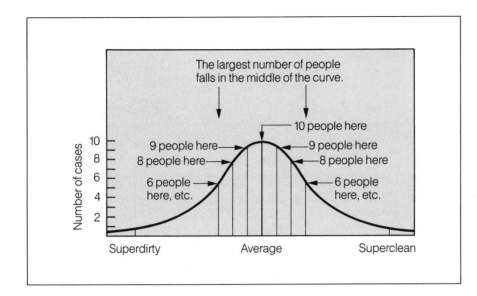

Figure A.9
Normal frequency distribution

and the very dull, one at each end of the curve, and the average in the middle.

Figure A.10 shows the percentage of subjects (persons, things, events, and so on) that would fall within a certain area of the curve if the curve were perfect. It is never perfect, but sometimes it comes close. The largest group of people fall into the middle (68 percent); 95 percent of the subjects are included within the second set of lines; and at 99 percent, the third set of lines, nearly everyone is accounted for. For example, 68 per-

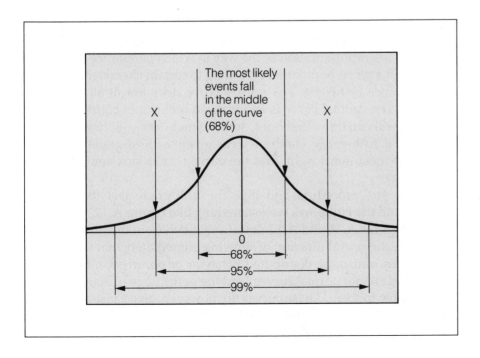

Figure A.10
Breakdown of normal curve

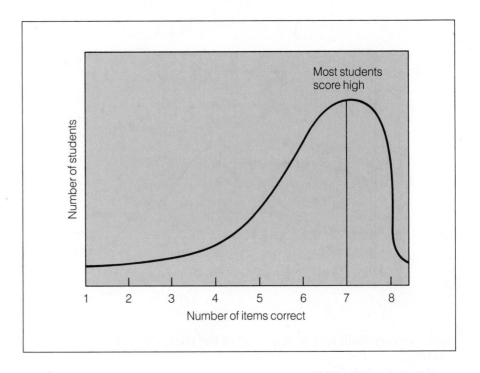

cent of a typical group is average clean. (In other words, if we had studied and categorized 100 individuals along the curve, 68 of them would fall between the two lines indicated.) All people vary somewhat, but they can be classified according to these individual differences. Some are cleaner than others, some brighter than others.

The student new to psychology usually finds the concepts of statistics somewhat difficult to grasp at first. The purpose of this discussion has been to acquaint you in a general way with a distribution curve. The normal curve is a representation of the way in which people are distributed throughout a given population according to certain characteristics, such as intelligence or height. The normal curve does not fit all situations, however. The normal curve is an idealized one, so, of course, the psychologist will run into other ones, some of them very oddly shaped. For example, if fifth-grade children were given a third-grade test, they would get most items right, and the curve would look something like Figure A.11.

Reverse the procedure and give the fifth-grade test to the third-graders, and the curve will look something like Figure A.12.

Since Figures A.11 and A.12 deviate so much from the normal curve, they serve the useful function of showing immediately that we are dealing with an unusually distributed behavior or occurrence. So, the last two curves are not normal curves, and the percentages discussed earlier do not apply to them. These curves do, however, give a visual representation of many numbers pertaining to grouped individuals, and they can quickly supply a general idea of performance, removing the need for

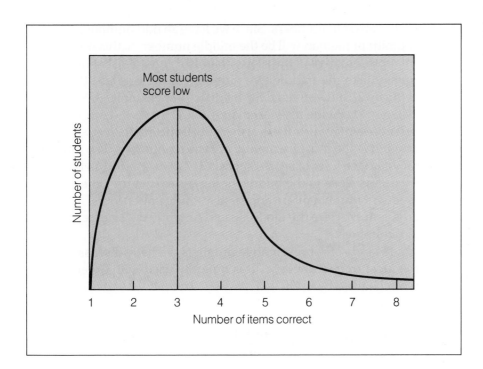

Figure A.12
Test results of third-graders given fifth-grade test

Most students score low

Number of students

Number of items correct

tedious research into the specific numbers obtained for each subject. Since all these kinds of curves are used so frequently, it is important that you grasp the general idea of what these curves are, how they are constructed, and how you read them.

Mean, Median, and Mode: Representative Numbers

Three other mathematical measures are used in psychology to condense information into accessible form. If we had five scores of 25, 26, 24, 24, and 21, for example, we could get a number that would closely represent all these numbers by adding them together and dividing by the number of entries (5). The result, 24, is very close to representing all these numbers, and this number is called the arithmetical **mean**—in everyday language, it is called the average.

These numbers present no problem; but, if we took the scores 3, 5, 6, 7, and 30 and figured the mean, we'd obtain 10.2, which would not be very representative of the many small scores we have (four out of five are below 10). The major problem with the mean, therefore, is that it can be inflated by a few extremely high or low numbers. This problem is sometimes an advantage, since the mean is sensitive to extreme scores and includes them in its calculation. As you will see, neither the median nor the mode takes extreme numbers into consideration. In the case of the numbers we have just listed, we can get the best possible representative number by using what is called the **median**, or halfway mark—the midpoint of a list of ordered numbers. Since we have an odd number of digits (5), the midpoint or median will be the middle number, 6; this number is much more representative of the scores than 10.2. If your list of numbers is even, merely take the middle two numbers in the list, add them together, divide by 2, and you have the median. (For example: 3, 5, 5, 6, 7, 30. Add: 5 + 6 = 11; divide by 2. Median = 5.5.)

The third representative numerical measure is the **mode**. It is very simply calculated: It is the most frequently appearing number. The mode is adequate if you have a set of scores such as 3, 7, 9, 9, 12, and 14 because the mode 9 occurs close to the middle of the series. On the other hand, the most frequent number might appear at a strange place in the list: 3, 3, 3, 9, 9, 12, 14, and 17. Here the mode is 3 and certainly does not represent the group of numbers.

Of the three kinds of representative numbers we have discussed, the mean is the most frequently used. It is typically used with other statistics, but it can be used by itself.

Probability, Chance, and Odds

We consider next the topics of probability, chance, and odds, since almost all the studies mentioned in this book are based on mathematical measures (statistics) that relate to probability and chance.

For example, consider that the basic issue in extrasensory perception is whether individuals even have such power. To show how statistics might help determine whether this power exists, suppose that we were to predict that the next flip of a coin would be heads, and indeed it was. Would you then agree that we had special powers of prediction? Hardly—but why not? Simply because our prediction could have come true just by chance. In other words, a single prediction had a 50-50 chance of being right. We could have predicted tails and been correct; that is, we could have been correct just by chance.

No one knows what chance is; we do, however, assume that certain fixed laws operate in the universe and influence, for example, the roll of dice. In addition to these laws, there is chance itself: the unknown factors influencing the roll, which might be the tilt of the floor, the particles in the air, the angle of the hand, and so on. Even though the mechanical laws operate, unknown or chance factors constantly enter into any occurrence. So, at any given time, almost anything could occur just by chance maybe once, maybe even twice, or possibly a few more times. But suppose we could correctly predict the roll of dice 99 percent of the time for 1,000 throws. We assume you would then give us the credit we deserve for our special abilities. Why? Because something other than chance must be operating.

The same considerations apply to studying extrasensory perception or even the problem of finding that a person is a delinquent and comes from a broken home. We might be able to guess a card someone is holding just by chance alone. Or the delinquent may come from a broken home just by chance, and there might be no relationship between the home and the child's later behavior. We need a statistic that will determine just how far-fetched it is to assume that chance is operating. If, for example, we were to apply a statistic to our 99-percent-correct predictions of dice rolls, we would find that the idea that chance alone is working *this often* is quite remote. In fact, we can be almost certain that something other than chance is operating, even if it is nothing more than our having loaded the dice. How far the results of a given study are removed from the effects of chance are reported numerically in the same fashion as other statistics are. We will get to this in a moment, but first it might be worthwhile to start the discussion all over again with another example to clarify these concepts.

One universal fact about human beings is that not everyone behaves in the same way. How, then, is it possible to make *any* statements about human behavior? We have already discussed correlation, but other statistical methods also give information about experimental findings. Suppose, for example, that we were to take the weights of a group of men found loitering on the corner somewhere and noted them to be 150, 165, 140, 160, and 325. Immediately we are struck by the highly deviant weight of 325, something expected very rarely. Also, we begin to speculate on how this man became so heavy. Maybe a glandular problem, maybe overeating. No one, however, tries to speculate on how a man comes to weigh 140 or 160 pounds. There's nothing unusual about it.

Reverse the situation. A group of experimenters think they have found a drug that induces weight increase. They administer it to a group of four males and then examine them ten years later, finding that their weights are 140, 150, 180, and 175. Assuming that their physiques correspond roughly to these weights, we can conclude that this is a very ineffective drug for increasing weight. Using another drug, the experimenters find ten years later that the subjects weigh 325, 298, 310, and 170. These heavier weights are extremely rare. Because of this rarity, the researchers can entertain the hypothesis that the drug induces weight gain. Chance might have given them one unusual weight, but it is highly unlikely that they would obtain three out of four strikingly deviant weights just by chance. In other words, the likelihood of this event occurring just by chance is remote. The scientist is always trying to demonstrate that the results obtained would be highly improbable if chance was the only factor operating.

Psychological experiments, including social studies, ESP experiments, intelligence testing, predictions of group behavior, and so on, never produce 100 percent rare events, just as the last study did not: 170 is not an unusual weight. On the other hand, the psychologist is looking for results that approach statistical rarity. The best way to understand this is to return to coin tossing.

In coin tossing, using a fairly new and untampered-with coin, the **probability**, or odds, that you will get either heads or tails is, in lay terminology, 50-50 (in statistical language, $p = .50$, where p stands for "probability"). In other words, *in theory*, every 100 tosses of a coin should yield 50 heads and 50 tails. In actuality, for any given set of 100 coin tossings, you might get 40 heads, 60 tails; 55 heads, 45 tails; and so on. Chance (unknown or accidental) factors are operating to give slight variations in the number of heads or tails. The nature of these chance factors is unspecified, but they are assumed *not* to operate in a consistent fashion; in other words, they temporarily influence the appearance of heads a few more times, or tails a few more times, eventually canceling one another out to result in overall figures close to 50-50.

If you have any money riding on the flips and they come up 20 tails and 80 heads, you should investigate the coin immediately on the grounds that something other than chance is operating—for example, a weighted coin. The discrepancy is too far removed from what normally occurs just by chance.

This is exactly what experimenters do: They look for results that are very remote from chance, just as it is very remote that 20 tails and 80 heads would occur merely from chance. (Note that it *is* physically possible for this to happen, but so rare as to be considered improbable.) It is more logical to search for a reason—a loaded coin—than to assume chance is the cause.

It is interesting to see what happens if you toss 10 different coins 1,024 times. First of all, even with so many coins, the law of probability will still work. We could expect 5 heads and 5 tails from the 10 coins more often than any other combination; next most probable would be 4 heads and 6 tails or 6 heads and 4 tails. Something to be expected *very* rarely would be 10 tails or 10 heads. Figure A.13 shows a curve that quite closely represents the results obtained from throwing a group of 10 coins 1,024 times. You will note that a toss of 10 heads or 10 tails comes up only once in 1,024 tosses. The odds are 1,024 to 1 of getting either 10 heads or 10 tails.

Figure A.13 is the normal curve again, and we can mark off the percentage of occurrences on the curve (Figure A.14). Take the combination of 10 heads. The point on the curve where it falls (indicated by the arrow that points off the page) is beyond the 99 percent level of the curve, actually a little beyond the 99.9 percent point, meaning that over 99.9 percent of all other combinations fall below this point on the curve. Looked at another way, 10 heads leaves only .1 percent (one-tenth of 1 percent) of the curve.

The whole curve, 100 percent, is going to equal 1.00 when the percentage is changed to a decimal (1.00). To find out how much of the curve representing 10 heads is left, we change 99.9 percent to .999 and subtract it from 1.00(0); .001 is the remainder. This figure as a fraction is $\frac{1}{1,000}$ and means that one time in 1,000 (actually, in our case, $\frac{1}{1,024}$) could this occur by chance alone. Thus, it is *extremely* rare.

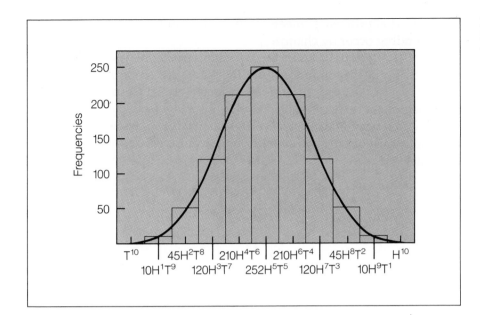

Figure A.13
Normal frequency distribution in coin tossing

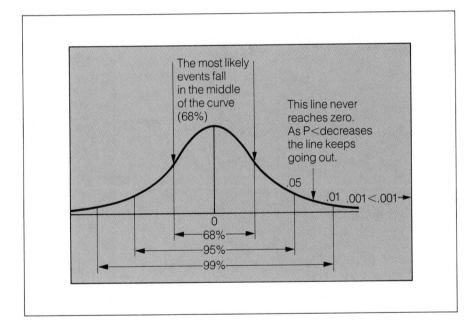

Figure A.14
Breakdown of normal curve

In the sciences, even though we know that events *could* conceivably occur with a *p* (probability) of .001 and still be chance, such an event is so rare that scientists assume that the result is more likely caused by the variable studied than by chance. Thus, if scientists find that statistics demonstrate that what they found in a study could occur only once in 1,000 times just by chance alone, they assume that chance is not the important factor. Another way of saying this is that the results reached the

.001 level of **significance**, meaning that only 1 out of 1,000 times would such a finding occur by chance.

The .001, .01, and .05 levels are typically agreed on by scientists as indicating significant (important) findings, and are reported in scientific studies as $p = .001$, $p = .01$; $p = .05$, respectively. The experimenter decides before the experiment what significance will be acceptable. For most studies, a significance level of .05 is considered good enough, but if the results turn out to be even more significant, say .01 or .001, so much the better.

Glossary

Acetylcholine   Neurotransmitter that regulates basic bodily processes such as movement.

Achievement tests   Tests that measure the amount of specific material remembered from the classroom.

Acoustic memory   A very brief sound memory that can be sent to the STM.

Acupuncture   A system of pain relief that involves inserting needles into the skin.

Adrenal glands   Glands that secrete the chemical adrenaline that prepares the body for an emergency or important activity.

Adrenaline   The chemical that prepares the body for emergency activity by increasing blood pressure, breathing rate, and energy level.

Afterimage   The firing of the cones not used while viewing something steadily in order to bring the visual system back in balance.

Agoraphobia   The fear of leaving a familiar environment, especially home.

Alcoholic withdrawal delirium   The "horrors" that can result from severe alcoholism; includes weakness, anxiety, cramps, hallucinations.

Alpha waves   Stage 1, fairly alert brain waves occurring just before going to sleep; relaxed.

Alzheimer's disease   The loss of chemical nerve cell transmitters and other damage to nerve transmission that result in mental deterioration.

Amnesia   The blocking of older memories and loss of new ones.

Androgens   Hormones that control sexual interest in both males and females.

Androgyny   The quality of having both masculine and feminine characteristics.

Anorexia nervosa   An eating disorder that involves severe loss of weight from excessive dieting or use of laxatives.

Antecedents   Information and beliefs we have beforehand about another.

Antibodies   Cells that fight off invading foreign bodies that might prove injurious; part of the immune system.

Antisocial personality disorder   The name of the disorder that the sociopath has, in which the person is in constant conflict with the law and seems to have no conscience.

Anxiety   A generalized feeling that something is wrong and disaster is imminent.

Anxiety disorder   Living in a continued, destructive state of anxiety.

Applied psychologists   Those who make direct use of the findings of research psychologists, deal directly with clients.

Approach-approach conflict   A choice between two attractive alternatives.

Approach-avoidance conflict   A conflict in which one part of the situation is attractive, but the other part is not; the choice is whether to do or not do something.

Aptitude   One's special skills as measured by an aptitude test.

Aptitude tests   Tests that measure one's special skills (in carpentry, medicine, and so forth).

Asthma   Muscle spasms and tissue swelling in the air tubes of the lungs.

Astrology   The prediction of behavior based on the positions of the planets and stars.

Attention   Alert focusing on material to be retained.

Attribution theory   A theory about the process by which we form opinions about another, by which we explain another's behavior.

Audition   The sense of hearing.

Auditory nerve   Bundle of nerves carrying sound to the brain.

Aversive conditioning   A behavioral technique in which unpleasantness is associated with acts that are to be avoided.

Avoidance-avoidance conflict   A choice between two unattractive alternatives.

Awfulize   To see things in the worst possible light; Ellis's term.

Axon   The part of the neuron that carries messages away from the nerve cell to the dendrites on another nerve cell.

Barnum effect   Stating the obvious as if it comes from special knowledge.

Behavioral therapy   Therapy that uses principles of learning to alter the person's behavior that is causing trouble.

Behaviorism   A personality theory that focuses on acts or behaviors rather than on consciousness or unconsciousness; Skinner and Bandura are examples of behavioral psychologists.

Behaviorists   Those who believe we are the product of associations.

Belongingness needs   Part of Maslow's hierarchy of needs: friendship, closeness with another.

Beta waves   Rapid brain waves; appear when a person is awake.

Binocular disparity   The difference between the visual image provided by each eye. When the images are brought together in the brain, they provide a sense of depth.

Biofeedback   A method of mental control in which a machine attached to the body records events going on (for example, high blood pressure) so that the individual can change them.

Biological clocks   Internal chemical units that control parts of the body and are regulated by nature.

Bipolar disorder   A major affective disorder with up and down swings of moods from "high" to "low."

Blind spot   The portion of the retina through which the optic nerve exits and where there are no receptors for light waves.

Blood-sugar level   The amount of sugar contained in the blood, which indicates the level of hunger.

Break set   To come up with unusual, unexpected ideas; to use something in a different way than it is normally used.

Brightness constancy   The human visual network's ability to keep brightness constant as an object changes environments; accomplished by taking an average.

Bulimia   A disorder that involves trying to avoid gaining weight by throwing up or using laxatives.

Cannon-Bard theory   Theory of emotion stating that the bodily reaction and the emotional response to an event occur at the same time.

Case study method   Research that collects information about a person's background, usually for psychological treatment.

Catharsis   The supposed ability to get rid of aggressive energy by viewing others acting aggressively.

Cerebellum   The portion of the lower brain that coordinates and organizes bodily movements for balance and accuracy.

Cerebral arteriosclerosis   A blockage of blood vessels, especially to the brain, that results in the loss of mental faculties.

Cerebral cortex   The 100-billion-nerve-cell unit that covers the lower brain and controls very high-level thought.

Chaining   Reinforcing the connection between different shaped acts.

Chemical dependence   The same as substance abuse; the use of drugs in excess in order to alter consciousness.

Chemotherapy   The use of drugs to relieve psychological disturbance.

Chronobiology   The study of forces that control the body at different times of the day, month, or year.

Chunking   Putting things into "chunks" so that items learned are in categories, rather than separately.

Cilia   Tiny hairs that receive odor molecules; act as receptors in the nose.

Circadian rhythm   Sequences of behavioral changes that occur every 24 hours.

Clang association   Psychotic speech in which words are rhymed.

Classical conditioning   Ivan Pavlov's method of conditioning in which associations are made between a natural stimulus and a learned, neutral stimulus.

Client-centered therapy   Rogers's humanistic approach; reflects belief that the client is more important than the therapist.

Clinical psychologists   Those who deal with emotional disturbances of any kind; may work with formal mental patients.

Clique   A very tightly knit group with limited membership and strict rules of behavior; normally middle class and tied in with school activities.

Closure   The process of filling in the missing details of what is viewed.

Cochlea   A snail-shaped part of the ear, filled with fluid and small hairs that vibrate to incoming sound.

Cognition   Symbolic thought processes.

Cognitive   Concerning the brain or mind.

Cognitive approach (to learning)   A way of learning based on abstract mental processes and previous knowledge.

Cognitive behavior therapy   Therapy in which thoughts are used to control emotions and behaviors.

Cognitive development   The ways in which thinking and reasoning grow and change.

Cognitive dissonance   A contradiction between actions or events and beliefs, which must be reconciled or justified.

Cognitive map   A mental image of where one is located in space.

Cognitive psychology   The study of how humans use mental processes to handle problems or develop certain personality characteristics.

Cognitive strategy   An organized mental task designed to convince the brain that all is well.

Cognitive theory (Schachter)   A theory of emotions stating that we label a bodily response by giving it the name of an emotion we think we are feeling.

Collective unconscious   Jung's term for the portion of a person that contains ideas (such as hero, mother, and so on) shared by the whole human race.

Color constancy   The ability to perceive an object as the same color regardless of the environment.

Compulsion   A symbolic, ritualized behavior that a person must keep acting out in order to avoid anxiety.

Concrete operations stage   Piaget's third stage of child development in which the child understands that there is a real world with real objects, which exist apart from the child and which can be manipulated.

Conditioned response   A response to a stimulus that is brought about by learning—for example, salivating at the word "pickle."

Conditioned stimulus   A previously neutral stimulus that has been associated with a natural (or unconditioned) stimulus.

Conditioning   Making an association between an event and something positive or negative by repeated exposure.

Cone   A visual receptor in the eye that responds during daylight; receives color.

Conflict   A problem that demands a choice between alternatives in order to be resolved.

Consciousness   The awareness of, or the possibility of knowing, what is happening inside or outside the organism.

Consequences   Our emotional responses and expectations regarding another.

Conservation   Piaget's term for the idea that some of an object's characteristics can be changed while others remain the same.

Consolidation   The process of strengthening a memory and its parts over time until they are very solid.

Construct   A belief in something that cannot be seen or touched but that seems to exist.

Contact comfort   The satisfaction obtained from pleasant, soft stimulation.

Continuous reinforcement   Reinforcement that is given each time a behavior occurs.

Control group   The group that does not participate in the critical part of the experiment.

Conventional level   Kohlberg's middle stage of moral development in which moral reasoning is based on the expectations of others regarding what is right or wrong.

Cornea   The clear outer covering of the eye behind which is fluid.

Corpus callosum   The massive bundle of nerve fibers that connects the two hemispheres of the brain.

Counseling psychologists   Those who deal mostly with problems not fitting into the formal classifications of mental disturbance.

Creativity   The mental processes that result in original, workable ideas.

Critical period   A specific time of development that is the only time when a particular skill can begin to develop or an association can occur.

Cross-sectional method   A method of research that looks at different age groups in order to understand changes that occur during the life span.

Crowding   A psychological feeling of too little space.

Crowds   Large groups with loose rules and changeable memberships.

Curiosity motive   A drive that moves a person to see new and different things.

Cutaneous receptors   The nerve receptors in the skin that account for the sense of touch.

Dark Ages   400 A.D.–900 A.D.; period of chaos and civil wars when intellectual progress stopped.

Decibels   A measure of how loud a sound is (its intensity).

Defense mechanisms   Techniques used to remain psychologically stable, or in balance.

Deindividuation   A loss of one's sense of individuality and responsibility when in a group.

Delta waves   Slow, lazy, deep-sleep brain waves.

Delusion   A belief in something (for example, that you are a king or queen) that is not true.

Dendrite   The part of the nerve cell that receives information from the axons of other nerve cells.

Denial   The process of refusing to admit that there is a problem.

Density   The actual number of people per square foot in a given space.

Dependent variable   That which changes as a result of what the experimenter does.

Depth perception   The ability to see objects in space.

Diagnostic and Statistical Manual of Mental Disorders III   A book that classifies the symptoms of mental problems into formal categories.

Diffusion   Marcia's term for the state of having no clear idea of one's identity nor attempting to find that identity.

Diffusion of responsibility   For an individual member of a group, the idea that responsibility for others is spread out among all group members.

Discrimination learning   Learning to tell the difference between one event or object and another; the reverse of generalization.

Dissociative disorders   Nonpsychotic disorders in which a part of one's life becomes disconnected from other parts; amnesia; multiple personality.

Distraction   The cognitive strategy that consists of thinking of something else during pain.

Distress   The stress that is nonproductive and that causes physical problems.

Dominance   In each individual, the dominance or control of either the right or left brain hemisphere, which controls the majority of actions performed.

Dopamine   The brain chemical present in excess in schizophrenics, which causes nerve cells to fire too rapidly and leads to thought and speech confusion.

Double approach-avoidance conflict   A choice between alternatives, both of which have good and bad parts.

Drive   Forces that push an organism into action.

Dysthymic disorder   A moderate, nonpsychotic depression.

Eardrum   A piece of skin stretched over the entrance to the ear; vibrates to sound.

Early adolescence   The period from 11 to 14 years of age.

Early maturer   Someone who develops one and a half years or more ahead of average growth.

Eclecticism   The process of making your own system by borrowing from two or more other systems.

Ego   Freud's term for the "self."

Eidetic imagery   An iconic memory lasting a minute or so that keeps images "in front of the person" so objects can be counted or analyzed; also called "photographic memory."

Elaboration   The process of attaching a maximum number of associations to a basic concept or other material to be learned so that it can be retrieved more easily.

Electroconvulsive therapy (ECT)   Therapy in which an electrical shock is sent through the brain to try to reduce symptoms of mental disturbance.

Emotion   A state of the body causing feelings of hope, fear, love, and so on.

Empty-nest period   The time of life when the children are grown and leave; for some people, leads to feelings of uselessness and depression.

Encounter groups   Therapy in which normal people are brought together to become more sensitive to others' problems as well as to themselves.

Endocrine system   The system of all the glands and their chemical messages taken together.

Endorphins   Morphine-like substances produced naturally within the body.

Entrainment   Altering the body's free-running cycle to fit one's own needs.

Environment   A person's surroundings, which have an influence on a person's characteristics and development.

Estrogen   The hormone that controls the female reproductive cycle.

Eustress   The stress that motivates us to do something worthwhile.

Evaluation apprehension   The concern about how others will judge us; we make our behavior conform to what we think they will approve of.

Experimental group   The group on which the critical part of the experiment is performed.

Extended family   Nuclear family plus other relatives living in the same home.

Extinction   The gradual loss of an association over time.

Extrasensory perception   The receipt of information without the aid of the "normal" senses such as hearing, seeing, feeling, and so on.

Extrinsic motivation   A reward from outside the organism for certain behavior.

Feral children   Wild, untamed children.

Fidelity   Erikson's term for being faithful to one's ideals and values; loyalty.

Field experiments   Research that takes place outside the laboratory.

Fight or flight reaction   The body's reaction to a crisis; these are the only two possibilities for action.

Fixed interval schedule   Reinforcement occurs after a fixed amount of time has passed.

Fixed ratio schedule   Reinforcement occurs after the desired act is performed a specific number of times.

Flight of ideas   A confused psychotic speech in which thoughts and speech go in all directions with no unifying idea.

Foreclosure   Marcia's term for the state of accepting the identity and values an adolescent was given in childhood.

Forgetting   An increase in errors when trying to bring material back from memory.

Forgetting curve Graphic representation of speed and amount of forgetting that occurs.

Formal operations stage Piaget's fourth stage of child development in which the ability to deal with the highly symbolic, abstract thoughts found in logic, math, philosophy, and ethics begins to appear; complex thought processes.

Free association Freudian process of saying whatever comes to mind; technique used in psychoanalysis to uncover the unconscious.

Free-running cycles Cycles set up by biological clocks that are under their own control.

Frontal association area The forward portion of the brain that engages in elaborate associations or mental connections; plays an important part in integrating personality and in complex thoughts.

Frustration The blocking or hindering of goals we are seeking.

Fully functioning individual Rogers's term for someone who has become what he or she should be.

Gang A rebellious, antisocial group with strict rules but not connected with accepted social organizations such as a school.

Gender The sex of an individual, male or female.

Gender role behavior Acts that reflect society's view of what is appropriate for males versus what is appropriate for females.

General adaptation syndrome The sequence of behavior that occurs in reaction to prolonged stress. It is divided into stages: alarm reaction, preparation for an attack; stage of resistance, trying to restore balance; and exhaustion, giving up the battle.

Generalization A behavior that spreads from one situation to a similar one.

Gerontology The branch of psychology that studies the aging process and the problems of those who are older.

Glands Units of the body that contain the hormones.

Glucose Another name for sugar in the blood.

Gonads The sex glands that make sperm or eggs for reproduction.

Group identity versus isolation Erikson's idea that early adolescents either belong to a group or feel lost (isolated).

Group intelligence tests IQ tests administered to many people at one time; test is highly verbal and uses paper and pencil.

Group therapy Therapy in which more than one person at a time is treated.

Growth cycles Patterns of development in which some areas develop more rapidly and some more slowly, but all in a way that's preplanned by nature.

Growth hormone The hormone controlled by the pituitary that regulates the growth process.

Growth spurt The rapid, temporary increase in growth during puberty.

Hair cells Same as cilia; tiny hairs that receive odor molecules; act as receptors in the nose.

Hallucinating Seeing or hearing things that are not physically present.

Halo effect The situation where a person comes off well in class or in an interview, even though this is not his or her "real" personality.

Hemisphere One-half of the two halves of the brain; the right hemisphere controls the left side of the body, the left hemisphere controls the right side.

Heredity Characteristics obtained directly from the genes.

Hierarchy of needs A system that ranks needs one above the other with the most basic needs for physical survival at the bottom of the pyramid.

Hormones Bodily chemicals that control physical growth and changes, sexuality, and emotional responses.

Hospices Places where terminally ill people can live out their lives in comfort and away from a hospital.

Humanism A personality theory that places emphasis on the positive potential of the person; Rogers and Maslow are examples of humanistic psychologists.

Humanistic Believing that people are basically good and capable of helping themselves.

Humanistic therapy Therapy that emphasizes the individual's own ability to heal himself or herself with some assistance.

Hypnosis A state of suggestion in which attention is focused on certain objects, acts, or feelings.

Hypothalamus A part of the brain that regulates basic needs such as hunger and thirst, as well as emotions such as pleasure, fear, rage and sexual desire.

Hypothesis A statement of the results that the experimenter expects; an educated guess as to what the results will be.

Iconic memory A very brief visual memory that can be sent to the STM.

Id Freud's term for the part of the unconscious that contains our animal impulses.

Ideal self Rogers's term for the goal of each person's development; perfection.

Identical twins Two people who come from the same egg in the mother; hence, they have the same heredity.

Identification The process of modeling behavior patterns after (usually) a member of the same sex.

Identity A sense of oneself as a unique person.

Identity achievement Marcia's term for the state of having developed well-defined personal values and self-concepts.

Identity confusion Erikson's term for an uncertainty about who one is or where one is going.

Illusion An inaccurate perception.

Illusory correlations Connections that seem very strong in one's mind but that don't really exist.

Imitation learning The process of learning behaviors by viewing others and imitating them.

Immune system The body's method for fighting disease or injury.

Immunization An attempt to train a person beforehand to resist persuasion or propaganda.

Imprinting A process that occurs at a preset time in an animal's development, when the animal's brain is ready to receive a belief or behavior.

Incubus attack Also called a night terror, a horrible nightmare occurring during NREM sleep when the body is not prepared for it.

Independent variable That which the experimenter does that has an effect on the dependent variable.

Individual intelligence tests IQ tests administered on a one-to-one basis—one examiner to one test taker.

Information processing The methods by which we take in, analyze, store, and retrieve material in memory.

Insomnia The inability to get enough sleep.

Intelligence The ability to understand and adapt to the environment by using a combination of inherited abilities and learning experiences.

Intelligence quotient A measure of brightness obtained by comparing mental age with physical age.

Intensity In hearing, how loud a sound is.

Interference theory The belief that we forget because new and old material conflict (interfere) with one another.

Internalize To take as part of ourselves the attitudes or beliefs of others.

Internalized sentences The opinions we form of ourselves by listening to our own inner voice; Ellis's term.

Interview A research method that involves studying people face to face and asking questions.

Intrinsic motivation Satisfaction that comes from within the individual for certain behavior.

Introspection The process of looking into yourself and describing what is there.

Iris A colored circular muscle that opens and closes, forming larger and smaller circles to control the amount of light getting into the eye.

James-Lange theory For emotion, first the body responds, *then* one feels the emotion.

Late adolescence The period from 16 to 19 years of age.

Late maturer Someone who develops one and a half years or more behind average growth.

Learning curve A gradual upward curve representing increased retention of material as the result of learning.

Lens The part of the eye that focuses an object on the back of the eye.

Libido Freudian term for internal energy forces that continuously seek discharge.

Longitudinal method A method of research that studies the same group of people over an extended period of time.

Long-term memory The memory system that retains information for days, weeks, months, decades.

Lower brain Basic "animal" units common to animals and humans that regulate basic functions such as breathing.

Major affective disorders Serious disturbances of affect, or emotion; person's moods go *very* high or *very* low.

Major depression A psychosis involving mammoth depression, loss of appetite, hopelessness, thoughts of death.

Mania An affective psychosis involving extreme agitation and restlessness.

Manipulation motive The drive that moves a person to handle and use objects in the environment.

Maturation The automatic, orderly, sequential process of physical and mental development.

Mediation A form of self-control in which the outside world is cut off from consciousness.

Menopause The "change of life" period for women when menstruation and ovulation stop; sometimes accompanied by major physical symptoms, such as dizziness and "hot flashes."

Menstrual cycles Monthly cycles that revolve around the elimination of the lining of the female uterus because it has not been fertilized.

Mental age The level of intellectual functioning in years, which is associated with chronological age.

Mental retardation Subaverage intellectual functioning in which a person is not able to perform at the level appropriate for his or her age.

Metabolism The speed with which the body operates or the speed with which it uses up energy.

Middle adolescence The period from 14 to 16 years of age.

Middle Ages 900 A.D.–1400 A.D.; period of little science.

Midlife crisis A time of upheaval and loss of purpose that occurs to some people around the age of 40 years.

Migraine headache A headache resulting from an insufficient supply of the brain chemical serotonin.

Mnemonic devices Unusual mental associations used to help recall things from memory.

Modeling Bandura's term for learning by imitating others.

Moratorium A term used by both Erikson and Marcia to describe the adolescent's delay in making the commitments normally expected of adults.

Motivation The need to seek a goal, such as food, water, friends, and so on.

Motor strip The rectangular strip running down the side of the brain that controls all bodily movements (called motor functions).

Müller-Lyer illusion A visual illusion in which one of two lines seems longer than the other but really isn't.

Multiple personality The division of a person into two (possibly more) separate personalities that can act independently.

Muscle contraction headaches Headaches from holding oneself in a fixed position, causing the muscles to spasm and putting pressure on the nerves.

Narcolepsy Disorder in which a person falls instantly into sleep no matter what is going on in the environment.

Naturalistic observation A research method that involves studying subjects without their being aware of being watched.

Nature/nurture Contrasting views of how we gain certain characteristics: by means of heredity, or because of our environment.

Negative identity Marcia's term for those who are bad or are troublemakers as a result of blocking growth using foreclosure.

Negative reinforcement Reinforcement that stops something unpleasant; for example, nagging ceases if we do a chore.

Negative transfer An interference with learning due to dissimilarities between two otherwise similar tasks.

Neo-Freudians Those psychoanalysts who broke away from Freud to emphasize social forces in the unconscious.

Neurobiological Viewing behavior as the result of biology plus nerve cells.

Neuron A nerve cell that transmits electrical and chemical information (via neurotransmitters) throughout the body.

Neurotransmitters Chemicals in the endings of nerve cells that send information across the synapse.

Nightmare Frightening dream during REM sleep.

Nondirective therapy Rogers's system of reflecting and bringing together whatever the client exposes.

Nonpsychotic disorders Disorders characterized by severe discomfort or inefficiency from which the person seeks relief.

Norms Patterns of test answers from different types of people.

NREM sleep Non–rapid eye movement sleep; sleep involving partial thoughts, images, or stories, poor organization; not dream sleep.

Nuclear family Parents and children living in the same house.

Object permanence Piaget's term for the awareness that specific objects are real and part of the world.

Observational learning A form of social learning in which the organism observes and imitates the behavior of others.

Obsession An endless preoccupation with an urge or thought.

Obsessive compulsive disorder Having continued thoughts (obsession) about performing a certain act over and over (compulsion).

Olfaction   The sense of smell.

Olfactory bulbs   Units that receive odor molecules and communicate them to the brain.

Operant conditioning   Conditioning that results from one's actions and the consequences they cause.

Opiates   Sedatives; drugs that reduce body functioning.

Ovaries   The female sex gland; make eggs.

Overlearning   The process of learning something beyond one perfect recitation so that the forgetting curve will have no effect; the development of perfect retention.

Panic disorder   A type of anxiety disorder in which one cannot relax and is plagued by frequent and overwhelming attacks of anxiety.

Paranoia   The belief that others are out to get you.

Partial reinforcement schedule   Reinforcement that is not given each time an act is performed.

Perception   A person's interpretation of what an incoming sensory message means.

Performance scale   IQ test items that try to bypass verbal material and focus on problem solving without words.

Persona   Jung's term for a "mask" people wear to hide what they really are or feel.

Personal space   Human territoriality; amount of space we define as belonging to us.

Personality   A person's broad, long-lasting patterns of behavior.

Personality disorder   A disorder in which the person is neither neurotic nor psychotic, but the personality is clearly disturbed.

Personality inventory   A list of items about a person's beliefs, habits, hopes, needs, and desires.

Personality traits   The more or less permanent personality characteristics that an individual has.

Phantom-limb pain   Severe pain that feels as if it is coming from a missing limb.

Pheromones   Odor chemicals that communicate a message.

Philosophy   The attempt to understand behavior by using logic and reason.

Phobic disorder   A type of anxiety disorder in which a person becomes disabled and overwhelmed by fear in the presence of certain objects or events.

Physical dependence   A craving by the body itself for a drug.

Physiological needs   The bottom level of Maslow's hierarchy of needs: hunger and thirst.

Pitch   How high or low a sound is.

Pituitary gland   The master gland of the body that activates the hypothalamus and controls other glands; produces a hormone that regulates growth and maturation.

Placebo   A "medicine" that has no active ingredients and works by the power of suggestion.

Placebo effect   Physical reaction to the power of suggestion.

Polygraph   A lie detector; machine used to measure physiological changes in a person.

Positive reinforcement   Reinforcement that occurs when we do something that adds to or increases what we want.

Positive transfer   A transfer of learning that results from similarities between two tasks.

Postconventional level   Kohlberg's term for the highest stages of moral development involving personal ethics and human rights.

Preconventional level   Kohlberg's early stage of moral development in which morality is determined by the sheer power of outside authority.

Prejudice   A bias that leads to treating people unfairly; ignoring the real person involved.

Premenstrual syndrome (PMS)   Anxiety, irritability, and mental confusion resulting from monthly female hormonal changes.

Preoperational stage   Piaget's second stage of child development in which the child is so self-involved that other points of view are not understood.

Primary reinforcement   Something necessary for survival that is used as a reward.

Principle learning   A method of learning in which an overall view (principle) or the material to be learned is developed so that the material is better organized.

Projection   The process of attributing our thoughts to someone else.

Projective tests   Tests measuring inner feelings projected onto a vague stimulus, such as an ink blot or unclear picture.

Psychedelic   A drug that distorts or confuses the user's perception of the world.

Psychiatric nurses   Registered nurses with special education in psychiatric medicine.

Psychiatric social workers   Mental health workers with a degree in social work; help patients and families deal with problems.

Psychiatrists   Medical doctors whose speciality is in mental health.

Psychoanalysis   System of therapy used by Freud and his followers that emphasizes the study of the unconscious.

Psychogenic amnesia   A dissociative disorder in which traumatic events "disappear" from memory.

Psychological dependence   A craving by the psyche for a drug, although the body doesn't demand it.

Psychological tests   Objective assessment of what people know; how they act, think, and feel; and what their goals are through observation and measurement.

Psychology   The scientific study of human and animal behavior.

Psychosurgery   Surgery that destroys part of the brain to make the patient calmer, freer of symptoms.

Psychotherapies   Broad term for any method used to try to help people with emotional and psychological problems.

Psychotic disorders   Disorders that involve a serious inability to think rationally and to perceive the world accurately.

Psychotic episodes   Periods of psychotic behavior that can alternate with periods of relative coherence and calm.

Puberty   The time of sexual maturation.

Pupil   The opening in the eye.

Rational emotive therapy   Treatment centering on getting emotions under control by using reason; Ellis's term.

Rationalization   The process of explaining away a problem so that we don't have to accept the blame.

Recall   The ability to bring back and integrate many specific learned details.

Recognition   The ability to pick the correct object or event from a list containing the correct answer.

Redefinition   The cognitive strategy that consists of talking ourselves into believing that an incoming stimulation is different from what it is.

Reinforcement   Events that strengthen a behavior by leading to a desirable result.

Reference group   A group with which one identifies and that provides standards of behavior.

Reflex   An automatic behavior of the body involving movement that is activated through the spinal cord without using the higher brain.

Regression The process of going back in behavior and thought to a period when one was taken care of as a child; childish behavior.

Reliability The ability of a test to give the same results over a period of time.

REM rebound Increase in the number of dreams after being deprived of them.

REM sleep Rapid-eye-movement sleep when we dream.

Renaissance The "rebirth" period of 1400 A.D.–1700 A.D., during which Greek thought reappeared and much scientific exploration took place.

Repression The process of pushing unwanted or painful memories or feelings into the unconscious.

Research psychologists Those who study the origin, cause, or results of certain behaviors.

Reticular activating system/reticular formation The alertness control center of the brain that regulates the activity level of the body.

Reticular formation The unit in the inner brain that registers and controls activity level, increases excitement, and helps generate sleep.

Retina The back of the eye, which contains millions of receptors for light.

Reverse halo The situation where a person has skills but covers them over, or distracts others from seeing them, by doing unacceptable things.

Reversibility Piaget's term for the idea that a relationship that goes in one direction can go in the other direction also.

Reversible figure An illusion in which the same object is seen as two alternate figures—first one, then the other.

Risky shift phenomenon The situation where the danger of an act is split among the members of a group; hence, it is smaller for each person.

Rite of passage The socially recognized movement from adolescence into adulthood; requires some ritual.

Rod A visual receptor most sensitive to the violet-purple wavelengths; very sensitive for night vision; "sees" only black and white.

Rorschach test Ink blot projective test developed by Hermann Rorschach.

Safety needs Part of Maslow's hierarchy of needs; shelter, nest egg of money.

Sample A group that represents a larger group.

Scapegoating Blaming someone else for one's own problem.

Schedules of reinforcement Different methods of reinforcing.

Schema An organized and systematic approach to answering questions or solving problems.

Schizophrenia The most serious mental disturbance, involving loss of contact with reality, thought disorders, hallucinations, and delusions.

Secondary reinforcer Anything that comes to represent a primary reinforcer, such as money bringing food.

Selective forgetting "Forgetting" only things that are very traumatic.

Self-actualization The top of Maslow's hierarchy of needs: establishing meaningful goals and a purpose in life; bringing one's life to its fullest potential.

Self-esteem The feeling that you are worthwhile and useful.

Self-esteem needs Part of Maslow's hierarchy of needs: liking and respecting yourself, feeling important and useful.

Senile A broad, often misused term referring to a loss of mental faculties as a result of aging.

Sensation The process of receiving information from the environment.

Sensorimotor stage Piaget's first stage of child development in which word symbols, movements, and objects in the environment are tied together.

Sensory deprivation A kind of torture that consists of removing all external sensations from the victim.

Sensory memory system Direct receivers of information from the environment—for example, iconic, acoustic.

Sensory strip The rectangular band running down the side of the brain that registers and provides all sensation.

Separation anxiety The baby's fear of being away from the parent; the desire to avoid strangers; appears from approximately 9 to 18 months after birth.

Serotonin The brain chemical that in excess leads to mania, in too low concentrations to depression.

Set A tendency to solve problems in the same old way over and over.

Set point The body-regulating mechanism that determines a person's ideal weight.

Shaping The process of developing a part of a whole learning sequence.

Short-term memory (STM) The memory system that retains information for a few seconds to a few minutes.

Similarity A perceptual cue in which we group like things together.

Simple phobia A major anxiety that arises when one is faced with a specific object, such as a snake, dog, elevator, and so on.

Situational assessment The process of looking at how the circumstances surrounding an event influence how people respond to that event.

Size constancy The ability to retain the size of an object regardless of where it is located.

Sleep apnea A condition in which breathing stops while one is asleep, waking the person.

Social contracts Kohlberg's term for agreements based on the concept of what's "best for everyone."

Social entrainment (of the sleep cycle) Fitting sleep and dreams to your social schedule.

Social learning All learning that occurs in a social situation.

Sociopath Someone with a personality disorder who is in constant conflict with the law and seems to have no conscience.

Space constancy The ability to keep objects in the environment steady.

Spatial ability The ability to view objects mentally as they exist in the environment, to imagine how they would look if moved about (rotated) in space.

Spinal cord The part of the body that functions as an automatic "brain" in its own right and is a relay station for impulses to and from the higher brain.

SQ3R Survey, question, read, recite, and review; a study technique that helps one organize, understand, and remember new material.

Standoutishness Doing something or wearing something at an interview that is so startling that it detracts from one's real abilities.

Stanford-Binet test The original intelligence test developed by Alfred Binet and perfected at Stanford University.

State-dependent learning The fact that material learned in one chemical state is best reproduced when the same state occurs again.

Stereotype   A fixed set of beliefs about a person or group that may or may not be accurate.

Stimulus generalization   A response spread from one specific stimulus to other stimuli that resemble the original.

Strategies   Methods for solving problems, usually involving cognitive maps.

Stress   The physical strain that results from demands or changes in the environment.

Stress hormone   A special chemical that signals the adrenal glands to activate the body.

Strong-Campbell Interest Inventory   The most used interest test; based on answers of people successful in certain fields.

Subconscious   Consciousness just below our present awareness.

Subjects   People or animals on whom the experiment is conducted.

Subliminal perception   Stimulation presented below the level of consciousness.

Substance abuse   The use of drugs to excess in order to alter consciousness.

Sudden-death phenomenon   Death resulting from panic and overload of the major nerve going to the heart.

Superego   Freud's term for the part of the unconscious that is roughly synonymous with conscience.

Survey   A method of research using questions on feelings, opinions, or behavior patterns.

Synapse   The junction point of two or more neurons; the connection is made by neurotransmitters.

Synergistic effect   The result of taking two drugs in combination, which makes each more potent than either one by itself.

Systematic desensitization   A behavioral technique in which the therapist step by step increases the patient's anxiety and counters it by association with relaxation in a step-by-step sequence.

Taste receptors   Chemical receptors on the tongue that decode molecules of food or drink to identify them.

Territoriality   Attachment to a fixed amount of space set aside by and "belonging to" a member of a species.

Testes   The male sex gland; makes sperm.

Thalamus   The portion of the lower brain that functions primarily as a central relay station for incoming and outgoing messages from the body to the brain and the brain to the body.

Thanatology   The study of death and of methods for coping with it.

Theory of multiple intelligences   The assumption that, besides an "IQ," each of us has special skills—music, carpentry, design, and so forth—at which we are proficient.

Thought disorder   A serious distortion of the ability to think or speak.

Thyroid gland   The gland that controls and regulates the speed of bodily processes, called metabolism.

Token economy   A behavioral technique in which rewards for desired acts are accumulated through tokens, which represent a form of money.

Tolerance   The need to take larger and larger dosages of a drug while still only getting the same effect as from the original dose.

Trance   Another word for the state of deep relaxation that can occur during hypnosis.

Transfer of training   A learning process in which learning is moved from one task to another based on similarities between the tasks.

Transference   The process in which the patient transfers the emotional conflicts of earlier years onto the therapist.

Type A personality   People who are always operating at full speed, are impatient, and are filled with distress.

Type B personality   People who are open to change, flexible, enjoy life, and have low levels of stress.

Twilight state   Time just before we fall into sleep.

Ulcer   Wound in the intestine or stomach resulting from severe irritation.

Unconditional positive regard   A principle of humanistic therapy in which the client's feelings and thoughts are accepted for whatever they are; Carl Rogers's term.

Unconditioned response   An automatic response to a particular natural stimulus, such as salivation to meat.

Unconditioned stimulus   A stimulus that automatically elicits a response, such as meat causing salivation.

Unconscious   The portion of a person's mind that contains thoughts or desires not directly known to the person; believed by psychoanalysts to affect or control our behavior.

Universal ethical principles   Kohlberg's term for concepts such as justice and honor.

Validity   Whether a test measures what it is supposed to measure.

Variable interval schedule   Reinforcement occurs after a varying amount of time if a desired act occurs.

Variable ratio schedule   Reinforcement occurs after a desired behavior occurs, but a different number of the desired acts is required each time.

Variables   Factors that change in an experiment.

Verbal scale   IQ test items that rely heavily on word comprehension and usage.

Visual area   The area at the back of the brain that interprets everything we see.

Visual cliff   A large table with Plexiglas, used to demonstrate depth perception in small children.

Visual texture   Depth perception based on how rough or smooth objects appear.

Vocational interest test   A test that attempts to predict a good occupational area for an individual.

Wechsler Adult Intelligence Scale (WAIS)   An intelligence test that provides three IQs: verbal, performance, and a combined (total) IQ.

White light   Light as it originates from the sun or a bulb before it is broken into different frequencies.

Word salad   Speech in which words are mixed together incoherently.

Bibliography

Aaronson, B. S. (1972). Color perception and effect. *Amer. J. Clin. Hyp.*, *14*, 38–43.

Adams, A. B. (1969). *Eternal quest: The story of the great naturalists.* New York: Putnam's.

Adams, H. E., Feuerstein, M., & Fowler, J. L. (1980). Migraine headache: Review of parameters, etiology, and intervention. *Psychol. Bull.*, *87*, 217–237.

Anastasi, A. (1982). *Psychological testing* (5th ed.). New York: Macmillan.

Anderson, J. R. (1983). *The architecture of cognition.* Cambridge, MA: Harvard University Press.

Anderson, R. D. (1970). The history of witchcraft: A review with some psychiatric comments. *Amer. J. Psychiat.*, *126*, 1727–1735.

Andrewartha, H. G. (1961). *Introduction to the study of animal populations.* Chicago: University of Chicago Press.

Annett, M. (1978). Throwing loaded and unloaded dice. *Beh. Brain Sci.*, *1*, 278–279.

Arkes, H. R., & Garske, J. P. (1982). *Psychological theory of motivation* (2d ed.). Monterey, CA: Brooks/Cole.

Asch, S. E. (1952). *Social psychology.* Englewood Cliffs, NJ: Prentice-Hall.

Asher, L. (1980, August). Genetic alcoholism? *Psychol. Today.*

Axelrod, J., & Reisine, T. D. (1984). Stress hormones: Their interaction and regulation. *Science*, *224*, 452–459.

Bagby, J. W. (1968). Quoted in J. D. Frank, The face of the enemy. *Psychol. Today*, *2*, 24–29.

Bahrick, H. P., Bahrick, P. O., & Wittlinger, R. P. (1974). Long-term memory: Those unforgettable high school days. *Psychol. Today*, *8*(7).

Balay, J., & Shevrin, H. (1988). The subliminal psychodynamic activation method. *Amer. Psychol.*, *43*, 161–174.

Baltes, R. B., Reese, H. W., & Lipsitt, L. P. (1980). Life-span developmental psychology. *Ann. Rev. Psychol.*, *31*, 65–110.

Bandura, A., Ross, D., & Ross, S. (1963). Imitation of film-mediated aggressive models. *J. Abnor. Soc. Psychol.*, *66*, 3–11.

Bandura, A., & Walters, R. (1963). *Social learning and personality development.* New York: Holt, Rinehart and Winston.

Barber, T. X. (1969). An empirically based foundation of hypnotism. *Amer. J. Clin. Hypn.*, *12*, 100–130.

Barker, J. C., & Miller, M. B. (1969). Quoted in T. Wolpe, *The Practice of Behavior Theory.* New York: Pergamon Press.

Barron, F., & Harrington, D. M. (1981). Creativity, intelligence, and personality. *Ann. Rev. Psychol.*, *32*, 439–476.

Barton, E. M., Baltes, M. M., & Orzech, M. J. (1980). Etiology of dependence in older nursing home residents during morning care: The role of staff behavior. *J. Person. & Soc. Psychol.*, *38*, 423–431.

Bartoshuk, L. (1978). Gustatory system. In B. Masterton (Ed.), *The handbook of behavioral neurobiology* (Vol. 1). New York: Plenum.

Bauer, D. H. (1976). An exploratory study of developmental changes in children's fears. *J. Child. Psychol. Psychiat.*, *17*, 69–74.

Beauchamp, G. K. (1987). The human preference for excess salt. *Amer. Sci.*, *75*(1).

Beck, A. T. (1967). *Depression.* New York: Harper & Row.

———. (1972). *Depression: Causes and treatment.* Philadelphia: University of Pennsylvania Press.

Beck, J. (1975). The perception of surface color. *Sci. Amer.*, *233*(2).

Beckwith, J., & Woodruff, M. (1984). Achievement in mathematics. *Science*, *223*, 1247.

Beecher, H. K. (1956). Relationship of significance of wound to the pain experienced. *J. Amer. Med. Assn.*, *161*, 1609–1613.

Bell, R. Q. (1979). Parent, child, and reciprocal influences. *Amer. Psychol.*, *34*, 821–826.

Bell, R. R. (1983). *Marriage and family interaction* (6th ed.). Homewood, IL: Dorsey Press.

Bellack, A. J., Rozensky, R., & Schwartz, J. (1973). Self-monitoring as an adjunct to a behavioral weight reduction program. *Proceed. 81st Ann. Conv. Amer. Psychol. Assn.*

Bem, S. L. (1975). Sex role adaptability: One consequence of psychological androgyny. *J. Pers. Soc. Psychol.*, *31*, 634–643.

Benbow, C. P., & Stanley, J. C. (1983). Sex differences in mathematical reasoning ability: More facts. *Science*, *222*, 1029–1031.

———. (1985). Quoted in "The left hand of math and verbal talent." *Sci. News*, *127*, 263.

Benedict, R. (1934). *Patterns of culture.* Boston: Houghton Mifflin.

Benjaminsen, S. (1981). Stressful life events preceding the onset of neurotic depression. *Psychol. Med.*, *11*, 369–378.

Bennett, W., & Gurin, J. (1982). *The Dieter's Dilemma.* New York: Basic Books.

Bergland, R. (1985). *The fabric of mind.* New York: Viking Press.

Berkowitz, L., & Green, R. G. (1967). Stimulus qualities of the target of aggression: A further study. *J. Personal. Soc. Psychol.*, *5*, 364–368.

Berman, P. W. (1980). Are women more responsive than men to the young? A review of developmental and situational variables. *Psychol. Bull.*, *88*, 668–695.

Bernard, J. (1981). The good-provider role: Its rise and fall. *Amer. Psychologist*, *36*, 1–12.

Bernard, L. C. (1980). Multivariate analysis of new sex role formulations and personality. *J. Pers. and Soc. Psychol.*, *38*, 323–336.

Bickerton, D. (1984). The language bioprogram hypotheses. *Brain Beh. Sci.*, *7*, 173–221.

Biller, H. B. (1970). Father absence and the personality development of the male child. *Develop. Psychol.*, *2*, 181–201.

Birren, J. E. (1983). Aging in America: Roles for psychology. *Amer. Psychol.*, *38*, 298–299.

Blackman, S., & Catalina, D. (1973). The moon and the emergency room. *Percept. Mot. Skills*, *37*, 624–626.

Blasi, A. (1980). Bridging moral cognition and moral action: A critical review of the literature. *Psychol. Bull.*, *88*, 1–45.

Block, J. M. (1973). Conceptions of sex role: Some cross-cultural and longitudinal perspectives. *Amer. Psychol.*, *28*, 512–526.

Blum, K. (1984). *Handbook of abusable drugs*. New York: Gardner Press.

Blum, K. (1988). Personal communication.

Bolles, R. D. (1969). The role of eye movements in Müller-Lyer illusion. *Percept. Psychophy.*, *6*, 175–176.

Bond, E. A. (1960). Tenth-grade abilities and achievements. Quoted in L. J. Cronbach, *Essentials of psychological testing* (2d ed.). New York: Harper & Row.

Boorstin, D. J. (1983). *The discoverers*. New York: Random House.

Bouchard, T. J., Jr. (1983). Twins. *Yrbk. Sci. and the Future. Encyclopaedia Britannica*.

Bower, B. (1985). Neuroleptic backlash. *Sci. News*, *128*(3).

Bower, G. H. (1981). Mood and memory. *Amer. Psychol.*, *36*, 129–148.

Bower, G. H., & Karlin, M. B. (1974). Depth of processing of faces and recognition memory. *J. Exper. Psychol.*, *103*, 751–759.

Bower, G. H., & Winzenz, D. (1969). Group structure, coding, and memory for digit series. *J. Exp. Psychol. Monogr.*, *80*(2), pt. 2.

Bozarth, M. A., & Wise, R. A. (1984). Anatomically distinct opiate receptor fields mediate reward and physical dependence. *Science*, *229*, 516–517.

Brasch, R. (1967). *How did it begin?* New York: McKay.

Braudel, F. (1981). *The structures of everyday life* (Vol. 1). (S. Reynolds, Trans.). New York: Harper & Row.

Breggin, P. R. (1983). *Psychiatric drugs: Hazards to the brain*. New York: Springer.

———. (1984). Electroshock therapy and brain damage: The acute organic brain syndrome as treatment. *Brain Beh. Sci.*, *7*, 24–25.

Bringmann, W. G., & Tweney, R. D. (Eds.). (1980). *Wundt studies: A centennial collection*. Toronto, Canada: Hogrefe.

Brislin, R. W. (1983). Cross-cultural research in psychology. *Ann. Rev. Psychol.*, *34*, 363–400.

Brody, E. M. (1974). Aging and family personality: A developmental view. *Fam. Process*, *3*, 23–37.

Brody, J. E. (1988). Studies unmask origins of brutal migraines. *New York Times*, October 11.

Brody, M. S. (1962). Prognosis and results of psychoanalysis. In J. H. Nodine and J. H. Moyer (Eds.), *Psychosomatic medicine*. Philadelphia: Lea and Febiger.

Brome, V. (1967). *Freud and his early circle*. New York: William Morrow.

Bromley, D. B. (1974). *The psychology of human aging* (2d ed.). Baltimore: Penguin Books.

Brown, H. (1976). *Brain and behavior*. New York: Oxford University Press.

Brown, J. M., & Chaves, J. F. (1980). *Cognitive activity, pain perception, and hypnotic susceptibility in chronic pain patients*. Paper Amer. Psychol. Anns., Montreal.

Brown, R. (1973). *A first language*. Cambridge, MA: Harvard University Press.

Brownell, K. (1984). Quoted in "Physical factors explored in dieting, type A behavior." *APA Monitor*, *15*(2).

Bruner, J. S. (1968). Foreword. In A. R. Luria, *The mind of a mnemonist*. New York: Basic Books.

Bryan, J. H., & Test, M. A. (1969). Models and helping: Naturalistic studies in aiding behavior. Quoted in P. H. Mussen and M. R. Rosensweig (Eds.), *Annual review of psychology*. Palo Alto, CA: Annual Review.

Bryer, K. B. (1979). The Amish way of death: A study of family support systems. *Amer. Psychol.*, *34*, 255–261.

Buckhout, R., Figueroa, D., & Hoff, E. (1972, November). *Psychology and eyewitness identification: A preliminary report*. Ctr. Responsive Psychol. Rep. (CR–1).

Budzynski, T. H. (1976). Biofeedback and the twilight states of consciousness. In G. E. Schwartz and D. Shapiro (Eds.), *Consciousness and self-regulation I*. New York: Plenum.

Bullock, A. (1953). *Hitler: A study in tyranny*. New York: Harper & Row.

Bureau of Census. (1983). *Current population reports*. P-25, no. 949.

———. (1984). *Current population reports*. P-23, no. 128.

Burger, J. M., & Arkin, R. M. (1980). Prediction, control, and learned helplessness. *J. Pers. Soc. Psychol.*, *38*, 483–491.

Burros, M. (1988, February 23). Women: Out of the house but not out of the kitchen. *New York Times*, 1, 18.

Buss, A. H. (1966). *Psychopathology*. New York: Wiley.

Calhoun, J. B. (1962). Population density and social pathology. *Sci. Amer.*, *206*, 139–148.

Campbell, A. (1975). *Measuring the perceived quality of life*. New York: Russell Sage Foundation.

Cannon, W. B. (1939). *The wisdom of the body*. New York: Norton.

———. (1942). Voodoo death. *Amer. Anthropol.*, *44*, 169.

Caplan, P. J. (1984). The myth of women's masochism. *Amer. Psychol.*, *40*, 786–799.

Carrington, P. (1972). Dreams and schizophrenia. *Arch. Gen. Psychiat.*, *26*, 343–350.

Carskadon, M. A., Harvey, K., Duke, P., Anders, T. F., Litt, I. F., & Dement, W. C. (1980). Pubertal changes in daytime sleepiness. *Sleep*, *2*, 453–460.

Carver, R. P. (1971). *Sense and nonsense in speed reading*. Silver Springs, MD: Revrac Publications.

Case, R. B. (1985). Quoted in "Type A's maybe now you can relax." *Science 85*, *6*(5).

Cash, T. F., & Janda, L. H. (1984). The eye of the beholder. *Psychol. Today*, *18*(12).

Casler, L. (1976). The "consciousness problem" is not the problem. *Percep. Mot. Skills*, *42*, 227–232.

Chaves, J. F., & Barber, T. X. (1974). Acupuncture analgesia: A six-factor theory. *Psychoenergetic Syst.*, *1*, 11–21.

Chertkoff, J. M., & Conley, M. (1967). Opening offer and frequency of concession as bargaining strategies. *J. Pers. Soc. Psychol.*, *7*, 181–185.

Chomsky, N. (1980). Rules and representations. *Beh. Brain Sci.*, *3*, 1–15.

Cialdini, R. B., Petty, R. E., & Cacioppo, J. T. (1981). Attitude and attitude change. *Ann. Rev. Psychol.*, *32*, 357–404.

Clausen, J. (1975). The social meeaning of differential physical and sexual maturation. In S. Dragastin and G. Elder, Jr. (Eds.), *Adolescence and the life cycle*. New York: Halsted Press.

Clark, R. W. (1980). *Freud: The man and the cause*. New York: Random House.

Cleland, C. C., Case, J., & Manaster, G. J. (1980). IQs and etiologies: The two-group approach to mental retardation. *Bull. Psychon. Soc.*, *15*, 413–415.

Coates, B., Anderson, E., & Hartup, W. (1972). Interrelations in the attachment behavior of human infants. *Develop. Psychol.*, 6, 218–230.

Coe, W. C., & Ryken, K. (1979). Hypnosis and risks to human subjects. *Amer. Psychol.*, 34, 673–681.

Cohen, D. B. (1979). Remembering and forgetting dreaming. In J. F. Kihlstrom and F. J. Evans (Eds.), *Functional disorders of memory*. Hillsdale, NJ: Erlbaum.

———. (1980a). REM dreaming as an adaptive process. Mimeographed paper, revised from APSS address. Received 1980.

———. (1980b). Adaptive capabilities of the nervous system. In P. S. McConnell, G. J. Boer, H. J. Romijn, N. E. van de Poll, and M. A. Corner (Eds.), *Progress in brain research*. New York: Elsevier/North Holland Biomedical Press.

Cohen, S. (1980). Aftereffects of stress on human performance and social behavior: A review of research and theory. *Psychol. Bull.*, 88, 82–108.

Coile, D. C., & Miller, N. E. (1984). How radical animal activists try to mislead humane people. *Amer. Psychol.*, 39, 700–701.

Coleman, R. M. (1986). *Wide awake at 3:00 A.M.* New York: W. H. Freeman.

Collette-Pratt, C. (1976). Attitudinal predictors of devaluation of old age in a multigenerational sample. *J. Geron.*, 31, 193–197.

Collins, W. A., & Zimmerman, S. A. (1975). Convergent and divergent social cues: Effects of televised aggression on children. *Comm. Res.*, 2, 331–346.

Colombo, J. (1982). The critical period concept: Research, methodology, and theoretical issues. *Psychol. Bull.*, 91, 260–275.

Comstock, G., Chaffee, S., Katzman, N., McCombs, M., & Roberts, D. (1978). *Television and human behavior*. New York: Columbia University Press.

Conger, J. C., Conger, A. J., Costanzo, P. R., Wright, K. L., & Matter, J. A. (1980). The effect of social cues on the eating behavior of obese and normal subjects. *J. Pers.*, 48, 258–271.

Conger, J. J., & Peterson, A. C. (1984). *Adolescents and youth*. New York: Harper & Row.

Cooper, E., & Tahoda, M. (1964). Quoted in W. W. Lambert and W. E. Lambert, *Social psychology*. Englewood Cliffs, NJ: Prentice-Hall.

Corballis, M. C., & Morgan, M. J. (1978). On the biological basis of human laterality: Evidence for a maturational left-right gradient. *Behav. Brain Sci.*, 1, 261–269.

Costa, P. T., Jr., & McCrae, R. R. (1986). Cross-sectional studies of personality in a national sample: 1. Development and validation of survey measures. *Psychol. Aging*, 1, 140–143.

Costa, P. T., Jr., Zonderman, A. B., McCrae, R. R., Cornoni-Huntley, Locke, B. Z., & Barbano, H. E. (1987). Longitudinal analysis of psychological well-being in a national sample: Stability of mean levels. *J. Gerontol.*, 42, 50–55.

Cowan, N. (1984). On short and long auditory stores. *Psychol. Bull.*, 96, 341–370.

Cowart, B. J. (1981). Development of taste perception in humans: Sensitivity and preference throughout the life span. *Psychol. Bull.*, 90, 43–73.

Cox, V. C., Paulus, P. B., & McCain, G. (1984). Prison crowding research: The relevance for prison housing standards and a general approach regarding crwoding phenomena. *Amer. Psychol.*, 39, 1148–1160.

Craik, F. I. M. (1979). Human memory. *Ann. Rev. Psychol.*, 30, 63–102.

Crick, F. H. C. (1983). Thinking about the brain. *The brain*. San Francisco: W. H. Freeman.

Cronbach, L. J. (1960). *Essentials of psychological testing* (2d ed.). New York: Harper & Row.

———. (1980). *Essentials of psychological testing* (4th ed.). New York: Harper & Row.

Crosby, F., Bromley, S., & Saxe, L. (1980). Recent unobtrusive studies of black and white discrimination and prejudice: A literature review. *Psychol. Bull.*, 87, 546–563.

Curtiss, S. (1977). *Genie: A psycholinguistic study of a modern-day "wild child."* New York: Academic Press.

Daniels, D. (1986). Differential experiences of siblings in the same family as predictors of adolescent sibling personality differences. *J. Pers. Soc. Psychol.*, 51, 339–346.

Davenport, H. W. (1982). Why the stomach does not digest itself. *Sci. Amer.*, 226(1).

Davis, K. (1972). The American family in relation to demographic change. In C. R. Westoff and R. Parke (Eds.), *Demographic and social aspects of population growth*: 1. Washington, DC: Bureau of Census.

Davis, K. E. (1985). Near and dear: Friendship and love compared. *Psychol. Today*, 19(2).

Dean, S. J., Martin, R. B., & Steiner, D. (1968). Mediational control of the GSR. *J. Exp. Res. Personal.*, 3, 71–76.

Deaux, K. (1985). Sex and gender. *Ann. Rev. Psychol.*, 36, 49–81.

DeBold, J. F. (1983). Quoted in "Masculine/feminine behavior: New views." *Sci. News*, 124, 326.

Degler, C. N. (1980). *At odds.* New York: Oxford University Press.

Delgado, J. M. R. (1969). *Physical control of the mind*. New York: Harper & Row.

Dement, W. C. (1974). *Some must watch while some must sleep*. San Francisco: W. H. Freeman.

———. (1979). Normal sleep and sleep disorders. In G. Usdin and J. M. Lewis (Eds.), *Psychiatry in general practice*. New York: McGraw-Hill.

Denton, D. (1983). *The hunger for salt*. New York: Springer-Verlag.

Depue, R. A., Slater, J. F., Wolfstetter-Kausch, H., Klein, D., Goplerud, E., & Farr, D. (1981). A behavioral paradigm for identifying persons at risk for bipolar depressive disorder: A conceptual framework and five validation studies. *J. Abn. Psychol. Monog.*, 90, 381–437.

Derryberry, J. S. (1983). Quoted in "Scientists give nod to sleeping pills." *Sci. News*, 124, 342.

Deutsch, A. (1946). *The mentally ill in America* (2d ed.). New York: Columbia University Press.

Deutsch, J. A. (1973). *Physiological psychology* (2d ed.). Homewood, IL: Dorsey Press.

Diagnostic and Statistical Manual of Mental Disorders (3d ed.). (1980). Washington, DC: American Psychiatric Association.

Diener, E. (1976). Effects of prior destructive behavior, anonymity, and group presence on deindividuation and aggression. *J. Pers. Soc. Psychol.*, 33, 497–507.

Diener, E., Fraser, S. C., Beaman, A. L., & Kelem, R. T. (1976). Effects of deindividuation variables on stealing among Halloween trick-or-treaters. *J. Pers. Soc. Psychol.*, 33, 178–183.

Diener, E., & Woody, L. W. (1981). Television violence, conflict, realism, and action. *Comm. Res.*, 8, 281–306.

Dohrenwend, B. S., Dohrenwend, B. P., Link, B., & Neugebauer, R. (1979). Epidemiology and genetics of schizophrenia. *Soc. Biol., 26*, 142–153.

Doob, A. N., & Climie, J. R. (1972). Delay of measurement and the effects of film violence. *J. Exp. Soc. Psychol., 8*, 136–142.

Dunlop, R. (1965). *Doctors of the American frontier.* Garden City, NY: Doubleday.

Dunn, A. J. (1980). Neurochemistry of learning and memory: An evaluation of recent data. *Ann. Rev. Psychol., 31*, 343–390.

Dunn-Rankin, E. D. (1978). The visual characteristics of words. *Sci. Amer., 238*(1).

Dweck, C. S., Goets, T. E., & Strauss, N. L. (1980). Sex differences in learned helplessness: 4. An experimental and naturalistic study of failure generalisation and its mediators. *J. Pers. & Soc. Psychol., 38*, 441–452.

Eagly, A. H. (1978). Sex differences in influencibility. *Psychol. Bull., 85*, 86–116.

Eagly, A. H., & Himmelfarb, S. (1978). Attitudes and opinions. *Ann. Rev. Psychol., 29*, 517–554.

Edinger, J. A., & Paterson, M. L. (1983). Nonverbal involvement and social control. *Psychol. Bull., 93*, 30–56.

Ehrhardt, A. (1979). Biological sex differences: A developmental perspective. *Master lectures on issues of sex and gender in psychology.* (Tape 15/12). Washington, DC: American Psychological Association.

Eisdorfer, C. (1983). Conceptual models of aging. *Amer. Psychol., 38*, 197–202.

Eisenberg, N., & Lennon, R. (1983). Sex differences in empathy and related capacities. *Psychol. Bull., 94*, 100–131.

Eisenberger, R. (1972). Explanation of rewards that do not reduce tissue needs. *Psychol. Bull., 77*, 319–339.

Eisler, R. M., & Williams, W. V. (1972). A comparison of preadmission characteristics of patients selected for long- or short-term psychiatric treatment. *J. Clin. Psychol., 28*, 209–213.

Elkind, D. (1978). *The child's reality: Three developmental themes.* Hillsdale, NJ: Erlbaum.

Ellenberger, H. F. (1970). *The discovery of the unconscious.* New York: Basic Books.

Ellis, A. (1980). Rational-emotive theory and cognitive behavior therapy: Similarities and differences. *Cog. Ther. & Res., 4*, 325–340.

Emery, R. E. (1982). Interparental conflict and the children of discord and divorce. *Psychol. Bull., 92*, 310–330.

Emlen, S. T. (1975). The stellar-orientation system of a migratory bird. *Sci. Amer., 233*(2).

Engen, T. (1987). Remembering odors and their names. *Amer. Sci., 75*(5).

Erikson, E. H. (1968). *Identity: Youth and crisis.* New York: Norton.

Eron, L. D. (1980). Prescriptions for reduction of aggression. *Amer. Psychol., 35*, 244–252.

———. (1983). Quoted in "Parental behavior, TV habits, IQ predict aggression." *Sci. News, 124*, 148.

Eron, L. D., & Huesman, L. R. (1985). Quoted in "Once a bully, always. . . ." *Psychol. Today, 19*(7).

Evans, C., & Evans, P. (Eds.). *Landscapes of the night.* New York: Viking Press.

Evans, G. W. (1980). Environmental cognition. *Psychol. Bull., 88*, 259–287.

Evans, G. W., & Howard, R. B. (1973). Personal space. *Psychol. Bull., 80*, 334–344.

Falbo, T., & Peplau, L. A. (1980). Power stategies in intimate relationships. *J. Pers. & Soc. Psychol., 38*, 618–628.

Fancher, R. E. (1979). *Pioneers of psychology.* New York: Norton.

Farber, M. L. (1968). *Theory of suicide.* New York: Funk & Wagnalls.

Farley, J., & Alkon, D. J. (1985). Cellular mechanisms of learning, memory, and information storage. *Ann. Rev. Psychol., 36*, 419–494.

Farr, L. (1975). Peddling the pedestal. *New Times, 5*(8).

Feingold, A. (1988). Cognitive gender differences are disappearing. *Amer. Psychol., 43*, 95–103.

Festinger, L. (1957). *A theory of cognitive dissonance.* Stanford, CA: Stanford University Press.

Fingarett, H. (1988). *Heavy drinking.* Berkeley: University of California Press.

Fishman, S. M., & Sheehan, D. W. (1985). Anxiety and panic: Their cause and treatment. *Psychol. Today, 19*(4).

Flexner, J. T. (1974). *Washington: The indispensable man.* New York: New American Library.

Fobes, J. C., & Smock, C. C. (1981). Sensory capacities of marine mammals. *Psychol. Bull., 89*, 288–307.

Fox, M. W. (Ed.). (1968). *Abnormal behavior in animals.* Philadelphia: Saunders.

———. (1980a, July 27). Animal bulletin. In "Animal doctor." *St. Louis Post Dispatch*, pp.

———. (1980b). *The soul of the wolf.* Boston: Little, Brown.

———. (1983). Humane ethics and animal rights. *Int. J. Stud. Anim. Prob., 4*, 286–289.

Frank, G. (1966). *The Boston strangler.* New York: New American Library.

Frank, J. D. (1968). The face of the enemy. *Psychol. Today, 2*, 24–29.

———. (1971). Therapeutic factors in psychotherapy. *Amer. J. of Psychother., 25*, 350–361.

———. (1974). *Persuasion and healing: A comparative study of psychotherapy.* Baltimore, MD: Johns Hopkins University Press.

Franzoi, S. L. (1985). Quoted in "The things they do for love." *Sci. News, 127*, 398.

Freedman, D. A., & Brown, S. L. (1968). On the role of somasthetic stimulation in the development of psychic structure. *Psychoanal. Quart., 37*, 418–438.

Freedman, J. L. (1984). Effect of television violence on aggressiveness. *Psychol. Bull., 96*, 227–246.

Freedman, J. L., & Fraser, S. C. (1966). Compliance without pressure. *J. Personal. Soc. Psychol., 4*, 196–202.

Freeman, C. (1985). Quoted in "The patients' perspective on ECT." *Sci. News, 127*, 74.

Freud, S. (1938). The history of the psychoanalytic movement. In A. A. Brill (Ed.), *The basic writings of Sigmund Freud.* New York: Random House.

Friedman, H. S., & Booth-Kewley, S. (1987). The "disease-prone" personality. *Amer. Psychol., 42*, 539–555.

Friedman, M. (1984). Quoted in "Type A: A change of heart and mind." *Sci. News, 126*, 109.

Friedman, M., & Rosenman, R. (1974). *Type A behavior and your heart.* New York: Knopf.

Frumkin, R. M. (1961). Beauty. In A. Ellis and A. Abarbanal (Eds.), *The encyclopedia of sexual behavior.* New York: Hawthorne Books.

Furst, C. J. (1979). The inside and outside of eidetic imagery. *Beh. Brain Sci.*, *2*, 602–603.

Gagnon, D. (1986). *Videogames and special skills.* Mimeograph from author.

Gardner, H. (1983). *Frames of mind: The theory of multiple intelligences.* New York: Basic Books.

Garfield, S. L. (1981). Psychotherapy: A 40-year appraisal. *Amer. Psychol.*, *36*, 174–183.

Gazzaniga, M. S. (1970). *The bisected brain.* Englewood Cliffs, NJ: Prentice-Hall.

Geddes, L. A., & Newberg, D. C. (1977). Cuff pressure oscillations in the measurement of relative blood pressure. *Psychophysio.*, *14*, 198–202.

Geen, R. (1977). The catharsis of aggression: An evaluation of a hypothesis. In L. Berkowitz (Ed.), *Advances in experimental social psychology.* New York: Academic Press.

Geschwind, N. (1983). Quoted in Kolata, G. Math genius may have hormonal basis. *Science*, *222*, 1312.

Getzels, J. W., & Jackson, P. W. (1962). *Creativity and intelligence.* New York: Wiley.

Gibson, E. J., & Walk, R. D. (1960). The visual cliff. *Sci. Amer.*, *202*(4).

Gilbert, S. (1985). Noise pollution. *Sci. Dig.*, *93*(3).

Gill, R., & Keats, D. (1980). Elements of intellectual competence: Judgements by Australian and Malay university students. *J. Cross-Cult. Psychol.*, *11*, 233–243.

Glick, P. C. (1977). Updating the life cycle of the family. *J. Marr. & Fam.*, *39*, 5–13.

Gold, M. S. (1985). Quoted in "Multiple drug use: A dangerous trend." *Sci. News*, *128*, 6.

Goldfried, M. R. (1980). Toward the delineation of therapeutic change principles. *Amer. Psychol.*, *35*, 991–999.

Goodall, J. (1971). *In the shadow of man.* Boston, MA: Houghton Mifflin.

Goodwin, J. S., Goodwin, J. M., & Garry, P. J. (1984). Quoted in "Food for thought in the elderly." *Sci. News*, *123*, 358.

Gough, H. G. (1960). *Manual for the California Psychological Inventory* (rev. ed.). Palo Alto, CA: Consulting Psychologists Press.

———. (1976). Studying creativity by means of word association tests. *J. Appl. Psychol.*, *61*, 348–353.

———. (1979). A creative personality scale for the Adjective Check List. *J. Pers. Soc. Psychol.*, *37*, 1398–1405.

Gould, J. (1985). Quoted in "To honeybees, a picture is worth a thousand line angles." *Sci. News*, *127*, 196.

Gould, J. L. (1984). Quoted in "Mind maps." *Sci. News*, *125*, 62–63.

Gould, R. (1975). Adult life stages: Growth toward self-tolerance. *Psychol. Today*, *8*(9).

Graber, E. (1988). Personal communication.

Graf, P., Squire, L. R., & Mandler, G. (1984). The information that amnesiac patients do not forget. *J. Exp. Psychol.: Lrn. Mem. & Cog.*, *10*, 164–178.

Graham, K., LaRocque, L., Yetman, R., Ross, J. G., & Guistra, E. (1980). Aggression and barroom environments. *J. Stud. Alcoh.*, *41*, 277–292.

Graham, P. A. (1984). Wanting it all. *Wilson Quart.*, *7*(1).

Grant, I., Sweetwood, H. L., Yager, J., & Gerst, M. (1981). Quality of life events in relation to psychiatric symptoms. *Arch. Gen. Psychiatr.*, *38*, 335–339.

Green, B. F. (1978). In defense of measurement. *Amer. Psychol.*, *33*, 664–670.

Green, R. (1974). *Sexual identity conflict in children and adults.* New York: Basic Books.

Greenough, W. (1985). Quoted in "The brain branches out." *Science 85*, *6*(5).

Gregory, R. L. (1968). Visual illusions. *Sci. Amer.*, *219*(5).

———. (1981). *Mind in science.* New York: Cambridge University Press.

Griffin, D. R. (1976). *The question of animal awareness.* New York: Rockefeller University Press.

Grinspoon, L. (1969). Marihuana. *Sci. Amer.*, *221*(6).

Gripp, R. F., & Magaro, P. A. (1971). A token economy program evaluation with untreated control ward comparisons. *Beh. Res. Ther.*, *9*, 137–149.

Gruenewald. D. (1971). Hypnotic techniques without hypnosis in the treatment of dual personality. *J. New Ment. Dis.*, *153*, 41–46.

Guilleminault, C., Pedley, T., & Dement, W. C. (1977). Sleepwalking and epilepsy. *Sleep Res.*, *6*, 170.

Gutmann, D. (1975). Parenthood: A key to the comparative study of the life cycle. In N. Datan and L. Ginsberg (Eds.), *Lifespan developmental psychology: Normative life crises.* New York: Academic Press.

Haber, R. N. (1970). How we remember what we were. *Sci. Amer.*, *222*(5).

Hall, C. S., Lindzey, G., Loehlin, J. C., & Manosevitz, M. (1985). *Introduction to theories of personality.* New York: Wiley.

Hall, G. (1980). Exposure learning in animals. *Psychol. Bull.*, *88*, 535–550.

Halpert, H. P. (1969). Public acceptance of the mentally ill. *Public Health Rep.*, *84*, 59–64.

Hamilton, D. L. (1979). A cognitive-attributional analysis of stereotyping. In L. Berkowitz (Ed.), *Advances in experimental social psychology.* New York: Academic Press.

Hamilton, D. L., & Rose, T. L. (1980). Illusory correlation and the maintenance of stereotypic beliefs. *J. Pers. Soc. Psychol.*, *39*, 832–845.

Hamilton, E. (1942). *The Greek way.* New York: Norton.

Harlow, H. F. (1959). Love in infant monkeys. *Sci. Amer.*, *22*(6).

Harlow, H. F., Blazek, N., & McClearn, G. (1956). Manipulatory motivation in the infant rhesus monkey. *J. Comp. Physiol. Psychol.*, *49*, 444–448.

Harmon, L. D. (1973). The recognition of faces. *Sci. Amer.*, *229*(5).

Harper, R. A. (1968). *Psychoanalysis and psychotherapy: 36 systems.* Englewood Cliffs, NJ: Prentice-Hall.

Hartmann, E. (1973). *The functions of sleep.* New Haven, CT: Yale University Press.

———. (1984). *The nightmare.* New York: Basic Books.

Hartmann, E., & Brewer, V. (1976). When is more or less sleep required? A study of variable sleepers. *Comp. Psychiatr.*, *17*, 275–284.

Haugeland, J. (1978). The nature and plausibility of cognitivism. *Behav. Brain Sci.*, *1*, 215–225.

Hawgood, J. A. (1967). *America's western frontiers.* New York: Knopf.

Hayflick, L. (1979). The cell biology of human aging. *Sci. Amer.*, *242*(1), 58–65.

Hearn, C. B., & Seeman, J. (1971). Personality integration and perception of interpersonal relationships. *J. Pers. Soc. Psychol.*, *2*, 138–143.

Hebb, D. O., & Donderi, D. C. (1987). *Textbook of Psychology*. Hillsdale NJ: Erlbaum.

Heide, F. J. (1985). Relaxation: The storm before the calm. *Psychol. Today*, 19(4).

Heinemann, L. G. (1970). Visual phenomena in a long sensory deprivation. *Percept. Mot. Skills*, 30, 563–570.

Hetherington, E. M. (1965). A developmental study of the effects of sex on the dominant parent on sex-role preference, identification, and imitation in children. *J. Personal Soc. Psychol.*, 2, 188–194.

Hilgard, E. R. (1974). Weapon against pain. *Psychol. Today*, 8(6).

———. (1980). Consciousness in contemporary psychology. *Ann. Rev. Psychol.*, 31, 1–26.

Hilgard, E. R., & Hilgard, J. R. (1975). *Hypnosis in the relief of pain*. Los Angeles: Daufmann.

Hoffman, L. W. (1977). Changes in family roles, socialization, and sex differences. *Amer. Psychol.*, 32, 644–657.

Hofling, C. K., Brotzman, E., Dalrymple, S., Graves, N., & Pierce, C. M. (1966). An experimental study in nurse-physician relationships. *J. Nerv. Ment. Dis.*, 143, 171–180.

Holden, C. (1980). Twins reunited. *Science 80*, 55–59.

Hollingsworth, H. L. (1922). *Judging human character*. New York: Appleton-Century-Crofts.

Holmes, D. S. (1984). Meditation and somatic arousal reduction. *Amer. Psychol.*, 39, 1–10.

Holmes, T. H., & Rahe, R. H. (1967). The social readjustment rating scale. *J. Psychosom. Res.*, 11, 213–218.

Honts, C., Hodes, R., & Raskin, D. (1985). Quoted in "Beat that lie detector!" *Psychol. Today*, 19(6).

Horney, K. (1950). *Neurosis and human growth*. New York: Norton.

Horton, D. L., & Mills, C. B. (1984). Human learning and memory. *Ann. Rev. Psychol.*, 35, 361–394.

Horton, P., & Miller, D. (1972). The etiology of multiple personality. *Comp. Psychiatr.*, 13(2).

Howells, W. (1962). *The heathens: Primitive man and his religions*. New York: Doubleday.

Hulicka, I. M. (1978). Cognitive functioning of older adults. *Master lectures on the psychology of aging*. Tape 14/15. Washington, DC: American Psychological Association.

Hurvich, L. M. (1974). Opponent processes as a model of neural organization. *Amer. Psychol.*, 29, 88–102.

Imara, M. (1975). Dying as the last stage of growth. In E. Kübler-Ross (Ed.), *Death, the final stage of growth*. Englewood Cliffs, NJ: Prentice-Hall.

Institute for Social Research. (1984). University of Michigan.

Isaacson, R. L., & Pribram, K. H. (1975). *The hippocampus*. New York: Plenum.

Isner, J. M. (1987). Interviewed in "Cocaine cardiology: Problems, mysteries." *Sci. News*, 131(5).

Itard, J. M. G. (1932). *The wild boy of Aveyron*. New York: Appleton-Century-Crofts.

Jackson, D. D. (1984). If women needed a quick pick-me-up, Lydia provided one. *Smithsonian*, 15(4).

Jacobs, B. L. (1987). How hallucinogenic drugs work. *Amer. Sci.*, 75, 386–392.

Jacobson, W. J., & Doran, R. L. (1985). Quoted in "Girls and science: The gap remains." *Psychol. Today*, 19(6).

James, T. M. (1985). The trade. *Wilson Quart.*, 9(1).

Jansen, D. G., & Nickles, L. A. (1973). Variables that differentiate between single and multiple admission psychiatric patients at a state hospital over a five-year period. *J. Clin. Psychol.*, 29, 83–85.

Jarvik, L. F. (1975). Thoughts on the psychobiology of aging. *Amer. Psychol.*, 30, 576–583.

Jarvik, L. F., & Cohen, D. (1973). A biobehavioral approach to intellectual changes with aging. In C. E. Eisdorfer and M. P. Lawton (Eds.), *The psychology of adult development and aging*. Washington, DC: American Psychological Association.

Jay, R. (1987). *Learned pigs & fireproof women*. New York: Villard Books.

Jaynes, J. (1976). *The origin of consciousness in the breakdown of the bicameral mind*. Boston: Houghton Mifflin.

Jemmott, J. B., III, & Locke, S. E. (1984). Psychosocial factors, immunologic mediation, and human susceptibility to infectious diseases: How much do we know? *Psychol. Bull.*, 95, 79–108.

Jensen, R. A., Martinez, J. L., McGaugh, J. L., Messing, R. B., & Vasquez, B. J. (1980). The psychobiology of aging. In G. J. Maletta and F. J. Pirossolo (Eds.), *The aging nervous system*. New York: Praeger.

Jerison, H. J. (1976). Paleoneurology and the evolution of mind. *Sci. Amer.*, 234(1).

Jones, M. C. (1924). A laboratory study of fear: The case of Peter. *Pedagog. Semin.*, 31, 308–315.

———. (1974). Albert, Peter, and John B. Watson. *Amer. Psychol.*, 29, 581–583.

Jones, R. M. (1970). *The new psychology of dreaming*. New York: Grune & Stratton.

Jouandet, M., & Gazzaniga, M. S. (1979). The frontal lobes. In M. S. Gazzaniga (Ed.), *Handbook of behavioral neurobiology*. New York: Plenum.

Jung, C. G. (1933). *Modern man in search of a soul*. New York: Harcourt Brace Jovanovich.

———. (1958). Transformation symbolism in the mass. In V. S. de-Laszio (Ed.), *Psyche and symbol: A selection of writings of C. G. Jung*. New York: Doubleday.

Kagan, J. (1975). Resilience in cognitive development. *Ethos*, 3, 231–247.

———. (1979). Family experience and the child's development. *Amer. Psychol.*, 34, 886–891.

———. (1984). *The nature of the child*. New York: Basic Books.

Kahn, E., Fisher, C., Edwards, A., & Davis, D. (1972). Psychophysiology of night terrors and nightmares. *Proceed. 80th Annual Conv. Amer. Psychol. Assn.*

Kahn, L. S. (1980). The dynamics of scapegoating: The expulsion of evil. *Psychother. Theory Res. Pract.*, 17, 79–84.

Kaluger, G., & Kaluger, M. F. (1984). *Human development*. St. Louis: Times Mirror/Mosby.

Kamin, L. J. (1978). Comment on Munsinger's review of adoption studies. *Psychol. Bull.*, 85, 194–201.

———. Inbreeding depression and I.Q. *Psychol. Bull.*, 87, 469–478.

Kamil, A. C., & Roitblat, H. L. (1985). The ecology of foraging behavior: Implications for animal learning and memory. *Ann. Rev. Psychol.*, 36, 141–169.

Kammerman, M. (Ed.). (1977). *Sensory isolation and personality change*. Springfield, IL: Thomas.

Kamerman, S. (1986, February). *Infant care usage in the United States*. Report to the National Academy of Sciences Ad Hoc committee on policy issues in child care for infants and toddlers. Washington, DC.

Kanfer, F. H., Karoly, P., & Newman, A. (1975). Reduction in children's fear of the dark by competence-related and situational threat-related verbal cues. *J. Clin. Psychol.*, 43, 251–258.

Kapatos, G., & Gold, R. M. (1972). Tongue cooling during drinking: A regulator of water intake in rats. *Science*, 176, 685–686.

Kaplan, R. M. (1982). Nader's raid on the testing industry. *Amer. Psychol.*, 37, 15–23.

Kary, S. (1984). Personal communication. (My thanks to Dr. Kary for his suggestion.)

Kastenbaum, R., & Costa, P. T. (1977). Psychological perspectives on death. *Ann. Rev. Psychol.*, 28, 225–249.

Katkin, E. S. (1985). Polygraph testing, psychological research and public policy. *Amer. Psychol.*, 40, 346–347.

Katz, D., & Braley, K. (1958). Verbal stereotypes and racial prejudice. In E. Maccoby, T. Newcomb, and E. Hautley (Eds.), *Readings in social psychology*. New York: Holt, Rinehart and Winston.

Kavanaugh, R. E. (1974). *Facing death*. Baltimore: Penguin Books.

Keeton, W. T. (1974). The mystery of pigeon homing. *Sci. Amer.*, 231(6).

Kellogg, R. T. (1980). Is conscious attention necessary for long-term storage? *J. Exp. Psychol. Hum. Lrn. Mem.*, 6, 379–390.

Kellogg, W. N., & Kellogg, L. A. (1933). *The ape and the child*. New York: McGraw-Hill.

Kernberg, O. F., Bernstein, C. S., Coyne, R., Applebaum, D. A., Horwitz, H., & Voth, T. J. (1972). Psychotherapy and psychoanalysis: Final report of the Menninger Foundation's psychotherapy research project. *Bull. Menninger Clin.*, 36, 1–276.

Kesner, R. P., & Conner, H. S. (1972). Independence of short- and long-term memory: A neural system analysis. *Science*, 176, 432–434.

Kidd, K. K. (1985). Quoted in "Depression and the family." *Sci. News*, 127, 360.

Kinsbourne, M., & Wood, F. (1975). Short-term memory processes and the amnesia syndrome. In D. Deutsch and J. Deutsch (Eds.), *Short-term memory*. New York: Academic Press.

Klatzky, R. L. (1980). *Human memory: Structures and processes* (2d ed.). San Francisco: W. H. Freeman.

———. (1984). *Memory and awareness: An information processing perspective*. New York: W. H. Freeman.

Kline, M. V. (1972). The production of antisocial behavior through hypnosis: New clinical data. *Int. J. Clin. Exp. Hyp.*, 2, 80–94.

Kobasa, S. C., Hilker, R. R., & Maddi, S. R. (1979). Who stays healthy under stress? *J. Occ. Med.*, 21, 595–598.

Kobasa, S. C., Maddi, S. R., & Kahn, S. (1980). Intrinsic motivation and health. In H. I. Day (Ed.), *Advances in intrinsic motivation and aesthetics*. New York: Plenum.

———. (1981). *Hardiness and health: A prospective study*. Mimeograph received from authors.

Kohlberg, L. (1963). Moral development and identification. In H. W. Stevenson (Ed.), *Yearbook of the national society for the study of education: 1. Child psychology*. Chicago: University of Chicago Press.

Kokkinidis, L. K., & Anisman, H. (1980). Amphetamine models of paranoid schizophrenia: An overview and elaboration of animal experimentation. *Psychol. Bull.*, 88, 551–579.

Kolata, G. (1983). Math genius may have hormonal basis. *Science*, 222, 1312.

Kolodny, R. C., Masters, W. H., Kolodner, R. M., & Toro, G. (1974). Depression of plasma testosterone levels after chronic intensive marijuana use. *New Eng. J. Med.*, 290, 872–874.

Krantz, D. S., & Manuck, S. B. (1985). Acute psychophysiologic reactivity and risk of cardiovascular disease: A review and methodologic critique. *Psychol. Bull.*, 96, 435–464.

Krasnoff, A. G. (1981). The sex difference in self-assessed fears. *Sex Roles*, 7, 19–23.

Kübler-Ross, E. (1969). *On death and dying*. New York: Macmillan.

———. (1975). *Death: The final stage of growth*. Englewood Cliffs, NJ: Prentice-Hall.

Kuehn, J. L., & Crinella, F. M. (1969). Sensitivity training: Interpersonal "overkill" and other problems. *Amer. J. Psychiat.*, 126, 840–845.

Lachman, S. J. (1983). Psychophysiological interpretation of voodoo illness and voodoo death. *Omega*, 13, 345–360.

Lamb, M. E. (1979). Paternal influences and the father's role. *Amer. Psychol.*, 34, 938–943.

Lambert, N. M., Hartsough, C. S., & Zimmerman, I. L. (1976). The comparative predictive efficiency of intellectual and nonintellectual components of high school functioning. *Amer. J. Orthopsychiat.*, 46, 109–122.

Lambert, W. W., & Lambert, W. E. (1964). *Social psychology*. Englewood Cliffs, NJ: Prentice-Hall.

Land, E. H. (1977). The retinex theory of color vision. *Sci. Amer.*, 237(6).

Landsbaum, J. B., & Willis, R. H. (1971). Conformity in early and late adolescence. *Develop. Psychol.*, 4, 334–347.

Lang, P. J., & Melamed, B. G. (1969). Case report: Avoidance conditioning therapy of an infant with chronic rumative vomiting. *J. Abnorm. Psychol.*, 74, 1–8.

Latané, B., & Darley, J. M. (1970). *The unresponsive bystander: Why doesn't he help?* Englewood Cliffs, NJ: Prentice-Hall.

Laurence, J. R. (1983). Hypnotically created memory among highly hypnotizable subjects. *Science*, 222, 523–524.

Lazarus, R. S. (1974). *The riddle of man*. Englewood Cliffs, NJ: Prentice-Hall.

Lazarus, R. S., & Folkman, S. (1984). *Stress, appraisal, and coping*. New York: Springer.

Lebovitz, P. S. (1972). Feminine behavior in boys: Aspects of its outcome. *Amer. J. Psychiat.*, 128, 1283–1289.

Lerner, R. M., & Frank, P. (1974). Relations of race and sex to supermarket helping behavior. *J. Soc. Psychol.*, 94, 201–203.

Lerner, R. M., & Hultsch, D. E. (1983). *Human development: A life-span perspective*. New York: McGraw-Hill.

Levine, J. D., & Gordon, N. C. (1985). Quoted in "The subtle strength of placebos." *Sci. News*, 127, 25.

Levine, R. V., West, L. J., & Reiss, H. T. (1980). Perceptions of time and punctuality in the United States and Brazil. *J. Pers. Soc. Psychol.*, 38, 541–550.

Levinson, D., Vaillant, G., & Gould, R. (1975). Adult life cycles. *APA Monitor*, 6(9 & 10).

Levinson, D. J. (1978). *The seasons of a man's life*. New York: Knopf.

Lewinsohn, P. M., Mischel, W., Chaplin, W., & Barton, R. (1980). Social competence and depression: The role of illusory self-perceptions. *J. Abn. Psychol.*, 89, 203–212.

Libet, B., Gleason, C. A., Wright, W. W., & Pearl, D. K. (1983). Time of conscious intention to act in relation to onset of cerebral activity (readiness-potential). *Brain*, 106, 623–642.

Lifton, R. (1961). *Thought reform and the psychology of totalism*. New York: Norton.

Liljefors, I., & Rahe, R. H. (1970). An identical twin study of psychosocial factors in coronary heart disease in Sweden. *Psychosom. Med.*, 32, 523–542.

Linville, P. W., & Jones, E. E. (1980). Polarized appraisals of out-group members. *J. Pers. Soc. Psychol., 38,* 689–703.

Lipton, D. S., & Marel, R. (1980). The white adolescent's drug odyssey. *Youth and Society, 11,* 397–413.

Livson, F. B. (1976). Patterns of personality development in middle-aged women: A longitudinal study. *Int'l. J. Aging & Human Devel., 7,* 107–115.

Llinas, R., & Pellionisa, A. (1979). Brain modeling by tensor networks theory and computer simulation. The cerebellum: Distributed processor for predictive coordination. *Neuroscience, 4.*

Lloyd, M. (1985). *Adolescence.* New York: Harper & Row.

Loeb, G. E. (1985). The functional replacement of the ear. *Sci. Amer., 252*(2).

Loftus, E. F. (1980). The malleability of human memory. *Amer. Sci., 67,* 312–320.

———. (1984). Eyewitnesses: Essential but unreliable. *Psychol. Today, 181*(2).

Lombroso-Ferrero, G. (1911). *Criminal man.* New York: Putnam's.

Lopez, B. H. (1978). *Of wolves and men.* New York: Scribner's.

Loque, A. W. (1986). *The psychology of eating and drinking.* New York: W. H. Freeman.

Lorenz, K. (1952). *King Solomon's ring.* New York: Crowell.

———. (1963). *On aggression.* New York: Harcourt Brace Jovanovich.

Lorenz, M. (1961). Problems posed by schizophrenic language. *Arch. Gen. Psychiat., 4,* 603–610.

Luce, G. G. (1971). *Body time.* New York: Random House.

Luria, A. R. (1968). *The mind of a mnemonist.* New York: Basic Books.

Lyell, R. G. (1984). Personal communication.

Lykken, D. T. (1981). *A tremor in the blood.* New York: McGraw-Hill.

———. (1987). An alternate explanation for low or zero sib correlations. *Beh. Brain Sci., 10,* 31.

Lynch, G., & Baudry, M. (1984). The biochemistry of memory: A new and specific hypothesis. *Science, 225,* 1057–1063.

Maccoby, E. E., & Jacklin, C. N. (1974). *The psychology of sex differences.* Stanford, CA: Stanford University Press.

Mackenzie, B. (1984). Explaining race differences in IQ. *Amer. Psychol., 39,* 1214–1233.

Maddison, S., Wood, R. J., Rolls, E. T., Rolls, B. J., & Gibbs, J. (1980). Drinking in the rhesus monkey: Peripheral factors. *J. Comp. Physiol. Psychol., 94,* 365–374.

Malinowski, B. (1929). *The sexual life of savages in northwestern Melanesia.* New York: Harcourt Brace Jovanovich.

Mandler, G. (1984). *Mind and body: Psychology of emotion and stress.* New York: Norton.

Mandler, J. M., & Ritchey, G. H. (1977). Long-term memory for pictures. *J. Exp. Psychol.: Hum. Lrn. Mem., 3,* 386–396.

Manning, A. (1967). *An introduction to anaimal behavior.* Reading, MA: Addison-Wesley.

Marcia, J. E. (1980). Identity in adolescence. In J. Adelson (Ed.), *Handbook of adolescent psychology.* New York: Wiley.

Margules, D. L., & Olds, J. (1962). Identical "feeding" and "rewarding" systems in the lateral hypothalamus of rats. *Science, 135,* 374–375.

Marks, I. (1979). Conditioning models for clinical syndromes are out of date. *Beh. Brain Sci., 2,* 175–176.

Martinez, J. L., Jr., Jensen, R. A., Messing, R. B., Vasquez, B. J.,

Soumireau-Mourat, S., Geddes, D., Laing, K. C., & McGaugh, J. L. (1980). Central and peripheral actions of amphetamine on memory storage. *Brain Res., 182,* 157–166.

Martinez, J. L., Jr., Jensen, R. A., Vasquez, B. J., Lacob, J. S., McGaugh, J. L., & Purdy, R. E. (1979). Acquisition deficits induced by sodium nitrite in rats and mice. *Psychopharm., 60,* 221–228.

Maslow, A. H. (1954). *Motivation and personality.* New York: Harper & Row.

———. (1968). *Toward a psychology of being* (2d ed.). New York: D. Van Nostrand.

Massaro, D. W. (1970). Forgetting: Interference or decay? *J. Exp. Psychol., 83,* 238–243.

Matarazzo, J. D. (1985). Psychotherapy. In G. A. Kimble and K. Schlesinger (Eds.), *Topics in the history of psychology.* Hillsdale, NJ: Erlbaum.

Matson, F. W. (1964). *The broken image.* New York: Braziller.

Maxwell, J. (1969). *Skimming and scanning improvement.* New York: McGraw-Hill.

McCaul, K. D., & Malott, J. M. (1984). Distraction and coping with pain. *Psychol. Bull., 95,* 516–533.

McClelland, D. C. (1973). Testing for competence rather than for "intelligence." *Amer. Psychol., 28,* 1–14.

McClelland, D. C., Atkinson, J. W., Clark, R. A., & Lowell, E. L. (1953). *The achievement motive.* New York: Appleton-Century-Crofts.

McCloskey, M., & Zaragonza, M. (1985). Quoted in "How malleable are eyewitness memories?" *Sci. News, 127,* 164.

McConnell, J. V., Cutler, R. L., & McNeil, E. B. (1958). Subliminal stimulation: An overview. *Amer. Psychol., 13,* 229–242.

McCullough, D. (1982). *The great bridge.* New York: Simon & Schuster.

McFarland, D. (Ed.). (1981). *The Oxford companion to animal behaviour.* New York: Oxford University Press.

McGaugh, J. L. (1983). Hormonal influences on memory. *Ann. Rev. Psychol., 34,* 297–324.

McGee, M. (1980). Faith, fantasy, and flowers: A content analysis of the American sympathy card. *Omega, 11,* 25–35.

McGill, M. E. (1980). *The 40- to 60-year-old male.* New York: Simon & Schuster.

McGlynn, F. D., & O'Brien, L. (1972). The semiautomated treatment of a phobia: A case study. *J. Clin. Psychol., 28,* 228–230.

McGrath, R. D. (1985, February 26–28). The myth of frontier violence. *Harpers.*

McGuire, W. J. (1964). Inducing resistance to persuasion: Some contemporary approaches. In L. Berkowitz (Ed.), *Advances in experimental social psychology.* New York: Academic Press.

McMahon, F. B., & McMahon, J. W. (1983). *Abnormal behavior: Psychology's view.* Homewood, IL: Dorsey Press.

McMahon, J. (1987). [Untitled John Wesley Hardin poem.]

Meador, B. D., & Rogers, C. R. (1973). Client-centered therapy. In R. Corsini (Ed.), *Current psychotherapy.* Itasca, IL: Peacock.

Meece, J. L., Parsons, J. E., Kaczala, C. M., Goff, S. B., & Futterman, R. (1982). Sex differences in math achievement: Toward a model of academic choice. *Psychol. Bull., 91,* 324–348.

Meehl, P. E. (1956). Wanted—a good cookbook. *Amer. Psychol., 11,* 262–272.

Melnechuk, T. (1983). The dream machine. *Psychol. Today, 17*(11).

Melzack, R. (1987). Interview in "Pain's Gatekeeper." *Psychol. Today, 21*(8).

Melzack, R., & Wall, P. D. (1982). *The challenge of pain.* New York: Basic Books.

Merz, W. R., & Rutherford, B. M. (1972). Differential teacher regard for creative students and achieving students. *Calif. J. Educ. Res., 23,* 83–90.

Milgram, S. (1977). *The individual in a social world.* Reading, MA: Addison-Wesley.

Miller, G. A. (1962). *Psychology: The science of mental life.* New York: Harper & Row.

Miller, G. S. (1956). The magical number seven plus or minus two: Some limits ono our capacity for processing information. *Psychol. Rev., 63,* 81–96.

Miller, J. A. (1983). Lessons from the lab. *Sci. News, 124,* 394–396.

Miller, N. E. (1985). Rx: Biofeedback. *Psychol. Today, 19*(2).

Miller, R. C., & Berman, J. S. (1983). The efficacy of cognitive behavior therapies: A quantitative review of the research evidence. *Psychol. Bull., 9,* 39–53.

Miller, W. R., & Orr, J. (1980). Nature and sequence of neuropsychological deficits in alcoholics. *J. Stud. Alco., 41,* 325–337.

Millodot, M. (1982). Accommodation and refraction of the eye. In H. B. Barlow and J. D. Mollon (Eds.), *The senses.* New York: Cambridge University Press.

Mollon, J. D. (1982). Colour vision and colour blindness. In H. B. Barlow and J. D. Mollon (Eds.), *The senses.* New York: Cambridge University Press.

Money, J. (1974). Differentiation of gender identity. *Master lectures on physiological psychology.* Tape. Washington, DC: American Psychological Association.

———. (1980). *Love and love sickness.* Baltimore: Johns Hopkins University Press.

Monk, T. H. (1983). Quoted in "Clocks for mind and body." *Sci. News, 10,* 154.

Montagu, A. (1964). *Man's most dangerous myth: The fallacy of race* (4th ed.). New York: World.

———. (1974). Aggression and the evolution of man. In R. E. Whalen (Ed.), *The neuropsychology of agression.* New York: Plenum.

Moore, T. E. (1984). Subliminal delusion. *Psychol. Today, 19*(7).

Moore-Ede, M. C. (1986, December 26). [Interview.] *New York Times,* pp.

Moore-Ede, M. C., Sulzman, F. M., & Fuller, C. A. (1982). *The clocks that time us.* Cambridge, MA: Harvard University Press.

Morgan, D. (1984, February 20). If you want good schools, stop doting on a test like the SAT. *Washington Post Nat. Week. Edition,* pp.

Moroney, W. F., & Zenhausern, R. J. (1972). Detection of deception as a function of galvanic skin response recording methodology. *J. Psychol., 80,* 255–262.

Mosher, L. R., Gunderson, J. G., & Buchsbaum, S. (1973). Special report: Schizophrenia, 1972. *Schiz. Bull., 7.*

Moss, C. S. (1965). *Hypnosis in perspective.* New York: Macmillan.

Mossip, C. E. (1977, April). *Hemispheric specialization as seen in children's perception of faces.* Paper presented at meeting of Eastern Psychological Association, Boston.

Moyer, K. E. (1975). *The psychobiology of aggression.* New York: Harper & Row.

Mueller, C. G. (1979). Some origins of psychology as science. *Ann. Rev. Psychol., 30,* 9–29.

Munroe, R. L., & Munroe, R. H. (1971). Male pregnancy symptoms and cross identity in three societies. *J. Soc. Psychol., 84,* 11–25.

Munsinger, H. (1975). The adopted child's IQ: A critical review. *Psychol. Bull., 82,* 623–659.

Muntz, W. (1981). Color vision. In D. McFarland (Ed.), *The Oxford companion to animal behaviour.* New York: Oxford University Press.

Murphy, G., & Kovach, J. (1972). *Historical introduction to modern psychology.* New York: Harcourt Brace Jovanovich.

Muse, K. (1985). Quoted in "Medical root for PMS found." *Sci. News, 127,* 24.

Muuss, R. E. (1975). *Theories of adolescence* (3d ed.). New York: Random House.

Myers, D. G. (1983). *Social psychology.* New York: McGraw-Hill.

Myers, J. J. (1984). Right hemisphere language: Science or fiction? *Amer. Psychol., 39,* 315–319.

Nassau, K. (1980). The causes of color. *Sci. Amer., 243*(4).

Neufeld, R. W. J., & Davidson, P. O. (1971). The effects of various and cognitive rehearsals on pain tolerance. *J. Psychosom. Res., 15,* 329–335.

Neugarten, B. L. (1976). Adaptation and the life cycle. *Coun. Psychol., 6,* 16–20.

———. (1977). Personality changes in adulthood. *Master lectures on brain-behavior relationships.* Tape 14/16. Washington, DC: American Psychological Association.

———. (1980, June). Must everything be a midlife crisis? *Prime Times,* pp.

Newcomb, T. (1963). Persistence and repression of changed attitudes: Long-range studies. *J. Soc. Issues, 19,* 3–14.

Newman, B. M., & Newman, P. R. (1984). *Development through life: A psychosocial approach.* Homewood, IL: Dorsey Press.

Newton, I. (1952). Optics, book 3. In R. M. Hutchins (Ed.), *Great books of the Western world,* no. 34. Chicago: Encyclopaedia Britannica.

Nias, D. K. (1979). Marital choice: Matching or complementation? In M. Cook and G. Wilson (Eds.), *Love and attraction.* New York: Pergamon Press.

Nicholson, J. (1984). *Men and women: How different are they?* New York: Oxford University Press.

Nicholson, R. A., & Berman, J. S. (1983). Is follow-up necessary in evaluating psychotherapy? *Psychol. Bull., 93,* 261–278.

Nielsen, A. C. (1985, February 18). Survey quoted in *U.S. News & World Report,* pp.

Nizer, L. (1966). *The jury returns.* New York: Doubleday.

Normann, R. A., Perlman, I., Kolb, K., Jones, J., & Daly, S. J. (1984). Direct excitory interactions between cones of different spectral types in the turtle retina. *Science, 224,* 625–627.

Nourse, A. E. (1964). *The body.* New York: Time.

O'Kelly, L. I., & Muckler, F. A. (1955). *Introduction to psychopathology.* Englewood Cliffs, NJ: Prentice-Hall.

Olds, J. (1956). Pleasure centers in the brain. *Sci. Amer., 195*(4).

Olton, D. S. (1978). Characteristics of spatial memory. In S. H. Hulse, H. F. Fowler, and W. K. Honig (Eds.), *Cognitive aspects of animal behavior.* Hillsdale, NJ: Erlbaum.

———. (1979). Mazes, maps and memory. *Amer. Psychol., 34,* 583–596.

Opton, E., Jr. (1979). A psychologist takes a closer look at the recent landmark *Larry P.* opinion. *APA Monitor, 10*(12).

Orlinsky, D. E., Howard, K. I., & Hill, J. A. (1970). The patient's concerns in psychotherapy. *J. Clin. Psychol., 26,* 104–111.

Ornstein, R. E. (1977). *The psychology of consciousness* (2d ed.). New York: Harcourt Brace Jovanovich.

Ornstein, R., & Sobel, D. (1987). *The healing brain: A new perspective on the brain and health.* New York: Simon & Schuster.

Oster, G. (1970). Phosphenes. *Sci. Amer.*, *222*(2).

Oswald, I. (1966). *Sleep.* Baltimore: Penguin Books.

Owen, D. (1983, May). The last days of ETS. *Harper's*, 21–37.

Owens, J., Bower, G. H., & Black, J. B. (1979). The "soap opera" effect in story recall. *Mem. Cogn.*, *7*, 185–191.

Parke, R. (1983). Quoted in "Researchers make room for father." *APA Monitor*, *14*(12).

Parkin, A. J. (1987). *Memory and Amnesia: An introduction.* New York: Blackwell.

Patterson, K. E., & Baddeley, A. D. (1977). When face recognition fails. *J. Exper. Psychol.: Hum. Lrn. Mem.*, *3*, 406–417.

Pearce, P. L. (1980). Strangers, travelers, and Greyhound terminals: A study of small-scale helping behaviors. *J. Pers. Soc. Psychol.*, *38*, 935–940.

Pearlin, L. I. (1975). Sex roles and depression. In N. Datan and L. Ginsberg (Eds.), *Life-span developmental psychology: Normative life crises.* New York: Academic Press.

Penfield, W. (1959). The interpretive cortex. *Science*, *129*(6).

Pengelley, E. T., & Asmundson, S. J. (1971). Annual biological clocks. *Sci. Amer.*, *224*(4).

Perry, J. S., & Slemp, S. R. (1980). Differences among three adult age groups in their attitudes toward self and others. *J. Genetic Psychol.*, *136*, 275–279.

Peskin, H. (1973). Influence of the developmental schedule of puberty and early development. *J. Youth Adol.*, *2*, 273–290.

Petersen, A. (1987). Those gangly years. *Psychol. Today*, *21*(9), 28–34.

Phillips, J. L., Jr. (1969). *The origins of intellect: Piaget's theory.* San Francisco: W. H. Freeman.

Phillips, J. S., & Bierman, K. L. (1981). Clinical psychology: Individual methods. *Ann. Rev. Psychol.*, *32*, 405–438.

Piaget, J. (1929). *The child's conception of the world.* New York: Harcourt Brace Jovanovich.

Pittner, M. S., & Houston, B. K. (1980). Response to stress, cognitive coping strategies, and the type A behavior pattern. *J. Pers. Soc. Psychol.*, *39*, 147–157.

Plomin, R., & Daniels, D. (1987). Why are children in the same family so different from one another? *Beh. Brain Sci.*, *10*, 1–16.

Plomin, R., De Fries, J. C., & McClearn, G. E. (1980). *Behavioral genetics: A primer.* San Francisco: W. H. Freeman.

Poggio, G. F., & Fischer, B. (1977). Binocular interaction and depth sensitivity of striate and prestriate cortical neurons of behaving rhesus monkeys. *J. Neurophysiol.*, *40*, 139–145.

Poggio, T. (1984). Vision by man and machine. *Sci. Amer.*, *250*(4).

Pokorny, A. D., & Mefferd, R. B. (1966). Geomagnetic fluctuation and disturbed behavior. *J. Nerv. Ment. Dis.*, *143*, 140–151.

Pope, H. G., Jr., & Katz, D. L. (1987). Of muscles and mania. *Psychol. Today*, *21*(9).

Posner, M., Klein, R., Summers, J., & Buggie, S. (1973). On the selection of signals. *Mem. Cogn.*, *1*, 2–12.

Premack, D., & Woodruff, G. (1978). Does the chimpanzee have a theory of mind? *Beh. Brain Sci.*, *1*, 515–526.

Prescott, J. W. (1979, December). Alienation of affection. *Psychol. Today*, p. 124.

Preston, S. H. (1984). Children and the elderly in the U.S. *Sci. Amer.*, *10*(13).

Pribram, K. H. (1971). *Languages of the brain: Experimental paradoxes and principles in neuropsychology.* Englewood Cliffs, NJ: Prentice-Hall.

Probst, T., Krafczyk, S., & Brandt, T. (1984). Interaction between perceived self-motion and object motion impairs vehicle guidance. *Science*, *225*, 536–538.

Quattrone, G. A. (1985). On the congruity between internal states and action. *Psychol. Bull.*, *98*, 3–40.

Rachlin, H. (1985). Pain and behavior. *Beh. Brain Sci.*, *8*, 42–53.

Rapoport, J. L. (1989). *The boy who couldn't stop washing: The experience and treatment of obsessive-compulsive disorders.* New York: Dutton.

Reedy, M. N. (1983). Personality and aging. In D. S. Woodruff and J. E. Birren (Eds.), *Aging: Scientific perspectives and social issues* (2d ed.). Monterey, CA: Brooks/Cole.

Reis, H. T., Nezlek, J., & Wheeler, L. (1980). Physical attractiveness in social interaction. *J. Pers. & Soc. Psychol.*, *38*, 604–617.

Reisman, J. M. (1966). *The development of clinical psychology.* Englewood Cliffs, NJ: Prentice-Hall.

Rennie, T. (1972). Prognosis in manic depressive psychosis. *Amer. J. Psychiatr.*, *98*, 801–814.

Restak, R. (1984). *The brain.* New York: Bantam Books.

Richardson, D., Vinsel, A., & Taylor, S. P. (1980). Female aggression as a function of attitudes toward women. *Sex Roles*, *6*, 265–271.

Rivlin, R., & Gravelle, K. (1984). *Deciphering the senses.* New York: Simon & Schuster.

Roberts, D. F., & Backen, D. M. (1981). Mass communication effects. *Amer. Rev. Psychol.*, *32*, 307–356.

Robinson, F. P. (1941). *Effective behavior.* New York: Harper & Row.

Robinson, H., & Robinson, N. (1970). Mental retardation. In P. H. Mussen (Ed.), *Carmichael's manual of child psychology* (3d ed.). New York: Wiley.

Rodin, J. (1984). A sense of control. *Psychol. Today*, *18*(12).

Rogers, C. R. (1951). *Client-centered therapy: Its current practice, implications and theory.* Boston: Houghton Mifflin.

———. (1961). *On becoming a person–A therapist's view of psychotherapy.* Boston: Houghton Mifflin.

Rogers, R. W., & Thistlethwaite, D. L. (1969). An analysis of active and passive defenses inducing resistance to persuasion. *J. Per. Soc. Psychol.*, *11*, 301–308.

Romagnano, M. A., & Hamill, R. W. (1984). Spinal sympathetic pathway: An enkephalin ladder. *Science*, *225*, 737–739.

Rorabaugh, W. J. (1979). *The alcoholic republic.* New York: Oxford University Press.

Rosenfeld, A. (1985). Stretching the span. *Wilson Quart.*, *9*(1).

Rosenzweig, M. (1962). The mechanisms of hunger and thirst. In L. Postman (Ed.), *Psychology in the making.* New York: Knopf.

Rosenzweig, M. R. (1984). Experience, memory, and the brain. *Amer. Psychol.*, *39*, 365–376.

Rosenzweig, M. R., Bennett, E. L., & Diaond, M. C. (1972). Brain changes in response to experience. *Sci. Amer.*, *226*(2).

Rotton, J., & Kelly, I. W. (1985). Much ado about the full moon: A meta-analysis of lunar-lunacy research. *Psychol. Bull.*, *97*, 286–306.

Rugg, M. (1985). Quoted in "Does the brain trigger an immune response?" *Science 85*, *6*(2).

Rule, B. G., & Nesdale, A. R. (1976). Emotional arousal and aggressive behavior. *Psychol. Bull.*, *83*, 851–863.

Russell, J. A., & Ward, L. M. (1984). Environmental psychology. *Ann. Rev. Psychol.*, 33, 651–688.

Russell, M. J., Switz, G. M., & Thompson, K. (1977, June). Olfactory influences on the human menstrual cycle. Paper. Amer. Assn. Advan. Sci.

Rust, S. M., & Black, K. A. (1972). The application of two mnemonic techniques following rote memorization of a free recall task. *J. Psychol.*, 80, 247–253.

Rust, V. D. (1984). What can we learn from others? *Wilson Quart.*, 7(1).

Ruttenber, A. J., & Luke, J. L. (1984). Heroin-related deaths: New epidemiologic insights. *Science*, 226, 14–20.

Sadker, M., & Sadker, D. (1985). Sexism in the schoolroom of the '80s. *Psychol. Today*, 19(3).

Sagan, C. (1977). *The dragons of Eden*. New York: Random House.

Sagar, H. A., & Schofield, J. W. (1980). Racial and behavioral cues in black and white children's perceptions of ambiguously aggressive acts. *J. Pers. Soc. Psychol.*, 39, 590–598.

Samuelson, F. (1980). J. B. Watson's Little Albert, Cyril Burt's twins, and the need for a critical science. *Amer. Psychol.*, 35, 619–625.

Sarason, S. B., Mandler, G., & Craighill, P. G. (1952). The effect of differential instructions on anxiety and learning. *J. Abnorm. Soc. Psychol.*, 47, 561.

Scarf, M. (1977). Husbands in crisis. In L. Allman and D. Jaffe (Eds.), *Readings in adult psychology: Contemporary perspectives*. New York: Harper & Row.

Schachter, S., & Rodin, J. (Eds.). (1974). *Obese humans and rats*. Potomac, MD: Erlbaum.

Schachter, S., & Singer, J. (1962). Cognitive, social, and psychological determinants of emotional state. *Psychol. Rev.*, 29, 379–399.

Schaie, K. W. (Ed.). (1983). *Longitudinal studies of adult psychological development*. New York: Adult Development and Aging.

Schein, E. H., Schneider, I., & Barker, C. H. (1961). *Coercive persuasion*. New York: Norton.

Schettino, A. P., & Borden, R. J. (1976). Sex differences in response to naturalistic crowding: Affective reactions to group size and group density. *Pers. & Soc. Psychol. Bull.*, 2, 67–70.

Schleifer, S. J. (1985). Quoted in "Severe depression depresses immunity." *Sci. News*, 127, 100.

Schuckit, M. A. (1980, August). Cited in L. Asher, Genetic alcoholism? *Psychol. Today*.

Schulman, R. E., & London, P. (1963). Hypnosis and verbal learning. *J. Abnorm. Soc. Psychol.*, 67, 363.

Schultz, D. P. (1969). *A history of modern psychology*. New York: Academic Press.

Schwartz, G. E. (1979). The brain as a health care system. In G. Stone, N. Adler, and F. Cohen (Eds.), *Health psychology*. San Francisco: Jossey-Bass.

Schwartz, J. C. (1979b). Childhood origins of psychopathology. *Amer. Psychol.*, 34, 879–885.

Schwartz, R. (1980). How rich a theory of mind? *Beh. Brain Sci.*, 3, 616–618.

Schwartz, S. H., & Gottlieb, A. (1980). Bystander anonymity and reactions to emergencies. *J. Pers. Soc. Psychol.*, 39, 418–430.

Schwartz, W. J. (1984). Quoted in "Fetuses watch the clock." *Sci. News*, 126, 266.

Scovern, A. W., & Kilmann, P. R. (1980). Status of electroconvulsive therapy: Review of the outcome literature. *Psychol. Bull.*, 87, 260–303.

Sears, R. R., Maccoby, E. E., & Levin, H. (1966). Development of the gender role. In F. A. Beach (Ed.), *Sex and behavior*. New York: Wiley.

Seedman, A., & Hellman, P., (1974). *Chief!* New York: Arthur Fields Books.

Seevers, M. (1968). Use, misuse, and abuse of amphetamine-type drugs from the medical viewpoint. In J. Russo (Ed.), *Amphetamine abuse*. Springfield, IL: Thomas.

Selcer, R. U., & Hilton, I. R. (1972). Cultural differences in the acquisition of sex roles. *Proceed. 80th Ann. Conv. Amer. Psychol. Assn.*

Seligman, M. E. P. (1971). Phobias and preparedness. *Beh. Ther.*, 2, 307–320.

Selye, J. (1956). *The stress of life*. New York: McGraw-Hill.

Senk, S., & Usiskin, Z. (1984). Quoted in "Inventing gender differences." *Science 85*, 6(5).

Sheldon, W. H. (1936). *The varieties of temperament: A psychology of constitutional differences*. New York: Harper & Row.

Sheridan, C. L., & King, R. G., Jr. (1972). Obedience to authority with an authentic victim. *Proceed. 80th Ann. Conv. Amer. Psychol. Assn.*

Sherif, C. W. (1982). Social and psychological bases of social psychology. In A. G. Kraut (Ed.), *The G. Stanley Hall lecture series* (Vol. 2). Washington, DC: American Psychological Association.

Sherman, M. (1938). Verbalization and language symbols in personality adjustment. *Amer. J. Psychiat.*, 75, 621–640.

Sherrod, D. (1982). *Social psychology*. New York: Random House.

Shinn, M. (1978). Father absence and children's cognitive development. *Psychol. Bull.*, 85, 295–324.

Shotland, R. L. (1985). When bystanders just stand by. *Psychol. Today*, 19(6).

Sidorowicz, L. S., & Lunney, G. S. (1980). Baby X revisited. *Sex Roles*, 6, 67–73.

Siegel, R. K. (1983). Quoted in "Natural highs in natural habitats." *Sci. News*, 124, 300–301.

———. (1985). Quoted in "Cocaine use: Disturbing signs." *Sci. News*, 128(14).

Simons, A. D. (1984). Quoted in "Changing ideas in depression." *Sci. News*, 125, 58.

Simons, M. (1987, February 13). Brazil's health crisis: The plague is just one part. *New York Times*, p.

Skinner, B. F. (1957). *Verbal behavior*. Englewood Cliffs, NJ: Prentice-Hall.

———. (1967). Autobiography. In E. G. Boring and Lindzey (Eds.), *A history of psychology in autobiography*. Englewood Cliffs, NJ: Prentice-Hall.

———. (1983). Intellectual self-management in old age. *Amer. Psychol.*, 38, 239–254.

Sloane, B. (1983). Health care: Physical and mental. In D. S. Woodruff and J. E. Birren (Eds.), *Aging: Scientific perspectives and social issues* (2d ed.). Monterey, CA: Brooks/Cole.

Smith, D. O. (1984). Quoted in "Aging at the nerve-muscle junction." *Sci. News*, 125, 376.

Smith, R. J., Griffith, J. E., Griffith, H. K., & Steger, M. J. (1980). When is a stereotype a stereotype? *Psychol. Rep.*, 46, 643–651.

Snarey, J. R. (1985). Cross-cultural universality of social-moral development: A critical review of Kohlbergian research. *Psychol. Bull.*, 97, 202–232.

Snow, C. P. (1966). *Variety of men*. New York: Scribner's.

Snyder, S. (1980). *Biological aspects of mental disorder*. New York: Oxford University Press.

Snyder, S. H. (1984). Drug and neurotransmitter receptors in the brain. *Science, 224,* 22–31.

———. (1986). *Drugs and the brain*. New York: W. H. Freeman.

Sommer, R. (1969). *Personal space: The behavioral basis of design*. Englewood Cliffs, NJ: Prentice-Hall.

Spain, D., and Bianchi, S. M. (1983, May). How women have changed. *Amer. Demogr.*

Spanos, N. P. (1986). Hypnotic behavior: A social-psychological interpretation. *Beh. Brain Sci., 9,* 449–467.

Spear, N. E. (1978). *The processes of memories: Forgetting and retention*. Hillsdale, NJ: Erlbaum.

Spitz, R. A. (1946). Hospitalism: A follow-up report. *Psychoanal, Study Child, 2,* 113–117.

Springer, S. P., & Deutsch, G. (1985). *Left brain, right brain*. New York: W. H. Freeman.

Squire, L. (1985). Quoted in "ECT: New studies on how, why, who." *APA Monitor, 16*(3).

Square, L. R. (1987). *Memory and brain*. New York: Oxford University Press.

Starr, R. H. (1979). Child abuse. *Amer. Psychol., 34,* 872–878.

Statistical Abstracts of the United States. (1986). Washington, DC: U.S. Government Printing Office.

Steinberg, L. (1987). Bound to bicker. *Psychol. Today, 21*(9).

Stephens, R., & Cottrell, E. (1972). A follow-up study of 200 narcotic addicts committed for treatment under the Narcotic Addict Rehabilitation act (NARA). *Brit. J. Addict., 67,* 45–53.

Stern, P. C. (1984, January). Saving energy: The human dimension. *Technology Rev.* (Mass. Inst. Technology).

Sternberg, R. J. (1984). Reinventing psychology. *Wilson Quart., 8*(5).

Stewart, A. J., & Winter, D. G. (1974). Self-definition and social definition in women. *J. Pers., 42,* 238–259.

Stewart, T. D. (1969). Fossil evidence of human violence. *Transaction, 6,* 48–53.

Stillings, N. A., Feinstein, M. H., Garfield, J. L., Rissland, E. L., Rosenbaum, D. A., Weisler, S. E., & Baker-Ward, L. (1987). *Cognitive science: An introduction*. Cambridge, MA: MIT Press.

Stokols, D. (1978). A typology of crowding experiences. In A. Baum and Y. Epstein (Eds.), *Human response to crowding*. Hillsdale, NJ: Erlbaum.

Stone, I. (1980). *The origin*. Franklin Center, PA: Franklin Library.

Strauss, J. S. (1979). Social and cultural influences on psychopathology. *Ann. Rev. Psychol., 30,* 397–415.

Suomi, S. J. (1983). Social development in rhesus monkeys: Consideration of individual differences. In A. Oliverio and M. Zappella (Eds.), *The behavior of human infants*. New York: Plenum Press.

Swaab, D. F., & Fliers, E. (1984). Quoted in "Sex differences found in human brains." *Sci. News, 127,* 341.

Swartz, K. B., & Rosenblum, L. A. (1980). Operant responding by bonnet macaques for color videotape recordings of a social stimuli. *Anim. Learn. Behav., 8,* 322–331.

Szasz, T. S. (1961). *The myth of mental illness: Foundations of a theory of personal conduct*. New York: Harper & Row.

Tabakoff, B., Melchoir, C. L., & Hoffman, P. (1984). Factors in ethanol tolerance. *Science, 224,* 523.

Taub, J. M., & Berger, R. J. (1976). Extended sleep and performance: The Rip Van Winkle effect. *Psychon. Sci., 16,* 204–265.

Taylor, M. C., & Hall, J. A. (1982). Psychological androgyny: Theories, methods, and conclusions. *Psychol. Bull., 92,* 347–366.

Tebbel, J. (1974). *The media in America*. New York: Crowell.

Tesser, A. (1978). Self-generated attitude change. *Adv. Exp. Soc. Psychol., 11,* 289–338.

Thomas, K. (1983). *Man and the natural world*. New York: Pantheon Books.

Thompson, J. K., Jarvie, G. J., Lahey, B. B., & Cureton, K. J. (1982). Exercise and obesity: Etiology, physiology, and intervention. *Psychol. Bull., 91,* 55–79.

Thompson, R. F. (1967). *Foundations of physiological psychology*. New York: Harper & Row.

Thorndike, E. L. (1920). A constant error in psychological testing. *J. Appl. Psychol., 4,* 25–29.

Tinbergen, N. (1969). *Herring gull's world*. New York: Basic Books.

Tolman, E. C., Ritchie, B. F., & Kalish, D. (1946). Studies in spatial learning. *J. Exp. Psychol., 36,* 221–229.

Torrance, E. P. (1979). Unique needs of the creative child and adult. *Nat. Soc. Study Educ. Yrbk., 78,* 352–371.

———. (1980). Creativity and futurism in education: Retooling. *Education, 100,* 298–311.

Tosteson, D. C. (1981). Lithium and mania. *Sci. Amer., 244*(4).

Traxler, A. J. (1979). Let's get gerontologized: Developing a sensitivity to aging. In *The multipurpose senior center concept: A training manual for practitioners working with the aging*. Springfield, IL: Illinois Department on Aging.

Traxler, A. J., & Linksvayer, R. D. (1973). Attitudes and age-related stress periods in adulthood. *Proceedings, APA Convention,* 779–780.

Traxler, A. T. (1988). Personal communication.

Tulving, E., & Partay, J. E. (1962). Concurrent effects of contextual constraint and word frequency on immediate recall and learning of verbal material. *Canad. J. Psychol., 16,* 83–95.

Turkington, C. (1984, Janauary). Ideology affects approach taken to alleviate PMS. *APA Monitor.*

Turner, S. M., Beidel, D. C., & Nathan, R. S. (1985). Biological factors in obsessive-compulsive disorders. *Psychol. Bull., 97,* 430–450.

Ullmann, L., & Krasner, L. (1969, 1975). *A psychological approach to abnormal behavior*. Englewood Cliffs, NJ: Prentice-Hall.

Vaillant, G. E., & Milofsky, E. S. (1982). The etiology of alcoholism. *Amer. Psychol., 37,* 494–503.

Valenstein, E. S. (1973). *Brain control: A critical examination of brain stimulation and psychosurgery*. New York: Wiley.

Vetter, H. (1969). *Language behavior and psychopathology*. Chicago: Rand McNally.

Von Frisch, K. (1963). *Man and the living world*. New York: Harcourt Brace Jovanovich.

Wadden T. A., & Anderson, C. H. (1982). The clinical use of hypnosis. *Psychol. Bull., 91,* 215–243.

Wallace, R. K., & Benson, H. (1972). The physiology of meditation. *Sci. Amer., 225*(2).

Wallach, M., Kogan, N., & Bem, O. (1962). Group influence on individual risk taking. *J. Abnor. Soc. Psychol., 9,* 101–106.

Waller, M. B., McBride, W. J., Gatto, G. J., Lumeng, L., & Li, Ting-Kai. (1984). Intragastric self-infusion of ethanol by ethanol-preferring and -nonpreferring lines of rats. *Science, 225,* 78–79.

Walsh, W. B., & Betz, N. E. (1985). *Tests and assessment*. Englewood Cliffs, NJ: Prentice-Hall.

Webb, W. B. (1982). Quoted in "Staying up." *Psychol. Today*, 16(3).

Webb, W. B., & Agnew, H. W. (1974). Sleep and waking in a time-free environment. *Aerosp. Med.*, 45, 617–622.

Webb, W. B., & Cartwright, R. D. (1978). Sleep and dreams. *Ann. Rev. Psychol.*, 29, 223–252.

Weber, A. L., Cary, M. S., Conner, N., & Keyes, P. (1980). Human non-24-hour sleep-wake cycles in an everyday environment. *Sleep*, 2, 347–354.

Wechsler, D. (1975). Intelligence defined and undefined: A relativistic appraisal. *Amer. Psychol.*, 30, 135–139.

——. (1981). *WAIS-R manual*. New York: Psychological Corporation and Harcourt Brace Jovanovich.

Weinberger, D. A., Schwartz, G. E., & Davidson, R. J. (1979). Low-anxious, high-anxious, and repressive coping styles: Psychometric patterns and behavioral and physiological responses to stress. *J. Abn. Psychol.*, 88, 369–380.

Weiner, B. (1985). "Spontaneous" causal thinking. *Psychol. Bull.*, 97, 74–84.

Weiner, R. D. (1984). Does electroconvulsive therapy cause brain damage? *Brain Beh. Sci.*, 7, 1–47.

Weisberg, P., & Waldrop, P. B. (1972). Fixed-interval work habits of Congress. *J. Appl. Behav. Anal.*, 5, 93–97.

Weisberg, R. W. (1986). *Creativity: Genius and other myths*. New York: W. H. Freeman.

Weisenberg, M. (1977). Cultural and racial reactions to pain. In M. Weisenberg (Ed.), *The control of pain*. New York: Psychological Dimensions.

Weiss, D. J., & Davidson, M. L. (1981). Test theory and methods. *Ann. Rev. Psychol.*, 32, 629–658.

Weiss, J. M. (1972). Psychological factors in stress and disease. *Sci. Amer.*, 226(6).

Weissman, M. M. (1985). Quoted in "Growing up with depression." *Sci. News*, 127, 344.

Wells, G. L. (1984). Do the eyes have it? More on expert eyewitness testimony. *Amer. Psychol.*, 39, 1064–1065.

Whalen, R. E., & Simon, N. G. (1984). Biological motivation. *Ann. Rev. Psychol.*, 35, 257–276.

White, G. L. (1980). Physical attractiveness and courtship. *J. Pers. Soc. Psychol.*, 39, 660–668.

White, R. D., & John, K. E. (1984, April 16). Teenagers agree with parents on drugs, politics, and sex. *Washington Post National Weekly*.

Williams G. (1987). *The age of miracles*. Chicago: Academy Publishers.

Windholz, G. (1987). Pavlov as a psychologist. *Biol. Sci.*, 22(3).

Winfree, A. T. (1987). *The timing of biological clocks*. New York: W. H. Freeman.

Winfrey, O. (1987, April 14). [Discussion.] "Oprah Winfrey Show."

Wolf, S. (1950). Effects of suggestion and conditioning on the action of chemical agents in human subjects. *J. Clin. Inves.*, 29, 100–109.

Wolf, S., & Wolff, H. G. (1947). *Human gastric function*. London: Oxford University Press.

Wolfe, D. A. (1985). Child-abusive parents: An empirical review and analysis. *Psychol. Bull.*, 97, 462–482.

Wolpe, J., & Lazarus, A. A. (1966). *Behavior therapy techniques: A guide to the treatment of neurosis*. Elmsford, NY: Pergamon Press.

Wong, D. F. (1985). Quoted in "Deciphering dopamine's decline." *Sci. News*, 127(1).

Woolfolk, R. L. (1985). What's at stake in the mental illness controversy? *Amer. Psychol.*, 40, 468.

Worchel, S., & Cooper, J. (1983). *Understanding social psychology*. Homewood, IL: Dorsey Press.

Wormser, R. (1962). *The story of the law*. New York: Simon & Schuster.

Wright, B. J., & Isenstein, V. R. (1975). *Psychological tests and minorities*. Rockville, MD: Nat. Inst. Ment. Health.

Wurtman, R. J. (1985). Alzheimer's disease. *Sci. Amer.*, 252(1).

Yalom, I. D., & Lieberman, M. A. (1971). A study of encounter group casualties. *Arch. Gen. Psychiat.*, 256, 16–30.

Yarnold, P. R., & Grimm, L. G. (1982). Time urgency among coronary-prone individuals. *J. Abnorm. Psychol.*, 91, 175–177.

Young, J. Z. (1978). *Programs of the brain*. New York: Oxford University Press.

Youtz, R. P. (1968). Can fingers "see" color? *Psychol. Today*, 1(9).

Zeichner, A., & Pihl, R. O. (1979). Effects of alcohol and behavior contingencies on human aggression. *J. Abn. Psychol.*, 88, 153–160.

Zelazo, P. R., Zelazo, N. A., & Kolb, S. (1972). "Walking" in the newborn. *Science*, 176, 314–315.

Zimbardo, P. G. (1972, April). Pathology of imprisonment. *Society*, 3–8.

Zubek, J. P., Hughes, G. R., & Shepard, J. M. (1971). A comparison of the effects of prolonged sensory deprivation and perceptual deprivation. *Can. J. Behav. Sci. Rev. Can. Sci. Comp.*, 3, 282–290.

Zuckerman, M., Larrance, D. T., Porac, J. F. A., & Blanck, P. D. (1980). Effects of fear of success on intrinsic motivation, causal attribution, and choice behavior. *J. Pers. & Soc. Psychol.*, 39, 503–513.

Zuckerman, M., & Wheeler, L. (1975). To dispel fantasies about the fantasy-based measure of fear of success. *Psychol. Bull.*, 82, 932–946.

Zung, W. W. K., & Green, F. L., Jr. (1974). Seasonal variation of suicide and depression. *Arch. Gen. Psychiat.*, 30, 89–91.

Index

incidence of, 416
intervention techniques, 419
myths about, 419
teenage, 417-18
and thyroid gland, 70-71
Superego, 351
Survey, 34
Symbolism, 110-11
Synapse, 63

Taste
bitterness detectors in, 92
buds, 92
and hereditary factors, 119
and hunger, 118
and need for salt, 92
and need for sugar, 92
and poisons, 92
types of, 92
Telepathy, 103
Testes, 114
Tests (psychological). *See also* Achievement
tests; Aptitude tests; Intelligence tests;
Personality tests; Vocational interest
tests
alternatives to, 388
and the Barnum effect, 391-92
definition of, 36, 375
ethics of, 389-90
and the halo effect, 388
interviews as, 388-89
purpose of, 374-75

situational assessments as, 389
validity of, 385-88
Thalamus, 60
Thanatology. *See* Death
Theories
behavioral, 15, 18-19
cognitive, 17-18, 19
humanistic, 16, 19
neurobiological, 13-15, 18
psychoanalytic, 16-17, 19
Theory, 126
Therapy. *See* Psychotherapy
Thirst, 119-20
Thyroid gland
definition of, 70
and metabolism, 70
and suicide, 70-71
Tolman, E. C., 180-81
Touch, 90
Trance, 153
Transfer, 194-95
negative, 195
positive, 194
of training, 194
Twins, 248-49
TV violence, 513-16

Ulcers, 430
Unconscious, 137-38, 349. *See also* Consciousness

Variable
definition, 28-29
dependent and independent, 30-31
Vision, 80-86. *See also* Eye
afterimages in, 86
in animals, 86
binocular disparity in, 97
color, 83, 84
and color defects, 84-86
night versus day, 83-84
structure of the eye and, 81-83
use of closure in, 98
visual texture in, 97-98
Visual cliff experiment, 96, 97
Vocational interest tests, 382-85
cautions about, 385
definition of, 382
Strong-Campbell Interest Inventory,
383-85

Washington, George, 8-9
Watson, John, 166-68, 269
Wechsler intelligence test(s), 224-27
for adults and children, 226
and emphasis on performance, 225, 226
history of, 224-26
performance scale in, 226
types of test items in, 225, 226
verbal scale in, 226
White light, 80
Wundt, Wilhelm, 12-13

Credits

Unit One **1** "Fabhorizont" by Willibrord Haas; reprinted by permission of the artist. **3** © Andrew J. Zito, The Image Bank. **7** ©Richard Weymouth Brooks, Photo Researchers. **11** Art Resource. **12** The Bettmann Archive. **15** (*top*) © Owen Franken, Stock Boston, (*bottom*) The Bettmann Archive. **16** (*top*) The Bettmann Archive. (*bottom*) The Bettmann Archive. **21** © Rogers, Monkmeyer. **25** © Lew Marrim, Monkmeyer. **28** The Bettmann Archive. **29** © Cathy Melloan, Click/Chicago. **31** (*top*) The Bettmann Archive. (*bottom*) © Rob Crandall, Stock Boston. **33** Ralph Morse, Life Magazine, © Time Inc. **42** © Rogers, Monkmeyer.

Unit Two **47** "Rotraute" by Willibrord Haas; reprinted by permission of the artist. **49** The Brookhaven National Laboratories. **55** (*left*) UPI. (*right*) © Howard Sochurek, Woodfin Camp. **56** © Thomas S. England, Photo Researchers. **62** © Pam Schuyler, Stock Boston. **66** © Lennart Nilsson, *Behond Man*, Little, Brown & Co. **70** © Michael Serino, The Picture Cube. **77** © Petit Format, Photo Researchers. **84** © Lennart Nilsson, *Behold Man*, Little, Brown & Company. **85** © Vince Streano, Click/Chicago. **94** © Owen Franken, Stock Boston. **96** © Ben Rose Photography. **97** © Enrico Feroelli, DOT. **97** The Bettmann Archive. **98** © Peter Menzel, Stock Boston. **101** Kaiser Porcelain Ltd. **102** The Bettmann Archive. **109** © Bernard Giani, Photo Researchers. **111** © Michael Grecco, Stock Boston. **113** (*top*) Courtesy of Dr. Neal Miller. (*left and middle*) UPI/Bettmann Newsphotos; (*right*) AP/Wide World Photos. **115** © Anthony Bannister, Animals, Animals. **118** AP/Wide World Photos. **121 122 123** Harry F. Harlow, University of Wisconsin, Primate Laboratory. **124** © Ted Polumbaum. **126** © Mike Rizza, The Picture Cube. **129** (*top*) © Keith Gunnar, Bruce Coleman, Inc. (*bottom*) © Tony Arriza, Bruce Coleman, Inc. **130** AP/Wide World. **135** © Chard Hutchings, Photo Edit. **138** © 1984 James R. Fisher, Photo Researchers. **143** © J. Allan Hobson and Hoffman-LaRoche, Inc. **146** Historical Pictures Service. **148** The Bettmann Archive. **152** The Bettmann Archive. **153** © Daemmrich, Stock Boston. **155** © Arlene Collins, Monkmeyer.

Unit Three **159** "Blausphare, schrag" by Willibrord Haas; reprinted by permission of the artist. **161** © Robert Brenner, PhotoEdit. **163** From "Case Report: Avoidance Conditioning Therapy of an Infant with Chronic Ruminative Vomiting" by P. J. Lang and B. G. Melamed, 1969 Journal of Abnormal Psychology. © by the American Psychological Association. **167** © David A Krathwohl, Stock Boston. **170** © Will Rapport, B. F. Skinner. **174** Stock Boston **178** Courtesy of Alfred Bandura, Stanford. **179** A. Bandura, D. Ross, and S. A. Ross, "Imitation of Film-mediated Aggressive Models," Journal of Abnormal and Social Psychology 68(1963)3–11. Copyright by the American Psychological Association Reprinted by permission. **180** © Kagan, Monkmeyer. **181** © Brian Seed, Click/Chicago. **183** ©Myrleen Ferguson, PhotoEdit. **189** © Christopher S. Johnson, Stock Boston. **194** © 1988 Tony Freeman, PhotoEdit. **195** © Richard Hutchings, InfoEdit. **203** © Bill Anderson, Monkmeyer. **207** © CRNI Science Photo Library, Photo Researchers. **209** AP/Wide World. **211** © Miro Vintoniv, Stock Boston. **212** © Larry Day. **219** © Paul Conklin, Monkmeyer. **221** (*left*) © Richard Hutchings, InfoEdit. (*right*) Historical Pictures Service, Inc. **226** © Peter Vandermark, Stock Boston. **234** Smithsonian Institution. **235** © Charles Gupton, Stock Boston. **238** (*top*) AP/Wide World. (*bottom*) The Bettmann Archive.

Unit Four **243** "Krottental," by Willibrord Haas; reprinted by permission of the artist. **245** © Freda Leinwand, Monkmeyer. **248** AP/Wide World Photos. **250** © Lionel Delevingne, Stock Boston. **251** © Gerry Cranham, Rapho/Photo Researchers. **253** Nina Leen, Life Magazine, Time, Inc. **254** PhotoEdit. **257** © Edward L. Miller, Stock Boston. **261** © Mimi Forsyth, Monkmeyer. **266** PhotoEdit. **268** © 1988 Tony Freeman, PhotoEdit. **269** © Sally Cassidy, The Picture Cube. **275** © Mimi Forsyth, Monkmeyer. **288** The Museum of Modern Art Film Stills Archive. **280** From Bachrach et al., "The Control of Eating Behavior in an Anorexic by Operant Conditioning Techniques" in Ullman & Krasner, Case Studies in Behavior Modification. Holt, Tinehart & Winston, 1965. Photos courtesy of A. E. Bachrach. **282** © Christopher Brown, Stock Boston. **282** © Ed Lettau, Photo Researchers. **284** © Sybil Shackman, Monkmeyer. **287** © 1989 Peter Glass, Monkmeyer. **289** © Mary Kate Denny, PhotoEdit. **290** © Bill Gillette, Stock Boston. **292** © Billy E. Barnes, Stock Boston. **297** © Richard Hutchings, InfoEdit. **299** © Alan Oddie, PhotoEdit. **300** (*left*) © 1989 Robert Brenner, PhotoEdit. (*right*) © Lew Merrim, Monkmeyer. **302** © 1988 Tony Freeman, PhotoEdit. **303** © Jeff Albertson, Stock Boston. **308** © Thomas Hopker, Woodfin Camp & Assoc. **311** © Richard Sobol, Stock Boston. **313** AP/Wide World. **316** © Michael Grecco, Stock Boston. **321** © 1988 Tony Freeman, PhotoEdit. **323** Historical Pictures Service. **324** The Bettmann Archive. **328** © L. S. Stepanowicz, The Picture Cube. **331** The Bettmann Archive. **333** © Alan Oddie, PhotoEdit. **335** © Billy E. Barnes, Jeroboam, Inc.

Unit Five **343** "Saima" by Willibrord Haas; reprinted by permission of the artist. **345** © Mark Richards, PhotoEdit. **348** National Library of Medicine, PhotoEdit. **354** The Granger Collection. **357** Courtesy of the Harvard University News Office. **357** © Ulrike Welsch, Stock Boston. **357** © Cary Wolinsky, Stock Boston. **361** (*top left*) © 1988 David Lissy, The Picture Cube. (*top right*) © Richard Hutchings, InfoEdit. (*middle*) © Judith Canty, Stock Boston. **364** © Yva Momatiuk 1976, Jeroboam. **373** © Robert V. Eckert, Jr., Stock Boston. **376** © Mimi Forsyth, Monkmeyer. **379** Reprinted by permission of the American Psychological Association. **388** (*left*) © Richard Hutchings, InfoEdit. (*middle*) © George Zimbel, Monkmeyer. (*right*) © S. Leatherwood, PhotoEdit. **391** Library of Congress. **395** © Gerard Fritz, Monkmeyer. **399** © St. Louis Post-Dispatch. **407** Courtesy Lester Grinspoon. **411** © Mark Richards, PhotoEdit. **414** © Arlene Collins, Monkmeyer. **418** © Charales Kennard, Stock Boston. **423** © 1987 David Lissy, The Picture Cube. **433** The Museum of Modern Art Film Still Archive. **436** © Paolo Koch, Rapho/Photo Researchers. **438** © Lew Merrim, Monkmeyer. **440** AP/Wide World.

Unit Six **447** "Orang-Keil" by Willibrord Haas; reprinted by permission of the artist. **449** © Richard Hutchings, InfoEdit. **452** © Owen Franken, Stock Boston. **457** © Bob Burch, Bruce Coleman, Inc. **458** © Cary Wolinsky, Stock Boston. **463** © Bill Bridges, Globe Photos. **463** © Loren Santow, Click/Chicago. **468** Derek Bayes, © Time, Inc. **477** © Rick Brown, Stock Boston. **481** Reuters/Bettmann Newsphotos. **482** © Billy E. Barnes, Jeroboam. **484** Courtesy of Albert Bandura. **490** © Abraham Menashe, Photo Researchers. **492** © Will McIntyre, Photo Researchers.

Unit Seven **501** "Gelber Durchblick" by Willibrord Haas; reprinted by permission of the artist. **503** © Billy Barnes, Jeroboam. **507** © 1988 Myrleen Ferguson, PhotoEdit. **511** AP/Wide World. **513** PhotoEdit. **514** PhotoEdit. **517** © Robert Brenner, PhotoEdit. **520** © 1988 Tony Freeman, PhotoEdit. **527** © Philip Jon Bailey, Jeroboam. **529** © Ellis Herwig, Stock Boston. **530** News Service, Stanford University. **531** © Kindra Clineff, The Picture Cube. **534** © Anna Flynn, Stock Boston. **536** From Opinions and social pressure by Solomon E. Asch. In Scientific American, November 1955.